Small Business Management
An Entrepreneurial Emphasis

Ninth Edition

Justin G. Longenecker
Baylor University

Carlos W. Moore
Baylor University

J. William Petty
Baylor University

COLLEGE DIVISION South Western Publishing Co.

Cincinnati Ohio

Acquisitions Editor: Randy G. Haubner
Developmental Editor: Carol A. Cromer
Production Editor: Sue Ellen Brown
Marketing Manager: Scott D. Person
Cover and Internal Designer: Joseph M. Devine
Internal Designer: Lesiak/Crampton Design
Photo Researcher: Kathryn A. Russell
Production House: WordCrafters Editorial Services, Inc.

GG70IA
Copyright © 1994
by South-Western Publishing Co.
Cincinnati, Ohio

3 4 5 6 7 KI 9 8 7 6 5

Printed in the United States of America

Library of Congress Cataloging-in-Publication Data
Longenecker, Justin Gooderl
    Small business management : an entrepreneurial emphasis / Justin
G. Longenecker, Carlos W. Moore, J. William Petty, — 9th ed.
        p. cm.
    Includes bibliographical references and index.
    ISBN 0-538-83045-X (alk. paper)
    1. Small business—Management.   I. Moore, Carlos W.   II. Petty,
J. William, 1942– .   III. Title.
HD62.7.L66   1994
658.02′2—dc20   93-27331
                                                                            CIP

International Thomson Publishing

South-Western Publishing Co. is an ITP Company. The ITP trademark is used
under license.

 This book is printed on acid-free paper that meets Environmental Protection
Agency standards for recycled paper.

ABOUT THE AUTHORS

JUSTIN G. LONGENECKER—BAYLOR UNIVERSITY

Justin Longenecker has taught a variety of graduate and undergraduate courses, including Small Business Management. His authorship of *Small Business Management, An Entrepreneurial Emphasis* began with the first edition of this book and continues with an active, extensive involvement in preparation of the present edition. He has authored a number of books and numerous articles in such journals as *Journal of Small Business Management, Academy of Management Review, Business Horizons,* and *Journal of Business Ethics.* Active in a number of professional organizations, he has served as president of the International Council for Small Business.

Dr. Longenecker attended Central College, a two-year college in McPherson, Kansas. He earned his bachelor's degree in Political Science from Seattle Pacific University, his M.B.A. from Ohio State University, and his Ph.D. from the University of Washington.

CARLOS W. MOORE—BAYLOR UNIVERSITY

Carlos W. Moore is the Edwin W. Streetman Professor of Marketing at Baylor University, where he has been an instructor for more than 20 years. He has been honored as a Distinguished Professor by the Hankamer School of Business, where he teaches both graduate and undergraduate courses. Professor Moore has authored articles in such journals as *Journal of Small Business Management, Journal of Business Ethics, Organizational Dynamics,* and *Accounting Horizons.* His authorship of this textbook began with its sixth edition.

Dr. Moore received an Associate Arts degree from Navarro Junior College in Corsicana, Texas, where he was later named Ex-Student of the Year. He earned a B.B.A. degree from The University of Texas at Austin, an M.B.A. from Baylor University, and a doctorate from Texas A & M University.

Besides his academic experience, Dr. Moore has business experience as co-owner of a small ranch and is a partner in a small-business consulting firm.

J. WILLIAM PETTY—BAYLOR UNIVERSITY

The ninth edition welcomes J. William Petty as the newest member of the authorship team. Dr. Petty is Professor of Finance and the W. W. Caruth Chairholder in Entrepreneurship in the Department of Finance at Baylor University. One of his primary responsibilities is teaching entrepreneurial finance, both at the undergraduate and graduate levels. He has also taught Financing the Small Firm at the University of Texas at Austin. He is a co-author of a leading corporate finance textbook and a co-author of *Financial Management of the Small Firm.* He is also a contributor to the *Portable MBA on Entrepreneurship.* In 1992, he served as the Program Chair for the annual meetings of the Academy of Small Business Finance. Professor Petty has published research in numerous academic and practitioner journals, including *Financial Management, Accounting Review, Journal of Financial and Quantitative Analysis, Journal of Managerial Finance,* and the *Journal of Small Business Finance.* He has served as a consultant to several small and middle-market companies.

Dr. Petty received his undergraduate degree in marketing from Abilene Christian University, and both his M.B.A. and Ph.D. in finance and accounting from The University of Texas at Austin. He is a C.P.A. in the State of Texas.

PREFACE

A NOTE TO THE TEACHER

For more than three decades, *Small Business Management, An Entrepreneurial Emphasis* has been the most widely used text in its field. In keeping with this tradition, we have prepared a ninth edition that incorporates the most current theory and practice related to starting and managing small firms. Reflecting our diverse academic fields of management, marketing, and finance, we have also attempted to provide a well-balanced treatment of small-business issues. In the preparation of the book, three primary standards have been used. First, we have made a strong effort to offer *completeness* in the treatment of each topic. Second, we have given readability a high priority; we have taken extra care to use a clear and concise writing style. Finally, frequent references have been made to real-world examples to help the student see the relevance of a concept.

We feel the balance between theory and practice offered by the text is the primary reason that IN-TELE-COM, a major producer of educational programs, has once again selected our text for use with its *Something Ventured* telecourse.

Ultimately, however, it is your evaluation that is most important to us. We sincerely want to know what you think. Please feel free to give any of us a call as you have questions or needs. We view ourselves as partners in this venture, and we will be sensitive to your wishes and desires whenever possible.

A NOTE TO THE STUDENT

As the authors of *Small Business Management, An Entrepreneurial Emphasis,* we realize that our success ought to be measured by the level of effectiveness in our presentation to you, the end user. While you most likely are not involved in the process of selecting which text will be used in your class, we still consider you to be our customer. Thus, we feel a strong desire to be sensitive to your needs to learn the concepts and ideas presented in the text. For this reason, we have made every effort to make the material understandable and relevant. We have tried to meet your needs in each chapter we have written.

REVISION HIGHLIGHTS OF THE NINTH EDITION

A number of specific changes have been made in the ninth edition that may not be obvious to the casual observer, but which should make the text even more beneficial than its predecessors. Among the revision highlights of this ninth edition are the following:

1. A new chapter (Chapter 3) emphasizes developing a competitive advantage and selecting a market niche.
2. The discussion of buying a business (Chapter 4) has been strengthened by an expanded explanation of methods of valuing a small firm.
3. The preparation of the business plan (Chapter 7) has been amplified to include a fuller treatment of the investor's perspective in examining such plans.
4. Chapter 10 provides a more complete presentation on determining the nature and amount of asset and financing requirements for a new venture.
5. A tutorial on finding the present value of future cash flows has been added in Appendix C.
6. Coverage of international marketing and its implications for small business has been expanded in Chapter 15.
7. Total quality management in all types of business operations has been made the primary focus of Chapter 18.
8. A new presentation on how to read financial statements that has been classroom proven to work well with students who are not accounting oriented is provided in Chapter 20.
9. Coverage of working capital management (Chapter 21) has been enhanced with special attention to cash-flow analysis.
10. A new chapter (Chapter 22) has been provided on using capital budgeting techniques within the small firm.
11. Chapter 23 has been completely rewritten to provide a thoroughly up-to-date treatment of the various types of computer-based technology applicable to small firms.

The preceding list of changes is not comprehensive. However, it does highlight the types of changes we have committed ourselves to making in order that the ninth edition will continue to reflect the very best that we have to offer.

KEY FEATURES OF THE TEXTBOOK

Small Business Management, An Entrepreneurial Emphasis, Ninth Edition, includes a number of features that facilitate student learning. The primary learning aids are:

1. A chapter "opener" (Spotlight on Small Business) that features a specific small-business firm in the context of that chapter.
2. A Looking Ahead section that presents active, measurable learning objectives and lists key terms and concepts for the chapter.
3. Small Business in Action reports that dramatize text material with experiences of real-world entrepreneurs.
4. Photographs, graphs, tables, and illustrations that communicate key concepts.
5. Definitions of key terms and concepts in the margins.
6. A Looking Back section for each chapter that reviews basic chapter topics.
7. Discussion Questions at the end of each chapter. Some questions review chapter content and some stimulate further thinking about chapter concepts.
8. Two short incidents (You Make the Call) to stimulate application of concepts developed in the chapter.
9. Experiential Exercises at the end of each chapter.
10. Annotated References to Small-Business Practices at the end of each chapter that identify and give a brief content description of articles describing applications of chapter topics.
11. Real-world cases at the end of the text. One case relates to each chapter of the book.
12. A glossary of terms used in the text.

INSTRUCTIONAL SUPPORT

The following supplements are available to assist in the teaching and learning process:

1. ***Student Learning Guide.*** This supplement presents key points of each textbook chapter, brief definitions, programmed self-reviews, creative exercises, and a series of pretests.
2. ***Instructor's Manual.*** To further facilitate instruction, a comprehensive *Instructor's Manual* is available. Each chapter of this manual contains lecture notes, sources of audio/video and other instructional materials, answers to

chapter discussion questions, comments on chapter "You Make the Call" situations, and suggestions for case and *Student Learning Guide* assignments. There are also separate sections devoted to teaching notes on the textbook cases, solutions to exercises in the *Student Learning Guide,* and transparency masters.

3. ***Color Transparencies.*** A set of over 100 color transparencies is available for use in the classroom discussion of chapter material. Many of these transparencies contain material not found in the textbook.

4. ***Videotapes.*** Since this textbook is used by IN-TELE-COM as part of their telecourse, *Something Ventured,* arrangements have been made for adopters to receive, at no cost, tapes from this video program. Contact your sales representative for details.

5. ***Test Bank.*** A comprehensive test bank includes true/false, multiple-choice, and discussion questions. All questions have been prepared by full-time instructors and carefully reviewed for clarity.

6. ***Computerized Test Bank.*** The complete test bank is available on easy-to-use diskettes. These MicroExam 4.0 diskettes are available for MS DOS® computers.

ACKNOWLEDGMENTS

In preparing the ninth edition, we have been aided by colleagues, students, business owners, and others in providing case materials in numerous other ways. For their helpful revision suggestions, we are especially grateful to the following individuals:

Guy Adamo
Berkeley College of Business

Robert J. Ash
Rancho Santiago College

Jerry E. Boles
Western Kentucky University

Richard P. Butler
Alverno College

Michael Crone
DeVry Institute of Technology

Norman Deunk
Central Michigan University

Bonnie Ann Dowd
Palomar College

Robert Edmondson
MiraCosta Community College

C. S. Everett
Des Moines Area Community College

Larry B. Hill
San Jacinto College Central

Donald W. Hucker
Cypress College

Roger J. Kashlak
Temple University

Roberta L. Kuhlman
Chaffey Community College

Joseph B. Lovell
California State University, San
  Bernardino

Donald D. Manning
Mesa State College

Susan J. Mitchell
Des Moines Area Community College

Joanne C. Murphy
Citrus College

E. Gladys Norman
Linn-Benton Community College

David Pecha
Northwestern Oklahoma State
  University

Gerald E. Smith
Vincennes University

Frederick A. Ware, Jr.
Valdosta State University

Arthur Yehle
Georgia College

We especially appreciate the contribution of Philip R. Carpenter. We also acknowledge the assistance of Fred S. Hulme, Jr., in the preparation of Chapter 23; the support of Mr. and Mrs. Edwin W. Streetman, the Hillcrest Foundation, and our Dean, Richard C. Scott; and the typing of Doris Kelly. We are especially indebted to H. N. Broom for the material that was shaped by his co-authorship over the first six editions. We also appreciate the understanding and support of our wives, Frances, Gwen, and Donna.

We also thank our friends at South-Western Publishing Co. They are truly professionals. We offer our personal expression of appreciation to Randy Haubner, our Acquisitions Editor, Carol Cromer, our Developmental Editor, and Sue Ellen Brown, our Production Editor.

As a final word, we express our sincere thanks to the many teachers who use *Small Business Management, An Entrepreneurial Emphasis* in the classroom—in both academic and professional settings. We thank you for letting us serve you.

Justin G. Longenecker
Carlos W. Moore
J. William Petty
Baylor University

BRIEF CONTENTS

xi

C O N T E N T S

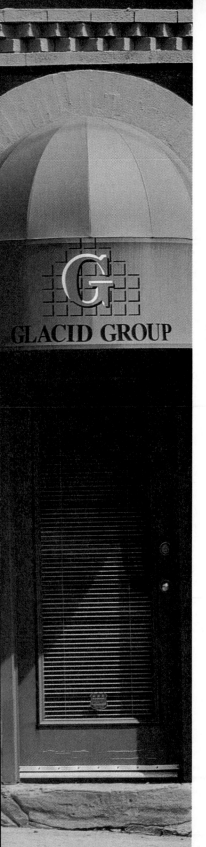

PART 4
SMALL BUSINESS MARKETING 297

PART 5
MANAGING SMALL BUSINESS
OPERATIONS 409

26 Working Within the Law 666

Regulation and Small-Business Opportunity 667   Regulation and Protection of the Marketplace 672   Business Agreements and the Law 682   The Challenge of Taxation 685

CASES

APPENDIXES

GLOSSARY 793

INDEX 807

ACKNOWLEDGMENTS 827

PART 1

Nature of Small Business

C H A P T E R 1

Entrepreneurs: The Energizers of Small Business

SPOTLIGHT ON SMALL BUSINESS

Michael Dell became an entrepreneur while he was a freshman at The University of Texas. He began selling computer parts by mail and was soon shipping $80,000 worth of them a month! The prospects were so attractive that he dropped out of school to devote full time to the business. In 1985, his company, Dell Computer Corporation, started selling IBM PC clones created with off-the-shelf parts and priced at less than $1,000. By 1993, annual sales of the company were expected to be near $2 billion.

Dell's entrepreneurial attitudes are evident in this explanation of his own thinking: "I never imagined myself being someone who worked his way up the ladder. . . . I wanted to control my own destiny and basically always felt I would be successful. I had a pretty strong inclination to create a business."

Youth was no barrier to Dell's success. He is a real entrepreneur, an "energizer," who started from "nowhere" to create a small business that quickly grew into a very big business. Are Dell's entrepreneurial skills sufficient to make Dell Computer Corporation—now the fourth largest personal computer maker in the United States—a powerful competitor in the big-business world of IBM, Apple, and Compaq? We can only wait and see.

Michael Dell—A College Student Entrepreneur

Source: The story above has been widely reported in the business press. The direct quotation is taken from Jeremy Main, "A Golden Age for Entrepreneurs," *FORTUNE,* Vol. 121, No. 4 (February 12, 1990), p. 120 © 1990 Time Inc. All rights reserved.

After studying this chapter, you should be able to:
1. Provide examples of highly successful entrepreneurs.
2. Name three rewards and three drawbacks of entrepreneurship.
3. Identify three characteristics often found in entrepreneurs.
4. Explain what factors indicate a readiness for entrepreneurship.
5. Identify ten types of entrepreneurial people or firms.

entrepreneur
need for achievement
internal locus of control
external locus of control
foreign refugee
corporate refugee
parental (paternal) refugee
feminist refugee

housewife refugee
society refugee
educational refugee
precipitating events
founders
general managers
franchisee

marginal firm
attractive small firm
high-potential venture
artisan entrepreneur
opportunistic entrepreneur
entrepreneurial team

Entrepreneurs are the folk heroes of modern business life. They provide jobs, introduce innovations, and spark economic growth. No longer do we view them as dull purveyors of groceries or auto parts. Instead, we see entrepreneurs as energizers who take risks necessary in a growing, productive economy. Each year, thousands of such individuals, from teenagers to senior citizens, launch new businesses of their own and thereby provide the dynamic leadership that leads to economic progress.

Although some writers restrict the term **entrepreneur** to founders of business firms, we use a broadened definition that includes all active owner-managers. This definition includes second-generation members of family-owned firms and owner-managers who buy out the founders of existing firms. However, the definition excludes salaried managers of large corporations, even those who are described as "entrepreneurial" because of their flair for innovation and their willingness to assume risk.[1]

Have you ever thought about your own prospects for entrepreneurship? For example, what kinds of opportunities exist? And how attractive are the rewards? Must entrepreneurs possess special characteristics in order to succeed? Is there a "right" time to launch a business? What kinds of entrepreneurs are there, and what kinds of businesses do they operate? This chapter will discuss these questions and thereby present an introduction to the formation and management of small firms.

entrepreneur
a person who starts up and/or operates a business

STORIES OF SUCCESSFUL ENTREPRENEURIAL "ENERGIZERS"

The reality of entrepreneurial opportunities can be communicated most vividly by giving examples of a few entrepreneurs who have succeeded. Reading these brief accounts of successful ventures should give you a "feel" for the potential that you can achieve if you dream of having your own business. Even though these ventures are unique in that each became a spectacular success, they can be highly informative. They demonstrate the continued existence of opportunities and show the vast potential for at least some new ventures. And you should realize that less spectacular business ventures can still provide highly attractive career options!

Cracker Barrel (Lebanon, TN)

The construction of interstate highways ruined many gasoline stations, motels, and other small businesses located on local roads. At the same time, the change presented business opportunities along the new routes. In the small town of Lebanon, Tennessee, ex-Marine Dan Evins saw the opportunity and responded to it by building a gasoline station combined with a restaurant and gift shop just off the interstate highway.[2] (After his Marine service, he had worked as a congressional aide and bank teller and then entered a family-owned oil company which operated some rural gasoline stations.)

In 1969, Evins borrowed $40,000 to build his first facility in Lebanon and called it the "Cracker Barrel." The restaurant featured "down-home" food—

Figure 1-1
Dan Evins of
Cracker Barrel Old
Country Store

biscuits, grits, country ham, and the like—at prices families could afford. The atmosphere was that of an old-fashioned country store.

The new firm prospered and earned a profit in its very first month. Evins sold off poorly located gas stations owned by the family and concentrated on the new type of business. By 1978, Evins had opened 15 Cracker Barrels, and by 1992, the number had reached 124. In the fiscal year ending August 2, 1991, Cracker Barrel Old Country Store, Inc., earned $23 million on revenues of $300 million.

Evins is a classic entrepreneur who responded to change in the highway system and capitalized on the opportunities presented by the change. By selling off the little gasoline stations, he faced up to the changing environment, refusing to drift downward with the declining market. By successfully meeting the needs of those traveling over interstate highways, he was able to achieve large financial rewards.

Federal Express (Memphis, TN)

With annual revenue in excess of $7 billion, Federal Express Corporation is no longer a small business! But Federal Express is a relatively new business, having

Figure 1-2
Frederick W. Smith, Founder of Federal Express

started operations in 1973. The company delivers parcels overnight to major cities all over the world. Its acquisition of the Flying Tiger cargo line in 1989 made it a truly international carrier. Using a hub-and-spokes pattern, its planes converge on Memphis nightly with incoming freight and then fly out with shipments to their respective home bases.

Federal Express originated in the mind of Frederick W. Smith, a student at Yale.[3] In 1965, he wrote a paper for an economics course proposing a new type of air freight service. According to his thesis, later proved successful by Federal Express, a company with its own planes dedicated to freight distribution should be superior to existing freight forwarders, who were limited by the shifting schedules of passenger airlines.

Smith's professor (who surely made a name for himself in the annals of business history) pointed out the fallacy of Smith's reasoning and gave the paper a C! But entrepreneurs are not deterred by professors or others who lack their vision of the future. After his subsequent distinguished tours of military duty in Vietnam, Smith "dusted off" the idea and persuaded enough people of its potential value to obtain financial backing.

This venture has been unique in many ways. It was forced to start with a fleet of planes that could cover the entire country. The founder also came from a wealthy family and was able, as well as willing, to risk a substantial part of the family fortune by investing several million dollars. Nevertheless, the capital requirements were great, and Smith found it necessary to obtain the major portion of the financing from the venture capital industry. Ultimately, over a dozen equity groups participated in three major rounds of financing.

Although the startup was unusual in many ways, it is especially significant in showing the ability of one person, a potential entrepreneur, to conceptualize an entirely new type of business by studying business methods and new trends. Smith's concept was implemented so successfully that it changed the very way in which business in America communicates and ships its freight.

Proctor and Gardner Advertising (Chicago, IL)

After earning an English degree at a small Alabama college, Barbara Gardner Proctor found a job as an advertising copywriter in Chicago.[4] As she gained experience in advertising, she also developed an appreciation for quality in advertising. One particular concept suggested for a TV commercial struck her as tasteless and offensive, and this difference of opinion led to her being fired.

Following her dismissal, Proctor applied to the Small Business Administration for a loan. She obtained $80,000 in this way and promptly opened her own agency in 1970.

Proctor and Gardner Advertising is still relatively small among advertising agencies, but it is well established and respected (having almost $11 million in billings in 1992). It specializes in advertising, public relations, and event management and counts Kraft Foods and Sears among its clients. Chicago's big

Figure 1-3
Barbara Gardner
Proctor, Founder of
Proctor and Gardner
Advertising

Jewel Food Stores chain credits Proctor with helping make its generic foods campaign a success in 1978.

Barbara Gardner Proctor, as an entrepreneur in the area of business services, succeeded by selecting a strategic niche in which she could compete effectively. The knowledge and skills that she developed as a salaried employee also contributed to the success of the agency.

Unlimited Entrepreneurial Opportunities

In a private enterprise system, any individual is free to enter business for himself or herself. In this chapter thus far, we have read of four different kinds of persons who took that step—a college student in Texas, an ex-Marine in Tennessee, a wealthy heir in Memphis, and an advertising copywriter in Chicago. In contrast to many others who have tried and failed, these individuals achieved outstanding success.

At any time, such potentially profitable opportunities exist in the environment. But these opportunities must be recognized and grasped by individuals with abilities and desire that are strong enough to assure success. The examples cited here can help you visualize the wide variety of opportunities that await you. Of course, there are thousands of variations and alternatives for independent business careers. In fact, you may achieve great success in business endeavors that are far different from those described here. In the varied types of entrepreneurship, there are a number of potential rewards. We turn now to a consideration of these benefits.

REWARDS AND DRAWBACKS OF ENTREPRENEURSHIP

Individuals are *pulled* toward entrepreneurship by a number of powerful incentives, or rewards (Figure 1-4). These rewards may be grouped, for the sake of simplicity, into three basic categories: profit, independence, and a satisfying life-style.

Profit

The financial return of any business must compensate its owner for investing his or her personal time (a salary equivalent) and personal savings (an interest and/or dividend equivalent) in the business before any "true" profits are realized. Entrepreneurs expect a return that will not only compensate them for the time and money they invest, but also reward them *well* for the risks and initiative they take in operating their own businesses. Not surprisingly, however, the profit incentive is a more powerful motivator for some entrepreneurs than for others. For example, Billy J. (Red) McCombs of San Antonio, Texas, has been described as a person who wanted to make as much money as possible. Even as

Figure 1-4
Entrepreneurial
Incentives

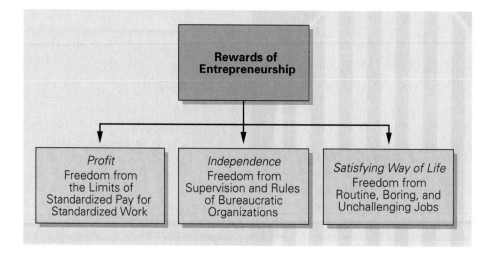

a boy, he displayed an entrepreneurial instinct and a strong desire to make money.

This single-mindedness baffled and sometimes distressed his gentle, middle-class parents. "When I was 11, I'd wash dishes in a cafe downtown from 4 P.M. until midnight and deliver newspapers at 5 A.M.," he recalls. "My mother would get tears in her eyes. 'You don't need to do this,' she'd say, and of course she was right. My father was an auto mechanic and we never wanted for anything. But I wanted to make money."[5]

Red McCombs' desire to make money led him into many entrepreneurial ventures. He invested his money in a chain of convenience stores, seven radio stations, oil exploration in two states, a contract drilling company, real estate, a Rolls-Royce dealership, and San Antonio's National Basketball Association franchise—the Spurs.

Red McCombs is an example of entrepreneurs who possess a strong interest in financial rewards. However, there are also those for whom profits are primarily a way of "keeping score." Such entrepreneurs may spend their profit on themselves or give it away, although most of them are not satisfied unless they make a "reasonable" profit. Indeed, some profit is necessary for survival because a firm that continues to lose money eventually becomes insolvent.

Independence

Freedom to operate independently is another reward of entrepreneurship. Its importance as a motivational factor is evidenced by a 1991 survey of small-business owners.[6] Thirty-eight percent of those who had left jobs at other companies said their main reason was that they wanted to be their own bosses. Like these entrepreneurs, many of us have a strong desire to make our own deci-

Figure 1-5
The Freedom to Operate Independently Is a Highly Motivating Factor in Entrepreneurship

sions, take risks, and reap the rewards for ourselves. Being one's own boss seems an attractive ideal.

The entrepreneurial desire for independence is evident in the experiences of entrepreneurs who sell out to large corporations and then stay on to run their firms as divisions of such corporations. Although some make the necessary adjustment, most find happiness elusive in these circumstances.

One entrepreneur who did not adjust well to the constraints of corporate life is Irwin Selinger. Selinger sold his medical supplies business to Squibb Corporation and continued on as chief executive. Following is a description of the conflict between this independent entrepreneur and the corporation:

"No one was a more gung-ho Squibb man than I was. I mean, my wife wore Opium perfume because it was made by a Squibb subsidiary."

Within months, the perfume didn't smell so sweet. A company officer criticized Selinger for flying coach, cautioning him that corporate executives flew first class. Then Selinger initiated an acquisition without so much as convening a committee. "I just went to the company president and said, 'Let's make a deal.'" Squibb was appalled. So was Selinger—at Squibb's reaction. "There are no bad guys in this story, just two cultures, two irreconcilable mentalities," he says.[7]

As a result of these differences, Selinger left Squibb Corporation and started a new firm with a line of medical instruments that Squibb had turned down. He was once again his own boss.

Of course, independence does not guarantee an easy life. Most entrepreneurs work very hard for long hours. But they do have the satisfaction of making their own decisions within the constraints imposed by economic and other environmental factors.

A Satisfying Way of Life

Entrepreneurs frequently speak of the personal satisfaction they experience in their own businesses. Some even refer to business as "fun." Part of this enjoyment may derive from the independence described above, but some of it also apparently comes from the peculiar nature of the business, the entrepreneur's role in the business, and the entrepreneur's opportunities to be of service.

In 1981, Larry Mahar took early retirement from a major advertising agency and, with his wife Hazel, embarked on a new business venture for the fun of it. They began to create and sell a product somewhat similar to greeting cards. However, their product was printed on parchment and was suitable for framing. They coined the name "Frameables" and the slogan, "When a mere card is not enough."

The Mahars loaded cards and display racks in their car and began calling on stores that looked as if they might sell greeting cards. For the first two years, they lost money, but since then their business has been thriving. They sell nearly 90,000 Frameables a year to retailers in five Northeastern states. Their personal satisfaction in operating the business is expressed in these words:

A lot of entrepreneurs want their business to be big. We have resisted bigness. We're more interested in enjoying what we do—just as long as we are making a nice living. We travel three days a week to meet with our customers; we know every one by name. We take our time, enjoy the scenery, and relax sometimes at quaint restaurants along the way.[8]

Drawbacks of Entrepreneurship

Although the rewards of entrepreneurship are enticing, there are also drawbacks and costs associated with business ownership. Starting and operating one's own business typically demands hard work, long hours, and much emotional energy. Many entrepreneurs describe their careers as exciting but very demanding. In fact, the strain of running a business is often listed as a reason for the breakup of entrepreneurial families.

The possibility of business failure is a constant threat to entrepreneurs. No one guarantees success or agrees to bail out a failing owner. As noted later in this chapter, entrepreneurs must assume a variety of risks related to failure. No one likes to be a loser, but that is always a possibility for one who starts a business.

In deciding upon an entrepreneurial career, therefore, you should look at both positive and negative aspects. The dangers noted here call for a degree of commitment and some sacrifice on your part if you expect to reap the rewards.

CHARACTERISTICS OF ENTREPRENEURS

A common stereotype of the entrepreneur emphasizes such characteristics as a high need for achievement, a willingness to take moderate risks, and a strong self-confidence. As we look at specific entrepreneurs, we see individuals who, for the most part, fit this image. In considering these qualities, however, we must express two words of caution. First, scientific proof of the importance of these characteristics is still lacking.[9] Second, there are exceptions to every rule, and individuals who do not "fit the mold" may still be successful entrepreneurs.

Need for Achievement

Psychologists recognize that people differ in the degree of their need for achievement. Individuals with a low need for achievement are those who seem to be contented with their present status. On the other hand, individuals with a high **need for achievement** like to compete with some standard of excellence and prefer to be personally responsible for their own assigned tasks.

A leader in the study of achievement motivation is David C. McClelland, a Harvard psychologist.[10] He discovered a positive correlation between the need for achievement and entrepreneurial activity. According to McClelland, those who become entrepreneurs have, on the average, a higher need for achieve-

need for achievement
a desire to succeed, where success is measured against a personal standard of excellence

ment than do members of the general population. While research continues to find that entrepreneurs are high achievers, the same characteristic has also been found in successful corporate executives.[11]

This drive for achievement is reflected in the ambitious individuals who start new firms and then guide them in their growth. In some families, such entrepreneurial drive is evident at a very early stage. For example, sometimes a child takes a paper route, subcontracts it to a younger brother or sister, and then tries another venture. Also, some college students take over or start various types of student-related businesses or businesses that can be operated while pursuing an academic program.

Willingness to Take Risks

The risks that entrepreneurs take in starting and/or operating their own businesses are varied. By investing their own money, they assume a financial risk. If they leave secure jobs, they risk their careers. The stress and time required in starting and running a business may also place their families at risk. And entrepreneurs who identify closely with particular business ventures assume psychic risk as they face the possibility of business failure.

David C. McClelland discovered in his studies that individuals with a high need for achievement also have moderate risk-taking propensities.[12] This means that they prefer risky situations in which they can exert some control on the outcome, in contrast to gambling situations in which the outcome depends on pure luck. This preference for moderate risk reflects self-confidence, the next entrepreneurial characteristic that will be discussed.

The extent to which entrepreneurs have a distinctive risk-taking propensity is still debatable. Some studies, for example, have found them to be similar to professional managers, while other studies have found them to have a greater willingness to assume risk.[13] This debate, however, should not be allowed to obscure the fact that entrepreneurs must be willing to assume risks. They typically place a great deal on the line when they choose to enter business for themselves.

Self-Confidence

Individuals who possess self-confidence feel they can meet the challenges that confront them. They have a sense of mastery over the types of problems they might encounter. Studies show that successful entrepreneurs tend to be self-reliant individuals who see the problems in launching a new venture but believe in their own ability to overcome these problems.

internal locus of control
believing that one's success depends upon one's own efforts

Some studies of entrepreneurs have measured the extent to which they are confident of their own abilities. According to J. B. Rotter, a psychologist, those who believe that their success depends upon their own efforts have an **internal locus of control.** In contrast, those who feel that their lives are controlled to a

B.C.   **BY JOHNNY HART**

By permission of Johnny Hart and Creators Syndicate, Inc.

© Creators Syndicate, Inc.

Figure 1-6
The Entrepreneur as "Refugee"

greater extent by luck or chance or fate have an **external locus of control.**[14] On the basis of research to date, it appears that entrepreneurs have a higher internal locus of control than is true of the population in general but that they may not differ significantly from other managers on this point.

external locus of control
believing that one's life is controlled more by luck or fate than by one's own efforts

A Need to Seek Refuge

Although most people go into business to obtain the rewards of entrepreneurship discussed earlier, there are some who become entrepreneurs to escape from some environmental factor. Professor Russell M. Knight of the University of Western Ontario has identified a number of environmental factors that encourage or "push" people to found new firms and has labeled such entrepreneurs as "refugees."[15]

In thinking about these kinds of "refugees," we should recognize that many entrepreneurs are motivated as much or more by entrepreneurial rewards than by an "escapist" mind set. Indeed, there is often a mixture of positive and negative considerations in this regard. Nevertheless, this characterization of some entrepreneurs as "refugees" does help clarify some important considerations involved in much entrepreneurial activity.

The "Foreign Refugee." There are many individuals who escape the political, religious, or economic constraints of their homelands by crossing national boundaries. Frequently such individuals face discrimination or handicaps in seeking salaried employment in the new country. As a result, many of them go into business for themselves.

foreign refugee
a person who leaves his or her native country and later becomes an entrepreneur

SMALL BUSINESS IN ACTION

"Foreign Refugee" to Entrepreneur

Immigrants who start new businesses are the "foreign refugees" who find a better life through their entrepreneurial endeavors. One such foreign refugee is Tuan Huynh, who was once a captain in the South Vietnamese army. Following the war in Vietnam and three years in a "re-indoctrination" camp, Huynh was reunited with his family and subsequently escaped with them, first to Indonesia and then, in 1980, to Dallas, Texas. In Dallas, Huynh found work as an auto mechanic, and his wife sewed at home for Dallas apparel manufacturers.

After five years, the family had saved $50,000 and was ready to launch a business named H&A Fashions. In just five years, this business had grown to the point that it employed 120 people and projected profits of nearly $1 million on sales of $35 million! Their customers included Sears Roebuck, Wal-Mart, and J C Penney. The spectacular success of this firm is a tribute to the remarkable entrepreneurial spirit and effort of one foreign refugee.

Source: "Surviving and Thriving," *Nation's Business*, Vol. 78, No. 3, p. 18. Reprinted by permission, *Nation's Business,* March 1990. Copyright 1990, U.S. Chamber of Commerce.

corporate refugee
a person who leaves big business to go into business for him- or herself

The "Corporate Refugee." Individuals who flee the bureaucratic environment of big business (or even medium-size business) by going into business for themselves are identified by Professor Knight as **corporate refugees.** Employees of large corporations often find the atmosphere, decisions, or relocations required by their jobs to be undesirable. Entrepreneurship provides an attractive alternative for many such individuals.

When IBM, in 1988, announced the transfer of IBM manufacturing from Boca Raton, Florida, to Raleigh, North Carolina, they offered either jobs at other locations or substantial sums of money to those who elected to resign or retire.[16] A number chose the latter option rather than following the corporate path of relocation, and they used the money to start businesses of their own. One of them, Don Bigando, opened an outlet serving "Texas Hot Weiners." Another, Gene Jones, turned his lifetime photography hobby into a business by opening a photography shop. A third employee, Bruce Dent, started a management consulting and training firm. These individuals avoided the disruption to personal life required by corporate transfers to new locations and, instead, became corporate refugees.

Other "Refugees."   Other types of "refugees" mentioned by Professor Knight are the following:

1. The **parental (paternal) refugee** who leaves a family business to show the parent that "I can do it alone."
2. The **feminist refugee** who experiences discrimination and elects to start a firm in which she can operate independently of male chauvinists.
3. The **housewife refugee** who starts her own business after her family is grown or at some other point when she can free herself from household responsibilities.
4. The **society refugee** who senses some alienation from the prevailing culture and expresses it by indulging in entrepreneurial activity—selling paintings to tourists or operating an energy-saving business.
5. The **educational refugee** who tires of an academic program and decides to go into business.

READINESS FOR ENTREPRENEURSHIP

Many people think about getting into business for themselves but are waiting for the right opportunity to come along. Others become so well established in careers that they tend to get "locked into" salaried employment.

Age and Entrepreneurial Opportunity

Education and experience are a part of the necessary preparation for most entrepreneurs. Although requirements vary with the nature and demands of a particular business, some type of "knowhow" is required. In addition, prospective entrepreneurs must build their financial resources in order to make initial investments.

Even though there are no hard and fast rules concerning the right age for starting a business, some age deterrents exist. As Figure 1-7 shows, young people are discouraged from entering entrepreneurial careers by inadequacies in preparation and resources. On the other hand, older people develop family, financial, and job commitments that make entrepreneurship seem too risky. They acquire interests in retirement programs and achieve promotion to positions of greater responsibility and higher salaries.

The ideal time appears to lie somewhere between these two periods, perhaps from the late 20s to the early 40s, when there is a balance between preparatory experiences on the one hand and family obligations on the other.

parental (paternal) refugee
a person who leaves a family business to prove his or her own entrepreneurial capabilities

feminist refugee
a woman who starts a firm in order to operate independently of male chauvinists

society refugee
a person who chooses to operate a business to escape societal expectations

housewife refugee
a woman who frees herself from household duties in order to start her own business

educational refugee
a person who tires of an academic program and decides to go into business

Figure 1-7
Age Concerns in
Starting a Business

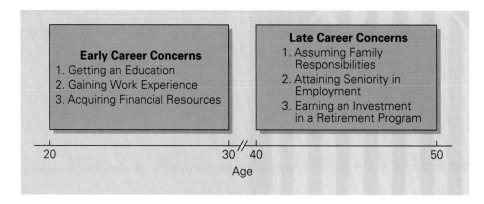

Obviously, there are exceptions to this generalization. Some teenagers start their own firms. And other persons, even at 50 or 60 years of age, walk away from successful careers in big business when they become excited by the prospects of entrepreneurship.

Precipitating Events

precipitating events
events, such as losing a job, which move individuals to become entrepreneurs

Many potential entrepreneurs never take the fateful step of launching their own business ventures. Some of those who actually make the move are stimulated by **precipitating events** such as job termination, job dissatisfaction, or unexpected opportunities.

Loss of a job, for example, caused Mary Anne Jackson to start her own business in Deerfield, Illinois.[17] Jackson was director of business and operations planning for Swift-Eckrich, a division of Beatrice Foods, until a leveraged buyout put her back in the job market in 1986. Well educated, with a bachelor's degree in accounting and a master's in business administration, she soon received attractive job offers. However, she decided instead to strike out on her own by producing nutritious meals in vacuum-sealed plastic pouches for children 2 to 10 years old. By 1991, the product was selling in a number of states, and sales were expected to reach $5 million. The loss of a corporate job had triggered her entry into a personally owned business.

Losing a job is only one of many types of experiences that may serve as a catalyst to "taking the plunge" as an entrepreneur. Some individuals become so disenchanted with formal academic programs that they simply walk away from the classroom and start new lives as entrepreneurs. Others become exasperated with the rebuffs or perceived injustices at the hands of superiors in large organizations and leave in disgust to start their own businesses.

In a more positive vein, prospective entrepreneurs may unexpectedly stumble across business opportunities. A friend may offer, for example, to sponsor an individual as an Amway distributor. Or a relative may suggest that the individual leave a salaried position and take over a family business.

Many prospective entrepreneurs, of course, simply plan for and seek out independent business opportunities. There is little in the way of a precipitating event involved in their decision to become entrepreneurs. We cannot say what proportion of new entrepreneurs make their move because of some particular event. However, many who launch new firms or otherwise go into business for themselves are obviously helped along by precipitating events.

Preparation for Entrepreneurial Careers

Proper preparation for entrepreneurship requires some mixture of education and experience. How much or what kind of each is necessary is notoriously difficult to specify. Different types of ventures call for different types of preparation. The background or skills needed to start a company to produce computer software are obviously different from those needed to open an automobile garage. There are also striking differences in the backgrounds of those who succeed in the same industry. For these reasons, we must be cautious in discussing qualifications, realizing there are exceptions to every rule.

Some fascinating entrepreneurial success stories feature individuals who dropped out of school to start their ventures. This should not lead one to conclude, however, that education is generally unimportant. As shown in Figure 1-8, the formal education of new owners is superior to that of the general adult

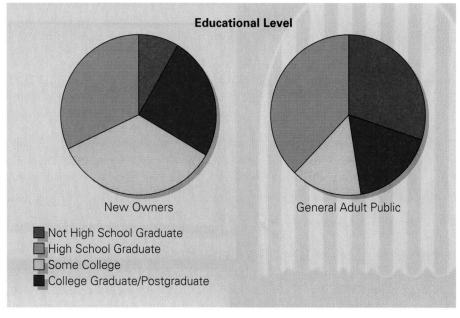

Figure 1-8
Education of New Business Owners and the Public

Source: Data developed and provided by the NFIB Foundation and sponsored by the American Express Travel Related Service Company, Inc.

public. This suggests that one should not expect success based on a substandard education.

In recent years, colleges and universities have greatly expanded their offerings in entrepreneurship and small business. The Wharton School was the first to offer a degree in entrepreneurship (in 1973).[18] Now thousands of students across the country are taking how-to-start-your-own-business courses. The usefulness of such courses is debated, some holding that entrepreneurs are born and not made or that early childhood influences are more important than education. Those who offer entrepreneurship courses believe that small-business education can contribute positively even though it will not be perfectly correlated with success.

What do business owners themselves perceive to be the contributors to success in small business? A study by A. B. Ibrahim and J. R. Goodwin identified three general factors that business owners regarded as important.[19] These factors were as follows:

1. *Entrepreneurial values* (including intuition, extroversion, risk taking, creativity, flexibility, a sense of independence, and a high value of time).
2. *Managerial skills* (including a niche strategy, effective management of cash flow, a simple but efficient budgetary system, pre-ownership experience, education, and a simple organization structure).
3. *Interpersonal skills* (including a good relationship with a credit officer or banker, good customer relations, and good employee relations).

Even though it is not possible to delineate educational and experiential requirements with great precision, we urge prospective entrepreneurs to maximize their preparation within the limits of their time and resources. At best, however, such preparation can never completely prepare one for the world of business ownership. Warren Buffett, the noted investor, has expressed it in this way: "Could you really explain to a fish what it's like to walk on land? One day on land is worth a thousand years of talking about it, and one day running a business has exactly the same kind of value."[20]

The message seems to be this: Get as much relevant education and experience as you can, but realize that you will still need a lot of on-the-job entrepreneurial training.

KINDS OF ENTREPRENEURSHIP

The field of small business encompasses a great variety of entrepreneurs and entrepreneurial ventures. This section examines this spectrum of entrepreneurship by identifying the varied types of people and firms that exist.

Women Entrepreneurs

The number of women becoming entrepreneurs has risen dramatically during the last two decades. Between 1982 and 1987, the number of women-owned businesses increased by 57.4 percent, with receipts of these businesses rising by 81.2 percent.[21] A study by economist David Birch, released in 1992, reported that women owned 28 percent of the businesses in the United States and that they employed 10 percent of the country's workers.[22] Women's business ownership has been expanding much more rapidly than men's business ownership, but women are expanding from a smaller base of ownership.

Women are not only starting more businesses than previously, but they are also starting businesses in nontraditional industries and starting them with ambitious plans for growth and profit. Not too many years ago, women entrepreneurs confined themselves, for the most part, to operating beauty shops, small clothing stores, or other establishments catering especially to women. Even though most women's business starts are still in services, women's ownership of construction firms rose by nearly 60 percent and their ownership of manufacturing firms more than doubled between 1982 and 1987.[23]

As one example of a woman entrepreneur in a nontraditional area, Carolyn Stradley runs an asphalt paving company, C&S Paving, in Atlanta, Georgia.[24] She started the business in 1979 with three employees, a pickup truck, and rented tools. By 1992, the staff of three had grown to as many as 32, depending on the season, and the firm grossed an estimated $3 million annually.

Women entrepreneurs obviously face problems common to all entrepreneurs. However, they must also contend with difficulties associated with their newness in entrepreneurial roles. Lack of access to credit has been a problem frequently cited by women who enter business. This is a troublesome area for

Figure 1-9
The Number of Women-Owned Businesses Is Expanding Rapidly

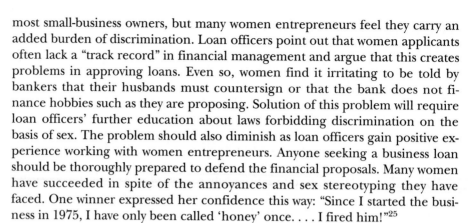

most small-business owners, but many women entrepreneurs feel they carry an added burden of discrimination. Loan officers point out that women applicants often lack a "track record" in financial management and argue that this creates problems in approving loans. Even so, women find it irritating to be told by bankers that their husbands must countersign or that the bank does not finance hobbies such as they are proposing. Solution of this problem will require loan officers' further education about laws forbidding discrimination on the basis of sex. The problem should also diminish as loan officers gain positive experience working with women entrepreneurs. Anyone seeking a business loan should be thoroughly prepared to defend the financial proposals. Many women have succeeded in spite of the annoyances and sex stereotyping they have faced. One winner expressed her confidence this way: "Since I started the business in 1975, I have only been called 'honey' once. . . . I fired him!"[25]

Another barrier for some women is the limited opportunity they find for business relationships with others in similar positions. It takes time and effort for them to gain full acceptance and to develop informal relationships with others in local, mostly male, business and professional groups. Women are attacking this problem by increasing their participation in predominantly male organizations and also by forming networks of their own—a female equivalent of the "old boy network."

Founders and Other Entrepreneurs

Although categories tend to overlap, entrepreneurial leadership may be classified into three types: founders, general managers, and franchisees.

Founding Entrepreneurs. Generally considered to be the "pure" entrepreneurs, **founders** may be inventors who initiate businesses on the basis of new or improved products or services. They may also be artisans who develop skills and then start their own firms. Or they may be enterprising individuals, often with marketing backgrounds, who draw upon the ideas of others in starting new firms. Whether acting as individuals or in groups, these people bring firms into existence by surveying the market, raising funds, and arranging for the necessary facilities. After the firm is launched, the founding entrepreneur may preside over the subsequent growth of the business or sell out and move on to other ventures.

founders
entrepreneurs who bring new firms into existence

General Managers. As new firms become well established, founders become less innovators and more administrators. Thus, we recognize another class of entrepreneurs called **general managers.** General managers preside over the operation of successful ongoing business firms. They manage the week-to-week and month-to-month production, marketing, and financial functions of small firms. The distinction between founders and general managers is often hazy. In some cases, small firms grow rapidly, and their orientation is more akin

general managers
entrepreneurs who function as administrators of their businesses

to the founding than to the management process. Nevertheless, it is helpful to distinguish those entrepreneurs who found and substantially change firms (the "movers and shakers") from those who direct the continuing operations of established firms.

Franchisees. It is helpful to recognize a third category of entrepreneurs—that of franchisees. **Franchisees** differ from general managers in the degree of their independence. Because of the constraints and guidance provided by contractual relationships with franchising organizations, franchisees function as limited entrepreneurs. Chapter 5 presents more information about franchisees.

> **franchisee**
> an entrepreneur whose power is limited by a contractual relationship with a franchising organization

High-Growth and Low-Growth Firms

Small-business ventures differ greatly in their potential for growth and profits. Some create millionaires, while others produce less spectacular results. To account for these differences, we may distinguish firms according to the following categories: marginal firms, attractive small companies, and high-potential ventures. In thinking about small business, one can easily fall into the trap of considering only one end of the spectrum. Some writers treat only the tiny, marginal firms whose owners barely survive, while others focus entirely on high-growth, high-technology firms. A balanced view must recognize the entire range of ventures with the varied problems and rewards presented by each point on the spectrum.

Marginal Firms. Very small dry cleaners, independent garages, beauty shops, service stations, appliance repair shops, and other small firms that provide very modest returns to their owners are **marginal firms.** We do not call them "marginal" because they are in danger of bankruptcy. Some marginal firms, it is true, are on "thin ice" financially, but the distinguishing feature is their limited ability to generate significant profits. Entrepreneurs devote personal effort to such ventures and receive a profit return that does little more than compensate them for their time. Part-time businesses typically fall into this category of marginal firms.

> **marginal firm**
> any small firm that provides insignificant profits to its owner(s)

Attractive Small Companies. In contrast to marginal firms, numerous **attractive small firms** offer substantial rewards to their owners. Entrepreneurial income from these ventures may easily range from $50,000 to $200,000 annually. These are the strong segment of small business—the "good" firms that can provide rewarding careers.

> **attractive small firm**
> any small firm that provides substantial profits to its owner(s)

High-Potential Ventures. A few firms have such great prospects for growth that they may be called **high-potential ventures.** Frequently these are also high-technology ventures. At the time of the firm's founding, the owners often anticipate rapid growth, a possible merger, or "going public" within a few

> **high-potential venture**
> a firm that has great prospects for growth

years. Some of the more spectacular examples within recent years include Microsoft, Wal-Mart, McDonald's, and Toys 'R' Us. In addition to such widely recognized successes, there are at any time thousands of less-well-known ventures being launched and experiencing rapid growth. Entrepreneurial ventures of this type appeal to many engineers, professional managers, and venture capitalists who see the potential rewards and exciting prospects.

Artisan Entrepreneurs and Opportunistic Entrepreneurs

Perhaps because of their varied backgrounds, entrepreneurs display great variation in their styles of doing business. They analyze problems and approach decision making in drastically different ways. Norman R. Smith has suggested two basic entrepreneurial patterns: artisan entrepreneurs and opportunistic entrepreneurs.[26]

artisan entrepreneur
a person who starts a business with primarily technical skills, and little business knowledge

The Artisan Entrepreneur. According to Smith, the education of the **artisan entrepreneur** is limited to technical training. Such entrepreneurs have technical job experience, but they lack good communication skills. Their approach to business decision making is characterized by the following features:

Figure 1-10
This Neon Sign Maker Exemplifies the Artisan Entrepreneur

1. They are paternalistic. (This means they direct their businesses much as they might direct their own families.)
2. They are reluctant to delegate authority.
3. They use few (one or two) capital sources to create their firms.
4. They define marketing strategy in terms of the traditional price, quality, and company reputation.
5. Their sales efforts are primarily personal.
6. Their time orientation is short, with little planning for future growth or change.

The mechanic who starts an independent garage and the beautician who operates a beauty shop illustrate the artisan entrepreneur.

The Opportunistic Entrepreneur. Smith's definition of the **opportunistic entrepreneur** is one who has supplemented technical education by studying such nontechnical subjects as economics, law, or English. Opportunistic entrepreneurs avoid paternalism, delegate authority as necessary for growth, employ various marketing strategies and types of sales efforts, obtain original capitalization from more than two sources, and plan for future growth. An example of the opportunistic entrepreneur is the small building contractor and developer who uses a relatively sophisticated approach to management. Because of the complexity of the industry, successful contractors use careful record keeping, proper budgeting, precise bidding, and systematic marketing research.

opportunistic entrepreneur
an entrepreneur who enters business with both sophisticated managerial skills and technical knowledge

In Smith's model of entrepreneurial styles, we see two extremes of managerial approach. At one end, we find an artisan in an entrepreneurial position. At the other end, we find a well-educated and experienced manager. The former "flies by the seat of the pants," and the latter uses systematic management procedures and something resembling a scientific management approach. In practice, of course, the distribution of entrepreneurial styles is less polarized than suggested by the model, with entrepreneurs scattered along a continuum in terms of their managerial sophistication. This book is intended to help you move toward the opportunistic end and away from the artisan end of the continuum.

Entrepreneurial Teams

In the discussion thus far, we have assumed that entrepreneurs are individuals. And, of course, this is usually the case. However, the entrepreneurial team is another possibility that is becoming popular, particularly in ventures of substantial size. An **entrepreneurial team** is formed by bringing together two or more individuals to function in the capacity of entrepreneurs.

entrepreneurial team
two or more people who work together as entrepreneurs

By forming a team, founders can secure a broader range of managerial talents than is otherwise possible. For example, a person with manufacturing experience can team up with a person who has marketing experience. The need for such diversified experience is particularly acute in creating new high-technology businesses.

One study of 890 company founders found that 39.1 percent had one or more full-time partners.[27] Even though the study underrepresented very small firms, it does suggest that founding teams are not unusual.

LOOKING BACK

1. Entrepreneurial opportunities are unlimited, as evidenced by various dramatic success stories of successful entrepreneurs.
2. Entrepreneurial rewards include profits, independence, and a satisfying way of life.
3. Individuals who become entrepreneurs have a high need for achievement, a willingness to take moderate risks, and a high degree of self-confidence.
4. The period between a person's late 20s and early 40s is the period in which entry into entrepreneurial careers tends to be easiest. Although individuals prepare for entrepreneurship by gaining education and experience, their entry into business is often triggered by precipitating events such as losing a job.
5. Entrepreneurship includes various kinds of entrepreneurs (women entrepreneurs, founding entrepreneurs, general manager entrepreneurs, franchisees, artisan entrepreneurs, opportunistic entrepreneurs, and entrepreneurial teams) and various kinds of ventures (marginal firms, attractive small firms, and high-potential ventures).

DISCUSSION QUESTIONS

1. What is meant by the term *entrepreneur*?
2. When we read the outstanding success stories at the beginning of the chapter, we realize they are exceptions to the rule. What, then, is their significance in illustrating entrepreneurial opportunity? Are these stories misleading?
3. Some corporate executives receive annual compensation in excess of $3 million. Profits of most small businesses are much less. How, then, can profits constitute a meaningful incentive for entrepreneurs?
4. What is the most significant reason for following an independent business career by the entrepreneur whom you know best?
5. The rewards of profit, independence, and a satisfying way of life attract individuals to entrepreneurial careers. What problems might be anticipated if an entrepreneur were to become obsessed with one of these rewards, that is, have an excessive desire for profit or independence or a satisfying way of life?
6. In view of the fact that entrepreneurs must satisfy customers, employees, bankers, and others, are they really independent? Explain the nature of their independence as a reward for self-employment.
7. What is shown by the studies of David C. McClelland regarding an entrepreneur's need for achievement?

8. Explain the internal locus of control and its significance for entrepreneurship.
9. On the basis of your own knowledge, can you identify a "foreign refugee" who is an entrepreneur?
10. What are the societal implications of the growth trend in women's entrepreneurship?
11. Why is the period from the late 20s to the early 40s in a person's life considered to be the best time for becoming an entrepreneur?
12. What is a precipitating event? Give some examples.
13. What is the difference between a marginal firm and a high-potential venture?
14. Distinguish between an artisan entrepreneur and an opportunistic entrepreneur.
15. What is the advantage of using an entrepreneurial team?

YOU MAKE THE CALL

Situation 1

Following is a statement of an entrepreneur in which he attempts to explain and justify his orientation toward slow growth in his business:

I limit my growth pace and make every effort to service my present customers in the manner they deserve. I have some peer pressure to do otherwise by following the advice of experts—that is, to take on partners and debt to facilitate rapid growth in sales and market share. When tempted by such thoughts, I think about what I might gain. Perhaps I could make more money, but I would also expect a lot more problems. Also, I think it might interfere somewhat with my family relationships, which are very important to me.

Questions
1. Should this venture be regarded as entrepreneurial? Is the owner a true entrepreneur?
2. Do you admire or dislike the philosophy expressed here? Is the owner really doing what is best for his family?
3. What kinds of problems is this owner avoiding?

Situation 2

When Amy Clark was growing up, her father had owned several service stations where she learned to pump gas and developed some knowledge of station operation. When she graduated from high school, Amy entered business college and trained to be a secretary. She married soon after school, and her husband also entered the service station business. Amy has decided she would like to operate a station of her own. A station with three service bays and facilities for minor auto repair is available if she can persuade the oil company—the same company that franchises her husband's station—that she is qualified to have a franchise.

Clark has expressed her philosophy as follows: "I'm a person who likes to get things done. I like to keep excelling and do bigger and better things than I've ever done before. I guess that's why I'd like to have a station of my own."

Questions
1. Evaluate Amy Clark's qualifications for the proposed venture. Should the oil company accept her as a dealer?
2. As a woman entrepreneur, what problems may she anticipate in relationships with customers, employees, the sponsoring oil company, and her family?

EXPERIENTIAL EXERCISES

1. Analyze your own education and experience as qualifications for entrepreneurship. Identify your greatest strengths and weaknesses.
2. Explain your own interest in each entrepreneurial reward—profit, independence, satisfying way of life, or other. Point out which of these is most significant for you personally and tell why.
3. Interview one entrepreneur who has started a business, asking for information regarding that entrepreneur's background and age at the time the business was started. In the report of your interview, show whether the entrepreneur was in any sense a "refugee" and how the timing of the startup related to the "ideal" time explained in this chapter.
4. Interview a female entrepreneur and report on what problems, if any, she has encountered because she is a woman.

REFERENCES TO SMALL-BUSINESS PRACTICES

Barrier, Michael, "What Does a Smell Look Like?" *Nation's Business,* Vol. 79, No. 3 (March 1991), pp. 57–59.
    This article tells the story of two women who started a flourishing business in a small town in Arkansas.
Brokaw, Leslie, "The Founders," *Inc.,* Vol. 13, No. 12 (December 1991), pp. 116–119.
    A number of founders of highly successful firms respond to a question about what made them start their businesses.
Buchalter, Gail, "The Nonconformist," *Forbes,* Vol. 148, No. 10 (October 28, 1991), p. 200.
    An entrepreneur with a strong sense of individualism first opened a commodities trading firm and later took over a bankrupt company with a good product and made the firm successful.
"Two Women Who Combine Old Values with New Dreams," *Nation's Business,* Vol. 78, No. 6 (June 1990), pp. 13–15.
    An entrepreneurial team was formed by two women in Seattle, Washington, to manufacture distinctive merchandise. One of the principals is a product designer, and the other handles the business side.

ENDNOTES

1. For an extended discussion of the nature of entrepreneurship, see William B. Gartner, "What Are We Talking About When We Talk About Entrepreneurship?" *Journal of Business Venturing,* Vol. 5, No. 1 (January 1990), pp. 15–28; also see Justin G. Longenecker and John E. Schoen, "The Essence of Entrepreneurship," *Journal of Small Business Management,* Vol. 13 (July 1975), pp. 26–32.

2. Toddi Gutner, "Nostalgia Sells," *Forbes*, Vol. 149, No. 9 (April 27, 1992), pp. 102–103. Adapted from FORBES magazine by permission. © Forbes Inc. 1992.

3. The account given here is drawn from a number of sources. For a report on the expansion of the business internationally, see "Vindicated," *Forbes*, Vol. 148, No. 13 (December 9, 1991), pp. 198–202. For an account of the founding of the firm, see "Frederick W. Smith of Federal Express: He Didn't Get There Overnight," *Inc.*, Vol. 6, No. 4 (April 1984), pp. 88–89.

4. The account of Proctor and Gardner Advertising is taken from a telephone conversation with a company official in 1992; *Standard Directory of Advertising Agencies (1991);* and Jill Bettner and Christine Donahue, "Now They're Not Laughing," *Forbes*, Vol. 132, No. 12 (November 21, 1983), p. 124.

5. "Red McCombs: Making Money's Fun," *Forbes*, Vol. 126 (September 15, 1980), p. 124.

6. "Poll: Most Like Being Own Boss," *USA Today* (May 6, 1991). For a scholarly study confirming the importance of a quest for independence as a motivational factor, see Marco Virarelli: "The Birth of New Enterprises," *Small Business Economics,* Vol. 3, No. 3 (September 1991), pp. 215–223.

7. "Two-Timer: The Once and Future CEO," *Inc.*, Vol. 8, No. 5 (May 1986), pp. 58–60.

8. Larry Mahar, "A Second Career for the Fun of It," *Nation's Business*, Vol. 79, No. 1, p. 10. Reprinted by permission, *Nation's Business*, January 1991. Copyright 1991, U.S. Chamber of Commerce.

9. For a review of this topic, see Robert H. Brockhaus, Sr., and Pamela S. Horwitz, "The Psychology of the Entrepreneur," in Donald L. Sexton and Raymond W. Smilor (eds.), *The Art and Science of Entrepreneurship* (Cambridge: Ballinger Publishing Company, 1986), pp. 25–48; and Peter B. Robinson, David B. Stimpson, Jonathan C. Huefner, and H. Keith Hunt, "An Attitude Approach to the Prediction of Entrepreneurship," *Entrepreneurship Theory and Practice,* Vol. 15, No. 4 (Summer 1991), pp. 13–31.

10. David C. McClelland, *The Achieving Society* (New York: The Free Press, 1961). Also see David C. McClelland and David G. Winter, *Motivating Economic Achievement* (New York: The Free Press, 1969) and Bradley R. Johnson, "Toward a Multidimensional Model of Entrepreneurship: The Case of Achievement Motivation and the Entrepreneur," *Entrepreneurship Theory and Practice*, Vol. 14, No. 3 (Spring 1990), pp. 39–54.

11. Robert H. Rockhaus, Sr., and Pamela S. Horwitz, *op. cit.*, p. 27.

12. David C. McClelland, *The Achieving Society*, Chapter 6.

13. See Robert H. Brockhaus, Sr., and Pamela S. Horwitz, *op. cit.*; and Rita Gunther McGrath, Ian C. MacMillan, and Sari Scheinberg, "Elitists, Risk-Takers, and Rugged Individualists? An Exploratory Analysis of Cultural Differences between Entrepreneurs and Non-Entrepreneurs," *Journal of Business Venturing*, Vol. 7, No. 2 (March 1992), pp. 115–135.

14. J. B. Rotter, "Generalized Expectancies for Internal Versus External Control of Reinforcement," *Psychological Monographs*, 1966a. A more recent review is given in Robert H. Brockhaus, Sr., and Pamela S. Horwitz, *op. cit.*, pp. 25–48.

15. Russell M. Knight, "Entrepreneurship in Canada," a paper presented at the Annual Conference of the International Council for Small Business, Asilomar, CA, June 22–25, 1980.

16. Leigh Hunt, "Middle Managers Take Off on Their Own," *In Business*, Vol. 11, No. 2 (March/April 1989), pp. 36–38.

17. Bob Weinstein, "Mom Knows Best," *Entrepreneurial Woman*, Vol. 2, No. 4 (May 1991), pp. 46–49.

18. "The Three Rs," *Venture*, Vol. 10, No. 6 (June 1988), pp. 55–56.

19. A. B. Ibrahim and J. R. Goodwin, "Perceived Causes of Success in Small Business," *American Journal of Small Business*, Vol. 11, No. 2 (Fall 1986), pp. 41–50.

20. "Your Toes Know," *In Business*, Vol. 10, No. 3 (May–June 1988), p. 6.

21. *The State of Small Business: A Report of the President 1991* (Washington: U.S. Government Printing Office, 1991), p. 250.

22. "Women Entrepreneurs: 'A Pretty Big Game,'" *Nation's Business*, Vol. 80, No. 8 (August 1992), p. 53.

23. *The State of Small Business*, p. 253.

24. "Street Wise," *Entrepreneur*, Vol. 20, No. 1 (January 1992), pp. 308–313.

25. Robert D. Hisrich and Candida G. Brush, *The Woman Entrepreneur* (Lexington, MA: Lexington Books, 1986), p. 18.

26. Norman R. Smith, *The Entrepreneur and His Firm: The Relationship Between Type of Man and Type of Company* (East Lansing: Bureau of Business and Economic Research, Michigan State University, 1967). Also see Norman R. Smith and John B. Miner, "Type of Entrepreneur, Type of Firm, and Managerial Motivation: Implications for Organizationl Life Cycle Theory," *Strategic Management Journal,* Vol. 4, No. 4 (October–December 1983), pp. 325–340; and Carolyn Y. Woo, Arnold C. Cooper, and William C. Dunkelberg, "The Development and Interpretation of Entrepreneurial Typologies," *Journal of Business Venturing,* Vol. 6, No. 2 (March 1991), pp. 93–114.

27. Arnold C. Cooper and William C. Dunkelberg, "Influences upon Entrepreneurship—A Large-Scale Study," paper presented to Academy of Management, San Diego, CA, August 4, 1981.

CHAPTER 2

Small Business: Vital Component of the Economy

SPOTLIGHT ON SMALL BUSINESS

Aggressive small firms can still compete effectively with large corporations, even in declining industries. The Butterick Company, founded in 1863, is an example of just such a competitive firm in the clothing pattern business, a declining industry. More than a century after its founding, Butterick languished as an obscure division of American Can Company. In 1983, two of the divisional managers, John Lehmann and William P. Wilson (who later retired) bought the business from American Can for $12.5 million, all but $500,000 of it borrowed money. Butterick once again became an independently owned business.

John Lehmann, Butterick CEO

The new owners immediately began to make changes in Butterick's operation. They slashed inventory and cut out workers. They consolidated five printing and distribution plants into a single plant. Speaking of the difference between the new operation and that of the former corporate owners, Lehmann said, "We were more careful about how we spent our own money than about how we spent theirs." The new owners invested in computerized design systems, stepped up promotion, and diversified into the greeting card business.

The surge of entrepreneurship put new life into the business. Butterick's market share climbed from 22 percent to 28 percent. The $12-million loan was paid off in two years. Just five years after purchase of the business, the company was valued at more than ten times its purchase price—a tribute to the competitive effectiveness of its new, independent owners!

Source: Jean Sherman Chatzky, "Reaping from Sewing," *Forbes*, Vol. 149, No. 11 (May 25, 1992), pp. 154–156. Adapted from FORBES magazine by permission. © Forbes Inc. 1992.

After studying this chapter, you should be able to:
1. Define small business and identify five criteria that may be used to measure the size of businesses.
2. Compare the importance of small business in the eight major industries.
3. Evaluate the trend in small-business activity.
4. Identify five special contributions of small business to society.
5. Discuss possible causes of business failure and evaluate the record of small-business failure.

size criteria	economic competition	failure rate
SBA standards	distribution function	Dun & Bradstreet
major industries	supply function	

It is easy to overestimate the importance of big business because of its high visibility. Small businesses seem dwarfed by such corporate giants as General Motors (756,000 employees), Citicorp ($146 billion in deposits), Prudential of America ($821 billion worth of insurance in force), and Exxon (over $5 billion of annual profits). Yet small firms, even though less conspicuous, are a vital component of our economy. In this chapter, we examine not only the extent of small-business activity but also the unique contributions of small businesses that help preserve our economic well-being. But first, we need to look at the criteria used to define small business.

DEFINITION OF SMALL BUSINESS

Specifying any size standard to define small business is necessarily arbitrary because people adopt different standards for different purposes. Legislators, for example, may exclude small firms from certain regulations and specify 10 employees as the cutoff point. Moreover, a business may be described as "small" when compared to larger firms, but "large" when compared to smaller ones. Most people, for example, would classify independently owned gasoline stations, neighborhood restaurants, and locally owned retail stores as small businesses. Similarly, most would agree that the major automobile manufacturers are big businesses. And firms of in-between sizes would be classified as large or small on the basis of individual viewpoints.

size criteria
criteria by which the size of a business is measured

Size Criteria

Even the criteria used to measure the size of businesses vary. Some criteria are applicable to all industrial areas, while others are relevant only to certain types of business. Examples of criteria used to measure size are:

1   Number of employees.
2. Volume of sales.
3. Value of assets.
4. Insurance in force.
5. Volume of deposits.

Although the first criterion listed above—number of employees—is the most widely used yardstick, the best criterion in any given case depends upon the user's purpose.

SBA Standards

The Small Business Administration (SBA) establishes size standards that determine eligibility for SBA loans and for special consideration in bidding on government contracts. In 1984, the SBA issued a revised set of standards, some of which are stated in terms of number of employees and others of which are stated in terms of sales volume. Some of these standards are shown in Table 2-1. Size standards for most nonmanufacturing industries are now expressed in terms of annual receipts. As you can see, $3.5 million is a common upper limit in the service and retail areas in which small business is strong. In mining and manufacturing, however, the SBA classifies firms with fewer than 500 employees as small.

SBA standards
the standards, determined by the Small Business Administration (SBA), by which the size of a business is measured

Type of Business	Sales Dollars or Number of Employees
Advertising Agencies	$ 3.5 million
Copper Ores Mining	500 employees
Employment Agencies	$ 3.5 million
Furniture Stores	$ 3.5 million
General Contractors—Single-family Houses	$17.0 million
Insurance Agents, Brokers, and Service	$ 3.5 million
Metal Can Manufacturing	1,000 employees
Mobile Home Dealers	$ 6.5 million
Newspaper Publishing and Printing	500 employees
Poultry Dressing Plants	500 employees
Radio and Television Repair Shops	$ 3.5 million
Radio Broadcasting	$ 3.5 million

Table 2-1
Examples of SBA Size Standards

Source: "Standard Industrial Classification Codes and Size Standards," *Code of Federal Regulations,* Title 13, Section 121.601, 1992.

Size Standards Used in This Book

To provide a clearer image of the small firm discussed in this book, we suggest the following general criteria for defining a small business:

1. Financing of the business is supplied by one individual or a small group. Only in a rare case would the business have more than 15 or 20 owners.
2. Except for its marketing function, the firm's operations are geographically localized.
3. Compared to the biggest firms in the industry, the business is small.
4. The number of employees in the business is usually fewer than 100.

Obviously, some small firms fail to meet *all* of the above standards. For example, a small executive search firm—a firm that helps corporate clients recruit managers from other organizations—may operate in many sections of the country and thereby fail to meet the second criterion. Nevertheless, the discussion of management concepts in this book is aimed primarily at the type of firm that fits the general pattern just described.

SMALL BUSINESS AS PRODUCER OF GOODS AND SERVICES

In this section, our purpose is to understand the contribution made by small business as part of our total economic system. The following questions will be answered:

1. In which industries does small business make its greatest contribution?
2. What proportion of our total economic output comes from small business?

Small Business in the Major Industries

major industries
the eight largest
groups of businesses

Small firms operate in all industries, but they differ greatly in their nature and importance from industry to industry. In thinking about their economic contribution, therefore, we first need to identify the major industries (as classified by the U.S. Department of Commerce) and note the types of small firms that function in these industries. The eight **major industries** and examples of small firms in each are as follows:

1. *Wholesale Trade*
   Wholesale drug companies
   Petroleum bulk stations
2. *Construction*
   General building contractors
   Electrical contractors

3. *Retail Trade*
   Hardware stores
   Restaurants
4. *Services*
   Travel agencies
   Beauty shops
5. *Finance, Insurance, and Real Estate*
   Local insurance agencies
   Real estate brokerage firms
6. *Mining*
   Sand and gravel companies
   Coal mines
7. *Transportation and Public Utilities*
   Taxicab companies
   Local radio stations
8. *Manufacturing*
   Bakeries
   Machine shops

Number of Small Businesses

Widely divergent statements about the number of U.S. businesses appear in print. You may read of 4 million business units in one account and 20 million in another! Much of the confusion arises from varying definitions of what constitutes a business.

The large numbers are typically based on Internal Revenue Service data. An estimated 20 million business tax returns were filed in 1990.[1] Does this mean that 20 million businesses exist? It all depends on the definition used. Many, probably most, business tax returns report business activities of an owner who has no employees. In many such cases, furthermore, the business activities are merely part-time, seasonal, or one-time activities. A homemaker, for example, may give piano lessons to two or three neighborhood children and file a business tax return to report the income.

Rather than including all businesses submitting tax returns, we have included in Table 2-2 only those enterprises which the Small Business Administration has in its data base. This data base contains all large corporations, but, at the lower end, it includes only those businesses having one or more employees, thereby excluding some self-employed individuals who submit tax returns.

As you can see, the vast majority of the four million businesses are small. Ninety-eight percent have fewer than 100 employees. Based on the number of business units, therefore, small business is the most common form of enterprise in the U.S. economy. These figures give a distorted view of the relative importance of small business, however, because of the huge number of very small firms.

Table 2-2
Number of
Enterprises by
Enterprise Size and
Major Industry,
1988

Industry	Total	Employment Size of Enterprise	
		Less than 100	100 or More
U.S. Total	4,004,743	3,910,798	93,945
Agriculture	115,206	114,330	876
Mining	32,560	31,818	742
Construction	559,139	554,123	5,016
Manufacturing	371,148	347,860	23,288
Transportation, Communications, Public Utilities	145,879	141,316	4,563
Wholesale Trade	426,106	420,395	5,711
Retail Trade	1,067,298	1,053,170	14,128
Finance, Insurance, Real Estate	300,785	293,681	7,104
Services	986,622	954,105	32,517

Source: *The State of Small Business: A Report of the President Transmitted to the Congress 1991* (Washington: U.S. Government Printing Office, 1991), pp. 80–81.

Relative Economic Importance of Small Business

The fact that numerous small firms appear in each industry does not tell us much about their relative importance. Small firms might be merely a tiny fringe in some industries. Or they may be so numerous and productive that their collective output exceeds that of large firms. The question before us is

Figure 2-1
Small Businesses
Such as This
Pizzeria Contribute a
Great Deal to the
Economy

this: What percentage of the economy's total output of goods and services comes from small business?

One simple way to measure this is to compare the number of employees who work in small firms with the number of employees who work in large firms. We can do this for each industry and for the economy as a whole. Figure 2-2 presents such a comparison.

As you can see, the small-business share of total U.S. employment is 35.0 percent, based on the 100-employee criterion, with an additional 15.1 percent

Figure 2-2
Percentage of Employees in Small Firms

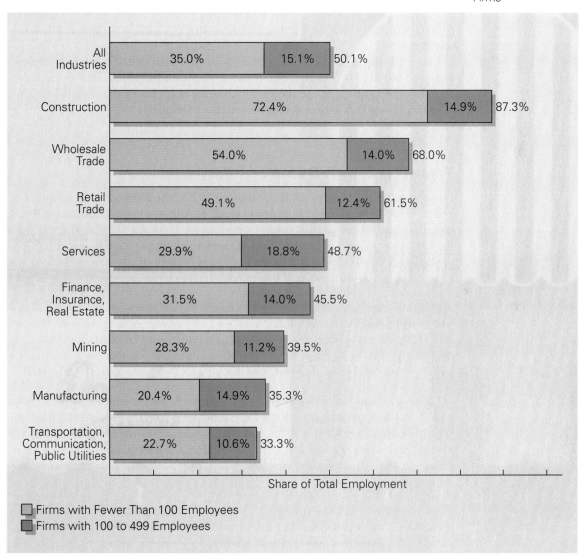

Source: *The State of Small Business: A Report of the President Transmitted to the Congress, 1991* (Washington: U.S. Government Printing Office, 1991), pp. 120–121.

added for firms with 100 to 499 employees, making a total of 50.1 percent based on the 500-employee criterion. Individual industries differ, naturally, from this overall average. In the construction industry, where small business is strongest, 87.3 percent of all employees work in firms with fewer than 500 employees. Assuming that all workers are equally productive, we can infer that 87.3 percent of that industry's output comes from small business.

In three of the industries portrayed in Figure 2-1, small business appears to be relatively more important than big business. These industries are construction, wholesale trade, and retail trade. In services and in finance, insurance, and real estate, small business is only slightly less important. In the other three industries, large business is clearly dominant. It is strongest in the transportation, communications, and public utilities category, with 66.7 percent of all employment.

For industry as a whole, as previously noted, firms with fewer than 500 employees account for 50.1 percent of the nation's employment and, presumably, the same percentage of the nation's output. It is apparent that much—roughly 50 percent—of U.S. business may be classified as small.

Trend in Small-Business Activity

For a number of decades prior to the mid-1970s, the share of total business accounted for by small firms had slowly eroded. Although small business still produced a major share of the nation's gross national product, it was gradually giving up some ground to big business. There is now evidence that small business is staging a comeback. Even popular business periodicals have observed the phenomenon, as seen in the following report from *The Economist*:

Despite ever-larger and noisier mergers, the biggest change coming over the world of business is that firms are getting smaller. The trend of a century is being reversed. Until the mid-1970s the size of firms everywhere grew; the numbers of self-employed fell . . . . No longer. Now it is the big firms that are shrinking and small ones that are on the rise. The trend is unmistakable—and businessmen and policymakers will ignore it at their peril.[2]

Research studies back up this contention. A major study by the International Institute for Labour Studies in Geneva, Switzerland, has examined the distribution of employment in the major industrial nations including the United States, Japan, and the United Kingdom.[3] This research revealed an increase in the share of total employment in small enterprises in these various countries.

What is remarkable about this finding is not that the recent growth in small unit employment shares has been enormous in all countries, but rather that the pattern of decline and then growth is so robust over such a wide sample of countries, sectors, size distributions, and institutions.[4]

Figure 2-3
New Technologies
Allow Businesses to
Produce More
Efficiently on a
Smaller Scale

Reasons for the more rapid growth of small firms are unclear. While we can only speculate at this point, factors such as those noted below may be contributing to this change.[5]

1. New technologies, such as numerically controlled machine tools, may permit efficient production on a smaller scale than formerly.
2. Greater flexibility is required as a result of increased global competition, a requirement that favors small firms.
3. Small firms may be more flexible in employing the increasing numbers of working mothers in the labor force.
4. Consumers may be coming to prefer personalized products over mass-produced goods, and this opens a door of opportunity for smaller business.

The resurgence of small business is also evident in the entrepreneurial boom in the United States. From 1950 to 1975, the number of new incorporations—a proxy for new business formation—merely kept pace with the growth of the economy. After 1975, however, the entrepreneurial pace picked up. In 1991, despite the recession, 630,000 companies incorporated—twice the rate of incorporations in 1975.[6] The spirit of entrepreneurship is obviously far from dead, and the effect has been to strengthen small business as a continuing, important part of the economy.

SPECIAL CONTRIBUTIONS OF SMALL BUSINESS

As part of the business community, small firms unquestionably contribute to our nation's economic welfare. They produce a substantial portion of our total goods and services. Thus, their general economic contribution is similar to that of big business. Small firms, however, possess some qualities that make them more than miniature versions of big business corporations. They make exceptional contributions as they provide new jobs, introduce innovations, stimulate competition, aid big business, and produce goods and services efficiently.

Providing New Jobs

Small businesses provide many of the job opportunities needed by a growing population and economy. In fact, it appears that small firms create the "lion's share" of new jobs, sometimes adding jobs while large corporations are "downsizing" and laying off employees. Between 1980 and 1986, firms with fewer than 20 employees accounted for more of the total job growth than did firms of 500 and more employees.[7]

The idea that small business generates more new jobs than big business originated in the research of David L. Birch in the early 1980s.[8] Even though this conclusion has been controversial, it has received support in some of the more recent research. Acs and Audretsch, for example, found that 1.3 million new jobs in manufacturing were created by small firms between 1976 and 1986, while the number of manufacturing jobs in large firms decreased by 100,000.[9] According to Acs and Audretsch, Birch's conclusion that the bulk of new jobs come from small enterprises has been largely substantiated.[10]

We should note that not all small firms grow at an even rate. Birch concludes that 12 to 15 percent of all small enterprises create most of the growth.

It is thus incorrect to speak of small enterprises as a uniformly expanding and active group. It is better to think of them as a large collection of seeds, a few of which sprout and become large plants. Their job-creating powers flow from the few, not the many.[11]

These firms continue to add jobs even as they grow out of their small-business size category. New jobs, therefore, come from the birth of new firms and their subsequent expansion. Also, some growth in employment comes from large corporations that expand and create additional jobs. The evidence presented here, however, reveals the special contribution of small business to job creation.

Introducing Innovation

New products that originate in the research laboratories of big business make a valuable contribution to our standard of living. There is a question, however, as to the relative importance of big business in achieving the truly significant innovations. The record shows that many scientific breakthroughs originated with independent inventors and small organizations. The following is a list of some twentieth-century examples of new products created by small firms:

Cat Box Filler: A Case of Nontechnical Innovation

Not all innovation is "high tech." Small firms often introduce into ordinary products practical improvements that appeal to purchasers of those products. One example is the development of cat box filler, a product that eliminates cats' biggest drawback as house pets. Some 27 million U.S. households own at least one cat, and many, if not most of them, have become users of this product.

Businesses are born under most unlikely circumstances. Forty years ago on a cold January day in Cassopolis, Michigan, Kay Draper's sandpile froze solid. As a result, she had to fill the cat's box with ashes, but the pet began tracking black smudges through the house. So Mrs. Draper scurried over to Ed Lowe for some sawdust. At 27, Lowe was just back from the war and struggling to keep his father's coal, ice, sawdust, and we-haul-anything business on its feet. In the trunk of his '43 Chevy coupe was some granulated dried mineral clay that he'd been trying, without much success, to sell to chicken farmers as nesting material.

"Try this," he said, pouring some of the absorbent clay in a paper bag and sending Mrs. Draper on her way. Soon she was back for more little bags. So were her friends. Lowe, tickled by the chance to make a few cents, decided to take a flier. He filled ten brown paper bags with clay, picked up a grease pencil, wrote two words on each bag, and took off down the road in his Chevy. Those words were KITTY LITTER.

Today Ed Lowe owns 13 homes (28 kitchens, and 19 fireplaces), 3,000 acres of land, an elegant yacht, a stable of quarter horses, and his own railroad. He also owns Edward Lowe Industries, the Indiana-based leader in the $350-million-a-year cat box filler industry. Sales of Lowe's Tidy Cat 3 and Kitty Litter brands were about $110 million last year. "This is a recession-proof business," he exults. "People will go without a lot of things before they'll go without their cats. And they're not going to have cats without litter."

In 1990, Edward Lowe Industries was sold to an entrepreneurial group led by Dan Good of Good Capital Company for $250 million.

1. Photocopiers
2. Insulin
3. Vacuum tube
4. Penicillin
5. Cottonpicker
6. Zipper
7. Automatic transmission
8. Jet engine
9. Helicopter
10. Power steering
11. Color film
12. Ball-point pen

It is interesting to note that research departments of big businesses tend to emphasize the improvement of existing products. In fact, it is quite likely that some ideas generated by personnel in big businesses are sidetracked because they are not related to existing products or because of their unusual nature. Unfortunately, preoccupation with an existing product can sometimes blind one to the value of a *new* idea. The jet engine, for example, had difficulty winning the attention of those who were accustomed to internal combustion engines.

Studies of innovation have shown the greater effectiveness of small firms in research and development. Figure 2-4, based on a study by Edwards and Gordon, shows that small firms are superior innovators in both increasing-employment and decreasing-employment industries. More recent research suggests that innovative activity tends to decrease as the level of concentration in an industry rises, thereby confirming the importance of small-firm innovation.[12]

Innovation contributes to productivity by providing better products and better methods of production. The millions of small firms that provide the centers of initiative and sources of innovation are thus in a position to help improve U.S. productivity.[13]

Figure 2-4
Innovations by
Employment Size of
Firm

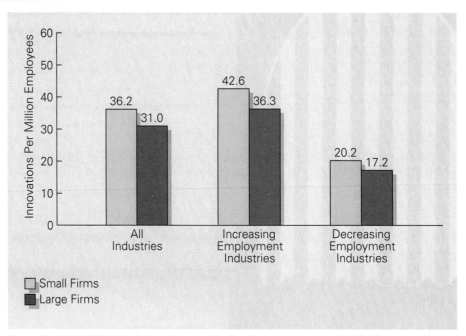

Source: *The State of Small Business: A Report of the President 1985* (Washington: U.S. Government Printing Office, 1985), p. 128; Keith L. Edwards and Theodore J. Gordon, "Characterization of Innovations Introduced on the U.S. Market in 1982" (Glastonbury, CT: Prepared for the U.S. Small Business Administration, Office of Advocacy, Under Award No. SBA-6050-OA-82, March 1984), p. 46.

Stimulating Economic Competition

Many economists, beginning with Adam Smith, have expounded the values inherent in **economic competition.** In a competitive business situation, individuals are driven by self-interest to act in a socially desirable manner. Competition acts as the regulator that transforms their selfishness into service.

economic competition
when businesses vie for sales

When producers consist of only a few big businesses, however, the customer is at their mercy. They may set high prices, withhold technological developments, exclude new competitors, or otherwise abuse their position of power. If competition is to have a "cutting edge," there is need for small firms.

The fall of Communist governments in Eastern Europe and the breakup of the USSR made possible a return to a competitive economic system there. Communism's economic system, lacking a free market and business competition, was a dismal failure. Scrapping that system of state-owned enterprise opened the way for independent business firms, many of them small firms, to compete and thereby to increase productivity and raise the standard of living.

Even China has taken steps to encourage the formation of small businesses as a means of stimulating economic growth. As China's leaders have in recent years introduced elements of capitalism, including privately owned businesses, the country has experienced a dramatic rise in living standards.[14] However, the Tienanmen Square massacre in 1989 and the severe restriction of human rights have slowed the country's movement toward a thoroughly competitive system.

Not every competitive effort of small firms is successful, but big business may be kept on its toes by small business. For example, a small jelly manufacturer, Sorrell Ridge of Port Reading, New Jersey, challenged giant Smucker's, whose commericals say, "With a name like Smucker's, it has to be good."[15] Tiny Sorrell Ridge introduced a line of no-sugar, all-natural fruit spreads and twitted its larger rival with its own commerical, "With a name like Smucker's, is it really so good? Sorrell Ridge—with 100% fruit, it has to be better." Smucker's soon introduced an all-fruit line of its own. Little companies like Sorrell Ridge keep larger companies like Smucker's keen.

However, there is no guarantee of competition in numbers alone. Many tiny firms may be no match for one large firm or for several firms that dominate an industry. Nevertheless, the existence of many healthy small businesses in an industry may be viewed as a desirable bulwark of the U.S. capitalistic system.

Aiding Big Business

The fact that some functions are more expertly performed by small business enables small firms to contribute to the success of larger ones. If small businesses were suddenly removed from the contemporary scene, big businesses would find themselves saddled with a myriad of activities that they could perform only inefficiently. Two functions that small business can often perform

Figure 2-5
Distribution of
Grocery Store
Produce Is One
Example of How
Small Business Can
Aid Larger
Companies

more efficiently than big business are the distribution function and the supply function.

distribution function
when small businesses link producers and customers

Distribution Function. Few large manufacturers find it desirable to own wholesale and retail outlets. Think, for example, of products like toiletries, books, lawnmowers, musical instruments, gasoline, food items, personal computers, office supplies, clothing, kitchen appliances, automobiles, tires, auto parts, furniture, and industrial supplies. Wholesale and retail establishments, many of them small, perform a valuable economic service by linking customers and producers of these products.

supply function
when small businesses act as suppliers and subcontractors for larger firms

Supply Function. Small businesses act as suppliers and subcontractors for large firms. Large firms recognize the growing importance of their suppliers by using terms like "partnership" and "strategic alliance" to describe the ideal working relationship. Japanese manufacturers have pioneered in developing strong relationships by working closely with trusted, long-term suppliers. To some extent, U.S. manufacturers are implementing this same approach, granting long-term contracts to suppliers in return for specified quality, lower prices, and cost-saving ideas.

In addition to supplying services directly to large corporations, small firms provide services to customers of big business. For example, they service automobiles, repair appliances, and clean carpets produced by large manufacturers.

Producing Goods and Services Efficiently

In considering the contributions of small business, we are concerned with an underlying question of small-business efficiency. Common sense tells us that the efficient size of business varies with the industry. We can easily recognize, for example, that big business is better in manufacturing automobiles but that small business is better in repairing them.

The continued existence of small business in a competitive economic system is in itself evidence of efficient small-business operation. If small firms were hopelessly inefficient and making no useful contribution, they would be forced out of business quickly by stronger competitors.

Although research has identified some cost advantages for small firms over big businesses, the economic evidence related to firm size and productivity is limited. The following summary points out some of the reasons for the relative strength of small business:

New contributions to the theory of business organization and operation suggest that small firms are less encumbered by the complex, multi-echelon decision-making structures that inhibit the flexibility and productivity of many large firms. Because the owners of small firms are often also their managers, small firms are less likely to be affected adversely by the separation of owners' interests from managerial control. Empirical evidence of small firm survival and productivity suggests that, where firm size is concerned, bigger is not necessarily better.[16]

Additional economic research will undoubtedly shed more light on the most effective combination of small and large businesses. In the meantime, we believe that small business contributes in a substantial way to the economic welfare of our society.

THE SMALL-BUSINESS FAILURE RECORD

A balanced view of small business in the economy requires us to consider also its darker side—that is, the record of business failure. While we wish to avoid pessimism, we must deal realistically with this matter.

Small-Business Failure Rate

Business failure data compiled by **Dun & Bradstreet, Inc.** have been used over the years to track the fortunes of business in general and small business in particular.[17] In general, the rate of failure has been low during periods of prosperity and high during economic recessions.

The frequent citation of failure data has tended to create an erroneous impression about the likelihood of failure.[18] In 1990, for example, 75 firms out of each 10,000 in Dun & Bradstreet's records (firms of all sizes) failed. This means

failure rate
the proportion of businesses that close with a loss to creditors

Dun & Bradstreet
a company that researches and publishes business information

SMALL BUSINESS IN ACTION

Efficient Operation by a Small Manufacturer

Small firms sometimes distinguish themselves by superior performance in highly competitive industries. One example is Fadal Engineering Company, a family-owned manufacturer of metalworking machines, whose performance has won the grudging admiration of large rivals in both the United States and Japan.

Compared with the machine tools catering to big manufacturers, Fadal's machine had fewer parts and simpler electronic controls. Also, Fadal offers preprogrammed functions and routines designed for smaller shops making anything from dental braces to guitar necks.

With Fadal, buyers get the Volkswagen Beetle of the industry. The machines are functional and durable, yet Fadal charges $74,500 for its main model, at least $15,000 less than the typical lowest-price competing machine *that does the same job. What's more, Fadal, with few exceptions, uses American-made, off-the-shelf parts, so repairs are generally a routine matter.*

Source: "Fadal's Attractions," October 22, 1990 issue of *Business Week*. Used by special permission © 1990.

that less than 1 percent failed. Viewed in this way, one can conclude that chances for success are excellent! The prospective entrepreneur should be encouraged to consider business ownership because of its bright prospects, rather than shun it because of fear of failure.

There are a number of reasons for the gap between the low Dun & Bradstreet failure rate and the much higher rates so often cited in the news media. Some of these are as follows:

1. A business may discontinue operations merely because profits are unsatisfactory. Dun & Bradstreet classifies discontinuances as failures only if there is a loss to creditors.
2. A business may close one branch office or store to consolidate operations, and this may appear to be a business failure.
3. A business may relocate, and the empty building with a "For Rent" sign may create an impression of failure.

The failure rate would vary, of course, if a different definition of failure were used. If discontinuances were considered failures, for example, the rate would be higher. Also, if only newly created businesses are considered, the failure rate is higher.

Recent research using the data base of the Small Business Administration has shown that 40 percent of new firms survive six or more years.[19] Moreover, most firms that do not survive are closed voluntarily, without loss to creditors. Furthermore, survival rates more than double for firms that grow. In fact, two out of three growing firms were found to survive six or more years.

Research by David L. Birch found that about three-quarters of the 1.1 million firms included in his study survived from 1983 to 1987.[20] The younger companies in the group studied were only slightly less likely than older companies to make it through the four-year period.

It is desirable, of course, that we learn from the experiences of those who fail. However, apprehension of failure should not be permitted to stifle inclinations toward independent business careers. While prospective entrepreneurs should understand that failure is possible, they should also recognize that the odds are far from overwhelming.

The Costs of Business Failure

The costs of business failure involve more than financial costs to the business owner and creditors. Costs include those of a psychological, social, and economic nature, too.

Loss of Entrepreneur's and Creditors' Capital. The owner of a business that fails suffers a loss of invested capital, either in whole or in part. This is always a financial setback to the individual concerned. In some cases, it means the loss of a person's lifetime savings! The entrepreneur's loss of capital is augmented by the losses of business creditors. Hence, the total capital loss is greater than the sum of the entrepreneurial losses in any one year.

Injurious Psychological Effects. Individuals who fail in business suffer a real blow to their self-esteem. The businesses they started with enthusiasm and high expectations of success have "gone under." Older entrepreneurs, in many cases, lack the vitality to recover from the blow. Many unsuccessful entrepreneurs simply relapse into employee status for the balance of their lives.

However, failure need not be totally devastating to entrepreneurs. They may recover from the failure and try again. Albert Shapero has offered these encouraging comments: "Many heroes of business failed at least once. Henry Ford failed twice. Maybe trying and failing is a better business education than going to a business school that has little concern with small business and entrepreneurship."[21] The key, therefore, is the response of the one who fails and that person's ability to learn from failure.

Social and Economic Losses. Assuming that a business opportunity existed, the failure of a firm means the elimination of its goods and services that the public needs and wants. Moreover, the number of jobs available in the community is reduced. The resulting unemployment of the entrepreneur and employees, if any, causes the community to suffer from the loss of a business payroll. Finally, the business that failed was a taxpayer that contributed to the tax support of schools, police and fire protection, and other governmental services.

CAUSES OF BUSINESS FAILURE

As shown in Table 2-3, Dun & Bradstreet cite "economic factors" as the leading cause of business failures—45 percent of the total. In this category, they include such factors as "inadequate sales," "insufficient profits," and "poor growth prospects." Another important category is "finance causes," which includes such components as "heavy operating expenses" and "insufficient capital."

The most intriguing class of failures is that of "experience causes"—contributing to 10.5 percent of the failures. These causes are obviously related to the quality of management, including as they do "lack of business knowledge," "lack of line experience," and "lack of managerial experience." Attributing the cause of failure to experience, therefore, is equivalent to saying failure results from substandard management.

Other, less-obvious causes cited by Dun & Bradstreet may also serve as masks for the underlying cause of managerial weakness. Such factors as "inadequate sales," "insufficient profits," and "heavy operating expenses" often serve as euphemisms for inferior management. The quality of management plays a major part in the majority of small-business failures.

Table 2-3
Causes of Business
Failure, 1990

Cause	Percentage of Failures
Neglect Causes	3.1
Disaster	1.6
Fraud	1.4
Economic Factors Causes	45.0
Experience Causes	10.5
Finance Causes	37.2
Strategy Causes	1.2

Source: *Business Failure Record* (New York: Dun & Bradstreet, Inc., 1992), p. 18.

LOOKING BACK

1. Definitions of small business are necessarily arbitrary and differ according to purpose. Although there are exceptions, we generally think of a business as small when it has one or a small group of investors, operates in a geographically restricted area, is small compared to the biggest firms in the industry, and has fewer than 100 employees. Size standards issued by the Small Business Administration relate to eligibility for SBA loans and to considerations in bidding for government contracts.

2. Small firms operate in all industrial areas but are particularly strong—in terms of number of employees on their payroll—in the fields of construction, wholesale trade, retail trade, and services.

3. The proportion of total business activity accounted for by small business is just over 50 percent.

4. Small businesses make several unique contributions to our economy. They provide a disproportionate share of new jobs needed for a growing labor force. They are responsible for introducing many innovations and originating such scientific breakthroughs as photocopiers and insulin. Small firms act as vigorous economic competitors and perform some business functions (such as distribution and supply) more expertly than large firms in many ways. Small firms can also produce goods and services more efficiently in some areas.

5. The rate of business failure is much lower than commonly believed—amounting in 1990 to less than one percent of the firms in Dun & Bradstreet's records. Although "economic factors" is cited as the most frequent reason for failure, it seems probable that management weakness is the leading underlying cause.

DISCUSSION QUESTIONS

1. In view of the numerous definitions of small business, how can you decide which definition is correct?

2. Of the businesses with which you are acquainted, which is the largest that you consider to be in the small-business category? Does it conform to the size standards used in this book?

3. On the basis of your acquaintance with small-business firms, give an example of a specific small firm in the field of transportation and other public utilities.

4. Suppose you decided to publish a tax advisory newsletter for small-business owners. How would you define your target market in terms of business size? What difference would this decision make?

5. What generalizations can you make about the relative importance of large and small business in the United States?

6. In which sectors of the economy is small business most important? What accounts for its strength in these areas?

7. As noted in this chapter, small business is stronger in some industries than in others. Would it be logical, therefore, for prospective entrepreneurs to concentrate their search for opportunities more in the strong small-business industries—for example, in wholesaling more than manufacturing?

8. What special contribution is made by small business in providing jobs?
9. How can you explain the unique contributions of small business to product innovation?
10. What changes would be necessary for Ford Motor Company to continue operation, if, for some strange reason, all firms with fewer than 500 employees were outlawed? Would the new arrangement be more or less efficient than the present one? Why?
11. In what way does small business serve as a bulwark of the capitalistic system?
12. List and describe some of the nonfinancial costs of business failure.
13. Explain the significance of the quality of management as a cause of failure.
14. What is the difference between saying that "most firms fail within five years" and that "most firms that fail do so within five years"? Which is more nearly correct? Based on the statistics on business failure, would you describe the prospects for new business starts as "bright" or "bleak"?
15. How can "economic factors," when cited as a cause of business failure, serve as a mask for other contributing causes?

YOU MAKE THE CALL

Situation 1

In the 1980s, a major food company began a push to increase its share of the nation's pickle market. To build market share, it used TV advertising and aggressive pricing. The price of its 46-ounce jar of pickles quickly dropped in one area from $1.89 to 79 cents—a price some believed was less than the cost of production. This meant strong price competition for a family business that had long dominated the pickle market in that area. This family firm, whose primary product is pickles, must now decide how to compete with a powerful national corporation whose annual sales volume amounts to billions of dollars.

Questions
1. How should the family business react to the price competition?
2. What advertising changes might be needed?
3. How can a family business survive in such a setting?

Situation 2

An entrepreneurial failure, that of Ron A. Berger, is described in the following account:

In 1979 Berger was hot. His four-year-old brainchild, Photo Factory, was pulling in $40 million a year. He had 57 stores in eight states, and he was rolling.

Then, suddenly, he was broke.

His business had been leveraged with a $1-million line of credit. Interest rates skyrocketed, and the bank called in his loan. Because Berger had personally guaranteed the loan, he was forced to declare personal bankruptcy. Overnight, Berger plummeted from a net worth of about $5 million to zip. Job searches and depression followed. "I couldn't come to grips with it," Berger says today. "I felt like a total failure. I questioned my own worth and every business decision I'd ever made."

Source: "Building on Failure," *Nation's Business*, Vol. 75, No. 4, p. 50. Reprinted by permission, *Nation's Business*, April 1987. Copyright 1987, U.S. Chamber of Commerce.

Questions
1. What was the cause of Berger's failure? Explain your answer.
2. What should he learn from this failure, and how should he deal with his feelings of failure?

EXPERIENTIAL EXERCISES

1. Visit a local firm and prepare a report showing the number of owners, geographical scope of operation, relative size in the industry, number of employees, and sales volume (if the firm will provide sales data). In your report, show the size of the firm (whether large or small) in terms of standards outlined in this chapter and the industry of which it is a part.
2. Interview a small-business owner-manager concerning the type of big-business competition faced by his or her firm and that owner-manager's "secrets of success" in competing with big business. Report on the insights offered by this entrepreneur.
3. Select a recent issue of *Inc.* and report on the types of new products or services being developed by small firms.
4. Select one section of 20 businesses in the Yellow Pages of the telephone directory, label each of these businesses as large or small on the basis of that limited information, and give your rationale or assumptions for your classification of each. Then call five of these firms and ask whether the firm is a large or small business. Compare the responses to your own classification.

REFERENCES TO SMALL-BUSINESS PRACTICES

"A Sweet Deal," *Inc.*, Vol. 13, No. 3 (March 1991), p. 12.
    An example of collaboration between a large corporation and small business—in this case between United Parcel Service of America and Mail Boxes Etc.
McElveen, Mary. "How Firms Coped After Hugo," *Nation's Business*, Vol. 78, No. 4 (April 1990), pp. 41–42.
    During an emergency, a number of small firms demonstrated the flexibility that is a virtue of small-business operation.
Nelton, Sharon. "Ten Key Threats to Success," *Nation's Business*, Vol. 80, No. 6 (June 1992), pp. 18–28.
    A discussion of factors that may lead to failure, with illustrations from a number of small firms.
"The Little Engineers That Could," *Business Week*, No. 3276 (July 27, 1992), p. 77.
    An account of an 18-mile railroad in New Mexico—a small firm in a big-business industry.

ENDNOTES

1. *The State of Small Business: A Report of the President 1991* (Washington: U.S. Government Printing Office, 1991), p. 20.

2. "The Rise and Rise of America's Small Firms," *The Economist* (January 21, 1989), p. 67.

3. W. Sengenberger, G. Loveman, and M. J. Piore (eds.), *The Re-emergence of Small Enterprises: Industrial Restructuring in Industrial Countries* (Geneva: International Institute for Labour Studies, 1990).

4. Gary Loveman and Werner Sengenberger, "The Re-emergence of Small-Scale Production: An International Comparison," *Small Business Economics,* Vol. 3, No. 1 (March 1991), p. 7.

5. The factors noted here are included in Zoltan J. Acs and David B. Audretsch, *Innovation and Small Firms* (Cambridge: The MIT Press, 1990), pp. 3–5.

6. Tatiana Pouschine and Manjeet Kripalani, "I Got Tired of Forcing Myself To Go to the Office," *Forbes,* Vol. 149, No. 11 (May 25, 1992), p. 104.

7. *The State of Small Business: A Report of the President 1988* (Washington: U.S. Government Printing Office, 1988), p. 38.

8. *The Contribution of Small Enterprise to Growth and Employment* (Cambridge: Program on Neighborhood and Regional Change, Massachusetts Institute of Technology, undated).

9. Acs and Audretsch, p. 151.

10. *Ibid.,* p. 2.

11. *The Contribution of Small Enterprise to Growth and Employment,* p. 10.

12. Zoltan J. Acs and David B. Audretsch, *Innovation and Small Firms* (Cambridge: The MIT Press, 1990), p. 59. Also see a National Science Foundation study in U.S. Congress, Senate, Joint Hearings before the Select Committee on Small Business and other committees, *Small Business and Innovation,* August 9–10, 1978, p. 7.

13. For an extended discussion of small-business contributions to productivity in manufacturing including numerous examples, see Joel Kotkin, "The Great American Revival," *Inc.,* Vol. 10, No. 2 (February 1988), pp. 52–63. For a more technical analysis, see John A. Hansen, "Innovation, Firm Size, and Firm Age," *Small Business Economics,* Vol. 4, No. 1 (March 1992), pp. 37–44.

14. "Capitalism in China," *Business Week,* No. 2876 (January 14, 1985), pp. 53–59.

15. "Sorrell Ridge Makes Smucker Pucker," *Forbes,* Vol. 143, No. 12 (June 12, 1989), pp. 166–168.

16. *The State of Small Business: A Report of the President 1987* (Washington: U.S. Government Printing Office, 1987), p. 105.

17. The most comprehensive statistics pertaining to failure and changes in rate of failure are collected by Dun & Bradstreet, a business firm devoted to the analysis and rating of the credit standing of other firms. Failures, as defined by Dun & Bradstreet, include only those discontinuances that involve loss to creditors; voluntarily liquidated firms with all debts paid are excluded.

18. Professor M. Z. Massel of De Paul University argues that writers generally have become so preoccupied with the minority of firms that fail that they paint an unnecessarily pessimistic picture of chances for success in business. See Michael Z. Massel, "It's Easier to Slay a Dragon Than Kill a Myth," *Journal of Small Business Management,* Vol. 16, No. 3 (July 1978), pp. 44–49.

19. Bruce D. Phillips and Bruce A. Kirchoff, "Formation, Growth and Survival: Small Firm Dynamics in the U.S. Economy," *Small Business Economics,* Vol. 1 (1989), pp. 65–74.

20. David L. Birch, "Live Fast, Die Young," *Inc.,* Vol. 10, No. 8 (August 1988), p. 23.

21. Albert Shapero, "Numbers That Lie," *Inc.,* Vol. 3, No. 5 (May 1981), p. 16.

P A R T 2

Entrepreneurial
Opportunities

CHAPTER 3

Competitive Advantage: Niche Strategy and Customer Service

Sheri Poe

SPOTLIGHT ON SMALL BUSINESS

Another athletic shoe in a market already filled with giant manufacturers? You must be kidding! This reaction from potential investors forced Sheri Poe to leverage her house in 1987 and borrow money from family and friends to launch Rykä, Inc. Poe had tried almost every brand of athletic shoes during years of working out, only to suffer severe lower-back and knee pain that were being caused by her sneakers. She concluded that existing women's athletic shoes were only sized-down versions of men's shoes. Poe believed an "entrepreneur could carve out a niche that the big guys have overlooked." Her company developed "a fitness shoe built specifically for a woman, a patented design for better shock absorption and durability."

The shoe was introduced at a trade show in 1988. Poe says, "As a new manufacturer in a big industry, we had a realistic fear that established companies would target us and market us right out of business." The strategy Rykä used to combat the threat was one which did not challenge the established shoe companies on all fronts but only in a narrow niche. Rykä had started with shoe designs for several applications—running, tennis, and so on. However, Poe "cut back to aerobic shoes because we wanted to stay focused and didn't have the budget to build several different markets at once," she says. Poe recognized the key to success is to target a strong niche and stay focused.

During 1991, sales at Rykä reached $8 million. The Rykä business venture is an example of how niche marketing can work for a small firm, allowing it to step into the land of giants.

Source: Sheri Poe, "To Compete With Giants, Choose Your Niche," *Nation's Business*, Vol. 80, No. 7, p. 6. Excerpted by permission from *Nation's Business*, July 1992. Copyright 1992 U.S. Chamber of Commerce.

After studying this chapter, you should be able to:
1. Discuss the forces that determine the nature and degree of competition within an industry.
2. Identify and compare two strategy options for building competitive advantage.
3. Describe three types of market segmentation strategies.
4. Explain the concept of niche marketing and its importance to small business.
5. Recognize the importance of customer service to successful operation of a small business.

competitive advantage
market segmentation
unsegmented strategy
multisegmentation
  strategy
single-segmentation
  strategy

market
segmentation variables
benefit variables
demographic variables
niche marketing

target marketing
strategic decision
customer-satisfaction
  strategy
total quality management

Business strategy is concerned with decisions which shape the very nature of the small firm. Small business strategy may just "happen," or it may result from careful thought about the mission of the firm. The latter is obviously preferable in building a successful small business.

By nature, most entrepreneurs are unaccustomed to systematic investigation of the kind required to develop strategy, and they typically have difficulty finding an appropriate starting point. Nevertheless, after examining opportunities, risks, and resources, the successful strategist must decide on alternatives and develop a basic strategy. Following the adoption of a strategy, the entrepreneur must implement and then periodically evaluate the strategy in a new round of strategic decision making. Finally, strategic plans should be reduced to writing to insure completion of the strategy-determination process and to provide a basis for subsequent planning. The firm's overall strategy should be translated into detailed plans of action.

These brief introductory comments regarding small business strategy demonstrate the complexity of strategy development. Therefore, it is not surprising that meaningful strategy creation requires a commitment by the entrepreneur to devote considerable time and energy to the process. This chapter describes key building blocks for the development of a small firm's basic strategy. These include the concepts of competitive advantage, market segmentation, target marketing, and customer service management. Additional examples of strategic planning are discussed in later chapters.

COMPETITIVE STRATEGY

Entrepreneurs are often confronted with two myths surrounding new venture creation. One is that most good business opportunities are already gone. The other is that small firms cannot compete well with big companies. Both these ideas need to be purged from the entrepreneur's mind! They are the exception, not the rule. Nevertheless, existing companies, large and small, do not typically welcome a new competitor. As one well-respected author, Karl H. Vesper, puts it:

Established companies do their best to maintain proprietary shields . . . to ward off prospective as well as existing competitors. Consequently, the entrepreneur who would create a new competitor to attack them needs some sort of "entry wedge," or strategic competitive advantage for breaking into the established pattern of commercial activity.[1]

Before choosing these "entry wedges," it is important for the entrepreneur to understand the basic nature of competition he or she faces. Only then can a competitive advantage be developed properly. A **competitive advantage** exists when a firm has a marketing idea that is seen by its target market as better than a competitor's idea.

competitive advantage
a marketing idea that is seen by its target market as better than a competitor's idea

The Basic Nature of Competition

The experiences of small firms included in *Inc.* magazine's 1992 list of the United States' fastest-growing private companies (The *Inc.* 500), typify the competitive and constantly changing environment of the marketplace. Consider the following three firms and their competitive situations:

Gary Gagliardi, a Seattle software consultant, begins to create and sell accounting programs for businesses. The marketplace is teeming with competitors, but Gagliardi's new company shoots to the top, displacing the industry leader. Before long, big customers such as Marriott Corp. are placing orders. Sales for fiscal 1991: $5 million, with profits in the 6%-to-10% range.

Dennis and Ann Pence leave high-powered careers in New York City for the wilds of northern Idaho. They start a catalog company selling nature-oriented gifts. Its success is startling: $11 million in revenues last year, an estimated $20 million this year. Profits hover around 16%.

Max Duncan loses his job as a drilling engineer; he is one more casualty of the mid-1980s slump in South Texas oil. Duncan gives the energy business one last shot, starting a company to make specialty chemicals for drillers. Incredibly—because better-established companies are scrambling to get out of this market—he strikes pay dirt. Last year Duncan's company topped $6 million in sales.[2]

Each of these businesses successfully competed within their respective industry. Each studied its competition and developed a sound strategy. But what are the basic forces in a competitive market? How does each force relate to the degree of competition in an industry?

There are a number of ingredients that determine the level of competition within an industry. Several typologies have been developed to categorize these competitive forces. One conceptualization is presented by Michael Porter in his book *Competitive Advantage.* He identifies five forces which determine the nature and degree of competition in an industry: (1) the entry of new competitors, (2) the threat of substitutes, (3) the bargaining power of buyers, (4) the bargaining power of suppliers, and (5) the rivalry among existing competitors. Figure 3-1 depicts these factors as pieces of a jigsaw puzzle.

These five market forces collectively determine the ability of a firm, whether it is large or small, to earn a return on its investment. Obviously, all industries are not alike; therefore, a single competitive strategy will not fit all situations. Although Porter identifies numerous factors which characterize industry structure and in turn influence these five competitive forces, he also briefly summarizes the influence of the five forces on competitive advantage as follows:

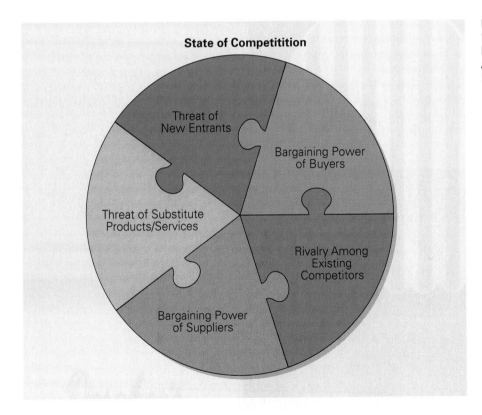

Figure 3-1
Puzzle Parts to Determine Industry Attractiveness and Profitability

Buyer power influences the prices that firms can charge, for example, as does the threat of substitution. The power of buyers can also influence cost and investment, because powerful buyers demand costly service. The bargaining power of suppliers determines the cost of raw materials and other inputs. The intensity of rivalry influences prices as well as the costs of competing in areas such as plant, product development, advertising, and sales force. The threat of entry places a limit on prices, and shapes the investment required to deter entrants.[3]

The better entrepreneurs understand the underlying forces of competitive pressure, the better they will be able to assess market opportunities or threats. Obviously, different forces will dominate industry competition depending on the particular circumstances. Therefore, the goal of entrepreneurs is to recognize and understand these forces so they can position the venture to best cope with the industry environment. Porter has identified five "fatal flaws" which plague entrepreneurs' strategic thinking regarding their competitive situation. These are:

1. *Misreading industry attractiveness*—The most attractive industry may not be the fastest growing or the most glamorous.
2. *Possessing no true competitive advantage*—Imitation of rivals is both hard and risky and is the opposite of competitive advantage.
3. *Pursuing a competitive advantage that is not sustainable*—Be sure your competitive advantage cannot be quickly imitated.
4. *Compromising a strategy in order to grow faster*—Losing a focus on the competitive advantage for the benefit of short-run growth can be a problem.
5. *Not making your strategy explicit and not communicating it to your employees*—Failure to make the strategy clear to the employees will typically result in inconsistent actions. A written strategy that is verbalized frequently helps prevent this flaw.[4]

Figure 3-2
Merlin Metalworks Inc. Finds Its Competitive Advantage in Product Differentiation—a Strong, Lightweight Bicycle Frame Favored by Racing Cyclists

The remaining sections of this chapter will focus on the first three of these flaws—those that relate directly to the development and maintenance of a competitive advantage. If entrepreneurs correctly understand industry potential, create a true competitive advantage, and maintain that advantage, they will greatly enhance the likelihood of success! The next section examines competitive strategy options.

Competitive Strategy Options

There are two broad-based options for building a firm's competitive advantage in the marketplace. One option involves creating a cost advantage. The other involves creating a marketing advantage.

Cost Advantage. The cost advantage strategy requires the entrepreneur to become the lowest cost producer within the market. The sources of this advantage are quite varied and can range from low-cost labor to efficiency in operations. For example, Max Duncan, founder of Integrity Industries in Kingsville, Texas, created a cost competitive advantage by locating his new chemical blending plant in a vacant facility where he persuaded the owner to sign on as a partner. Then:

> *He found an experienced sales manager willing to take another third of the company in lieu of a year's salary. Duncan bought used equipment for "pennies on the dollar;" he ordered free samples from chemical companies for his initial raw materials . . . .*
>
> *Duncan quickly found customers. The reason was simple: his costs were so low that he could charge 10% to 20% less than the competition . . . . "We're able to make healthy profit margins and keep prices low by maintaining extreme efficiency in operation," he explains.*[5]

Since 1987, Integrity Industries has grown eightfold but has not abandoned its key cost advantage. Another example of a cost advantage is found in the strategy of Stanley Anderson, the owner of ProCard, Inc., in Golden, Colorado. After 30 years in banking, Anderson "saw a niche in the giant category of low-dollar procurement (corporate purchasing transactions)." ProCard looks like an ordinary credit card, but provides the corporate customer with significantly better reporting and a 20 percent reduction in costs. Anderson is projecting 1992 revenues of $3 million.[6]

Marketing Advantage. The second strategy option for building a competitive advantage is achieving a marketing advantage. This requires efforts which differentiate the entrepreneur's product or service. A firm which is able to create and sustain a differentiation will be a successful performer in the marketplace. The uniqueness of the product or service can be real or simply a result of consumer perceptions. A wide variety of marketing tactics lead to product/service differentiation. These range from quality improvement to product design.

A famous example of product differentiation was hatched in the successful family business of Frank Perdue that began back in the 1950s. Perdue had taken over his parents' chicken farm in Maryland and needed a clear strategy for the future. He decided to stop competing on price and start competing on product differentiation—which he obtained by a unique and attractive packaging of chicken.

Chicken in those days was, well, just chicken; everyone was selling the same commodity and, because there was a glut of producers, prices were consistently low. But our Maryland farmer figured out that by packaging his product uniformly and attractively, he could give his customers something different; he could give them a better feeling about the product's quality and distinguish his chicken from that of his competitors.[7]

Perdue also realized he could mold his competitive advantage by building a brand name and image through extensive advertising. Obviously, his strategy worked!

Another example of creating a competitive advantage through marketing is provided by the innovative product design of inventor Henry Artis. Artis entered the home garden composting market with a new product design. Traditional composters were designed as fixed rectangular bins. A stationary design requires periodic "stirring" to introduce oxygen into the leaves, grass clippings, and discarded food. Still other designs use elevated tubes that are rotated with a hand-operated crank. Artis's idea, called a TumbleBug, features a giant hollow plastic ball that can be rolled across the yard to achieve the necessary agitation to create compost. Selling at a relatively expensive $169, Artis's product provides "better looks, no odors, higher temperatures, and faster composting."[8] This venture relies on product differentiation rather than price for its competitive advantage.

MARKET SEGMENTATION STRATEGIES

Previously discussed competitive advantage strategies—cost and marketing—are based on the assumption that the marketplace has homogeneous characteristics. A different strategy is one which focuses on a more narrow market within an industry. Michael Porter refers to this competitive strategy as a "focus" strategy. Both cost and marketing advantages can be achieved within narrow market segments as well.

Within marketing circles, this "focus" strategy is generally called **market segmentation**. Formally defined, it is "the process of dividing the total market for a product or service into groups with similar needs such that each group is likely

market segmentation
dividing a market into several smaller groups with similar needs

to respond favorably to a specific marketing strategy."[9] A small business may view its market in either general or focus terms. The personal-computer industry is a good example of real-world market segmentation. Traditionally, computer manufacturers practiced very little market segmentation. But recently, as corporate demand has stagnated, the personal-computer industry has been divided into focused fragments such as small businesses, home use, and portables. "People had been shooting into the middle and missing the market," says William C. Michels, vice-president at consultants Booz, Allen Hamilton, Inc.[10]

How far can the entrepreneur take market segmentation? Consider how the Coca-Cola Company has segmented the market for Coke. By one count, this company has 24 variations! Theoretically, each of these has a unique target market. Below is a list of these Coke brands:[11]

New Coke	Coke Classic
Diet New Coke	Diet Coke Classic
Low-Caffeine New Coke	Low-Caffeine Coke Classic
Low-Caffeine Diet New Coke	Low-Caffeine Diet Coke Classic
Caffeine-Free New Coke	Caffeine-Free Coke Classic
Caffeine-Free Diet New Coke	Caffeine-Free Diet Coke Classic
Cherry New Coke	Cherry Coke Classic
Diet Cherry New Coke	Diet Cherry Coke Classic
Low-Caffeine Cherry New Coke	Low-Caffeine Cherry Coke Classic
Low-Caffeine Diet Cherry New Coke	Low-Caffeine Diet Cherry Coke Classic
Caffeine-Free Cherry New Coke	Caffeine-Free Cherry Coke Classic
Caffeine-Free Diet Cherry New Coke	Caffeine-Free Diet Cherry Coke Classic

The Need for Market Segmentation

If a business had control of the only known water supply in the world, its sales volume would be huge. This business would not be concerned about differences in personal preferences for taste, color, or temperature. It would consider its customers to be *one* market. As long as the water product was "wet," it would satisfy everyone. However, if someone else discovered a second water supply, the view of the market would change. The first business might discover that sales were drying up and turn to a modified strategy. The new approach could well emerge from an understanding of consumer behavior.

In the real world, a number of preferences for liquid drinks exist. What may seem to be a homogeneous market is actually heterogeneous. The different preferences may take a number of forms. Some preferences may relate to the way consumers react to the taste or to the container. Other preferences may relate to the price of the liquid drink or to the availability of "specials." Preferences might also be uncovered with respect to different distribution strategies or to certain promotional tones and techniques. In other words, markets may actually be composed of several submarkets.

Types of Market Segmentation Strategies

The three types of market segmentation strategies discussed in this section are the unsegmented approach, the multisegmentation approach, and the single-segmentation approach. These strategies can best be illustrated by using an example of a hypothetical firm—the Community Writing Company.

The Unsegmented Strategy. When a business defines the total market as its target market, it is following an **unsegmented strategy.** "Mass marketing" is a term frequently used for this approach. This strategy can be successful occasionally, but it assumes that all buying units desire the same general benefit from the product or service. This may hold true for water but probably not for shoes, which satisfy numerous needs through many styles, prices, colors, and sizes. With an unsegmented strategy, the firm would develop a single marketing mix, which means one combination of the product, price, promotion, and distribution plan. For the unsegmented strategy of Community Writing Company, see Figure 3-3. Community Writing Company's product is a lead pencil that is sold at the one price of 79 cents and is communicated with a single promotional and distribution plan. Notice how the marketing mix is aimed at everybody.

The Multisegmentation Strategy. With a view of the market that recognizes individual segments that have different preferences, a firm is in a position to tailor-make different strategies. A firm may think that two or more homogeneous market segments can be profitable. If it develops a unique marketing mix for each segment it will be following a **multisegmentation strategy.**

Let us now assume that Community Writing Company has discovered three

unsegmented strategy
a business defines the total market as its target market

multisegmentation strategy
a business recognizes different preferences of individual market segments and develops a unique marketing mix for each

Figure 3-3
An Unsegmented Market Strategy with Its Single Marketing Mix

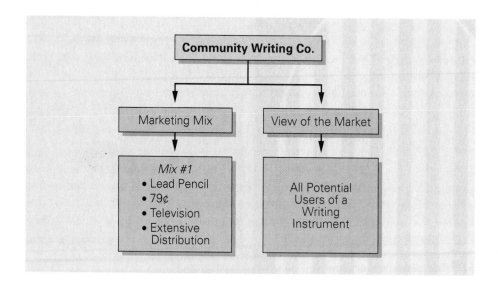

separate market segments: students, professors, and executives. Following the multisegmentation approach, the company develops three mixes, which might be based on differences in pricing, promotion, distribution, or the product itself, as shown in Figure 3-4. Mix #1 consists of selling felt-tip pens to students through vending machines at the slightly higher-than-normal price of $1.00 and supporting this effort with a promotional campaign in campus newspapers. With Mix #2, the company might market the same pen to universities for use by professors. Professional magazines are the only promotion used in this mix, distribution is direct from the factory, and the product price of 49 cents is ex-

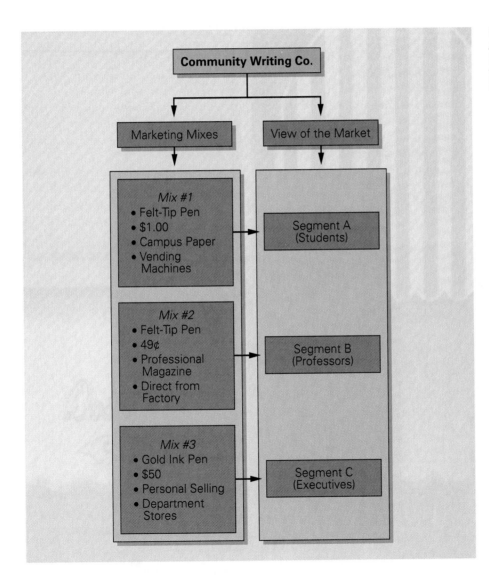

Figure 3-4
A Segmented
Market Strategy
with Multiple
Marketing Mixes

tremely low. Finally, with Mix #3, which is aimed at corporate executives, the product is a solid gold fountain pen sold only in exclusive department stores. It is promoted by personal selling and carries the extremely high price of $50. Although students might conceivably buy the solid gold pens for classroom writing, they are not viewed as members of this target market.

Notice the dramatic differences in the three marketing mixes. Small businesses, however, tend to postpone the use of multisegmentation strategies because of the risk of spreading resources too thinly among several marketing efforts.

single-segmentation strategy

a business recognizes the existence of several distinct market segments, but pursues only the most profitable segment

The Single-Segmentation Strategy. When a firm recognizes that several distinct market segments exist but chooses to concentrate on reaching only one segment, it is following a **single-segmentation strategy.** The segment selected will be one that the business feels will be most profitable.

This was the strategy of Larry Meyer when he started Monograms Plus in 1988, "because I saw a large void in the marketplace for a while-you-wait monogramming business," he explains. The franchise has expanded quickly by "capitalizing on this niche."[12] He used the single-segmentation strategy to build a reputation among the target market that he feels will spread to other markets as he expands his services.

Community Writing Company, our hypothetical example, selects the student market segment when pursuing a single-segmentation approach, as shown in Figure 3-5.

Figure 3-5
A Segmented
Market Strategy
with a Single
Marketing Mix

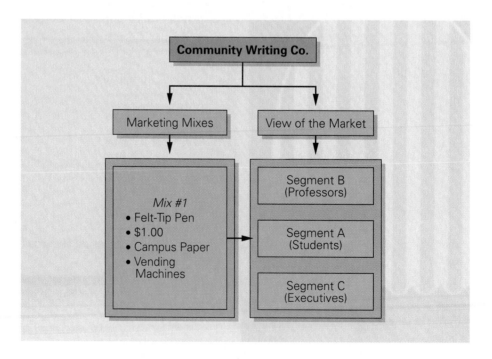

The single-segmentation approach is probably the best strategy for small businesses during initial marketing efforts. This approach allows them to specialize and make better use of their more limited resources. Then, when a reputation has been built, it is easier for them to enter new markets. A single-segmentation approach has become known in recent years as "niche" marketing strategy. Because of its popularity and potential value to a small firm's success, we will devote a later section to niche marketing.

Segmentation Variables. A firm's market could be defined very simply as "anyone who is alive"! However, this is too broad to be useful even for a firm that follows an unsegmented approach. We define a **market** as a group of customers or potential customers who have purchasing power and unsatisfied needs. With any type of market analysis, some degree of segmentation must be made. Notice in Figure 3-2, which represents an unsegmented market strategy, that the market is not everyone in the universe—just those who might use writing instruments.

In order to divide the total market into appropriate segments, a business must consider segmentation variables. Basically, **segmentation variables** are labels that identify the particular dimensions that are thought to distinguish one form of market demand from another. Two particular sets of segmentation variables that represent the major dimensions of a market are benefit variables and demographic variables.

Benefit Variables. Our definition of a market highlighted the unsatisfied needs of customers. **Benefit variables** are related to customer needs in that they are used to divide and identify segments of a market according to the benefits sought by customers. For example, the toothpaste market has several benefit segments. The principal benefit to parents may be cavity prevention for their young children. On the other hand, the principal benefit to a teenager might be fresh breath. In both cases, toothpaste is the product, but it has two different markets.

In our hypothetical example for Community Writing Company, the market is subdivided according to the benefit variables of convenience and economy. This is illustrated in Figure 3-6.

Demographic Variables. Benefit variables alone are insufficient for market analysis. It is impossible to implement forecasting and marketing strategy without defining the market further. Therefore, small businesses commonly use demographics as part of market segmentation. Typical demographics are age, marital status, sex, occupation, and income. Remember again our definition of a market—customers with purchasing power and unsatisfied needs. Thus, **demographic variables** refer to certain characteristics that describe customers and their purchasing power. One recent study found the most widely employed segmentation methods among small firms to be demographic, geographic, benefits sought, marketing attributes, extent of usage, and the time of use.[13]

market
a group of customers who have purchasing power and unsatisfied needs

segmentation variables
the parameters used to distinguish one form of market demand from another

benefit variables
variables that distinguish market segments according to the benefits sought by customers

demographic variables
characteristics that describe customers and their purchasing power

Figure 3-6
Combined Demographic and Benefit Segmentation Variables

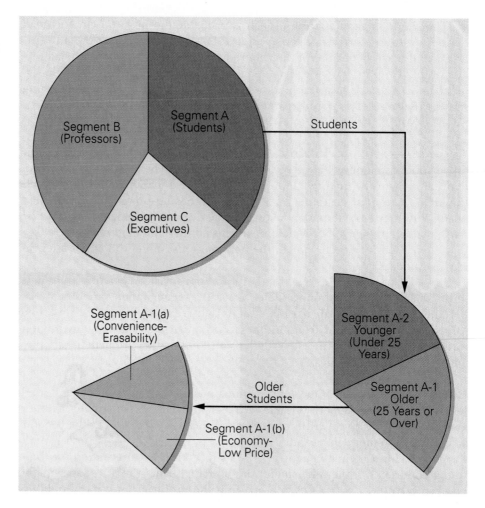

Figure 3-6 shows the market scenario for Community Writing Company where the demographic variables of occupation and age have been used to profile the potential market segments. Segment A-1(a) represents older students who are seeking convenience in a writing instrument. Segment A-1(b) represents older students who want a low-priced writing instrument.

NICHE MARKETING

niche marketing (target marketing)
choosing marketing segments not adequately served by competitors

Niche marketing or **target marketing** is a special form of market strategy in which entrepreneurs try to isolate themselves from competitors by targeting special market segments. The strategy can be developed through any element of marketing—price, product design, service, packaging, and so on. Target marketing can be effective in both domestic and international markets.

Table 3-1
Extent of Use of
Target Marketing by
Industry

Industry	Number of Firms in Study	Number Employing Target Marketing	Percentage Employing Target Marketing
Retailing	316	212*	67.1
Service	127	61	48.0
Manufacturing	42	31*	73.8
Wholesaling	22	11	50.0
Other	12	5	41.7

*Denotes a frequency that is statistically larger than the expected frequency, according to a chi-square test at the .05 level.
Source: Robin T. Peterson, "Small Business Usage of Target Marketing," *Journal of Small Business Management,* Vol. 29, No. 4 (October 1991), p. 82.

A target market strategy is particularly attractive to any small firm that is building a competitive advantage and also trying to escape direct competition with industry giants. One research study found extensive use of target marketing among small firms which were clients of consulting programs operated by Small Business Institutes. Some of the key statistics from the study are shown in Table 3-1. The study also found that, of the firms employing less than 100 persons, 81 percent use target marketing.

Selecting a Market Niche

Many new ventures fail because of poor market positioning or lack of a perceived advantage by customers in their target market. To minimize this chance

Figure 3-7
This Sushi Restaurant Targets the Growing Market of Customers Who Enjoy Eating Raw Fish

of failure, an entrepreneur should consider the benefits of exploiting gaps or niches in a market. The choice of a niche strategy by a small firm is suggested by, but not restricted to, the following marketing activities:[14]

- Strict concentration on a single market segment.
- Concentration on a single product.
- Reliance on close customer contact and intuitive knowledge of the market.
- Restriction to a single geographical region.
- Emphasis on substantive superiority of the product.

If a firm's strategy focuses on a unique target market, it must also use marketing tactics that match this strategy. Consider the following example of a marketing-niche strategy and related marketing tactics:

Sue and Jim Acres operate the Blue Ribbon Car Wash in an affluent part of the city. They do not market their car wash to the general public, and the general public would not typically frequent it anyway. This is because of both the cost and the nature of the service provided. Charging more than thirty dollars for a wash job and fifty for a wash and wax, Blue Ribbon caters only to owners of Audis, Cadillacs, and Lincolns. Cars are accepted by appointment only and must be left for at least four hours. The car is washed by hand using only top quality cleaners and waxes, and it is cleaned and vacuumed inside. A fabric protector is applied if desired. Wheels are scrubbed and wire wheels are carefully attended to—if necessary with a toothbrush. For an additional charge, the engine compartment can be cleaned, the trunk can be vacuumed, and the oil can be changed. Sue reports that business is brisk—six cars a day. Some owners wait as long as two weeks for an appointment.[15]

Notice how the pricing strategy of Blue Ribbon Car Wash reflects the uniqueness of the service. Also, by requiring appointments, it creates an air of exclusiveness—not just anyone can drive in and get the service.

By selecting a particular niche, an entrepreneur thereby decides upon the basic direction of the firm. Because such a choice affects the very nature of the business, we call it a **strategic decision**. A firm's overall strategy is formulated, therefore, as its leader decides how it will relate to its environment—particularly to the customers and competitors in that environment.

Selection of a very specialized market is, of course, not the only possible strategy for a small firm. Nevertheless, finding a niche that can be exploited is a popular strategy. It allows a small firm to operate in the "crack" between larger competitors. If a small firm chooses to go "head-to-head" in competition with other businesses, particularly large corporations, it must be prepared to distinguish itself in some way—for example, by attention to detail, highly personal service, or speed of service—in order to make itself a formidable competitor.[16]

The following products and services are recent examples of niche marketing by creative entrepreneurs:

- Malcolm Swenson runs a company based in Grantham, New Hampshire, which is a stone construction consulting firm. They help developers and their architects select and buy the right stones.[17]

strategic decision
a decision regarding the direction a firm will take in relating to its customers and competitors

S M A L L   B U S I N E S S   I N   A C T I O N

New Product Waits on Marketing Strategy

In 1987, Bill Sanford became the president of Steris Corporation after being hired by a venture capital firm the year before to evaluate the company for potential investment. Sanford was a marketing specialist, but he inherited a firm with a great new product and "not a whit of marketing strategy."

The product is a sterilizing system for endoscopes that reduces the sterilization time from 10 hours to 20 minutes. While the system's inventor, Ray Kralovic, worked on the system, Sanford was conducting research to determine a target market. The market niche selected was hospitals. More specifically, the system would be targeted to operating room nurses. Sanford's reasons were as follows:

"First of all, you know where they are. Second, they know all about sterilization, so you don't have to educate them. Third, they have tremendous discretionary budgets since they generate vast revenues" for their hospitals . . . [N]urses . . . "wield incredible power in recommending equipment like this."

The company has used trade magazine advertising, direct mail campaigns, and booths at nurses' association meetings to promote the product. The system sells for just under $10,000.

Source: Frank Bentayou, "Fertile Ground for Sterilization." *VENTURE, For Entrepreneurial Business Owners & Investors,* October, 1988.

- In Beverly Hills, California, entrepreneur Richard Myers . . . opened a Rodeo Drive store that sells nothing but technically advanced makeup and shaving mirrors.[18]
- In New York, Arlen Lessin runs a firm that advises large corporations only on "managing innovation."[19]
- Earth's Best, Inc., founded by Arme and Ron Koss, produces organic baby food.[20]
- Sam Scheinberg, founder of Seaberg, designed and produces a new kind of splint that is malleable, reusable, and suited for people or pets.[21]
- Bob Roch developed drive-thru windshield wiper replacement booths so drivers can pull up and have their wipers changed within three minutes.[22]
- Steven Rowse helped his family business roll out the first juice-only vending machine. Veryfine has become the industry leader in the "healthy beverage" business.[23]

Maintaining Niche Potential

Those firms that adopt a niche strategy tread a narrow line between maintaining a protected market and attracting competition. Michael Porter, in his book

Competitive Strategy, cautions that a segmented market (focus strategy) can erode when:

1. The focus strategy is imitated.
2. The target segment becomes structurally unattractive due to erosion of the structure, or demand simply disappears.
3. The segment's differences from other segments narrow.
4. New firms subsegment the industry.

An example of the first situation is Minnetonka, a small firm widely recognized as the first to introduce liquid hand soap. Its brand was Softsoap. Its huge success quickly attracted several of the industry giants including Procter & Gamble. Minnetonka's competitive advantage was soon washed away. Some writers believe the company focused too much on the advantages of liquid soap in general and not enough on the particular benefits of Softsoap. Regardless, it lost its competitive advantage.

The following cases of "niching" should help demonstrate several positioning strategies that have been successfully maintained by small firms:

While Prodigy has spent an estimated $1 billion to create a mass market for on-line information services, tiny America Online, Inc. has created a profitable business by mining niches . . . Unlike Prodigy, America Online became profitable just two years after its launch . . . With its niche strategy, America Online will probably never catch up in size . . . But its market-building approach has endless possibilities.[24]

Daniel and Marylou Marsh Sanders started Ecosport, Inc. in December 1990 to sell clothes made from cotton that is cultivated without toxic pesticides, herbicides, or defoliants and is processed without bleach. They say their sales this year will exceed $4 million.[25]

Larry Flax and Richard Rosenfield . . . are the founders of the California Pizza Kitchen chain—restaurants that offer what one reviewer calls "a trendy menu of pasta and designer pizzas" . . . The service is courteous and efficient, the food arrives quickly, and the tab typically hovers between $10 and $11 per person. "We're in a niche where there are not many players," Rosenfield says . . . Average annual sales per restaurant are now $3 million.[26]

Technical Salvage & Environmental Engineering, Inc. opened a lamp-recycling facility . . . as regulators lengthen their list of dangerous substances . . . "This is a niche recycling market that has just seen the light of day" . . . The target of the new rules is the mercury that escapes into the environment when fluorescent tubes are crushed and buried in landfills or burned in incinerators.[27]

Clearly, niche marketing does not guarantee a competitive advantage forever. But small firms can extend their prosperity by developing competitive clout.[28] One marketing textbook lists four "military-type" principles for maintaining a competitive advantage. These are:[29]

1. Concentrate resources where they will have the greatest effect because a small firm's resources are limited.
2. Take the initiative by acting rather than reacting to environmental changes.
3. Maneuver resources so that overall objectives are accomplished in a coordinated fashion.
4. Plan with enough flexibility to anticipate both environmental change and competitive actions.

CUSTOMER SERVICE MANAGEMENT

There are many tactics a firm can adopt to gain a real competitive advantage. Several of these tactics were described in the real-world experiences of the small firms mentioned in the previous sections. Now we direct attention to perhaps the most important tactic for providing unique opportunities in every small firm—customer service. The following three characteristics of customer service form the motivation for this belief:

1. Customer satisfaction is not a means to achieve a certain goal; rather, it *is* the goal.
2. Customer service can provide a competitive edge.
3. Small firms are potentially in a much better position to achieve customer satisfaction than are big businesses.

Figure 3-8
Danny Wegman Is President of Wegmans Food Markets, a Chain Noted for Its Dedication to Customer Satisfaction

These three characteristics, particularly the last one, suggest that *all* small-business managers should incorporate customer service management into their firms. A small business that ignores customer service is jeopardizing its chances for success!

Customer Satisfaction—The Key Ingredient

The use of outstanding customer service to earn a competitive advantage is certainly not new. Longtime retailer Stanley Marcus, of Dallas-based Neiman-Marcus, is famous for his commitment to customer service.

What is new to small firms is the wide recognition that customer service is smart business. In 1986, the Gallup Organization polled executives of 615 companies on the importance of several factors contributing to the success of businesses. Almost one-half of the respondents picked service quality as the number one factor! Another survey by a private consulting firm pointed out three major causes of service dissatisfaction:

- *About 20 percent of dissatisfaction is caused by the attitude or performance of employees.*
- *About 40 percent of dissatisfaction is caused by companies whose structure, rules, or operating procedures are not designed for customer satisfaction. . . . "The person who deals with the consumer must have the authority to help the consumer in almost any way possible, without always transferring him or her to someone else."*
- *. . . 40 percent of dissatisfaction is caused by customers who misuse products or don't read directions.*[30]

According to Bonnie Jansen, associate director of the division of information at the U.S. Office of Consumer Affairs, consumers are "sick and tired of being battered around; they're sick of getting poor service all the time."[31]

What is the special message of these statistics for small business? The answer is that small firms are *potentially* in a much better position to achieve customer satisfaction than are big businesses! Why? Reread the three causes of customer dissatisfaction found in the private consulting firm survey. Ask yourself if the problems are not reduced by having fewer employees in a firm. For example, with fewer employees, a small firm can vest authority for dealing with complaints in each employee. On the other hand, a large business will usually charge a single individual or department with that responsibility.

Consider the following two firms' success with customer service tactics. Sewell Village Cadillac, a car dealer in Dallas, Texas, is famous for its customer service. Its owner, Carl Sewell, began its service journey in 1967 when Sewell Village was in third place among all Dallas Cadillac dealers—there were only three. Sewell " . . . realized that most people didn't like doing business with car dealers . . . They looked forward to seeing us about as much as they did going to the dentist," he says. Therefore, he simply began asking customers what they didn't like about car dealers. Three points of major dissatisfaction were identified. These issues and Sewell's response are:[32]

Issue:	*Response:*
a. Usual service hours of car dealerships—8:00 to 5:00, Monday through Friday— are inconvenient.	a. Sewell Village Cadillac service department opens at 7:30 A.M., closes at 8:00 P.M. and is open all day Saturday.
b. Hated being without a car while it is in the shop.	b. Customers at Sewell Village Cadillac are given a free car to use; today the loaner fleet numbers 281 cars.
c. Disliked having to bring their car back to get a repair done right.	c. Instituted a customer service system to monitor every service transaction.

Another company known for its emphasis on customer satisfaction is "Bugs" Burger Bug Killers (BBBK) of Miami, Florida. This business was started by Alvin L. "Bugs" Burger in 1960 and later sold to Johnson's Wax. Mr. Burger built the pest-extermination company on this service guarantee to hotel and restaurant clients:

You don't owe one penny until all pests on your premises have been eradicated.

If you are ever dissatisfied with BBBK's service, you will receive a refund for up to 12 months of the company's services—plus fees for another exterminator of your choice for the next year.

If a guest spots a pest on your premises, BBBK will pay for the guest's meal or room, send a letter of apology, and pay for a future meal or stay.

If your facility is closed down due to the presence of roaches or rodents, BBBK will pay any fines, as well as all lost profits, plus $5,000.[33]

Customer service can provide a competitive edge for small firms regardless of the nature of the business. A **customer-satisfaction strategy** is a marketing plan that emphasizes the goal of customer service. It applies to consumer products and services as well as industrial products. There is no reason why customer service should be the exception rather than the rule.

High levels of customer service do not come cheaply. There is definitely a cost associated with offering superior service before, during, and after a sale. However, many customers are willing to pay for good service. These costs can be reflected in a product's or service's price, and they can sometimes be scheduled separately based on the amount of service requested.

David and Linda West, owners of San Luis Sourdough Co., in San Luis Obispo, California, subscribe to this philosophy. They price according to how much service their supermarket and specialty-food-store clients require. "If a supermarket is happy to have the bread dropped off at the back door, the wholesale price is 97¢. If the store wants to be able to return day-old bread for

customer-satisfaction strategy
a marketing plan that emphasizes customer service

full credit, the cost is $1.02 a loaf." The Wests figure the price covers the cost of the service.[34]

TOTAL QUALITY MANAGEMENT

total quality management (TQM)
popular quality control programs based on Japanese quality control methods

Total quality management (TQM) is an umbrella term encompassing the quality control programs which have become popular in U.S. businesses in the past several years.[35] TQM is rooted in the superior product quality of Japanese products in the 1970s. Large U.S. manufacturers fought the Japanese challenge with similar quality control programs.

Increasingly, small manufacturing firms are feeling the impact of TQM, partly due to pressure from the big companies which they supply. Also, smaller firms are interested in TQM principles because they recognize the potential for creating a better competitive advantage. TQM concepts, therefore, extend beyond manufacturing to firms offering final consumer products and services. We will briefly examine the elements of a TQM program related to offering final consumer products and services. (TQM as it relates to production and operations management is analyzed in Chapter 18.)

Quality improvement starts with the culture of the organization. Consider the remarks of Jim Zawacki, owner and president of Grand Rapids Spring & Wire Products, in Grand Rapids, Michigan—a small firm with 160 employees. Zawacki believes, "getting people to understand why we're in business," and building "trust, relationships, integrity, and communication," are the keys to developing the appropriate corporate culture for TQM. His firm is seeing results. Over the past five years, on-time delivery has gone from 60 percent to over 95 percent.[36]

Entrepreneurs should place top priority on creating and controlling quality customer service. One recent study indicates small firms are keenly aware of the importance of customer service when they compete with big business. As can be seen in Figure 3-9, approximately 70 percent of the small firms surveyed mentioned "customer service" as a preferred competitive tactic. Also note that "quality of employees" was mentioned quite frequently. Obviously, employees are critical ingredients in a quality customer service program.

Making customer service and satisfaction the number one priority is not necessarily as natural as it might seem. Business has used the phrase "the customer is always right" for decades, but have U.S. businesses achieved a high level of customer satisfaction? Consider the following summarized survey results. Companies of all sizes were included in this survey, and one-half of the companies had 500 or fewer employees. Is it fair to say there is room to improve customer satisfaction?

- Only 57 percent rate "meeting customer needs" as their number one priority.
- In 62 percent of the companies, not everyone is aware of what customers do with the company's product or service.

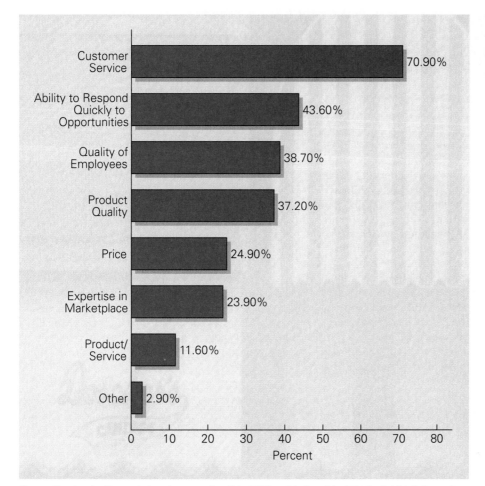

Figure 3-9
Areas in Which Small Companies Believe They Have an Advantage Over Big-Company Competitors

Source: Reprinted with permission, *Inc.* magazine (July 1990), p. 94. Copyright 1990 by Goldhirsh Group, Inc., 38 Commercial Wharf, Boston, MA 02110.

- Fewer than half of new products and services are developed or improved based on customer suggestions and complaints, despite an MIT study showing that the best innovations come from customers.
- Only 59 percent of the respondents contact lost customers; 7 percent do nothing when they lose a customer.
- In some companies (17 percent), not even salespeople talk to customers. It gets worse for senior management (22 percent don't talk to them), marketing (29 percent), and R&D (67 percent).
- Only 60 percent report they base their competitive strategy primarily on "attention to customer needs." (And they say that only 29 percent of their competitors emphasize this.)
- Thirty-three percent say their marketing strategy aims to produce business from new, as opposed to repeat, customers.[37]

SMALL BUSINESS IN ACTION

Try My Service On For Size

A marketing strategy emphasizing good customer service should provide the entrepreneur with a distinct advantage. An excellent example is the quality service policies of small-business owner Gail Sundling. Sundling operates Delmar Bootery in Albany, New York, where she is a 1992 state designee in the Blue Chip Enterprise program. (The program is jointly sponsored by Connecticut Mutual Life Insurance Co., the U.S. Chamber of Commerce, and *Nation's Business* magazine.) "I give my people on the floor every bit of my authority," to keep the customers happy, she says. Sundling estimates the cost of retaining a customer to be one-fifth of what it takes to gain a new one.

Several customer service techniques have worked well for her store. For example, anyone who buys a pair of shoes at her bootery gets free shoe shines for the life of the shoes. Sundling has learned that this policy not only creates goodwill but results in customers purchasing a lot of extras when they come in for a free shine.

Source: Bradford McKee, "If the Shoe Fits, They'll Be Back," *Nation's Business,* Vol. 80, No. 7, p. 8. Excerpted by permission from *Nation's Business,* July 1992. Copyright 1992 U.S. Chamber of Commerce.

Evaluating Customer Service

The delivery of customer service begins with an understanding of customer attitudes. Typically, a gap is found between these attitudes and the level of service being offered in any given industry. Most customers of auto repair shops, restaurants, retail stores, and other businesses recognize weaknesses in the service they receive from these firms. This, indeed, presents an opportunity to the small firm that is able to excel in its management of customer service.

Often, there are problems with the delivery of good service. Employees do not always share the owner's dedication to service. Therefore, employee attitudes must be changed before customers can receive maximum service. Scott Hanson recognized this in his management of Hanson Galleries in Sausalito, California. He works with his salespeople—called "art consultants"—to educate them in the difference between "selling a customer and servicing a client." It has worked. The best consultants make nearly $1 million in sales each year.[38]

Problems with customer service are recognized in a number of ways. Probably the most common is through customer complaints. Every firm strives to eliminate customer complaints. When they occur, however, they should be analyzed carefully to discover possible weaknesses in customer service. Customer hotlines should be available whenever possible.

Managers can also learn about customer service problems through personal observations and undercover techniques. A manager can evaluate service by talking directly to customers or by playing that role anonymously—for example, by a telephone call to one's own business. Also, there are professional undercover shopping services that play the customer role for business clients and make service evaluations.[39] Some restaurants and motels invite feedback on customer service by providing comment cards to customers.

1. The major forces that determine the level of competition in the marketplace are: (1) the entry of new competitors, (2) the threat of substitutes, (3) the bargaining power of buyers, (4) the bargaining power of suppliers, and (5) the rivalry among existing competitors.
2. A firm's competitive advantage can be built with a cost or marketing advantage. Product differentiation is frequently used as a means to gain a marketing advantage.
3. Market segmentation, sometimes called a "focus" strategy, is the process of dividing the total market for a product or service into groups with similar needs such that each group is likely to respond favorably to a specific marketing strategy. The three types of market segmentation strategy are the unsegmented approach, the multisegmentation approach, and the single-segmentation approach. Selecting a niche market is a special segmentation strategy that small firms can use successfully.
4. It is important that small firms use outstanding service to gain a competitive advantage. Small firms are potentially in a much better position to achieve a customer-satisfaction strategy. Total Quality Management is a term describing programs devoted to creating and controlling quality products and customer service.

DISCUSSION QUESTIONS

1. Think of one purchase experience in which you were extremely displeased. What was the primary reason for your dissatisfaction?
2. What are the two basic strategy options for creating a competitive advantage discussed in the chapter?
3. What advantages, if any, does a small firm have in creating a competitive advantage?
4. What are the five forces which dictate competition in any industry? How do they relate to the level of competition?
5. Explain the primary purpose of market segmentation. What are some examples that you can give?
6. Explain the difference, if any, between a multi- and single-segmentation strategy. Which one may be more appealing to a small firm? Why?
7. Discuss the need for market segmentation.

8. What types of variables are used for market segmentation? Would a small firm use the same variables as a large business? Why or why not?
9. Explain what is meant by niche marketing.
10. Give some examples of niche marketing in addition to those given in the chapter.
11. Discuss the role of quality customer service in the creation of a competitive advantage.
12. Think of a recent customer service policy you have encountered in your own consumer behavior. What made it a special event?
13. What is meant by the phrase "total quality management"?
14. Do you believe customer service quality is better or worse in small firms? Why?
15. Discuss how you have handled or would handle customer complaints with an employee or the complaining customer.

YOU MAKE THE CALL

Situation 1

Carolyn Duty has developed an idea for reusable shopping bags made from heavy twill poly-cotton canvas. There are six bags in a set. One of the bags has two Velcro straps that hold the remaining five bags when they are rolled up. "I designed the bags in a compact unit to take back and forth to the store with as little hassle as possible," says Duty. "The key in my mind was convenience for the shopper."

Duty has met with grocery store executives about distributing her bags. She has also been developing school markets that would sell the bags as fundraising projects. The retail price for the six bags is $34.95.

Questions
1. Is Mrs. Duty using a market segmentation strategy? Why or why not?
2. What type of market niche do you think she can successfully reach with this product? Why?
3. What types of quality concerns should she have regarding her product?

Source: Nora Goldstein, "Finding Your Niche," *In Business,* Vol. 13, No. 2 (March–April 1991), pp. 50–51.

Situation 2

Amy Wright is the owner of Fit Wright Shoes, a manufacturer of footwear located in Alice, Texas. Her company has pledged that all customers will have a lifetime replacement guarantee on all footwear bought from the company.

This guarantee applies to the entire shoe, even though parts of the product are made by another company.

Questions
1. Do you think a lifetime guarantee is too generous for this kind of product? Why or why not?

2. What impact will this policy have on quality standards in the company? Be specific.
3. What alternative customer service policies would you suggest?

EXPERIENTIAL EXERCISES

1. Select a recent issue of a business publication and report on the type of target market strategy you believe they use.
2. Visit a local small-business retailer and ask the manager to describe their customer service policies.
3. Select a new product that most of the class knows about. Divide into three or more groups, and write a brief description of what you believe is the best target market for that product. Be specific in your market profile. Read the description to the class.
4. Interview several of your friends to determine what personal experiences they can recount related to their satisfaction or dissatisfaction with a shopping experience in a small retail firm. Summarize their stories and report to the class.

REFERENCES TO SMALL-BUSINESS PRACTICES

Case, John. "The Time Machine," *Inc.,* Vol. 12, No. 6 (June 1990), pp. 48–55.
    This article is devoted to the strategy of Electronic Liquid Fillers, which achieved success with a strategy of delivering products to the customer faster than competitors.
Fuller, Charles. "King of the Mountain," *Entrepreneur,* Vol. 19, No. 4 (April 1991), pp. 173–177.
    In this article the growth of a bicycle business is followed from its early days to its current million-dollar sales level. The firm's niche is high-end quality products that pay attention to customer needs.
Henricks, Mark. "Satisfaction Guaranteed," *Entrepreneur,* Vol. 19, No. 5 (May 1991), pp. 120–125.
    This article discusses the importance of after-sale support to consumer satisfaction. The experiences of several companies are used to illustrate the service recommendations.
Posner, Bruce, "Growth Strategies," *Inc.,* Vol. 13, No. 12 (December 1991), pp. 110–112.
    This article describes several fast-growing companies that used varied strategies to achieve success.
Sellers, Patricia. "What Customers Really Want," *Fortune,* Vol. 121, No. 6 (June 4, 1990), pp. 58–68.
    The importance of service to customer and employee retention is discussed in this article. There are numerous suggestions for hiring and training employees who want to serve customers.

ENDNOTES

    1. Karl H. Vesper, *New Venture Strategies,* Revised Edition (Englewood Cliffs, NJ: Prentice-Hall, 1990), p. 192.
    2. John Case, "How To Launch An Inc. 500 Company," *Inc.,* Vol. 14, No. 10 (October 1992), p. 91.
    3. See Michael E. Porter, *Competitive Advantage* (New York: The Free Press, 1985), p. 5.

4. Michael E. Porter, "Know Your Place," *Inc.*, Vol. 13, No. 9 (September 1992), pp. 90–93.

5. Case, *op. cit.*

6. "Companies Can Now Say, 'Charge It!'," *Inc.*, Vol. 14, No. 8 (August 1992), p. 27.

7. Peter Davis, "Strategy is the Key to Staying in the Game," *Family Business* (June 1990), p. 11.

8. John Pierson, "There's Mulch Ado About Composting in the Round," *The Wall Street Journal* (December 2, 1992), p. B1.

9. For an excellent discussion of the relationship of marketing concepts to entrepreneurship, see Gerald E. Hills and Raymond W. LaForge, "Research at the Marketing Interface to Advance Entrepreneurship Theory," *Entrepreneurship Theory and Practice*, Vol. 16, No. 36 (Spring 1992), pp. 33–59.

10. Catherine Arnst, "PC Makers Head For 'SOHO'," *Business Week*, No. 3285 (September 28, 1992), p. 125.

11. "Ultimate in Product Segmentation," *Advertising Age* (September 23, 1985), p. 18.

12. "Initial Profits," *Entrepreneur*, Vol. 18, No. 3 (March 1990), p. 165.

13. Robin T. Peterson, "Small Business Usage of Target Marketing," *Journal of Small Business Management*, Vol. 29, No. 4 (October 1991), p. 81.

14. Ronald E. Merrill and Henry D. Sedgwick, *The New Venture Handbook* (New York: AMACOM, 1987), pp. 107–108.

15. Charles R. Stoner and Fred L. Fry, *Strategic Planning in the Small Business* (Cincinnati: South-Western Publishing Co., 1987), p. 109.

16. For an excellent discussion of the success of marketing strategies in established markets, see John L. Wood and Stanley F. Stasch, "How Small Share Firms Can Uncover Winning Strategies," *The Journal of Business Strategy*, Vol. 9, No. 5 (September–October 1988), pp. 26–31.

17. Udayan Gupta, "Narrowest Niches Can Yield Comfortable Profit Margin," *The Wall Street Journal* (September 26, 1990), p. B2.

18. *Ibid.*

19. *Ibid.*

20. Mary Beth Grover, "Brown Rice for Babies," *Forbes*, Vol. 147, No. 6 (March 18, 1992), pp. 63–64.

21. Merritt Des Voigne, "Starting On a Gum Wrapper," *Nation's Business*, Vol. 80, No. 7 (July 1992), p. 21.

22. Karen Fadel, "Different Strokes," *Entrepreneur*, Vol. 19, No. 4 (April 1991), p. 104.

23. Alan Radding, "Veryfine," *Advertising Age* (July 6, 1992), p. S-6.

24. Mark Lewyn, "For America Online, Nothing Is Nice as a Niche," *Business Week*, No. 3283 (September 14, 1992), p. 100.

25. "Some 'Green' Clothes for 'Green' Consumers," *The Wall Street Journal* (September 29, 1992), p. B1.

26. Michael Barrier, "Designer Pizza At Off-The-Rack Prices," *Nation's Business*, Vol. 79, No. 3 (March 1991), p. 13.

27. Eugene Carlson, "Regulations on Fluorescent Lamp Kindle New Industry," *The Wall Street Journal* (August 31, 1992), p. B2

28. For an interesting discussion of such tactics, see Edward P. DiMingo, "Marketing Strategies for Small-Share Players," *The Journal of Business Strategy*, Vol. 11, No. 1 (January/February 1990), pp. 26–30.

29. Henry Assael, *Marketing Principles & Strategy* (Hinsdale, IL: The Dryden Press, 1990), p. 100.

30. Scott Matulis, "The Customer Is King," *Entrepreneur*, Vol. 16, No. 9 (September 1988), p. 69.

31. *Ibid.*, p. 65.

32. Carl Sewell and Paul B. Brown, "Customers For Life," *Family Business*, Vol. 1, No. 10 (November 1990), pp. 39–40.

33. Christopher W.L. Hart, "The Power of Unconditional Service Guarantees," *Harvard Business Review*, Vol. 66, No. 4 (July–August 1988), p. 54.

34. Paul B. Brown, "You Get What You Pay For," *Inc.,* Vol. 12, No. 10 (October 1990), p. 155.

35. For an overview of the principles of TQM, see Richard J. Schonberger, "Is Strategy Strategic? Impact of Total Quality Management on Strategy," *Academy of Management Executive,* Vol. 6, No. 3 (1992), pp. 80–87.

36. Patricia A. Galagan, "How To Get Your TQM Training On Track," *Nation's Business,* Vol. 80, No. 10 (October 1992), p. 26.

37. Joan Koob Cannre with Donald Caplin, *Keeping Customers For Life* (New York,: AMACOM, 1991), p. 237.

38. Tom Richman, "Come Again," *Inc.,* Vol. 11, No. 4 (April 1989), pp. 177–178.

39. Mark Stevens, "Learn Your Firm's Inside Story," *Nation's Business,* Vol. 77, No. 8 (August 1989), pp. 59–60.

CHAPTER 4

Startup and Buyout Opportunities

SPOTLIGHT ON SMALL BUSINESS

Douglas Foreman

For Douglas Foreman, a diet was the beginning of a new business. Foreman, trying to lose weight, cut back on some foods, but didn't want to give up his favorite snack—tortilla chips. At that time, all commercial chips were fried. Foreman tried *baking* a batch at home and was so pleased with the results, he suggested the method to chip makers. Meeting disinterest, Foreman decided to make and market the chips himself.

Foreman wanted it to appear that he had a going business. So, he bought $200 worth of cellophane bags, custom-made labels, and a heat sealer. He baked enough chips to fill two bags and took them to a local health food supermarket. Demand grew, and Foreman increased production and also added a line of low-fat dips and sauces.

Foreman's startup capital came from friends, family, and the sale of his own restaurant business. Then a customer and two entrepreneurs bought shares of the company, Guiltless Gourmet, Inc. Expansion has been funded, in part, by a Small Business Administration loan. Foreman now owns 30 percent of the three-year-old business, and the worth of this share alone is estimated at around $2 million.

Source: Toni Mack, "Tortilla Wizard," *Forbes,* Vol. 150, No. 2 (July 20, 1992), pp. 88–89. Adapted from FORBES magazine by permission. © Forbes Inc. 1992.

After studying this chapter, you should be able to:
1. Give three reasons for developing a startup business.
2. Describe five forces that influence whether an idea is a good investment opportunity.
3. Discuss pros and cons of buying an existing business.
4. Summarize four basic approaches for determining a fair value for a business.

startup
buyout
Type A startup ideas
Type B startup ideas
Type C startup ideas
serendipity
asset-based valuation approach

modified book value approach
replacement value approach
liquidation value approach
market-based valuation approach

earnings-based valuation approach
capitalization rate
cash-flow-based valuation
risk premium

This chapter and the two that follow explore four different types of small-business ownership opportunities: startups, buyouts, franchises, and family businesses. Figure 4-1 depicts each of these options.

Building a business from "scratch"—a **startup**—is the route most often thought of when discussing new-venture creation. There is no question that startups represent a significant opportunity for many entrepreneurs. However, even more individuals realize their entrepreneurial dreams through other alternatives—either purchasing an existing firm (**buyout**), franchising, or entering a family business.

The startup and buyout options for entering small business are examined in this chapter. Franchising is discussed in Chapter 5, and the family business is analyzed in Chapter 6.

startup
building a business from "scratch"

buyout
purchasing an existing business

THE STARTUP: CREATING A NEW BUSINESS

There are several possible reasons for developing a startup business, rather than pursuing other alternatives. Such reasons would include:

1. Invention of a new product or service that necessitates a new type of business.
2. Freedom to select the ideal location, equipment, products or services, employees, suppliers, and bankers.
3. Avoidance of undesirable precedents, policies, procedures, and legal commitments of existing firms.

Figure 4-1
Alternative Routes
to Small-Business
Ownership

Startup

Buyout

Franchising

Family Business

Assuming that one of these reasons exists, several issues must be considered: (1) What are the different types of startup ideas you should consider? (2) How do you identify a genuine opportunity? (3) What are some sources for new ideas? (4) How do you refine your idea? Lets look at each of these questions.

Kinds of Startup Ideas

The startup ideas depicted in Figure 4-2 portray different types of new-venture ideas. Note that the spotlights—the types of ideas—shed light on the entrepreneur's search for a startup opportunity.

Type A startup ideas
provide customers
with an existing
product not available in their market

Many startups are developed from **Type A ideas**—providing customers with a product or service that does not exist in their market but already exists somewhere else. An example would be a maid-service venture in a city that previously had no service of this type.

Type B startup ideas
provide customers
with a new product

Startups are also based on **Type B ideas**—a technically new process. One example is David Olson's startup, named STARS, based in Austin, Texas. He used satellite dish technology to form a mobile satellite transmitter and receiver business that he now uses to carry data and voice transmissions for such corporate clients as Tenneco, Inc.[1] Another example is a small Redwood City, California, company, Advanced Polymer Systems, Inc. The company has developed a microsponge technology allowing oils to be contained inside billions of

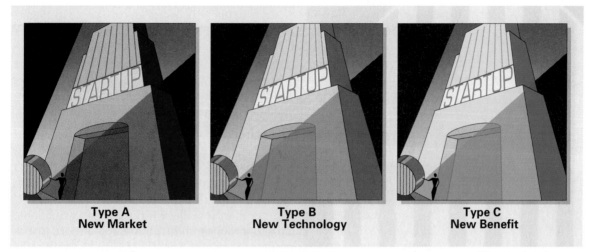

Figure 4-2
Types of Ideas That
Shed Light on
Startups

microscopic sponges. "It's a unique technology and it is applicable to a lot of different industries," states one investor.[2]

Type C startup ideas probably account for the largest number of all new-venture startups. These are concepts for performing old functions in new and improved ways. In fact, most new ventures, especially in service firms, are founded on "me, too" strategies, differentiating themselves through superior execution and better service. One example would be the baby stroller that Phil and Mary Baechler designed and now manufacture. It performs the function of transporting young children—nothing really new—but in an improved manner. It pushes more easily and is more difficult to overturn than previous designs. Their primary market is young parents who are joggers who want to push their babies as they run.[3]

Type C startup ideas provide customers with an improved product

Identifying and Evaluating
Investment Opportunities

Most of us at one time or another become convinced that we have a great idea for a startup business. At least from our perspective, we believe that others would find the product or service to have appeal. However, experience tells us that a good idea is not necessarily a good investment opportunity. In fact, there is a tendency for most of us to become infatuated with an idea, and underestimate the difficulty involved in developing market receptivity to our idea. To qualify as a good investment opportunity, our product must meet a real need with respect to functionality, quality, durability, and price. The opportunity ultimately depends on our ability to convince consumers (the market) of the benefits of the product or service. "Startups with products that do not serve clear and important needs cannot expect to be 'discovered' by enough customers to make a difference."[4] Only if the "discovery" occurs at a significant level do we have a good investment opportunity. Thus, the market determines whether an idea has potential as an investment opportunity. That is, only the marketplace will finally tell us whether the idea creates value for the end user of the product or service—value that the consumer is willing to pay for.

There are many forces that influence whether an idea is also a good opportunity. Some of the more fundamental requirements include the following:

1. The timing must be right. Opportunities arise in what some call "real time." The product or service concept may be a good one, but if the timing is not right, there is no viable investment opportunity. For an entrepreneur to seize an opportunity requires that the window of opportunity be opening, and remain open long enough to exploit the opportunity.
2. The proposed business must be able to achieve a durable or sustainable competitive advantage. Failure to understand the nature and importance of having a sustainable competitive advantage has resulted in the failure of many small firms. This issue deserves special attention.
3. The economics of the venture need to be rewarding and even forgiving, allowing for significant profit and growth potential. That is, the profit margin (profit as a percentage of sales) and return on investment (profit as a percentage of the size of the investment) must be attractive enough to allow for errors and mistakes, and still create significant economic benefits.
4. There must be a good fit of the entrepreneur with the opportunity. In other words, the opportunity must be captured and developed by someone who has the appropriate skills and experience, and who has access to the critical resources necessary to enable the venture to grow.
5. There must be no fatal flaw in the venture—that is, no circumstance or development that could in and of itself make the business a loser.

The foregoing criteria are also presented in Figure 4-3, where we identify somewhat more specifically the evaluation criteria for a startup venture. In either case, the point being made may be stated as follows: Beware of being deluded into thinking that an idea is a "natural," and cannot miss. The market can be a real disciplinarian for those who have not done their homework. However, for those who succeed at identifying a meaningful opportunity in a world of chaos and confusion, the rewards can be sizable.

Sources of Startup Ideas

Since startups begin with ideas, let us consider the circumstances that tend to spawn such new ideas. Several studies have addressed the question of where new product ideas for small-business startups originate. Figure 4-4 gives the results of a study conducted by the National Federation of Independent Business Foundation, which found that "prior work experience" accounted for 45 percent of the ideas for new businesses. The next highest source was "personal in-

Figure 4-3   Evaluation Criteria for a Startup Venture

Criterion	Attractiveness	
	Favorable	**Unfavorable**
Market Factors		
Need for the product	Well identified	Unfocused
Customers	Reachable; receptive	Unreachable; strong product loyalty for competitor
Value created by product or service for the customer	Significant	Not significant
Life of product	Use extends beyond time for customer to recover investment plus profit	To be used for a time less than that required for customer to recover investment
Market structure	Emerging industry; not highly competitive	Highly concentrated competition; mature or declining industry
Market size	$100 million sales or more	Unknown or less than $10 million sales or multibillion
Market growth rate	Growing by at least 30% annually	Contracting or growth less than 10% annually
Competitive Advantage		
Cost structure	Low-cost producer	No production cost advantage
Degree of control over:		
Price	Moderate to strong	Nonexistent
Costs	Moderate to strong	Nonexistent
Channels of supply	Moderate to strong	Nonexistent
Barriers to entry:		
Proprietary information or regulatory protection	Have or can develop	Not possible
Response/lead-time advantage	Resilient and responsive	Nonexistent
Legal, contractual advantage	Proprietary or exclusivity	Nonexistent
Contacts and networks	Well-developed	Limited
Economics		
Return on investment	25% or more; durable	Less than 15%; fragile
Investment requirements	Small to moderate amount; easily financed	Large amount; financed with difficulty
Time to break-even profits or to reach positive cashflows	Under 2 years	More than 3 years
Management Team Issues		
	Proven experience, with diverse skills among the management team	Solo entrepreneur with no related experience
Fatal Flaws Issue		
	None	One or more

Adapted from Jeffry A. Timmons, *New Venture Creation* (Homewood, IL: Irwin, 1990), p.76.

Figure 4-4
The New Idea Pie

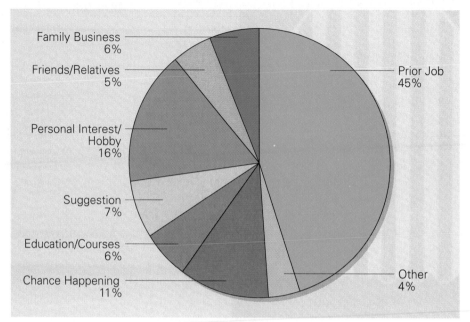

Source: Data developed and provided by The NFIB Foundation and sponsored by the American Express Travel Related Services Company, Inc.

terest and hobbies," for 16 percent of the total. A "chance happening" accounted for 11 percent of the new ideas reported in the research.

Let us consider in more detail the circumstances that tend to create new ideas. Since there are numerous possibilities (a new idea can come from virtually anywhere), we have developed four categories to examine: personal experience, hobbies, accidental discovery, and deliberate search.

Personal Experience. One basis for startup ideas is personal experience, which is obtained both at home and on the job. Consider "Saved By The Bell," a small business in New York City that handles a variety of chores for busy individuals. Started by Susan Bell in 1984, the company serves over 50 clients who pay a fee to get the grocery shopping done, pick up shirts at the laundry, or a variety of other household chores. The idea for her personal-service business came from her own experience. One day, while sitting on her apartment floor surrounded by notes on things to do, she "realized that there are a lot of other people like me—people who need a 'wife' to help them with the details of their lives."[5] Shortly after this experience, she started the business.

Also, from knowledge gleaned from their present or recent jobs, some employees see possibilities in modifying an existing product, improving a service, or duplicating a business concept in a different location. For example, a furniture salesperson may see the possibility of opening a new furniture store in a

S M A L L   B U S I N E S S   I N   A C T I O N

Bringing an Existing Product into Focus

Max Morris, at age 57, was unable to drive or work. He had suddenly developed cataracts. Unable to read without great difficulty, he began to experiment with various reading aids. And even after surgery, which restored his sight, he continued to work with more efficient ways to read.

Eventually he developed his Kwikscan system, which emphasizes keywords in a passage in boldface print. These keywords, when linked by the reader, form their own meaningful sentences. Morris obtained a patent for the process and then formed his own business, Micro-Books, Inc. But what should he publish?

"I knew how much of a problem reading is for many people today—and how few actually read books—yet some publications have vast audiences," he recalls. . . . "So we decided to publish a series of 'how-to' titles in Kwikscan that would sell for less than $2, and sell them *in supermarkets and other mass-market outlets."*

Later, however, Morris had a better idea—publish the Bible with the Kwikscan system. Since the Bible is the best-selling title of all time and is unprotected by copyright, Morris decided to give it a try. Working in the den of his home with his wife and two children, he turned the Kwikscan version of the New Testament into a reality.

Source: William G. Flanagan. "In the Beginning Was the WORD," *Forbes,* April 20, 1987, pp. 100–101. Forbes Inc., 1987. Excerpted from FORBES magazine by permission. © Forbes Inc. 1987.

different area of the city. The new store may follow the business strategy of the existing store, or it may feature different, restricted, or expanded lines of merchandise. It may also adopt credit or delivery policies that are more appealing to customers in that area. Work experience may well be the most productive of all sources of new-venture ideas.

Hobbies. Sometimes hobbies grow beyond their stature as hobbies to become businesses. For example, a coin collector who buys and sells coins to build a personal collection may easily become a coin dealer. In 1976, Eleanor Mills made one of her ceramic plates, adorned with handpainted sketches, for her sister. Friends and neighbors loved it and wanted to place orders. This was the beginning of Millscraft, The Plate Place. Today, Mrs. Mills works full time in the business.[6]

SMALL BUSINESS IN ACTION

An Idea Fits a Need

In August 1985, a women's shoe store by the name of Magnifete opened in downtown Cincinnati. The entrepreneur owner is Shelagh Watson, who recalls that her idea for the store started when "I couldn't find fashion shoes in my size—11½. That started me thinking about the concept of a women's shoe store that catered to the oversize range." That's what she started. Magnifete sold 6,500 pairs of shoes in 1986 and grossed over $367,000 in sales.

Watson wants customers in her store to be able to find large sizes in stock so they can try the shoes and take them home without special ordering. The store maintains 5,000 pairs of shoes in inventory.

Lacking business experience, Watson took a course in starting a business before she opened Magnifete. She also hired a consultant to help develop a business plan. Two years later, in 1987, Watson began franchising her store concept.

Source: Marcia King, "Having a Football," *Nation's Business,* Vol. 76, No. 2, p. 75. Reprinted by permission, *Nation's Business,* February 1988. Copyright 1988 U.S. Chamber of Commerce.

Hobbies are often turned into startups by business executives who retire. For example, Bob Howard, at age 58, retired from a corporate position in Scottsdale, Arizona, to pursue his tennis hobby full time. He now teaches tennis courses for senior players.[7]

serendipity
the faculty for making desirable discoveries by accident

Accidental Discovery. As a source of new startup ideas, accidental discovery involves something called **serendipity**—the faculty for making desirable discoveries by accident. Any person may stumble across a useful idea in the ordinary course of day-to-day living. This was true of Patty Ludwin, founder of Calamity Jeans and Jewels, in Canonsburg, Pennsylvania. Her firm sells jeans riddled with bullet holes. Her inspiration came when a sharpshooter girlfriend shot up a pair of her boyfriend's jeans in a lovers' spat. (He was not wearing the jeans at the time!) The man liked the "new" jeans even better than before. Currently, the bullet-hole jeans are sold through mail order.[8] Products like this are very faddish, but profits can be made while they are "hot."

Deliberate Search. A startup idea may also emerge from a prospective entrepreneur's deliberate search—a purposeful exploration to find a new idea. Entrepreneurs can survey their own capabilities and then look at the new products or services they are capable of producing, or they can first look for needs in the marketplace and then relate these to their own capabilities. The latter approach—beginning with a look at market needs—has apparently produced

Figure 4-5
A Hobby Such as
This Intricate Wood-
working Can Evolve
into a Business
Startup.

more successful startups, especially in the field of consumer goods and services, than the former.

Magazines and other periodicals are excellent sources of startup ideas. One way of generating startup ideas is by reading about the creativity of other entrepreneurs. For example, in most issues, *Inc.* magazine features many kinds of business opportunities in the section "The American Dream."

A deliberate search also helps in a general way by stimulating a readiness of mind. Prospective entrepreneurs who are thinking seriously about new-business ideas will be more receptive to new ideas from any source.

Since a truly creative person may find useful ideas in many different ways, the sources of new-venture ideas mentioned here are suggestive, not exhaustive. We encourage you to seek and reflect upon new-venture ideas in whatever circumstances you find yourself.

Refining a New-Venture Idea

A new-venture idea often requires an extended period of time for refinement and testing. This is particularly true for original inventions that require developmental work to make them operational. The need for refining a new idea is not limited to high-technology ventures, however. Almost any idea for a new business deserves careful study and typically requires modification as the aspiring entrepreneur moves toward opening day for the new business.

An example is found in the case of John Morse, who founded Fratelli's Ice Cream in Seattle. A course with Karl Vesper at the University of Washington required him to bring some practicality to his abstract ideas for this business.

"When I first mentioned the ice cream idea to Karl, he told me I was crazy. He pointed out that we had experience bordering on weeks, no contacts, and that we'd be up against big hitters," says Morse. "The idea was 99% inspiration and 1% thought. Karl forced me to think it through." Responding to Vesper's challenges over the next two years, Morse finally signed an agreement with a local dairy to produce Fratelli's ice cream. "They had 76 years of experience—and connections," he says. Today he annually sells $1 million of ice cream in three states.[9]

The process of preparing a business plan, as discussed later in this book, helps the individual to think through an idea and consider all aspects of a proposed business. Outside experts can be used to review the business plan, and their questions and suggestions can help to improve it. For example, the founders of a rotary-drill venture had the initial strategy to price their products below the competition even though they had a superior product innovation in a growing market.[10] Outside experts persuaded them to price 10 percent over the competition, and this decision contributed significantly to later profits.

BUYING AN EXISTING BUSINESS

Would-be entrepreneurs can choose to buy an existing business as an alternative to buying a franchise, starting from scratch, or joining a family business. This decision should be made only after careful consideration of the advantages and disadvantages of buying an established business.

Reasons for Buying an Existing Business

All decisions in life have pros and cons. The decision to buy an existing business is no exception. A listing of some of these pros and cons follows.[11]

Pros

1. Prior successful operation of a business increases your chances of success with the same business.
2. Prior successful operation provides the location of the business previously selected and in use.
3. If the business has been profitable or is headed toward profit, you will be profitable sooner than if you start up your own business.
4. The amount of planning that may be necessary for an ongoing business will probably be less than that for a new business.

5. You will already have established customers or clientele.
6. You will already have established suppliers and will not have to look for them.
7. You may already have inventory on hand and will not lose the time necessary for selecting, ordering, and waiting for the order to arrive before you can make your first sales.
8. Necessary equipment is probably already on hand.
9. Financing will be necessary for the single transaction of purchasing the business.
10. You may be able to buy the business at a bargain price.
11. You will acquire the benefit of the experience of the prior owner.
12. If employees are on board, they are probably already experienced in the business.
13. You may be able to finance all or part of the purchase price through a note to the owner.
14. Existing records of the business may help you and guide you in running the business.

Cons

1. You will inherit any bad will that exists because of the way the business has been managed.
2. The employees who are currently working for the company may not be the best or the best for you and the way you manage.
3. The image of the business is already established. If it is a poor image, it will be difficult to change.
4. Precedents have already been set by the previous owners. They may be difficult to change.
5. Modernization may be needed.
6. The purchase price may create a burden on future cash flow and profitability.
7. It is possible that you can overpay due to misrepresentation or an inaccurate appraisal of what the business is worth.
8. The business location may be a drawback.

This list of the pros and cons of buying an existing business can be condensed into three main considerations in the decision to purchase an existing business: (1) reduction of uncertainties, (2) acquisition of ongoing operations and relationships, and (3) a bargain price. We will examine each of these in more detail.

Reduction of Uncertainties. A successful going concern has demonstrated an ability to attract customers, control costs, and make a profit. Although future operations may be different, the firm's past record shows what it can do under actual market conditions. For example, the satisfactory location of a going concern eliminates one major uncertainty. Although traffic counts are useful in assessing the value of a potential location, the acid test comes when a business opens its doors at that location. This test has already been met in the case of an existing firm. The results are available in the form of sales and profit data.

Acquisition of Ongoing Operations and Relationships. The buyer of an existing business typically acquires its personnel, inventories, physical facilities, established banking connections, and ongoing relationships with trade suppliers. Consider the time and effort otherwise required in acquiring them "from scratch." Of course, this situation is an advantage only under certain conditions. For example, the firm's skilled, experienced employees constitute a valuable asset only if they will continue to work for the new owner. The physical facilities must not be obsolete, and the relationships with banks and suppliers must be healthy.

A Bargain Price. A going business may become available at what seems to be a low price. Whether it is actually a "good buy" must be determined by the prospective new owner. The price may appear low, but several factors could make the "bargain price" anything but a bargain. For example, the business may be losing money; the location may be deteriorating; or the seller may intend to reopen another business as a competitor. However, the business may indeed be a bargain and turn out to be a wise investment.

Finding a Business to Buy

Frequently in the course of day-to-day living and business contacts, a would-be buyer comes across an opportunity to buy an existing business. For example, a sales representative for a manufacturer or a wholesaler may be offered an opportunity to buy a customer's retail business. In other cases, the would-be buyer may need to search for a business to buy.

Other sources of business leads include suppliers, distributors, trade associations, and even bankers, who may know of business firms available for purchase. Also, realtors—particularly those who specialize in the sale of business firms and business properties—can provide leads. In addition, there are specialized brokers, called "matchmakers," who handle all the arrangements in closing a buyout. At least 2,000 such matchmakers handle mergers and acquisitions of small and mid-sized companies.

Investigating and Evaluating the Existing Business

Regardless of the source of business leads, each opportunity requires a background investigation and careful evaluation. As a preliminary step, the buyer needs to acquire information about the business. Some of this information can be obtained through personal observation or discussion with the seller. Also important is talking with other parties such as suppliers, bankers, and possibly customers of the business. Although some of this investigation requires personal checking, the buyer can also seek the help of outside experts. The two most valuable sources of assistance in this regard are accountants and lawyers. However, the prospective buyer should not relinquish the final decision to the "experts." Too often, advisors have a bias for the acquisition to be completed. For one thing, their fees may be more if the business is acquired. While advisors are usually valuable in these situations, especially where the buyer is inexperienced, the final consequences of purchasing a business, be they good or bad, are borne by the buyer. As a result, it is a mistake to assume that the "professionals" are infallible. They will not be the ones to pay the price if the decision to buy proves to be a mistake. Seek advice and counsel, but the decision is too important to entrust to someone else. Also, it is wise to seek out others who have acquired a business, to learn from their experience. Their perspective will be different from that of a consultant, and it brings some balance to the counsel received.

The seller's real reasons for selling a going business may or may not be disclosed. Robert Haas, general partner of Intercapco, a venture capital firm, expresses this concern by saying, "When somebody puts a company on the market, you wonder why they are trying to get rid of it. Either the company is not doing well, or it has a skeleton in the closet that will affect its future performance."[12] The buyer must be wary, therefore, of taking the seller's explanations at face value. Here, for example, are some of the most common reasons why owners offer their businesses for sale:

1. Old age or illness.
2. Desire to relocate in a different section of the country.
3. Decision to accept a position with another company.
4. Unprofitability of the business.
5. Discontinuance of an exclusive sales franchise.

The buyer will also be interested in the history of the business and the direction in which it is moving. To form a clear idea of the firm's value, however, the buyer must eventually examine the financial data pertaining to its operation. Although valuation is not a science, the entrepreneur must decide how much the business is worth. A logical starting point is an independent audit of the firm offered for sale.

The Independent Audit. The major purpose of an independent audit is to reveal the accuracy and completeness of the financial statements of the business. It also determines whether the seller has used acceptable accounting procedures in depreciating equipment and in valuing inventory. If financial statements are available for the past five or ten years, or even longer, the buyer can obtain some idea of trends for the business.

Adjustment of Audited Statements. Even audited statements may be misleading and require "normalizing" to obtain a realistic picture of the business. For example, business owners sometimes understate business income in an effort to minimize taxable income. On the other hand, expenses, such as employee training or advertising, may be reduced to abnormally low levels, in an effort to make the income look good in the hopes of selling the business.

Other items that may need adjustment include personal or family expenses and wage or salary payments. For example, costs related to the family use of business vehicles frequently appear as a business expense. In some situations, family members receive excessive compensation or none at all. "I don't touch 80 percent of the businesses . . . even when you have the books and records, it's a fiction . . . the owners hide the perks," cautions Stanley Salmore, a Beverly Hills business broker.[13] All items must be examined carefully to be sure that they relate to the business and are realistic. Figure 4-6 shows an income statement that has been adjusted by a prospective buyer. Notice carefully the reasons for the adjustments that have been made. Naturally, many other adjustments can be performed.

The buyer should also scrutinize the seller's balance sheet to see whether asset book values are realistic. Property often appreciates in value after it is recorded on the books.[14] In other cases, physical facilities or inventory or receivables decline in value so that their actual worth is less than their inflated book value.

Valuation of the Business

At some point in deciding whether or not to buy a company, you must decide what you believe to be a fair value for the firm. Let us begin with a word of caution. Valuing a company is not easy or exact. Officers of the Corporate Investment Business Brokers describe the situation as follows:

A lot of [small businesses] are still run out of shoe boxes . . . . What to do? Ask to examine federal tax returns and state sales tax statements . . . . You can gain a better fix on the business by looking through invoices and receipts with both customers and suppliers, as well as bank statements.[15]

asset-based valuation approach
the value of a business determined by examining the value of its assets

While numerous techniques of valuing a company are used, they are typically derivations of four basic approaches: (1) asset-based valuations, (2) market-based valuations, (3) earnings-based valuations, and (4) cash-flow-based valuations. The basic ideas of these approaches are explained in the following sections.

modified book value approach
the value of a business determined by adjusting book value to reflect differences between the historical cost and the current value of the asset

Asset-Based Valuation. The **asset-based valuation approach** assumes that the value of a firm can be determined by examining the value of the underlying assets of the business. Three variations of this approach include estimating (1) a modified book value, (2) the replacement value of the assets, and (3) the assets' liquidation value. The **modified-book value approach** uses the firm's book value, as shown in the balance sheet, and adjusts this value to reflect any obvious differences between the historical cost of an asset and its current value. For instance, marketable securities held by the firm may have a to-

Figure 4-6   Income Statement as Adjusted by Prospective Buyer

Original Income Statement			Required Adjustments	Adjusted Income Statement	
Estimated sales	$172,000			$172,000	
Cost of goods sold	84,240			84,240	
Gross profit		$87,760			$87,760
Operating expenses:					
Rent	$20,000		Rental agreement will expire in six months; Rent is expected to increase 20 percent.	$24,000	
Salaries	19,860			19,860	
Telephone	990			990	
Advertising	11,285			11,285	
Utilities	2,580			2,580	
Insurance	1,200		Property is underinsured; Adequate coverage will double present cost.	2,400	
Professional services	1,200			1,200	
Credit card expense	1,860		Amount of credit card expense is unreasonably large; Approximately $1,400 of this amount should be classified as personal expense.	460	
Miscellaneous	1,250	60,225		1,250	$64,025
Net income		$27,535			$23,735

tally different market value than the historical book value. The same may be true for real estate. The second asset-based approach, the **replacement value approach,** attempts to determine what it would cost to replace each of the firm's assets. The third method, the **liquidation value approach,** estimates the amount of money that could be received if the firm ended its operations and liquidated the individual assets.

The asset-based approaches are not held in high esteem. Using historical costs from the balance sheet may bear little relationship to the current value of the assets. The book value of an asset was never intended to measure present value. While making adjustments for this misapplication may be better than no recognition of the inherent weakness, it is building an estimate of value on a bad foundation. Also, all three techniques fail to recognize the firm as a going concern. However, while we acknowledge the weakness of this approach, it is still frequently used in conjunction with other methods, just to be "conserva-

replacement value approach
the value of a business based on the cost to replace the firm's assets

liquidation value approach
the value of a business based on the money available if the firm were to liquidate its assets

Figure 4-7
Entrepreneurs
Study Business
Records to
Determine the
Valuation of a
Business

tive." Its a bit like an old habit that is hard to break. The only possible exception to this criticism is in valuing firms that either are in the natural resources industry or the securities industry.

Market-Based Valuation. The **market-based valuation approach** relies on the marketplace in estimating a firm's value. The method looks at the actual sales prices (market values) of similar firms, relative to their net income and to their book value of equity.[16] In using sales prices or market values for valuing a company, we seek out firms that are "comparable" to the one being valued and compute the price-earnings ratio and/or the market-value-to-book-value ratio for these comparable companies. We then apply these ratios to estimate our prospective company's value if it had the same price-earnings or market-to-book values as the similar firms that were recently sold.

The approach is not as easy as it might appear, because it is not always easy to find a company that is a good comparison in every way. It is not enough simply to find a firm in the same industry, although that might provide a rough approximation. Instead, we need to find a company that is in the same or similar type business and that has similar growth rates, financial structure, asset turnover ratios (sales/total assets), and comparable profit margins (profits/sales). However, in this regard, there is considerable published information about company purchases. For instance, *Mergerstat Review* publishes the price for all company sales that were announced in the public media. Also, many of the larger accounting firms have departments that may be able to give some insight as to the selling price of comparable companies.

Example: Assume that we are considering the purchase of the Aberdeen Company, which recently had net income of $80,000 and a book value of eq-

market-based valuation approach
the value of a business based on the sale prices of comparable firms

uity of $300,000. We are interested in knowing what a "fair price" would be for the company. We have located three comparable firms that recently sold on average for six times the firms' net income. That is,

$$\frac{\text{Firm market value}}{\text{Net income}} = 6$$

Also, these firms' market-to-book values, on average, were 1.5, measured as follows:

$$\frac{\text{Firm market value}}{\text{Equity book value}} = 1.5$$

Using this information, we may estimate the market value of Aberdeen's equity in the following ways:

$$\frac{\text{Aberdeen market value}}{\text{Aberdeen net income}} = 6$$

$$\frac{\text{Aberdeen}}{\text{market value}} = 6 \times \left(\frac{\text{Aberdeen}}{\text{net income}} \right)$$

Given Aberdeen's net income of $80,000, we would estimate its equity market value (the owner's value) to be $480,000:

$$\frac{\text{Aberdeen}}{\text{market value}} = 6 \times \$80,000$$
$$= \$480,000$$

Next, using the market-value-to-book-value-of-equity ratio, we would estimate Aberdeen's equity to be worth $450,000, calculated as follows:

$$\frac{\text{Aberdeen market value}}{\text{Aberdeen equity book value}} = 1.5$$

$$\text{Aberdeen market value} = 1.5 \times \left(\begin{array}{c} \text{equity} \\ \text{book} \\ \text{value} \end{array} \right)$$
$$= 1.5 \times \$300,000$$
$$= \$450,000$$

Thus, using the market-based valuation methods, we could reasonably argue that the market value of Aberdeen Company's equity ownership, a price we might be willing to pay for the firm, is between $450,000 and $480,000.

Earnings-Based Valuation. We now take a different perspective, where the value of a firm is determined not by the historical or replacement costs nor by market comparables, but by the future returns from the investment. We want to determine the value of the firm based on its ability to pro-

earnings-based valuation approach
the value of a business based on its potential future income

capitalization rate
a figure, determined by the riskiness of current earnings and the expected growth rate of earnings, used to assess the earnings-based value of a business

duce future income or profits—thus, the name, **earnings-based valuation approach.**

Different procedures are used in valuing a company based upon its earnings, but the underlying concept is generally the same: determine a "normalized earnings" figure and divide this amount by a **capitalization rate.** Firm value using this technique is measured as follows:

$$\text{Firm's value} = \frac{\text{normalized earnings}}{\text{capitalization rate}}$$

By "normalized earnings," we mean that the earnings should be adjusted for any unusual items, such as a one-time loss on the sale of real estate, or the consequence of a fire. Also, we should be certain that all relevant expenses are included, such as a fair salary for the owner's time.

The appropriate capitalization rate is determined by the riskiness of the earnings, and the expected growth rate of these earnings in the future. The relationships are as follows:

1. The more (less) *risky* the business, the higher (lower) the *capitalization rate* to be used, and as a consequence, the lower (higher) the firm's *equity value.*
2. The higher (lower) the *projected growth rate* in future earnings, the lower (higher) the *capitalization rate* to be used, and therefore the higher (lower) the *value.*

The foregoing relationships are presented graphically in Figure 4-8.

In practice, the capitalization rate is determined largely by "rules of thumb," based upon conventional wisdom and the experience of the person

Figure 4-8
Determinants of a Firm's Capitalization Rate

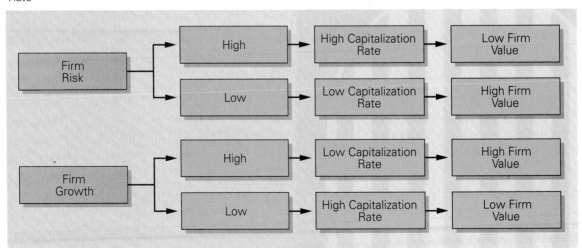

doing the valuation. For example, the capitalization rates for some types of firms might be something as follows:

- Small, well-established business, but vulnerable to recessions   15%
- Small companies requiring average executive ability but in a highly competitive environment   25%
- Firms that depend on the special, often unusual skill of one, or of a small group of managers   50%

For example, assume that the "normalized earnings" for a company is $130,000, before deducting anything for the owner's salary, and that a fair salary for the owner's time would be $50,000. Using the earnings-capitalization technique, we would capitalize the $80,000 in earnings ($130,000 – $50,000). If we use a 20 percent capitalization rate, we would value the firm at $400,000, calculated as follows:

$$\text{Firm's value} = \frac{\text{normalized earnings}}{\text{capitalization rate}}$$

$$= \frac{\$80,000}{0.20}$$

$$= \$400,000$$

Cash-Flow-Based Valuation. The foregoing earnings-based valuation approach, while extremely popular in practice, presents a conceptual problem for us—it considers earnings, rather than cash flows, as the item to be valued. The market value of a firm should be based on future cash flows, and not its reported earnings, especially not a single year of earnings. Valuing a firm is just too complex an issue to be captured in a single earnings figure. For one thing, there are simply too many ways to affect the firm's earnings favorably (through generally accepted accounting principles) that have no effect on future cash flows, or, even worse, may result in reduced cash flows.

Think of buying a business as similar to investing in a savings account in a bank. In a savings account, you are interested in the cash (capital) you have to put in the account and the future cash flows you will receive in the form of interest. In like manner, when you buy a company, you should be interested in future cash flows received relative to capital invested. In a **cash-flow-based valuation,** you then compare your expected rate of return on investment (the interest rate promised by the bank) with your required rate of return to know if the investment (savings account) is satisfactory.

In measuring the present value of a company's future cash flows, you must decide on an appropriate discount rate, or required rate of return.[17] This rate is not the same as the capitalization rate used when you capitalize earnings. The capitalization rate is used to convert the current or normalized earnings into value. A required rate of return is used as a discount rate applicable to a stream of projected future cash flows. The required rate of return is the opportunity cost of the funds, where you think, "If I do not make this investment

cash-flow-based valuation
the value of a business determined by a comparison of the expected and required rates of return on the investment

(buy this company), what is the best rate of return that I could earn on another investment having a similar level of risk?" The answer to this question gives you the appropriate discount rate to be used in valuing future cash flows.

The required rate of return also equals the existing risk-free rate in the capital markets, such as the rate earned on short-term U.S. government securities, plus a return premium for assuming risk. In other words,

$$\frac{\text{Required}}{\text{rate of return}} = \frac{\text{risk-free}}{\text{rate}} + \frac{\text{risk}}{\text{premium}}$$

For instance, assume the current rate on U.S. Treasury Bills, a short-term government security, is 4 percent. If for a given investment, such as buying a company, your risk premium is 15 percent, then your required rate of return ought to be 19 percent (4% + 15%).

How you estimate the risk premium is clearly an important ingredient to determining the required rate of return. One source of information is Ibbotson and Sinquefield, who have calculated the actual rates of return for different portfolios of stocks and bonds for each year over the 1926–1991 time period.[18] (They provide rates of return for subperiods, as well.) These annualized returns are presented in Figure 4-9 for two common-stock portfolios; first, for all common stocks listed on the New York Stock Exchange and, second, for the "small companies" listed on the Exchange.[19] Also, you see the returns for a portfolio of long-term corporate bonds and for government securities—both long-term government bonds and short-term U.S. Treasury Bills. The difference between the average annualized return for a given portfolio and the risk-free rate, or the U.S. Treasury Bill rate, is the **risk premium** earned by the investor. For instance, the risk premium for the portfolio of common stocks is 8.6 percent (12.4 percent common stock average annualized return minus 3.8 percent average return for U.S. Treasury Bills). The third column shows the standard deviation of the returns, which is a measure of the volatility of the returns over the years. The standard deviation is a measure of the riskiness of the portfolio of assets. The riskiness of the different portfolios is also shown graphically in the corresponding return frequency distributions.

Figure 4-9 shows a definite relationship between average returns and risk; that is, the greater the average returns, the greater the risk. Consider this as you think about buying a truly small company. As a rational person, you should not invest in a small firm unless you can expect to earn a risk premium of more than 13.7 percent (17.5 percent for small-company stocks less 3.8 percent for Treasury Bills)—that being the risk premium offered by the smaller companies listed on the New York Stock Exchange (see Figure 4-9, Column 2, Line 2). In fact, for most small firms, the rate should be significantly more. Suggested returns to be required above and beyond the risk-free rate are presented in Figure 4-10. As you look at the different risk categories, you will see that categories 3, 4, and 5 apply to small companies. Thus, the risk premium should, according to one experienced appraiser, be at least 16 percent, and as much as 30 percent, depending on the riskiness of the firm being valued. Given your re-

risk premium

the difference between the average annualized return and the risk-free rate of return on a given investment

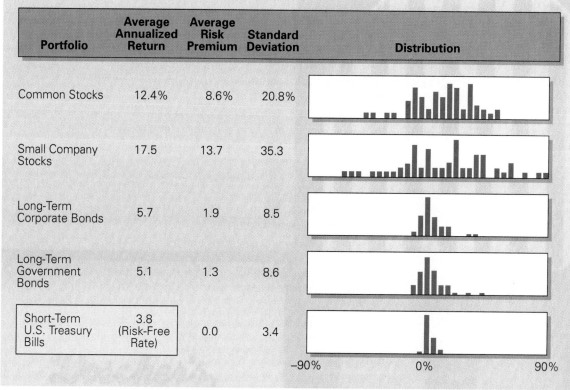

Portfolio	Average Annualized Return	Average Risk Premium	Standard Deviation	Distribution
Common Stocks	12.4%	8.6%	20.8%	
Small Company Stocks	17.5	13.7	35.3	
Long-Term Corporate Bonds	5.7	1.9	8.5	
Long-Term Government Bonds	5.1	1.3	8.6	
Short-Term U.S. Treasury Bills	3.8 (Risk-Free Rate)	0.0	3.4	

Source: *Stocks, Bonds, Bills, and Inflation 1993 Yearbook* ™, Ibbotson Associates, Chicago (annually updates work by Roger G. Ibbotson and Rex A. Sinquefield). Used with permission. All rights reserved.

Figure 4-9
Average Annual Returns and Standard Deviations: 1926–1991

quired rate of return for valuing a company, you can then use the rate to calculate the present value of the firm's future cash flows.

Although not the most popular approach, valuing a company based on the present value of its future cash flows makes a lot of sense. However, while being the best valuation technique conceptually, it is a relatively involved procedure, and beyond the scope of this text.[20]

Nonquantitative Factors to Consider in Valuing a Business

In addition to the quantitative methods of valuation, there are a number of other factors to consider in evaluating an existing business. Although they are indirectly related to the company's future cash flows and financial position, they deserve mentioning. Some of these factors are:

1. *Competition.* The prospective buyer should look into the extent, intensity, and location of competing businesses. In particular, the buyer should check

Figure 4-10
Risk Premium
Categories
Suggested by
James H. Schilt

Category	Description	Risk Premium
1	Established businesses with a strong trade position that are well financed, have depth in management, have stable past earnings, and whose future is highly predictable.	6–10%
2	Established businesses in a more competitive industry that are well financed, have depth in management, have stable past earnings, and whose future is fairly predictable.	11–15%
3	Businesses in a highly competitive industry that require little capital to enter, have no management depth, and have a high element of risk, although past record may be good.	16–20%
4	Small businesses that depend upon the special skill of one or two people. Larger established businesses that are highly cyclical in nature. In both cases, future earnings may be expected to deviate widely from projections.	21–25%
5	Small "one person" businesses of a personal services nature, where the transferability of the income stream is in question.	26–30%

Source: James H. Schilt, "Selection of Capitalization Rates—Revisited," *Business Valuation Review* American Society of Appraisers, P.O. Box 17265, Washington, DC 20041 (June, 1991), p. 51.

to see whether the business in question is gaining or losing in the race with competitors.

2. *Market.* The adequacy of the market to maintain all competing business units, including the one to be purchased, should be determined. This entails market research, study of census data, and personal, on-the-spot observation at each competitor's place of business.

3. *Future community developments.* Examples of community developments planned for the future include:
   a. Changes in zoning ordinances already enacted but not yet in effect.
   b. Land condemnation suits for construction of a public building, municipally operated parking lot, or public park.
   c. Change from two-way traffic flow to one-way traffic.
   d. Discontinuance of bus routes that will eliminate public transportation for customers and employees.

4. *Legal commitments.* These may include contingent liabilities, unsettled lawsuits, delinquent tax payments, missed payrolls, overdue rent or installment payments, and mortgages of record against any of the real property acquired.

Figure 4-11
Present Market and
Competition Must
Be Considered in
Valuing a Business.
Suburban Expan-
sions Stimulate
Business, as Shown
in This Shopping
Center.

5. *Union contracts.* The prospective buyer should determine what type of labor agreement, if any, is in force, as well as the quality of the firm's employee relations.

6. *Buildings.* The quality of the buildings housing the business, particularly the fire hazard involved, should be checked. In addition, the buyer should determine whether there are restrictions on access to the building. For example, is there access to the building without crossing the property of another? If necessary, a right of way should be negotiated before the purchase contract is closed.

7. *Future national emergencies.* The buyer should determine the potential impact of possible future national emergencies such as price and wage controls, energy shortages, human-resources shortages, raw-material shortages, and the like.

8. *Product prices.* The prospective owner should compare the prices of the seller's products with manufacturers' or wholesalers' catalogs or prices of competing products in the locality. This is necessary to assure full and fair pricing of goods whose sales are reported on the seller's financial statements.

Negotiating and Closing the Deal

The purchase price of the business is determined by negotiation between buyer and seller. Although the calculated value is not the price of the business, it gives the buyer an estimated value to use in negotiating price. Typically, the buyer tries to purchase the firm for something less than the full estimated value. Likewise, the seller tries to get more than the estimated value.

An important part of this negotiation is the terms of purchase. In many

Let's Make a Deal

Cash up front is sometimes the preferred method in a buyout deal because the seller-entrepreneur wants to fund another new venture. "If I were interested in stock, I'd be in the stock market," says Laurence Smith, who sold his Boston-based Associated Mobile X-Ray Services, Inc., in 1984. Smith remained with the new owners on salary.

In other buyouts, the sellers may not want all cash. Consider the situation of Jan and Al Williams when they sold their Bio Clinic Company in Southern California. When they sold their firm, they were getting a divorce and each had different objectives for the sale. "I wanted stock," says Jan; "My husband wanted as much cash as possible." The purchaser wanted to give all cash, but after a long negotiation gave cash to Al and stock to Jan.

Source: Sandra Salmans, "Cutting the Deal" *Venture* (January 1988).

cases, the buyer is unable to pay the full price in cash and must seek extended terms. The seller may also be concerned about taxes on the profit from the sale. Terms may be more attractive to the buyer and seller as the amount of the down payment is reduced and/or the length of the repayment period is extended.

As in the purchase of real estate, the purchase of a business is closed at a specific time. The closing may be handled, for example, by a title company or an attorney. Preferably the closing should occur under the direction of an independent third party. If the seller's attorney is suggested as the closing agent, the buyer should exercise caution. Regardless of the closing arrangements, the buyer should never go through a closing without extensive consultation with a qualified attorney.

A number of important documents are completed during the closing. These include a bill of sale, certifications as to taxing and other governmental authorities, and agreements pertaining to future payments and related guarantees to the seller. Also, if you purchase the firm, be certain to apply for a federal identification number and a new state identification number. Otherwise, you may be responsible for past obligations associated with the old numbers.

1. There are many alternatives for starting a small business, but these options can usually be grouped into one of four categories: startups, buyouts, franchising, and joining a family business.
2. The many different types of startup ideas can generally be classified into one of three groups: existing concepts redirected to new markets, technologically derived ideas, and ideas to perform existing functions in a new and improved manner.
3. A good idea is not necessarily a good investment opportunity. In fact, if you do not have a competitive advantage when you start a business or buy one, you probably will not make a good return on your investment.
4. Ideas for new startups come from many different sources, including personal experiences, hobbies, accidental discovery, and deliberate search. Such ideas require study and refinement before the business is launched.
5. A number of reasons exist for buying a business. Fewer uncertainties are involved than in launching an entirely new firm. Also, the facilities, personnel, and other elements of a going business are already assembled. The business may also be available at a bargain price.
6. Several techniques can be used in valuing an existing company. These include (1) asset-based valuation, such as replacement value or liquidation value, (2) market-based valuation, (3) earnings-based valuation, and (4) present value of the firm's future cash flows.

DISCUSSION QUESTIONS

1. Why would an entrepreneur prefer to launch an entirely new venture rather than buy an existing firm?
2. Describe a business that grew out of the entrepreneur's hobby and one that resulted from the entrepreneur's work experience.
3. Suggest a product or a service not currently available that might lead to a new small business. How safe would it be to launch a new small business depending solely on that one new product or service? Why?
4. Classify the business of a mobile car service that changes oil and filters in parking lots according to the Figure 4-2 categories. Can you think of a similar but different service that might fit the other two categories? Explain.
5. Do you perceive any ethical questions when an entrepreneur bases a startup on someone else's new-venture idea? Explain.
6. What are the advantages and disadvantages of using a business broker when considering a buyout?
7. What are the advantages of purchasing an existing business with all cash up front? What are the disadvantages?
8. Suppose that a business firm available for purchase has shown an average net profit of $40,000 for the past five years. During these years, the amount of profit fluctuated between $20,000 and $60,000. The business is in a highly competitive industry and requires only a small capital outlay to enter the business. Thus, the

barriers of entry are low. State your assumptions and then calculate the value that you might use in negotiating the purchase price.

9. Contrast the market-based valuation approach with the earnings-based approach. Which is easier to apply? Which is the most appropriate?

10. Try finding a business venture that failed, one you know about personally or read about in the press, and see if you can relate the reason for failure to our criteria for evaluating a new venture presented in Figure 4-3.

11. Using the earnings-capitalization technique, value the following companies:
    a. The normalized net income is $50,000, and the business requires average executive ability—and at the same time a comparatively small capital investment. Established goodwill, however, is of distinct importance.
    b. The normalized net income is $80,000, and the firm is a small industrial business in a highly competitive industry, and requires a relatively small capital outlay. Anyone with little capital may enter the industry.
    c. The normalized net income is $30,000, and the business depends on the special skills of a small group of managers. The business is highly competitive and the mortality rate in the industry is relatively high.
    d. The normalized net income is $60,000; the firm is a personal service business. Little if any capital is required. The earnings of the enterprise are the reflection of the owner's skill; the owner is not likely to be able to create "an organization" which can successfully "carry on."

12. Describe the relationship between a firm's capitalization rate and (1) the riskiness of the firm, and (2) the prospects of firm growth.

13. Differentiate between a capitalization rate and a required rate of return.

14. What is the present risk-free rate, as reported in *The Wall Street Journal*? Select a small company and, using Figure 4-9, estimate what you believe to be an appropriate risk premium and total required rate of return if you were to buy the company.

YOU MAKE THE CALL

Situation 1

After selling his small computer business, James Stroder set out on an 18-month sailboat trip with his wife and young children. He had founded the business several years earlier, and it had become a million-dollar enterprise. Now, he was looking for a new venture.

While giving his two sons reading lessons on board the sailboat—they each had slight reading disabilities—he had an inspiration for a new company. Stroder wondered why a computer could not be programmed to drill students in special-education classes who needed repetition to recognize and pronounce new words correctly.

Based on an article in *The Wall Street Journal.* [Names are fictitious.]

Questions
1. How would you classify Stroder's startup idea?
2. What source of a new idea, according to this book, would describe Stroder's circumstance?

3. Do you think Stroder might develop his idea with a startup rather than a buyout? Why?

Situation 2

Four years after starting their business, Bill and Janet Brown began to have thoughts of selling out. Their business, Bucket-To-Go, had been extremely successful, as indicated by an average 50 percent increase in revenue each of its years in existence. Their business began when Bill turned his hobby of making wooden buckets into a full-time business. The buckets were marketed nationwide in gift shops and garden centers.

Sam Kline learned of the buyout opportunity after contacting a business broker. Kline wanted to retire from corporate life and thought this business was an excellent opportunity.

Questions
1. Which valuation technique would you suggest Kline use to value the business? Why?
2. What accounting information should Kline consider? What adjustments might be required?
3. What qualitative information should Kline evaluate?

EXPERIENTIAL EXERCISES

1. Research small-business periodicals in your school's library and locate five or six new startups that have been profiled by the magazines. Report to the class, describing the source of the ideas.
2. Consult the Yellow Pages of your local telephone directory to locate the name of a business broker. Contact the business broker and report to the class on how that broker values businesses.
3. Select a certain startup that you are personally familiar with and then write out a description of your experiential and educational background and evaluate the exent to which it would qualify you to operate that startup.
4. Consult your local newspaper's new-business listings and then contact one of the firms to arrange a personal interview. Report to the class on how the new-business idea originated. Classify the type of new-business idea according to Figure 4-2.

REFERENCES TO SMALL-BUSINESS PRACTICES

Brokkaw, Leslie. "The Truth About Startups," *Inc.*, Vol. 13, No. 4 (April 1991), pp. 52–67.
  Interviews owners of several recent startup companies. Gives good examples of what these firms found to be important.
Galant, Debbie. "The Stuff Dreams Are Made Of." *Venture*, Vol. 10, No. 1 (January 1988), pp. 52–56.
  This article describes several entrepreneurs who have turned their hobbies into successful businesses. The pros and cons of building a business from a hobby are examined through the entrepreneurs' experiences.

Harrell, Wilson. "Entrepreneurial Terror." *Inc.*, Vol. 9, No. 2 (February 1987), pp. 74–76.

The author of this article shares his own personal terror as he explains his entrepreneurial experiences.

Johansen, John A. "Setting the Price of a Small Company," *In Business,* Vol. 10, No. 6 (November–December 1988), pp. 42–44.

The article discusses the factors that affect firm value and then provides a step-by-step example of using discounted cash flows to value a firm.

Kotite, Erika. "Reinventing the Wheel Part I." *Entrepreneur,* Vol. 16, No. 7 (July 1988), pp. 54–59.

The theme of this article is that "anything that has been done can be done better." The background of the idea to develop a cloth diaper with all the convenience of a disposable diaper is recounted. How the idea for a new bicycle seat came about is also described.

"Small Business," *The Wall Street Journal* (October 16, 1992).

A supplement that provides a series of timely articles on starting and operating a small business.

ENDNOTES

1. Paulette Thomas, "The Big Idea," *The Wall Street Journal* (June 10, 1988).

2. Jerry E. Bishop, "Tiny Sponges Try to Capture a Big Role in Many Products," *The Wall Street Journal* (June 20, 1986), p. 19.

3. Rachell Orr, "Merrily They Roll Along," *Nation's Business,* Vol. 75, No. 11 (November 1987), p. 65.

4. Amar Bhide, "Small Money Entrepreneurship," Unpublished manuscript, January 5, 1992.

5. Georganne Fiumara, "Busy Woman Needs 'Wife,'" *Family Circle,* Vol. 101, No. 12 (September 1, 1988), p. 30.

6. Ellen M. Weber, "Retirees Go to Work for Themselves," *USA Today,* (August 21, 1986), p. 1.

7. Earl C. Gottschalk, Jr., "More Ex-Managers Seek to Turn Hobbies into Full-Time Businesses," *The Wall Street Journal* (December 23, 1986), p. 21.

8. Laurie Kretchmar, "Taking a Pop at the Jeans Market," *Venture,* Vol. 10, No. 6 (June 1988), p. 10.

9. Stephen Robinett, "What Schools Can Teach Entrepreneurs," *Venture,* Vol. 7, No. 2 (February 1985), p. 58.

10. Jeffry A. Timmons, "A Business Plan Is More Than a Financing Device," *Harvard Business Review,* Vol. 58, No. 2 (March–April 1980), p. 30.

11. William A. Cohen, *The Entrepreneur and Small Business Problem Solver* (New York: John Wiley & Sons, 1983), pp. 126–127. Copyright © 1983, John Wiley & Sons. Reprinted by permission of John Wiley & Sons, Inc.

12. Ronald Tanner, "When It's Better to Buy," *Venture,* Vol. 6, No. 6 (June 1984), p. 76.

13. Stanford L. Jacobs, "Asian Immigrants Build Fortune in U.S. by Buying Cash Firms," *The Wall Street Journal* (October 1, 1984), p. 29.

14. Standard accounting practice requires land, for example, to be recorded at cost. No adjustments are subsequently made to recognize its increasing or decreasing value. When real estate values are changing substantially, therefore, the amounts shown on the books do not correspond with reality.

15. John A. Byrne, "The Business of Business," *Forbes,* Vol. 134, No. 4 (August 13, 1984), p. 112.

16. The book value of a firm's equity is equal to the owner's historical investment in the firm. It includes the investments made in the business by the owners plus the profits that have

been retained within the company instead of being distributed to the owners.

17. If you are not familiar with the concept and process of discounting cash flows to their present value, you might want to read Appendix A of the text.

18. R. G. Ibbotson and R. A. Sinquefield, *Stocks, Bonds, Bills, and Inflation* (Chicago: Dow Jones-Irwin, 1991).

19. These "small companies" are not exactly what you or I may think of as small. Small companies in this case are those that represent the smallest of the large. To be exact, they are the bottom quartile in terms of size of the firms listed on the New York Stock Exchange.

20. If you would like to extend your study on valuing a company based on the present value of a company's future cash flows, see Alfred Rappaport, *Creating Shareholder Value* (New York: The Free Press, 1986).

Franchising

Greg Muzzillo

SPOTLIGHT ON SMALL BUSINESS

Successful small-business ventures are not limited to glamorous startups involving innovative new and spectacular products. Many times they simply result from recognizing a need and providing ordinary products to receptive customers through appropriate marketing strategies. ProForma, started by entrepreneur Greg Muzzillo, is an excellent example. He developed his business by using existing products and formulating a successful marketing program, which he began franchising in 1985. ProForma franchisees market business forms and office supplies by acting as intermediaries between commercial printers and ultimate users.

Muzzillo started ProForma in 1978 after he and a college friend pooled their resources and bought an answering machine to enable them to use their apartment for their business. In 1985 ProForma won the Small Business Administration National "Business of the Year" award. By 1991, ProForma achieved $22 million in sales representing almost 100 franchisees.

Source: Personal communication with the franchisor, 1992.

After studying this chapter, you should be able to:
1. Describe three types of franchising systems and give examples of opportunities they offer for entrepreneurs.
2. Discuss the pros and cons of buying a franchise.
3. Outline the steps in evaluating franchise opportunities.
4. Identify benefits and drawbacks of becoming a franchisor.
5. Discuss trends in franchising.

franchising
franchisee
franchisor
franchise contract
franchise

product and trade name
   franchising
business format franchising
piggyback franchising
master franchising

subfranchising
System A franchising
System B franchising
System C franchising
disclosure document

franchising
a marketing system in which one party conducts business as an individual owner according to methods and terms specified by another party

franchisee
the party in a franchise contract whose power is limited by the franchising organization

franchisor
the party in a franchise contract who specifies the methods and terms to be followed by the other party

franchise contract
the legal agreement between franchisor and franchisee

franchise
the privileges in a franchise contract

product and trade name franchising
a franchise relationship granting the right to use a widely recognized product or name

Chapter 4 explained the new-business alternatives of creating an entirely new venture or buying an existing business—startups and buyouts. This chapter examines a third alternative—beginning a business with franchising.

The franchising concept helps thousands of entrepreneurs realize their business-ownership dreams each year. Initially, let us examine the language and structure of franchising.

FRANCHISING TERMINOLOGY

The term *franchising* is defined in many ways. In this text, we use a broad definition to encompass its wide diversity. **Franchising** is a marketing system revolving around a two-party legal agreement whereby one party (the **franchisee**) is granted the privilege to conduct business as an individual owner but is required to operate according to methods and terms specified by the other party (the **franchisor**). The legal agreement is known as the **franchise contract,** and the privileges it contains are called the **franchise.**

The potential value of any franchising arrangement is determined by the rights contained in the franchise contract. The extent and importance of these rights are quite varied. For example, a potential franchisee may desire the right to use a widely recognized product or name. The term commonly used to describe this relationship between supplier and dealer is **product and trade name franchising.** Gasoline service stations and soft drink bottlers are typical examples. Product and trade name franchising consistently accounts for over two-thirds of all franchise sales but less than one-third of all franchise businesses.[1]

Alternatively, the potential franchisee may seek an entire marketing system and an ongoing process of assistance and guidance. This type of relationship is referred to as **business format franchising.** The volume of sales and number of franchise units owned through business format franchising have increased steadily since the early 1970s. Fast-food outlets and business services are examples of this type of franchising.

Piggyback franchising refers to the operation of a retail franchise within the physical facilities of a host store. Examples would be a cookie franchise doing business inside an Arby's fast-food outlet or a car-phone franchise within an automobile dealership. This form of franchising benefits both parties. The host store is able to add a new product line, and the franchisee obtains a location near the customers.

Another franchising strategy gaining widespread usage is **master franchising** or **subfranchising.** A master franchisor is an individual who has a continuing contractual relationship with a franchisor to sell its franchises. This independent businessperson is a type of sales agent. Master franchisors are responsible for finding new franchisees within a specified territory. Sometimes they will even provide support services such as training and warehousing traditionally provided by the franchisor.

TYPES OF FRANCHISING SYSTEMS

Three types, or levels, of franchising systems offer opportunities for entrepreneurs. Figure 5-1 depicts each of these systems and provides examples. In **System A,** the producer/creator (the franchisor) grants a franchise to a wholesaler (the franchisee). This system is often used in the soft-drink industry. Dr Pepper and Coca-Cola are examples of System A franchisors.

In the second level, designated as **System B,** the wholesaler is the franchisor. This system prevails among supermarkets and general merchandising stores. Ben Franklin and Ace Hardware are examples of System B franchisors.

The third type, **System C,** is the most widely used. In this system the producer/creator is franchisor and the retailer is the franchisee. Automobile dealerships and gasoline service stations are prototypes of this system. In recent years, this system also has been used successfully by many fast-food outlets and printing services. Notable examples of System C franchisors are Burger King and Kwik-Kopy.

BUYING A FRANCHISE

"Look before you leap" is an old adage that should be heeded by potential franchisees. Entrepreneurial enthusiasm should not cloud your eyes to the realities, both good and bad, of franchising. Therefore, we shall first look at the advantages of buying a franchise and then examine the limitations of franchising. Study these topics carefully, and remember them when you are evaluating a franchise.

business format franchising
the franchisee obtains an entire marketing system and ongoing guidance from the franchisor

piggyback franchising
the operation of a retail franchise within the physical facilities of a host store

master franchising (subfranchising)
a master franchisor has a continuing contractual relationship with a franchisor to sell its franchises

System A franchising
a producer grants a franchise to a wholesaler

System B franchising
a wholesaler is franchisor

System C franchising
a producer is franchisor and a retailer is franchisee

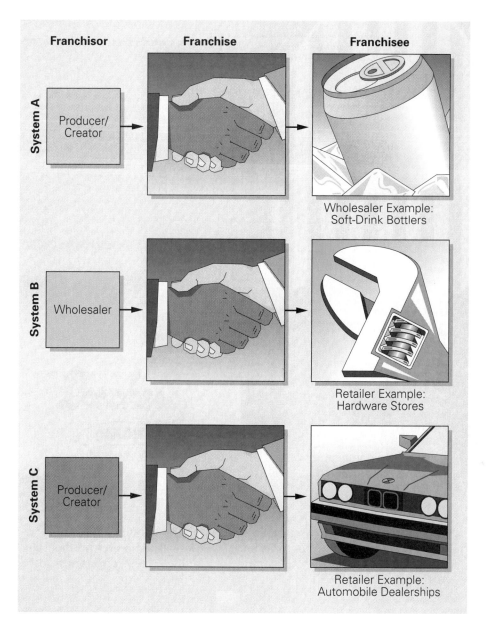

Figure 5-1
Alternative
Franchising
Systems

The Pros and Cons of Franchising

The choice of franchising over alternative methods of starting your own business ultimately is based on adding up the pluses and minuses of franchising after considering the entrepreneur's personal goals and aspirations. Figure 5-2 depicts the major considerations for this evaluation. Franchising obviously will

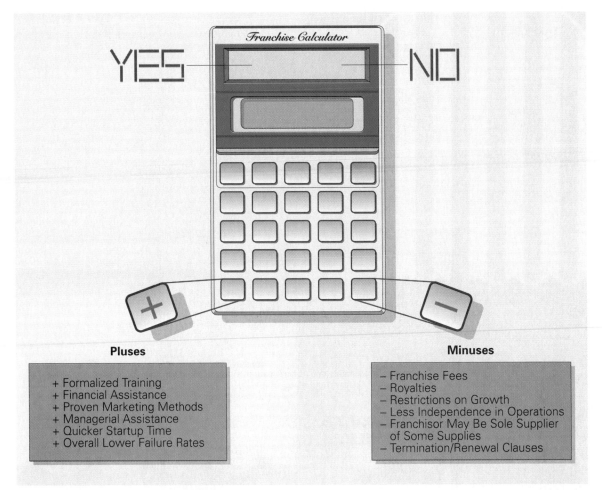

Figure 5-2
Major Pluses and
Minuses in the
Franchising
Calculation

not be the choice for all prospective entrepreneurs, because each consideration will carry different weight for different individuals. However, in their particular circumstances, many people find the franchise form of business to be
the best choice.[2]

Advantages of Franchising

A franchise is attractive for many reasons. Three advantages in particular warrant further analysis. A franchise can offer the entrepreneur (1) formal training, (2) financial assistance, and (3) marketing and management benefits.
Naturally, all franchises may not be equally strong on all these points. But it is
these advantages which motivate many persons to consider the franchise
arrangement.

Formal Training. The importance of formal training received from the franchisor is underlined by the managerial weakness of many small entrepreneurs. To the extent that this weakness can be overcome, therefore, the training program offered by the franchisor constitutes a major benefit.

The value and the effectiveness of training are evident from the records of business failures, a large majority of which are caused by deficiencies in management. For example, franchisors such as McDonald's and Kentucky Fried Chicken reputedly have never experienced a failure. Some franchisors admit to purchasing a weak operating franchisee to keep it from going under, thereby maintaining their image. However, there appears to be little question that the failure rate for independent small businesses in general is much higher than for franchised businesses in particular.

Operating as a franchisee, however, in no way guarantees success. A particular franchisor may offer unsatisfactory training. The franchisee may not apply the training correctly or may fail for some other reason.

Initial Training. Training by the franchisor often begins with an initial period of a few days or a few weeks at a central training school or at another established location. For example, the Holiday Inn franchise chain operates the hotel industry's largest training center, Holiday Inn University, which was built in 1972 at a cost of $5 million. Initial training programs cover not only the operating procedures to be used by the business, but also broader topics such as record keeping, inventory control, insurance, and human relations.

The Mister Donut franchise requires an initial training course of four weeks, including such topics as doughnut making, accounting and controls, advertising and merchanding, scheduling of labor and production, purchasing, and so on. Naturally, the nature of the product and the type of business affect the amount and type of training required in the franchised business. In most cases, training constitutes an important advantage of the franchising system and permits individuals who have had little training and education to start and succeed in businesses of their own.

Continuing Guidance. Initial training is ordinarily supplemented with subsequent training and guidance. This may involve refresher courses and/or training by a traveling representative who visits the franchisee's business from time to time. The franchisee may also receive manuals and other printed materials that provide guidance for the business. However, guidance shades into control, so that in particular cases it may be difficult to distinguish the two. The franchisor normally places a considerable emphasis upon observing strict controls. Still, much of the continued training goes far beyond the application of controls. While some franchising systems have developed excellent training programs, this is by no means universal. Some unscrupulous promoters falsely promise satisfactory training.

Figure 5-3 displays selected listings from the U.S. Department of Commerce publication entitled *Franchise Opportunities Handbook*. This handbook contains a

SMALL BUSINESS IN ACTION

Kwik-Kopy Campus

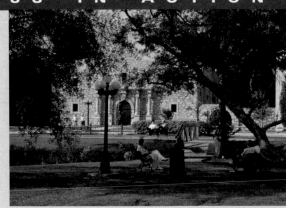

One of the major reasons for buying a Kwik-Kopy franchise according to Robin Averitt, the company's training director, is good training. Kwik-Kopy's training covers the technical aspects of running a printing business as well as the standard topics of accounting, computers and leadership. However, Kwik-Kopy's training facility is unique. Located near Houston, Texas, the Kwik-Kopy campus looks like an amusement park with a full-size replica of the Texas Alamo. The 69-year-old founder of the company, Bud Hadfield, likes to do things differently. Trainees also like to have fun.

But franchise trainees quickly realize that the three-week training program is hard. Classes usually start at 7:00 A.M. and conclude at 6:00 P.M., Mondays through Fridays, and they continue for a half-day on Saturdays. It is not much time to train the franchisees, but it is not mission impossible.

The training program must be working. Kwik-Kopy has 1,000 franchises spread over eight countries.

As reported in Greg Hassell, "Kan-do Atmosphere Key to Success of Kwik-Kopy," *Houston Chronicle* (August 3, 1990), p. 2C.

comprehensive listing of franchisors with a brief statement about the nature and requirements of each franchise. Notice the description of training provided by the four franchises listed. (Notice also that one of the franchisors in Figure 5-3 is ProForma, Inc., the franchise featured at the beginning of this chapter in the "Spotlight on Small Business.")

Financial Assistance. The costs of starting an independent business are often high and the prospective entrepreneur's sources of capital quite limited. The entrepreneur's standing as a prospective borrower is weakest at this point. By teaming up with a franchising organization, the aspiring franchisee may enhance the likelihood of obtaining financial assistance.

If the franchising organization considers the applicant to be a suitable prospect with a high probability of success, it frequently extends a helping hand financially. For example, the franchisee seldom is required to pay the complete cost of establishing the business. In addition, the beginning franchisee is normally given a payment schedule that can be met through successful operation. Also, the franchisor may permit delay in payments for products or supplies obtained from the parent organization, thus increasing the franchisee's working capital.

Figure 5-3   Informational Profile of Selected Franchises

*KWIK-KOPY CORPORATION
1 Kwik-Kopy Lane, P.O. Box 777
Cypress, Texas 77429
Director—Marketing

Description of Operation: A Kwik-Kopy Center franchise offers a system for production and sale of high quality printing, duplicating, copying, bindery and attendant services on rapid time schedules tailored to meet the customers' desire. The franchise includes volume buying discounts on the purchase of equipment, microcomputer hardware with specialized business systems software, furniture, fixtures and supplies, market research, site selection, negotiation of real estate leases, equipment operation, public relations, sales and advertising programs, start-up assistance, and continued support service in technical and business management problems over the entire 25-year term of the franchise agreement.

Number of Franchisees: Approximately over 1,000 in 42 States, Canada, United Kingdom, Australia, South Africa and Israel.

In Business Since: 1967

Equity Capital Needed: Minimum cash requirement of approximately $40,000–$50,000.

Financial Assistance Available: Third party financing available.

Training Provided: Completion of an intensive 2 week training course is provided by Kwik-Kopy Corporation at its management training center and is required prior to opening a Kwik-Kopy Center. Additional 1 week on-the-job training in the franchise owner's place of business during and after start-up is also provided. Training includes equipment operation, accounting, advertising sales and business methods in Kwik-Kopy Center operations. Pre- and post-training video tapes on business procedures, operation and maintenance of equipment, sales and advertising programs are supplied to each franchise owner.

Managerial Assistance Available: The company provides continued support services to its franchise owners for the term of the franchise agreement, including management counsel, advertising and training of new employees. Assistance and counseling is available to all franchise owners by telephone through nationwide toll-free WATS lines available to all franchise owners.

*MCDONALD'S CORPORATION
Kroc Drive
Oakbrook, Illinois 60521
Licensing Department

Description of Operation: McDonald's Corporation operates and directs a successful nationwide chain of quick service restaurants serving a moderately priced menu. Emphasis is on quick, efficient service, high quality food, and cleanliness. The standard menu consists of hamburgers, cheeseburgers, fish sandwiches, French fries, apple pie, shakes, breakfast menu, and assorted beverages.

Number of Franchisees: Over 2,000 in the United States

In Business Since: 1955

Equity Capital Needed: Varies.

Conventional Franchise: 40 percent of total cost (approximately $610,000), which must be from personal unencumbered funds to lease a new restaurant; approximately $40,000 to lease an existing restaurant.

Business Facilities Lease: $66,000 from nonborrowed funds.

Financial Assistance Available: None

Training Provided: Prospective franchisees are required to complete a structured training program that includes approximately 18–24 months of in-store training (on a part-time basis) and 5 weeks of classroom training.

Managerial Assistance Available: Operations, training, maintenance, accounting and equipment manuals provided. Company makes available promotional advertising material plus field representative consultation and assistance.

(Continued on next page)

Figure 5-3   Informational Profile of Selected Franchises (*Continued*)

NOVUS WINDSHIELD REPAIR
AND SCRATCH REMOVAL
10425 Hampshire Avenue South
Minneapolis, Minnesota 55438
Gerald E. Keinath, President

Description of Operation: Using the exclusive NOVUS patented process, professionally trained franchisees repair, rather than replace, stone-damaged windshields. NOVUS franchisees are the experts in windshield repair and offer a money-saving service to fleets, insurance companies, government agencies, and consumers. Franchisees work out of their home or from a fixed location. NOVUS has also developed a process for removing scratches from windshields and other laminated glass.

Number of Franchisees: 600

In Business Since: 1972

Equity Capital Needed: Approximately $10,000

Financial Assistance Available: None

Training Provided: 5 day factory training at the NOVUS international headquarters includes technical training, sales and marketing classes and seminars on general business operations.

Managerial Assistance Available: Ongoing technical sales assistance provided by professional staff. Newsletters, conventions, regional meetings, and ongoing research and development are included.

*PROFORMA, INC.
4705 Van Epps Road
Cleveland, Ohio 44131
John Campbell, Director of Franchise
Development

Description of Operation: Business products. Distributors of business forms, commercial printing, office supplies, computer supplies. This is not a quick print shop or retail operation.

Number of Franchisees: 105 in 27 States

In Business Since: 1978, franchising started 1985

Equity Capital Needed: $75,000-$100,000

Financial Assistance Available: None

Training Provided: 1 week intensive training program covering industry/product knowledge and selling skills, ongoing field support.

Managerial Assistance Available: Franchise owner does not need to hire any administrative employees because most administrative functions are performed by franchisor. Franchisor answers franchisee's telephone (toll free number), generates billings, does computer input, logs cash receipts, and generates monthly business reports. Continuous managerial advice is available from an experienced team of professionals in selling, product knowledge, manufacturer sourcing, and administration.

Source: U.S. Department of Commerce, *Franchise Opportunities Handbook* (Washington: U.S. Government Printing Office, 1991).

Association with a well-established franchisor may also improve the new franchisee's credit standing with a bank. The reputation of the franchising organization and the managerial and financial controls that it provides serve to recommend the new franchisee to a banker. Also, the franchisor frequently will cosign notes with a local bank, thus guaranteeing the franchisee's loan.

Marketing and Management Benefits. Most franchised products and services are widely known and accepted. For example, customers will read-

SMALL BUSINESS IN ACTION

Smart Money on Franchising

Rarely will an entrepreneur have enough personal funds to cover the total startup cost of a new business. The entrepreneur will probably seek additional financing from friends, individual investors, banks, or government programs. Fortunately, an entrepreneur pursuing a franchise has another potential source of funds—the franchisor.

"There is much more franchisor-assisted financing going on than ever before," says Les Rager, a franchise consultant, "because franchisors realize that in order to add units, they are going to have to offer some form of help to prospective franchisees." For example, a franchisor can provide financial assistance by waiving the franchise fee, providing equipment-leasing programs, and making special arrangements with external lending institutions. The following two examples show how franchisors have assisted franchisees:

> John Graves, founder and president of Bike Line, a franchise headquartered in West Chester, PA, . . . sends [a potential franchisee] to Bike Line's in-house financial advisor . . .

[who] assesses the candidate's credit worthiness and recommends the next steps. "We actively talk with their banks, and we have our banks to vouch for us as the franchisor," says Graves.

> American Recycling, a franchise that specializes in recycling metals, offers its franchisees a program in which the equipment may be leased with an option to buy. "We have made arrangements with various equipment lessors, and our franchisees usually work out a five-year lease with an option to buy," says Harvey Matarasso, vice-president of sales for the franchise.

In the past, franchising was frequently thought of as a somewhat risky business venture, but today the financial lending industry views franchising as a solid investment opportunity. "The smart money on Wall Street is watching franchising," says Carol Hance, a financial strategic adviser. Therefore, the potential franchisee's search for funds should be easier than before, particularly if he or she includes the franchisor in the search.

Source: Meg Whittemore, "Financing Your Franchise," *Nation's Business,* Vol. 80, No. 9, pp. 51–57. Excerpted by permission from *Nation's Business,* September 1992. Copyright 1992, U.S. Chamber of Commerce.

---

ily buy McDonald's hamburgers or Baskin-Robbins ice cream because they know the reputation of these products. Travelers may recognize a restaurant or a motel because of its name, type of roof, or some other feature. The travelers may turn into a Denny's Restaurant or a Holiday Inn because of their previous experience and the knowledge that they can depend upon the food and service that these outlets provide. Thus, franchising offers both a proven successful line of business and product or service identification.

The entrepreneur who enters a franchising agreement acquires the right to use the franchisor's nationally advertised trademark or brand name. This serves to identify the local enterprise with the widely recognized product or service.

Figure 5-4
Selecting a
Franchise with a
Famous Name Such
as Wendy's Gives
the Entrepreneur
Marketing and
Management
Benefits

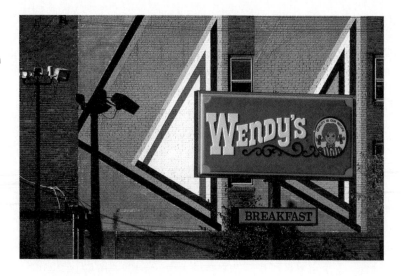

Of course, the value of product identification differs with the type of product or service and the extent to which it has received widespread promotion. In any case, the franchisor maintains the value of its name by continued advertising and promotion.

In addition to offering a proven successful line of business and readily identifiable products or services, franchisors have developed and tested their methods of marketing and management. The standard operating manuals and procedures they supply have permitted other entrepreneurs to operate successfully. This is one reason why franchisors insist upon the observance of standardized methods of operation and performance. If some franchises were allowed to operate at substandard levels, they could easily destroy the customer's confidence in the entire system.

The existence of proven products and methods, however, does not guarantee that a franchised business will succeed. For example, what the franchisor's marketing research techniques showed to be a satisfactory location may turn out to be inferior. Or the franchisee may lack ambition or perseverance. Yet the fact that a franchisor can show a record of successful operation proves that the system can work and has worked elsewhere.

Limitations of Franchising

Franchising is like a coin—it has two sides. We have examined the positive side of franchising, but we must look on the other side of the coin and examine its negative side. In particular, three shortcomings permeate the franchise form of business. These are (1) the cost of a franchise, (2) the restrictions on growth that can accompany a franchise contract, and (3) the loss of absolute independence on the part of the franchisee.

Cost of a Franchise. The total franchise cost consists of several components. Only after all of these cost components have been examined can a realistic picture be drawn. The cost of a franchise begins with the franchise fee. Generally speaking, higher fees will be required by the well-known franchisors.

Other costs include royalty payments, promotion costs, inventory and supplies costs, and building and equipment costs. When these costs are considered with the franchise fee, the total investment may look surprisingly large. A McDonald's franchise may require over $600,000 in startup costs. Other franchises, such as the NOVUS Windshield Repair franchise, which operates out of a car, require approximately $10,000. (See Figure 5.3, page 118.) In addition to startup costs, it is often recommended that funds be available for at least six months to cover pre-opening expenses, training expenses, personal expenses, and emergencies.[3]

If entrepreneurs could earn the same income independently, they would save the amount of these fees and some of the other costs. However, objecting to paying the fees is not valid if the franchisor provides the benefits previously described. In that case, franchisees are merely paying for the advantages of their relationship with the franchisor. This may be a good investment indeed.

Restrictions on Growth. A basic way to achieve business growth is to expand the existing sales territory. However, many franchise contracts restrict the franchisee to a defined sales territory, thereby eliminating this form of growth. Usually, the franchisor agrees not to grant another franchise to operate within the same territory. The potential franchisee, therefore, should weigh territorial limitation against the advantages cited earlier.

Loss of Absolute Independence. Frequently, individuals leave salaried employment for entrepreneurship because they dislike working under the direct supervision and control of others. By entering into a franchise relationship, such individuals may simply find that a different pattern of close control over personal endeavors has taken over. The franchisee does surrender a considerable amount of independence upon signing a franchise agreement.

Even though the franchisor's control of business operations may be helpful in assuring success, regulation may be unpleasant to an entrepreneur who cherishes independence. In addition, some franchise contracts go to extremes by covering unimportant details or specifying practices that are more helpful to others in the chain than to the local operation. Thus, as an operator of a franchised business, the entrepreneur occupies the position of a semi-independent businessperson.

EVALUATING FRANCHISE OPPORTUNITIES

Once an interest in becoming a franchisee emerges, much remains to be done before the dream materializes. The prospective franchisee must locate the right opportunity, investigate the franchise, and examine the franchise contract carefully.

Locating a Franchise Opportunity

With the growth of franchising over the years, the task of initially locating opportunities has become easier. Sources of franchise opportunities are promoted widely.

Often an entrepreneur's interest in franchising is sparked by franchisor advertisements in newspapers or magazines. These advertisements generally have headlines that appeal to the financial and personal rewards sought by the entrepreneur. *The Wall Street Journal, Entrepreneur, In Business,* and *Inc.* are examples of publications that include information on franchise opportunities. Figure 5-5 is an advertisement from *The Wall Street Journal.*

Investigating the Franchise Offer

The nature of the commitment required in franchising justifies a careful investigation. A franchised business typically involves a substantial investment, possibly many thousands of dollars. Furthermore, the business relationship is one that may be expected to continue over a period of years.

Ordinarily, the investigation process is a two-way effort. The franchisor wishes to investigate the franchisee, and the franchisee obviously wishes to evaluate the franchisor and the type of opportunity offered. Time is required for this kind of investigation. One should be skeptical of a franchisor who pressures a franchisee to sign at once without allowing for proper investigation.

What should be the prospective entrepreneur's next step after becoming aware of a franchising opportunity? What sources of information are available? Do governmental agencies provide information on franchising? These and other questions should be considered as the entrepreneur evaluates franchising. Basically, three sources of information should be tapped: First, there are the franchisors themselves; second, there are existing and previous franchisees; third, there are several third-party sources.

The Franchisor as a Source of Information. The most logical source of the greatest amount of information about a franchise is the franchisor. Obviously, information provided by a franchisor must be viewed in light of its purpose—to promote a franchise. However, there is no quicker source of information than this.

There are several ways to obtain information from a franchisor. The franchisor can be contacted directly, or information can be requested by responding to "reader service cards"—a service provided by most business magazines. Notice in Figure 5-5 the toll-free telephone number at the bottom of the advertisement for ProForma. The authors called the number and, within a few days,

Figure 5-5
ProForma
Newspaper Ad

The Corporate Alternative

Jeff Jellison
*Sales Representative
Eastman Kodak*

Sam Dixon
*Vice-President, Sales
Armira, Inc.*

Will Quinn
*Senior Vice President
Hewitt, Coleman &
Assoc., Inc.*

These sales and marketing executives have left their corporate positions to enjoy the success of owning their own business products franchise.

If you're ready to reap the rewards of developing your own business . . .

ProForma Offers:

■ **A Business-to-Business Opportunity**
■ **Products and Services Every Business Needs**
■ **Low Initial Overhead**
■ **High Repeat Sales**
■ **Unlimited Growth Potential**
■ **Comprehensive Training and Ongoing Support**
■ **Less than $50K investment**

Call today to learn more about ProForma and the opportunity to secure your future in the $135 billion business products industry.

PROFORMA®

1-800-825-1525

Source: Courtesy of ProForma.

received an attractive brochure describing ProForma, an application form, and a cover letter from their marketing representative. These three items are the items typically received in an initial contact. Additionally, the response included the history of the company as shown in Figure 5-6.

Financial data are sometimes provided in this kind of information packet. However, it is important for potential franchisees to remember that many of the financial figures are only estimates. Profit claims are becoming more common, partly because tough economic times make it difficult to sell a franchise without giving potential franchisees some idea of what they can earn.[4] Reputable franchisors are careful not to represent that any franchisee can expect to attain certain levels of sales, gross income, or profits. After a potential

Figure 5-6 History of ProForma

THE HISTORY OF PROFORMA

1977 GROUNDWORK FOR PROFORMA LAID.

Gregory P. Muzzillo graduates from Baldwin-Wallace College and begins working as an accountant in the firm of Deloitte, Haskins & Sells CPA.

1978 MUZZILLO STARTS PROFORMA.

Quickly disillusioned with working for others, Greg and a friend from college pool their resources ($200), buy an answering machine and begin ProForma in the apartment they share.

1979 SALES SOON TOP $250,000!

With more than 300 clients, ProForma grows daily and success becomes a welcome inevitability. For that success to continue, Muzzillo realizes he needs a strategy to carry him into the new decade.

1980 MARKETING STRATEGY OPENS DOOR TO UNLIMITED OPPORTUNITY!

With the assumption that marketing makes the company, ProForma refines the strategic sales techniques and presentations, giving growth to "the closing machine" technique and creating an atmosphere of perpetual growth.

1981 TOTAL GROSS SALES TOP MILLION DOLLAR MARK!

ProForma's ability to service customers allows the company to develop a stronghold in the Cleveland, Ohio market. Additional product lines are sought.

1982 AS SALES DOUBLE, THE BUSINESS FORMS INDUSTRY TAKES NOTICE NATIONWIDE.

The sales force doubles to six, ProForma diversifies adding office supplies to their growing product and service portfolio. Muzzillo considers alternative routes for expansion.

1983 INC. MAGAZINE CITES PROFORMA AS ONE OF AMERICA'S 500 FASTEST GROWING PRIVATE COMPANIES.

With a five-year sales growth rate of 629 percent, sales reach an all-time high of $3.5 million and staff grows to 25.

1984 PROFORMA NAMED TO INC. MAGAZINE 500 FOR SECOND YEAR!

Again one of the fastest growing companies in America, ProForma climbs 33 places in the list with a sales growth rate of 765 percent and becomes the only company in the business forms industry to make the list twice.

1985 PROFORMA WINS 1985 SMALL BUSINESS ADMINISTRATION NATIONAL "BUSINESS OF THE YEAR" AWARD.

Muzzillo is invited to Washington, D.C. by President Ronald Reagan to receive SBA Award. Cited a third year by INC., ProForma purchases DeCapite's Office Furniture and diversifies its product line further. In December ProForma begins franchising its successful concept.

1986 PROFORMA GOES NATIONAL.

Through centralized computerized inventory, accounting management and publicity services, ProForma performs bookkeeping and public relations services for franchise owners. Fifteen franchises sold in 10 states.

1987 PROFORMA MAKES VENTURE MAGAZINE LIST OF TOP 50 HOTTEST AND GROWING NEW FRANCHISES.

As the only Cleveland-based franchisor to make this listing, the company is rated in the top 50 of the 389 new franchises that began operation that year. Sixty four franchises in 25 states by year end.

1988 PROFORMA MAKES VENTURE MAGAZINE LIST OF TOP 100 FASTEST GROWING FRANCHISORS NATIONWIDE.

After only 2 years of franchising, ProForma is recognized for its dynamic unit growth nationwide. ProForma continues to attract past Presidents, Vice-Presidents and Marketing Executives from major corporations to its growing franchise network. ProForma is also named to the Weatherhead 100 list in recognition of having one of the fastest growing companies in Northeast Ohio. ProForma begins 1989 with 83 franchises in 28 states.

1989 PROFORMA INTRODUCES PROFORMAX.

Recognizing the need for a service which provides companies an ability to have their paperwork simplified, ordering process streamlined and distribution of products handled through a central distribution facility, ProForma introduced ProFormax. Franchisees are immediately successful in offering this service to companies such as Revlon, Weyerhauser, Chevron, Wells Fargo and Macy's.

1990 PROFORMA INTRODUCES PROFORMA DIRECT

ProForma Direct offers large corporations an opportunity to capitalize on their existing client base through additional product lines of the ProForma Franchise System. As an adjunct to their products and/or services, ProForma Direct allows a company to offer business forms and other related product lines in order to enhance its profitability and broaden its service in existing accounts. ProForma targets resellers, software developers, associations, etc. for its ProForma Direct program.

1991 PROFORMA GOES INTERNATIONAL

ProForma's successful expansion in the U.S. causes recognition in Canada and it establishes franchises in the province of Ontario, Canada. With this expansion, ProForma continues as the leading franchisor in the business product industry and the only distributor network with international status.

Source: Courtesy of ProForma.

franchisee has expressed further interest in a franchise by completing the application form and the franchisor has tentatively qualified the entrepreneur, a meeting is usually arranged to discuss the disclosure document. A **disclosure document** (see Figure 5-7) is a detailed statement of such information as the franchisor's finances, experience, size, and involvement in litigation. The document must inform potential franchisees of any restrictions, costs, and provisions for renewal or cancellation of the franchise.

disclosure document financial data required by the Federal Trade Commission to be made available to all investors.

The disclosure document is required by the Federal Trade Commission, and failure to make it available subjects the franchisor to possible fines. The document, called the Uniform Franchise Offering Circular (UFOC), is somewhat technical, and some prospective entrepreneurs mistakenly fail either to read it or get professional assistance.[5] All disclosure statements must carry a certain statement (see box) on the front page that advises the reader to study it and show it to an accountant or lawyer.

INFORMATION FOR PROSPECTIVE FRANCHISES REQUIRED BY FEDERAL TRADE COMMISSION

To protect you, we've required your franchisor to give you this information. We haven't checked it, and don't know if it's correct. It should help you make up your mind. Study it carefully. While it includes some information about your contract, you can't rely on it alone to understand your contract. Read all of your contract carefully. Buying a franchise is a complicated investment. Take your time to decide. If possible, show your contract and this information to an advisor, like a lawyer or an accountant. If you find anything you think may be wrong or anything important that's been left out, you should let us know about it. It may be against the law. There may also be laws on franchising in your state. Ask your state agencies about them.

Existing Franchisees as a Source of Evaluation. There may be no better source of franchise facts than existing franchisees. Sometimes the location of a franchise may preclude a visit to the business site. However, a simple telephone call can provide the viewpoint of someone in the position you are considering. If possible, also talk with franchisees who have left the business. They can offer valuable input about their decision.

Government and Trade Sources of Franchise Information. State and federal governments are valuable sources of franchising information. Since most states require registration of franchises, a prospective franchise should not overlook state offices for assistance. The federal government publishes *Franchise Opportunities Handbook.* The information in Figure 5-3 is taken from this publication. The *Franchise Opportunities Guide* is published by

Figure 5-7
Sections of Uniform
Franchise Offering
Circular (UFOC)

1. The Franchisor

2. Identity and Business Experience of Persons Affiliated with the Franchisor; Franchise Brokers

3. Litigation

4. Bankruptcy

5. Franchisee's Initial Franchise Fee or Other Initial Payment

6. Other Fees

7. Franchisee's Initial Investment

8. Obligations of Franchisee to Purchase or Lease from Designated Sources

9. Obligations of Franchisee to Purchase or Lease in Accordance with Specifications or from Approved Suppliers

10. Financing Arrangements

11. Obligations of the Franchisor

12. Exclusive Area of Territory

13. Trademarks, Service Marks, Trade Names, Logotypes, and Commercial Symbols

14. Patents and Copyrights

15. Obligations of the Franchisee to Participate in the Actual Operation of the Franchise Business

16. Restrictions on Goods and Services Offered by Franchisee

17. Renewal, Termination, Repurchase, Modification, and Assignment of the Franchise Agreement and Related Information

18. Arrangements with Public Figures

19. Actual, Average, Projected, or Forecasted Franchisee Sales, Profits, or Earnings

20. Information Regarding Franchisees or the Franchisor

21. Financial Statements

22. Contracts:
Franchise Agreement
Subfranchise Agreement
Sublease

23. Acknowledgments of Receipt by Prospective Franchisee

Source: Actual franchise offering prospectus.

the International Franchise Association (IFA). The IFA is a nonprofit trade association of more than 550 franchisors that sponsors legal and government affairs symposiums, franchise management workshops, franchisor-franchisee relations seminars, and trade shows. The IFA is highly selective and not all companies applying for membership are accepted.

Business Publications as Sources of Franchise Information.

Many business publications include articles on specific franchisors, and several include regular features on franchising. *Entrepreneur, Inc., Nation's Business,* and *The Wall Street Journal,* to name a few, can be found in most libraries.

Continuing with our hypothetical evaluation of the ProForma franchise, we researched several business publications and in the process located two informative articles describing ProForma and its operating strategy.[6] Frequently, material provided in articles is not available through the franchisor's own promotions or in the governmental information. Articles in these publications will often give an extensive profile of franchise problems and strategy changes. The third-party coverage of the franchise adds credibility to the information in the article.

Franchise Consultants.

In recent years franchise consultants have appeared in the marketplace to assist individuals seeking franchise opportunities. Some of these consulting firms present seminars on choosing the right franchise. One such firm is Franchise Seminars, Inc., of Minneapolis, Minnesota.

As in choosing any type of consultant, the prospective franchisee needs to select a reputable consultant. Since franchise consultants are not necessarily attorneys, a recognized franchise attorney should be used to evaluate all legal documents.

Examining the Franchise Contract

The basic features of the relationship between the franchisor and the franchisee are embodied in the franchise contract. The contract is typically a complex document, often running several pages. Because of its extreme importance in furnishing the legal basis for the franchised business, no franchise contract should ever be signed by the franchisee without legal counsel. As a matter of fact, many reputable franchisors insist that the franchisee have legal counsel before signing the agreement. An attorney would be useful in anticipating trouble and in noting objectionable features of the franchise contract.

In addition to consulting an attorney, as a prospective franchisee you should use as many other sources of help as possible. In particular, you should discuss the franchise proposal with a banker, going over it in as much detail as possible. You should also obtain the services of a professional accounting firm in examining the franchisor's statements of projected sales, operating expenses, and net income. The accountant can give valuable help in evaluating the quality of these estimates and in discovering projections that may be unlikely to occur.

One of the most important features of the contract is the provision relating to termination and transfer of the franchise. Some franchisors have been accused of devising agreements that permit arbitrary cancellation. Of course, it is reasonable for the franchisor to have legal protection in the event that a franchisee fails to obtain a satisfactory level of operation or to maintain satisfactory quality standards. However, the prospective franchisee should avoid contract provisions that contain overly strict cancellation policies. Similarly, the rights of the franchisee to sell the business to a third party should be clearly stipulated. Any franchisor who can restrict the sale of the business to a third party can assume ownership of the business at an unreasonable price. The right of the franchisee to renew the contract after the business has been built up to a successful operating level should also be clearly stated in the contract.

The American Arbitration Association reported in a 1990 study that franchising disputes had increased fivefold since 1981. The Association attributes this rise both to the growth in franchising and to agreements to resolve disputes out of court. Most of the recent arbitration cases involve contract termination, unpaid fees, and territorial rights.[7]

Being Wary of Franchising Frauds

Every industry has its share of shady operations, and franchising is no exception. Unscrupulous fast-buck artists offer a wide variety of fraudulent schemes to attract the investment of unsuspecting individuals. The franchisor in such cases is merely interested in obtaining the capital investment of the franchisee and not in a continuing relationship.

The possibility of such fraudulent schemes requires alertness on the part of prospective franchisees. Only careful investigation of the company and the product can distinguish between fraudulent operators and legitimate franchising opportunities. Sometimes even careful investigation is not enough. Consider the following situation:

Rose Gregg found out first-hand. The 35-year-old single mother from Cincinnati invested all of her modest savings two years ago with American Legal Distributors, an Atlanta concern that billed itself as a provider of prepaid legal services. She saw the business—marketing the company's services in local shopping malls—as work that would let her spend more time with her son, who has cerebral palsy.

"They had the biggest booth at the show, surrounded by legitimate franchises I recognized," she says. "I spent a week in a training seminar. I talked to other people who said they'd been successful. They even sent a bouquet of flowers after I invested."

That was all she got. Ms. Gregg was one of 375 people bilked out of more than $3 million by American Legal, with individual losses ranging from Ms. Gregg's $5,500 nest egg to more than $25,000, according to court documents. The scam's organizer, Harold H. Pasley, was sentenced last month to 15 years in prison, while four "singers," people who were paid to pose as successful franchisees, also received stiff sentences. James C.

Strayhorn, Mr. Pasley's attorney, says his client disputes the charges and intends to pursue an appeal of his sentence.[8]

SELLING A FRANCHISE

Franchising contains opportunities on both sides of the fence. We have already presented the franchising story from the viewpoint of the potential franchisee. Now we shall briefly look through the eyes of the potential franchisor.

Why would a businessperson wish to become a franchisor? At least three general benefits can be identified.

1. *Reduced capital requirements.* Franchising allows you to expand without diluting your capital. The firm involved in franchising, in effect, through fee and royalty arrangements, borrows capital from the franchisee for channel development and thus has lower capital requirements than does the wholly owned chain.
2. *Increased management motivation.* Franchisees, as independent businesspeople, are probably more highly motivated than salaried employees because of profit incentives and their vested interest in the business. Since franchising is decentralized, the franchisor is less susceptible to labor-organizing efforts than are centralized organizations.
3. *Speed of expansion.* Franchising lets a business enter many more markets much more quickly than it could using only its own resources.

There are also distinct drawbacks associated with franchising from the franchisor's perspective. At least three of these can be isolated:

1. *Reduction in control.* A franchisor's right of control is greatly reduced in the franchising form of business. This is a major concern for most franchisors.
2. *Sharing of profits.* Only part of the profits from the franchise operation belongs to the franchisor.
3. *Increasing operating support.* There is generally more expense associated with nurturing the ongoing franchise relationships—providing accounting and legal services—than there is with centralized organization.

Amid the older and highly successful large franchisors, such as McDonald's, are many small businesses that are finding success as franchisors. For example, David Martin, president of Steak-Out, made the transition from an independent to a franchised business. The steak and burger home-delivery franchise is based in Huntsville, Alabama. In 1987, Martin and his wife, Rhonda, who is operations manager, decided to franchise. The Martin's closely followed the advice of their franchising consultant, and the franchise has grown to 17 locations.[9]

Franchising has undoubtedly enabled many individuals to enter business who otherwise would never have escaped the necessity of salaried employment. Thus, franchising has contributed to the development of many successful small businesses.

The Shoe May Not Fit

In 1986, Shelagh Watson chose to pursue expansion of her shoe store business through franchising. She had started Magnifete in downtown Cincinnati, Ohio, only a year earlier. Her store specializes in hard-to-find women's oversized shoes. After $367,000 in gross sales in 1986, sales reached $600,000 in 1987. In light of this success, Watson opened two more company stores and began to market franchises through national trade shows.

Now, six years later and after $250,000 in expenses, Watson has closed the franchise company. She says her entry into franchising was pre-mature. "Our franchisee profile was not working . . . the people who were interested wanted to be absentee owners, or couldn't get the financing, or thought they would turn a 15 percent profit in the first year," says Watson. Watson was also concerned with the potential for franchise litigation over the life of a franchise contract. "I'd rather say that this [franchise program] was a nice research project for a quarter of a million dollars than be in a lawsuit for a million or more because we hadn't supported [the franchisee] properly."

After pulling out of franchising, Watson introduced a catalog of oversized shoes, and sales have increased by 30 percent.

Source: Meg Whittemore, "Is There a Franchise in Your Future?" *Nation's Business*, Vol. 80, No. 6, p. 63. Adapted by permission from *Nation's Business*, June 1992. Copyright 1992, U.S. Chamber of Commerce.

TRENDS IN FRANCHISING

The growth pattern for franchised businesses historically has been steady. One of the first franchise arrangements involved a relationship between Singer Sewing Machine Company and its dealers during the nineteenth century. Post-World-War-II franchise growth was based on the expansion of the franchising principle into areas such as motels, variety shops, drugstores, and employment agencies. Then came the boom in the 1960s and 1970s, which featured franchising of fast-food outlets. Franchising growth continued into the 1980s. The International Franchise Association predicts that half of all retail sales will be franchise sales by the end of this century.

A major trend in franchising during the past decade has been the exporting of U.S. franchises. Canada has provided the biggest market for U.S. franchisors, although Continental Europe and Japan have also been extremely receptive to U.S. franchises. The most noteworthy international franchising event in recent years was the opening of a McDonald's restaurant in 1990 in Moscow. Technically, the restaurant was a joint venture between McDonald's Canada and the Moscow city authorities, but it did bring international attention to a major franchising organization.[10]

Figure 5-8
The Growth of Franchising—From
Singer Sewing Machine Company
in the Nineteenth Century to Global
Fast Food in the 1990s (Here,
McDonald's in Amsterdam)

International franchising is a two-way street. There are an increasing number of foreign companies operating franchises in the United States. For example:

- Ceiling Doctor International, Inc., based in Toronto, has sold 16 ceiling and wall-cleaning franchises in the U.S. since 1987.
- Moneysworth & Best Shoe Repair, Inc., also of Toronto, last year opened its first U.S. shoe repair outlet. Meanwhile, the company sold 17 more U.S. franchises.
- Fastframe USA, Inc., a . . . franchisor controlled by British shareholders, has opened 89 U.S. franchises, offering custom framing and related service.[11]
- Body Shop International PLC which entered the U.S. in 1988 with a store in Manhattan, has established 98 U.S. stores, most of which are franchises.[12]

The most popular approach to international franchising is through master franchising or subfranchising, which we described earlier in this chapter. Master franchising is a franchise sales and management system that creates master franchisors who have the authority to sell and supervise individual franchises. Master franchisees, in effect, establish minifranchise companies of their own. "Subfranchising is the only method we consider when developing a new foreign market," says Dennis Steinman, director of international development for National Video, Inc. "It gives us tight control over a market, but at the same time it gives the subfranchisor enough autonomy so we don't have to look over his shoulder all the time."[13]

A franchisor must be careful to select master franchisors who understand the market, its language and political system, and other factors of the local culture. Startup costs may be higher in many foreign markets, but this is usually offset by less competition and large population bases.

LOOKING BACK

1. Three basic types of franchising systems are System A, in which the franchisor is a producer and the franchisee is a wholesaler; System B, in which the franchisor is a wholesaler and the franchisee is a retailer; and System C, in which the franchisor is a producer and the franchisee is a retailer. The most widely used is System C.

2. Franchising provides three main advantages to the franchisee: formal training, financial assistance, and marketing and managerial expertise—all provided by the franchisor. Franchising also has its disadvantages. These include its costs, restrictions on growth, and loss of independence.

3. A franchise should be carefully evaluated before signing an agreement. Useful information can be obtained from the franchisor and nonfranchisor sources such as business magazines, other franchisees, governmental agencies, and private professionals.

4. Reduced capital requirements, increased management motivation, and speed of expansion are three reasons for becoming a franchisor. Drawbacks are reduction in control, sharing of profits, and increasing operating support.

5. The future of franchising continues to look bright at home and abroad. Many foreign firms are franchising in the United States.

DISCUSSION QUESTIONS

1. What makes franchising different from other forms of business? Be specific.
2. What is the difference between trade name franchising and business format franchising? Which one accounts for the majority of franchising activity?
3. Explain the three types of franchising systems. Which is most widely used?
4. Discuss the advantages and disadvantages of franchising from the viewpoints of the potential franchisee and the potential franchisor.
5. Should franchise information provided by a franchisor be discounted? Why or why not?

6. Do you believe the government-required disclosure document is useful to franchise evaluation? Defend your position.

7. Evaluate "loss of control" as a disadvantage of franchising from the franchisor's perspective.

8. What is the advantage of a franchisor's developing a prototype?

9. What are some reasons, in addition to those listed in the chapter, why an entrepreneur would consider franchising a new-business concept?

10. What are some of the trends that support a forecast of increased growth of franchising in the 1990s? Discuss.

11. Discuss how subfranchising is used in foreign franchising.

12. What types of restrictions on franchisee independence do you believe might be included in a typical franchise contract?

13. What problems could result when consulting previous franchisees in the process of evaluating a franchise?

14. What types of franchise information could you expect to obtain from business magazines that you would not secure from the franchisor?

15. Why are not all new businesses franchised?

YOU MAKE THE CALL

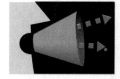

Situation 1

While still a student in college in 1992, Adrian Johnson began his first business venture. He took his idea for a laundromat to a local bank and brought back a $90,000 loan. After finding a suitable site close to his campus, he signed a 10-year lease and opened for business. Over the first three days, the business averaged over 1,000 customers per day.

The attraction of Adrian's laundromat was its different and unique atmosphere. The business was carpeted, with oak paneling and brass fittings. There was a snack bar and a big-screen TV for patrons to enjoy while waiting for their laundry. Within a week of opening day, Adrian had an offer to sell his business at twice his investment. He rejected the offer in favor of the possibility of franchising his business concept.

Questions
1. Do you think Adrian's business concept can be franchised successfully? Why or why not?
2. Would the subfranchising concept work for this type of business?
3. If Adrian does indeed franchise his business, what types of training and support systems would you recommend he provide to franchisees?

Situation 2

Hard times in the agricultural commodities market led broker Bill Landers to leave his independent business and look for new opportunities. This time around Bill was committed to going into business with his wife Gwen and their teenage son and daughter. His goal was to keep the family close and reduce the stress in their lives. In his previous job as a broker, Bill would leave home early and return late, with little time for his wife or children.

Before leaving his job, Bill looked at several franchise opportunities. One he and Gwen were seriously considering was a custom-framing franchise that had been in existence for over 10 years and had almost 100 stores nationwide. However, the Landers were concerned about their lack of experience in this area and also about how long it would take to get the business going.

Questions
1. How important should prior experience be in the Landers's decision?
2. What other characteristics of the franchise should they investigate? What sources for this information would you recommend?
3. Can they reasonably expect a different life-style with a franchise? Explain.

EXPERIENTIAL EXERCISES

1. Interview a franchisee from the local community. Try to contact the owner-manager of a widely recognized retail franchise such as McDonald's. Ask the person to explain how he or she obtained the franchise and the advantages of franchising over starting a business from scratch.
2. Find a franchise advertisement in a recent issue of a business magazine. Research the franchise and report back to class with your findings.
3. Consider the potential for a hypothetical new fast-food restaurant to be located next to the campus. (Be as specific about the assumed location as you can.) Divide into two groups. Ask one group to favor a franchised operation and the other to support a nonfranchised business. Plan a debate on the merits of each operations for the next class meeting.
4. Report in class on the articles cited in the References to Small-Business Practices in this chapter.

REFERENCES TO SMALL-BUSINESS PRACTICES

Caminiti, Susan. "Look Who Likes Franchising Now." *FORTUNE,* Vol. 124, No. 7 (September 23, 1991), pp. 125–130.
> This article tells the story of corporate refugees entering the franchising experience. Many are victims of the recession while others are simply tired of the executive life and desire to be their own boss.

Huber, Janean. "R-E-S-P-E-C-T." *Entrepreneur,* Vol. 20, No. 1 (January 1992), pp. 117–123.
> Described in this article are four businesses which used franchising to remove the "Mom and Pop" mystique of a small business. The industries are vinyl repair, housekeeping services, decorative glass, and mailing services. Franchising is described as a key to public acceptance of a business.

Huffman, Frances. "ABCs of Business Opportunities." *Entrepreneur,* Vol. 18, No. 7 (July 1990), pp. 102–106.
> This article makes a distinction between franchised and nonfranchised business opportunities. The argument is made that a nonfranchised business opportunity can be more attractive to an entrepreneur.

Stodder, Gayle Sato. "Fear of Franchising." *Entrepreneurial Women,* Vol. 2, No. 6 (July/August 1991), pp. 48–51.

This article summarizes conversations with independent business women regarding their reasons to consider and not to consider buying a franchise. Independence, creativity, and financial considerations appear to be common denominators for most of their reasons.

Urbanski, Al. "The Franchise Option." *Sales and Marketing Management,* Vol. 140, No. 2 (February 1988), pp. 28–33.

This article provides a profile of several franchisees and the franchise businesses they own and operate. Each entrepreneur in the article was previously in a corporate sales position. A change of life-style was the principal reason for going into franchising.

ENDNOTES

1. "Franchising in the U.S. Economy: Prospects and Problems," Committee on Small Business, House of Representatives (Washington: U.S. Government Printing Office, 1990), p. 3.

2. For an empirical study of franchising advantages, see Alden Peterson and Rajiv P. Dant, "Perceived Advantages of the Franchise Option from the Franchisee Perspective: Empirical Insights from a Service Franchise," *Journal of Small Business Management,* Vol. 28, No. 3 (July 1990), pp. 46–61.

3. For further discussion of franchise financing, see Andrew Sherman, "Financing the Franchise," *Nation's Business,* Vol. 75, No. 10 (October 1987), pp. 41–44.

4. See Jeffrey A. Tannenbaum, "More Franchisers Include Profit Claims in Pitches," *The Wall Street Journal,* (August 20, 1991), p. B1.

5. An excellent article describing the UFOC is David J. Kaufmann, "The First Step," *Entrepreneur,* Vol. 20, No. 1 (January 1992), pp. 90–97.

6. One article was in *USA Today* and the other in *FORTUNE.*

7. "Arbitration Cases Soar in Franchising Industry," *The Wall Street Journal,* (July 25, 1990), p. B1.

8. John R. Wilke, "Fraudulent Franchisers Are Growing," *The Wall Street Journal* (September 21, 1990), p. B1.

9. Meg Whittemore, "A Consultant Who Has Gone the Distance," *Nation's Business,* Vol. 78, No. 5 (May 1990), p. 70.

10. *Op. cit.,* "Franchising in the U.S. Economy: Prospects and Problems," p. 19.

11. Jeffrey A. Tannenbaum, "Foreign Franchisers Entering U.S. in Greater Numbers," *The Wall Street Journal* (June 11, 1990), p. B2.

12. Valerie Reitman, "Success of Body Shop Natural Cosmetics Attracts Imitators to the Scent of Profits," *The Wall Street Journal* (September 4, 1992), pp. B1, B4.

13. John F. Porsinos, "New Worlds to Franchise," *Venture,* Vol. 9, No. 11 (November 1987), p. 50.

CHAPTER 6

Family Business Opportunities

SPOTLIGHT ON SMALL BUSINESS

Married couple Karl Friberg and Lyn Peterson have chosen a nontraditional lifestyle by running their own firm, Motif Designs—a thriving home furnishings business. When they started a wallpaper store outside New York City in 1975, Friberg worked for Citibank and Peterson was an interior designer. (Earlier, Peterson had worked as a waitress to put Friberg through Harvard Business School.) Their tiny shop grew rapidly and expanded to include design and manufacture of wallpaper.

The division of labor was relatively clearcut, with Peterson running the design studio and Friberg providing business management. As the firm grew, they added other relatives— Peterson's father, a cousin, and others. Four children were born to Friberg and Peterson during these years of business growth.

Business activities often intrude on family life. Their home, for example, is used as a showpiece for their wallpaper and fabric lines, having appeared in such magazines as *Better Homes and Gardens* and *House Beautiful.* This means that rooms must often be revamped for photo shoots. On one occasion, the baby's room was repapered three times in a single day! Another child came home from preschool to find that his bed had disappeared!

The couple works hard to maintain a strong family and to keep business disagreements from destroying the marriage relationship. Peterson explains their strategy as follows: "Because it's so difficult for a husband and wife to work together, we've always tried to treat each other much more courteously and kindly—both at home and in the office—than couples and business partners usually do."

Friberg and Peterson and the Staff of Motif Designs

Source: Jill Andresky Fraser, "The New American Dream," *Inc.*, Vol. 12, No. 4, pp. 42–51. Reprinted with permission, *Inc.* magazine, April 1990. Copyright 1990 by Goldhirsh Group, Inc., 38 Commercial Wharf, Boston, MA 02110.

After studying this chapter, you should be able to:
1. Discuss the factors that make a family business unique.
2. Describe advantages and difficulties that arise in family businesses.
3. Identify two ways families may formalize the review of family business concerns.
4. Explain seven stages in the process of succession in a family business.

family business	cultural family pattern	family retreat
family and business over-lap	cultural governance pattern	family council
cultural business pattern	cultural configuration	stages in succession
		transfer of ownership

The preceding chapters have identified three routes to entrepreneurship—starting a new business, buying a going concern, and franchising. This chapter examines a fourth alternative open to many young people—that of joining the family business.

The founder of a small business often wishes to pass it on to a son or daughter. As a result, ownership may remain in the family for two, three, or more generations. Younger members of such families often have the opportunity to enter the firm with the expectation of some day taking over its leadership. An intelligent decision concerning this type of entrepreneurial path should be based on some understanding of the dynamics of the family business. This chapter examines some of the distinctive features that set the family business apart as a special type of entrepreneurial alternative.

THE FAMILY BUSINESS: A UNIQUE INSTITUTION

A number of features distinguish the family firm from other types of small businesses. In its decision making and culture, for example, we observe a mixture of family and business values. This section examines the family business as a unique type of institution.

What Is a Family Business?

To speak of a **family business** is to imply ownership or other involvement of two or more family members in the life and functioning of that business. The nature and extent of that involvement varies. In some firms, family members may work full time or part time. In a small restaurant, for example, the entrepreneur may serve as host and manager, the spouse may keep the books, and the children may work in the kitchen or as servers.

family business
involvement of family members in the functioning of a business

A business also comes to be distinguished as a family business when it passes from one generation to another. For example, Thompson's Plumbing Supply may be headed by Bill Thompson, Jr., son of the founder, who is now deceased. His son, Bill Thompson III, has started to work on the sales floor, after serving in the stockroom during his high school years. He is the heir apparent who will someday replace his father. People in the community recognize Thompson's Plumbing Supply as a family business.

Most family businesses, and the type we are concerned with in this book, are small. However, family considerations may continue to be important even when these businesses become large corporations. Companies such as Wal-Mart Stores, Levi Strauss and Company, Ford Motor Company, and Marriott Corporation are still recognized, to some extent, as family businesses.

Family and Business Overlap

family and business overlap
the intersection of family concerns and business interests in a family business

The family business is composed of both a family and a business. Although these are separate institutions—each with its own members, goals, and values—they are brought into a condition of overlap in the family firm.

Families and businesses exist for fundamentally different reasons.[1] The family's primary function relates to the care and nurture of family members, whereas the business is concerned with the production or distribution of goods and/or services. The family's goal is the fullest possible development of each member, regardless of limitations in ability, and the provision of equal opportunities and rewards for each member. The business goal is profitability and survival. There is a possibility for either harmony or conflict in these goals, but it is obvious that they are not identical. In the short run, what is best for the family may or may not be what is best for the business.

Figure 6-1
The Overlap of Family Concerns and Business Interests

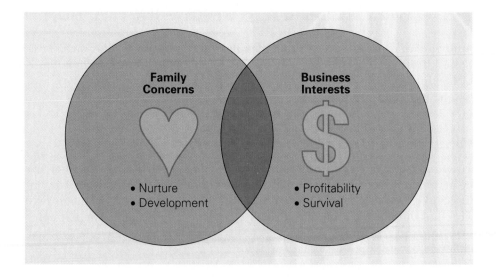

The overlap is reflected in numerous tensions and potential conflicts that arise between the business and the family. In the "Spotlight on Small Business" at the beginning of this chapter, we saw the impact of the firm's interior decorators as they modified the living quarters of the family for business purposes. Relationships among family members in a business are more sensitive than they are among unrelated employees. For example, a father may become angry at a son who consistently arrives late, but disciplining or firing the son is much more serious than disciplining or firing a nonfamily employee.

Business Decisions and Family Decisions

The overlap of family concerns and business interests complicates the management process in the family firm. Many decisions impact both business and family. Consider, for example, a performance review session between a parent-boss and a child-subordinate. Even with nonfamily employees, performance review discussions can be potential minefields. The overlay of family relationships vastly increases the complexity of the review process.

Which comes first, the family or the business? In theory at least, most opt for the family. Few business owners would knowingly allow the business to destroy the family. In practice, however, the resolution of such tensions becomes difficult. For example, a parent, motivated by a sense of family responsibility, may become so absorbed in the business that he or she spends insufficient time with the children.

If the business is to survive, its interests cannot be unduly compromised to satisfy family wishes. Firms that grow must recognize the need for professional management and the necessary limitations on family concerns. An example is found in the experience of Pierre DuPont:

As far as Pierre was concerned, the large firm did not have the obligation to provide the family with jobs; instead, it should ensure them of large dividends. Of course, when the firm expanded, there would be increased employment opportunities for younger relatives.[2]

The health and survival of the family business requires a proper balancing of business and family interests. Otherwise, results will be unsatisfactory to both the business and the family.

Advantages of Family Involvement in the Business

Problems associated with family businesses can easily blind young people to the advantages deriving from family participation in the business. There *are* values associated with family involvement, and these should be recognized and used in the family firm.

One primary benefit comes from the strength of family relationships. Members of the family are drawn to the business because of family ties, and they tend to stick with the business through "thick and thin." A downturn in

Figure 6-2
Siblings Hamish,
Cynthia, and
Arjester Reed,
Owners of
Branches Medical
Inc., of Lauderhill,
Florida, Exemplify
the Benefits of
Strong Family Ties
in a Business

business fortunes might cause nonfamily managers to seek greener pastures
elsewhere. A son or daughter, however, is reluctant to leave. The family name,
the family welfare, and possibly the family fortune are at stake. In addition, a
person's reputation as a family member may be at stake. Can he or she continue the business that Mom or Grandfather built?

Family members may also sacrifice income needed in the business. Rather
than draw large salaries or high dividends, they permit such resources to remain in the business for current needs. Many families have gone without a new
car or new furniture long enough to let the new business get started or to get
through a period of financial stress.

Some family businesses use the family theme in advertising to distinguish
themselves from their competitors. Such advertising campaigns attempt to convey the fact that family-owned firms have a strong commitment to the business,
high ethical standards, and a personal commitment to serving their customers.

Family firms also possess certain features that can contribute to superior
business decision making. To achieve their full potential, family businesses
must develop some key advantages. According to Peter Davis, director of the
Wharton Applied Research Center at the Wharton School in Philadelphia,
three such advantages are the following:[3]

1. *Preserving the humanity of the workplace.* A family business can easily demonstrate higher levels of concern and caring for individuals than are found in
   the typical corporation.

Business Benefits from Family Relationships

One benefit deriving from family relationships is the willingness of family members to sacrifice during times of crisis. Here is the way that Computerware, Inc., a computer retailer run by four brothers, their parents, and one outsider, drew on that strength during down cycles:

> Budget tightening, says president and eldest brother John Kovalcik, Jr., was easier to impose on family members. First went perks like afternoons of golf. Next were the company credit cards, so that managers had to fill out T&E forms for reimbursement of expenses. Salaries were frozen for everyone in the company, and the seven owners took 10% pay cuts.
>
> "It was just done, and it was accepted," says Kovalcik. "Our family said, 'OK, we'll pitch in.' And this was a good amount of our income; what we earn right now isn't even within industry standards."

Source: Leslie Brokaw, "Why Family Businesses Are Best," *Inc.*, Vol. 14, No. 3, p. 74. Reprinted with permission, *Inc.* magazine, March 1992. Copyright 1992 by Goldhirsh Group, Inc., 38 Commercial Wharf, Boston, MA 02110.

2. *Focusing on the long run.* A family business can take the long-run view more easily than corporate managers who are being judged on year-to-year results.
3. *Emphasizing quality.* Family businesses have long maintained a tradition of providing quality and value to the consumer.

The Culture of the Family Business

The imprint of its founder is often evident in the family firm. The founder may emphasize values that become part of the business and family code. Observance of such values becomes a matter of family pride. Of course, the founder cannot merely impose his or her values upon the organization. As Edgar H. Schein, a noted social psychologist, points out, these basic assumptions can become part of the culture only if they work and become accepted by the group.[4]

The founder, for example, may develop the business by catering to customer needs in a special way. Customer service becomes a guiding principle for the business, and legends may be passed on to illustrate the extreme measures taken by the founder to satisfy customer needs. Any business operates according to some set of values, but the family business follows with special care those values clearly emphasized by the founding family.

In addition to regarding culture as a collection of individual values and practices, we can also look at it as the arrangement of such values and practices

cultural business pattern
a system of beliefs and practices pertaining to business operations of a family firm

cultural family pattern
a set of beliefs and behaviors pertaining to family relationships in a family firm

cultural governance pattern
a set of beliefs and behaviors pertaining to governance of a family firm

cultural configuration
the total culture of the family firm that is made up of the firm's business, family, and governance patterns

into cultural patterns. This means that any given family firm has a grouping of beliefs and behaviors that makes it like some other family firms but also sets it apart from others. By carefully examining the cultural pattern of a specific family business, therefore, we may be able to recognize it as a particular type of culture found in many family firms.

W. Gibb Dyer, Jr., a professor at Brigham Young University, has identified a set of cultural patterns that apply to three facets of family firms: the business itself, the family, and the governance (board of directors) of the business.[5] These patterns are outlined in Figure 6-3. The **business pattern, family pattern,** and **governance pattern** presumably combine to form an overall **cultural configuration** that constitutes a family firm's total culture.

In the early stages of a family business, according to Dyer, a common cultural configuration includes a paternalistic business culture, a patriarchal family culture, and a rubber-stamp board of directors. To simplify, this means that family relationships are more important than professional skill, that the founder is the undisputed head of the clan, and that the board automatically supports the founder's decisions.

Nonfamily Members in a Family Firm

Even those employees who are not family members are nevertheless affected by family considerations. In some cases their opportunities for promotion are less-

Figure 6-3
Cultural Configuration of a Family Firm

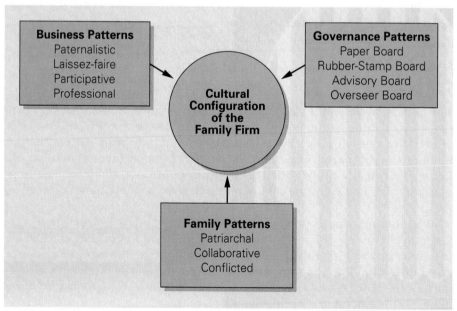

Source: W. Gibb Dyer, Jr., *Cultural Change in Family Firms* (San Francisco: Jossey-Bass Publishers, 1986), p. 22.

ened by the presence of family members who seem to have the "inside track" for promotion. What parent is going to promote an outsider over a competent daughter or son who is being groomed for future leadership? The potential for advancement of nonfamily members, therefore, may be limited, and they may experience a sense of unfairness and frustration.

The extent of such limitation will depend on the number of family members active in the business and the number of managerial or professional positions in the business to which a nonfamily member might aspire. It will also depend on the extent to which the owner demands competence in management and maintains an atmosphere of fairness in supervision. To avoid a stifling atmosphere, the owner should make clear the extent of opportunity that does exist for the nonfamily member and identify the positions, if any, that are reserved for family members.

Nonfamily members may also be caught in the crossfire between family members who are competing with each other. Family feuds in family businesses make it difficult for outsiders to maintain strict neutrality. If a nonfamily employee is perceived as siding with one contender, he or she will lose the support of other family members. Some hard-working employees no doubt feel they deserve hazard pay for working in a firm plagued by an unusual amount of family conflict.

FAMILY ROLES AND RELATIONSHIPS

As noted earlier, a family business involves the overlapping of two institutions—a family and a business. This fact makes the family firm incredibly difficult to manage. This section examines a few of the numerous possible family roles and relationships that contribute to the complexity of such a firm.

Mom or Dad, the Founder

A common figure in the family business is the man or woman who founds the firm and plans to pass it on to a son or a daughter. In most cases, the business and the family grow simultaneously. Some founders achieve a delicate balance between their business and family responsibilities. In other situations, parents must exert great diligence to squeeze out time for weekends and vacation time with the children.

Entrepreneurs who have sons and daughters typically think in terms of passing the business on to the next generation of the family. Parental concerns in this process include the following:

1. Does my son or daughter possess the temperament and ability necessary for business leadership?
2. How can I, the founder, motivate my son or daughter to take an interest in the business?

3. What type of education and experience will be most helpful in preparing my son or daughter for leadership?
4. What timetable should I follow in employing and promoting my son or daughter?
5. How can I avoid favoritism in managing and developing my son or daughter?
6. How can I prevent the business relationship from damaging or destroying the parent-child relationship?

Of all relationships in the family business, the parent-child relationship (especially the father-son relationship) has been most sensitive and troublesome. The problem has been recognized informally for generations. In more recent years, counseling has developed, seminars have been created, and books have been written about such relationships. In spite of extensive discussion, however, the parent-child relationship continues to perplex numerous families involved in family businesses.

Couples in Business

Some family businesses involve husband-wife teams. Their roles may vary depending on their backgrounds and expertise. In some cases, the husband serves as general manager and the wife runs the office. In other cases, the wife functions as operations manager and the husband keeps the books. Whatever the arrangement, both parties are an integral part of the business.

A potential advantage of the husband-wife team is the opportunity it provides for them to share more of their life. For some couples, however, the potential benefits tend to become eclipsed by problems related to the business. Differences of opinion about business matters may carry over into family life. And the energies of both parties may be so dissipated by their work in a struggling family firm that little zest remains for a strong family life.

One couple who have experienced both the joys and strains of working together as business partners are Adele Bihn and Murray P. Heinrich of San Jose, California.[6] After 12 years of marriage and collaboration in their business, Data Marketing, Inc., they are described as "still blissfully happy." Adele, mother of their four children, owns 50 percent of the company and serves as president. Murray owns the other 50 percent and heads up product research. To maintain their happiness, they must deal with strains imposed by the business. They have worked together to resolve these pressures by using a variety of methods, including semiannual visits with a marriage counselor, annual away-from-work business strategy sessions, Saturday morning breakfast dates with just the two of them, and annual separate vacations. Their experience shows that entrepreneurial couples can maintain good marriages, but it also shows that such couples may need to devote special effort to both business and family concerns.

Sons and Daughters

Should sons and daughters be groomed for the family business, or should they pursue careers of their own choosing? This is a basic question facing the entrepreneurial family. A natural tendency is to think in terms of a family business career and to push the son or daughter, either openly or subtly, in that direction. Little thought, indeed, may be given to the basic issues involved.

One question is that of talent, aptitude, and temperament. The offspring may be a "chip off the old block," but the offspring may also be an individual with different bents and aspirations. The son or daughter may prefer music or medicine to the world of business. He or she may fit the business mold very poorly. It is also possible that the abilities of the son or daughter may simply be insufficient for the leadership role. (Of course, a child's talents may be underestimated by parents simply because there has been little opportunity for development.)

A second issue is that of freedom. We live in a society that values the rights of individuals to choose their own careers and way of life. If the entrepreneur wishes to recognize this value—a value that is typically embraced by the son or daughter—that son or daughter must be granted the freedom to select a career of his or her own choosing.

The son or daughter may feel a need to go outside the family business, for a time at least, to prove that "I can make it on my own." To build self-esteem, the young person may wish to operate independently of the family. Going back to the family business immediately may seem stifling—"continuing to feel like a little kid with Dad telling me what to do."

If the family business is profitable, it does provide opportunities. The son or daughter may well give serious consideration to accepting such a challenge. If the relationship is to be satisfactory, however, family pressure must be minimized. Both parties must recognize the choice as a business decision, as well as a family decision—a decision that may conceivably be reversed. In the case of a

Figure 6-4
Following the Founder's Footsteps

WINTHROP® by Dick Cavalli

WINTHROP reprinted by permission of NEA, Inc.

large family, another problem arises if the business is not large enough to support all of the children who wish to join it.

Sibling Cooperation, Sibling Rivalry

In families with a number of children, two or more of them may become involved in the family firm. This depends, of course, on the interests of the individual children. In some cases, parents feel themselves fortunate if even one child elects to stay with the family firm. Nevertheless, it is not unusual for two or more, sometimes all, of the children to take positions in the family business. Even those who do not work in the business may be more than casual observers on the sidelines because of their stake as heirs or partial owners.

At best, the children work as a smoothly functioning team, each contributing services according to his or her respective abilities. Just as some families experience excellent cooperation and unity in their family relationships, so family businesses can benefit from effective collaboration among brothers and sisters.

But just as there are squabbles within the family, so can there be sibling rivalry within the business. Business issues tend to generate competition, and this affects family as well as nonfamily members. Two siblings, for example, may disagree about business policy or about their respective roles in the business.

Sibling rivalry has been identified as a problem in the operation of Johnson Products Company, a Chicago hair-products manufacturer and one of the largest black-owned companies in the United States.[7] Twenty-seven-year-old Joan M. Johnson clashed with her 40-year-old brother, Eric G. Johnson, who served as president, over her role in the business. The conflict led to Eric's resignation in 1992 and the subsequent elevation of Joan to a newly created "office of the president." Their father and company founder, George E. Johnson, had resigned as chairman and given up his stake in the company as part of a divorce settlement in 1989. Their mother, Joan B. Johnson, owns 61 percent of the company and serves as chairman.

In-Laws in and out of the Business

As sons and daughters marry, the daughters-in-law and sons-in-law become significant actors in the family business drama. Some of them may be directly involved when one, a son-in-law, for example, is employed in the family firm. If a son or daughter is also employed in the same firm, the potential for rivalry and conflict is present. How are the performance and progress of a son-in-law to be rewarded equitably as compared with the performance and progress of a son or daughter?

For a time, effective collaboration may be achieved by assigning family members to different branches or roles within the company. Eventually, the competition for top leadership will require decisions that distinguish among sons, daughters, sons-in-law, and daughters-in-law employed in the business.

Being fair and retaining family loyalty become difficult as the number of family employees increases.

Sons, daughters, sons-in-law, and daughters-in-law who are on the sidelines are also participants with an important stake in the business. For example, they may be married to someone on the family payroll. Whatever the relationship, the view from the sideline has both a family and a business dimension. A decision by a parent affecting one member is seen from the sideline as a family *and* a business decision. The parent is giving the nod to a daughter or a son-in-law, and that is more than merely promoting another employee in a business. Both the business and the family come to involve highly sensitive relationships.

The Entrepreneur's Spouse

One of the most critical roles in the family business drama is that of the entrepreneur's spouse. Traditionally and typically, this is the entrepreneur's wife and the mother of his children. However, women are increasingly becoming entrepreneurs and many husbands have also assumed the role of a entrepreneur's spouse.

A spouse plays a supporting role to the entrepreneur's career; as parent, she or he helps prepare their children for possible careers in the family business. This leads to a need for communication between spouse and entrepreneur. The spouse can contribute by being a good listener. To do so, the spouse needs to hear what's going on in the business; otherwise, the spouse feels detached and must compete for attention. The spouse can offer understanding and act as a sounding board only if there is communication on matters of such obvious importance to them both individually and as a family.

It is easy for the spouse to function as "worrier" for the family business. This is particularly true if there is insufficient communication about business matters. One spouse said:

I've told my husband that I have an active imagination—very active. If he doesn't tell me what's going on in the business, well, then I'm going to imagine what's going on and blow it all out of proportion. When things are looking dark, I'd rather know the worst than know nothing.[8]

The spouse also serves as mediator in relationships between the entrepreneur and the children. Comments such as the following may illustrate the nature of this function:

- "John, don't you think that Junior may have worked long enough as a stockperson in the warehouse?"
- "Junior, your father is going to be very disappointed if you don't come back to the business after your graduation."
- "John, do you really think it is fair to move Stanley into that new office? After all, Junior is older and has been working a year longer."
- "Junior, what did you say to your father today that upset him?"

Ideally, the entrepreneur and spouse form a team committed to the success of both the family and the family business. They share with each other in the processes that affect the fortunes of each. Since such teamwork does not occur automatically, it requires a collaborative effort by both parties to the marriage.

Family Retreats and Family Councils

family retreat
a gathering of family members, usually at a remote location, to discuss family business matters

Some families have formalized the review of family business concerns by holding family retreats and/or creating family councils. A **family retreat** is a gathering of family members, usually at a remote location, to discuss family business matters. Even though the process is formalized to the extent of convening discussion sessions, an attempt is made to create an informal atmosphere. Nancy Bowman-Upton, Director of the Institute for Family Business at Baylor University, has conducted many retreats for business families. She has described the general purpose and approach to family retreats as follows:

The purpose of the retreat is to provide a forum for introspection, problem solving and policy making. For some participants this will be their first opportunity to talk about their concerns in a nonconfrontational atmosphere. It is also a time to celebrate the family and enhance its inner strength.

A retreat usually lasts two days and is held far enough away so you won't be disturbed or tempted to go to the office. Every member of the family, including in-laws, should be invited.[9]

family council
an organized group of family members who gather periodically to discuss family-related business issues

Such a retreat could result in the formation of a family council. A **family council** would involve family gatherings on a periodic basis, thereby providing continuity in the discussion of family issues related to the business.

The prospect of sitting down together to discuss family business matters sometimes appears threatening to members of the family. Some families tend to avoid extensive communication because of the fear that it would stir up trouble. They assume that decision making that occurs quietly or secretly will preserve harmony. Unfortunately, such an approach may conceal serious differences that become increasingly troublesome. Family retreats and family councils are designed to open lines of communication and to bring about understanding and agreement on family-business issues.

Since getting started in such discussions is difficult, family leaders often invite an outside expert or facilitator to lead early sessions. The facilitator can help develop an agenda and establish ground rules for discussion. By moderating early sessions, the facilitator can help to develop a positive tone that emphasizes family achievements and encourages rational consideration of sensitive issues. Families which hold such meetings often speak of the joy of sharing family values and stories of past family experiences. In this way, the meetings can strengthen the family as well as the business.

THE PROCESS OF SUCCESSION

The task of preparing family members for careers and turning the business over to them is difficult and sometimes frustrating. Professional and managerial requirements tend to become intertwined with family feelings and interests. This section looks at the development and transfer process and some of the difficulties associated with it.

Available Family Talent

A stream can rise no higher than its source, and the family firm can be no more brilliant than its leader. The business is dependent, therefore, upon the quality of leadership talent provided by the family. If the available talent is deficient, the entrepreneur must provide outside leadership or supplement family talent in some way. Otherwise, the business will suffer decline under the leadership of the second- or third-generation family members.

The question of competency of family members presents both a critical and delicate issue. With experience, individuals can improve their abilities; so, younger people cannot be judged too harshly too early. Furthermore, potential successors may be held back by the reluctance of a parent-owner to delegate realistically to them.

Perhaps the most appropriate philosophy is to recognize the right of family members to prove themselves. A period of testing may occur either in the family business or in another organization. As children show themselves to be capa-

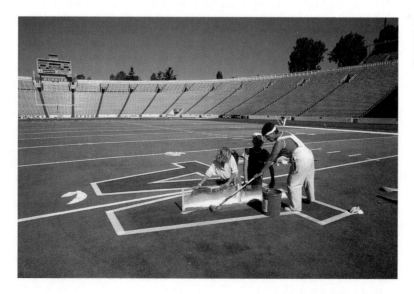

Figure 6-5
Learning the Family
Business from the
Ground Up

ble, they earn the right to increased leadership responsibility. If potential successors are found, through a process of fair assessment, to have inadequate leadership abilities, preservation of the family business and even the welfare of family members demand that they be passed over for promotion. The appointment of competent outsiders to these jobs, if necessary, increases the value of the firm to all family members who have an ownership interest in it.

Stages in the Process of Succession

Sons or daughters do not typically assume leadership of a family firm in a moment of time. Dad or Mom does not step down on Friday with the daughter or son taking over Monday morning. Instead, a long, drawn-out process of preparation and transition is customary—a process that extends over years and often decades. You may visualize this process as a series of **stages in succession** as portrayed in Figure 6-6.[10]

stages in succession
the process of transition of power from parent to child in a family business

Pre-Business Stage. In Stage I, the successor becomes acquainted with the business as a part of growing up. The child accompanies the parent to the office or store or warehouse, or plays with equipment related to the business. There is no formal planning of the youngster's preparation in this early period in which he or she might be only four or five years of age. This first stage forms a boundary that precedes the more deliberate process of socialization.

Introductory Stage. Stage II includes experiences that occur before the successor is old enough to begin part-time work in the family business. It differs from Stage I in that family members deliberately introduce the child to certain people associated directly or indirectly with the firm and to other aspects of the business. The parent explains the difference between a front loader and a backhoe or introduces the child to the firm's banker.

Introductory Functional Stage. In Stage III, the son or daughter begins to function as a part-time employee. This often occurs during vacation periods or after the school day is completed. During this time, the son or daughter develops an acquaintance with some of the key individuals employed in the firm. Often, such work begins in the warehouse or office or production department and may involve assignments in various functional areas as time goes on. The introductory functional stage includes the educational preparation and the experience the son or daughter gains in other organizations.

Functional Stage. Stage IV begins when the successor enters full-time employment, typically following the completion of an educational program. Prior to moving into a management position, the successor may work as an accountant, a salesperson, or an inventory clerk and possibly gain experience in a number of such positions.

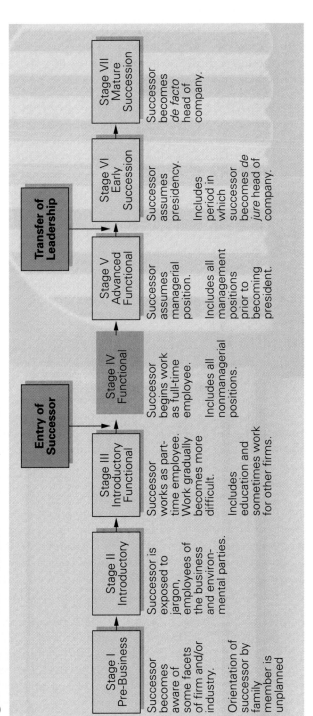

Figure 6-6 A Model of Succession in a Family Business

Stage I Pre-Business	Stage II Introductory	Stage III Introductory Functional	Stage IV Functional	Stage V Advanced Functional	Stage VI Early Succession	Stage VII Mature Succession
Successor becomes aware of some facets of firm and/or industry.	Successor is exposed to jargon, employees of the business and environmental parties.	Successor works as part-time employee. Work gradually becomes more difficult.	Successor begins work as full-time employee.	Successor assumes managerial position.	Successor assumes presidency.	Successor becomes *de facto* head of company.
Orientation of successor by family member is unplanned		Includes education and sometimes work for other firms.	Includes all nonmanagerial positions.	Includes all management positions prior to becoming president.	Includes period in which successor becomes *de jure* head of company.	

Entry of Successor

Transfer of Leadership

Advanced Functional Stage. As the successor assumes supervisory duties, he or she enters the advanced functional stage, or Stage V. The management positions in this stage involve directing the work of others but not the overall management of the firm.

Early Succession Stage. In Stage VI, the son or daughter is named president or general manager of the business. At this point, he or she presumably exercises overall direction of the business, but the parent is still in the background. The leadership role of an organization does not transfer as easily or absolutely as does the leadership title. The successor has not necessarily mastered the complexities of the presidency, and the predecessor may be reluctant to give up all decision making.

Mature Succession Stage. Stage VII is reached when the transition process is complete. The successor is leader in fact as well as in name. In some cases, this does not occur until the predecessor dies. Perhaps optimistically, we assume progress on the part of the successor and regard Stage VII as beginning two years after the successor assumes the presidency of the firm.

Reluctant Parents and Ambitious Children

Let us assume the business founder is a father who is preparing his son or daughter to take over the family firm. The founder's attachment to the business must not be underestimated. Not only is he tied to the firm financially—it is probably his primary if not his only major investment—but he is also tied to it emotionally. The business is "his baby," and he is understandably reluctant to entrust its future to one who is immature and unproven. (Unfortunately, parents often have a way of seeing their children as immature long after their years of adolescence.)

The child may be ambitious, possibly well educated, and insightful regarding the business. His or her tendency to push ahead—to try something new—often conflicts with the father's caution. As a result, the child may see the father as excessively conservative, stubborn, and unwilling to change.

A recent research study examined 18 family-owned businesses in which daughters worked as managers with their fathers. Interviews with family members produced this picture of the daughters' positions:

In 90% of the cases, the daughters reported having to contend with carryover, conflict, and ambiguity in their business roles in the firm and as daughters. While the majority of the women interviewed had previously worked in other organizations, and had developed their identities as businesswomen, they discovered that when they joined the family business they were torn between their roles as daughter and their business roles. They found their relationships with the boss transformed, since the boss was not only the boss, but the father as well. These daughters reported that they often found themselves reduced to the role of "daddy's little girl" (and in a few cases, "mommy's little girl"), in spite of their best intentions.[11]

SMALL BUSINESS IN ACTION

Reluctant Father and Ambitious Daughter

Children often feel they are ready to take control before their parents are ready to acknowledge it. This is true of Tasco Corporation, a Miami-based distributor of optical products such as telescopes and rifle scopes. The intensity of the father's and daughter's feelings is evident in this account:

> On one side is George Rosenfield, 68, who founded the company some 40 years ago. A proud man, Rosenfield steadfastly refuses to say what will happen to the company when he leaves. He says he's in perfectly fine health, and he's not going anywhere.
>
> In the other corner is Rosenfield's daughter, Sheryl Rosenfield. Headstrong, 39 years old and eager to take charge of the company, Sheryl has worked at Tasco for her entire 17-year business career and currently carries the title of executive vice president. At the very

> least, she would like to become a partner with her dad. She figures she's entitled.
>
> Dad disagrees. "I'm still in charge, and she doesn't seem to understand it," says he. "You can't run a business where two people are in charge." Retorts Sheryl: "Dad's ideal daughter is one who would be there for him but one who wouldn't want the throne. That's not me."

Source: Dyan Machan, "'It Would Be Stupid to Quit Now,'" *FORBES,* Vol. 145, No. 7 (April 2, 1990), pp. 178–180. Excerpted from *FORBES* magazine by permission. © Forbes Inc. 1990.

At the root of many such difficulties is a lack of a clear understanding between father and child. They work together without a map showing where they are going. Children in the business, and also their spouses, may have expectations about progress that, in terms of the founder's thinking, are totally unrealistic. The successor tends to sense such problems much more acutely than does his or her father. But much of the problem could be avoided if a full discussion about the development process took place.

Cultural Patterns and Leadership Succession

The process of passing the leadership reins from one generation to another is complicated by, and interwoven with, changes in the family business culture. To appreciate this point, think about the paternalistic-patriarchal culture mentioned earlier in the chapter—a culture that is quite common in the early days of a family business. Changing conditions may render that culture ineffective. As a family business grows, it requires a greater measure of professional expertise. Thus, the firm is pressured to break from the paternalistic mold that gave first priority to family authority and less attention to professional abilities. Likewise, aging of the founder and maturation of the founder's children tend to weaken the patriarchal family culture with its one dominant source of authority—a parent who "always knows best."

Succession may occur, therefore, against the backdrop of a changing culture. In fact, leadership change may itself play an important role in introducing or bringing about changes in the culture and making a break with traditional methods of operation. To some extent, the successor may act as a change agent as he or she assumes decision-making authority. For example, a son or daughter with a college degree may eliminate musty managerial practices and substitute a more professional approach.

As W. Gibb Dyer, Jr., has pointed out, each generation faces its own set of cultural challenges.[12] In the first generation, there are centralized decision-making practices that increasingly lead to inefficiency in operation. The challenge is to retain the founder's values without losing effectiveness in operation. In the second and third generations, the founder's departure creates a vacuum that can lead to family conflicts and power struggles or to collaboration. The challenge is to work together in ways that preserve family relationships and also protect the business. In each stage of succession, the leadership goal is to preserve the best of the existing culture while eliminating its most serious defects.

Transferring Ownership

transfer of ownership
the final step in conveyance of power from parent to child, that of distributing ownership of the business

A final and often complex step in the succession process is the **transfer of ownership** in the family firm. Questions of inheritance affect not only the successor or potential successor in management, but also other family members with no involvement in the family business. In distributing their family estate, parents typically wish to treat all their children fairly, both those involved in the business and those on the outside.

One of the most difficult decisions is that of determining the future ownership of the business. If there are several children, for example, should they all receive equal shares? On the surface, this seems to be the fairest approach. However, such an arrangement may play havoc with the future functioning of the business. Suppose that each of five children receives a 20 percent ownership share when only one of them is active in the business. The child active in the business—the successor—becomes a minority stockholder completely at the mercy of relatives on the outside.

Ideally, the entrepreneur is able to arrange his or her personal holdings so that he or she creates wealth outside the business as well as within it. In this way, he or she may be able to bequeath comparable shares to all heirs while allowing business control to remain with the child or children active in the business.

Tax considerations are relevant, of course, and they tend to favor gradual transfer of ownership to all heirs. As noted above, however, this arrangement may be inconsistent with future efficient operation of the business. Tax laws cannot be allowed to dominate decisions about transferring ownership without regard for these other practical considerations.

Planning and discussing the transfer of ownership is not easy, but such action is recommended. Over a period of time, the owner must reflect seriously on family talents and interests as they relate to the future of the firm. The plan for transfer of ownership can then be "firmed up" and modified as necessary when it is discussed with the children or other potential heirs.

One such arrangement was worked out by a warehouse distributor in the tire industry.[13] The distributor's son and probable successor was active in the business. The distributor's daughter was married to a college professor at a small southern university. Believing the business to be their most valuable asset, the owner and his wife were concerned that both the daughter and the son receive a fair share. Initially, the parents decided to give the real estate to the daughter and the business itself to the son, who would then pay rent to his sister. After discussing the matter with both children, however, they developed a better plan whereby the business property and the business itself would both go to the son. The daughter would receive all nonbusiness assets plus an instrument of debt by the son to his sister which was intended to balance the monetary values. In this way, they devised a plan that was not only fair but also workable in terms of the operation and management of the firm.

Good Management in the Process of Succession

Good management is necessary for the success of any business, and the family firm is no exception.[14] Significant deviations for family reasons from what we might call good management practices, therefore, will only serve to weaken the firm. Such a course of action would run counter to the interests of both the firm and the family. In concluding this discussion of succession, we should recall and emphasize those management concepts which are particularly relevant to the family firm.

The first concept relates to the competence of professional and managerial personnel. A family firm cannot afford to accept and support family members who are incompetent or who lack the potential for development.

Second, the extent of opportunities for nonfamily members and any limitations on those opportunities should be spelled out. They should know and not have to wonder whether they can aspire to promotion to key positions in the firm.

Third, favoritism in personnel decisions must be avoided. If possible, the evaluation of family members should involve the judgment of nonfamily members—those in supervisory positions, outside members of the board of directors, or managers of other companies in which family members work for a time.

Fourth, plans for succession, steps in professional development, and intentions regarding changes in ownership should be developed and discussed openly. Founders who recognize the need for managing the process of succession can work out plans carefully rather than drift haphazardly. Lack of knowledge regarding plans and intentions of key participants creates uncertainty and possible suspicion. This planning process can begin as the founder or the presiding family member shares his or her dream for the family firm and family participation it it.

The family firm is a business—a competitive business. The observance of these and other fundamental precepts of management will help the business to thrive and permit the family to function as a family. Disregard of such considerations will pose a threat to the business and impose strains on family relationships.

LOOKING BACK

1. A family business is one in which the family has a special involvement. Such a business involves an overlapping of business interests (production and profitability) and family interests (care and nurturing).

2. A family business often benefits from the strong commitment of family members to the welfare of the business and the ability of management to focus on human potential, quality, and long-run decisions. Potential weaknesses include a tendency to place family interests before business interests.

3. The culture of a family business includes three segments: the business culture (e.g., paternalistic), the family culture (e.g., patriarchal), and the governance or board-of-directors culture (e.g., rubber-stamp board). Changes in culture often occur as leadership passes from one generation to another.

4. It is difficult to provide strong motivation for nonfamily employees whose promotional opportunities are limited. This problem can be minimized by open communication concerning the extent of these opportunities.

5. A primary family relationship is that between the founder and the son or daughter who may succeed the founder in the business. Sons, daughters, in-laws, and sometimes other relatives have the possibility for collaboration or conflict with the founder and among themselves in the operation of the business. The role of the founder's spouse is especially important, often as a mediator between the founder and other family members. Family retreats and family councils are used by some families to enhance communication and deal openly with family roles and interests related to the business.

6. Succession is typically a long-term process starting early in the successor's life. Tension often exists between the founder and the successor as the latter gains experience and becomes qualified to make business decisions independently. Transfer of ownership involves issues of placing control in the hands of the successor, being fair to all heirs, and facing tax consequences. A carefully formulated plan is helpful in the proper resolution of these issues.

DISCUSSION QUESTIONS

1. How would you define a family business? How does the size of the business affect your definition?

2. A computer software company began operation with a three-member management team that included skills in engineering, finance, and general business. Is this a family business? What might cause it to be classified as a family business or to become a family business?

3. Suppose that an entrepreneur's son-in-law is employed in a family firm. What conflict might possibly occur between family interests and business interests in the career of this son-in-law?

4. Suppose that you, as founder of a business, have a vacancy in the position of sales manager. You realize that sales may suffer somewhat if you promote your son from sales representative to sales manager. However, you would like to see your son make some progress and earn a higher salary to support his wife and young daughter. How would you go about making this decision? Would you promote your son?

5. To what extent should business interests be compromised or sacrificed because of family considerations?

6. What benefits result from family involvement in a business?

7. Why does a first-generation family business tend to have a paternalistic business culture and a patriarchal family culture?

8. Assume that you are an ambitious, nonfamily manager in a family firm and that one of your peers is a son or daughter of the founder. What, if anything, would keep you interested in pursuing your career with this company?

9. On the basis of your own observations, describe a founder-son or founder-daughter relationship in a family business. What strengths or weaknesses do you see in that relationship?

10. Does the involvement of both husband and wife in a family business strengthen or weaken their family relationship? Can you cite any situations you have observed to support your answer?

11. Should a son or daughter feel an obligation to carry on a family business? What is the source of such a feeling?

12. Identify and describe the stages outlined in the model of succession shown in Figure 6-6.

13. What steps can be taken to minimize conflict between parent and child in family business decisions?

14. As a recent graduate in business administration, you are headed back to the family business. As a result of your education, you have become aware of some outdated business practices in the family firm. In spite of them, the business is showing a good return on investment. Should you "rock the boat"? How should you proceed in correcting what you see as obsolete traditions?

15. Should estate tax laws or other factors be given greater weight than family concerns in decisions about transferring ownership of a family business from one generation to another? Why?

YOU MAKE THE CALL

Situation 1

The three Dorsett brothers are barely speaking to each other. "Phone for you" is about all they have to say.

It hasn't always been like this. For more than 30 years, Tom, Harry, and Bob Dorsett have run the successful manufacturing business founded by their father. For most of that time, they have gotten along rather well. They've had their differences and arguments, but important decisions were thrashed out until a consensus was reached.

Each brother has two children in the business. Tom's oldest son manages the plant, Harry's oldest daughter keeps the books, and Bob's oldest son is a rising outside salesman. The younger children are learning the ropes in lower-level positions.

The problem? Compensation. Each brother feels that his own children are underpaid and that some of his nieces and nephews are overpaid. After violent arguments, the Dorsett brothers just quit talking while each continued to smolder.

The six younger-generation cousins are still on speaking terms, however. Despite the differences that exist among them, they manage to get along with one another. They range in age from 41 down to 25.

The business is in a slump but not yet in danger. Because the brothers aren't talking, important business decisions are being postponed.

The family is stuck. What can be done?

Source: "Anger Over Money Silences Brothers," *Nation's Business,* Vol. 78, No. 10, p. 62. Reprinted by permission, Nation's Business, October 1990. Copyright 1990, U.S. Chamber of Commerce.

Questions
1. Why do you think the cousins get along better than their fathers?
2. How might this conflict over compensation be resolved?

Situation 2

Harrison Stevens, second-generation president of a family heating and air conditioning business, was concerned about his 19-year-old son, Barry, who worked as a full-time employee in the firm. Although Barry had made it through high school, he had not distinguished himself as a student or shown interest in further education. He was somewhat indifferent in his attitude toward his work, although he did reasonably, or at least minimally, satisfactory work. In the view of his father, Barry was immature and more interested in riding motorcycles than in building a business.

Harrison Stevens wanted to provide his son with an opportunity for personal development. This could begin, as he saw it, by learning to work hard. If he liked the work and showed promise, he might eventually be groomed to take over the business. His father also held a faint hope that hard work might eventually inspire Barry to get a college education.

In trying to achieve these goals, Harrison Stevens sensed two problems. First, Barry obviously lacked proper motivation. The second problem related to his supervision. Supervisors seemed reluctant to be exacting in their demands on

Barry. Rather than making him toe the line, they allowed him to get by with marginal performance. It may have been their apprehension that they might antagonize the boss by being too hard on his son.

Questions
1. In view of Barry's shortcomings, should Harrison Stevens seriously consider him as a potential successor?
2. How can Barry be motivated? Can Harrison Stevens do anything more to improve the situation, or does the responsibility lie with Barry?
3. How can the quality of Barry's supervision be improved so that his work experience will be more productive?

EXPERIENTIAL EXERCISES

1. Interview a college student who has grown up in a family business concerning the way that he or she may have been trained or educated, both formally and informally, for entry into the business. Prepare a brief report, relating your findings to the stages of succession shown in Figure 6-6.
2. Interview a college student who has grown up in a family business concerning parental attitudes toward his or her possible entry into the business. Submit a one-page report showing the extent of pressure to enter the business and the direct or indirect ways in which expectations were communicated.
3. Locate a family business and prepare a brief report on its history, including its founding, family involvement, and any leadership changes that have occurred.
4. Most libraries have biographies or histories pertaining to families in business or the family businesses themselves. Read and report on one such book.

REFERENCES TO SMALL-BUSINESS PRACTICES

Alster, Norm. "A Third-Generation Galvin Moves Up," *Forbes,* Vol. 145, No. 9 (April 30, 1990), pp. 57–62.
    This article describes the developing career of the grandson of Motorola founder Paul Galvin and his upward movement in the company.
Cropper, Carol M. "Lots of Horses But No Horse Sense," *Forbes,* Vol. 149, No. 4 (February 17, 1992), pp. 78–79.
    This story tells how family-owned Calumet Farm, a jewel among Kentucky horse farms, was destroyed by later generations of the family.
Kreisler-Bomben, Kristin von. "How To Operate a Family-Owned Business," *Entrepreneur,* Vol. 19, No. 2 (February 1991), pp. 56–59.
    The competition between family interests and business interests in The Coffee Beanery, a Michigan franchisor, is described.
Marsh, Barbara. "Daughters Find That Fathers Still Resist Passing the Family Business On To Them," *The Wall Street Journal* (April 14, 1992) p. B-1.
    This account describes the frustrations of daughters in working toward taking over family businesses from their fathers.

McManus, Kevin. "Whose Company Is This Anyway?" *Family Business* (February 1990), pp. 29–33.

A family council was established to keep the business in the family and to help Challenge Machinery Company deal with family issues.

ENDNOTES

1. This distinction between family and business is carefully examined in Ivan Lansberg, "Managing Human Resources in Family Firms: The Problem of Institutional Overlap," *Organizational Dynamics*, Vol. 12 (Summer 1983), pp. 39–46; and Elaine Kepner, "The Family and the Firm: A Coevolutionary Perspective," *Organizational Dynamics*, Vol. 12 (Summer 1983), pp. 57–70.

2. Pat B. Alcorn, *Success and Survival in the Family Owned Business* (New York: McGraw-Hill Book Company, 1982), p. 107.

3. Peter Davis, "Realizing the Potential of the Family Business," *Organizational Dynamics*, Vol. 12 (Summer 1983), pp. 53–54.

4. Edgar H. Schein, "The Role of the Founder in Creating Organizational Culture," *Organizational Dynamics*, Vol. 12 (Summer 1983), pp. 13–28.

5. W. Gibb Dyer, Jr., *Cultural Change in Family Firms* (San Francisco: Jossey-Bass Publishers, 1986), Chapter 2.

6. Marie-Jeanne Juilland, "The Good, the Bad, and the Ugly," *Venture*, Vol. 10, No. 1 (January 1988), p. 42.

7. "Brawl in the Family at Johnson Products," *Business Week*, No. 3257 (March 23, 1992), p. 34.

8. Katy Danco, *From the Other Side of the Bed: A Woman Looks at Life in the Family Business* (Cleveland: The Center for Family Business, 1981), p. 21.

9. Nancy Bowman-Upton, *Transferring Management in a Family-owned Business* (Washington: U.S. Small Business Administration, 1991), p. 6.

10. For an earlier extended treatment of this topic, see Justin G. Longenecker and John E. Schoen, "Management Succession in the Family Business," *Journal of Small Business Management*, Vol. 16 (July 1978), pp. 1–6.

11. Colette Dumas, "Integrating the Daughter into Family Business Management," *Entrepreneurship Theory and Practice*, Vol. 16, No. 4 (Summer 1992), p. 47.

12. W. Gibb Dyer, Jr., *op. cit.*, pp. 57–58.

13. Leon A. Danco, *Inside the Family Business* (Cleveland: The Center for Family Business, 1980), pp. 198–199.

14. For an excellent treatment of leadership transition in a family firm, see John L. Ward, *Keeping the Family Business Healthy* (San Francisco: Jossey-Bass Publishers, 1987), Chapter 8.

PART 3

Preparing the Business Plan

Creating a Formal Business Plan

Nonplanners who succeed in spite of lack of planning may later recognize the wisdom of planning. This is true of Julie and Bill Brice, a brother-and-sister team who used $10,000 of their own money to buy two faltering frozen yogurt stores.

"We just winged it" in the beginning, Julie Brice recalls. "When you are in school, you think you are invincible." But winging it soon grew too complicated for the Brices as they expanded their business to four stores within the first year.

Julie soon signed up for an entrepreneurship course at Southern Methodist University. At the end of the semester, she emerged with a business plan. Planning continued as the business expanded into a nationwide franchise network of more than 120 I Can't Believe It's Yogurt stores. In hindsight, Julie conceded the value of preliminary planning. "If I had to start over again, I definitely would do a business plan to take a look at all the opportunities, the positives and the negatives," she says.

Source: Roger Thompson, "Business Plans: Myths and Reality," *Nation's Business,* Vol. 76, No. 8 (August 1988), pp. 16–23.

Julie and Bill Brice

After studying this chapter, you should be able to:
1. State the reasons for preparing a business plan and explain how the plan is used.
2. Describe how to prepare a business plan.
3. Identify features of a business plan that appeal to investors.
4. Outline the content of a business plan.

business plan   marketing plan   financial plan
executive summary   management plan   pro formas
products and services   operating plan   legal plan
   plan

An early, important step in the launching of any business is preparation of a business plan. Obviously, a plan of some type exists in the mind of any person who is thinking about a new business venture. However, this is a weak substitute for a written business plan. This chapter covers the transformation of those often vague ideas into a written document that lays the groundwork for the proposed venture.

NEED FOR A BUSINESS PLAN

Prospective entrepreneurs tend to neglect the planning stage of a new venture. They are eager to get started, and they do not always realize the importance of a written plan. They may also lack sufficient funds or necessary expertise to conduct an adequate feasibility study.

The **business plan** describes the new-venture idea and projects the marketing, operational, and financial aspects of the proposed business for the first three to five years. Its preparation permits analysis of the proposal and helps the prospective entrepreneur avoid a downhill path that leads from wild enthusiasm to disillusionment to failure. Although this chapter explains the planning process and presents an outline for a business plan, you should use the ideas presented throughout this book and particularly those in Chapters 8 through 11 when preparing such a plan.

business plan
a document containing the basic business idea and all the related considerations in starting a new business

What Is a Business Plan?

If you were to consider starting your own business, an advisor might tell you to begin by preparing a business plan. This plan would present your basic business idea and all related operating, marketing, financial, and managerial considerations. In a sense, it would represent your "game plan." It would crystallize the dreams and hopes that provide your motivation. Whatever the name, it should lay out your idea, describe where you are, and point out where you want to go and how you propose to get there.

The business plan is in a sense the entrepreneur's "first creation." For anything we build, be it a house or a business, there are always two creations, first mentally and then physically. That is, there can be no second creation without there being a first creation. Certainly some things happen as mere chance events where there are not two creations, but seldom are they anything of lasting importance. Also, the plan, to be successful, must be based on a market need for the product or service.

The business plan may present a proposal for launching an entirely new business. More commonly, perhaps, it may present a plan for a major expansion of a firm that has already started operation. For example, an entrepreneur may open a small local business and see the possibility of opening additional branches or extending its success in other ways. The plan may also be a response to some change in the external environment (government, demographic, industry, etc.) that may lead to new opportunities.

More mature businesses also prepare strategic and operational plans that contain many of the features described in this chapter. In fact, planning should be a continuing process in the management of any business. That is, the plan may also be used internally by the owners to more efficiently manage the business on an on-going basis. The concepts presented in this chapter are not limited, therefore, to businesses that are just beginning operation.

Benefits of Preparing a Business Plan

Any activity that is initiated without adequate preparation tends to be haphazard and unsuccessful. This is particularly true of such a complex process as initiating a new business. Although planning is a mental process, it must go beyond the realm of thought. Thinking about a proposed business becomes more rigorous as rough ideas must be crystallized and quantified on paper. The written plan is essential to assure the systematic coverage of all important features of the new business. The plan becomes our "model" of what we want to happen. It captures our understanding of the important variables in the success or failure of our business. Someone has said, "If you cannot model the problem, you do not understand it." That is, modeling or planning helps us to focus on some of the important issues and activities that must be addressed if we are to be effective.

One benefit derived from preparing a formal written plan is the discipline provided for the prospective entrepreneur. For example, in order to prepare a written statement about marketing strategy, you must perform some market research. Likewise, a study of financing requirements will require a review of receipts and expenditures month by month. Even good business ideas may fail because of negative cash flow. In short, business plan preparation forces a prospective entrepreneur to exercise the discipline that good managers must possess.

Using the Business Plan Internally in Managing

A business plan is more than a device for raising funds. More fundamentally, it is a basis for operating a business. Figure 7-1 shows the various users of the business plan. In it, an entrepreneur charts the course for a new firm. As we just noted, the process of formulating the plan can uncover weaknesses or alert the entrepreneur to sources of possible danger. The well-conceived plan thus offers a sound basis for operation.

The goals identified in the business plan become targets for operating control. If the new firm substantially exceeds or falls short of these goals, the entrepreneur must act. The plan itself may require modification, or other management action may be needed.

The business plan also provides a basis for communicating the business mission to insiders, the employees of the firm. Some, indeed, suggest that it can be used as a tool in recruiting key personnel.

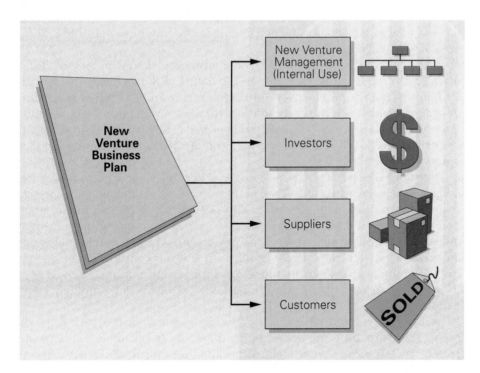

Figure 7-1
Users of Business Plans

Figure 7-2
Working with a
Bank Loan Officer
Requires a Business
Plan

The Business Plan and Outsiders

Investors and lenders are the primary, although not the only, outside users of business plans. Almost anyone starting a business faces the task of raising financial resources to supplement personal savings. Unless the entrepreneur has a "rich uncle" who will supply funds, he or she must appeal to bankers, individual investors, venture capitalists, or other sources. The business plan is the entrepreneur's "calling card."

Both lenders and investors can use the business plan to gain an idea of the business, the type of product or service, the nature of the market, and the qualifications of the entrepreneur or entrepreneurial team. A venture capital firm or other sophisticated investor would not think of investing in a new business without seeing a properly prepared business plan. The plan can also be helpful in establishing a good relationship with a commercial bank, a relationship that is important for a new firm.

The business plan is not, however, a legal document for actually raising the needed capital. When it comes time to solicit investors for money, a prospectus, or "offering memorandum," is used. This document contains all the information needed to satisfy the federal and state security laws for warning potential investors as to the possible risks of the investment. As a consequence, it is not an effective marketing document by which to sell your concept. Thus, you first use the business plan to create interest in your startup venture, followed by a formal offering memorandum to those investors who seem genuinely interested.

Relationships with nonfinancial outside groups may also benefit from exposing those groups to the business plan. Suppliers, for example, extend trade credit, which is often an important part of the firm's financial plan. A well-prepared business plan may be helpful in gaining a supplier's trust and quickly securing favorable credit terms. Occasionally, a business plan can also improve sales prospects—for example, by convincing a potential customer that a new firm is likely to be around to service a product or to continue as a procurement source.

HOW TO PREPARE A BUSINESS PLAN

Preparation of a business plan is a difficult, frustrating, and often unrewarding task, as reflected in the following quotation:

Here's a financing riddle: What costs upwards of $5,000 to prepare, commands a few moments of an investor's time, and fails 98% of the time?

Answer: The typical business plan.[1]

Understanding the Investor's Perspective

If you are to use the business plan to raise capital, you must understand the investor's basic perspective. You must see the world as the investor sees the world; that is, you must think as the investor thinks. For most entrepreneurs, this is more easily said than done. The entrepreneur generally perceives a new venture very differently from the investor. The entrepreneur will characteristically focus on the upside potential of the startup; what will happen if everything goes right. The prospective investor, on the other hand, plays the role of the skeptic, thinking more about what could go wrong. Failure not only to understand but also to appreciate the difference in perspectives greatly increases the chance of the investor's rejecting the plan.

At the most basic level, the potential investor who might read your business plan has a single goal: maximize the potential return on investment through the cash flows that will be received from the investment, while minimizing the personal risk exposure. Even venture capitalists, who are thought to be the great risk takers, want to minimize their risk in an investment. They will be looking, as will any informed investor, for ways to have the entrepreneur share as much of the risk as possible.

Given the fundamental differences between the investor and the entrepreneur, the important question becomes: How do you write a business plan that will capture the prospective investor's interest? There is no easy answer, but two things we know for certain. First, investors have a short attention span. Second, there are certain things known to have general appeal to investors, and other things that are almost certainly unappealing.

The Five-Minute Reader

The venture capitalist has been called "the five-minute reader," to indicate someone who spends only a few moments to glance at a business plan.[2] Very few plans are read in detail from cover to cover. Far too many proposals are received by the typical venture capital firm to permit such careful examination. George Kalan, managing general partner of Orien Ventures Inc., New Caanan, Connecticut, has been quoted as follows: "We got 750 plans last year and made 11 deals. I look at the executive summary, and if it's clearly out of our scope, in a few minutes we send it back with a no-thank-you letter."[3]

The speed with which business plans are reviewed means that they must be designed to communicate effectively even to the speed reader. They must not sacrifice thoroughness, however, or substitute a few snappy phrases for basic factual information. After all, someone is going to read the plan carefully if it ever succeeds. To get that careful reading, however, the plan must first gain the interest of the reader, and it must be formulated with that purpose in mind. This raises the question as to what features of a plan make it appealing to investors.

Business Plans That Attract Investors

To appeal effectively to prospective investors, the plan cannot be extremely long or encyclopedic in detail. Plans should seldom exceed 40 pages in length. Those who work with venture capitalists have reported their tendency to go for brief reports and to avoid those that take too long to read. It follows also that the general appearance of the report should be attractive and that it should be well organized, with numbered pages and a table of contents.

Venture capitalists are more market-oriented than product-oriented, and there is a reason for this orientation. They realize that most inventions, even those patented, never earn a dime for the inventors. It is desirable for budding entrepreneurs to join prospective investors in their concern about market prospects. See Figure 7-3 for a listing of special features in successful business plans.

Factors that presumably interest investors are the following:[4]

- Evidence of customer acceptance of the venture's product or service.
- An appreciation of investors' needs, through recognition of their particular financial-return goals.
- Evidence of focus, through concentration on only a limited number of products or services.
- Proprietary position, as expressed in the form of patents, copyrights, and trademarks.

Prospective investors may also be unimpressed by a business plan. Some of the features that create unfavorable reactions are the following:[5]

- Infatuation with the product or service rather than familiarity with and awareness of marketplace needs.
- Financial projections at odds with accepted industry ranges.
- Growth projections out of touch with reality.
- Custom or applications engineering, which make substantial growth difficult.

Figure 7-3
Plans That Succeed

Based on their experience with the MIT Enterprise Forum, Stanley R. Rich and David E. Gumpert have identified the type of plan that wins funding. (The MIT Enterprise Forum sponsors sessions in which prospective entrepreneurs present business plans to panels of venture capitalists, bankers, marketing specialists, and other experts.) Following are the "winning" features:

- It must be arranged appropriately, with an executive summary, a table of contents, and its chapters in the right order.

- It must be the right length and have the right appearance—not too long and not too short, not too fancy and not too plain.

- It must give a sense of what the founders and the company expect to accomplish three to seven years into the future.

- It must explain in quantitative and qualitative terms the benefit to the user of the company's products or services.

- It must present hard evidence of the marketability of the products or services.

- It must justify financially the means chosen to sell the products or services.

- It must explain and justify the level of product development which has been achieved and describe in appropriate detail the manufacturing process and associated costs.

- It must portray the partners as a team of experienced managers with complementary business skills.

- It must suggest as high an overall "rating" as possible of the venture's product development and team sophistication.

- It must contain believable financial projections, with the key data explained and documented.

- It must show how investors can cash out in three to seven years, with appropriate capital appreciation.

- It must be presented to the most potentially receptive financiers possible to avoid wasting precious time as company funds dwindle.

- It must be easily and concisely explainable in a well-orchestrated oral presentation.

Source: "Plans That Succeed" (pp. 2–3) and dialogue on pp. 126–127 from *Business Plans That Win $$$: Lessons from the MIT Enterprise Forum* by Stanley R. Rich and David E. Gumpert. Reprinted by permission of Sterling Lord Literistic, Inc. Copyright © 1985 by Stanley R. Rich and David E. Gumpert.

Computer-Aided Business Planning

The computer facilitates preparation of the business plan. Its word-processing capabilities, for example, can speed up the writing of narrative sections of the report, such as the description of the product and the review of key management personnel. By using a word-processing software package, the planner can

S M A L L   B U S I N E S S   I N   A C T I O N

Plans That Are Too Long

By using a computer, a prospective entrepreneur can easily generate reams of material—sometimes too many pages. An official of a venture capital firm has complained about this tendency as noted here:

"There's this horrible disease going around right now," says Robert J. Crowley, vice-president of Massachusetts Technology Development Corp., a state-owned venture firm. "It's called spreadsheet-itis. It's the most common ailment in business plans today." And the venture capitalists blame word processors and spreadsheet software. . . . Recently, Crowley received a 98-page plan: 48 pages of spreadsheets, 30 pages of technology description, and 20 pages on management. He was horrified. Most venture capitalists say plans should run no longer than 40 pages. "Word processors allow you to just ramble on," continues Crowley, "because there's no person, no secretary, saying, "You want me to retype what?"'

Source: Reprinted with permission, *Inc.* magazine (February 1987). Copyright 1987 by Goldhirsh Group, Inc., 38 Commercial Wharf, Boston, MA 02110.

begin with an original version of the narrative, go through a series of drafts as corrections and refinements are made, and print out a final plan as it is to be presented to investors or others. Several such word-processing packages are described in Chapter 23.

The computer is an even more helpful tool in preparing the financial statements needed in the plan. Since the various parts of a financial plan are interwoven in many ways, a change in one item—sales volume or interest rate or cost of equipment, for example—will cause ripples to run through the entire plan. If the planner wishes to check out a number of assumptions, this requires a long, tedious set of calculations. By using a computer spreadsheet, the planner can accomplish this task electronically. A computer spreadsheet enables a planner to experiment with various scenarios and quickly ascertain their effect on the firm's balance sheet, operating profits, and cash flows.

Format and Writing Suggestions

The quality of a completed business plan is obviously dependent on the quality of the underlying business concept. A defective venture idea cannot be rescued by good writing. A good venture concept may be destroyed, however, by writing that fails to communicate.

The business plan must be clearly written, and relatively short, typically under 40 pages. Use the plan to give credibility to your ideas. When you make a claim, such as a promise to provide superior service or regarding the attractiveness of the market, offer strong supporting evidence for your position. Above all, make sure the plan is believable.

Skills of written communication are necessary to present the business concept in an accurate, comprehensible, and enthusiastic way. Space does not permit discussion of general writing principles here. Nevertheless, it may be useful to include some practical suggestions specifically related to the business plan. Following are some hints given by the public accounting firm Arthur Anderson and Company in their booklet, *An Entrepreneur's Guide to Developing a Business Plan:*

1. *Provide a table of contents and tab each section for easy reference.*
2. *Use a typewritten 8½" × 11" format and photocopy the plan to minimize costs. Use a looseleaf binder to package the plan and to facilitate future revisions.*
3. *To add interest and improve comprehension—especially by prospective investors who lack the day-to-day familiarity that your management team has—use charts, graphs, diagrams, tabular summaries, and other visual aids.*
4. *You almost certainly will want prospective investors, as well as your management team, to treat your plan confidentially, so indicate on the cover and again on the title page of the plan that all information is proprietary and confidential. Number each copy of the plan and account for each outstanding copy by filing the recipient's memorandum of receipt.*
5. *Given the particularly sensitive nature of startup operations based on advanced technology, it is entirely possible that many entrepreneurs will be reluctant to divulge certain information—details of a technological design, for example, or highly sensitive specifics of marketing strategy—even to a prospective investor. In that situation, you still can put together a highly effective document to support your funding proposal by presenting appropriate extracts from your internal business plan.*
6. *As you complete major sections of the plan, ask carefully chosen third parties—entrepreneurs who have themselves raised capital successfully, accountants, lawyers and others—to give their perspectives on the quality, clarity, reasonableness, and thoroughness of the plan. After you pull the entire plan together, ask these independent reviewers for final comments before you reproduce and distribute the plan.*[6]

Assistance in Preparing a Business Plan

The founder of a business is most notably a "doer." Such a person often lacks the breadth of experience and know-how needed in planning. Consequently, he or she must supplement personal knowledge and personal skills by obtaining the assistance of outsiders or adding individuals with planning skills to the management team.

Securing help in plan preparation does not relieve the founder of direct involvement. The founder must be the primary planner simply because it is his or her plan. The founder's basic ideas are necessary to produce a plan that is realistic and believable. Furthermore, the plan may eventually require defense and interpretation to outsiders. An entrepreneur can be prepared for such a presentation only by having complete familiarity with the plan.

However, after the owner has the basics of the plan in place, outside help to finish and polish the plan is appropriate and wise. Outside professionals who can provide assistance include the following:

1. *Attorneys,* who can make sure that the company has necessary patent protection, review contracts, consult on liability and environmental concerns, and advise on the best form of legal organization.

Figure 7-4
Experts Help Design a Floor Plan Before This Entrepreneur Can Proceed with the Business Plan

2. *Marketing specialists,* who can perform market analysis and evaluate market acceptance of a new product.
3. *Engineering and production experts,* who can perform product development, determine technical feasibility of products, and assist in plant layout and production planning.
4. *Accounting firms,* which can guide in developing the written plan, assist in making financial projections, and advise in establishing a system of financial control.
5. *Incubator organizations,* which offer space for fledgling companies and supply management counsel in structuring new businesses. (Incubators are discussed at greater length in Chapters 9 and 16.)

CONTENT OF A BUSINESS PLAN

A prospective entrepreneur needs a guide to follow in preparing a business plan. Although there is no one standard format in general use, there are many similarities among the general frameworks proposed for business plans. Figure 7-5 presents a simple condensation of the major segments common to many of

Figure 7-5
Overview of a Business Plan

Executive Summary: A one- to three-page overview of the total business plan. Written after the other sections are completed, it highlights their significant points and, ideally, creates enough excitement to motivate the reader to read on.

General Company Description: Explains the type of company and gives its history if it already exists. Tells whether it is a manufacturing, retail, service, or other type of business.

Products and Services Plan: Describes the product and/or service and points out any unique features. Explains why people will buy the product or service.

Marketing Plan: Shows who will be your customers and what type of competition you will face. Outlines your marketing strategy and specifies what will give you a competitive edge.

Management Plan: Identifies the "key players"—the active investors, management team, and directors. Cites the experience and competence they possess.

Operating Plan: Explains the type of manufacturing or operating system you will use. Describes the facilities, labor, raw materials, and processing requirements.

Financial Plan: Specifies financial needs and contemplated sources of financing. Presents projections of revenues, costs, and profits.

Legal Plan: Shows the proposed type of legal organization—for example, proprietorship, partnership, or corporation. Points out special, relevant legal considerations.

Appendix: Provides supplementary materials to the plan.

these organizing patterns. Its special value lies in the excellent bird's-eye view it gives. Before becoming immersed in the details of a plan, you can form a general idea of the various segments of a plan and how they are related to each other.

Segments of a Business Plan

With an overview of the business plan at hand (Figure 7-5), let's consider each part of the plan, along with figures that identify some of the important questions that must be answered. A business plan for each new venture is unique. Therefore, we are unable to cover every question to be addressed; however, we do ask some of the questions common to many business plans.

executive summary
an overview of the entire business plan

Executive Summary. This section is crucial in getting the attention of the five-minute reader. It must, therefore, convey a clear picture of the proposed venture and, at the same time, create a sense of excitement regarding its prospects. This means that it must be written and rewritten to achieve clarity and interest. Even though it comes at the beginning of the business plan, it summarizes the total plan and must be written last. A sample executive summary for an all-natural baby and children's food company is shown in Figure 7-6.

General Company Description. The body of the business plan begins with a brief description of the company itself. If the firm is already in existence, its history is included. By examining this section, the reader will know, for example, whether the company is engaged in retailing or construction or some other line of business, where the business is located, and whether it is serving a local or international market. In many cases, issues noted in the legal plan—especially the form of organization—are incorporated into this section of the plan. See Figure 7-7 for some important questions to be addressed in this section of the plan.

products and services plan
a description of the product or service to be provided and an explanation of its merits

Products and Services Plan. As implied by the title, this section discusses the products and/or services to be offered to customers. If a new or unique physical product is involved and a working model or prototype is available, a photograph should be included. Investors will naturally show the greatest interest in products that have been developed, tested, and found to be functional. Any innovative features should be identified and patent protection, if any, explained. In many instances, of course, the product or service may be similar to that offered by competitors—for example, starting an electrical contracting firm. However, any special features should be clearly identified. See Figure 7-8 for important questions to be answered in this section of the plan. Chapter 8 discusses this topic at greater length.

Figure 7-6
Executive Summary
for Good Foods
Incorporated

This business plan has been developed to present Good Foods Incorporated (referred to as GFI or The Company) to prospective investors and to assist in raising the $700,000 of equity capital needed to begin the sale of its initial products and finish development of its complete product line.

The Company

GFI is a startup business with three principals presently involved in its development. The principal contact is Judith Appel of Nature's Best, Inc., 24 Woodland Road, Great Neck, New York (516-555-5321).

During the past three years, GFI's principals have researched and developed a line of unique children's food products based on the holistic health concept—if the whole body is supplied with proper nutrition, it will, in many cases, remain healthy and free of disease.

Holism is the theory that living organisms should be viewed and treated as whole beings and not merely as the sum of different parts. The holistic concept, which *Health Food Consumer* determined is widely accepted among adult consumers of health foods, is new to the child-care field.

Hence, GFI plans to take advantage of the opportunities for market development and penetration that its principals are confident exist. GFI also believes that the existing baby-food industry pays only cursory attention to providing high-quality, nutritious products, and that the limited number of truly healthy and nutritious baby foods creates a market void that GFI can successfully fill.

Based on the detailed financial projections prepared by The Company's management, it is estimated that $700,000 of equity investment is required to begin The Company's operations successfully. The funds received will be used to finance initial marketing activities, complete development of The Company's product line, and provide working capital during the first two years of operation.

Market Potential

GFI's market research shows that the United States is entering a "mini baby boom" that will increase the potential market base for its products. This increase, combined with an expected future 25 percent annual growth rate of the $2.4 billion health food industry, as estimated by *Health Foods Business* in 1985, will increase the demand for GFI's products. Additionally, health food products are more frequently being sold in supermarkets, which is increasing product visibility and should help to increase popularity.

The Company will approach the marketplace primarily through health food stores and nature-food centers in major supermarket chain stores, initially in the Northeast and California. Acceptance of the GFI concept in these areas will enable The Company to expand to a national market.

The specific target markets GFI will approach through these outlets are:

Parents who are concerned about their health and their children's health and who thus demand higher and more nutritionally balanced foods and products.

Operators of child-care centers who provide meals to children.

Figure 7-6
(Continued)

Major Milestones

Approximately two-thirds of GFI's product line is ready to market. The remaining one-third is expected to be completed within one year.

Distinctive Competence

GFI is uniquely positioned to take advantage of this market opportunity due to the managerial and field expertise of its founders, and its products' distinct benefits.

Judith Appel, George Knapp, MD, and Samuel Knapp, MD, all possess several years of experience in the child-care industry. Ms. Appel is a nutritionist and has served as director for the Children's Hospital for Special Services in White Plains, New York. In addition, she has nine years of business experience, first as marketing director for Healthy Harvest Foods in Yonkers, New York, then as owner/president of Nature's Best, Inc. Both of the Doctors Knapp have worked extensively with children, in hospital-based and private practices.

Together, the principals have spent the last three years developing, refining, testing, and selling GFI's products through Nature's Best, Inc., the retail outlet in Great Neck, a Long Island suburb of New York City.

GFI's product line will satisfy the market demand for a natural, nutritious children's food. The maximum amount of nutrients will be retained in the food, providing children with more nutritional benefit than most products presently on the market. The menu items chosen will reflect the tastes most preferred by children. A broad product line will also provide a diverse meal plan.

Financial Summary

Based on detailed financial projections prepared by GFI, if The Company receives the required $700,000 in funding, it will operate profitably by year three. The following is a summary of projected financial information (dollars in thousands).

	Year 1	Year 2	Year 3	Year 4	Year 5
Sales	$1,216	$1,520	$2,653	$4,021	$5,661
Gross margin	50%	50%	50%	50%	50%
Net income after tax	$(380)	$(304)	$15	$404	$633
Net income after tax/sales	—	—	0.6%	10.0%	11.2%
Return/equity	0.0%	0.0%	10.8%	73.9%	53.6%
Return/assets	0.0%	0.0%	2.6%	44.5%	36.2%

Source: Eric Siegel, Loren Schultz, Brian Ford, and Jay Bornstein, *The Ernst & Young Business Plan Guide,* pp. 47–50. Copyright © 1993, John Wiley & Sons. Reprinted by permission of John Wiley & Sons, Inc.

Figure 7-7
General Company
Description Ques-
tions

1. Is this a startup, buyout, or expansion?

2. Has this business started operation?

3. What is the firm's mission statement?

4. When and where was this business started?

5. What is the basic nature and activity of the business?

6. What is its primary product or service?

7. What customers are served?

8. Is this company in manufacturing, retailing, service, or another type of industry?

9. What is the current and projected state of this industry?

10. What is the company's stage of development—"seed stage," full product line, or what?

11. What are its objectives?

12. Does the company intend to become a publicly traded company or an acquisition candidate?

13. What is the history of this company?

14. What achievements have been made to date?

15. What changes have been made in structure or ownership?

16. What is the firm's distinctive competence?

Marketing Plan. As stated earlier, prospective investors and lenders attach a high priority to market considerations. A product may be well engineered but unwanted by customers. The business plan, therefore, must identify user benefits and the type of market that exists. Depending upon the type of product or service, you may be able not only to identify but also to quantify the user's financial benefit—for example, by showing how quickly a user can recover the cost of a product through savings in operating cost. Of course, benefits may also take the form of convenience, time saving, greater attractiveness, better health, and so on.

marketing plan
a description of potential customers and competitors, and the marketing strategy to be used

The business plan should follow the establishment of user benefits by documenting the existence of customer interest, and showing that a market exists and that customers are ready to buy the product or service. The market analysis must be carried to the point that a reasonable estimate of demand can be achieved. Estimates of demand must be analytically sound and based on more than assumptions if they are to be accepted as credible by prospective investors. The marketing plan must also examine the competition and present elements of the proposed marketing strategy—for example, by specifying the type of sales force and methods of promotion and advertising that will be used. See

Figure 7-8
Products and
Services Plan
Questions

1. What product or service is being offered?

2. What does the product look like?

3. What is the stage of product development?

4. What are the unique characteristics of the product or service?

5. What are its special advantages?

6. What additional products or services are contemplated?

7. What legal protection applies—patents, copyrights, or trademarks?

8. What government regulatory approval is needed?

9. How does the product relate to the state of the art for such products?

10. What are the dangers of obsolescence?

11. What dangers are related to style or fashion change?

12. What liabilities may be involved?

13. How has the product been tested or evaluated?

14. How does the product or service compare with products or services of competitors?

15. What makes this firm's service superior?

Figure 7-9 for key questions to be answered in this section of the plan. Chapter 8 presents a fuller discussion of the marketing plan.

management plan
a description of the
"key players" in a
new business, and
their experience
and qualifications

Management Plan. Prospective investors look for well-managed companies. Unfortunately, the ability to conceive an idea for a new venture is no guarantee of managerial ability. The plan, therefore, must detail the organizational arrangements and the backgrounds of those who will fill key positions in the proposed firm.

Ideally, investors desire to see a well-balanced management team, one that includes financial and marketing expertise as well as production experience and inventive talent. Managerial experience in related enterprises and in other startup situations is particularly valuable in the eyes of outsiders reading the business plan. See Figure 7-10 (on page 180) for some critical questions to be answered in this section of the plan. The factors involved in preparing the management plan are discussed more fully in Chapter 9.

operating plan
a description of the
facilities, labor, raw
materials, and processing requirements of a new
business

Operating Plan. This section of the plan shows how you will produce the product or provide the service. It touches on such items as location and facilities—how much space you will need and what type of equipment you will require. The importance of the operating plan varies from venture to venture, but this plan is necessary even for firms providing services. The operating plan

Figure 7-9
Marketing Plan
Questions

Market Analysis

1. What is your target market?

2. What is the size of your target market?

3. What market segments exist?

4. What is the profile of your target customer?

5. How will customers benefit by using your product or service?

6. What share of the market do you expect to get?

7. What are the market trends and market potential?

8. What are the reactions of prospective customers?

9. How will your location benefit your customers?

Competition

1. Who are your strongest competitors?

2. Is their business growing or declining?

3. How does your business compare with that of competitors?

4. On what basis will you compete?

5. What is the future outlook of your competitors?

Marketing Strategy

1. How will you attract customers?

2. How will you identify prospective customers?

3. What type of selling effort will you use?

4. What channels of distribution will you use?

5. In what geographic areas will you sell?

6. Will you export to other countries?

7. What type of sales force will you employ?

8. What special selling skills will be required?

9. What selling procedures will be used?

10. How will you compensate your sales force?

11. What type of sales promotion and advertising will you use?

12. What pricing policy will you follow?

13. What credit and collection policy will you follow?

14. What warranties and guarantees will you offer?

15. How do your marketing policies compare with those of competitors?

16. How will you handle seasonal peaks in the business environment?

Figure 7-10
Management Plan
Questions

1. Who are members of the management team?

2. What are the skills, education, and experience of each?

3. What other active investors or directors are involved, and what are their qualifications?

4. What vacant positions exist, and what are the plans to fill them?

5. What consultants will be used, and what are their qualifications?

6. What is the compensation package of each key person?

7. How is the ownership distributed?

8. How will employees be selected and rewarded?

9. What style of management will be used?

10. How will personnel be motivated?

11. How will creativity be encouraged?

12. How will commitment and loyalty be developed?

13. How will new employees be trained?

14. Who is responsible for job descriptions and employee evaluations?

15. What time frame has been developed to accomplish the company's objectives?

should explain the proposed approach to assuring production quality, controlling inventory, using subcontracting, or meeting other special problems related to raw materials. See Figure 7-11 for some important questions to be answered in this section of the plan. This area is treated at greater length in Chapter 9.

financial plan
an account of the financial needs and sources of financing and projection of revenues, costs, and profits of a new business

pro formas
a business's projected financial statements

Financial Plan. The financial analysis constitutes another crucial section of the business plan. In it, the entrepreneur presents projections of the company's financial statements, or **pro forma statements,** over the next five years or even longer. The forecasts include balance sheets, income statements, cash flow statements, and break-even analysis. These pro formas, as they are called, should be prepared on a monthly basis for the first year, quarterly for the second and third years, and annually for the remaining years. It is vitally important that the financial projections be supported by well-substantiated assumptions and explanations on how the projections and costs are determined.

While all the financial statements are important, we should give special attention to understanding the cash flows, because a business may be profitable, but fail miserably at producing positive cash flows. Through the cash flow statement, we will see the sources of cash—how much will be raised from investors and how much will be generated from operations. It also shows how much money will be devoted to such investments as inventories and equipment.

Figure 7-11
Operating Plan
Questions

1. How will you produce your product or service?
2. What production will be accomplished by subcontracting?
3. What production or operating facilities will be used?
4. What is the capacity of these facilities?
5. How can capacity be expanded?
6. What methods of production will be used?
7. What type of plant layout will be used?
8. What production control procedures will be used?
9. What quality control system will be used?
10. How will inventory be controlled?
11. What is the environmental impact of the business?
12. What are the advantages and disadvantages of the location?
13. What production or operating advantages exist?
14. What are the labor requirements?
15. What are the major production costs?
16. What materials or components are critical to production?
17. What sources of supply exist?
18. What will be the production cost at each level of operation?

Within this section, the plan should indicate clearly how much cash is needed by the prospective investors, and the intended purpose for the money. Lastly, the investor needs to be told how and when he or she may expect to cash out of the investment. Most investors want to invest in a privately-held company for only a finite time period. They want to know what mechanism will be available for their exiting the company. Experience tells them that the eventual return on their investment will be largely dependent on their ability to cash out of the investment. See Figure 7-12 for important questions to be answered in this section of the plan. The preparation of pro forma financial statements and the process of raising the needed capital are discussed more fully in Chapters 10 and 20.

Legal Plan. In the legal plan, the entrepreneur sets out the form of organization. The three major alternatives are proprietorship, partnership, and corporation. There are variations, however, that deserve consideration. A special type of corporation, for example, may serve to minimize federal taxes paid by the firm and its owners. As noted earlier, the legal plan does not necessarily stand as a totally separate section of the business plan but is often made a part

legal plan
a description of the legal form of organization and related legal matters

Figure 7-12
Financial Plan

1. What assumptions are used for financial projections?

2. What revenue level is projected by months and years?

3. What expenses are projected by months and years?

4. What profits are projected by months and years?

5. What cash flow is projected by months and years?

6. What financial position exists now, and what is anticipated at various points during the next five years?

7. When will the business break even?

8. What financial resources are required now?

9. What additional funds will be required?

10. How will these funds be used?

11. How much has been invested and loaned by the principals?

12. What additional potential sources will be explored?

13. What proportions of funding will be debt and equity?

14. What type of financial participation is being offered?

of the general company description. The legal issues are important, however, and deserve careful consideration. See Figure 7-13 for important questions to be answered in this section. These issues are discussed further in Chapter 11.

Appendix. The appendix should contain various supporting materials and attachments that are not primary issues but complement the reader's understanding of the plan. These would include items of interest that were referenced in the text of the business plan. Examples would include: résumés of the key investors and managers; photographs of products, facilities, and building; professional references; market research studies; pertinent published research; signed contracts of sales; and other such materials.

Sample Plans and Plan-Preparation Manuals

A prospective entrepreneur typically likes to see a sample plan and have specific guidelines for preparing a plan. Used carefully, such aids can facilitate the planning process. You should be cautious, however, about trying to follow another plan too closely by changing the numbers and adapting it for another venture. Each business is unique, and your plan should capture the essence of your specific business.

By exercising caution, however, you can benefit by referring to manuals that are now available. Most, if not all, major accounting firms have compiled

Figure 7-13
Legal Plan
Questions

1. Will the business function as a proprietorship?

2. Will the business function as a general or limited partnership?

3. Will the business function as a regular corporation or Subchapter S corporation?

4. What are the legal liability implications of the form of organization chosen?

5. What are the tax advantages and disadvantages of this form of organization?

6. Where is the corporation chartered?

7. What was the date of incorporation?

8. What attorney or legal firm has been selected to represent the firm?

9. What type of relationship exists with this attorney or law firm?

10. What legal issues are presently or potentially significant?

11. What licenses/permits may be required?

12. What insurance will be taken out on the business, the employees, and so forth?

manuals on preparation of business plans. Private publishers and other groups have also issued books, manuals, and workbooks on this subject, and many of these publications contain sample plans. A number of such sources are listed below. This list is by no means exhaustive, but merely suggestive in indicating the types of publications available.

The Ernst & Young Business Plan Guide, by Eric Siegel, Loren Schultz, Brian Ford, and Jay Bornstein (New York: John Wiley and Sons, 1993)

The Business Plan: A Touche Ross Guide to Writing an Effective Business Plan (Los Angeles: Touche Ross, 1991)

An Entrepreneur's Guide to Developing a Business Plan (Chicago: Arthur Anderson and Company, 1990)

The Business Plan, by Michael O'Donnell (Natick, MA: Lord Publishing, Inc., 1988)

The Business Planning Guide, by David Bangs, Jr. (Dover, NH: Upstart Publishing Company, 1992)

How to Write a Successful Business Plan, by Julie K. Brooks (New York: American Management Association, 1987)

Business Plans That Win $$$: Lessons from the MIT Forums, by Stanley R. Rich and David Gumpert (New York: Harper & Row, 1985)

LOOKING BACK

1. Preparing a business plan forces the prospective entrepreneur to examine a business idea systematically and to deal with potential difficulties before they happen. It can be used internally as the basis for operating the business and externally as a device for raising funds or explaining the business to others.

2. A business plan should be well organized, have a table of contents, and make extensive use of charts, graphs, diagrams, tabular summaries, or other visual aids. A computer can be used in preparing the narrative sections and also, more importantly, in developing the financial section. Outside professional assistance in preparing the plan can also be obtained.

3. Investors like brief reports that are more market-oriented than product-oriented. Such reports must contain believable financial projections and portray the management team as experienced and capable of directing the venture.

4. A business plan should begin with an executive summary, which presents highlights of the overall plan for the busy reader. After the executive summary, the plan devotes sections to a general company description, products/services, marketing plan, management plan, operating plan, financial plan, legal plan, and an appendix.

DISCUSSION QUESTIONS

1. Sometimes an investor will put money into a new business even though it lacks a business plan. Would this be riskier in a very small (less than $1 million sales) business or in a somewhat larger (more than $25 million sales) business? Why?

2. A business plan was described in this chapter as a "game plan." What features of such a plan justify this label?

3. Suppose a student plans to start a very small sideline business—one that will require less than a $200 investment. Is there any point in preparing a written business plan? Why?

4. What benefits are associated with the preparation of a written new-venture plan? Who uses it?

5. Why do entrepreneurs tend to neglect initial planning? Why would you personally be most tempted to neglect it?

6. In what way could a business plan be used in recruiting key management personnel?

7. Recall the statement that the venture capitalist is a "five-minute reader." Would a really intelligent investor make decisions based on such a hasty review of business plans? Is it possible they are acting like financial wizards while throwing money away?

8. Venture capitalists were described as being more market-oriented than product-oriented. What does this mean? What is the logic behind this orientation?

9. Why shouldn't longer business plans be better than shorter ones in view of the fact that more data and supporting analysis can be included?
10. What advantages are realized by using a computer in preparing narrative sections of a business plan? In preparing the financial section?
11. Evaluate the "Format and Writing Suggestions" for preparing a business plan presented in this chapter. Would these suggestions apply equally well to the preparation of reports or papers for a college class?
12. In selling a new type of production tool, how might you quantify user benefit?
13. The founders of Apple Computer, Inc., eventually left or were forced out of the company's management. What implications does this have for the management section of a business plan?
14. If the income statement in a business plan shows the business will be profitable, what is the need for a cash flow forecast?

YOU MAKE THE CALL

Situation 1

New ventures are occasionally more successful than projected in their initial business plans. One example relates to Compaq Computer Corporation. Ben Rosen and L. J. Sevin invested in this company even though they had reservations about its projected sales volume. They were then astonished by the excellent results.

In 1982, Rosen and partner L. J. Sevin, a couple of lucky guys, invested in a company then called Gateway Technology Inc. Gateway's plan said the company would make a portable computer compatible with IBM's personal computer and would sell 20,000 machines for $35 million in its first year—"Which we didn't believe for a moment," says Rosen. The sales projection for the second year was even more outrageous: $198 million. "Can you imagine seeing a business plan like this for a company going head-on against IBM, and projecting $198 million?" he asks. He and Sevin told the fledgling company to scale down its projections.

Gateway later changed its name to Compaq Computer Corp. In its first year the company sold an estimated 50,000 machines, more than twice the plan's forecast, for $111 million. In the second year Compaq's sales were $329 million.

Source: Reprinted with permission, *Inc.* magazine (February 1987). Copyright © 1987 by Goldhirsh Group, Inc., 38 Commercial Wharf, Boston, MA 02110.

Questions
1. In view of the major error in projected sales, what benefits, if any, may have been realized through initial planning?
2. What implications for preparation of a business plan are found in the investors' skepticism concerning sales projections?
3. In view of the circumstances in this case, do you think that entrepreneurs or investors are likely to be more nearly accurate and realistic in projections in new business plans? Why?

Situation 2

A young journalist contemplated launching a new magazine that would feature wildlife, plant life, and the scenic beauty of nature throughout the world. The prospective entrepreneur intended that each issue would contain several feature articles such as the dangers and benefits of forest fires, features of Rocky Mountain National Park, wildflowers found at high altitudes, danger of acid rain, and so on. It would make extensive use of color photographs, but its articles would also contain discussions that were scientifically correct and interestingly written. Unlike *National Geographic,* the proposed publication would avoid articles dealing with the general culture and confine itself to topics closely related to nature itself. Suppose you are a venture capitalist examining a business plan prepared by this journalist.

Questions
1. What are the most urgent questions you wish to have answered in the marketing plan?
2. What details would you look for in the management plan?
3. Do you think this business plan would need to raise closer to $10,000 or $10 million in invested funds? Why?
4. At first glance, are you inclined to accept or reject the proposal? Why?

EXPERIENTIAL EXERCISES

1. Assume that you wish to start a business to produce and sell a device to hold down picnic table cloths so that they will not blow in the wind. Prepare a one-page outline of the marketing section of a business plan for this business. Be as specific and comprehensive as possible.
2. A former chef wishes to start a temporary help business to supply kitchen help (banquet chefs, sauce cooks, bakers, meat cutters, and so on) to restaurants that are short of staff during busy periods. Prepare a one-page report showing which section or sections of its business plan would be most crucial and why it or they would be most crucial.
3. Suppose you wish to start a tutoring service for students in college elementary accounting courses. Outline on one page the benefits that you would realize by preparing a written business plan.
4. Interview a person who has started a business within the past five years. Prepare a report showing the extent to which the founder engaged in preliminary planning and the founder's views about the value of business plans.

REFERENCES TO SMALL BUSINESS PRACTICES

Broome, J. Tol, Jr. "How to Write a Business Plan," *Nation's Business* (February 1993), pp. 29, 30.
   The article identifies some of the important questions to address in preparing a business plan and warns about common mistakes made in plans.

Gumpert, David E. *How to Really Create a Successful Business Plan,* Inc. Business, 1990.

   This book contains actual business plans for such firms as Pizza Hut and Ben & Jerry's.

Hand, Jason. "'They Told Us to Focus,'" *Forbes,* Vol. 142, No. 10 (October 31, 1988), pp. 134–136.

   This article describes the history of Etak, Inc., a company whose first plan was a product plan scratched on the back of an envelope. The company produces computerized navigational systems for cars, but it almost failed because of an error in the marketing plan.

Kuratko, Donald F. "Demystifying the Business Plan Process: An Introductory Guide," *Small Business Forum,* Vol. 8, No. 3 (Winter 1990/1991), pp. 33–40.

   The article provides an overview of the content of a business plan and suggestions in the preparation of the plan. It also suggests resources that may be helpful in developing a business plan.

ENDNOTES

   1. Warren Strugatch, "Wooing That Crucial Business Plan Reader," *Venture,* Vol. 10, No. 5 (May 1988), p. 80.

   2. Joseph R. Mancuso, *How To Start, Finance, and Manage Your Own Small Business,* Revised Edition (Englewood Cliffs, NJ: Prentice-Hall, Inc., 1984), p. 56.

   3. Warren Strugatch, *op. cit.,* p. 80.

   4. Stanley R. Rich and David E. Gumpert, *Business Plans That Win $$$: Lessons from the MIT Forums* (New York: Harper & Row, Publishers, 1985), p. 22.

   5. *Ibid.,* p. 23.

   6. *An Entrepreneur's Guide to Developing a Business Plan* (Chicago: Arthur Anderson and Company, 1990), p. 10.

CHAPTER 8

Building the Marketing Plan

Entrepreneurs need to understand as much as possible about a target market prior to developing the marketing plan. Marketing research is the tool to collect this information.

Although there are many sources of market information, one of the most important is customers. Failing to survey customers and potential customers is a major mistake. Fortunately, there are several simple and inexpensive research tools for collecting customer comments.

Christopher Fish, owner of Northwest Industrial Coatings (NIC) in White City, Oregon, can attest to this fact. He conducted a simple customer survey four years ago and learned about customer satisfaction:

Christopher Fish

But while Fish's questionnaire showed that his customers were satisfied with the quality of NIC's work, they were finding it hard to place orders [by telephone]. "We were surprised that the phone lines were so tied up. On our end things seemed to be rolling along smoothly with four lines," says Fish.

In response to this information, NIC installed new telephone and fax lines. NIC has continued to conduct customer surveys to assist in developing their marketing plan.

Source: Kim T. Gordon, "Tuning In To Your Customers," *Independent Business*, Vol. 4, No. 1 (January–February 1993), p. 24.

After studying this chapter, you should be able to:
1. Identify core marketing activities.
2. List and evaluate three distinct marketing philosophies.
3. Explain the benefits and techniques of collecting marketing information.
4. Describe how market potential is determined.
5. Outline the elements of a formal marketing plan.

small-business marketing	sales forecast	direct forecasting
marketing research	breakdown process	indirect forecasting
secondary data	buildup process	customer profile
primary data		

Entrepreneurs need formal marketing plans not only to convince potential investors of the worth of the venture, but also to guide in the initial days and months of operation. Unfortunately, many entrepreneurs will work on the cart and neglect the horse—develop the product but neglect the marketing plan that will pull the product into the market.

Consider the following conversation between a first-time entrepreneur and a market consultant:

"Do you have a marketing plan?"

"No," she answered, "but we have a great product, and we know that once people see it they will buy it."

"How do you know that?" I asked. "Did you do some consumer research?"

"No, but all our friends told us it was a fantastic idea that would sell like hotcakes."[1]

UNDERSTANDING MARKETING ACTIVITIES

Before we describe the formal marketing plan, we must first examine small-business marketing more generally. What should be the goals of all marketing efforts? What activities are within the scope of small-business marketing? How can marketing research help the entrepreneur understand the market? How can sales be forecasted? Answers to these questions will help the entrepreneur to understand the role of marketing in a new venture and the specific activities that must be conducted in the process of developing the formal marketing plan. A business cannot rely on a good financial strategy or a sound organizational plan as a substitute for good marketing.[2]

Scope of Marketing Activities

At one time, marketing was viewed only as the performance of business activities that affect the flow of goods and services from producer to consumer or user. Notice that this old definition emphasizes distribution. Unfortunately, many entrepreneurs today continue to view marketing in this manner. Others see marketing as nothing more than selling. Actually, marketing is much more. Many marketing activities occur even before a product is produced and ready for distribution and sale! In order to portray the complete scope of marketing, we will use a broader definition. **Small-business marketing** consists of those business activities that relate directly to identifying target markets; determining target market potential; and preparing, communicating, and delivering a bundle of satisfaction to these markets.

small-business marketing
identifying target markets, assessing their potential, and delivering satisfaction

This modern definition reveals the marketing activities and marketing strategy that are essential to every small business. This relationship is depicted in Figure 8-1. Notice that the marketing activities reflect the key components in our definition of small-business marketing. Likewise, marketing strategy evolves from these marketing activities. Market segmentation, market research, and sales forecasting are integral parts of market analysis. Product, pricing, promotion, and distribution plans result in the firm's marketing mix.

Adopting a Marketing Philosophy

A person's philosophy will naturally influence the tactics used to achieve a particular goal. For example, a football coach who believes in "three yards and a cloud of dust" uses the running attack as the major offensive weapon. Similarly, an entrepreneur must choose between major marketing philosophies. The philosophy adopted will shape the firm's marketing activities.

Figure 8-1
Scope of Marketing Activities

Definition of Marketing	Marketing Activities	Strategy Benefit
Identifying Target Markets Determining Target Market Potential	Market Segmentation Market Research Sales Forecasting	Market Analysis
Preparing a Bundle of Satisfaction Communicating a Bundle of Satisfaction Delivering a Bundle of Satisfaction	Product Planning Pricing Planning Promotion Planning Distribution Planning	Marketing Mix

Types of Marketing Philosophies.

Historically, three distinct marketing philosophies have been evident among firms. These are commonly referred to as production-oriented, sales-oriented, and consumer-oriented philosophies. From the late nineteenth century to the present, big business has shifted its marketing emphasis from production to sales to a consumer orientation. Is this same evolution necessary within a single small business? The answer is no. It need not be. Indeed, it should not be. Is one philosophy more consistent with success? The answer is yes. No matter what the type of business, nothing is better than a consumer orientation!

Each philosophy may occasionally permit success. However, the consumer orientation is preferable because it not only recognizes production-efficiency goals and professional selling, but also adds concern for the customer's satisfaction. In effect, a firm that adopts a consumer orientation considers the consumer as both the beginning and the end for its exchange transactions. Remember, customer satisfaction is not a means to achieving a certain goal; rather, it *is* the goal!

Factors That Influence a Marketing Philosophy.

Why have many small firms failed to adopt a consumer orientation? The answer lies in three crucial factors. First, the state of competition affects a firm's orientation. If there is little or no competition and if demand exceeds supply, a firm's activities will likely emphasize production efficiency. Usually this is a temporary situation.

Second, small-business managers show a wide range of interests and abilities in gathering market-related information and interpreting consumer char-

Figure 8-2
This Plant Nursery Owner Knows That a Consumer Orientation Is the Best Marketing Philosophy

acteristics. For example, some small-business managers are strongest in production and weakest in sales. Naturally, production considerations receive their primary attention.

Third, some managers are merely shortsighted. A sales-oriented philosophy, for example, is a shortsighted approach to marketing. Emphasis on "moving" merchandise can often create customer dissatisfaction if high-pressure selling is used with little regard for customers' needs. On the other hand, a consumer orientation contributes to long-range survival by emphasizing customer satisfaction.

COLLECTING MARKETING INFORMATION

Entrepreneurs can make marketing decisions based on intuition alone, or they can base their judgment on sound marketing information. It is often a good idea to put entrepreneurial enthusiasm on "hold" until market research facts are evaluated. According to Elaine Romanelli, director of the Center for Entrepreneurial Studies at Duke University, "A lot of [entrepreneurs] think, 'I experience a need and so does everyone else.'"[3] The availability of research information in no way guarantees good marketing decisions, but it is a major ingredient.

A survey of 173 small to midsize companies around the United States demonstrated that these firms use a variety of sources of market research for new products and services. As shown by Figure 8-3, current customers, networking, and gut instinct are the top three sources of market information.

Nature of Marketing Research for Small Business

marketing research
gathering, processing, reporting, and interpreting marketing information

Marketing research may be defined as the gathering, processing, reporting, and interpreting of marketing information. A small business typically conducts less marketing research than a big business.

Part of the reason for this situation is cost. Another factor is a lack of understanding of the marketing research process. Our coverage of marketing research will emphasize the more widely used practical techniques that small-business firms can use as they analyze their market and make other operating decisions.

Evaluating the cost of research against the expected benefits is a step that the small-business manager should consider. Although this is a difficult task, some basic logic will show that marketing research can be conducted within resource limits.

Figure 8-3
Top Sources of
Market Research for
New Products

Source: *Inc.*, Vol. 14, No. 6 (June 1992), p. 108. Reprinted with permission, *Inc.* magazine, June 1992. Copyright 1992 by Goldhirsh Group, Inc., 38 Commercial Wharf, Boston, MA 02110.

Misconceptions About Marketing Research

Many entrepreneurs avoid marketing research, not fully understanding what it can do for them. Four common misconceptions related to marketing research are described by one author as myths:[4]

- *The "survey myopia" myth.* With its random samples, questionnaires, computer printouts, and statistical analyses, marketing research is synonymous with field survey research.
- *The "big bucks" myth.* Marketing research is so expensive that it can only be used by the wealthiest organizations, and then only for their major decisions.
- *The "sophisticated researcher" myth.* Since research involves complex and advanced technology, only trained experts can and should pursue it.
- *The "most research is not read" myth.* A very high proportion of marketing research is irrelevant to managers or is simply confirming what they already know.

The entrepreneur should recognize these myths and thereby be more open to gathering marketing information.

Nondisposable Research

Good market information is often the key to the successful introduction of a new product. The experience of Culley Davis, founder of Vencor International, in Carlsbad, California, is a testimony to this fact. Davis relied on market research to evaluate and perfect a self-fastening, all-cloth, washable diaper and also to select an appropriate target market.

Davis's product idea originated with his brother-in-law, who sold Davis the product rights for $1,000 after he became tired of working on the concept. Davis went through nine different prototypes, testing each with willing mothers until, three and one-half years later, he was ready to market the product. The primary advantages of the product, named Didee Snug, are its Velcro fas-

tenings and the retention of its prefolded shape even after washing.

Davis selected the final consumer market as his target market primarily because of its size—estimated according to his research to be a $3-billion industry. He estimated that supplying a baby with disposable diapers for 30 months cost some $2,000 more than cloth diapers. Research also showed that many babies were allergic to materials used in disposable diapers. These considerations prompted Davis to tap the consumer market first, rather than other market segments such as hospitals and other medical facilities.

Davis says, "A lot of us dream about things, but putting it to work is another story." He also analyzed market potential in other countries, where he found that customers have a limited product selection.

Source: Erika Kotite, "Reinventing the Wheel Part I." *Entrepreneur*, Vol. 16, No. 7 (July 1988). Reprinted with permission from *Entrepreneur* magazine, July 1988.

Steps in the Marketing Research Procedure

A knowledge of good research procedures benefits the small-business manager. It helps in evaluating the validity of research done by others and in guiding the manager's own efforts. The various steps in the marketing research procedure include identifying the problem, searching for secondary data and primary data, and interpreting and reporting the information gathered.

Identifying the Problem. The first step in marketing research is to define precisely the informational requirements of the decision to be made. Although this may seem too obvious to mention, the fact is that customer needs or wants are too often investigated without sufficient definition. If the problem is not defined clearly, the information gathered will be useless. For example, Figure 8-4 displays a survey questionnaire developed to ascertain information for a producer of wooden pallets. In this situation, the problem was defined as a lack of information about wooden pallet demand among *current users*. With this precise definition, the survey was designed to concentrate only on this class of customer.

Figure 8-4
Questionnaire for a
Mail Survey

QUESTIONNAIRE

Special Note. If you would like to receive information on our wooden pallets once production is started, please check the square below and write in your current mailing address.

I would like to receive this information ☐
Address: _____
_____

1. Does your business currently use wooden pallets? (If   Yes _____
   No, skip to Question 7.)   No _____

2. What percentage of your wooden pallet needs require
   Expendable Pallets (pallets used only one time)?   0–25% _____
                                                              26–50% _____
                                                              51–75% _____
                                                             76–100% _____

3. For each of the following types of wooden pallets, please indicate the approximate quantity you require each year.

Type	*Quantity*
Pallet Bins (All Sizes)	_____
Pallet Bases (All Sizes)	_____
Other (Please Specify)	_____

4. Please indicate which one of the following statements best describes your firm's buying patterns for wooden pallets. (Please check only one.)
   Purchase each month . . . .   _____
   Purchase about twice a year . . . .   _____
   Purchase only once a year . . . .   _____

5. Approximately how close to your business site is your major supplier of wooden pallets?
   Less than 20 miles . . . .   _____
   20 to 50 miles . . . .   _____
   51 to 80 miles . . . .   _____
   81 to 120 miles . . . .   _____
   121 to 150 miles . . . .   _____
   Over 150 miles . . . .   _____

6. What suggestions would you make to help us provide wooden pallets to better meet your needs?

   _____

7. Please indicate the major products of your firm.

   _____
   _____

Please mail the questionnaire in the enclosed self-addressed envelope.
THANK YOU FOR YOUR COOPERATION!!!

Searching for Secondary Data. Information that has already been compiled is known as **secondary data.** Generally speaking, secondary data are less expensive to gather than new data. Therefore, the small business should exhaust all the available sources of secondary data before going further into the research process. Marketing decisions often can be made entirely with secondary data.

secondary data
information that has
been previously
compiled

Secondary data may be internal or external. *Internal* secondary data consist of information that exists within the small business. *External* secondary data abound in numerous periodicals, trade associations, private informational services, and government publications. A helpful source of external data for the small business is the Small Business Administration. This agency publishes extensive bibliographies relating to many decision areas, including market analysis.

Unfortunately, several problems accompany the use of secondary data. One problem is that such data may be outdated and, therefore, less useful. Another problem is that the units of measure in the secondary data may not fit the current problem. For example, a firm's market might consist of individuals with incomes between $20,000 and $25,000, while the secondary data show the number of individuals with incomes between $15,000 and $25,000. Finally, the question of credibility is always present. Some sources of secondary data are less trustworthy than others. Publication of the data does not in itself make the data valid and reliable!

Searching for Primary Data. If the secondary data are insufficient, a search for new information, or **primary data,** is the next step. Several techniques can be used in accumulating primary data. These techniques are often classified as observational methods and questioning methods. Observational methods avoid contact with respondents, while questioning methods involve respondents in varying degrees.

primary data
new information
gathered through
various methods

Observational Methods. Observation is probably the oldest form of research in existence. Indeed, learning by observing is quite a common occurrence. Thus, it is hardly surprising that observation can provide useful information for small businesses, too. Observational methods can be used very economically. Further, they avoid a potential bias that results from a respondent's contact with an interviewer during questioning.

Observation can be conducted by a human or a mechanical observer. The small-firm manager can easily use the less sophisticated personal observation method. The major kinds of mechanical observation devices are usually beyond the budget of most small businesses. A major disadvantage of observational methods is that they are limited to descriptive studies.

Questioning Methods. Both surveys and experimentation are questioning methods that involve contact with respondents. Surveys include contact by mail, telephone, and personal interviews. Mail surveys are often used when respondents are widely dispersed; however, these are characterized by low response rates. Telephone surveys and personal interview surveys involve verbal communication with respondents and provide higher response rates. Personal interview surveys are more expensive than mail and telephone surveys. Moreover, individuals often are reluctant to grant personal interviews because they feel that a sales pitch is forthcoming.

Developing a Questionnaire. A questionnaire is the basic instrument for guiding the researcher and the respondent when surveys are being taken. The questionnaire should be developed carefully and pretested before it is used in the market. Several major considerations in designing a questionnaire are listed below:

1. Ask questions that relate to the decision under consideration. An "interesting" question may not be relevant. Assume an answer to each question, and then ask yourself how you would use that information. This provides a good test of relevance.
2. Select a form of question that is appropriate for the subject and the conditions of the survey. Open-ended and multiple-choice questions are two popular forms.
3. Carefully consider the order of the questions. The wrong sequence can cause biases in answers to later questions.
4. Ask the more sensitive questions near the end of the questionnaire. Age and income, for example, are usually sensitive subjects.
5. Carefully select the words of each question. They should be as simple, clear, and objective as possible.

The one-page questionnaire shown in Figure 8-4 was developed for a small business by one of the authors of this textbook. The firm's research problem was to assess the market potential for its new product—wooden pallets. Potential users of wooden pallets were identified and mailed the one-page questionnaire. Notice the use of both multiple-choice and open-ended questions in this questionnaire. Responses to Item 6 were particularly useful for this firm.

Interpreting the Information. After the necessary data have been accumulated, they should be transformed into usable information. Large quantities of data are only facts without a home. They must be organized and molded into meaningful information. Numerous methods of summarizing and simplifying information for users include tables, charts, and other graphic methods. Descriptive statistics, such as the mean, mode, and median, are most helpful during this step in the research procedure. Inexpensive personal computer software is now available to perform statistical calculations and generate report-quality graphics. Some of these programs are identified in Chapter 23.

DETERMINING MARKET POTENTIAL

A small business can be successful only if a market exists for its product or service. Analyzing a market is particularly important prior to starting a business. Without it, the entrepreneur enters the marketplace much like a high diver who leaves the board without checking the depth of the water. Many types of information from numerous sources are required for a market analysis. See Figure 8-5 for an example of market analysis or new venture.

Components of a Market

The term "market" means different things to different people. Sometimes it simply refers to a location where buying and selling take place, as when we hear, "She went to the market." On other occasions the term is used to describe selling efforts, as when business managers say, "We must market this product aggressively." Still another meaning is the one we use in this chapter. We define a market as a group of *customers* or potential customers who have *purchasing power* and *unsatisfied needs.*

Notice carefully the three components of our definition of a market. First, a market must have a buying unit, or customers. These units may be individuals or business entities. For example, consumer products are sold to individuals and industrial products are sold to business users. Thus, a market is more than a geographic area. It must contain potential customers.

Second, customers in a market must have purchasing power. Assessing the level of purchasing power in a potential market is very important. Customers who have unsatisfied needs but who lack money and/or credit are poor markets because they have nothing to offer in exchange for a product or service. In such a situation, no transactions can occur.

Third, a market must contain buying units with unsatisfied needs. Final consumers, for instance, will not buy unless they are motivated to do so. Motivation can occur only when an individual has unsatisfied needs. It would be difficult, for example, to sell tent dehumidifiers to desert nomads!

In light of our definition of a market, therefore, determining market potential is the process of locating and investigating buying units that have purchasing power and needs that can be satisfied with the product or service that the entrepreneur can offer.

The Sales Forecast

sales forecast
the prediction of how much will be purchased by a market for a defined period of time

Formally defined, a **sales forecast** is the prediction of how much of a product or service will be purchased by a market for a defined time period. The sales forecast can be stated in terms of dollars and/or units.

Notice that a sales forecast revolves around a specific market. This means that the market should be defined as precisely as possible. The market description forms the forecasting boundary. For example, consider the sales forecast

Figure 8-5
Determining Market
Potential for a Small
Restaurant

Many business owners think of [market potential] information as meaningless if their market is small and relatively local, but they may be mistaken.

Take the case of a restaurateur who decided to build a new restaurant in a small New England city. He learned that the state university had an excellent business college that offered in-depth assistance to entrepreneurs at very low cost as a means of training students in market research.

As a first step, the students developed basic market information from U.S. Census studies. "County Business Patterns," the Census Bureau's county-by-county summaries of business activity and establishments, and the "Census of Retail Trade" gave them the number of restaurants in the target county and each surrounding county—five in all—that they defined as the overall market area. Using this data, as well as room- and meal-tax information from the state department of taxation, the students put a dollar figure on the amount local people spent eating out.

As a second step the students determined the average family income for the market area, available from "Characteristics of the Population," also published by the Census Bureau. From these various studies, they were able to calculate the average annual amount and percentage of total income spent per family on outside meals.

Comparing this figure with the national average and making adjustments for the relatively high family income of the market area, the students determined that families were spending considerably less on outside meals than would normally be expected. The reason, they concluded, was a shortage of attractive, upscale restaurants in the market area.

With the help of the restaurateur and his staff, the students visited every restaurant in the market area, writing a brief profile of the decor, pricing, cuisine, number of seats, location and ambience of every competitive facility. This further supported the quantitative information they had developed and also confirmed that restaurants appealing to upper-income families were in short supply.

Further census research uncovered some facts well known to market researchers: The number of upper-income families has been growing rapidly and is expected to grow in the future far more rapidly than middle- or lower-income families. This national trend was paralleled locally and lent authority to the restaurateur's plans. It was one of the factors considered by the bankers who eventually lent the money needed for the restaurateur's new establishment.

Part of the student project was to forecast the volume that a restaurant aimed at upper-income families would do in future years. The projections gave the entrepreneur and his staff information they needed to help determine the number of seats and the prices they could charge.

The total cost of the study was well under $5,000. In no way did it suffer from the fact that relatively inexperienced students did the work; it was a study that any professional would have been proud of.

Source: James S. Howard, "Build Your Company on Customer Needs." Reprinted from the July/August 1989 issue of *D&B Reports,* the Dun & Bradstreet Magazine for Small Business Management.

SMALL BUSINESS IN ACTION

Ethnic Marketing

Ethnic marketing is a type of competitive strategy which strives to fulfill the needs of consumers segmented by racial and ethnic profiles. These minority markets are providing increasing opportunities for small businesses wanting to serve niche markets.

One entrepreneur who has responded to the demands within the Asian-American markets is Michael Ghafouri, who launched Kayla in 1990 as a fashionable women's salon for makeup and cosmetics. "In my travels, I realized that Asians buy a tremendous amount of cosmetic products," says Ghafouri, a former Max Factor executive. "We are no different from any other company, with one exception. We identified these gaps, and we came up with the solution."

Ghafouri learned the tastes and preferences of other Asians by listening to customers. After two years of operation, Kayla's sales reached $8 million.

Source: Adapted from William Dunn,"The Move Toward Ethnic Marketing," *Nation's Business,* Vol. 80, No. 7, pp. 39–41. Excerpted by permission, *Nation's Business,* July 1992. Copyright 1992, U.S. Chamber of Commerce.

for a manual shaving device. If the market for this product is described simply as "men," the potential sales forecast would be extremely large. A more precise definition, such as "men between the ages of 15 and 25 who are dissatisfied with electric shavers," will result in a smaller but more useful forecast.

Also note that the sales forecast implies a defined time period. One sales forecast may cover a year or less, while another extends over several, maybe five years. Both the short-term and the long-term forecasts are needed in the entrepreneur's business plan.

Importance of Forecasting

The sales forecast is a critical component of the business plan for assessing the feasibility of a new venture. If the market is insufficient, the business is destined

Figure 8-6
A Sales Forecast Is Necessary in Planning Such Business Activities as Maintaining Inventories in This Auto Parts Store

for failure. The sales forecast is also useful in other areas of business planning. Production schedules, inventory policies, and personnel decisions—to name a few—all start with the sales forecast. Obviously, forecasts can never be perfect. Furthermore, the entrepreneur should remember that forecasts can be in error in either of two ways—an underestimation or an overestimation of potential sales.

A recent survey of sales executives among small companies found the following:[5]

- *About 40 percent of the respondents estimated that their sales forecasts were 75–89 percent accurate; 23 percent said they were 90–94 percent accurate.*
- *Over 90 percent stated that no consultants were used in sales forecasting.*
- *Secondary purposes for their sales forecast were budget preparation, setting quotas for salespeople, determining advertising and sales promotion expenditures, hiring personnel, advance purchasing of raw materials and parts, and making cash forecasts.*

These statistics indicate both the importance of sales forecasting and the tendency for entrepreneurs to shoulder the entire burden of developing the forecast.

Limitations to Forecasting

For a number of practical reasons, forecasting is used more successfully by large firms than by small companies. First, the entrepreneur's forecasting circumstances are unique. Inexperience coupled with a new idea represents the most difficult forecasting situation, as depicted in Figure 8-7. An ongoing business that needs only an updated forecast for its existing product is in the most

S M A L L   B U S I N E S S   I N   A C T I O N

Learning to Forecast

Sales forecasting is vital to a complete venture business plan. It also continues to be important to guide ongoing marketing activities. An important characteristic of successful forecasting for any small firm is employee participation. For example, consider the forecasting process of Alan Burkhard, CEO of The Placers, Inc., which is a temporary-personnel and job search firm based in Wilmington, Delaware.

At The Placers, the forecasting process runs from October to December each year, and every employee is involved. Burkhard implemented the current forecasting process after several early years of forecasting which never worked out. The five essential phases of his forecasting system are summarized as follows:

1. *The preplanning session:* An initial all-day meeting with the senior management team to set the overall tone and context that will guide the process is held in mid-October. Issues such as current market trends and competitive developments are discussed.
2. *The leadership session:* The executive vice-president of operations meets next with the company's "leadership" team—the 12 employees who supervise offices or departments. This group generates actual numbers for sales and expenditures reflecting the overall "picture" of the market set by senior management.
3. *The research process:* During November, all employees, guided by a worksheet, project how many temporaries will be placed at each location, corresponding billing rates, and operating expenses. To obtain good numbers, salespeople are encouraged to telephone major clients.
4. *Collation of results:* Department heads collect each employee's projections and enter the numbers into the company computer. Burkhard and his management team analyze this data and suggest changes where appropriate.
5. *The final forecast:* By December, the final forecast is compiled and then circulated to each employee by the first of the next year.

On a weekly basis, all salespeople are sent budget updates comparing forecasted sales with actual results. "We tell people we expect them to stay on target. And, if they're not meeting their forecasted numbers, they've got to figure out why not, how they can adjust their performance, and whether variances represent problems for the business," says Burkhard.

Source: Jill Andresky Fraser, "On Target," *Inc.*, Vol. 13, No. 4 (April 1991), pp. 113–114. Reprinted with permission, *Inc.* magazine, April 1991. Copyright 1991 by Goldhirsh Group, Inc., 38 Commercial Wharf, Boston, MA 02110.

favorable forecasting position. Second, the small-business manager may be unfamiliar with methods of quantitative analysis. This is not to say that all forecasting must be quantitatively oriented. Qualitative forecasting is helpful and may be sufficient. However, quantitative methods have proven their value in forecasting over and over again.

Third, the small-business entrepreneur is ordinarily not familiar with the forecasting process, and it is unlikely that the small firm employs a forecaster.

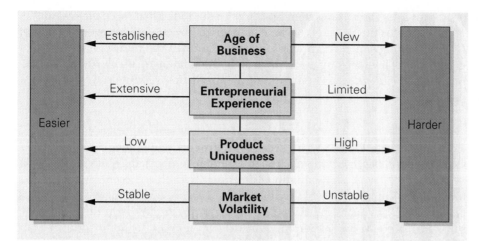

Figure 8-7
Dimensions of
Forecasting
Difficulty

To overcome these deficiencies, some small firms attempt to keep in touch with industry trends through contacts with their trade association. From the standpoint of its professional staff members, the trade association is frequently better qualified to engage in business forecasting. Also, small-business entrepreneurs provide themselves with current information about business trends by regularly reading trade publications and economic newsletters such as the *Kiplinger Washington Letter, Business Week,* and *The Wall Street Journal.*

Government publications, such as *Survey of Current Business, Federal Reserve Bulletin,* and *Monthly Labor Review,* are also of interest in a general way. Then there is the possibility of subscribing to professional forecasting services, which provide forecasts of general business conditions or specific forecasts for given industries.

Despite limitations, a small business should not slight the forecasting task. Remember how important the sales outlook is to the business plan when obtaining financing! The statement "We can sell as many as we can produce" does not satisfy the information requirements of potential investors.

One business consultant described entrepreneurs' lack of forecasting concern by saying, "They don't know if the market needs it, but they are in love with it . . . they don't know the market potential, they don't know the market size. I ask how many they need to sell to break even . . . and they don't know."[6]

Steps in the Forecasting Process

Estimating market demand with a sales forecast is a multistep process. Typically, the sales forecast is a composite of several individual forecasts. The process of sales forecasting then must merge the individual forecasts properly.

The forecasting process can be characterized by two important dimensions: (1) the point at which the process is started, and (2) the nature of the predicting variable. The starting point is usually designated by the terms *breakdown process* or *buildup process*. The nature of the predicting variable is denoted by either *direct* forecasting or *indirect* forecasting.

The Starting Point. The **breakdown process,** sometimes called a "chain-ratio" method, begins with a macro-level variable and systematically works down to the sales forecast. This method is frequently used for consumer products forecasting. The macro-level variable might be a population figure for the targeted market. By using percentages, the appropriate link is built to generate the sales forecast. For example, consider the market segment identified in Chapter 3, Figure 3-6, by our hypothetical company, Community Writing Co. The targeted market is older students (25 years of age or over) seeking convenience/erasability in their writing instrument. Furthermore, assume that the initial geographic target is the state of Idaho. Table 8-1 outlines the breakdown process. Obviously, the more "links" in the forecasting chain, the greater the potential for error.

The **buildup process** calls for identifying all potential buyers in a market's submarkets and then adding up the estimated demand. For example, a local dry-cleaning firm forecasting demand for cleaning high school athletic letter jackets might first estimate its market share as 20 percent within each school. Then, by determining the number of high school athletes obtaining a letter jacket in each area school—maybe from the school yearbook—a total could be forecasted.

The buildup method is especially helpful for industrial goods forecasting. Census of Manufacturers data are often used to estimate potential. The information can be segmented with the Standard Industrial Classification (SIC) code. This classification system identifies potential industrial customers by SIC code, allowing the forecaster to locate information on number of establishments, location, number of employees, and annual sales. By summing this information for several relevant SIC codes, a sales potential can be constructed.

The Predicting Variable. In **direct forecasting,** sales is used as the predicting variable. This is the simplest form of forecasting. Many times, however, sales cannot be predicted directly. In this case other variables related to sales must be forecast. **Indirect forecasting** takes place when these other forecasts are used to project the sales forecast. For example, a firm may lack information about industry sales of baby cribs but may have data on births. The figures for births can help forecast industry sales for baby cribs.

breakdown process
a forecasting method that begins with a macro-level variable and works down to the sales forecast

buildup process
a forecasting method that identifies all potential buyers in submarkets and adds up the estimated demand

direct forecasting
a forecasting method that uses sales as the predicting variable

indirect forecasting
a forecasting method that uses variables related to sales to project the sales forecast

Table 8-1
Sales Forecasting with the Breakdown Method

	Linking Variable	Reference	Estimating Value	Market Potential*
a.	Idaho State Population	U.S. Census of Population		1,000,000
b.	State Population in Target Age Category	*Sales & Marketing Management Survey of Buying Power*	12%	120,000
c.	Target Age Enrolled in College and Universities	Idaho Department of Education	30%	36,000
d.	Target Age College Students Preferring Convenience Over Price	Student Survey in Marketing Research Class	50%	18,000
e.	"Convenience-Oriented" Students Likely to Purchase New Felt-tip Pen within Next Month	Personal Telephone Interview by Entrepreneur	75%	13,500
f.	People Who Say They Are Likely to Purchase Who Actually Buy	Article in *Journal of Consumer Research*	35%	4,725
g.	Average Number of Pens Bought per Year	Personal Experience of Entrepreneur	4 units	18,900
	SALES FORECAST FOR IDAHO			18,900 units

*Figures in this column, b–g, are derived by multiplying the percentage or number in the estimatimg value column times the amount on the previous line of the market potential column.

DESIGNING THE FORMAL MARKETING PLAN

After preliminary marketing analysis is completed—such as market research, market analysis, and sales forecasting—the entrepreneur is ready to construct the formal marketing plan. A general guide to various components of a marketing plan was presented in Figure 7-9 of Chapter 7. When questions in that outline are answered sufficiently, the entrepreneur will have the necessary information to write the final document.

It is important to remember that each business venture is different and therefore each marketing plan will be unique. An entrepreneur should not feel that he or she must develop a cloned version of someone else's plan.

The marketing plan should include sections on market analysis, competition, and marketing strategy. In the following paragraphs we will describe the major elements of the formal marketing plan. A detailed discussion of marketing activities for both new and ongoing small businesses is provided in Part IV of this book.

Market Analysis

customer profile
a description of potential customers

In this initial section of the marketing plan, the entrepreneur should discuss target market customers. The description of potential customers is commonly called a **customer profile.** Information compiled with market research—both secondary and primary data—can be used to construct this profile. A detailed discussion of the major customer benefits characterizing the new product or service should be included. Obviously, these benefits must be reasonable and consistent with statements in the "Products and Services" section of the business plan.

If an entrepreneur envisions several target markets, then each segment must have its corresponding customer profile. Likewise, several target markets necessitate an equal number of different marketing strategies.

Another major element of market analysis is the sales forecast. It is usually desirable to include more than one sales forecast—"most likely," "pessimistic," and "optimistic." This provides investors and the entrepreneur with three sales scenarios upon which to base their evaluation.

As pointed out earlier in this chapter, forecasting sales for a new venture is extremely difficult. Assumptions will be necessary but should be minimized. The forecasting method should be noted and supported by empirical data wherever feasible.

Competition

Frequently, entrepreneurs ignore the reality of competition for their new ventures. Apparently they believe that the marketplace contains no close substitutes or that their success will not attract other entrepreneurs! Stephen J. Warner, president of Merrill Lynch Venture Capital, Inc., New York, states that investors want to see a section on competition to demonstrate that an entrepreneur has considered his or her competition. He says, "I'm very pleased when I see a section on the competition that's well done . . . . I'm very worried when it's missing."[7]

Existing competitive firms should be studied carefully. They should be profiled, and the names of key management personnel should be included. A brief discussion of competitors' overall strengths and weaknesses should be a part of this section. Also, a list of related products currently marketed or being tested by competitors should be noted. An assessment and explanation of the likelihood that each of these firms will enter the entrepreneur's target market should be made. Consider the competitive situation of Worthington Foods, Inc., of Worthington, Ohio:

Worthington is a pioneer in fat-free foods but its growth has attracted competition. From 1987 to 1991, Worthington's sales doubled, to $70 million, but profit margins have been squeezed below that of other specialty food companies such as McCormick and J.M. Smucker. In part this is because the competitors are huge companies with marketing muscle.[8]

SMALL BUSINESS IN ACTION

A Prisoner to Competition

The reality of competition is sometimes found in strange places—even behind bars. Several small companies, producing products ranging from draperies to audio cables, are facing a marketing disadvantage due to the government contracts given Federal Prison Industries, Inc., which is a government corporation operating under the name Unicor.

The traditional prison-shop operation of stamping out license plates has evolved into a "professional-looking catalog listing 150 products in 46 industries." Small firms contend the prison industry is encroaching unfairly on their potential markets. Richard Secter, Unicor's chief executive, says a recent market study found Unicor's impact on the private sector to be "insignificant."

However, Stephen Heller, who operates Hil-tronics, a family business in Stony Point, New York, contends prison-made products are forcing the shutdown of his company. Hiltronics makes one product—audio cable used in airplanes and helicopters. Its military orders have dropped to one from two dozen four years ago.

Also, Thomas W. Raftery, Inc., a drapery manufacturer in Hartford, Connecticut, saw its government sales slide last year after Unicor began bidding on government drapery orders. "We became pretty dependent on the federal market, [and] they simply took the customers away from us," says Gary Rigolletti, Raftery's president.

Small business is lobbying for a change, according to Leslie Aubin, a representative of the Na-tional Federation of Independent Business. "It's fine for prisoners to have factories. . . . We're just asking for a level playing field," she says.

Source: Eugene Carlson, "Some Small Companies Find Competition Is in Prisons," *The Wall Street Journal* (December 9, 1991), p. B2. Reprinted by permission of *The Wall Street Journal*, © 1991 Dow Jones & Company, Inc. All Rights Reserved Worldwide.

Marketing Strategy

A well-prepared market analysis and a discussion of competition are important to the formal marketing plan. But this section—covering marketing strategy—is the most detailed and, in many respects, subject to the closest scrutiny by potential investors. Strategy plots the course of marketing action that will activate the entrepreneur's venture.

There are four areas of marketing strategy that should be addressed within the marketing plan. First, the plan includes marketing decisions that transform the basic product or service idea into a "total product." Second, the plan includes promotional decisions that will communicate the necessary information to target markets. Third, there are decisions regarding the distribution of a product to customers. Finally, there are pricing decisions that will set an acceptable value on the total product or service.

Obviously, the nature of a new venture has a direct bearing on the emphasis given to each of these areas. For example, a service business will not have the same distribution problems as a product business. Also, the promotional challenge facing a new retail store is quite different from that of a new manufacturer. Despite these differences, we can still offer a generalized format for presenting marketing strategy in a business plan.

The Total Product/Service. Within this section of the marketing plan, the entrepreneur needs to include the product or service name and why it was selected. Any legal protection that has been initiated or currently exists should be explained. It is very important to explain the logic of the name selected. An entrepreneur's family name, for certain products or services, may make a positive contribution to sales. In other situations, a descriptive name that suggests a benefit of the product may be more desirable. Regardless of the strategy of the name, it should be defended.

Other components of the total product, such as the package, should be presented via a drawing. Sometimes it may be desirable to use professional packaging consultants to develop the package. One such consultant expresses the importance of packaging to the total product by saying, "It's not something you add on at the last moment. The consumer doesn't think of the package as a separate entity when he picks up the product but sees it as a part of the product itself."[9]

Customer service plans such as warranties and repair policies need to be discussed also. These elements of the marketing plan should be tied directly to the customer-satisfaction emphasis of the venture.

Promotional Plans. This section should cover the entrepreneur's approach to creating customer awareness of the product or service and motivating customers to buy. The entrepreneur has many options. Personal selling and advertising are two of the most popular alternatives.

If personal selling is appropriate, the plan should outline how many salespeople will be employed and how they will be compensated. Plans for training the sales force should be mentioned. If advertising is to be used, a listing of the specific media should be included and the advertising themes described.

Often it is advisable to seek the services of a small advertising agency. In this case, the name and credentials of the agency should be discussed. A brief mention of successful campaigns supervised by the agency can add to the value of this section of the marketing plan.

Distribution Plans. Quite often, new ventures will use established intermediaries to structure their channels of distribution. This strategy expedites distribution and reduces investment.

How these intermediaries will be convinced to carry the new product should be explained. If the business plans to license its product or service, this strategy should also be covered in this section.

Some new retail ventures require fixed locations; others require mobile stores. The layouts and configurations of these retail stores should be planned as explained in the next chapter.

Figure 8-8
Promotional Plans
May Include the
Services of an
Advertising Agency

Sometimes a new business begins with exporting. When this is the strategy, the marketing plan must discuss the relevant laws and regulations governing exporting. Knowledge of exchange rates and distribution options must be reflected by the material included in this section.

Pricing Plans. At the very minimum, a price must reflect the costs of bringing a product or service to the customer. Therefore, this section of the plan must include a schedule of both production and marketing costs. It is advisable to label each of these costs as either fixed or variable so that break-even computations can be generated for alternative prices. The sales figures from the market analysis section were obviously forecasted assuming a certain sales price. Naturally, the analysis in this section should be consistent with the forecasting methods of the market analysis section.

However, setting a price based exclusively on break-even ignores other aspects of pricing. If the entrepreneur truly has a unique niche, she or he may be able to charge a premium price—at least for initial operating periods.

The closest competitor should be studied to learn what that firm is charging. The new product or service will most likely have to be in a reasonable range of that price. One pricing consultant gives this advice: "Being on the high end is pretty good, because you can always fall back . . . . In the long run, however, the market is going to tell you what your pricing should be."[10]

1. The three major marketing management philosophies are production-oriented, sales-oriented, and consumer-oriented. The consumer-oriented philosophy is the essence of the marketing concept. Entrepreneurs need to adopt a strategic position that includes an emphasis on customer service and satisfaction.

2. The first step in the marketing research procedure is to identify accurately the problem to be solved. The second step is to search for secondary and primary data, which are two forms of marketing information. Data are collected by observational and questioning methods. Finally, the data are interpreted and prepared for use in the business plan.

3. Estimating market demand with a sales forecast involves a multistep process. The starting point of the sales forecast can be designated as a buildup process or a breakdown process. Direct forecasting and indirect forecasting are two basic forms of forecasting sales. Forecasting techniques are usually classified in two ways: qualitative techniques and quantitative techniques.

5. A formal marketing plan is the component of the overall business plan that describes the marketing plan of action. It covers a description of the market, competition, and marketing strategy.

DISCUSSION QUESTIONS

1. Can you think of one purchase experience in which you were completely satisfied? If so, explain the circumstances surrounding that purchase. If not, what made a purchase less than satisfactory?

2. Do you believe that small businesses can achieve a higher level of customer satisfaction than big businesses? Why or why not?

3. What research methods would you use to measure the number of males with brown eyes at your school?

4. What research method would you use to determine whether or not a warranty helped product sales? Be specific.

5. Explain why the three components in our definition of a market must be viewed as having a multiplicative relationship rather than an additive relationship.

6. Explain the concept of a market niche as it might relate to an entrepreneur's desire to market a new poison-alert product. The device emits an electronic warning whenever a cabinet or drawer containing harmful materials is opened.

7. Why is it so important to understand the target market? What difference would it make if the entrepreneur simply ignored the characteristics of market customers?

8. How do the three marketing management philosophies differ? Select a consumer product and discuss your marketing tactics for each philosophy.

9. Summarize the market research process that the student research team followed when they determined the market potential for the restaurant entrepreneur as described in the chapter.

10. Assume that your instructor desired to design this course using benefit variables. What various types of benefits do you believe exist for your classmates (consumers)? How would this influence your instructor's course requirements?

11. Assume that you are planning to market a new facial tissue product. Write a detailed market profile of your target customers. Use benefit and demographic variables in your profile. Then change one or more of these variables. How would this change the marketing mix?

12. Distinguish between direct sales forecasting and indirect sales forecasting. Give examples.

13. What promotional techniques do you feel would be most effective to promote a new retail clothing store to its customers?

14. Comment on the statement "You get what you pay for" when you buy any product.

15. Select several new product names from recent issues of a magazine and discuss how conducive the names will be to marketing.

YOU MAKE THE CALL

Situation 1

James Mitchell was born and raised in the cattle country of southern Oklahoma, where he continued to ranch for almost 20 years until falling beef prices in the mid-1970s drove him out of business. After a brief try at the restaurant business, Mitchell, now age 64, wants to try a venture in the car-care service business.

His business will be an automobile inspection-sticker service. There is currently no other business of this type in the city of 150,000 residents where he lives, and he has leased a good location adjacent to a major traffic artery of the city. Mitchell does not plan to do mechanical work other than minor jobs necessary to get a car up to inspection standards, such as fuse and headlight replacements. Since the state mandates that automobiles pass an inspection yearly, he feels market demand will be stable.

Questions

1. Write a brief description of what you see as Mitchell's strategic marketing position. Do you think it is a worthy strategy? Why or why not?
2. What methods of marketing research can Mitchell use to gather helpful marketing information?
3. What name might be appropriate for Mitchell's business? What forms of promotion should be in his marketing plan?
4. What type of pricing strategy would you suggest Mitchell adopt? Why?

Situation 2

Mary Wilson is a 31-year-old wife and mother who wants to start a business. She has no previous business experience but has an idea to market an animal grooming service using a pizza delivery concept. In other words, when a customer calls, she will arrive, in a van, in less than 30 minutes and provide the grooming service.

Many of her friends think the idea is unusual, and they usually smile and remark, "Oh, really?" However, Wilson is not discouraged; she is setting out to purchase the van and necessary grooming equipment.

Questions
1. What target market or markets can you identify for Mrs. Wilson? How could she forecast sales for her service in each market?
2. What advantage do you see in her service compared to existing grooming businesses?
3. What business name and what promotional strategy would you suggest to Mrs. Wilson?

EXPERIENTIAL EXERCISES

1. Interview a local small-business manager to determine what he or she believes is (are) the competitive advantage(s) offered by the business.
2. Select a recent issue of a business publication and report on the marketing strategy described in one of the articles.
3. Interview a local small-business manager to determine the type of market research, if any, he or she uses.
4. Visit a local small-business retailer and observe its marketing efforts—such as salesperson style, store atmosphere, and warranty policies. Report to the class and make recommendations for improving these efforts for greater customer satisfaction.

REFERENCES TO SMALL-BUSINESS PRACTICES

Brown, Paul B. "Fame," *Inc.,* Vol. 10, No. 8 (August 1988), pp. 43–48.
   The "star" status of several entrepreneurs is profiled in this article. The majority of the entrepreneurs attribute their success to a customer orientation.
Brown, Paul B. "On the Cheap," *Inc.,* Vol. 10, No. 2 (February 1988), pp. 108–110.
   This article describes the inexpensive marketing information used by an entrepreneur opening a men's specialty store. The two most valuable sources of information were his own retailing experience and data developed and paid for by others—secondary data.
Cole, Wendy. "You're Only As Good As Your Last Meal," *Venture,* Vol. 10, No. 2 (February 1988), pp. 55–58.
   The problems of a weak marketing plan are described by a restaurant owner. Other management problems that lead to failure are also discussed.
Gilbert, Nathaniel. "Breaking In," *Entrepreneur,* Vol. 18, No. 12 (December 1990), pp. 147–153.
   This article discusses 10 ways to monitor competitive activities. The negative experience of one entrepreneur who did not consider the competition properly is described.
Jones, Arthur. "'CI' versus Spy," *Financial World* (April 28, 1992), pp. 62–64.
   This article discusses the difficulty in gathering information on the competition. The owner of a consulting firm that helps companies establish their competition intelligence units describes the differences between competition intelligence and spying.

ENDNOTES

1. Wilson Harrell, "But Will It Fly?" *Inc.,* Vol. 9, No. 1 (January 1987), p. 85.

2. An excellent article describing the role of marketing in entrepreneurship is Gerald E. Hills and Raymond W. LaForge, "Research at the Marketing Interface to Advance Entrepre-neurship Theory," *Entrepreneurship Theory and Practice,* Vol. 16, No. 3 (Spring 1992), pp. 33–59.

3. Marie-Jeanne Juilland, "A Bright Idea Isn't Enough," *Venture,* Vol. 10, No. 4 (April 1988), p. 78.

4. Alan R. Andreasen, "Cost-Conscious Marketing Research," *Harvard Business Review,* Vol. 61, No. 4 (July–August 1983), p. 74.

5. Excerpted from Harry R. White, *Sales Forecasting: Timesaving and Profit-Making Strategies That Work* (Glenview, IL: Scott, Foresman and Company, 1984), Chapter 3.

6. Kevin McDermott, "Selling High Technology," *D&B Reports,* Vol. 35, No. 5 (September–October 1987), p. 36.

7. Warren Strugatch, "Wooing That Crucial Business Plan Reader," *Venture,* Vol. 10, No. 5 (May 1988), p. 81.

8. Richard Phalon, "Thin in the Wrong Places," *Forbes* (June 8, 1992), pp. 62–63.

9. Warren Strugatch, "Marketing By Design," *Venture,* Vol. 10, No. 10 (October 1988), p. 88.

10. Carol R. Riggs, "A Marketing Plan for Service Businesses," *D&B Reports,* Vol. 36, No. 5 (September–October 1988), p. 25.

CHAPTER 9

Planning the Management Team and Physical Facilities

SPOTLIGHT ON SMALL BUSINESS

What is the world's best location for a sailboarding business? It may be Corpus Christi, Texas. Mark Dulaney's MD Surf & Skate Shop is located there, and Dulaney is working to make Corpus Christi the nation's capital for the increasingly popular sport of sailboarding. Sailboarding is basically surfboarding with a sail, and Corpus Christi, with its good wind, big waves, warm water, and warm air, provides an excellent location for this sport. The city's competitive edge rests on these factors:

1. It is more accessible than Hawaii for most sailboarders.
2. It has better wind conditions than San Diego or Florida.
3. It has warmer water than San Francisco, Santa Barbara, or Hood River.
4. There are no dangerous reefs.

Mark Dulaney

The sport's annual U.S. Open has drawn live television coverage and brought thousands of spectators to Corpus Christi. As the sport continues to develop, MD Surf & Skate Shop should reap the benefits of its ideal location.

Source: Greg Fieg Pizano, "Dulaney Rode Right Wave: Skateboards and Sailboards Are Business," *Corpus Christi Caller-Times*, July 31, 1988, p. 20.

After studying this chapter, you should be able to:
1. Explain the value of a management team and the way in which it is assembled.
2. Identify the pivotal factors in choosing a location.
3. Compare the relative advantages of renting versus buying a building.
4. Describe the advantages and drawbacks in using homes and incubators as business locations.
5. Explain how efficiency is attained in the layout of small factories and retail stores.
6. Describe the nature of equipment and tooling needs of small factories and retail stores.

management team	product layout	general-purpose
zoning ordinance	grid pattern	equipment
business incubator	free-flow pattern	special-purpose
process layout	self-service layout	equipment

A business plan takes on a visible form as an entrepreneur assembles the human and physical resources needed to implement the plan. As a first step, the entrepreneur must find the people who are to help in running the business. In addition, the entrepreneur must select a location and arrange for the necessary building and equipment.

PLANNING THE MANAGEMENT TEAM

Unless a firm is extremely small, the founder will not be the only individual in a leadership role. The concept of a management team, therefore, is relevant. In general, the **management team**, as we envision it here, includes both managers and other professionals or key persons who help give the new company its general direction.

management team
managers and other key persons who give a company its general direction

Value of a Strong Management Team

The quality of a firm's management is generally recognized as vital in its effective operation. As we noted in Chapter 2, poor management is a significant contributor to business failure. Strong management can make the best of any business idea and provide the resources to make it work. Of course, even a highly competent management team cannot rescue a firm that is based on a totally weak business concept or has completely inadequate resources.

For some ventures, a team can be stronger than one individual entrepreneur. One reason is that a team can provide a diversity of talent to meet a diversity of staffing needs. This is particularly true for high-tech startups. Also, a team can provide greater assurance of continuity in that the departure of one team member would be less devastating than the departure of a sole entrepreneur.

The importance of management in the starting of a new venture is evident in the attitudes of venture capitalists who examine business plans. A review of the management team is one of their first steps in evaluating a business plan.

Building a Management Team

The management team includes individuals with supervisory responsibilities—for example, a financial manager who supervises a small office group. The team also includes others who play key roles in the business even though they are not supervisors. A new firm, for example, might begin with only one individual conducting its marketing effort. Because of the importance of the marketing function, that person would be a key member of the management team.

The type of competence needed in a management team depends upon the type of business and the nature of its operations. For example, a software development firm and a restaurant call for different types of business experience. Whatever the business, the small firm needs managers with an appropriate combination of educational background and experience. In evaluating the qualifications of those who will fill key positions, one needs to know whether an applicant is experienced in a related type of business, whether the experience has included any managerial responsibilities, and whether the individual has ever functioned as an entrepreneur.

Not all members of a management team need competence in all areas. The key is balance. Is one member competent in finance? Does another have an adequate marketing background?

The personal compatibility and cooperation of team members are also necessary for effective collaboration. Barbara J. Bird presents comments by four team members in a machine-fabrication business that portray an almost ideal climate of psychological safety and openness:

You never doubt about these guys. They put everything into their work. Their best. They're hard working, and they enjoy doing that.

Anybody fails we all fail. So we stay alert. . . . We have to so everybody can help before it happens.

Then it's safe. No one is saying you're stupid or thick headed. . . . It's like an objective exercise, never personal. No egos involved.

Every night we have a chance to talk. . . . If we can't be here together, we call each other. Share the day's news.[1]

In addition to identifying the key positions or individuals, the entrepreneur should carefully design the organizational structure. Relationships among the

Management Team— Key to Success

A well-chosen management team can give a new startup a powerful advantage. This was the case with Quantum Health Resources, which was started in 1988 as a supplier of drugs for hemophiliacs. Quantum delivered drugs directly to homes or treatment centers and also provided related services such as nursing care. In less than four years, the company was a resounding success with 254 full-time employees, 14 field offices nationwide, and annual sales of $77 million.

Much of the credit for its success goes to its management team. Doug Stickney, Quantum's CEO, and three of his associates at Western Medical Specialty Corporation found themselves unemployed when Western was sold. They started Quantum, and their managerial skills and knowledge were keys to its success. They already had excellent connections in the industry and knew physicians in this area of medicine. In addition, their experience enabled them to cover the various functional areas such as marketing, financing, and operations. A venture capitalist described Stickney as an extraordinary manager in terms of his ability to attract and motivate high-level people.

Source: Leslie Brokaw, "Older and Wiser," *Inc.*, Vol. 14, No. 1, pp. 51–54. Reprinted with permission, *Inc.* magazine, January 1992. Copyright 1992 by Goldhirsch Group, Inc., 38 Commercial Wharf, Boston, MA 02110.

various positions need to be understood. Although such relationships need not be worked out in great detail, it is desirable to have sufficient planning to permit orderly functioning of the enterprise and to avoid a jumble of responsibilities that invites conflict.

The management plan should be drafted in such a way as to provide for business growth. Unfilled positions should be specified. Job descriptions should spell out the duties and qualifications for such positions, and methods for selecting key employees should be explained. In a partnership, the partners need to look ahead to the possible breakup of the partnership.

The ownership share, if any, needs to be thought out carefully. Likewise, the compensation arrangements, including bonus systems or other incentive plans for key organization members, warrant scrutiny and planning.

Outside Professional Support

The managerial and professional talent of a new-venture management team can be supplemented by drawing upon outside assistance. This may take various forms. As one example, an active board of directors can provide counsel and guidance to the leadership group. Directors may be appointed on the basis of their business or technical expertise as well as on the basis of their financial investment. Selection and use of directors is discussed at greater length in Chapter 11.

A small firm may also "shore up" weak areas by carefully developing working relationships with external professional groups. Examples are the firm's relationships with a commercial bank, an attorney, and a certified public accounting firm. To some extent, reliance on such outside advisors can compensate for the absence of sufficient internal staffing.

Planning the company's leadership, then, should produce a team that is able to give competent direction to the new firm. It should be balanced in covering the various functional areas and in offering the right combination of education and experience. It may be comprised of both insiders and outside specialists.

Nonmanagerial Personnel

In many cases, the entrepreneur or the management team are the only employees when the business begins operations. However, additional personnel will be required as the business grows. The selection and training of such employees are treated in Chapter 17.

Human resources—the people involved in the business—require physical resources in the form of a place to work. We turn now to the business plan's coverage of these physical resources: a location, a building, and equipment.

SELECTING A LOCATION

Location is an integral part of the business plan. For most small businesses, a location decision is made only when the business is first established or purchased. Occasionally, however, a business considers relocation to reduce operating costs, get closer to its customers, or gain other advantages. Also, as a business expands, it sometimes becomes desirable to begin additional operations at other locations. The owner of a custom drapery shop, for example, may decide to open a second unit in another section of the same city or even in another city.

Importance of a Good Location

It is not the frequency but the lasting effects of location decisions that make them so important. Once the business is established, it is costly and often impractical, if not impossible, to "pull up stakes" and move. If the business depends upon a heavy flow of customer traffic, a shrewdly selected site that produces maximum sales will increase profits throughout its existence at that location. In contrast, a site with light traffic will reduce sales volume throughout the life of the business. If the choice is particularly poor, the business may never be able to "get off the ground," even with adequate financing and superior ability in purchasing and selling merchandise. This enduring effect is so clearly recognized by national chain-store organizations that they spend thousands of dollars investigating sites before establishing new stores.

The choice of a location is much more vital to some businesses than to others. For example, the site chosen for a dress shop can make or break it. In contrast, the exact location of a painting contractor is of relatively minor importance. Even painting contractors, however, may suffer from certain locational disadvantages. All cities have buildings that need painting, but some communities keep property in better condition and provide better opportunities for painters.

General Considerations in Choosing a Location

Only careful investigation will reveal the good and bad features of any particular location. Four general factors are important in this investigation. These factors are: personal preference, environmental conditions, resource availability, and customer accessibility. In a particular situation, one factor may be more important than the others, but each always has an influence. These factors and their impact on location decisions are depicted in Figure 9-2. Notice that the compass needle is influenced by all four factors. The needle is moving restlessly and unable to point to the best location until specific venture circumstances are provided.

Figure 9-1
If a Business Plan Calls for a Poor Location, Prospects for a Successful Venture are Weak

PEANUTS reprinted by permission of UFS, Inc.

Figure 9-2
The Compass Finds
the Optimum Loca-
tion by Responding
to the Relative
Importance of the
Four Factors for a
Particular Business

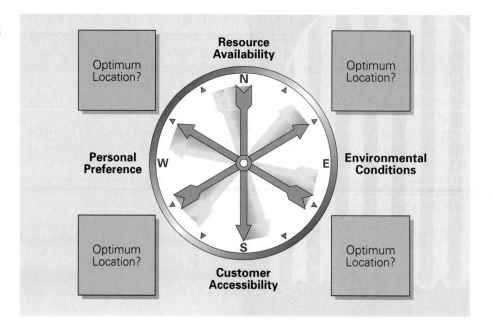

Personal Preference. As a practical matter, a prospective entrepreneur typically considers only the home community for locating the business. Frequently, the possibility of locating elsewhere never enters the mind. Home community preference, of course, is not the only personal factor influencing location.

Choosing one's hometown for personal reasons is not necessarily illogical. In fact, there are certain advantages. For one thing, the individual generally accepts and appreciates the atmosphere of the home community, whether it is a small town or a large city. From a practical business standpoint, the entrepreneur can more easily establish credit. The hometown banker can be dealt with more confidently, and other businesspersons may be of great service in helping evaluate a given opportunity. If customers come from the same locality, the prospective entrepreneur has probably a better idea of their tastes and peculiarities than an outsider would have. Relatives and friends may also be one's first customers and may help to advertise one's services. The establishment of a beauty shop in the home community would illustrate a number of these advantages.

Personal preferences, however, should not be allowed to cancel out location weaknesses, even though such preferences may logically be a primary factor. Just because an individual has always lived in a given town does not automatically make it a satisfactory business location!

Environmental Conditions. A small business must operate within the environmental conditions of its location. These conditions can hinder or promote success. For example, weather is an environmental factor that has traditionally influenced location decisions. Other environmental conditions, such as competition, laws, and public attitudes, to name a few, are all part of the business environment. The time to evaluate all these environmental conditions is prior to making a location decision.

Resource Availability. Resources associated with the location site are an important factor to consider when selecting a location. Land, water supply, labor supply, transportation facilities, and waste disposal are just a few of the site-related factors that have a bearing on location costs.

Raw materials and labor supply are particularly critical considerations to the location of a manufacturing business. The location compass in Figure 9-3 symbolizes the prominent role of resource availability to manufacturers. The compass needle has settled considerably and now points in one general direction—a location that favors resource availability. However, personal preference or environmental conditions may exert a stronger influence on the final location decision and thus offset some resource advantage.

Customer Accessibility. Sometimes the foremost consideration in selecting a location is customer accessibility. Retail outlets and service firms are

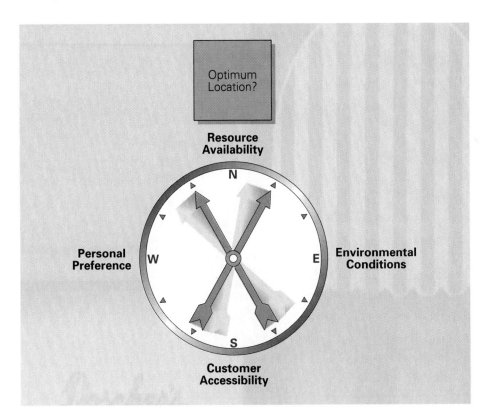

Figure 9-3
For Certain Businesses, Especially Manufacturers, Resource Availability Is a Primary Consideration in Choosing a Location

typical examples of businesses that must be located conveniently to customers. Figure 9-4 shows the compass needle settling in the general direction of the customer-accessibility variable, reflecting its importance in locating service/retail businesses. Once again, the precise location may be influenced more strongly by the variables of personal preference or environmental conditions.

Choice of Region

For some businesses—a barbershop or drugstore, for example—the choice of a region is simple. These businesses can operate successfully in most areas of the country. Other types of small business, however, need to analyze the problem of geographical location with extreme care. Their location decision need not be made entirely by chance.

Some markets for goods and services are restricted to specific regions. For example, a ski lodge is practical only in an area with slopes and snow, and a boat repair service must locate near the water. However, most new firms have the option of selecting any of several regions.

The impact of regional differences on a service firm can be illustrated by a

Figure 9-4
For Businesses Such as Retail and Service Firms, Customer Accessibility Is a Prime Consideration in Choosing a Location

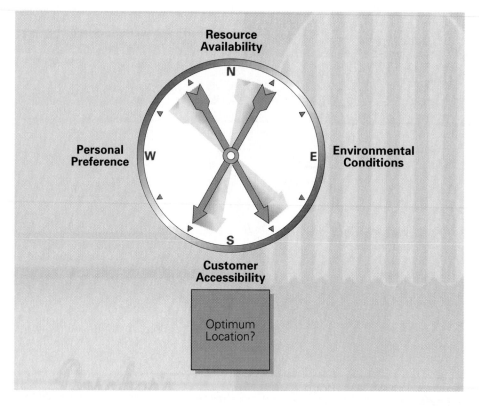

Figure 9-5
Foot Traffic Is
Important to Retail
Businesses That
Display Their Goods
on the Sidewalk

car-wash business. The owner of four car washes, George Rohtstein, points out
the effect of weather differences:

*"Go south, where the weather is more uniform," Rohtstein says, "and you've got an ideal
business—200 cars today, tomorrow and the next day." Up north, when it rains, when it
snows, the business collapses; when the weather clears, business booms. There was a lot of
rain in the Boston area last year, and the number of cars washed fell maybe 30 percent.*[2]

Nearness to the Market. Locating near the center of the market is desirable if other factors are approximately equal in importance. This is especially
true of industries in which the cost of shipping the finished product is high relative to its value. For example, packaged ice and soft drinks require production
facilities that are close to the consuming markets.

Availability of Raw Materials. If the required raw materials are not
abundantly available in all areas, the region in which these materials abound
offers special locational advantages. Bulky or heavy raw materials that lose
much of their bulk or weight in the manufacturing process are powerful forces
that affect location. The sawmill is an example of a plant that must stay close to
its raw materials in order to operate economically.

SMALL   BUSINESS   IN   ACTION

Exceptions to the Rule

The personal preferences of an entrepreneur can sometimes overshadow such location considerations as being near your customers. The Western Fair, founded by Judge R. W. Hailey, who is now deceased, is an excellent example of how there are exceptions to every rule.

The Fair is a specialty western store located in Lott, Texas, a small town of around 900 people. The store's sale of high-quality merchandise at a low price brings customers from all over the United States. Some days Lott will see five or six times its population in the Western Fair store. The outside appearance of the store is plain and the inside is stacked with merchandise.

The owner's grandson, Chester Springfield, manages the store, which has grown from a sales volume of $750,000 in 1956 to $2 million in 1991. Chester concedes that their operation isn't always run by the textbook, but things have seemed to work out okay.

Source: Personal conversation with Dr. Helen Ligon, daughter of the Western Fair founder.

Adequacy of Labor Supply. A manufacturer's labor requirements depend upon the nature of its production process. In some cases the need for semiskilled or unskilled labor justifies locating in a surplus labor area. Other firms find it desirable to seek a pool of highly skilled labor. In addition, wage rates, labor productivity, and a history of peaceful industrial relations are particularly important considerations for labor-intensive firms.

Choice of City

Choice of region and choice of city tend to overlap. The entrepreneur needs the right city in the right region. To make the best decision, he or she must analyze various cities in terms of the competitive situation, availability of support services, and other such factors.

A few years ago, Bob Freese and three colleagues from 3M Corporation in St. Paul, Minnesota, started a new high-tech firm, Alphatronix, to produce optical storage devices for computers. They were reluctant to locate in Minnesota because the cost of doing business was high. Also, they believed it might be difficult for a startup to lure professional talent to such a cold climate. Therefore, they made a careful nationwide search of cities to find the best spot for the new company.

Alphatronix's Bob Freese and his partners looked carefully at Kansas City, as well as at other finalists such as Washington, D.C., and Salt Lake City. Various cities scored high on one or another criterion. Washington had a well-developed high-tech infrastructure; it also had high costs and a mixed quality of life. Salt Lake City had moderate costs and a high quality of life, but transportation was a problem: reaching customers on the East Coast wouldn't be easy. The ultimate winner: Research Triangle Park, in the Raleigh-Durham area of North Carolina. "Other places in the country might look better in any given category," says Freese. "But when you begin looking at two or three criteria, this area just pops right up."[3]

The Research Triangle Park alone housed about 60 high-tech companies and was expanding into 2,000 undeveloped acres.

Some cities are growing in both population and business activity, and the income level of their citizens is advancing. In contrast, other cities are expanding slowly or even declining in population. Table 9-1 lists four rapidly growing cities and four declining cities. Most businesses would prefer to locate in an area with growing population.

Most small businesses are concerned about the nature and the amount of local competition. Manufacturers who serve a national market are an exception to this rule, but overcrowding can occur in the majority of small-business fields. The quality of competition also affects the desirability of a location. If existing businesses are not aggressive and do not offer the type of service reasonably expected by the customer, there is likely to be room for a newcomer.

Published data can be used to shed light upon this particular problem. The average population required to support a given type of business can be determined on a national or a regional basis. By comparing the situation in the given city with these averages, it is possible to get a better picture of the intensity of local competition.

Unfortunately, objective data of this type seldom produce unequivocal answers. There is no substitute for personal observation. In addition, the entrepreneur will do well to seek the opinion of those well acquainted with local

City	Percentage of Population Change
Mesa, AZ	+89%
Plano, TX	+78%
Irvine, CA	+78%
Las Vegas, NV	+57%
New Orleans, LA	−11%
St. Louis, MO	−12%
Detroit, MI	−15%
Gary, IN	−23%

Table 9-1
Cities Growing and Declining in Population, 1980–1990

Source. "Fastest Growth in West, South," USA TODAY, March 4, 1991, p. 9A. Copyright 1991, USA TODAY. Reprinted with permission.

business conditions. Wholesalers frequently have an excellent notion of the potential for additional retail establishments in a given line of business.

Local government can help or hinder a new business. In choosing a city, the prospective entrepreneur should be assured of satisfactory police and fire protection, streets, water and other utilities, street drainage, and public transportation. Unreasonably high local taxes or severely restrictive local ordinances are to be avoided. Some cities offer incentives, such as low-interest loans or a break in local property taxes, to new or expanding businesses.

Finally, the city might also qualify with respect to civic, cultural, religious, and recreational affairs that make it a better place in which to live and do business.

Choice of Site

After choosing a region and a city, the next step is to select a specific site for the business. Some critical factors to consider at this stage include costs, customer accessibility, neighborhood conditions, and the trend toward suburban development.

In selecting a site, some firms stress the operating costs and purchasing costs associated with a specific business site. Examples of these firms are most manufacturers, wholesalers, plumbing contractors, and painting contractors. It would be foolish for these firms to locate in high-rent districts.

Earlier we recognized customer accessibility as a consideration in selecting a location. This factor becomes critical when evaluating a specific site for many types of retail stores. For example, a shoe store or a drugstore may fail simply because it is on the wrong side of the street. Measurement of customer traffic—pedestrian or auto depending on the nature of the business—is helpful, therefore, in evaluating sites for some types of business. One individual in the car-wash business explains that a good location should have traffic moving at the right speed with ease of ingress and egress.[4] He suggests that a minimum of 20,000 to 30,000 cars per day going by at speeds of not more than 25 miles per hour is necessary for successful operation. Many state highway departments have statistics available on traffic counts for major roadways.

Some site locations present special problems because of deteriorating conditions or threat of natural disaster. During the Los Angeles riots of 1992, for example, many small-business buildings were totally destroyed. And during the mid-western floods in the summer of 1993 many small firms found themselves under several feet of water. While there are business opportunities in all areas, advantages and weaknesses must be evaluated.

The trend toward suburban shopping centers has been a significant development. Increasing suburban population, greater use of the family car, traffic congestion, lack of parking space downtown, and other factors have contributed to the relative decline of central business district activity in many cities. This shift in business has created problems in the downtown area, as well as offered opportunities in the suburbs. For the small retail business, a shopping center or other suburban location often presents a better opportunity than a downtown spot.

THE BUILDING AND ITS LAYOUT

The business plan should address the space in which the business will be housed. A new business ordinarily begins by occupying an existing building. An existing structure may make a given site either suitable or unsuitable. Thus, the location decision must be coupled with an analysis of building requirements.

Rent or Buy?

Assuming that a suitable, existing building is available, the founder must decide whether to rent or buy such a facility. Although ownership confers greater freedom in modifying and using a building, the advantages of renting usually outweigh these considerations. Two reasons why most new firms should rent are the following:

1. A large cash outlay is avoided. This is important for the new small firm, which typically lacks adequate financial resources.
2. Risk is reduced by avoiding substantial investment and by postponing commitments for building space until the success of the business is assured and the nature of building requirements is better known.

When entering into a leasing agreement, the renter should check the landlord's insurance policies to be sure there is proper coverage for various types of risks. If not, the renter should seek coverage under his or her own policy. It is also important to have the terms of the rental agreement reviewed by an attorney. A renter should not be unduly exposed to liability for damages that are caused by the gross negligence of others. An example has been cited of a firm that wished to rent just 300 square feet of storage space in a large complex of offices and shops.[5] On the sixth page of the landlord's standard lease was language that could have made the tenant responsible for the entire 30,000-square-foot complex if it burned down, regardless of blame!

Home-Based Businesses

Many small-business firms are based in their owners' homes. Rather than renting or buying a separate building, they house the business operation in a basement, garage, or spare room.

Some businesses can operate in the home because of their modest space demands. In 1988, for example, Christine Wells started a custom filtration equipment/service business for saltwater aquariums (Underwater FantaSea) in her home in Torrance, California.[6] She began by making a filtration system for her own aquarium and then responding to requests of friends who saw it and wanted similar systems. Her work space was her two-car garage. Some firms of this type are simply Stage I firms, or beginning firms, that move out of the home when growth makes it necessary. Others continue to operate in the home indefinitely. Wells plans to maintain her business as a small specialized service for the Los Angeles area and to remain in her home for the foreseeable future.

Many businesses operate in the home in order to blend business activities and family care. When her son, Jeffrey, was born in 1992, Jane Edgington wanted to be at home to care for him during his early life. Her solution was to give up her position as a marketing research director for a publishing company in the Chicago area. Using a computer in a spare bedroom, she set up business as a freelance research analyst in her own home.

To function successfully, owners of home-based businesses need to establish both spatial and nonspatial boundaries between the business and the home. Without boundaries, the home and the business can easily interfere with each other. An owner may establish boundaries, for example, by setting aside specific business space in the home and/or by scheduling definite hours for business matters. Client calls, indeed, may require the observance of regular business hours. The owner needs to protect the business from undue family or home interference and also to protect the home from unreasonable encroachment by the business. Since the owner never leaves the home to go to the office or place of business, he or she may find that either the business or the family absorbs every available waking moment.

zoning ordinances
local laws regulating land use

Zoning ordinances pose a potential problem for home-based businesses in some cities. Such local laws regulate the types of enterprises that are permitted to operate in various geographical areas. For example, some areas of a city may be zoned as residential, others as commercial, and still others as industrial. In Philadelphia, Wesley Morrison decided to operate a desktop publishing business, Delancey Press, from his apartment. He did not anticipate difficulty in getting a zoning variance. However, he encountered questions and delays prior to approval because city officials thought that "publishing" entailed whirring printing presses, forklift trucks, and other industrial equipment.

Space in a Business Incubator

business incubator
a facility that provides shared space, services, and management assistance to new businesses

In recent years, **business incubators** have sprung up in all areas of the country. Incubators are organizations that rent space to new businesses or to people wishing to start businesses. They are often located in recycled buildings such as abandoned warehouses or schools. They serve fledgling businesses by making space available, offering administrative services, and providing management advice. An incubator tenant can be fully operational the day after moving in, without buying phones, renting a copier, or hiring office employees.

The purpose of incubators is to see new businesses "hatch," grow, and leave the incubator. Most incubators, although not all, have some type of governmental or university sponsorship and are motivated by a desire to stimulate economic development.

Although the building space provided by incubators is significant, their greatest contribution lies in the business expertise and management assistance they provide. A more extensive discussion of incubators is included in Chapter 16.

Functional Requirements

When planning the initial building requirements, the entrepreneur must avoid commitments for a building space that is too large or too luxurious. At the same time, the space should not be too small or too austere for efficient operation. Buildings do not produce profits directly. They merely house the operations and personnel that produce the profits. Therefore, the ideal building is practical but not pretentious.

The general suitability of a building for a given type of business operation relates to its functional character. For example, the floor space of a restaurant should normally be on one level. Other important factors to consider are the shape, age, and condition of the building; fire hazards; heating and air conditioning; lighting and restroom facilities; and entrances and exits. Obviously, these factors carry different weights for a factory operation as compared with a wholesale or retail operation. In any case, the comfort, convenience, and safety of employees and customers of the business must not be overlooked.

Federal legislation, as discussed in Chapter 26, requires that places of business, even for small firms, be made accessible to individuals with physical disabilities. This may necessitate such modifications as widening doorways or building ramps.

Building Layout

Good layout involves an arrangement of physical facilities that contributes to efficiency of business operations. To provide a concise treatment of layout, we will limit our discussion to two different layout problems—layout for manufacturers (whose primary concern is production operations) and layout for retailers (whose primary concern is customer traffic).

Factory Layout. The factory layout presents a three-dimensional space problem. Overhead space may be utilized for power conduits, pipelines for exhaust systems, and the like. A proper design of storage areas and handling systems makes use of space near the ceiling. Space must be allowed also for the unobstructed movement of products from one location to another.

The ideal manufacturing process would have a straight-line, forward movement of materials from receiving room to shipping room. If this ideal cannot be realized for a given process, backtracking, sidetracking, and long hauls of materials can at least be minimized. This will reduce production delays.

Two contrasting types of layout are used in industrial firms. One of these is called **process layout** and has similar machines grouped together. Drill presses, for example, are separated from lathes in a machine shop using a process layout. The alternative is called a **product layout.** In a plant using product layout, special-purpose equipment is placed along a production line in the sequence that each piece of equipment is used in processing. The product is moved along from one work station to the next. The machines are located at the work stations where they are needed for the various stages of production.

Smaller plants that operate on a job-lot basis cannot use a product layout, because product layout demands too high a degree of standardization of both product and process. Thus, small machine shops are generally arranged on a process layout basis. Small firms with highly standardized products, such as dairies, bakeries, and car-wash firms, however, can use a product layout.

Retail Store Layout. The objectives for a retail store layout include the proper display of merchandise to maximize sales and customer convenience and service. Normally, the convenience and attractiveness of the surroundings contribute to a customer's continued patronage. An efficient layout also contributes to operating economy. A final objective is the protection of the store's equipment and merchandise. In achieving all these objectives, the flow of customer traffic must be anticipated and planned. A grid pattern and free-flow pattern of store layout are the two most widely used layout designs.[8]

The **grid pattern** is the plain, block-looking layout typical of supermarkets and hardware stores. It provides more merchandise exposure and simplifies security and cleaning. The **free-flow pattern** makes less efficient use of space but has greater visual appeal and allows customers to move in any direction at their own speed. The free-flow patterns result in curving aisles and greater flexibility in merchandise presentation.

Many retailers use a **self-service layout,** which permits customers direct access to the merchandise. Not only does self-service reduce the selling expense, but it also permits shoppers to examine the goods before buying. Today, practically all food merchandising follows this principle.

Some types of merchandise—for example, magazines and candy—are often purchased on an impulse basis. Impulse goods should be placed at points where customers can see them easily. Some such items are typically displayed near the cash register. Products that the customers will buy anyway and for which they come in specifically may be placed in less conspicuous spots. Bread and milk, for example, are located at the back of a food store. It is hoped that customers will buy other items as they walk down the store aisles.

Various areas of a retail store differ markedly in sales value. Customers typically turn to the right upon entering a store, and so the right front space is the most valuable. The second most valuable are the center front and right middle spaces. Department stores often place high-margin giftwares, cosmetics, and

---

process layout
factory layout that groups similar machines together

product layout
factory layout that arranges machines according to their role in the production process

grid pattern
a block-like type of retail store layout that provides good merchandise exposure and simple security and cleaning

free-flow pattern
a type of retail store layout that is visually appealing and gives customers freedom of movement

self-service layout
a retail store layout that gives customers direct access to merchandise

jewelry in these areas. The third most valuable are the left front and center middle spaces. And the left middle space is fourth in importance. Since the back areas are the least important so far as space value is concerned, most service facilities and the general office typically are found in the rear of a store. Certainly the best space should be given to departments or merchandise producing the greatest sales and profits. Finally, the first floor has greater space value than a second or higher floor in a multistory building.

EQUIPMENT AND TOOLING

The final step in arranging for physical facilities involves the purchase or lease of equipment and tooling. Here again, the types of equipment and tooling required obviously depend upon the nature of the business. We will limit our discussion of equipment needs to the two diverse fields of manufacturing and retailing. Of course, even within these two areas there is great variation in the required tools and equipment.

Factory Equipment

Machines in the factory may be either general-purpose or special-purpose in character. **General-purpose equipment** for metalworking includes lathes, drill presses, and milling machines. In a woodworking plant, general-purpose machines include ripsaws, planing mills, and lathes. In each case, jigs, fixtures, and other tooling items set up on the basic machine tools can be changed so that two or more shop operations can be accomplished. Bottling machines and automobile assembly-line equipment are examples of **special-purpose equipment.**

general-purpose equipment
machines that serve many functions in the production process

Advantages of General-Purpose Equipment. General-purpose equipment requires a minimum investment and is well adapted to a varied type of operation. Small machine shops and cabinet shops, for example, utilize this type of equipment. General-purpose equipment also contributes the necessary flexibility in industries in which the product is so new that the technology has not yet been well developed or in which there are frequent design changes in the product.

special-purpose equipment
machines designed to serve specialized functions in the production process

Advantages of Special-Purpose Equipment. Special-purpose equipment permits cost reduction where the technology is fully established and where a capacity operation is more or less assured by high sales volume. A milking machine in a dairy illustrates specialized equipment used by small firms. Nevertheless, a small firm cannot ordinarily and economically use special-purpose equipment unless it makes a standardized product on a fairly large scale.

Figure 9-6
General-Purpose Equipment, Such as Saws and Lathes, Provides Flexibility for This Cabinet Shop

Specialized machines using special-purpose tooling result in greater output per machine-hour operated. Hence, the labor cost per unit of product is lower. However, the initial cost of such equipment and tooling is much higher, and its scrap value is little or nothing due to its highly specialized function.

Retail Store Equipment

Small retailers must have merchandise display counters, storage racks, shelving, mirrors, seats for customers, customer push carts, cash registers, and various items necessary to facilitate selling. Such equipment may be costly but is usually less expensive than equipment for a factory operation.

If the store attempts to serve a high-income market, its fixtures typically should display the elegance and beauty expected by such customers. Polished mahogany and bronze fittings of showcases will lend a richness of atmosphere. Indirect lighting, thick rugs on the floor, and big easy chairs will also contribute to the air of luxury. In contrast, a store that caters to lower-income-bracket customers would find that luxurious fixtures create an atmosphere inconsistent with low prices. Therefore, such a store should concentrate on simplicity.

Automated Equipment

Automation, which takes many forms, has come into use in many small-business operations. For example, the use of computers is commonplace in businesses. Supermarkets and department stores use electronic devices to read product codes, thereby facilitating the sales, inventory control, and record-keeping processes.

Small manufacturing firms face greater difficulties, however, in using automated equipment. The major barrier to automation is found in short production runs. But if a small plant produces a given product in large volume, with infrequent changes in design, the owner should seriously consider the many benefits derived from automation. Among these are the following:

1. Operator errors are minimized.
2. Processing costs are lowered by speed of operation and machine efficiency.
3. Human resources are conserved while personnel skill requirements are upgraded.
4. Safety of manufacturing and handling operations is promoted.
5. Inventory requirements tend to be reduced because of faster processing:

1. The business plan should identify a competent and properly balanced management team. Outside professional assistance is often used to supplement the efforts of employed staff members.
2. The location specified in the business plan depends on four general considerations: personal preference, environmental conditions, resource availability, and customer accessibility. Their relative importance depends upon the nature of the business.
3. Most new firms rent rather than buy their building space. The primary reasons for renting are conservation of cash and reduction of risk.
4. Basements, garages, and spare rooms provide building space for many small businesses that are starting and for others that have limited space requirements. Business incubators also offer economical facility arrangements for many firms during their first one or two years of operation.
5. Proper layout depends upon the type of business. Manufacturing firms use layout patterns that facilitate production operations and provide for the efficient flow of materials. Retailers lay out building space in terms of customer needs and the flow of customer traffic.
6. Most small manufacturing firms use general-purpose equipment, although some have sufficient volume and a standardized operation, which permit the use of special-purpose equipment. The type of equipment and tooling in retail firms should be related to the general level and type of the business.

DISCUSSION QUESTIONS

1. Why do investors tend to favor a management team for a new business in preference to a lone entrepreneur? Is this preference justified?
2. Would you rather have your grade in a course be based on your own work or on that of a team of which you are a member? Why? What does your answer say, if anything, about the use of management teams in small businesses?
3. How much competence in financial management is needed by a business founder who has an experienced finance person on the management team?

4. Since most small-company boards of directors are little more than "rubber stamp" boards, how can they make a meaningful contribution to the management team of a new business? If you were an investor, would you consider a qualified director as an asset? Why?

5. Is the hometown of the business owner likely to be a good location? Why? Is it logical for an owner to allow personal preference to influence the decision on a business location? Why?

6. For the five small businesses that you know best, would you say that their locations were based upon the evaluation of location factors, chance, or something else?

7. In the selection of a region, what types of businesses should place greatest emphasis upon (a) markets, (b) raw materials, and (c) labor? Explain.

8. In the choice of specific sites, what types of businesses must show the greatest concern with customer accessibility? Why?

9. Suppose you were considering a location within an existing shopping mall. How would you go about evaluating the pedestrian traffic at that location? Be specific.

10. Under what conditions would it be most logical for a new firm to buy rather than rent a building for the business?

11. In a home-based business, there is typically some competition, if not conflict, between the interests of the home and the interests of the business. What would determine whether the danger is greater for the home or the business?

12. What is a business incubator and what advantages does it offer as a home for a new business?

13. When should the small manufacturer utilize process layout, and when product layout? Explain.

14. Discuss the conditions under which a new small manufacturer should buy general-purpose and special-purpose equipment?

15. Describe the unique problems concerning store layout and merchandise display that confront a new small jeweler.

YOU MAKE THE CALL

Situation 1

A husband-and-wife team operated small department stores in two midwestern towns with populations of about 2,000 each. Their clientele consisted of the primarily blue-collar and rural populations of those two areas. After several years of successful operation, they decided to open a third such store in a town of 5,000 people.

Most of the businesses in this larger town were located along a six-block-long strip—an area commonly referred to as "downtown." One attractive site for the store was situated in the middle of the business district, but the rental fee for that location was very high. Another available building had once been occupied by Montgomery Ward, but was vacated several years earlier. It was located at one end of the business district. Other businesses in the same block were a TV and appliance store and some service businesses. Two clothing stores were located in the next block—closer to the center of town. The rent for this latter site (the former Montgomery Ward store) was much more reasonable, a three-year lease was possible, and a local bank was willing to loan sufficient funds to accomplish necessary remodeling.

Questions

1. Does the location in the middle of the business district seem to be substantially better than the second site?
2. How might this owner evaluate the relative attractiveness of these two sites?
3. To what extent would the department store benefit from having the service businesses and a TV and appliance business in the same block?
4. What other market or demographic factors, if any, should the owners consider in opening a store in this town?

Situation 2

A business incubator rents space to a number of small firms that are beginning operation or are very young. In addition to supplying space, the incubator provides a receptionist, computer, conference room, paper cutter, and copy machine. In addition, it offers management counseling and assists new businesses in getting reduced advertising rates and reduced legal fees.

Two clients of the incubator are the following:

1. A jewelry repair, cleaning, and remounting service that does such work on a contract basis for pawn shops and jewelry stores.
2. A home health care company that employs a staff of nurses to visit the homes of elderly people who need daily care but who cannot afford or are not yet ready to go to a nursing home.

Questions

1. If these businesses did not use the special services provided by the incubator, would they still find it advantageous to locate in the center? What would make it logical or illogical for them?
2. Evaluate each of the services offered by the incubator in terms of its usefulness to these two businesses. Do the benefits seem to favor this location if rental costs are similar to rental costs for space outside the incubator?

EXPERIENTIAL EXERCISES

1. Prepare a one-page résumé of your own qualifications to launch a term-paper-typing business at your college or university. Add a critique that might be prepared by an investor evaluating your strengths and weaknesses as shown on the résumé.
2. Identify and evaluate a nearby site that is now vacant after a business closure. Point out the strengths and weaknesses of that location for the former business and comment on the part the location may have played in the closure.
3. Interview a small-business owner concerning the strengths and weaknesses of that owner's business location. Prepare a brief report summarizing your findings.

4. Visit three local retail stores and observe differences in their layouts and flow of customer traffic. Prepare a report describing the various patterns and explaining the advantages of the best pattern.

REFERENCES TO SMALL-BUSINESS PRACTICES

Bahls, Jane Easter. "Profit Zone," *Entrepreneur,* Vol. 19, No. 11 (November 1991), pp. 144–149.
Small businesses that have located advantageously in urban enterprise zones are described.
Brokaw, Leslie. "Can Carolyn Blakeslee Have It All?" *Inc.,* Vol. 13, No. 9 (September 1991), pp. 78–85.
This tells the story of Carolyn Blakeslee's efforts in starting a monthly publication, *ArtCalender,* and publishing it from her home in Virginia.
Finegan, Jay. "Grown in Montana," *Inc.,* Vol. 13, No. 1 (January 1991), pp. 62–69.
This article presents the story of an entrepreneur who located his tree nursery in Montana and includes an evaluation of that area for this type of business.
Kotte, Erika. "Behind the Scenes," *Entrepreneur,* Vol. 18, No. 5 (May 1990), pp. 89–92.
The approaches taken by several small businesses to buy computer equipment for their business needs are outlined.
Richman, Tom. "Beyond the Start-Up Team," *Inc.,* Vol. 9, No. 13 (December 1987), pp. 53–55.
This article reports on the effectiveness of the original management teams of several rapidly growing firms and the tendency for some companies to outgrow their original managers.

ENDNOTES

1. *Entrepreneurial Behavior,* by Barbara J. Bird (Glenview, IL: Scott, Foresman and Company, 1989), p. 213. Copyright 1989. Reprinted by permission of HarperCollins Publishers.

2. James Cook, "'It's Cheaper Than Going to a Shrink,'" *Forbes,* Vol. 145, No. 10 (May 14, 1990), p. 52.

3. John Case, "The Best Places in America To Own a Business," *Inc.,* Vol. 14, No. 8, p. 38. Reprinted with permission, *Inc.* magazine, August 1992. Copyright 1992 by Goldhirsh Group, Inc., 38 Commercial Wharf, Boston, MA 02110.

4. James Cook, *op. cit.,* p. 32.

5. Marisa Manley, "Look Before You Lease," *Inc.,* Vol. 8, No. 8 (August 1986), p. 91.

6. Kevin McLaughlin, "Home Advantage," *Entrepreneur,* Vol. 19, No. 9 (September 1991), p. 105.

7. Julie Fanselow, "Zoning Laws vs. Home Businesses," *Nation's Business,* Vol. 80, No. 8 (August 1992), pp. 35–36.

8. A discussion of these two layout patterns can be found in Barry Berman and Joel R. Evans, *Retail Management: A Strategic Approach,* 4th ed. (New York: Macmillan Publishing Co., 1989), Chapter 14.

C H A P T E R 10

Initial Financial Requirements and Sources of Financing

SPOTLIGHT ON SMALL BUSINESS

Meet F.R.O.Y.D., the product with perfect prospects. Sure, he's a homely guy, bright yellow with a big nose and a sheepish grin. Here's a list of folks who say this 13-inch toy looks like a winner: Hasbro, Coleco Industries, Fisher-Price, Tyco Toys, and Kenner Products.

And here's a list of folks who have turned down the chance to launch F.R.O.Y.D.: Hasbro, Coleco Industries, Fisher-Price, Tyco Toys, and Kenner Products.

Carolyn and Jeffrey Greene

F.R.O.Y.D. signifies "for reality of your dreams." It is supposed to remind children that they can be anything they want to be, if they work at it.

After seeking financing for the new venture from toy manufacturers and venture capitalists but receiving rejections, Carolyn Greene, F.R.O.Y.D.'s creator, and her husband and partner, Jeffrey Greene, decided that the money did not have to come from companies or institutions. It could come from individuals. They went back to the people they had met along the way—everyone who had said "great idea"—and asked them to buy stock in the company. It worked beautifully. Sixteen investors provided the needed $600,000.

The Greenes eventually had more than enough investors. The key was approaching individuals whose business experiences would suggest an appreciation for marketing or the character-development business. The firm's backers include senior executives in an advertising agency, a consumer products company, and a direct-mail business.

While the Greenes do not yet know if their company will be viable, their first round of financing worked wonderfully well.

Source: Ellyn E. Spragins, "Intelligent Money," *Inc.* magazine, Vol. 12, No. 6, pp. 106–107. Reprinted with permission, *Inc.* magazine (June 1990). Copyright 1990 by Goldhirsh Group, Inc., 38 Commercial Wharf, Boston, MA 02110.

After studying this chapter, you should be able to:
1. Forecast a new venture's profitability.
2. Analyze the nature and type of financial requirements of a new business.
3. Estimate the dollar amounts of required funds.
4. Identify sources of funds.

NEW TERMS AND CONCEPTS

current assets
working capital (circulating capital)
fixed assets
other assets
debt capital
short-term debt
long-term debt
accounts payable
accrued expenses
short-term notes
owners' equity capital

percentage-of-sales techniques
liquidity
spontaneous financing
external equity
profit retention
informal capital
internal equity
business angels
formal venture capitalists
line of credit

revolving credit agreement
term loan
chattel mortgage
real estate mortgage
small-business investment companies
venture capitalist
asset-based lending
factoring
private placement

If we were to ask owners of small businesses to identify their most pressing problem, the answers might include finding and retaining qualified employees, meeting the increasing cost of employee health care, and managing change. Also, the difficulty of acquiring the needed financing would invariably be cited as a critical problem. As noted by one entrepreneur, "The biggest problem facing small business, as I see it, is money; where to get it, how to get it, and where to get enough when you need it."[1]

FINANCING THE NEW VENTURE: THE BASIC QUESTIONS

While the acquisition of financing may seem intimidating, it need not be. It does require us to think carefully about the cash outflows needed to undertake a venture and where we might find the money to fund these cash expenditures.

Chapter 7 briefly examined financial issues that must be addressed in writing a business plan. This chapter explains how to find the answers to some of those questions. The discussion is organized into the following categories:

1. Forecasting a new company's profits.
2. Understanding the *nature* of the asset and financing requirements for a new firm.
3. Estimating the *amount* and *basic type* of the assets needed and financing required for the new venture.
4. Identifying and locating likely sources of financing.

The foregoing issues were addressed in Figure 7-12 (on page 182) when we presented the financial section of the business plan. One of the questions in Figure 7–12 that we will still postpone is the projection of the firm's cash flows. This important issue of projecting cash flows is covered in depth in Chapters 20 and 21.

PROFITABILITY AND FINANCING A NEW VENTURE

A key question for anyone starting a new business should be, "How profitable is the opportunity?" In Chapter 21, we will look at this issue in detail, with an eye for learning how and why a company achieves profitability. For now, however, we are interested in understanding the relationship between profits and financing the new business.

A company's profit is a primary source for financing future growth. The more profitable a company, the more funds it will have for growing the firm.[2] Thus, we need to know the factors that drive profits, so that we may make the needed profit projections. In this regard, a company's net income or net profits are dependent on four variables:

1. *Amount of sales.* Much that we project about a company's financial future is driven by the assumptions we make regarding future sales.
2. *Operating expenses.* Operating expenses include such expenses as the cost of goods sold and the expenses related to marketing and distributing the product. We will want, as best we can, to classify these expenses according to those that do not vary as sales increase or decrease (*fixed* operating expenses) versus those that change proportionally with sales (*variable* operating expenses).
3. *Interest expense.* When we borrow money, we agree to pay interest on the loan principal. For instance, if we borrow $25,000 for a full year and commit to pay 12 percent interest, our interest expense would be $3,000 for the year (12% × $25,000).
4. *Taxes.* The firm's taxes are, for the most part, a percentage of taxable income. The rate increases as the amount of income increases.

Let's consider an example to demonstrate how we would estimate a new venture's profits. We are contemplating a new business, Oakcrest Products, Inc., to make stair parts for more expensive homes. A newly developed lathe will permit the new firm to be more responsive to different design specifications, while doing so more cheaply than heretofore possible. In studying the market and the economics of the venture, we have made the following estimates for the first two years of operations:

1. Oakcrest expects to sell its product for $125 per unit, with total sales for the next two years as follows:

	Projected *Unit Sales*	*Projected* *Dollar Sales*
Year 1	2,000	$250,000
Year 2	3,200	$400,000

2. The fixed production costs are expected to be $100,000 per year, while the fixed operating expenses (marketing expenses, and administrative expenses) should be about $50,000. Thus, the total fixed operating costs will be $150,000.

3. The variable costs of producing the stair parts will be around 20 percent of dollar revenues (sales), and the variable operating expenses will be approximately 30 percent of dollar sales. In other words, given an expected $125 sales price, the combined variable costs per unit, both for producing the stair parts and for marketing the products will be $62.50 [(20% + 30%) × $125].

4. The bank has agreed to loan the firm $100,000 at an interest rate of 12 percent.

5. Assume the income tax rate will be 25 percent; that is, taxes will be 25 percent of earnings before tax (taxable income).

Given the foregoing assumptions, we may forecast Oakcrest's profits, as shown in Figure 10-1.

Figure 10-1
Oakcrest Products, Inc.—Projected Income Statements

	Year 1	Year 2	
Sales	$250,000	$400,000	*Line 1*
Cost of goods sold			
Fixed costs	$100,000	$100,000	*Line 2*
Variable costs (20% of sales)	50,000	80,000	*Line 3*
Total cost of goods sold	$150,000	$180,000	*Line 4*
Gross profits	$100,000	$220,000	*Line 5*
Operating expenses			
Fixed expenses	$50,000	$50,000	*Line 6*
Variable expenses (30% of sales)	75,000	120,000	*Line 7*
Total operating expenses	$125,000	$170,000	*Line 8*
Operating profits	–$25,000	$50,000	*Line 9*
Interest expenses (interest rate 12%)	12,000	12,000	*Line 10*
Earnings before tax	–$37,000	$38,000	*Line 11*
Taxes (25% of earnings before tax)	0	9,500	*Line 12*
Net income	–$37,000	$28,500	*Line 13*

In projecting the firm's net income, the following steps are taken:

1. We first compute the expected cost of goods sold (line 4) and the operating expenses (line 8) for the given level of sales. Subtracting these costs and expenses from the firm's sales gives us the company's *operating profits,* or *earnings before interest and taxes* (line 9).
2. We next calculate the interest expense for each year (line 10). In this case, the annual interest expense is $12,000 (12% × $100,000).
3. The final computation involves estimating income taxes, where the taxes are 25 percent of earnings before tax. However, we have a small complication resulting from the $37,000 loss in Year 1. Typically, when a company has a loss from its operations, the tax laws allow it to apply the loss against any income in other years. To keep things simple, we will assume that these losses are not carried forward to future years.[3]

The result of all our computations suggests that the firm will lose money in Year 1 in the amount of $37,000, followed by positive net income of $28,500 in Year 2.[4]

DETERMINING THE NATURE OF FINANCIAL REQUIREMENTS

The specific needs of a proposed business venture govern the nature of its initial financial requirements. If the firm is a food store, financial planning must provide for the store building, cash registers, shopping carts, shelving inventory, office equipment, and other items required in this type of operation. An analysis of capital requirements for this or any other type of business must consider how to finance (1) the needed investments and expenses incurred to start and grow the company, and (2) any personal expenses if the owner does not have other income for living purposes. Let's consider these two needs.

Startup Investment and Financing Requirements

To understand the financing requirements for a new company, visualize a balance sheet, as shown in Figure 10–2. The left side of the balance sheet shows the assets owned by the company, such as cash, accounts receivable, and equipment. The right side tells us who has provided the needed capital for the business.

A firm's assets are generally classified into one of three categories or types: (1) current assets, (2) fixed assets, and (3) other assets.

Current Assets. **Current assets** comprise the assets that are relatively liquid—that is, assets that will be converted into cash within the firm's operating cycle. The current asset items mainly include cash, accounts receivable, inventories, and prepaid expenses. Current assets represent the company's **working**

current assets
assets that will be converted into cash within a company's operating cycle

working capital (circulating capital)
a company's current assets

Figure 10-2
Balance Sheet
Components

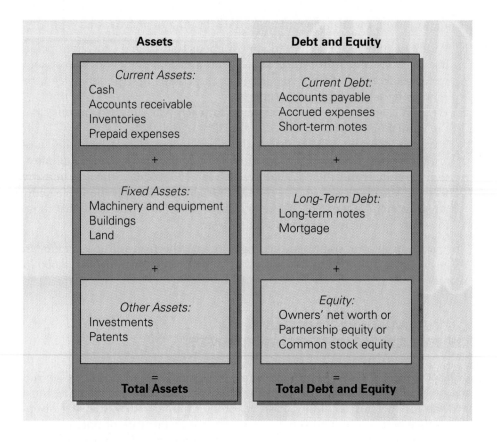

capital. The term **circulating capital** is sometimes applied to these items, emphasizing the constant cycle from cash to inventory to receivables to cash, and so on.

Cash. Every firm must have the cash essential for current business operations. Also, a reservoir of cash is needed because of the uneven flow of funds into the business (cash receipts) and out of the business (cash expenditures). The size of this reservoir is determined not only by the volume of sales, but also by the regularity of cash receipts and cash payments. Uncertainties exist because of unpredictable decisions by customers as to when they will pay their bills and because of emergencies that require substantial cash outlays. If an adequate cash balance is maintained, the firm can take such unexpected developments in stride. However, a firm could have too much cash. Since cash is a non-income-producing asset, there is a limit as to how much cash we want to keep on hand.

Accounts Receivable. The firm's accounts receivable consist of payments due from its customers. If the firm expects to sell on a credit basis—and in many lines of business this is necessary—provision must be made for financing receivables. The firm cannot afford to wait until its customers pay their bills before restocking its shelves.

Inventories. Although the relative importance of inventories differs considerably from one type of business to another, they often constitute a major part of the working capital. Seasonality of sales and production affects the size of the minimum inventory. Retail stores, for example, may find it desirable to carry a larger-than-normal inventory during the Christmas season.

Prepaid Expenses. When starting a company, we may need to prepay some of the expenses. For example, insurance premiums may be due before the business actually opens, or utility deposits may be demanded before the electricity at the business can be turned on. For accounting purposes, these expenses are initially recorded as current assets, and then shown as expenses during the year as used.

Fixed Assets. **Fixed assets** are the more permanent type assets that are intended for use in the business, rather than for sale. As shown in Figure 10-2, the fixed assets needed in a new business might include machinery and equipment, buildings, and land.

    The nature and size of the fixed-asset investment are determined by the type of business operation. A beauty shop, for example, might be equipped for

fixed assets
relatively permanent assets intended for use in the business

Figure 10-3
To Establish His Barbershop Business, the Owner Had to Invest in Furniture and Equipment

around $80,000 whereas a motel sometimes requires 50 or more times that amount. In any given kind of business, moreover, there is a minimum quantity or assortment of facilities needed for efficient operation. It would seldom be profitable, for example, to operate a motel with only one or two rooms. It is this principle, of course, that excludes small business from automobile manufacturing and other types of heavy industry.

A firm's flexibility is inversely related to its investment in fixed assets. Investments in land, buildings, and equipment involve long-term commitments. The inflexibility inherent in fixed-asset investment underscores the importance of a realistic evaluation of fixed-asset needs.

other assets

assets that are neither current nor fixed

Other Assets. The third category of assets—**other assets**—includes such items as intangible assets. Patents, copyrights, and goodwill are intangible assets. For the startup company, "other assets" could also include organizational costs—costs incurred in organizing and promoting the business. Such startup costs are shown as an "other asset" and then amortized as expenses in future years.

Funds for Personal Living Expenses

In many startup businesses, provision must also be made for the owner's personal living expenses during the initial period of operation. Whether or not these expenses are recognized as part of the business capitalization, they must be considered in the business financial plan. Inadequate provision for personal expenses will inevitably lead to a diversion of business assets and a departure from the financial plan. Thus, failure to incorporate these expenses into the plan raises a red flag to any prospective lender or investor in the firm.

Having studied the nature of the assets essential in starting and operating a company, we now shift our attention to the financing of these assets. We shall begin by describing the basic types of capital available for financing the new firm.

BASIC TYPES OF FINANCING

Financing comes from two basic sources: debt (liabilities) and ownership equity. Debt is money that is borrowed and that must be repaid at some predetermined date in the future. Ownership equity, on the other hand, represents the owners' investment in the company—money they have personally put into the firm without any specific date for repayment. As owners, they recover their investment by withdrawing money from the company or by selling their interest in the firm.

Debt Capital

As shown in Figure 10–2, **debt capital** is divided into (1) current or short term, and (2) long term. **Short-term liabilities (debt)** include money borrowed that must be repaid within the next 12 months; **long-term debt** comes due and payable some time after 12 months, depending on the terms of the loan. The short-term sources of debt may be classified as follows:

1. **Accounts payable.** Accounts payable represents credit extended by suppliers. If credit is provided, the purchaser may have 30 or 60 days before paying for the inventory. This form of credit extension or loan is also called trade credit.
2. **Accrued expenses.** Accrued expenses are those expenses that have been incurred, but not paid. For instance, employees may perform work, but payday may not come until next month.
3. **Short-term notes.** Short-term notes consist of amounts borrowed from a bank or other lending sources—for example, a 90-day note at the bank.

Short-term credit represents a primary source of financing for most smaller companies. Since small businesses have access to fewer sources of capital than their larger counterparts, they must rely more on short-term debt capital.

Long-term debt includes loans from banks or other sources of capital that loan on a long-term basis. If you borrow money for five years to buy equipment, you will sign an agreement (called a *note*) promising to repay the money in five years. Alternatively, you may borrow money to purchase real estate, such as a warehouse or office building. Such a loan may be for 30 years, and the lender uses the real estate as collateral for the loan. If the borrower is unable to repay the loan, the lender can take the real estate in settlement for the loan. This type of long-term loan is a called a *mortgage*.

Owners' Equity Capital

The **owners' equity capital** is simply the money the owners invest in the business. They are the residual owners, in that they receive money only if there is something left over after repaying the debtholders. Thus, if the company is liquidated, the creditors are paid first, and only then are the owners paid. Also, in each year, the creditors must be paid the interest on the debt before the owners can participate in the income from the business.

The amount of equity in a business is determined by (1) the amount of the owners' initial investment as well as any later investments in the business; and (2) the income retained within the business from its beginning to the present, less any withdrawals by the owners. Thus, the owners' equity consists of the following:

debt capital
business financing provided by a creditor

short-term debt
debt that must be repayed within 12 months

long-term debt
debt with a repayment term of more than 12 months

accounts payable
credit extended by suppliers

accrued expenses
expenses that have been incurred, but not paid

Short-term notes
amounts borrowed from a bank or other lending sources, and that must be repaid within 12 months

owners' equity capital
money the owners invest in a business

$$\left(\begin{array}{c}\text{owners' investment}\\\text{in the firm}\end{array}\right)+\left(\begin{array}{c}\text{profits retained}\\\text{within the firm}\end{array}\right)-\left(\begin{array}{c}\text{owners' withdrawals}\\\text{from the firm}\end{array}\right)$$

In summary, financing a new business entails raising debt capital and equity financing. However, knowing the basic types of capital is not enough. We must also estimate the *amount* of our asset requirements and decide how we will go about financing these needs. The next section helps us begin to answer these questions.

ESTIMATING THE AMOUNT OF FUNDS REQUIRED

When estimating the magnitude of capital requirements for a small business, the entrepreneur quickly feels the need for a "crystal ball." The uncertainties surrounding an entirely new venture make estimation difficult. Even for established businesses, forecasting is never exact. Nevertheless, when seeking initial capital, the entrepreneur must be ready to answer the questions, "How much, and for what purpose?"

The amount of capital needed by various types of new businesses varies considerably. High-technology companies, such as computer manufacturers, designers of semiconductor chips, and gene-splicing companies, often require several million dollars in initial financing. Most service businesses, on the other hand, require small amounts of initial capital.

A prospective entrepreneur may use a "double-barreled" approach to estimating capital requirements by (1) applying industry standard ratios to estimate dollar amounts, and (2) cross-checking the dollar amounts by break-even analysis and empirical investigation. Robert Morris Associates, Dun & Bradstreet, Inc., banks, trade associations, and other organizations compile industry standard ratios for numerous types of businesses. If no standard data can be located, then estimating capital requirements involves common sense and educated guesswork.

Estimating Asset Requirements

The key to effectively forecasting asset needs depends on an understanding of the relationship between projected sales and needed assets. A firm's sales is the primary driving force of future asset needs. That is, a sales increase causes an increase in a firm's asset needs, which in turn results in a need for more financing. These relationships are depicted graphically in Figure 10-4.

Stated differently, asset needs tend to follow sales increases. Consequently, a company's asset needs may be estimated as some percentage of sales. That is, given that we have estimated future sales, a ratio of assets to sales may be used to estimate asset requirements.

Figure 10-4
Sales-Asset-Financing
Relationships

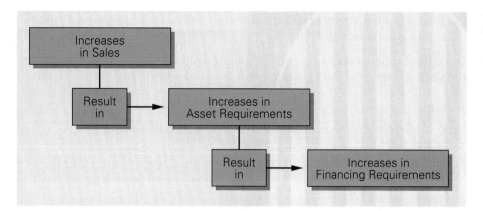

$$\text{Assets} = \text{sales} \times \left(\begin{array}{c}\text{assets as a} \\ \text{percentage of sales}\end{array}\right)$$

For example, if we believe that sales will be $1 million, and we know that within our industry, assets tend to run about 50 percent of sales, we could reasonably expect that the firm's asset requirements will be $500,000 (50% × $1,000,000).

While the asset-to-sales percentage will vary over time and with individual firms to some extent, the relationship tends to be relatively constant. For example, the asset-to-sales relationship for grocery stores is on average around 20 percent, compared to about 65 percent for an oil and gas company.

We may also use this method—the **percentage-of-sales technique**—to project the *individual* asset investments. For instance, we can expect there to be a relationship between the amount of accounts receivable and sales.

percentage-of-sales technique
a method to forecast asset and financing requirements

To illustrate how we could use the percentage-of-sales technique for forecasting purposes, consider the following example. Katie Dalton is planning to start a new business, Trailer Craft, Inc., to produce small trailers to be pulled behind motorcycles. After studying a similar company in a different state, she believes the business could generate sales of approximately $250,000 in the first year, and have significant growth potential in future years. Based on her investigation of the opportunity, she has also made the following projections:

1. The requirements for cash, accounts receivable, and inventories estimated as a percentage of sales for the first year are as follows:[5]

Assets	Percentage of Annual Sales
Cash	5%
Accounts receivable	10%
Inventories	25%

2. Dalton has searched for a manufacturing facility, and has found a suitable building for about $50,000.

Given the anticipated sales of $250,000 and the asset-to-sales relationships shown, the forecasted asset requirements for Trailer Craft, Inc. are as follows:

Cash	$12,500	(5% of sales)
Accounts receivable	25,000	(10% of sales)
Inventories	62,500	(25% of sales)
Total current assets	$100,000	
Fixed assets (machinery)	50,000	(Estimated market price)
Total assets	$150,000	

Thus, we could expect to need $150,000 in assets, some immediately and the rest as the firm continues in its first year of operation. While these amounts are only rough approximations, the estimates should be relatively close if we have identified the asset-to-sales relationships correctly and if sales materialize as expected.

Liquidity Considerations in Structuring Asset Needs: A Caveat

The need for adequate working capital deserves special emphasis. A common weakness in small-business financing is the disproportionately small investment in current assets relative to fixed assets. In such weakly financed firms, too much of the money is tied up in assets that are difficult to convert to cash. Danger arises from the fact that the business depends upon daily receipts to meet obligations coming due from day to day. If there is a slump in sales or if there are unexpected expenses, creditors may force the firm into bankruptcy.

The lack of flexibility associated with the purchase of fixed assets suggests the desirability of minimizing this type of investment. Often, for example, there is a choice between renting or buying property. For perhaps the majority of new small firms, renting provides the better alternative. A rental arrangement not only reduces the initial cash requirement but also provides the flexibility that is helpful if the business is more successful or less successful than anticipated.

Estimating Financing Requirements

We have used the relationship between assets and sales to estimate the firm's asset requirements. Someone, however, must provide the money to purchase these assets. In other words, for every dollar of assets, there must be a dollar of financing. We now want to focus on sources of financing, or what we call the firm's financial requirements.

Correctly forecasting a company's financial requirements requires an understanding of certain guidelines or principles of finance. Five such guidelines may be stated as follows:

1. *The more assets needed by a firm, the greater the financial requirements.* Thus, the faster a firm is growing in sales, the greater will be its asset requirements, and, consequently, the greater the pressure to find the needed financing.

2. *A company should finance its growth in a way that maintains a proper degree of liquidity.* In business, **liquidity** is the ability to meet maturing financial obligations as they come due. A conventional measurement of liquidity is the current ratio, which merely compares a firm's current assets (mainly cash, accounts receivable, and inventories) to its current or short-term debt (short-term liabilities). The current ratio is measured as follows:

$$\frac{\text{Current}}{\text{ratio}} = \frac{\text{current assets}}{\text{current liabilities}}$$

liquidity
the ability to meet maturing financial obligations as they come due

For instance, to insure that we have the ability to pay short-term debts as they come due, we might want to maintain a current ratio of two—that is, to have current assets that are twice as much as current liabilities.

3. *There is a limit to how much debt a firm can use in financing the business.* The amount of total debt is limited by the amount of equity provided by the owners. We cannot expect a bank to loan all the money needed to finance a company. Owners must put some of their own money into the venture. Thus, we may decide that at least half of the firm's financing should come from equity and the remaining half be financed with debt.

4. *Some short-term debt becomes available spontaneously as the firm grows.* Certain types of short-term debt are spontaneous in nature; thus the name **spontaneous financing.** That is, these sources will increase as a natural consequence of an increase in the firm's sales. For instance, as sales increase, we purchase more inventories and accounts payable increase. Typically, these spontaneous sources of financing follow a certain percentage of sales. For example, spontaneous sources of financing might average 10 percent of sales.

spontaneous financing
short-term debts that increase in relation to a firm's increasing sales

5. *There are two sources of equity capital: external and internal.* The equity ownership of a company comes initially from the owners making an investment in the firm. We think of these funds as **external equity.** After the company is in operation, additional equity may then come from **profit retention,** when profits are retained within the company rather than being distributed to the owners. This latter source is called **internal equity.** These funds come not from going to investors and raising capital, but from reinvesting the company's profits into the business—money that could have been distributed to the owners, but instead was reinvested for them.[6] For the small firm, internal equity, which is merely the retention of profits, is *the* primary source of equity for financing company growth.

external equity
equity ownership of a company that comes initially from the owners' investment

profit retention
the reinvestment of profits into a business

internal equity
equity that comes from the retention of profits within a company

In summary, we can say that:

$$\begin{pmatrix} \text{Total asset} \\ \text{requirements} \end{pmatrix} = \begin{pmatrix} \text{Total sources} \\ \text{of financing} \end{pmatrix}$$

and that

$$\begin{pmatrix} \text{Total sources} \\ \text{of financing} \end{pmatrix} = \begin{pmatrix} \text{spontaneous sources} \\ \text{of financing} \end{pmatrix} + \begin{pmatrix} \text{profits retained} \\ \text{within the business} \end{pmatrix} + \begin{pmatrix} \text{external sources} \\ \text{of financing} \end{pmatrix}$$

The foregoing equations capture the essence of forecasting financial requirements. If we understand these relationships, we will be prepared to forecast our firm's financial requirements. Let's return to the Trailer Craft, Inc. example, where we projected the asset requirements for the firm during its first year of operations. Assuming sales, as forecasted, of $250,000, we estimated the following asset requirements:

Cash	$12,500
Accounts receivable	25,000
Inventories	62,500
Total current assets	$100,000
Fixed assets (machinery)	50,000
Total assets	$150,000

In addition, Katie Dalton, as the prospective owner of the new company, has made the following observations:

1. Earnings after taxes will be about 12 percent of sales; that is, $250,000 of sales should result in after-tax profits of $30,000 (12% × $250,000).
2. Trailer Craft has negotiated with a supplier to extend credit on inventory purchases; as a result, accounts payable will average about 8 percent of sales.
3. Accruals should run approximately 4 percent of annual sales.
4. Dalton plans to invest $40,000 of her personal savings in the venture in return for 10,000 shares of common stock.[7]
5. The bank has agreed to provide a short-term line of credit to Trailer Craft of $20,000, which means the firm can borrow up to this amount as the need arises. However, as the firm has excess cash, it may choose to pay down the line of credit. For instance, during the spring and summer, business is particularly active. In these months, Trailer Craft may need to borrow the entire $20,000 for buying inventory and extending credit to customers. However, during the winter months, a slack time, less money will be needed, so the loan balance could possibly be reduced.
6. The bank has also agreed to help finance the purchase of the building to be used in manufacturing and warehousing the firm's product. Of the $50,000

cost for the facilities and equipment, the bank will loan the company $35,000, with the building serving as collateral for the loan. The loan will be a 25-year mortgage.

7. As conditions for the bank's agreeing to loan the money to Trailer Craft, Inc., the banker will impose two loan restrictions: (1) the firm's current ratio (current assets ÷ current liabilities) should not fall below 1.75, and (2) no more than 60 percent of the firm's financing should come from debt, including both short term and long term; that is, total debt relative to total assets should not be greater than 60 percent. Failure to comply with either of these terms would result in the bank loans coming due immediately.

From the foregoing information, we may estimate the financial sources for Trailer Craft, Inc. as follows:

1. Accounts payable: (8% × $250,000 sales) = $20,000
2. Accruals: (4% × $250,000 sales) = $10,000
3. Credit line: Per the agreement with the bank, Trailer Craft, Inc. may borrow up to $20,000. Any additional financing must come from other sources.
4. Long-term debt: The bank has agreed to loan Trailer Craft $35,000 for the purchase of the real estate.
5. Equity: By year end the firm's equity should be around $70,000. This consists of the $40,000 original investment in the company made by the owner, plus the projected $30,000 in profits after taxes for the year. The $30,000 is to be retained within the company and not distributed to the owner.

Based on the foregoing information, we may now formulate the projected debt and equity section of the balance sheet for Trailer Craft, Inc. The balance sheet also reflects the financial requirements for the firm for the first year of business. These financial requirements are shown in the bottom portion of Figure 10-5, which shows Trailer Craft's projected balance sheet.

Two comments need to be made about the final projected balance sheet in Figure 10-5. First, *sources must always equal uses,* and *assets must equal debt plus equity.* For Trailer Craft, Inc., asset requirements were estimated to be $150,000 by year end; thus, debt and equity must likewise equal $150,000. As a result, only $15,000 of the $20,000 credit line will be needed to bring the total debt and equity to $150,000. Second, if all goes as planned, Trailer Craft will be able to satisfy the banker's loan restrictions, both in terms of the current ratio and the debt-to-total asset relationship. From the balance sheet, we can compute these ratios as follows:

$$\frac{\text{Current}}{\text{ratio}} = \frac{\text{current assets}}{\text{current liabilities}} = \frac{\$100,000}{\$45,000} = 2.22$$

and

$$\frac{\text{Debt to}}{\text{total assets}} = \frac{\text{total debt}}{\text{total assets}} = \frac{\$80,000}{\$150,000} = 53.3\%$$

Figure 10-5
Trailer Craft, Inc.,
Projected Balance
Sheet at Year End

Assets		
Cash	$12,500	
Accounts receivable	25,000	
Inventories	62,500	
Total current assets	$100,000	
Fixed assets (machinery)	50,000	
Total assets	$150,000	
Debt and Equity		
Accounts payable	$20,000	(8% × $250,000 sales)
Accruals	10,000	(4% × $250,000 sales)
Credit line	15,000	(per bank agreement)
Total current liabilities	$45,000	
Long-term debt	35,000	(per bank agreement)
Total debt	$80,000	
Equity.		
Common stock	$40,000	(owner's investment)
Retained earnings	30,000	(12% × $250,000 sales)
Total equity	$70,000	
Total debt and equity	$150,000	

Hence, the current ratio would be 2.22, compared to a minimum requirement of 1.75, and the debt ratio would be 53.3 percent, compared to the maximum limit of 60 percent. Both outcomes would more than meet the bank's requirements.

A REVIEW OF WHAT WE HAVE LEARNED

We have now completed our instructions on forecasting profits and projecting asset needs and financing requirements for the firm. We have covered a considerable amount of information regarding financial planning for the new company. Thus, before continuing, it would be helpful to review the major ideas we have developed. They are as follows:

1. A company's *operating* profitability is determined by the dollar sales level achieved and the mix of fixed and variable operating expenses.
2. There are two basic types of capital used in financing a company. debt financing and equity ownership. Debt financing is classified either as short term or long term, depending upon when it matures. Also, some short-term debt is spontaneous in nature; that is, it increases as a natural consequence of the firm's growth in sales. Equity either comes from new investments in the firm by the owners or by retaining the firm's profits and reinvesting these funds in the company.
3. There is a direct relationship between sales growth and asset needs. As sales increase, more assets are required. As assets increase, more financing is required. We may use the *percentage-of-sales technique* to forecast asset needs and then to forecast financial requirements.
4. We must blend equity with debt in financing. As we increase the amount of debt, there must be a corresponding increase in the amount of equity, either through new investments in the firm by the owners or through retaining the profits in the business, which is a form of equity.

Our efforts to forecast profitability and to anticipate the firm's asset needs and financing requirements are complete. We are now ready to look at where we go to find the financing needed by a startup company.

FINDING SOURCES OF FUNDS

To this point, we have examined the nature of financial needs and ways to estimate how much funding is required. Now we turn our attention to locating the sources of these funds and establishing the necessary financial arrangements to obtain them.

The initial financing of a small business is quite often patterned after the typical personal financing plan. A prospective entrepreneur will first canvass personal savings and then those of family and friends. Only if these sources are inadequate will the entrepreneur turn to the more formal channels of financing such as banks and venture capitalists.

The major sources of equity financing are personal savings, venture capitalists, wealthy individuals (angels), and the securities market. The major sources of debt financing are individuals, commercial banks, government-assisted programs, business suppliers, and asset-based lenders. Of course, the use of these and other sources of funds is not limited to initial financing. They can also be tapped to finance growing day-to-day operating requirements and business expansion. Figure 10-6 gives a visual overview of the funding sources discussed in this chapter.

Figure 10-6
Locating Sources of
Funds

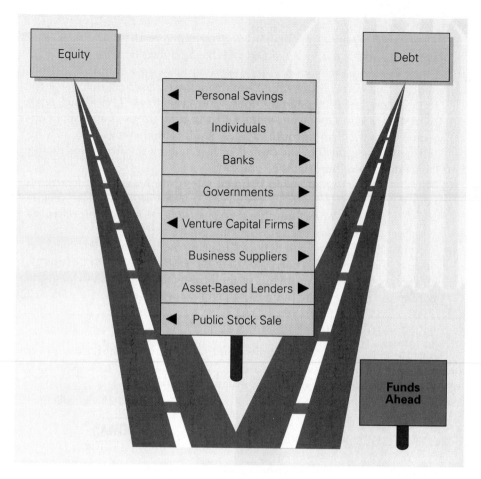

Individuals as Sources of Funds

The search for financial support should begin close to home. The budding entrepreneur essentially has three sources of early financing: (1) personal savings, (2) friends and relatives, and (3) private investors in the community.

Personal Savings. A financial plan that includes the entrepreneur's personal funds helps build confidence among potential investors. It is important, therefore, that the entrepreneur have some personal assets in the business. Indeed, the ownership equity for a beginning business typically comes from personal savings.

A study conducted by the National Federation of Independent Business found that personal savings is the most frequently used financing method.[8] Figure 10-7 shows that over 70 percent of the entrepreneurs in their study used personal savings when they purchased or started a business from scratch. The frequency of use of other financing sources is also displayed in Figure 10-7.

Figure 10-7   Sources of Financing to Start or Purchase a Business

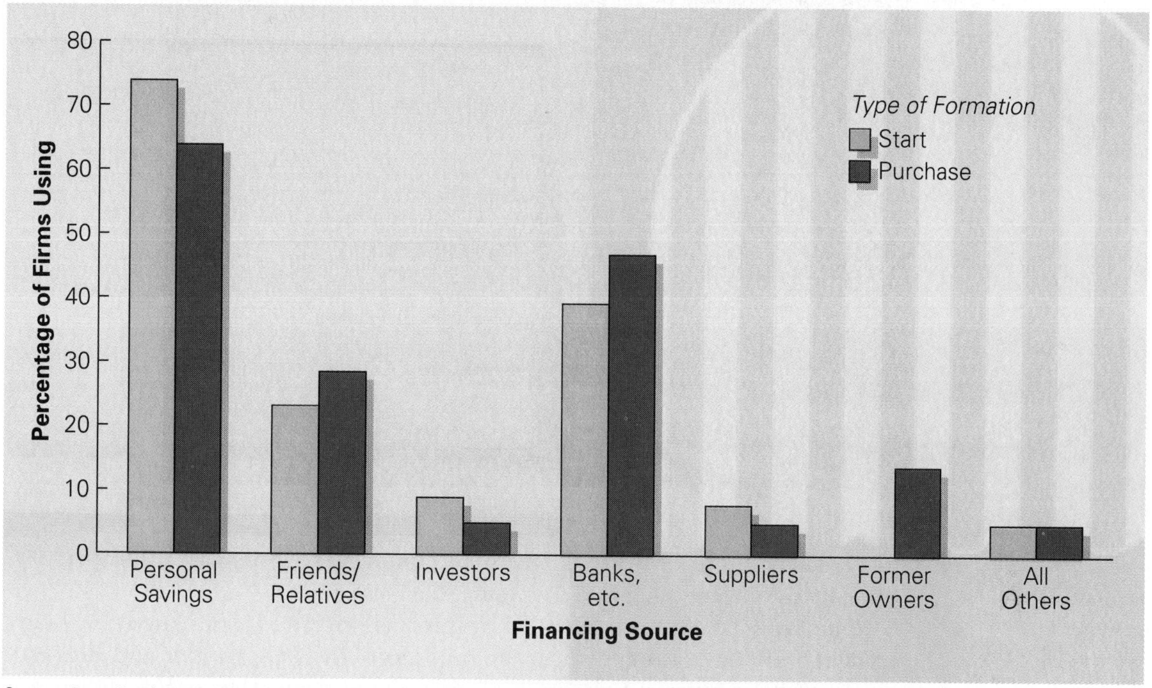

Source: Data developed and provided by The NFIB Foundation and sponsored by the American Express Travel Related Services Company, Inc.

Personal savings invested in the business eliminate the requirement of fixed interest charges and a definite repayment date. If profits fail to materialize exactly as expected, the business is not strapped with an immediate drain on capital.

Friends and Relatives. At times, loans from friends or relatives may be the only available source of new small-business financing. Friends and relatives can often be a shortcut to financing. As a Dallas banker put it, "If Momma's got the money, get it from her. She loves you. She knows you're great, and her interest rate is low."[9] However, friends and relatives who provide business loans sometimes feel that they have the right to interfere in the management of the business. Hard business times may also strain the bonds of friendship. If relatives and friends are indeed the only available source, the entrepreneur has no alternative. However, the financial plan should provide for repayment as soon as is practical.

Other Individual Investors. There is a large group of private individuals who invest in entrepreneurial ventures, including mostly persons who have moderate to significant business experience themselves, but also including affluent professionals, such as lawyers and physicians. This source of financing has come to be known as **informal capital,** in that there is no formal market

informal capital
investment in entrepreneurial ventures by private individuals

Figure 10-8
Entrepreneur Presents His Ideas to a "Business Angel" as a Potential Source of Financing

business angels
private investors who finance new, risky, small ventures

formal venture capitalists
individuals who formally create a firm for the purpose of investing in new growth companies

place where these individuals invest in companies. Somewhat appropriately, these investors have acquired the name, **business angels.**

The aggregate amount invested by informal investors is not known with any certainty; however, we know it to be very large. In 1988, Gaston and Bell estimated that each year some 720,000 individuals made almost 500,000 investments in high-risk ventures, with an average investment of about $67,000. Their findings suggested an annual flow of informal equity capital of $32.7 billion. During the same period, **formal venture capitalists,** those who have formally created a firm for the express purpose of investing in new growth companies, invested only $3 billion annually, with an average investment per business of about $1 million.[10]

The traditional path to locating angels is through contact with dealmakers such as business associates, accountants, and lawyers. A more recent approach involves formal angel networks or "clubs." One example is Venture Capital Network, Inc., in Boston. This network receives proposals from potential investors and entrepreneurs and, for a fee, attempts to find a match. These networks can increase the odds of finding an investor. However, "successful angels say it is best to try both formal and informal grapevines. . . ."[11] Other entrepreneurs continue to be the best source of help in identifying prospective informal or private investors.

Competing for informal capital is no easy task. Private investors can be very demanding; however, they can frequently contribute not only money to the venture, but also "know-how." A study by Freear, Sohl, and Wetzel inquired into the opinions of entrepreneurs regarding their experience with informal investors. Following are some things these entrepreneurs would do differently:[12]

1. They would try to raise more external equity funding earlier.
2. They would work to present their case for funding more effectively.

An Angel at Work

Bob McCray is an example of an angel. Having run his own company for 26 years, he eventually sold out for $50 million, and then began investing in other ventures.

*He's made four investments, each within 50 miles of his house. Like most angels, he in-*vests anywhere from $10,000 to $100,000 in a deal, and usually brings other angels into the picture. In return, the average angel seeks 30% per annum return on any investment, fully aware that up to half the companies he backs will fold.

Source: William Bryant Logan, "Finding Your Angel," *Venture,* Vol. 8, No. 3 (March 1986), p. 39.

3. They would try to find more investors and develop a broader mix of investors, with each investing smaller amounts.
4. They would be more careful in defining their relationships with individual investors before they finalize the terms of the agreement.

Commercial Banks as a Source of Funds

Commercial banks are the primary providers of debt capital to small companies. Although banks tend to limit their lending to working-capital needs of going concerns, some initial capital does come from this source.

Types of Bank Loans. There are three types of loans that bankers tend to make: lines of credit, term loans, and mortgages.

Line of Credit. A **line of credit** is an informal agreement or understanding between the borrower and the bank as to the maximum amount of credit the bank will provide the borrower at any one time. However, under this type of agreement, the bank is under no legal obligation to provide the stated capital. A similar arrangement that does legally commit the bank is a **revolving credit agreement.** The entrepreneur should arrange for a line of credit in advance of the actual need because banks extend credit only in situations about which they are well informed. Obtaining a loan on a spur-of-the-moment basis, therefore, is virtually impossible.[13]

Term loans. Given certain circumstances, banks will loan money on a five- to ten-year term. Usually these loans are used to finance equipment that has an economic useful life corresponding with the loan maturity date. Since the economic benefits of such an investment extend beyond one year, the bank is willing to loan on terms that more closely match the cash flows to be received from

line of credit
an informal agreement between borrower and bank as to the maximum amount of credit the bank will provide at any one time

revolving credit
a legal commitment by the bank to lend up to a maximum amount of credit

term loan
money lent on a five- to ten-year term, corresponding to the length of time the investment will bring in profits

the investment. It would be a mistake to borrow short term, such as for six months, when the money is to be used to buy equipment that is expected to be used for five years. Failure to match the loan payment terms with the expected cash inflows from the investment is a frequent cause of financial problems for many small firms.

chattel mortgage
a loan for which items of inventory or other moveable property serve as collateral

real estate mortgage
a long-term loan with real estate held as collateral

Mortgages. Mortgages, which represent a long-term source of debt capital, are of two types: chattel mortgages and real estate mortgages. A **chattel mortgage** is a loan where certain items of inventory or other moveable property serve as collateral for the loan. The borrower retains title to the inventory but cannot sell the inventory without the banker's consent. A **real estate mortgage** is a loan where real estate, such as land or a building, provides the collateral for the loan. Typically, these loans extend over 25 or 30 years.

What the Banker Expects of the Borrower. Obtaining a loan from a banker requires cultivation and personal selling. In this effort, there are several things to remember:

1. Do not call on a banker for a loan without an introduction by someone who already has a good relationship with the banker. Cold calling is not appropriate here.
2. Do not wait until there is a dire need for money. Such lack of planning is not perceived with favor by a prospective lender.
3. A banker is not an entrepreneur or a venture capitalist. Some bankers even have difficulty in understanding how the entrepreneur thinks. Thus, do not expect the banker to show the same enthusiasm you may have for the venture.
4. Work to develop alternative sources of debt capital; that is, visit with several banks. However, be sensitive as to how a banker feels about your courting more than one bank.

All bankers have two fundamental concerns when they make a loan. They examine any loan in terms of (1) how much income the loan will provide the bank, either in interest income and other forms of income, and (2) the chance that the borrower will default on the loan. The banker is not interested in taking large amounts of risk; thus, the loan agreement will be designed to reduce the risk to the bank.

In making a loan decision, a banker looks at the proverbial "Five Cs of Credit": (1) the borrower's *character,* (2) the borrower's *capacity* to repay the loan, (3) the *capital* being invested in the venture by the borrower, (4) the *conditions* of the industry and economy, and (5) the *collateral* available to secure the loan. Also, there are certain key questions that a banker needs answered before a loan will be made. Some of these questions include:

1. What is the strength and quality of the management team?
2. How has the firm performed financially?

3. What is the venture going to do with the money?
4. How much money is needed?
5. When and how will the money be paid back?
6. When is the money needed?
7. Does the borrower have a good public accountant and attorney?
8. Does the borrower already have a banking relationship?

Finally, a well-prepared business plan containing projections of cash flows and profits (and losses) and balance sheets is essential, because only with these projections can the borrower clearly demonstrate the need for the loan and how it can be repaid.

Selection of a Banker. The varied services provided by banks make the choice of a bank important. For the typical small firm, the provision of checking-account facilities and the extension of short-term (and possibly long-term) loans are the two most important services of a bank. Normally, loans are negotiated with the same bank in which the firm maintains its checking account. In addition, the firm may use the bank's safety deposit vault or its services in collecting notes or securing credit information. An experienced banker can also provide management advice, particularly in financial matters, to the beginning entrepreneur.

The factor of location limits the range of choices possible for the small firm. For reasons of convenience in making deposits and in conferring with the banker concerning loans and other matters, it is desirable that the bank be located in the same vicinity as the firm. Any bank is also interested in its home community and therefore tends to be sympathetic to the needs of business firms in the area. Except in very small communities, however, two or more local banks are available, thus permitting some freedom of choice.

Lending policies of banks are not uniform. Some bankers are extremely conservative, while others are more venturesome in the risks they will accept. If a small firm's loan application is neither obviously strong nor obviously weak, its prospects for approval depend as much upon the bank as upon the borrowing firm. Some banks actively seek small-business accounts. Differences in willingness to lend have been clearly established by research studies, as well as by the practical experience of many business borrowers.

Government-Sponsored Agencies as Source of Funds

There are several government programs that provide financing to small businesses. The availability of these funds varies with the economic condition of the nation and states.

Federal Government Sponsorship. The federal government has a longstanding reputation for helping new businesses get started. Some types of loans available through the Small Business Administration and Small Business Investment Companies are discussed in the next two sections.

Small Business Administration (SBA) Loans. There are two basic types of Small Business Administration business loans. Guaranty loans are made by private lenders and guaranteed up to 90 percent by the SBA. These loans are usually made through commercial banks. For loans exceeding $155,000, the guaranty percentage is 85 percent. A loan up to $750,000 can be guaranteed. To obtain a guaranty loan, the small business must submit the loan application to the lender—such as a bank—who, after initial review, will forward the loan application to the SBA. When approved, the lender closes the loan and disburses the funds.

The SBA also makes direct loans. This form of lending is available only after the small business has been unable to obtain a guaranty loan. This form of lending is much more limited and is usually for a maximum of $150,000.

The maximum maturity of SBA loans is 25 years. Interest rates are negotiated between the borrower and the lender but are subject to maximum rates set by the SBA. The SBA also requires assets to be pledged for security of the loan. Personal guarantees and liens on personal assets may also be required.

To qualify for an SBA loan, certain company size standards are imposed by the SBA. These size limitations are as follows:[14]

- *Manufacturing:* Maximum number of employees may range from 500 to 1,500, depending on the type of product manufactured.
- *Wholesaling:* Maximum number of employees may not exceed 100.
- *Services:* Annual receipts may not exceed $3.5 to $14.5 million, depending on the industry.
- *Retailing:* Annual receipts may not exceed $3.5 to $13.5 million, depending on the industry.
- *Construction:* General construction annual receipts may not exceed $9.5 to $17 million, depending on the industry.
- *Special Trade Construction:* Annual receipts may not exceed $7 million.
- *Agriculture:* Annual receipts may not exceed $0.5 to $3.5 million, depending on the industry.

small business investment companies
privately owned banks that supply capital to small businesses

Small Business Investment Companies (SBICs). In 1958, Congress passed the Small Business Investment Act. This act provides for the establishment of privately owned capital banks, SBICs, whose purpose is to provide long-term and/or equity capital to small businesses. SBICs are licensed and regulated by the Small Business Administration. They may obtain a substantial part of their capital from the SBA at attractive rates of interest.

Although SBICs may either lend funds or supply equity funds, the act was intended to place a strong emphasis upon equity financing. The SBIC that provides equity financing may do so either by directly purchasing the small firm's stock or, quite commonly, by purchasing the small firm's convertible debentures (bonds), which may be converted into stock at the option of the SBIC.

State and Local Government Sponsorships. State and local governments are increasingly becoming involved in financing new businesses. The nature of state financing varies from state to state, but each program is geared to augment other sources of funding.

California was one of the first states to create a business and industrial development corporation to lend money to new businesses. Michigan has also been very active in establishing a state funding program. "We are trying to get private seed funds going by giving them a little government boost," according to Steve Rohde, of the Michigan Strategic Fund.[15]

Some large cities are also providing funds for new-business ventures. For example, Des Moines, Iowa, has established a Golden Circle Loan Guarantee Fund to guarantee bank loans to small companies. Loan amounts are available up to $250,000.[16]

Venture Capital Firms as Sources of Funds

Technically speaking, anyone investing in a new-business venture is a venture capitalist. However, the term **venture capitalist** is usually associated with those corporations or partnerships which operate as investment groups. Each year more venture capital groups are being organized.

venture capitalist
an investor or investment group that invests in new-business ventures

Some venture capital companies provide management assistance to young businesses. They also can assist in later financing needs. One such venture capital firm is Onset, based in Palo Alto, California. Started in 1984, it had $5 million in capital two years later. It is what is called a seed or incubator fund. Entrepreneurs have access to capital, management skills, and product-design advice, all from one source.[17]

Special resource directories are available for the entrepreneur seeking venture capital. One such book, compiled by Stanley Pratt, lists over 800 venture capital sources plus several informative articles written by venture capitalists.[18]

While venture capital as a source of financing receives significant coverage by the business media, few small companies ever receive funding from this source of financing. Fewer than 1 percent of the business plans received by any venture capitalist are eventually funded. Joseph Horowitz, a general partner of U.S. Venture Partners, expressed the challenge of obtaining financing from his firm this way:

No idea gets far unless its promoter pursues it with obsession. If a person doesn't have a sense of urgency . . . then it's difficult to imagine it's going to get done at all . . . . You need people who understand the skills and discipline of running all facets of a business. . . . Ethics are absolutely essential . . . .[19]

Failure to receive funding from a venture capitalist does not necessarily suggest that the opportunity is not a good one. Often the venture is simply not a good fit for the venture capitalist. Venture capital is inappropriate for firms lacking:[20]

1. *Size.* Venture capitalists are seldom interested in making investments of less than $1 million. They simply have too much in the way of fixed research costs to afford investing in small deals.
2. *A proprietary advantage.* Unless the firm has some proprietary advantage, such as patents, many venture capitalists are not interested in investing.
3. *A well-defined road map.* Without a well-prepared business plan that speaks clearly to all the issues venture capitalists consider, there is little chance of getting a second look.
4. *Star founders.* Most small companies are founded by individuals who are high-energy persons with a dream, but have limited experience and may not have a graduate degree from a leading university. Venture capitalists want to invest in founders of a new business with extensive experience related to what they are doing and with excellent educational credentials. Trying to attract money from the venture capitalist by one who does not fit their "star" criteria will often prove difficult and frustrating.

So before trying to compete for venture capital financing, the entrepreneur should assess whether the firm and the management team is a good fit for the venture capitalist.

Business Suppliers as Sources of Funds

Companies with which a new firm has business dealings also represent a source of funds for the firm's merchandise inventory and equipment. Thus, both wholesalers and equipment manufacturers/suppliers can be used to provide trade credit (accounts payable) or equipment loans and leases.

Trade Credit (Accounts Payable). Credit extended by suppliers is of unusual importance to the beginning entrepreneur. In fact, trade (or mercantile) credit is the small firm's most widely used source of short-term funds. Trade credit is of short duration—30 days being the customary credit period. Most commonly, this type of credit involves an unsecured, open-book account. The supplier (seller) sends merchandise to the purchasing firm. The buying firm then sets up an account payable for the amount of the purchase.

The amount of trade credit available to a new firm depends upon the type of business and the supplier's confidence in the firm. For example, sunglass distributors provide business capital to retailers by granting extended payment dates on sales made at the start of a season. The retailers, in turn, sell to their customers during the season and make the bulk of their payments to the distributor at or near the end of the season. If the retailer's rate of stock turnover is greater than the scheduled payment for the goods, cash from sales may be obtained even before paying for the sunglasses.

Equipment Loans. Some small businesses—for example, restaurants— utilize equipment that may be purchased on an installment basis. A down pay-

ment of 25 to 35 percent is ordinarily required, and the contract period normally runs from three to five years. The equipment manufacturer or supplier typically extends credit on the basis of a conditional sales contract (or mortgage) on the equipment. During the loan period, the equipment cannot serve as collateral for a bank loan.

The small-business firm should be aware of the danger in contracting for so much equipment that it becomes impossible to meet installment payments. It is a mark of real management ability to recognize the limits in this type of borrowing.

Asset-Based Lending Companies as Sources of Funds

Asset-based lending is financing secured by working-capital assets. Usually, the assets used for security are accounts receivable or inventory. However, other assets such as equipment and real estate can be taken for loan collateral. Asset-based lending is a viable option for young, growing businesses that may be caught in a "cash-flow bind."

asset-based lending
financing secured by working-capital assets

factoring
obtaining cash by selling accounts receivable to another firm

There are several categories of asset-based loans, the oldest of which is factoring. **Factoring** is an option that makes cash available to the business *before* accounts receivable payments are received from customers. Under this option another firm, known as a factor, purchases the accounts receivable for their full value. The factor charges a servicing fee, usually 1 percent of the value of the receivables, and an interest charge on the money advanced. The interest charge may range from 2 percent to 3 percent above the prime rate, which is the interest rate that commercial banks charge their most creditworthy customers.

Stock Sales as a Source of Funds

Another way to obtain capital is through the sale of stock to individual investors beyond the scope of one's immediate acquaintances. This is commonly called "going public."[21] Going public provides both benefits and drawbacks. These have been identified by one public accounting firm as:[22]

Benefits
1. Improved financial conditions.
2. Using stock for acquisitions.
3. Using stock as an employee incentive.
4. Enhancing corporate prestige.
5. Diversification of owner's personal portfolio and estate planning.

Drawbacks
1. Loss of privacy and control.
2. Limiting management's freedom to act.
3. Costs.

Whether the owner is wise in declining to use outside equity financing depends upon the firm's long-range prospects. If there is an opportunity for substantial expansion on a continuing basis and if other sources are inadequate, the owner may logically decide to bring in other owners. Owning part of a larger business may be more profitable than owning all of a smaller business.

private placement
selling a firm's capital stock to selected individuals

Private Placement. One way to sell capital stock is through **private placement.** This means that the firm's capital stock is sold to selected individuals, who are most likely to be the firm's employees, the owner's acquaintances, local residents, customers, and suppliers. Private sale of stock is difficult because the new firm is not known and has no ready market for its securities. However, the entrepreneur avoids many requirements of the securities laws when a stock sale is restricted to a private placement.

Public Sale. Some small firms make their stock available to the general public. These are typically the larger small-business firms. The reason often

SMALL BUSINESS IN ACTION

Asset-Based Financing

Margaret Thacker owns and operates Official Products Co., Inc., a warehouse distributorship for automotive paint and body-shop supplies in Atlanta. She has always been careful to maintain a good relationship with her banker. However, in 1991, the bank tightened its credit requirements and increased the interest rate charged Thacker's firm, "because the company's sales ratios were not in compliance with our loan requirements." Thacker began looking for an alternative source of financing.

Started in 1945 by her father, Thacker's firm has annual sales of $9 million. Fortunately, she located and obtained an attractive revolving-loan agreement with an asset-based division of Textron Financial Corp. Textron Financial is a major financial-services company headquartered in Providence, Rhode Island; its asset-based division is in Atlanta.

The financing provided by Textron Financial has met Official Product's working capital needs.

According to Thacker, "A finance company is easier to get along with. It sees your needs. As long as the assets are there, Textron doesn't panic."

Source: Joan C. Szabo, "A Capital Option: Finance Companies." Excerpted by permission, *Nation's Business* (July 1992), p. 42. Copyright 1992, U.S. Chamber of Commerce.

cited for a public sale is the need for additional working capital or, less frequently, for other capital needs.

In undertaking the public sale of stock, the small firm subjects itself to greater public regulation. There are state regulations pertaining to the public sale of securities. The federal Securities and Exchange Commission (SEC) also exercises surveillance over such offerings.

Common stock may also be sold to underwriters, who guarantee the sale of securities. The compensation and fees paid to underwriters typically make the sale of securities in this manner expensive. The fees themselves may range from 10 percent to 30 percent, with 18 percent to 25 percent being typical. In addition, there are options and other fees that may run the actual costs higher. The reason for the high expense is, of course, the element of uncertainty and risk associated with public offerings of stock of small, relatively unknown firms.

Studies of public sale of stock by small firms reveal that small companies frequently make financial arrangements that are not sound. Indeed, the lack of knowledge on the part of small-firm owners often leads to arrangements with brokers or securities dealers that are not in the best interest of the small firms.

The condition of the financial markets at any given time has a direct bearing on the prospects for the sale of capital stock. Entrepreneurs found the early years of the 1980s to be strong for new-venture stock sales. Interest in new stocks ran hot and cold during the 1980s. In the early 1990s there have been renewed interests. The more recent interest is observed in new offerings such as Gupta Corporation, when the stock price doubled to $34 immediately after the offering. Market conditions do change, however, and therefore must be studied carefully. Consider the situation of MediVision, Inc., following the 500-point decline of the Dow in October, 1987.

The Boston-based operator of eye surgery centers was just a week away from filing a $30-million initial public offering (IPO). Rather than take a lower valuation in an IPO, MediVision rounded up . . . private debt financing . . . . "Debt money is no more expensive than the depletion we would have suffered had we gone public after October 19," explains Christopher Grant, Jr., chief financial officer of the four-year-old concern.[23]

There are differences in opinion regarding initial public offerings (IPOs) for startup companies. Some market professionals say IPOs should be avoided for new businesses because they lack operating histories.[24] In any case, the new venture can rarely make a successful initial public offering. Most new startups are simply too small and unimpressive at the beginning to attract serious public interest.

CONCLUDING THOUGHTS

We have covered a great amount of material in this chapter, but no more than is essential for understanding the financing of a new business. As concluding thoughts, we want to share with you some ideas of Amar Bhide, a professor at Harvard University, who spent extensive time interviewing owners of some of the high-growth companies in the United States.[25]

Interviewing owners and managers of the *Inc.* 500, which is *Inc.* magazine's compilation of the fastest-growing companies in the United States, Bhide learned that few of these high-growth companies had access to the venture capital markets. Instead, they were most often required to bootstrap their financing—that is, get it any way they could. Based on his many interviews, he offered the following recommendations to any aspiring entrepreneur who wants to start a business:

1. First, get operational. At some point, it is time to stop planning, and just make things happen.
2. Go for quick-break-even and high-cash-flow-generating projects whenever possible.

3. Fit growth goals to your available personal resources.
4. Have a preference for high-ticket, high-profit margin projects and services that can sustain direct personal selling.
5. Start up only with a product or service that satisfies a clear need.
6. Forget about needing a crack management team with all the textbook credentials. It can come as the venture develops.
7. Focus on cash—not profits, market share, or anything else.
8. Cultivate the banker.

LOOKING BACK

1. The profitability of a venture is determined by the level of sales achieved and the amount of its operating expenses.
2. Starting a venture requires us to find the needed funding for the company's asset requirements, as well as for personal living expenses incurred until the venture is underway and profitable.
3. We can rely on the asset-to-sales relationship to estimate the firm's investment or asset requirements.
4. Initial capital consists of owner capital and debt capital. Although there are successful businesses that started with all debt and no ownership equity, the conservative approach suggests that initial debt should not exceed one-third of total initial capital.
5. The major sources of funding are personal savings; other individuals, such as "angels"; commercial banks; government-sponsored agencies; venture capital firms; business suppliers; asset-based lenders; and stock sales.

DISCUSSION QUESTIONS

1. What determines a company's profitability?
2. Define the types of assets needed to start a new business.
3. Describe the process for estimating the amount of assets needed.
4. Why should personal expenses be included in the initial financing planning?
5. Suppose that a retailer's estimated sales are $900,000 and the standard sales-to-inventory ratio is 6. What dollar amount of inventory would be estimated for the new business?
6. Distinguish between owner capital and debt capital.
7. Distinguish between spontaneous and nonspontaneous debt financing and between internal and external equity capital.
8. How do you estimate a company's financial requirements?
9. What does a banker need to know in order to decide whether to make a loan?
10. Why might venture capital not be an appropriate source of financing for most small firms?
11. What are some of the major advantages and disadvantages of "going public"?
12. Explain how trade credit and equipment loans provide initial capital funding.
13. How does the federal government help with initial financing for a small business?

14. If you were starting a new business, where would you start looking for capital? Would your answer change if the nature of your new business was different?
15. Assume that you are starting a new business for the first time. What do you feel the greatest personal obstacles will be in obtaining funds for the new venture? Why?

YOU MAKE THE CALL

Situation 1

Mary Watson has been a mother and housewife for most of her married life. She is a creative person and has always had a special interest in arts and crafts projects. For the last several years, she has created her own craft projects at home, traveling to occasional arts and crafts shows to sell her wares.

Recently, she has decided to open an arts and crafts shop to sell supplies and finished crafts. She lives in a small rural community and knows of other women who produce various craft items that could supplement her own products. Watson believes a shop could be successful if several artists would display their work. She knows of a vacant building in the local town that would be an ideal location.

Watson's husband has been supportive of her idea and has promised to help with obtaining financing. However, he does not have the time or the patience to estimate the nature or quantity of the new venture's financial needs.

Questions
1. What do you see as the nature of Watson's financial requirements?
2. Is this venture too small to justify preparation of a financial plan? Why or why not?
3. Which sources of funds described in this chapter do you think would not be suitable for this venture? Explain your reasoning.

Situation 2

The Trailer Craft, Inc., example given in the chapter is an actual firm located in West Texas, however, some of the facts have been changed for reasons of confidentiality. In reality, Stuart Hall had just bought the company from its founding owners and was moving its operations to his home town when we were revising the text. Although we estimated the firm's asset needs and financing requirements in the chapter, we have no certainty that these projections will be realized. The numbers used represent the most-likely event. However, Mr. Hall also has made some projections that he considers to be the "worst-case" and "best-case" sales and profit projections. If things do not go well, the firm might only sell $150,000 in the first year, and earn 10 percent on each sales dollar. However, if the potential of the business is realized, Mr. Hall believes that sales could be as high as $400,000, with a profits-to-sales ratio of 15 percent. If Mr. Hall needs any additional financing beyond the existing line of credit, he conceivably could borrow another $5,000 in short-term debt from the bank by pledging some personal investments. Any more financing will need to come from Mr. Hall himself—increasing.his equity stake in the business.

Question

Assuming that all the other relationships hold, as given in the examples for Trailer Craft in the text, how will Mr. Hall's projections affect the balance sheet? Reconstruct the pro forma balance sheets, and compare your results with the original projected balance sheet shown in Figure 10-5 (on page 252).

EXPERIENTIAL EXERCISES

1.   Interview local small-business firms to determine how funds were obtained to start their businesses. Be sure you phrase questions so that they are not overly personal, and do not ask for specific dollar amounts. Report on your findings.
2.   Interview a local banker to discuss the bank's lending policies for small-business loans. Ask the banker to comment on the importance of a business plan to the bank's decision to loan money to a small business. Report on your findings.
3.   Review recent issues of *Entrepreneur, Inc.,* or *In Business,* and report on the financing arrangements of firms featured in these magazines.
4.   Interview a stockbroker or investment analyst and discuss his or her views regarding the sale of capital stock by a small business. Report on your findings.

REFERENCES TO SMALL-BUSINESS PRACTICES

Ang, James S. "Small Business Uniqueness and the Theory of Financial Management," *The Journal of Small Business Finance,* Vol. 1, No. 1 (Spring 1991), pp. 1–13.
    A presentation of the important concepts of finance as they relate to the small firm. The article helps us understand why small firms behave as they do when it comes to financial decisions.
Bhide, Amar. "Bootstrap Finance: The Art of Start-ups," *Harvard Business Review,* Vol.70, No. 6 (November–December 1992), pp.109–117
    Reports the results of extensive interviews with owner-managers of the *Inc.* 500, representing the fastest growing privately held firms in the United States. Looks at how these firms were financed.
Posner, Bruce G. "The 1-Page Loan Proposal," *Inc.,* Vol. 13, No. 9 (September 1991), pp. 73–75.
    Provides basic guidelines for submitting a loan request to a banker.
Posner, Bruce G. "How to Finance Anything," *Inc.,* Vol. 14, No. 4 (April 1992), pp. 51–62.
    Lists the possible asset needs of a small business and gives suggestions on how these needs might be financed.
Roderick, Pamela H. "Beyond Banks," *Entrepreneur,* Vol. 18, No. 6 (June 1990), pp. 159–163.
    Describes how a small firm can use a private placement as an important, but often overlooked, source of financing.
Whittemore, Meg. "Financing Your Franchise," *Nation's Business* (September 1992) pp. 51–58.

A "special guide" on how to finance a franchise operation. Also provides sources of information for financing a franchise.

ENDNOTES

1. "What Is the Most Pressing Concern for Small Business Today?" *Small Business Forum,* Vol. 10, No. 1 (Spring 1992), p. 86. (The article provides the answers given by ten business owners to this question.)

2. This statement is not totally accurate. As we shall see more clearly in Chapter 20, a firm may be highly profitable, but be cash poor. So we ought to be very careful about thinking that profits and cash are one and the same. They are not; however, we will reserve this issue for later.

3. This provision is explained more fully in the next chapter.

4. A question related to predicting a company's profits deals with measuring its break-even point. If we are investing in a startup company, we want to know how long it will take the firm to become profitable. Measuring a company's break-even point, while important from a financial perspective, is also needed in pricing the firm's product or services. The pricing issue is addressed in Chapter 13. We have chosen to defer our discussion about break-even analysis until that time.

5. Instead of representing the assets as a percentage of sales, we frequently express the asset-sales relationship as a turnover ratio. The turnover ratio is measured as (sales ÷ asset) instead of (asset ÷ sales). For example, instead of saying that inventories will be about 25 percent of sales, we could say that the inventories will "turn over" four times per year. That is,

$$\frac{\text{Sales}}{\text{Inventories}} = 4$$

In our example,

$$\frac{\$250,000}{\text{Inventories}} = 4$$

and therefore,

$$\text{Inventories} = \frac{\$250,000}{4} = \$62,500$$

Thus, inventories would equal $62,500; the same answer as before, but just calculated a bit differently.

6. We should be careful not to think of retained earnings as a big bucket of cash. As already noted, a company can have a large amount of earnings, and no cash to reinvest. More about this problem in Chapters 20 and 21.

7. The choice of a legal form of business is discussed in the next chapter. For now, we need only be aware that Dalton could have chosen between operating as a sole proprietorship or a corporation. For reasons to be explained later, she chose to form a corporation. Also, there is no economic rationale for 10,000 shares; it could just as easily have been 20,000 shares. In either case, the total value of the equity ownership would be the same; only the value per share would be different.

8. *Small Business Primer,* a publication of the NFIB Foundation, 1988, p. 13.

9. Sanford L. Jacobs, "Aspiring Entrepreneurs Learn Intricacies of Going It Alone," *The Wall Street Journal* (March 23, 1981), p. 23.

10. R. J. Gaston and S.E. Bell, *The Informal Supply of Capital* (Washington: Office of Economic Research, U.S. Small Business Administration, 1988).

11. Bradley Hitchings, "Finding Startups with Star Quality," *Business Week,* No. 2948 (May 26, 1986), p. 137.

12. John Freear, Jeff A. Sohl, and William E. Wetzel, "Raising Venture Capital: Entrepreneur's View of the Process," Paper presented at the Babson College Entrepreneurship Research Conference.

13. An interesting discussion of creating a line of credit with a bank can be found in Jeffrey L. Seglin, "Court a Banker Now, Borrow Money Later," *Venture,* Vol. 10, No. 8 (August 1988), pp. 65–68.

14. *Business Loans from the SBA* (Washington: U.S. Small Business Administration, June 1987).

15. Steven P. Galante, "States Cultivating Seed Funds to Spur Early Stage Ventures," *The Wall Street Journal* (January 12, 1987), p. 23.

16. Steven P. Galante, "Des Moines Has Its Own Way to Back Small-Business Loans," *The Wall Street Journal* (September 29, 1986), p. 37.

17. Udayan Gupta, "California Venture Capitalists Take Earlier Role in Start-Ups," *The Wall Street Journal* (February 3, 1986), p. 14.

18. Stanley Pratt, Ed., *Guide to Venture Capital Sources,* 13th ed. (Wellesley Hills, MA: Capital Publishing Company, 1989).

19. Peter Waldman, "Taking a Flier," *The Wall Street Journal* (June 10, 1988), p. 10R.

20. Amar Bhide, "Bootstrap Finance: The Art of Start-ups," *Harvard Business Review,* Vol. 70, No. 6 (November-December 1992), pp. 109–117. This article includes a complete discussion of the inappropriateness of venture capital for many small companies.

21. An excellent discussion of going public is contained in James M. Johnson and Robert E. Miller, "Going Public: Information for Small Business," *Journal of Small Business Management,* Vol. 23, No. 4 (October 1985), pp. 38–44.

22. Daniel R. Garner, Robert R. Owen, and Robert P. Conway, *The Ernst & Young Guide to Raising Capital* (New York: John Wiley & Sons, 1991), pp. 15–23.

23. Sallie Hofmeister, "Sailing on Stormy Seas," *Venture,* Vol. 10, No. 9 (September 1988), p. 23.

24. Francine Schwadel, "Stock Market Pros Offer Some Tips on Judging Initial Public Offerings," *The Wall Street Journal* (February 21, 1986), p. 21.

25. Amar Bhide, "Bootstrap Finance: The Art of Start-ups," *Harvard Business Review,* Vol. 70, No. 6 (November-December 1992), pp. 109–117.

CHAPTER 11

Choosing a Form of Ownership

SPOTLIGHT ON SMALL BUSINESS

Partnership relationships can be challenging because of differences in personal traits and management styles. Kenneth Ryan and Edward LeBeau, the owners and partners of Airmax, demonstrate how a difficult business relationship can survive, with some care and attention. Their company's sales increased nicely from 1986 to 1990. However, the two men who founded the firm indicate they underestimated the time and effort needed in maintaining an effective relationship.

Kenneth Ryan and Edward LeBeau

"We have a lot of common attitudes about how a business should be run," says LeBeau. *"And then there is the matter of style. . . ."* Ryan says he is impulsive and intuitive and would become *"impatient"* with LeBeau's more methodical, *"plodding"* way of working.

"In time," says Ryan, *"we found ourselves really disturbed with each other. The partnership was suffering, and we were going to end up splitting up. We wanted [the conflicts] stopped."*

LeBeau and Ryan decided to get help, calling on Kenneth Kaye, a Chicago psychologist, who counsels troubled business partnerships. Kaye helped the owners see that many of their problems were ones of perception. For example, "'plodding' is negative, but if we say 'careful' it sounds constructive," says Kaye, "and 'impulsive' can be viewed as 'energetic.'" He also taught them to take time out when talk gets heated. Ryan comments in jest: "Now, if only Ed would listen to everything I said and realize I was right about it. . . ."

Source: "Imperfect Partnerships: *Vive La Difference!*" Excerpted by permission, *Nation's Business,* Vol. 80, No. 5 (May 1992), p. 14. Copyright 1992, U.S. Chamber of Commerce.

After studying this chapter, you should be able to:
1. Identify common forms of legal organization.
2. Describe characteristics of the proprietorship option.
3. Describe characteristics of various types of partnerships.
4. Describe characteristics of a regular corporation and a Subchapter S corporation.
5. Identify factors to consider in making a choice between the different legal forms of business.
6. Explain how different legal forms of ownership are taxed.
7. Describe the role of boards of directors in small firms and the process for selecting good board members.

proprietorship	general partner	Section 1244 stock
unlimited liability	limited partner	board of directors
partnership	corporation	corporation charter
articles of partnership	legal entity	S corporation
agency power	stock certificate	C corporation
limited partnership	pre-emptive rights	advisory council

A number of legal and regulatory issues grow out of the initial business planning discussed in previous chapters. This chapter examines the major legal forms of business organization and the related issues of taxes.

FORMS OF LEGAL ORGANIZATION

Various legal forms of organization are available to organize small businesses. Several options are appropriate only for very specialized applications. A new form, the limited liability company, is now recognized in some states. However, we confine our attention here to the forms currently in wide use by small business. These forms are shown in Figure 11-1 as the proprietorship, the partnership, and the corporation. Within the partnership form, there are two basic types—the general partnership and the limited partnership. Also, in addition to the regular corporation, there is a legal form known as a Subchapter S corporation.

The proprietorship is the most popular form of business organization among small businesses. This popularity exists across all industries. Nevertheless, many small businesses operate as partnerships and as corporations, which suggests that there are circumstances that favor these forms. About 70 percent of the firms in the United States are sole proprietorships, 20 percent are corporations, and 10 percent are partnerships.[1]

Figure 11-1
Forms of Small-
Business Legal
Organization

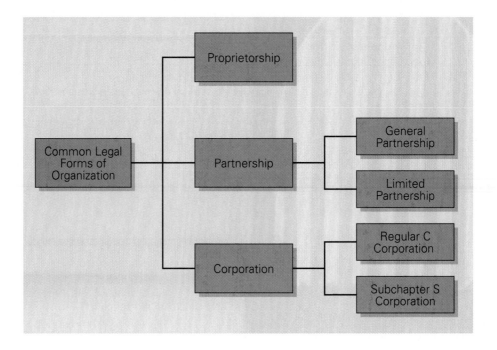

THE PROPRIETORSHIP OPTION

proprietorship
a business owned
and operated by one
person

The **proprietorship** is a business owned and operated by one person. The individual proprietor has title to all business assets, subject to the claims of creditors. He or she receives all profits but must also assume all losses, bear all risks, and pay all debts of the business. The proprietorship is the simplest and cheapest way to start operation and is frequently the most appropriate form for a new business. In the proprietorship, the owner is free from interference by partners, shareholders, directors, and officers.

However, the proprietorship lacks some of the advantages of other legal forms. For example, there are no limits on the owner's personal liability; an owner has **unlimited liability.** This means that the owner's personal assets outside the business can be taken by creditors if the business fails. In addition, proprietors are not employees and cannot receive some of the tax-free fringe benefits customarily provided by corporations—for example, insurance and hospitalization plans.

unlimited liability
liability that extends
beyond the assets of
the business

The death of an owner terminates the legal existence of a business that is organized as a proprietorship. The possibility of the owner's death may cloud relationships between the business and its creditors and employees. The need for a will is suggested because the assets of the business minus its liabilities belong to the heirs. In a will, the owner can give an executor the power to run the business for the heirs until they can take over or until it can be sold.

Figure 11-2
Sole Proprietor of a
Temporary Services
Agency

Another contingency that must be provided for is the possible incapacity of the proprietor. If he or she were badly hurt in an accident and unconscious for an extended period, the business could be ruined. The proprietor can guard against this by giving a legally competent person a power of attorney to carry on.

In some cases, the proprietorship option is virtually ruled out by the circumstances. For example, a high exposure to legal risks may require a legal form that provides greater protection against personal liability, as in the case of a manufacturer of potentially hazardous consumer products.

THE PARTNERSHIP OPTION

A **partnership** is a voluntary "association of two or more persons to carry on, as co-owners, a business for profit." Because of its voluntary nature, a partnership can be quickly set up without many of the legal procedures involved in creating a corporation. A partnership pools the managerial talents and capital of those joining together as business partners. However, partners have unlimited liability.

partnership
a voluntary association of two or more persons to carry on, as co-owners, a business for profit

Qualifications of Partners

Any person capable of contracting may legally become a business partner. Individuals may become partners without contributing to capital or sharing in the assets at the time of dissolution. Such persons are partners only as to management and profits.

Figure 11-3
Personal Compatibility Is an Important Consideration in Forming a Business Partnership

Aside from legal aspects, however, partnership formation deserves serious study. A strong partnership requires partners who are honest, healthy, capable, and compatible.

Operating as a partnership has its benefits, but it is also fraught with problems. In this regard, *Inc.* magazine surveyed individuals regarding their opinions about the partnership form of ownership.[2] Almost 60 percent of the respondents considered a partnership to be a "bad way to run a business." The respondents were also asked to identify what they believed to be good and bad qualities associated with the partnership form of business. The responses given are shown in Table 11-1.[3] Interestingly, few of the pros or cons are directly associated with financial matters. For instance, a mere 6 percent thought the dilution of equity was a good reason not to add a new partner. Instead, those disliking partnerships focused more on the deterioration of relationships. Many spoke of dishonesty at worst and differing priorities at best. The important point: Form a partnership carefully and only if it is clearly the best option when all matters are considered. Prospective partners should ask themselves the questions shown in Figure 11-4.

Rights and Duties of Partners

articles of partnership
a document that states explicitly the rights and duties of partners

Partners' rights and duties should be stated explicitly in written **articles of partnership.** These articles should be drawn up during the preoperating period and should cover the following items as a minimum:

1. Date of formation of the partnership.
2. Names and addresses of all partners.

Why is a partnership good?	Percentage Responding
Spreads the workload	55%
Spreads the emotional burden	41%
Buys executive talent not otherwise affordable	40%
Spreads the financial burden	33%
Makes company-building less lonely	26%

Why is a partnership bad?	Percentage Responding
Personal conflicts outweigh the benefits	60%
Partners never live up to one another's expectations	59%
Companies function better with one clear leader	53%
Dilutes equity too much	6%
You can't call your own shots	6%

Table 11-1
An Opinion Survey About the Partnership Form of Ownership

Source: "The *Inc.* FaxPoll: Are Partners Bad for Business?" *Inc.* magazine, Vol. 14, No. 2, p. 24. Reprinted with permission, Inc. magazine (February 1992). Copyright 1992 by Goldhirsh Group, Inc., 38 Commercial Wharf, Boston, MA 02110.

3. Statement of fact of partnership.
4. Statement of business purpose(s).
5. Duration of the business.
6. Name and location of business.
7. Amount invested by each partner.
8. Sharing ratio for profits and losses.
9. Partners' rights, if any, for withdrawals of funds for personal use.
10. Provision for accounting records and their accessibility to partners.
11. Specific duties of each partner.
12. Provision for dissolution and for sharing the net assets.
13. Restraint on partners' assumption of special obligations, such as endorsing the note of another.
14. Provision for protection of surviving partners, decedent's estate, and so forth.

Unless specified otherwise in the articles, a partner is generally recognized as having certain implicit rights. For example, partners share profits or losses equally if they have not agreed on a profit-and-loss sharing ratio.

In a partnership each partner has **agency power,** which means that a partner can bind all members of the firm. Good faith, together with reasonable care in the exercise of management duties, is required of all partners in a business. Since their relationship is fiduciary in character, a partner cannot com-

agency power
the right of a partner to bind all members of the firm

Figure 11-4
What to Find Out
Before Taking on a
New Partner

Would-be partners should ask questions for the purpose of clarifying expectations. Some important questions include the following:

1. WHAT'S OUR BUSINESS CONCEPT? This is a big, broad topic, and sometimes it helps to ask a third party to listen in, just to see if partners are on each other's wave length. First, you need to decide who will make the widgets and who will sell them. Then you need to talk about growth. Are we building the company to sell it, or are we after long-term growth? It's also important to discuss exactly how the business will be run. Do we want participative management, or will employees simply hunker down at machines and churn out parts? "If one guy is a fist pounder with a 'do-it-as-I-say' mentality and the other believes that people ought to feel good about their jobs, that probably represents an irreconcilable difference," says Sam Lane, a Fort Worth consultant who works with partners.

2. HOW ARE WE GOING TO STRUCTURE OWNERSHIP? It sounds great for two people to scratch out 50-50 on a cocktail napkin and leave it at that. But in practice, splitting the company down the middle can paralyze the business. If neither is willing to settle for 49%, then build some arbitration into your partnership agreement.

3. WHY DO WE NEED EACH OTHER? "I thought it would be much less scary with two of us," says Arthur Eisenberg, explaining his rationale for teaming up with Cap Pannell. That may be so, but bringing on a partner means sharing responsibility and authority. "If you are taking on a partner because you are afraid of going it alone, find some other way to handle the anxiety," advises Mardy Grothe, a psychologist.

4. HOW DO OUR LIFESTYLES DIFFER? The fact that one partner is single and the other has a family, for instance, can affect more than just the time each puts in. It may mean that one partner needs to pull more money out of the business. Or it may affect a partner's willingness to take risks with the company. "All of this stuff needs to get talked out," says Peter Wylie, a psychologist who works with Mardy Grothe. "The implications are profound."

Source: Joshua Hyatt, "Reconcilable Differences," *Inc.* magazine, Vol. 13, No. 4, p. 87. Reprinted with permission, Inc. magazine (April 1991). Copyright 1991 by Goldhirsh Group, Inc., 38 Commercial Wharf, Boston, MA 02110.

pete in business and remain a partner. Nor can a partner use business information solely for personal gain.

Termination of a Partnership

Death, incapacity, or withdrawal of any one of the partners ends a partnership and necessitates liquidation or reorganization of the business. Liquidation often results in substantial losses to all partners. It may be legally necessary, however, because a partnership is a close personal relationship of the parties that cannot be maintained against the will of any one of them.

This disadvantage may be partially overcome at the time a partnership is formed by stipulating in the articles of partnership that surviving partners can continue the business after buying the decedent's interest. This can be facilitated by having each partner carry life insurance, with the other partners named as beneficiaries.

The Limited Partnership

A small business sometimes finds it desirable to use a special form of partnership called the **limited partnership.** This form consists of at least one general partner and one or more limited partners. The **general partner** remains personally liable for the debts of the business. All **limited partners** have limited personal liability as long as they do not take an active role in the management of the partnership. In other words, limited partners risk only the capital which they invest in the business. Because of this feature, an individual with substantial personal assets can invest money in a limited partnership without exposing his or her total personal estate to liability claims that might arise through activities of the business. If a limited partner becomes active in management, the limited liability is lost.

To form a limited partnership, partners must file a certificate of limited partnership with the proper state office. State law governs this form of organization.

THE CORPORATION OPTION

In the *Dartmouth College* case of 1819, Chief Justice John Marshall of the United States Supreme Court defined a **corporation** as "an artificial being, invisible, intangible, and existing only in contemplation of the law." By these words the court recognized the corporation as a **legal entity.** This means that a corporation can sue and be sued, hold and sell property, and engage in business operations stipulated in the corporate charter.

The corporation is a creature of the state, being chartered under its laws. Its length of life is independent of its owners' (stockholders') lives. It is the corporation, and not its owners, that is liable for debts contracted by the corporation. Its directors and officers serve as agents to bind the corporation.

Rights and Status of Stockholders

Ownership in a corporation is evidenced by **stock certificates,** each of which stipulates the number of shares owned by a stockholder. An ownership interest does not confer a legal right to act for the firm or to share in its management. It does evidence the right to receive dividends in proportion to stockholdings—but only when they are properly declared by the board of directors.

limited partnership
a partnership of at least one general partner and one or more limited partners

general partner
the partner with unlimited liability in a general or limited partnership

limited partner
a partner who is not active in the management of a limited partnership and who therefore has limited personal liability

corporation
a business organization that exists as a legal entity

legal entity
a business organization that is recognized by the law as a separate legal being

stock certificate
a document specifying the number of shares owned by a stockholder

Figure 11-5
Corporate Executives Hold Impromptu Meeting in Foyer

Ownership of stock typically carries the right to buy new shares, in proportion to stock already owned, before the new stock is offered for public sale. This right is known as a **pre-emptive right.**

pre-emptive rights
rights of stockholders to buy new shares of a stock before it is offered for public sale

In the initial organization of a corporation, the owner does well to consider a type of stock known as **Section 1244 stock.** By issuing stock pursuant to Section 1244 of the Internal Revenue Code, the stockholder is somewhat protected in case of corporate failure. If the stock becomes worthless, the loss (up to $100,000 on a joint tax return) may be treated as an ordinary tax-deductible loss.[4]

Section 1244 stock
stock that protects the stockholder in the case of corporate failure

A common stockholder may ordinarily cast one vote per share in stockholders' meetings.[5] Thus, the stockholder indirectly participates in management by helping elect the directors. The **board of directors** is the governing body for corporate activity. It elects the firm's officers, who manage the enterprise with the help of management specialists. The directors also set or approve management policies, receive and consider reports on operating results from the officers, and declare dividends (if any).

board of directors
the governing body elected by the stockholders of a corporation

The legal status of stockholders and managers is fundamental, of course, but it may be overemphasized. In the case of many small corporations, the owners may also be directors and managing officers. The person who owns most or all of the stock can control the business as effectively as if it were a proprietorship. The corporate form is thus applicable to individual and family-owned businesses.

Major stockholders must be concerned with their working relationships, as well as their legal relationships, with other owners if they are active in the business. Cooperation among the entire owner-manager team of a new corporation is necessary for its survival. Legal technicalities are important, but they provide an inadequate basis for successful collaboration in the enterprise.

Limited Liability of Stockholders

One of the advantages of the corporate form of organization to owners is their limited liability. However, new small-business corporations often are in somewhat shaky financial circumstances during the early years of operation. As a result, the stockholders, few in number and active in management, frequently assume personal liability for the firm's debts by endorsing its notes. Also, courts may ignore the corporate entity and hold shareholders liable in certain unusual cases. Examples would be if personal and corporate funds are mixed together or if the corporation was formed to try to evade an existing obligation.

Death or Withdrawal of Stockholders

Unlike the partnership, ownership in a corporation is readily transferable. Exchange of shares of stock is all that is required to convey an ownership interest to a different individual.

In a large corporation, stock is being exchanged constantly without noticeable effect upon the operations of the business. In a small firm, however, the change of owners, though legally just as simple, may produce numerous complications. For instance, merely finding a buyer for the stock of a small firm may prove difficult. Also, a minority stockholder is vulnerable. To illustrate, suppose that two of the three equal shareholders in a business for one reason or another sold their stock to an outsider. The remaining stockholder would then be at the mercy of the outsider, who might decide to remove the former from any managerial post he or she happened to hold. In fact, a minority stockholder may be legally ousted from the board of directors and have no voice whatsoever in the management of the business.

The death of the majority stockholder could be equally unfortunate. An heir, executor, or purchaser of the stock might well insist upon direct control, with possible adverse effects for the other stockholders. To prevent problems of this nature from arising, legal arrangements should be made at the time of incorporation to provide for management continuity by surviving stockholders, as well as for fair treatment of heirs of a stockholder. As in the case of the partnership, mutual insurance may be carried to assure ability to buy out a decedent stockholder's interest. This arrangement would require an option for the corporation or surviving stockholders to: (1) purchase the decedent's stock ahead of outsiders, and (2) specify the method for determining the stock's price per share. A similar arrangement might be included to protect remaining stockholders if a given stockholder wished to retire from the business at any time.

SMALL BUSINESS IN ACTION

Minority Stockholder Beware

Wayne Ragan was a successful GMC truck dealer in Lubbock, Texas, but he sold the business in 1987. He later served as a consultant to several firms, both in and out of the trucking and automobile industry. Then, in 1989, a banker approached Ragan about helping the bank find new owners for a car dealership. The bank had extended credit to a dealership that later encountered financial difficulties. In an effort to protect its loan position, the bank wanted to bring in new owners.

Ragan called on Richard Harris, who had the financial means to buy the dealership and a possible interest in such an investment. They then visited with Mike Tarhill to see if he would have an interest in investing in the dealership and serving as its operating manager. The deal was struck. Harris and Tarhill were each to have 47 percent of the company's stock, and Ragan was to receive the remaining 6 percent of the stock for helping to put the deal together and for continued advising.

At the outset, everything worked well, and the firm appeared on its way back to profitability. However, Tarhill and Harris soon began having problems in working together. It finally reached a point where they could not agree on much of anything. Ragan became the mediator, trying to work out a plan they both could accept. After several months, when nothing else had worked, Ragan became convinced that the two men could not work together. Thus, he recommended that one of the men buy the other one's ownership in the company. However, Tarhill could not raise the necessary financing, but was unwilling to sell to Harris.

Ragan again tried to resolve the problems between the two men, but with no success. They each owned 47 percent, and neither was willing to change his position. At this point, Ragan met with Tarhill and urged him to let Harris purchase his interest in the business. Tarhill again refused. Ragan then told Tarhill, "Mike, you have not been successful at getting the financing to buy Harris's stock, so you need to let Harris buy you out. But if you will not, then at the stockholders' meeting this month, I will make a motion that you be dismissed as the operating manager and that your salary be terminated at the appropriate time. While I only own 6 percent of the company, we both know that Harris will vote with me." In response, Tarhill reluctantly agreed to begin looking for another dealership.

Ragan did make the motion at the next stockholders' meeting, and Tarhill was removed as the manager of the dealership. Fortunately, Ragan and Tarhill remained friends. However, this example demonstrates a fact of corporate life. Minority stockholders in a small firm can quickly lose any say in business decisions, even at times when they would most like to influence those decisions.

The Corporate Charter

corporation charter
the document that establishes a corporation's existence

To form a corporation, one or more persons must apply to the secretary of state for permission to incorporate. After preliminary steps, including payment of the incorporation fee, the written application is approved by the secretary of state and becomes the corporation's charter. In some states, the documents showing that the corporation exists are called articles of incorporation or a certificate of incorporation rather than a charter. A **corporation charter** typically provides for the following:

1. Name of the company.
2. Formal statement of its formation.
3. Purposes and powers—that is, type of business.
4. Location of principal office in the state of incorporation.
5. Duration (perpetual existence, 50-year life and renewable charter, or other).
6. Classes and preferences of classes of stock.
7. Number and par (or stated value) of shares of each class of stock authorized.
8. Voting privileges of each class of stock.
9. Names and addresses of incorporators and first year's directors.
10. Names and addresses of, and amounts subscribed by, each subscriber to capital stock.
11. Statement of limited liability of stockholders (if required specifically by state law).
12. Statement of alterations of directors' powers, if any, from the general corporation law of the state.

A corporation's charter should be brief, in accord with the law, and broad in the statement of the firm's powers. Details should be left to the bylaws. The charter application should be prepared by an attorney.

The Subchapter S Corporation

The name **S corporation** comes from Subchapter S of the Internal Revenue Code, which permits corporations to retain the limited-liability feature of regular corporations (**C corporations**) while being taxed as partnerships. A corporation's desire to obtain S corporation status is motivated entirely by tax considerations. To make the election, a corporation must meet certain eligibility requirements. The major requirements are as follows:

S corporation
a type of corporation that is taxed as a partnership

C corporation
a type of corporation that is taxed as a separate legal entity

- No more than 35 stockholders are allowed. Husband and wife count as one stockholder.
- All stockholders must be individuals or certain qualifying estates and trusts.
- There can be only one class of stock outstanding.
- It must be a domestic corporation.
- There can be no nonresident alien stockholders.
- The S corporation cannot own more than 79 percent of the stock of another corporation.

Once S status is elected by a corporation, it stops paying corporate income taxes and instead passes taxable income or loss to the stockholders. This allows stockholders to receive dividends from the corporation without double taxation on the corporation's profit—once as corporate tax and again as personal tax.

The 1986 Tax Reform Act has had considerable effect on the S corporation arrangement. Therefore, a competent tax attorney should be consulted before making the S status election. A sample of the limitations of S corporation status under the tax regulations are as follows:[6]

1. Except for certain exceptions, an S corporation must use the calendar year for tax reporting.
2. Only stockholder employees owning less than 5 percent of the S corporation can borrow from the corporation's pension and profit-sharing plans.
3. Medical-plan premiums paid by the S corporation and other fringe benefits received by stockholder employees are taxable income.
4. An S corporation may be required to pay corporate tax if its passive income exceeds 25 percent of gross receipts.

Despite these and other limitations, the S corporation has been particularly desirable because of tax advantages. Namely, the tax rates in the 1980s and early 1990s were lower for individuals than for C corporations. However, with the 1993 tax law changes, the tax rates for high-income individuals, including many owners of S corporations, are now higher than C corporation tax rates—thus decreasing the attractiveness of the S corporation.

CRITERIA FOR CHOOSING THE OWNERSHIP FORM

It should be apparent by now that it is not easy to choose the best form of ownership. A number of criteria must be considered, and some tradeoffs are necessary. Table 11-2 on pages 286 and 287 provides an overview of the more important criteria. The bottom row in the exhibit suggests a favored form of business organization, given the particular list of factors shown above. In examining the exhibit, the following observations are offered:

1. *Organizational costs.* The initial organizational costs increase as the formality of the organization increases. That is, sole proprietorships are typically less expensive to form than partnerships, and partnerships are usually less expensive to create than the corporation. However, this consideration is of minimum importance in the long term.
2. *Limited versus unlimited liability.* The sole proprietorship and the general partnership have the inherent disadvantage of unlimited liability. For these organizations, there is no distinction between business assets and the owner's personal assets. The creditors lending money to the business can require the owners to sell personal assets if the firm is financially unable to repay its loans. In contrast, both the limited partnership and the corporation limit the owner's liability to his or her investment in the company. However, if a corporation is small, its president is often required to guarantee a loan personally.
3. *Continuity.* The sole proprietorship is immediately dissolved upon the owner's death. Likewise, the general partnership is terminated upon the death or

withdrawal of a partner, unless stated otherwise in the partnership agreement. The corporation, on the other hand, offers the greatest degree of continuity. The status of the investor does not affect the corporation's existence.

4. *Transferability of ownership.* The ability to transfer ownership between persons is intrinsically neither good nor bad. Its desirability depends largely on the owners' preferences. In certain businesses, the owners may want the option to evaluate any prospective new investors. In other circumstances, unrestricted transferability may be preferred.

5. *Control.* The sole proprietor has absolute control of the firm. Control within the general partnership is normally based on the majority vote. An increase in the number of partners reduces each partner's voice in management. With the limited partnership, there is a separation of ownership from control. The general partner controls the firm's operations, but the limited partners generally have most of the ownership. Within the corporation, the control factor has two dimensions: (1) the formal control vested in the stockholders having the majority of the voting common shares, and (2) the functional control exercised by the corporate officers in conducting the daily operations. For the small corporation, these two controls usually rest in the same individuals.

6. *Raising new equity capital.* The corporation has a distinct advantage in raising new equity capital, owing to the ease of transferring ownership through the sale of common shares and the flexibility in dividing the shares. In contrast, the unlimited liabilities of the sole proprietorship and the general partnership deter raising equity capital from new investors. Between these extremes, the limited partnership does provide limited liability for the limited partners. This feature has a tendency to attract wealthy investors. However, the impracticality of having a large number of partners and the difficulty often encountered in selling an interest in a partnership makes the limited partnership less attractive than the corporation for raising large amounts of new equity capital.

7. *Income taxes.* Income taxes frequently have a major effect on an owner's selection of a legal business form. The sole proprietorship, partnership, and S corporation are not taxed as separate entities; the owners report business profits on their personal tax returns. The earnings from the company are taxable to the owner, regardless of whether these profits have been paid out to the owner. On the other hand, the C corporation is taxed as a separate and distinct entity. The corporation income is taxed again if and when it is distributed to the shareholder in the form of dividends.

The foregoing factors represent the main considerations in selecting a form of ownership. However, the relationship between income taxes and the legal form of ownership make it an especially important factor in choosing the legal form of ownership. In the next section, we will look more closely at taxes, particularly as they relate to the legal form of ownership.

Form of Organization	Organizational Requirements and Costs	Liability of the Owners	Continuity of the Business
Sole proprietorship	Minimum requirements: Generally no registration or filing fee.	Unlimited liability.	Dissolved upon proprietor's death.
General partnership	Minimum requirements; Generally no registration or filing fee. Written partnership agreement not legally required but is strongly suggested.	Unlimited liability.	Unless partnership agreement specifies differently, dissolved upon withdrawal or death of partner.
Limited partnership	Moderate requirements; Written certificate must be filed; must comply with state law.	General partners: Unlimited liability.	General partners: Same as general partnership.
		Limited partners: Liability limited to investment in company.	Limited partners: Withdrawal or death does not affect continuity of business.
Corporation	Most expensive and greatest requirements: Filing fees; compliance with state regulations for corporations.	Liability limited to investment in company.	Continuity of business unaffected by shareholder withdrawal or death.
Form of organization normally favored	Proprietorship or general partnership.	Limited partnership or corporation.	Corporation.

Table 11-2
Comparison of Legal Forms of Ownership

FEDERAL INCOME TAXES AND THE LEGAL FORM OF BUSINESS

To understand the income tax system, we must first answer the twofold question, "Who is responsible for paying taxes and how is the taxl liability ascertained?" In business, taxes are paid in the following ways:

1. Self-employed individuals who operate a business as a sole proprietorship report income from the business on their individual tax returns. They are then taxed at the rates set by the legislature for individuals. The present tax rates for a married couple reporting their income jointly are as follows:

Transferability of Ownership	Management Control	Attractiveness for Raising Capital	Income Taxes
May transfer ownership in company name and assets.	Absolute management freedom.	Limited to proprietor's personal capital.	Income from the business is taxed as personal income to the proprietor.
Requires the consent of all partners.	Majority vote of partners required for control.	Limited to partners' ability and desire to contribute capital.	Income from the business is taxed as personal income to the partners.
General partners: Same as general partnership.	General partners: Same as general partnership.	General partners: Same as general partnership.	General partners: Same as general partnership.
Limited partners: May sell interest in the company.	Limited partners: Not permitted any involvement in management.	Limited partners: Limited liability provides a stronger inducement in raising capital.	Limited partners: Same as general partnership.
Easily transferred by transferring shares of stock.	Shareholders have final control, but usually board of directors controls company policies.	Usually the most attractive form for raising capital.	The C corporation is taxed on its income and the stockholder is taxed if and when dividends are received. The S corporation is taxed as a partnership.
Depends upon the circumstances.	Depends upon the circumstances.	Corporation.	Depends upon the circumstances.

Amount of Taxable Income	Tax Rate
$0–$35,800	15%
$35,800–$86,500	28%
$86,500–$140,000	31%
$140,000–$250,000	36%
Over $250,000	36%

For example, assume a sole proprietor, who is married and files a joint return with a spouse, has taxable income of $150,000 from a business. The taxes owed on this income would be $39,751, computed as follows:

Income	×	Tax Rate	=	Taxes
$ 35,800	×	15%	=	$ 5,370
50,700	×	28%	=	14,196
53,500	×	31%	=	16,585
10,000	×	36%	=	3,600
$150,000				$39,751

2. A partnership reports the income it earns to the Internal Revenue Service, but it does not pay any taxes. The income is allocated to the owners according to their agreement. They each report their share of the partnership income on their personal tax returns and pay any taxes owed. So the partnership itself never pays taxes.

3. The corporation, as a separate legal entity, reports its income and pays any taxes related to these profits. The owners (stockholders) of the corporation need not report these earnings on their personal tax returns, except for any amounts paid to them by the corporation in the form of dividends. The current corporate tax rates are as follows:

Amount of Taxable Income	Tax Rate
$0–$50,000	15%
$50,001–$75,000	25%
Over $75,000	35%

An additional 5 percent tax is imposed on taxable income between $100,000 and $335,000.

For example, the tax liability for the T & W Corporation, which had $150,000 in taxable income, would be $42,500, calculated as follows:

Income	×	Tax Rate	=	Taxes
$ 50,000	×	15%	=	$ 7,500
25,000	×	25%	=	6,250
75,000	×	35%	=	26,250
$150,000				$40,000
Plus 5% surtax for income exceeding $100,000 (5% × $150,000–$100,000)				2,500
Total tax liability				$42,500

If the T&W Corporation paid a dividend to its owners in the amount of $40,000, the owners would need to report this dividend income when computing personal income taxes. Thus, we see the $40,000 being taxed twice, first as part of the corporation's income and then as part of the owner's personal income. However, this double taxation would be avoided if the firm were a Subchapter S corporation.

THE BOARD OF DIRECTORS IN SMALL CORPORATIONS

All too often, the majority stockholder (the entrepreneur) in a small corporation appoints a board of directors merely to fulfill a legal requirement. Such owners make little or no use of directors in managing their companies. In fact, an entrepreneur may actively resent efforts of managerial assistance from directors. When appointing directors, the entrepreneur tends to select personal friends, relatives, or other managers who are too busy to analyze situations and are not inclined to argue. In directors' meetings, the entrepreneur and other directors may simply engage in long-winded, innocuous discussions of broad general policies, leaving no time for serious, constructive questions. Some entrepreneurs, however, have found an active board to be both practical and beneficial.[7]

Contribution of Directors

A properly assembled board of directors can bring supplementary knowledge and broad experience to corporate management. The board should meet regularly to provide maximum assistance to the chief executive. Such board meetings should be conferences in which ideas are debated, strategies determined, and the pros and cons of policies explored. In this way, the chief executive is assisted by the experience of all the board members. Their combined knowledge makes possible more intelligent decisions on major issues.

Utilizing the experience of a board of directors does not mean that the chief executive of a small corporation is abdicating active control of its operations. Instead, it means merely that the chief executive is consulting with, and seeking the advice of, the board's members in order to draw upon a larger pool of business knowledge.

An active board of directors serves management in several important ways. The first of these, of course, is the board's review of major policy decisions. There is also the matter of advice on external business conditions and on proper reaction to the business cycle. Moreover, some directors are willing to provide individual advice informally, from time to time, on specific problems that arise. Here objectivity is the most valuable contribution of outside directors.

Outside directors may also serve the small firm by scrutinizing and questioning its ethical standards. S. Kumar Jain notes that "operating executives, without outside directors to question them, may rationalize unethical or illegal behavior as being in the best interest of the company."[8] With a strong board, the small firm gains greater credibility with the public as well as with the business and financial community.

Selection of Board Members

Many sources are available to the owner attempting to assemble a cooperative, experienced, able group of directors. The firm's attorney, banker, accountant,

S M A L L   B U S I N E S S   I N   A C T I O N

Use of Outside Board Members by Small Companies

A recent survey of the fastest-growing U.S. companies showed that most of them make only limited use of outside directors. For example, 43 percent of the companies do not have anyone outside the company serving on the board, and almost 60 percent have fewer than 20 percent of board members coming from outside the company.

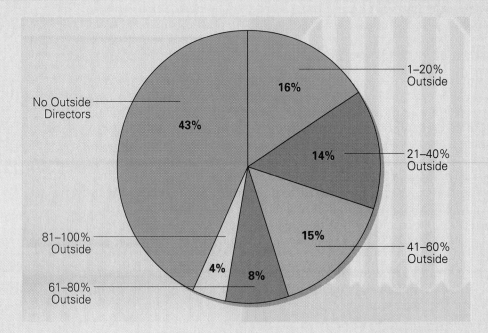

Source: *Inc.*, Vol. 12, No. 10, p. 151. Reprinted with permission, *Inc.* magazine (October 1990). Copyright © 1990 by Goldhirsh Group, Inc., 38 Commercial Wharf, Boston, MA 02110.

other business executives, and local management consultants might all be considered as potential directors. However, such individuals lack the independence needed for critical review of an entrepreneur's plans. Also, the owner is already paying for their expertise. For this reason, the owner needs to consider the value of an outside board—one with members whose income does not depend on the corporation.

SMALL BUSINESS IN ACTION

Outside Directors Are an Asset Inside Small Companies

For many small companies, outside directors, if they exist at all, are compliant and content to rubber-stamp the ideas of their friend, the board chairman. But the perspectives of nonmanagement, nonfamily directors bring fresh and independent thought to important questions for some companies. Kurtz Bros. Inc., a landscape materials business in Cuyahoga Falls, Ohio, is a good example.

When the family members who run it decided to diversify into industrial materials two years ago, they initially forgot to consult the outside directors. When the three non-family board members learned of the plan, "they were pretty tough on us," recalls Lisa Kurtz, the company's president. "They told us we were fracturing our organization, and that we should stick to our knitting," which for Kurtz Bros. consists of selling topsoil, mulch, and other landscaping supplies. The family officers reconsidered and liquidated the new unit.

Source: Eugene Carlson, "Outside Directors Are an Asset Inside Small Companies," *The Wall Street Journal,* October 30, 1992, p. B2. Reprinted by permission of The Wall Street Journal, © 1992 Dow Jones & Company, Inc. All Rights Reserved Worldwide.

The importance of selecting a truly independent group of board members is expressed in these comments:

Probably the strongest argument for adding outsiders to the family business board is to make qualified and objective confidants available to the chief executive. Too many family business directors seek to tell the CEO what he wants to hear. That is understandable if the directors are other family members, employees, or outsiders who depend on the family for income.[9]

The nature of the business and the needs of the firm will help determine the types of director qualifications needed. For example, a firm that faces a marketing problem may benefit greatly from the counsel of a board member with a marketing background. Business prominence in the community is not essential, although it may help give the company credibility and enable it to attract other well-qualified directors.

After deciding upon the qualifications needed, a business owner must seek suitable candidates. Suggestions may be obtained from the firm's accountants, attorney, banker, or other friends in the business community. Owners or managers of other, noncompeting small companies as well as second- and third-level executives in large companies are often willing to accept such positions. Some discreet checking of candidates is appropriate before offering them positions on the board.

Compensation of Directors

The amount of compensation paid to board members varies greatly, and some small firms pay no fees whatever. However, for smaller firms, a board member would generally be paid between $200 and $300 monthly for serving on a board. The commitment usually involves one meeting per month for a morning or afternoon. Board members also work at cultivating relationships within the community, an important activity. For the same services, a mid-sized company with about 500 employees might pay $400 or so per month.

The relatively modest compensation for the service of well-qualified directors suggests that financial compensation is not the only, or perhaps even the primary, motivation in attracting them. Some reasonable compensation appears appropriate, however, if directors are making an important contribution.

An Alternative: An Advisory Council

In recent years, increased attention has been directed to the legal responsibilities of directors. Outside directors may be held responsible for illegal company action even though they are not directly involved in wrongdoing. As a result of such legal pressures, some individuals are now reluctant to accept directorships.

advisory council
a group that advises rather than governs a corporation

One alternative that is used by some small companies is an **advisory council.** Rather than being elected as directors, qualified outsiders are asked to serve as advisers to the company. The group of outsiders then functions in much the same way as a board of directors, except that its actions are advisory only.

The following account illustrates the potential value of an advisory council:

In another case, a seven-year-old diversified manufacturing company incurred its first deficit, which the owner-manager deemed an exception that further growth would rectify. Council members noted, however, that many distant operations were out of control and apparently unprofitable. They persuaded the owner to shrink his business by more than one-half. Almost immediately, the business began generating profits. From its reduced scale, growth resumed—this time soundly planned, financed, and controlled.[10]

The legal liability of members of an advisory council is not completely clear.[11] However, a clear separation of the council from the board of directors is thought to lighten if not eliminate the personal liability of its members. Since it is advisory in nature, it may, consequently, pose less of a threat to the owner and possibly work more cooperatively than a conventional board.

LOOKING BACK

1. Various legal forms of organization are available to organize small businesses. The most common are the proprietorship, the partnership, and the corporation.

2. In a proprietorship the owner receives all profits and bears all losses. The principal limitation of this form is the owner's unlimited liability.

3. A general partnership should be established on the basis of a written partnership agreement. Partners can individually commit the partnership to binding contracts. In a limited partnership, general partners are personally liable for the debts of the business, while limited partners have limited personal liability as long as they do not take an active role in managing the business.

4. Corporations are particularly attractive because of their limited-liability feature. The fact that ownership is easily transferable makes them well suited for combining the capital of numerous owners. S corporations are corporations that enjoy a special tax status that permits them to avoid corporate tax by passing taxable gains and losses to individual stockholders.

5. Boards of directors can contribute to small corporations by offering counsel and assistance to their chief executives. To be most effective, members of the board must be properly qualified and be independent outsiders.

DISCUSSION QUESTIONS

1. Discuss the relative merits of the three major legal forms of organization.
2. Does the concept of limited liability apply to a proprietorship? Why or why not?
3. How does the death of the owner of a proprietorship affect the legal operation of the business?
4. Suppose a partnership is set up and operated without formal articles of partnership. What problems might arise? Explain.
5. What is the purpose of the articles of partnership?
6. Explain why the agency status of business partners is of great importance.
7. How does the death of an owner in a partnership affect the legal operation of the business?
8. What is a limited partnership, and how does it differ from a general partnership?
9. How does the death of an owner affect the legal operation of a corporation?
10. What is typically covered in a corporation charter?
11. What is a Subchapter S corporation, and what is its advantage?
12. Evaluate the three major forms of organization from the standpoint of management control by the owner and the sharing of the firm's profits.
13. How might a board of directors be of real value to management in a small corporation? What are the qualifications essential for a director? Is stock ownership in the firm a prerequisite?
14. What may account for the failure of most small corporations to use boards of directors as more than legal entities or rubber-stamp boards?

15. How do advisory councils differ from boards of directors? Which would you recommend to a small-company owner? Why?

YOU MAKE THE CALL

Situation 1

Ted Green and Mark Stroder became close friends as 16-year-old teenagers while both worked part time for Green's dad in his automotive parts store. After high school, Green went to college and Stroder joined the National Guard Reserve and devoted his efforts to supporting his weekend auto racing habit. Green continued his association with the automotive parts store by buying and managing two of his dad's stores.

In 1993, Green conceived the idea of starting a new business that would rebuild automobile starters, and he asked Stroder to be his partner in the venture. Stroder was somewhat concerned about working with Green because their personalities were so different. Green had been described as "outgoing and enthusiastic" while Stroder was "reserved and skeptical." However, Stroder was out of work at the time, and he agreed to the offer. He set up a small shop behind one of Green's automotive parts stores. Stroder did all the work; Green supplied the cash.

The "partners" realized the immediate need to decide on a legal form of organization. They had agreed to name the business "STARTOVER."

Questions

1. How relevant are the individual personalities to the success of this entrepreneurial team? Do you think Green and Stroder have a chance to survive their "partnership"? Why or why not?
2. Do you think being the same age is an advantage or disadvantage to this team?
3. Which legal form of organization would you propose for STARTOVER? Why?
4. If Stroder and Green decide to incorporate, would they qualify as an S corporation? If so, would you recommend this option? Why or why not?

Situation 2

For years, a small distributor of welding materials followed the practice of most small firms in treating the board of directors as a legal necessity. The board was composed of two co-owners and a retired steel company executive, but it was not a working board. The company was profitable and had been run with informal, traditional management methods.

The majority owner, after attending a seminar, decided that a board might be useful for more than legal or cosmetic purposes. Based on this thinking, he invited two outsiders—both division heads of larger corporations—to join the board. This brought the membership of the board to five and, in the thinking of the majority owner, should open up the business to new ideas.

Questions:
1. Can two outside board members in a group of five make any real difference in the way it operates?
2. Evaluate the owner's choices for board members.
3. What will determine the usefulness or effectiveness of this board? Do you predict that it will be useful? Why?

EXPERIENTIAL EXERCISES

1. Interview an attorney whose practice includes small-business clients. Inquire about the legal considerations in choosing the form of organization for a new business. Report your findings to the class.
2. Interview the owners of a local partnership business. Inquire about their partnership agreements. Report your findings to the class.
3. Interview the owner of a small business in your community. If possible, select one who has recently opened for business. Inquire about what licenses and permits the owner was required to obtain. Report your findings to the class.
4. Discuss with a corporate director, attorney, banker, or business owner the contributions of directors to small firms. Prepare a brief report of your findings. If you discover a particularly well-informed individual, suggest that person to your instructor as a possible speaker.

REFERENCES TO SMALL-BUSINESS PRACTICES

Danco, Leon. "Do Boards of Directors Really Help Small Business?" *Small Business Forum,* Vol. 9, No. 3 (Winter 1991/1992), pp. 88–90.
> This article explains how to use a board of directors to gain the benefit of insights from people outside of the firm.

Hyatt, Joshua. "Reconcilable Differences," *Inc.,* Vol. 13, No. 4 (April 1991), pp. 78–87.
> Describes the problems frequently encountered by individuals who form a partnership. These are rarely matters of basic strategy, but more often small differences that accumulate over time.

Rutman, Gail. "Should You Go Corporate?" *Nation's Business,* Vol. 78, No. 5 (May 1990), pp. 46–48.
> Explains the advantages and disadvantages of an S corporation and looks at the requirements to qualify for this form of legal entity. It provides some good examples to help make the presentation understandable.

Ward, John L. "Recruiting the Board for You," *Family Business,* Vol. 3, No. 1 (Winter 1992), pp. 37–43.
> Explains how to recruit a board that can contribute to the strategic needs of a firm.

ENDNOTES

1. U.S. Internal Revenue Service, *Statistics of Income, Corporation Income Tax Returns, and Statistics of Income Bulletin,* 1991.

2. "The *Inc.* FaxPoll: Are Partners Bad for Business?" *Inc.,* Vol. 14, No. 2 (February 1992), p. 24.

3. Some of the respondents who said the partnership was a bad way to run a business did find some redeeming qualities of a partnership. In like manner, the advocates for a partnership did note some inherently bad qualities. Thus, the matter is not simply black and white.

4. Ordinary income is income earned in the ordinary course of business, as well as earned income, such as salary. Capital gains and losses are gains or losses incurred from the sale of property not used in the ordinary course of business. For example, if we sell some Procter & Gamble stock that we own, any gain or loss from the sale is defined by the tax laws as a capital gain or loss, depending on whether we sell it for more or less than what we paid for the stock. For tax purposes, any capital losses may only be deducted from capital gains and may not be shown as a deduction against ordinary income. However, 1244 stock is an exception where any capital loss may be deducted against ordinary income.

5. Stock may be either preferred stock or common stock; however, we only consider common stock for now. Small firms seldom issue preferred stock.

6. Based on discussions in Ted S. Frost, "Opting for 'S' Status," *D & B Reports,* November/December 1987, p. 6.

7. For a number of excellent articles on boards of directors for small firms, see the special issue of *Family Business Review,* Vol. 1, No. 3 (Fall 1988).

8. S. Kumar Jain, "Look to Outsiders to Strengthen Small Business Boards," *Harvard Business Review,* Vol. 58, No. 4 (July–August 1980), p. 166.

9. Gardner W. Heidrick, "Selecting Outside Directors," *Family Business Review,* Vol. 1, No. 3 (Fall 1988), p. 271. Copyright 1988 by Jossey-Bass Inc., Publishers.

10. Harold W. Fox, "Growing Concerns: Quasi-boards—Useful Small Business Confidants," *Harvard Business Review,* Vol. 60, No. 1 (January–February 1982), p. 164.

11. Fred A. Tillman, "Commentary on Legal Liability: Organizing the Advisory Council," *Family Business Review,* Vol. 1, No. 3 (Fall 1988), pp. 287–288.

PART 4

Small Business Marketing

Consumer Behavior and Product/Service Strategy

SPOTLIGHT ON SMALL BUSINESS

A carefully planned focus strategy helps new firms achieve competitive advantage. However, problems can arise when inexperienced entrepreneurs embark on new growth strategies. This happened to Bob and Susan Goldstein after they built Lick Your Chops, Inc., a tiny Yorktown Heights store, into a successful pet-food chain. The firm grew from one store in 1979 to six stores ten years later. Two years later, the Goldsteins had resigned as the company's top officers. What happened?

The Goldsteins began their business by targeting a special market niche—customers who needed a dog food to prevent and help treat animal illness. Veterinarian Bob Goldstein and his wife "got the idea after he concocted a diet of brown rice, vegetables, fresh meat, mineral-free water, and vitamins that healed their golden retriever's crippling arthritis." Financing for their startup came from the sale of their veterinary clinic, a home-equity loan, and a small group of outside investors.

Bob and Susan Goldstein

These financial backers persuaded the Goldsteins to shift their marketing emphasis from retail stores to a direct-mail delivery service. A year later the unprofitable home-delivery program was abandoned for another new focus—wholesale distribution. Although sales from the wholesaling operation grew quickly, the company still lost money. The Goldsteins "knew little about the highly competitive, low-margin wholesale-food market. And, they now acknowledge, they made serious mistakes." Unfortunately, most of the capital for these new marketing efforts came from a single outside investor who eventually acquired ownership of the company. In February, 1991, this investor forced the Goldsteins to resign.

One year later, the Goldsteins started over with a venture called Earth Animal —a retail health-food store for pets in Westport, Connecticut. The Goldsteins say, ". . . they have learned not to wander. Focus is so key."

Source: Michael Selz, "Losing Control," *The Wall Street Journal* (October 16, 1992), pp. R6 and R7. Reprinted by permission of *The Wall Street Journal*, © 1992 Dow Jones & Company, Inc. All Rights Reserved Worldwide.

After studying this chapter, you should be able to:
1. Explain three concepts of consumer behavior.
2. Identify product strategies for small business.
3. Name and explain two tools for strategy management.
4. Discuss ways of completing a firm's total bundle of satisfaction.

LOOKING AHEAD

evaluative criteria	attitude	product line
evoked set	culture	product item
cognitive dissonance	social classes	product mix consistency
needs	reference group	product strategy
perception	opinion leader	brand
perceptual categorization	product	warranty
motivations	product mix	

NEW TERMS AND CONCEPTS

In Chapter 8, Building the Marketing Plan, we examined several marketing considerations which have a direct impact on creating sales—adopting a marketing philosophy, collecting marketing information, and determining market potential. We also presented an outline of the components of a comprehensive marketing plan—product/service strategy, pricing strategy, promotional strategy, and distribution strategy. This part of the book (Chapters 12–15) develops each of these components more fully.

This chapter begins by examining concepts of consumer behavior. This discussion is followed by an analysis of product strategies for small firms. Finally, we discuss the elements of a firm's product/service mix which complete a firm's total bundle of satisfaction. As you read and study this chapter, remember that all components of a marketing strategy begin and end with customer satisfaction.

CONCEPTS OF CONSUMER BEHAVIOR

The small-business manager must understand certain realities of consumer behavior. This is, however, a difficult task because the subject matter is complex. The following presentation isolates only essential concepts for the small-business situation. The most successful small-business manager of the future may well be the best student of consumer behavior! Figure 12-1 contains a model of consumer behavior structured around three major topics: decision-making processes, psychological concepts, and sociological concepts.

Figure 12-1
Simplified Con-
sumer Behavior
Model

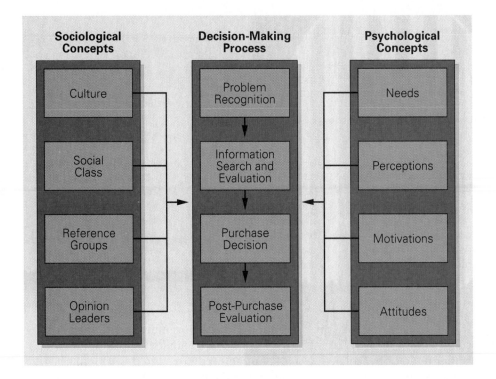

Consumer Decision Making

One theory about human information processing holds that humans are problem solvers. According to this theory, the stages of consumer decision making are:

1. Problem recognition.
2. Information search and evaluation.
3. Purchase decision.
4. Post-purchase evaluation.

We will use this framework to examine consumer decision making.[1]

Problem Recognition. A consumer must recognize his or her "problem" before purchase behavior is begun. This process cannot be avoided. As obvious as this should be, many small firms appear to develop marketing strategy as if consumers are functioning at later stages. In reality, the consumers may have not yet recognized a problem!

A generally accepted definition of problem recognition is "the mental state of a consumer where a significant difference is recognized between his or her current state of affairs and some ideal state." Figure 12-2 depicts the problem-definition state. Some "problems" are simply routine conditions of depletion,

Figure 12-2
Components of the Problem Recognition State

such as the need for food when lunch time arrives. Other problems occur much less frequently and may evolve slowly over time. The desire to replace the family automobile, for example, may take many years.

There are many factors that influence the recognition of a problem by consumers. Some of these influence the actual state of affairs, and others influence the desired state. A few examples are:

1. Changing financial status.
2. Household characteristics.
3. Normal depletion.
4. Product/service performance.
5. Past decisions.
6. Availability of products.

Once a market's problem recognition situation is understood, the entrepreneur can decide what marketing strategy is appropriate. In some situations, the small firm manager will need to *influence* problem recognition. For example, consider the situation facing Bron-Shoe Company. This family-owned firm has been bronzing baby shoes for over 60 years, but today's "upscale parents now view such keepsakes as passé. Instead, they buy camcorders to preserve the memories of a video generation." Bron-Shoe is trying to influence consumers' desired state by contracting with independent sales representatives to go door-to-door to increase visibility of its product.[2]

In other situations, the small-firm manager will simply *react* to problem recognition. This is what Safeguard Business Systems, Inc., is doing. It is moving from marketing only manual accounting systems materials—such as its

One-Write check writing systems—into selling computer forms and accounting software to their small-business customers.[3] Research shows that small-business owners are continually recognizing how the state of their actual accounting system is not "up to" their desired state. This creates demand that Safeguard can pursue.

Information Search and Evaluation. The second stage in the consumer decision process involves consumers' activities to collect and evaluate appropriate information from both internal and external sources. The principal goal of search activity is to establish **evaluative criteria**—the features or characteristics of products or services which are used to compare brands. The small-firm manager should understand which evaluative criteria are most likely to be selected by customers.

Evoked set is the term used to describe brands which a person is both aware of and also willing to consider as a solution to a purchase problem. The initial challenge for the new firm is to gain market *awareness* for its products or services. Only then is it possible for the brand to enter the consumer's evoked set.

Consider the awareness challenge facing entrepreneur Sheryl Leach, the creator of the video character Barney the Dinosaur. She has learned that breaking into a stronghold of world-famous names such as Big Bird and Winnie-the-

evaluative criteria
the features of products that are used to compare brands

evoked set
brands that a person is both aware of and willing to consider as a solution to a purchase problem

Figure 12-3
TV Show *Barney and Friends* Exemplifies the Importance of Gaining Market Awareness

Pooh is a major awareness problem. Her small firm produced three kids' videos in 1988 featuring the Barney character which were distributed to Toys "R" Us stores, but sitting on the shelf next to Disney and Sesame Street videos, "the [Barney] tapes mostly gathered dust. What we didn't realize is that exposure is so important," Ms. Leach said. She later used a free distribution of videos to area preschools and day-care centers. Sales started up immediately. By 1991 sales had surpassed $3.2 million. Currently, Barney is the star of PBS's *Barney and Friends*.[4]

The decision process to buy a new product will naturally take longer than decision activities involving a known product. For example, an industrial-equipment dealer may find it necessary to call on a prospective new customer for a new product over a period of months before making the first sale.

Purchase Decisions. Once consumers have evaluated brands in their evoked set and made their choice, they must still decide on how and where to make the purchase. A substantial volume of retail sales now come from non-store settings such as catalog and television shopping. These outlets have created a complex and challenging environment within which to develop a marketing strategy—particularly distribution decisions. Consumers recognize many different advantages and disadvantages to alternate shopping outlets. This makes it difficult for the small firm to devise correct strategy. Sometimes, however, a simple recognition of these factors can be helpful. Consider the following profile of in-home shopping.[5]

Advantages

- Time savings: may reduce shopping and travel time.
- Time flexibility: can generally be done at any time of the day.
- Effort savings: less physical effort of travel, driving, and so forth.
- Psychological convenience: no frustrations with clerks, crowds, parking.
- Social risk reduction: no embarrassment when buying personal items or appearing "dumb" or "vain" to salespeople and others.
- Wide assortment: catalogs often have a much wider assortment than many stores.
- Entertainment: television shopping and, to a lesser extent, catalog shopping may be viewed as entertaining or fun.

Disadvantages

- Gratification delay: delivery takes time.
- Reduced social contacts: store shopping provides social contacts that many enjoy.
- Reduced personal attention: in-home shopping can seldom provide one-on-one advice (except for door-to-door sales such as Avon).
- Increased product risk: one cannot physically examine items.
- Difficulty in comparing brands.

Of course, not every purchase decision is planned *prior* to entering a store or looking at a mail-order catalog. Studies have shown that over 50 percent of most purchases from traditional retail outlets are not decided prior to entering the store. This behavior places tremendous importance on store layout, sales personnel, point-of-purchase displays, and so forth.

Post-Purchase Evaluation. The consumer-decision process does not terminate with a purchase. A small firm that desires repeat purchases from customers—and they all should—needs to understand post-purchase behavior.[6] There are several consumer activities during post-purchase evaluation. This process is depicted in Figure 12-4. We will briefly comment on two of these activities—post-purchase dissonance and consumer complaints.

 cognitive dissonance the tension that occurs when a customer has "second thoughts" after a purchase

Post-purchase dissonance is commonly called **cognitive dissonance.** This is the tension occurring *immediately* following a purchase decision. It exists where customers have "second thoughts" as to the wisdom of a purchase. This anxiety is obviously uncomfortable to consumers and, if left "untreated," may negatively influence product evaluation and customer satisfaction. Small firms need to manage cognitive dissonance among their customers in whatever way is effective. This is what Clarke Otten, president of Professional Swedish Car Repair in Atlanta, Georgia, does with his customers. He allocates an hour or more each day to telephone recent customers to find out if they are happy with the car-repair service they received.[7]

In Chapter 3, it was noted that U.S. consumers frequently experience dissatisfaction in their relationships with businesses. What do these consumers do when they are displeased? Figure 12-5 shows that consumers have several options when dealing with their dissatisfaction. Six of the seven options threaten repeat sales. Only one—a private complaint to the offending business—is desirable. These odds are not encouraging. It does, once again, emphasize the importance of quality customer service—both before and after a sale. One source contends that "ninety-one percent of all dissatisfied customers will not buy again and each one will tell at least nine other people about their bad experience."[8]

Psychological Concepts

Figure 12-4
Post-Purchase Activities of Consumer

The next component of our consumer behavior model contains psychological concepts. Psychological factors in consumer behavior models may be labeled as

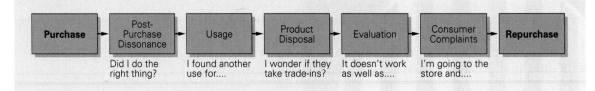

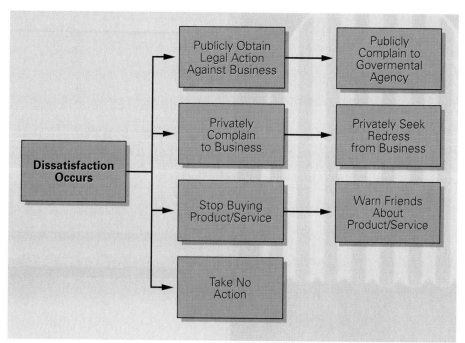

Figure 12-5
Avenues to Deal with Product/Service Dissatisfaction

Source: Adapted from J. Singh, "Consumer Complaint Intentions and Behavior," *Journal of Marketing* (January 1988), pp. 93–107.

hypothetical because they cannot be seen or touched. By the process of inference, however, several factors have been identified. The four factors, as shown in Figure 12-1, page 300, that have the greatest relevance to small business are needs, perceptions, motivations, and attitudes.

Needs. We define **needs** as the basic seeds of (and the starting point for) all behavior. Without needs, there would be no behavior. There are many lists of consumer needs, but the major points we wish to convey do not require an extensive listing.[9] Needs are either physiological, social, psychological, or spiritual.

needs
the starting point for all behavior

Needs are never completely satisfied. This favorable characteristic of needs assures the continued existence of business. A complicating characteristic of needs is the way they function together in generating behavior. In other words, various "seeds" (remember the definition) can blossom together. This makes it more difficult to understand which need is being satisfied by a specific product or service. Nevertheless, a careful assessment of the need-behavior connection can be very helpful in developing marketing strategy. For example, many food products in supermarkets are purchased by consumers to satisfy physiological needs. But food is also selected in status restaurants to satisfy social and/or psychological needs. A need-based strategy would add a different flavor to the marketing strategy in each of these two situations.

Figure 12-6
Psychological and
Social Needs Play
an Important Role in
Consumer
Purchases. These
Young Women
Model the Latest in
Teenage Fashion,
the "Grunge" Look

perception
the individual
processes that give
meaning to the stim-
uli that confront
consumers

**perceptual
categorization**
the perceptual
process of grouping
similar things to
manage huge quan-
tities of incoming
stimuli

Perception. Our second psychological factor is perception. **Perception** describes those individual processes which ultimately give meaning to the stimuli
that confront consumers. The "meaning" is not easily understood, however. It
may be severely distorted or entirely blocked. Perception by customers can
screen a small firm's marketing effort and make it ineffective.

Perception is a two-sided coin. It depends on the characteristics of both the
stimulus and the perceiver. For example, it is known that consumers attempt to
manage huge quantities of incoming stimuli by a process of **perceptual categorization.** This means that things that are similar are perceived as belonging together. Therefore, if a small business wishes to position its product alongside an
existing brand and have it accepted as a comparable product, its marketing mix
should reflect an awareness of perceptual categorization. A similar price can be
used to communicate similar quality. A package design with a similar color
scheme may also be used to convey the identical meaning. These techniques will
help the customer fit the new product into the desired product category.

Firms that select a family brand name for a new product rely on perceptual
categorization to "presell" the new product. On the other hand, if the new
product is generically different or of a different quality, a unique brand name
may be selected to avoid perceptual categorization.

If an individual has strong brand loyalty to a product, it is difficult for other
brands to penetrate that person's perceptual barriers. Competing brands will

likely experience distorted images because of the individual's attitude. The perceptual mood presents a unique communication challenge.

Motivations. Unsatisfied needs create tension within an individual. When this tension reaches a certain level, a person becomes uncomfortable and attempts to reduce the tension.

We are all familiar with "hunger pains." These are manifestations of tension created by an unsatisfied physiological need. What is it that directs a person to seek food so the "hunger pains" can be relieved? The answer is motivation. **Motivations** are goal-directed forces within humans that organize and give direction to tension caused by unsatisfied needs. Marketers cannot create needs, but they can create and offer unique motivations to consumers. If an acceptable reason for purchasing is provided, it will probably be internalized as a motivating force. The key for the marketer is to determine which motivation the consumer will perceive as an acceptable solution for the "hunger pains." The answer is found in analyzing the other consumer behavior variables.

motivations
forces that give direction and organization to the tension of unsatisfied needs

Each of the other three classes of needs—social, psychological, and spiritual—is similarly connected to behavior via motivations. For example, when a person's social needs create tension due to incomplete satisfaction, a firm may show how its product can fulfill those needs by providing acceptable social motivations to that person. A campus clothing store might promote the styles that communicate that a college student has obtained group membership.

Understanding motivations is not easy. Several motives may be present in each situation. Many times the motivations are subconscious, but they must be investigated if the marketing effort is to have an improved chance for success.

Attitudes. Like the other psychological variables, attitudes cannot be observed, but all persons know that they have attitudes. Do attitudes imply knowledge? Do they imply a feeling of good/bad or favorable/unfavorable? Does an attitude have a direct impact on behavior? If you answered "yes" to all these questions, you were correct each time. An **attitude** is an enduring opinion that is based on a combination of knowledge, feeling, and behavioral tendency.

attitude
an enduring opinion based on a combination of knowledge, feeling, and behavioral tendency

An attitude can be an obstacle or a catalyst in bringing a customer to your product. Armed with an understanding of the structure of an attitude, the marketer can approach the consumer more intelligently.

Sociological Concepts

The last component of our consumer behavior model covers sociological concepts. Among these social influences are culture, social class, reference groups, and opinion leaders. Notice that each of the sociological concepts in Figure 12-1 on page 300 represents different degrees of people aggregation. Starting with culture, we see large masses of people. Then we see smaller groups—social classes and reference groups—until we find a single individual who exerts influence, the opinion leader.

culture
a group's social heritage, including behavior patterns and values

Culture. A group's social heritage is called its **culture.** This heritage has a tremendous impact on the purchase and use of products. Marketing managers will often overlook the cultural variable because its influences are so neatly concealed within the society. Cultural influence is somewhat like the presence of air. You really do not think about its function until you are in water over your head! Then you realize the role that air has played in your existence. On the other hand, international marketers who have experienced more than one culture can readily attest to the reality of cultural influence.

It is the prescriptive nature of culture that most concerns the marketing manager. Cultural norms create a range of product-related, acceptable behavior that influences consumers in what they buy. Culture does change, however. It adapts slowly to new situations. Therefore, what works today as a marketing strategy may not work a few years later.

An investigation of culture with a narrower definitional boundary, such as age, religious preference, ethnic orientation, or geographical location, is called *subcultural analysis.* Here, too, the unique patterns of behavior and social relationships concern the marketing manager. For example, the needs and motivations of the youth subculture are far different from those of the senior-citizen subculture. Certain food preferences are unique to Jewish culture. If small-business managers familiarize themselves with cultures and subcultures, they can prepare better marketing mixes.

social classes
divisions in a society with different levels of social prestige

Social Class. Another sociological concept in consumer behavior is social class. **Social classes** describe divisions in a society with different levels of social prestige. There are important implications for marketing in a social-class system. Different life-styles correlate with the different levels of social prestige, and products are often symbols of life-styles.

Unlike a caste system, a social-class system provides for upward mobility. The status position of parents does not permanently fix the social class of their child. Occupation is probably the single most important determinant of social class. Other determinants that are used in social-class research include possessions, source of income, and education.

For some products, such as consumer packaged goods, social-class analysis will probably not be very useful. For others, such as home furnishings, it may help to explain variations in shopping and communication patterns.

reference group
a group that influences individual behavior

Reference Groups. Although social class could, by definition, be considered to be a reference group, we are more generally concerned with small groups such as the family, the work group, a neighborhood group, or a recreational group. Not every group is a reference group. **Reference groups** are only those groups from which an individual allows influence to be exerted upon his or her behavior.

The existence of group influence is well established. The challenge to the marketer is to understand why this influence occurs and how the influence can be used to promote the sale of a product. Individuals tend to accept group influence for the benefits perceived. These perceived benefits allow the influencers to use various kinds of power. Five widely recognized forms of power are reward, coercive, expert, referent, and legitimate. Each of these power forms is available to the marketer.

Reward power and coercive power relate to a group's ability to give and to withhold rewards. Rewards can be material or psychological. Recognition and praise are typical psychological rewards. A Tupperware party is a good example of a marketing technique that takes advantage of reward power and coercive power. The ever-present possibility of pleasing or displeasing the hostess-friend tends to encourage the guest to buy.

Referent power and expert power involve neither rewards nor punishments. These types of power exist because an individual attaches a unique importance to being like the group or perceives the group as being in a more knowledgeable position than the individual. Referent power causes consumers to conform to the group's behavior and to choose products selected by the group's members. Children will often be influenced by referent power. Marketers can create a desire for products by using cleverly designed advertisements or packages.

Also, consider the strategy of BertSherm Products, Inc., which markets Fun 'n Fresh deodorant sticks targeted to seven- to twelve-year-olds. Cleveland, Ohio, entrepreneur Philip B. Davis has been selling his product with a campaign, "Be Cool in School." Children admit they purchase the deodorant not because of body odor but rather because the deodorant makes them feel like an adult.[10]

Legitimate power involves the sanction of what one ought to do. We saw legitimate power at the cultural level when we talked about the prescriptive nature of culture. This type of power can also be used at a smaller group level.

Opinion Leaders. The concept of opinion leaders is largely a communication idea. According to this concept, consumers receive a significant amount of information through individuals called opinion leaders. Thus, an **opinion leader** is a group member playing a key communications role.

Generally speaking, opinion leaders are knowledgeable, visible, and exposed to the mass media. A small-business firm can enhance its own product and image by identifying with such leaders. For example, a farm-supply dealer may promote agricultural products in a community by arranging demonstrations on the farms of outstanding farmers. These farmers are the community's opinion leaders. Also, department stores may use attractive students as models in showing campus fashions.

opinion leader
a group leader who plays a key communications role

PRODUCT STRATEGIES FOR SMALL BUSINESS

Small-business managers are often weak in their understanding of product strategy issues. This creates ineffectiveness and conflict in the marketing effort. The following sections examine product strategy terminology and alternatives.

Product/Service Terminology

There is confusion in marketing circles regarding the language of marketing strategy. In particular, some authors challenge the usage of the phrase "product marketing" to include services. Traditionally, marketers have used the word "product" as a generic term describing both goods and services. More recently, there has been a debate that goods marketing and services marketing are distinctly different.

This debate is relevant to our discussion of strategy because there is a favorable future for small business in the services sector. Consider the assessment of one researcher:

Over half of all service-sector employment and output now originates in 5.5 million small businesses, which account for 99 percent of the sector's enterprises. In addition, the service sector is assuming an increasingly significant role in U.S. economic growth, accounting for 76 percent of the work force. . . .[11]

When we examine this debate, we find that the argument for a significant distinction between the two takes place on several dimensions. As shown in Figure 12-7, these dimensions are tangibility, production and consumption time separation, and standardization.[12] For example, a pencil would fit the "pure goods" end of the scale and a haircut would fit the "pure services" end. The major implication of this debate is that services present challenges to strategy development that are different from those of goods.

Although we recognize the benefit of examining the marketing of services as a unique form of marketing, space limitations in this book require us to include the services area within the more comprehensive category of product marketing. A **product,** then, will be considered to include the total "bundle of

product
the "bundle of satisfaction" offered to customers in an exchange transaction

Figure 12-7
Contrast of Services and Goods Marketing

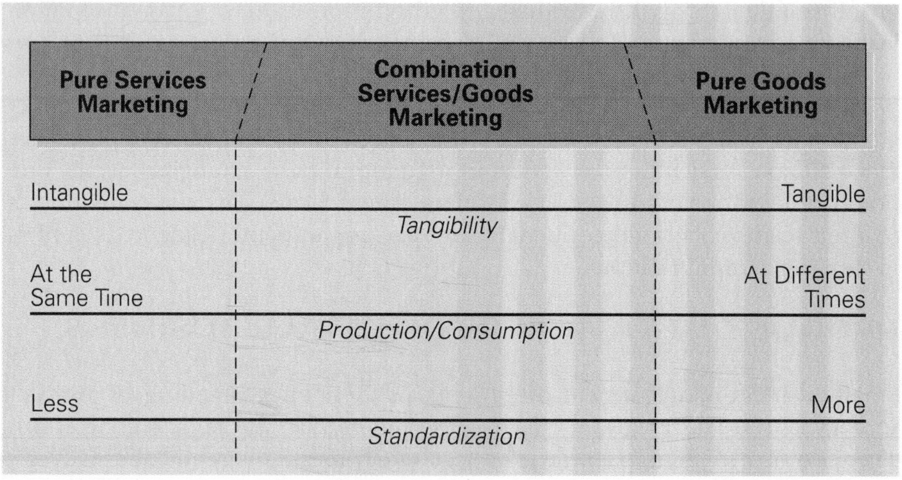

Pure Services Marketing	Combination Services/Goods Marketing	Pure Goods Marketing
Intangible	*Tangibility*	Tangible
At the Same Time	*Production/Consumption*	At Different Times
Less	*Standardization*	More

"satisfaction" that is offered to customers in an exchange transaction—whether it be a good or a service.

Such a product includes not only the main element of the "bundle," which is the physical product itself, but also complementary components such as packaging. Of course, the physical product is usually the most important component. But sometimes the main element of a product is perceived by customers to be like that of all other products. The complementary components can then become the most important features of the product. For example, a particular cake mix brand may be preferred by consumers, not because it is a better mix, but because of the toll-free telephone number on the package that can be called for baking hints.

A **product mix** is the collection of product lines within a firm's ownership and control. A **product line** is the sum of the individual product items that are related. The relationship is usually defined generically. Two brands of bar soap would be two product items in one product line. A **product item** is the lowest common denominator in a product mix. It is the individual item.

The more items in a product line, the more depth it has. The more product lines in a product mix, the greater the breadth of the product mix. **Product mix consistency** refers to the closeness, or similarity, of the product lines. **Product strategy** describes the manner in which the product component of the marketing mix is used to achieve the objectives of a firm.

product mix
a firm's total product lines

product line
the sum of the individual product items that are related

product item
the lowest common denominator in the product mix—the individual item

product mix consistency
the similarity of product lines

product strategy
the way a product is used to achieve a firm's objectives

Product Strategy Alternatives

The overall product strategy alternatives of a small business can be grouped into the following eight categories:

1. Initial product/initial market.
2. Initial product/new market.
3. Modified product/initial market.
4. Modified product/new market.
5. New related product/initial market.
6. New related product/new market.
7. New unrelated product/initial market.
8. New unrelated product/new market.

Each alternative represents a different approach to product strategy. Some strategies can be pursued concurrently. Usually, however, the small firm will find that it will pursue the alternatives in basically the order listed above. Keep this premise in mind as you read about each one. Figure 12-8 displays each of these strategies in matrix format.

Initial Product/Initial Market. In the earliest stage of a new venture, the "initial product/initial market" product strategy is followed. Most entrepreneurs start with one product. Growth can be achieved under this strategy in

Product Dimension

Market Dimension		Initial Product	Modified Product	New *Related* Product	New *Unrelated* Product
	Initial Market Segment	**1.** Convince current customers to use more. Find new customers within the same market. Promote new uses for the product.	**3.** Convince current customers to use more. Find new customers within the same market. Promote new uses for the product.	**5.** Convince current customers to use more. Find new customers within the same market. Promote new uses for the product.	**7.** Convince current customers to use more. Find new customers within the same market. Promote new uses for the product.
	New Market Segment	**2.** Convince current customers to use more. Find new customers within the same market. Promote new uses for the product.	**4.** Convince current customers to use more. Find new customers within the same market. Promote new uses for the product.	**6.** Convince current customers to use more. Find new customers within the same market. Promote new uses for the product.	**8.** Convince current customers to use more. Find new customers within the same market. Promote new uses for the product.

Note: The three substrategies —"Convince current customers to use more," "Find more customers," and "Promote new uses for product"— are identical strategies applied within separate target markets.

Figure 12-8
Product Strategy Matrix

three ways. First, current customers can be encouraged to use more of the product. Second, new customers within the same market can be sold on the product. Third, current customers can be educated to use the existing product for additional purposes, thereby increasing demand. An example is Minnetonka's Softsoap, which was originally positioned as a replacement for bar soap. More recently, it has been promoted as a gift item and a skin-care product. As indicated in Figure 12-8, these same three growth strategies can be applied within each of the remaining target markets.

Initial Product/New Market. An extension of the first alternative is the "initial product/new market" product strategy. With a small additional commitment in resources, a current product can often be targeted to a new market. Taking a floor-cleaning compound from the commercial market into the home market would be an example. Marketing the same product abroad after first selling it domestically would also be an example of this strategy.

Modified Product/Initial Market. Customers seemingly anticipate the emergence of "new, improved" products. With the "modified product/initial market" strategy, the existing product can be either replaced, gradually phased out, or left in the product mix. If the existing product is to be retained, the impact on sales of the modified product must be carefully assessed. It does little good to make an existing product obsolete unless the modified product has a larger profit margin. The product modification can involve a very minor change. For example, adding colored specks to a detergent can give the product a "new" and sales-attractive appeal. Some people, of course, would question the social value of such "improvements."

Another example of modifying an existing product for the same target market is found in the Saf-T-Loc brake. This design, for supermarket shopping carts, was developed by Steve Kovac. When his brake is attached to the wheels, the cart can be conveniently secured. Kovac designed the new product in response to studies that indicated more than $100 million of car damage occurs each year from runaway shopping carts in parking lots.[13]

Modified Product/New Market. A modified product can also be used to reach a new market. The only difference in the "modified product/new market" strategy from the previous one is its appeal to a new market segment. For example, a furniture manufacturer currently selling finished furniture to customers might market unfinished furniture to the "do-it-yourself" market.

New Related Product/Initial Market. Current, satisfied customers make good markets for new additions to the product assortment of a small business. Many products can be added that are more than product modifications but are still similar to the existing products. These new products are considered to be similar when they have a generic relationship. For example, Zoom Telephonics originally produced a speed-dialer which was introduced in 1981. Three years later, sales were over $5 million. Changes in the telephone industry depressed its demand among final consumers. However, Zoom has successfully responded with a new related product—a modem.[14]

New Related Product/New Market. Going after a different market with a new but similar product is still another product strategy. This approach is particularly appropriate when there is concern that the new product may reduce sales of the existing product in a current market. For example, a firm producing wood-burning stoves for home use might introduce a new gas-burning furnace targeted for use in office buildings.

As another example, a few cotton farmers are targeting the "green" products market with a new organic cotton—cotton grown with no chemical fertilizers, herbicides, or insecticides.[15] The fiber from this organically grown product is processed by special textile manufacturers and used in unbleached and undyed wearing apparel and mattresses.

New Unrelated Product/Initial Market. A product strategy that includes a new product generically different from existing products can be very

Figure 12-9
Targeting the "Green" Market with Organically Grown Cotton—An Example of the New Related Product-New Market Strategy

risky. However, the "new unrelated product/initial market" strategy is sometimes used by small businesses, especially when the new product fits existing distribution and sales systems. For example, a local dealer selling Italian sewing machines may add a line of microwave ovens.

New Unrelated Product/New Market. The final product strategy occurs when a new unrelated product is added to the product mix to serve a new market. This strategy has the most risk among all the alternatives since the business is attempting to market an unfamiliar product to an unfamiliar market. For example, one electrical equipment service business added a private employment agency.

With this product strategy, however, a hedge can be built against volatile shifts in market demand. If the business is selling snowshoes and suntan lotion, it hopes that demand will be high in one market at all times.

BASIC CONCEPTS FOR STRATEGY MANAGEMENT

The management of the firm's product mix is guided by many considerations. For example, competition, market demand, and pricing flexibility are important influences.

Two marketing concepts are extremely useful to the small-business manager in any efforts to control and develop the firm's product mix. These are the

SMALL BUSINESS IN ACTION

Adding to the Product Line

Most new businesses are launched with a single product or service. When successful, such ventures typically attract competitors. Too often, entrepreneurs are complacent and slow to react to this competition. Others are wiser and embark on a diversification strategy before sales of the initial product begin to level off.

Such was the strategy used by Kevin Howe, president of DacSoftware, based in Dallas, Texas. Its computer software, named Dac-Easy, was launched in 1985. The integrated accounting package was offered on one floppy disk and priced at an unbelievably low $50.00. It was an immediate success! But Howe did not rest easy. He knew the importance of "not falling in love with success."

"I had always been conscious of the perils of being a one-track pony," he says. "With the creation of Dac-Easy, the company had produced its one death-defying act. So the question was what do we do next? How do we keep the momentum going?"

The answer was diversification. His strategy was to keep current customers coming back rather than relying entirely on new customers. Howe now estimates that 40 percent of DacSoftware's

revenues are from repeat customers. Dac-Easy add-ons have been introduced each year.

Howe is pleased with his early diversification strategy and points to an array of products and more than 300,000 customers and says, "I think I'll be the last vendor in my industry to be hurt in a recession."

Source: Adapted from Karen Berney, "If At First You Do Succeed," *Nation's Business,* Vol. 76, No. 6 (June 1988), pp. 14–20. Copyright 1988, U.S. Chamber of Commerce.

product development curve and the product life cycle. Both of these concepts provide concise summaries of activities or circumstances relating to the management of the product mix.

The Product Development Curve

A major responsibility of the entrepreneur is to recognize, prepare, and implement any of the product strategy alternatives discussed earlier. Many of these strategies require a structured mechanism for new-product development. In big business, committees or even entire departments are created for that purpose. In a small business this responsibility will usually rest with the entrepreneur.

The entrepreneur usually views new-product development as a mountainous task. Therefore, we show the product development curve in Figure 12-10 in the form of a mountain. The left slope of the mountain represents the gathering of a large number of ideas. Beginning at the mountain peak, these ideas are screened as you move down the right slope until the base of the mountain—the retention of one product ready to be introduced into the marketplace—is reached. In our discussion, we emphasize product development by manufacturers rather than distributors.

Idea Accumulation. The first phase of the product development curve, labeled *Idea Accumulation,* shows the need to increase the number of ideas under consideration. New products start with new-product ideas, and these ideas have varied origins. Some of the many possible sources of ideas are:

1. Sales, engineering, or other personnel within the firm.
2. Government-owned patents, which are generally available on a royalty-free basis.
3. Privately owned patents listed in the *Official Gazette* of the U.S. Patent Office.
4. Other small companies that may be available for acquisition or merger.

Figure 12-10
The Product
Development Curve

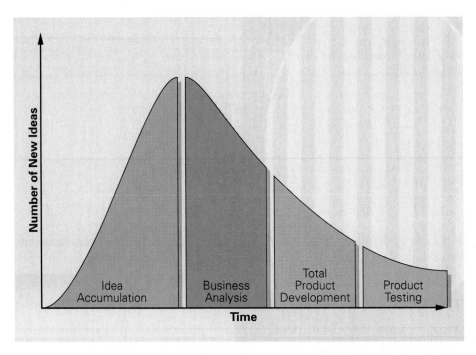

5. Competitors' products and advertising.
6. Requests and suggestions from customers.

Business Analysis. *Business Analysis* is the next stage in the process. Every new-product idea must be carefully analyzed in relation to several considerations.

Relationship to Existing Product Line. Any product to be added should be consistent with, or properly related to, the existing product line. For example, a new product may be designed to fill a gap in the company's product line or in the price range of the products it currently manufactures. If the product is completely new, it should normally have at least a family relationship to existing products. Otherwise, the new products may call for drastic and costly changes in manufacturing methods, distribution channels, type of promotion, or manner of personal selling.

Cost of Development and Introduction. One problem in adding new products is the cost of development and introduction. The capital outlays may be considerable. These include expenditures for design and development, market research to establish sales potential and company volume potential, advertising and sales promotion, patents, and the equipment and tooling that must be added. It may be from one to three years before profits may be realized on the sale of the contemplated new or altered product.

Personnel and Facilities. Obviously, having adequate skilled personnel, managers, and production equipment is better than having to add personnel and buy equipment. Hence, introducing new products is typically more logical if the personnel and the required equipment are already available.

Competition and Market Acceptance. Still another factor to be considered is the character of the market and the potential competition facing the proposed product. Competition must not be too severe. Some authorities, for example, think that new products can be introduced successfully only if a 5 percent share of the total market can be secured. The ideal solution, of course, is to offer a sufficiently different product or one in a cost and price bracket that avoids direct competition.

Total Product Development. The next stage, *Total Product Development,* entails the planning for suitable branding, packaging, and other supporting efforts such as pricing and promotion. After these components are considered, many new-product ideas may be discarded.

Product Testing. The last step in the product development curve is *Product Testing.* This means that the physical product should be proven to perform correctly. While the product can be evaluated in a laboratory setting, a test of market reaction to the total product should also be conducted. This test can be performed only in the marketplace.

The Product Life Cycle

Another valuable concept for managing the product mix is the product life cycle. Our portrayal of the product life cycle in Figure 12-11 takes the shape of a roller-coaster ride. This is actually the way many entrepreneurs describe their experiences with the life cycle of their products. The initial stages are characterized by a slow and upward movement. The stay at the top is exciting but relatively brief. Then, suddenly the decline begins, and the movement down is fast.

The product life cycle gives the small-business manager a valuable planning tool. Promotional, pricing, and distribution policies can all be adjusted to reflect a product's position on the curve.

When a small business is committed to the product development concept, it can look forward to expanding its product mix successfully and to staying above the nemesis of the "roller-coaster ride" pictured in Figure 12-11.

COMPLETING THE TOTAL BUNDLE OF SATISFACTION

A major responsibility of marketing is to transform a basic product into a total product. An idea for a unique new writing pen that has already been developed

Figure 12-11
The Product Life Cycle

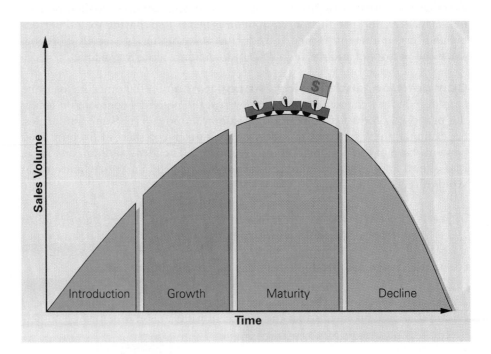

Applying the Product Life Cycle Concept

It is extremely difficult for some entrepreneurs to focus on new-product development while their existing products are selling like hotcakes! These entrepreneurs need to realize that nothing lasts forever and, therefore, preparations should be made for the time when demand slackens. The product life cycle concept is applicable to this problem. One small-business manager who has successfully applied the concept is Thomas L. Venable, chairman of Spectrum Control, in Erie, Pennsylvania. Venable's assessment of the problem is expressed as follows:

It's amazing, isn't it? . . . companies get so caught up pushing products out the door . . .

they're totally unprepared for the moment when demand slackens or a better mousetrap comes along.

Spectrum makes technology-based business products such as "filters" to prevent garage-door openers from activating other home electronic devices. In this industry, change is inevitable. Therefore, Spectrum, under Venable's leadership, has used the product life cycle to plan for new products.

The success of the planning tool at Spectrum Control has been reflected in its earnings. "The whole idea behind the process is to avoid crises," says Venable. "You want to be ready to go with the second product just as the first one is about to die off."

Source: "The Eternal Second Act." Reprinted with permission, *Inc.* magazine (June 1988). Copyright © 1988 by Goldhirsh Group, Inc., 38 Commercial Wharf, Boston, MA 02110.

into a physical reality is still not ready for the marketplace. The total product, in this example, would incorporate more than the materials molded into the shape of the new pen. To be marketable, the basic product must be named, have a package, perhaps have a warranty, and be supported by other product components. We will now examine a few of these components.

Branding

An identification for a product is termed a **brand**. A brand includes both the identification which can be verbalized and that which cannot. The name Xerox is a brand, as are the "golden arches" of McDonald's. A name and a trademark are important to the image of the business and its products. Therefore, considerable attention should be given to every decision in a branding strategy.

In general, there are five rules to follow in naming a product:

1. *Select a name that is easy to pronounce.* You want customers to remember your product. Help them with a name that can be spoken easily. An entrepreneur's own name should be carefully evaluated to be sure it is acceptable.

brand
a verbal or symbolic means of identifying a product

The founder of a major fast-food chain used his daughter's name for the company. Her name? Wendy. The name of the business? Wendy's.

2. *Choose a descriptive name.* A name that is suggestive of the major benefit of the product can be extremely helpful. The name Elephant for a computer memory disk correctly suggests a desirable benefit. The name Rocky Road would be a poor selection for a mattress!

3. *Use a name that can have legal protection.* Be careful that you select a name that can be defended successfully. This is sometimes difficult, but do not risk litigation by copying someone else's brand name. A new soft drink named Prof. Pepper would likely be contested by the Dr Pepper company. An attorney who specializes in trademarks should be hired to run a search for a same or confusingly similar tradename and to register your tradename.

4. *Consider names that have promotional possibilities.* Exceedingly long names are not, for example, compatible with good copy design on billboards, where space is at such a premium. A competitor of the McDonald's hamburger chain is called Wuv's. This name will easily fit on any billboard.

5. *Select a name that can be used on several product lines of a similar nature.* Many times customer goodwill is lost when a name doesn't fit a new line. A company producing a furniture polish called Slick-Surface could not easily use the same name for its new sidewalk surfacing compound which purports to increase traction.

A small business also should carefully select its trademark. The mark should be unique, easy to remember, and related to the product.

Trademark registration for products in interstate commerce is handled through the U.S. Patent and Trademark Office under the authority of the Lanham Trademark Act. This act also covers the registration of service marks, certification marks, and collective marks. Further discussion of trademarks and legal ramifications is deferred to Chapter 26.

Once a trademark is selected by a small business, it is important to protect its use. Two rules can help. One is to be sure the name is not carelessly used in place of the generic name. For example, the Xerox company never wants a person to say that he or she is "xeroxing" something. Second, the business should inform the public that the brand is a brand by labeling it with the symbol ™ or, if the mark has been registered with the Trademark Office, the symbol ®. If the trademark is unusual or written in a special form, it is easier to protect.

Packaging

Packaging is another important part of the total product. In addition to protecting the basic product, packaging is also a significant tool for increasing the value of the total product. Consider for a moment some of the products you purchase. Do you buy them primarily because of preference for the package design and/or color?

Innovative packaging is frequently the deciding factor for consumers. If a product, otherwise, is relatively the same as the competition, the package may be the unique characteristic that makes the sale.

Labeling

Another part of the total product is its label. Labeling is particularly important to manufacturers, who apply most labels. A label serves several purposes. It often shows the brand, particularly when branding the basic product would be undesirable. For example, a furniture brand is typically shown on a label and not on the basic product. On some products, visibility of the brand label is highly desirable. Calvin Klein jeans would probably not sell as well with the name labeled only inside the jeans.

A label is also an important informative tool for the small business. It can include information on product care. It can inform consumers how to use the product correctly. It can even include information on how to dispose of the product.

Laws on labeling requirements should be consulted carefully. Be innovative in your labeling information. Include information that goes beyond the specified minimum legal requirements.

Warranties

A **warranty** is simply a promise that a product will do certain things or meet certain standards. It may be expressed (written or spoken) or implied. All sellers make an implied warranty that the seller's title to the product is good. A "merchant" seller, who deals in goods of the kind in question, makes the additional implied warranty that the goods are fit for the ordinary purposes for which they are sold. A written warranty on a product is not always necessary. As a matter of fact, many firms operate without written warranties. They are concerned that a written warranty will only serve to confuse customers and make them suspicious.

The Magnuson-Moss Warranty Act of 1974 has had an impact on warranty practices. This law covers several warranty areas, including warranty terminology. The most notable provisions affecting terminology relate to the use of the terms "Full" and "Limited" on an express warranty for a product that costs over $15.00. In order to give the Full Warranty designation, the warranty must state certain minimum standards such as replacement or full refund after reasonable attempts at repair. Warranties not meeting all the minimum standards must carry the Limited Warranty title.

Warranties are important for products that are innovative, relatively expensive, purchased infrequently, relatively complex to repair, and positioned as high-quality goods. The major considerations that help decide the merits of a warranty policy are:

warranty
a promise that a product will do certain things

1. Costs.
2. Service capability.
3. Competitive practices.
4. Customer perceptions.
5. Legal implications.

LOOKING BACK

1. The stages of consumer decision making include problem recognition, information search and evaluation, the decision to purchase, and post-purchase evaluation.
2. The eight product strategy alternatives are initial product/initial market, initial product/new market, modified product/initial market, modified product/new market, new related product/initial market, new related product/new market, new unrelated product/initial market, and new unrelated product/new market.
3. Two concepts useful to the management of the product mix are the product development curve and the product life cycle. The product development curve consists of four phases: idea accumulation, business analysis, total product development, and product testing. The product life cycle consists of four stages: introduction, growth, maturity, and decline.
4. When choosing a brand name, the entrepreneur should follow five basic rules. Packaging can be used for protection, promotion, and opening new markets. Labels are informative tools for the marketer. A warranty is a promise that a product will do certain things or meet certain standards.

DISCUSSION QUESTIONS

1. What is the meaning of the statement "Customer satisfaction is not a means to achieve a certain goal, but, rather, it *is* the goal"?
2. How can a small firm know whether it is providing sufficient customer service? Be specific.
3. Do you feel that small firms in general provide better customer service? Why or why not?
4. Select a magazine advertisement and analyze it for perceptual techniques.
5. Select a magazine advertisement and analyze it for the use of reference-group influence and cultural uniqueness.
6. Give some examples of the way in which legitimate power is used in marketing.
7. What kinds of consumer behavior occur in the post-purchase stage? Be specific.
8. What are the three ways to achieve additional growth within each of the market strategies?
9. How does the new related product/new market strategy differ from the new unrelated product/new market strategy? Give examples.

10. A manufacturer of power lawn mowers is considering the addition of a line of home barbecue equipment. What factors would be important in a decision of this type?

11. List some of the major activities in the business analysis stage of the product development curve.

12. Select two product names and evaluate each with the five rules for naming a product listed in this chapter.

13. Would a small business desire to have its name considered to be the generic name for the product area? Defend your position.

14. For what type of firm is the packaging of products most important? For what firms is it unimportant?

15. How important do you believe warranties are in selling products? Discuss.

YOU MAKE THE CALL

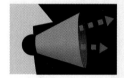

Situation 1

Paul McKinney is the owner and operator of a small restaurant located in the downtown area of Oklahoma City, Oklahoma. McKinney is a college graduate with a major in accounting. His ability to analyze and control costs has been a major factor in keeping his five-year-old venture out of the red.

The restaurant is located in an old but newly remodeled downtown building. His business is built on the strategy of high volume and low overhead. However, space limitations provide seating for only 25 to 30 people at one time. McKinney is concerned that customers stay too long after their meal, thereby tying up seating. He has considered using a buzzer system to remind customers that it is time to move on. He is concerned that this method is too obvious and may create customer dissatisfaction.

Questions

1. What is your opinion regarding McKinney's proposed buzzer system?
2. What other suggestions to help increase turnover can you make? Why are these ideas better?
3. What type of diversification strategy would be consistent with McKinney's restaurant business? Be specific.

Situation 2

In 1980, Chris Longfelder opened a cosmetics store with her savings of $500 and a $10,000 bank loan. The focus of her appeal was on price. One of her newspaper ads urged, "If you're tired of overpriced department store cosmetics, visit Generic Makeup." The first store was profitable, and Longfelder opened a second Generic Makeup store only four months later.

In 1986, a study of customer attitudes revealed a number of negative attitudes about her company. Some customers felt the products were leftovers and must be lower quality. Furthermore, she found that price was not the major reason customers came to her store—service, selection, and store atmosphere were all mentioned more frequently.

Longfelder has decided to change the name of her store. Two names are candidates: Kriselle and Faces.

Source: Tom Watson, "Retailer Adds Profits and 'New Faces,' " *In Business*, Vol. 10, No. 1 (January–February 1988), pp. 26–27. Reprinted from *In Business* magazine (Box 323, Emmaus, PA 18049).

Questions

1. Do you believe a name change is warranted? If so, what other factors make you feel this way?
2. What factors should be evaluated in making the choice between the two names under consideration?
3. Could the perceived need to change names have been avoided? How?

EXPERIENTIAL EXERCISES

1. Obtain permission from a local mall to conduct shopper interviews. Ask customers about their major service complaints. Report your findings.
2. Over a period of two or three days, carefully note your own shopping experiences. Summarize what you consider to be the best customer service you received.
3. Visit a local retail store and observe brand names, package designs, labels, and warranties. Report your thoughts to the class.
4. Consider your most recent purchase. Relate the decision-making process you used to the four stages of decision making presented in the textbook. Report your conclusions.

REFERENCES TO SMALL-BUSINESS PRACTICES

Daescher, William F. "A Lesson in Competitiveness,' *D & B Reports*, Vol. 37, No. 2 (March/April 1988).
    A small office supply company is used as an example of how a firm can remain competitive through diversification and customer service.
Huffman, Frances. "Services," *Entrepreneur*, Vol. 16, No. 9 (September 1988), pp. 91–98.
    Six service firms are profiled in this article. Each business has been successful in providing a special service in a unique manner.
Larson, Erik. "Forever Young," *Inc.*, Vol. 10, No. 7 (July 1988), pp. 50–62.
    This article provides an intriguing account of how a new business starting as a simple ice-cream parlor has diversified while retaining its unusual commitment to the needs of its employees and community.
Mamis, Robert A. "Real Service," *Inc.*, Vol. 11, No. 5 (May 1989), pp. 80–89.
    A mail-order company that has provided extensive customer service is profiled in this article.

Posner, Bruce G. "Growth Strategies," *Inc.*, Vol. 13, No. 12 (December 1991), pp. 109–112.
> This article looks at how six different growth companies exploited their niche.

Ross, Marilyn and Tom. "Diversify to Multiply," *Independent Business,* Vol. 3, No. 5 (September–October 1992), pp. 42–45.
> This article provides a look at several small firms and their diversification strategies. The businesses featured range from a cafe to a vacuum cleaner shop.

ENDNOTES

1. For a more detailed presentation of consumer decision making, see Michael R. Solomon, *Consumer Behavior* (Needham Heights, MA: Allyn and Bacon, 1992), Chapter 8.

2. James S. Hirsch, "Bron-Shoe Tries to Polish Image of an Old-Line Business," *The Wall Street Journal* (May 9, 1991), p. B2.

3. David J. Jefferson, "Manual-Ledger Maker's Strategy: Sell to the Small," *The Wall Street Journal* (September 26, 1991), p. B2.

4. Karen Blumenthal, "How Barney the Dinosaur Beat Extinction, Is Now Rich," *The Wall Street Journal* (February 28, 1992), p. B2; Mimi Swartz, "Invasion of the Giant Purple Dinosaur," *Texas Monthly* (April 1993), p. 176.

5. Del I. Hawkins, Roger J. Best, and Kenneth A. Coney, *Consumer Behavior Implications for Marketing Strategy,* 5th ed. (Homewood, IL: Richard D. Irwin, 1992), p. 523.

6. Some sources estimate about 65 percent of a business's income is from repeat customers. See, for example, Program 112 of *Something Ventured,* produced by Southern California Consortium (now called Intelecom. Phone [818] 796-7300).

7. "Presidential Hot Line," *Inc.*, Vol. 13, No. 2 (February 1991), p. 76.

8. *Something Ventured, op. cit.*

9. Hawkins, *op. cit.*, Chapter 10.

10. Timothy L. O'Brien, "BertSherm Aims Its Deodorant at Pre-Adolescent Set," *The Wall Street Journal* (July 16, 1992), p. B2.

11. Joan C. Szabo, "Slower Growth Expected for the Service Sector," *Nation's Business,* Vol. 77, No. 1 (January 1989), p. 12.

12. For a more detailed presentation of the uniqueness of services, see Charles W. Lamb, Joseph F. Hair, Jr., and Carl McDaniel, *Principles of Marketing* (Cincinnati, OH: South-Western Publishing Co., 1992), Chapter 21.

13. "Making Shopping Carts Safer for Kids and Cars," *The Wall Street Journal,* March 17, 1992, p. B1.

14. John R. Wilkie, "In Niches, Necessity Can Be the Mother of Reinvention," *The Wall Street Journal* (April 30, 1991), p. B2.

15. See Calvin Pigg, "Organic Cotton: A Mix of Old and New," *Southwest Farm Press* (September 17, 1992), p. 14.

CHAPTER 13

Pricing and Credit Strategies

SPOTLIGHT ON SMALL BUSINESS

Charles Bennett

Sometimes entrepreneurs can successfully price their product well above costs due to the uniqueness of the item. Such is the case for Charles Bennett, of Branford, Connecticut, who sells a car wax, named Zymöl, at prices well above costs.

Bennett and his wife Donna, an analyst at a pharmaceutical company, adapted a homemade wax formula they discovered while vacationing in Germany. Using their electric coffeepot as a vat, they eventually decided on the Zymöl ingredients. An 8-ounce jar of the wax was originally priced at $19.95 but later increased to $40!

It takes a certain amount of brass to ask $40 for an 8-ounce jar of wax good for a dozen wax jobs. A 9.5-ounce can of Turtle Wax, by comparison, sells for about $7.50. Add to Bennett's basic 8-ounce jar some car cleaners and a towel and you've got a Zymöl starter kit, priced at $100. At the higher end, there's Zymöl Concours at $150 per 8-ounce jar, and Zymöl Destiny, priced at $450.

Does Bennett's wax create a winning shine? Simply ask the six winners at the 1990 Pebble Beach Car Show. Their cars were all shined with Zymöl.

Source: Jerry Flint, "Fruit Salad Car Wax," *Forbes,* Vol. 149, No. 9, pp. 126–129. Excerpted by permission of FORBES magazine, April 27, 1992. © Forbes Inc., 1992.

After studying this chapter, you should be able to:
1. Discuss cost and demand considerations in pricing.
2. Apply a break-even analysis to pricing.
3. Explain several pricing strategies and calculate markups.
4. Identify kinds of consumer and trade credit.
5. Discuss factors involved in managing credit activity.

price	elasticity of demand	open charge account
credit	elastic demand	installment account
profit	inelastic demand	revolving charge account
total cost	penetration pricing	trade-credit agencies
total variable costs	skimming-price strategy	credit bureau
total fixed costs	price line	aging schedule
average pricing	consumer credit	bad-debt ratio
prestige pricing	trade credit	

A product or service is not ready for sale until it is priced, and, increasingly, pricing must be augmented by credit. The **price** of a product or service is the seller's measure of what he or she is willing to receive in exchange for transferring ownership or use of that product or service. **Credit** involves an agreement that payment for a product or service will be made at some later date.

Price and credit decisions are vital to small firms because such decisions directly impact the revenue and cash flow stream of the business. Also, initial pricing and credit decisions are important because customers dislike price increases and often react negatively to more restrictive credit policy changes. Therefore, care should be exercised when first making these decisions to reduce the likelihood of such changes. This chapter examines both the pricing and credit decisions of the small firm.

PRICING ACTIVITIES

Pricing is the systematic determination of the right price for a product. While setting just any price is easy, systematic pricing is complex and difficult. Before we examine the process of pricing for the small business, let us first consider why this process is important.

Importance of Pricing

The revenue of a small business is a direct reflection of two components: sales volume and product price. In a real sense, then, the product price is half of one side of the revenue equation. A small change in price can drastically influence total revenue. For emphasis, consider the following situations.[1]

price
a seller's measure of what he or she is willing to receive in exchange for transferring ownership of a product or service

credit
an agreement to delay payment for a product or service

Situation A

Quantity sold	×	Price per unit	=	Revenue
250,000	×	$3.00	=	$750,000

Situation B

Quantity sold	×	Price per unit	=	Revenue
250,000	×	$2.80	=	$700,000

The price per unit in Situation B is only 20 cents lower than in Situation A. However, the total reduction in revenue is $50,000! Thus, a small business can lose revenue unnecessarily if a price is set too low.

Another reason pricing is important is that price has an indirect effect on sales quantity. In the examples just given, quantity sold was assumed to be independent of price—which it may well be for a change in price from $3.00 to $2.80. However, a larger change, up or down, from $3.00 might change the quantity sold.

Pricing, therefore, has a double influence on total sales revenue. It is important *directly* as one part of the revenue equation and *indirectly* through its impact on quantity demanded.

Cost Considerations in Pricing

total cost

cost of goods sold, selling expenses, and general administrative expenses

In a successful business, price must be sufficient to cover total cost plus some margin of profit. **Total cost** includes three components. The first is the cost of goods (or services) offered for sale. An appliance dealer, for example, must include in the price the cost of the appliance and freight charges. The second component is the selling cost. This includes the direct cost of the salesperson's

Figure 13-1
Merchandisers Consider the Three Components of Total Cost in Determining How to Price Their Products

time as well as the cost of advertising and sales promotion. The third component is the general overhead cost applicable to the given product. Included in
this cost are such items as office supplies, utilities, taxes, office salaries, and
management salaries. **Profit** is the necessary payment for entrepreneurial services and the risk of doing business.

Another cost consideration concerns the way costs behave as the quantity
marketed increases or decreases. **Total variable costs** are those that increase as
the quantity marketed increases. Sales commission costs and material costs for
production are typical variable costs. These are incurred as a product is made
and sold. **Total fixed costs** are those that remain constant at different levels of
quantity sold. An advertising campaign expenditure and factory equipment
cost would be fixed costs.

By understanding the behavior of these different kinds of costs, a small-
business manager can avoid pricing below costs. If all costs are considered, in-
correctly, to behave in the same way, pricing can be inappropriate. Small businesses often disregard differences between fixed and variable costs and treat
them identically for pricing. This can be a dangerous practice. An approach
called **average pricing** is an example of this disregard. Average pricing occurs
when the total cost over a previous period is divided by the quantity sold in that
period. The resulting average cost is then used to set the current price.

Consider the cost structure of a hypothetical firm selling 25,000 units of a
product in 1994 at a sales price of $8.00 each (Figure 13-2). The average unit
cost at the 1994 sales volume of 25,000 units is $5.00 ($125,000 ÷ 25,000). The
$3.00 markup on the average cost provides a satisfactory margin at this sales
volume.

However, consider the profit impact if next year's sales reach only 10,000
units and the selling price has been set at the same $3.00 markup based on
1994's average cost (Figure 13-3). At the lower sales volume (10,000 units), the
average unit cost has increased to $9.50 ($95,000 ÷ 10,000). Such a procedure
overlooks the reality of a higher average cost at a lower sales level. This is, of
course, due to a constant fixed cost spread over fewer units.

Profit
revenues minus
expenses

total variable costs
costs that vary with
the quantity mar-
keted

total fixed costs
costs that remain
constant as the
quantity sold varies

average pricing
a pricing approach
using average cost as
a basis to set price

Year 1994

Sales Revenue		$200,000
(25,000 units @ $8.00)		
Total Costs:		
Fixed Costs	$75,000	
Variable Costs ($2 per unit)	50,000	125,000
Gross Margin		$ 75,000

Figure 13-2
Hypothetical Firm
Cost Structure,
1994

Figure 13-3
Hypothetical Firm
Cost Structure,
1995

Year 1995		
Sales Revenue		$80,000
(10,000 units @ $8.00)		
Total Costs:		
Fixed Costs	$75,000	
Variable Costs ($2 per unit)	20,000	95,000
Gross Margin		$(15,000)

Demand Considerations in Pricing

Cost considerations provide a floor below which a price would not be set for normal pricing purposes. Cost analysis does not tell the small-business manager how far the "right" price should exceed that minimum figure. Only after considering the nature of demand can this be determined.

Demand Factors. Several factors affect the demand for a product or service. One is the appeal of the product itself. If consumers perceive the product as an important solution to their unsatisfied needs, there will be demand.

Only in rare cases are identical products and services offered by competing firms. In many cases the products are dissimilar in some way. Even when products are similar, the accompanying services typically differ. Speed of service, credit terms, delivery arrangements, personal attention by a top executive, and willingness to stand behind the product or service are but a few of the areas that distinguish one product from another. The pricing implications depend on whether the small firm is inferior or superior in these respects to its competitors. Certainly, there is no absolute imperative for the small business to conform slavishly to the prices of others. Its unique combination of goods and services may well justify a premium price.

Another factor that has a major influence on demand is the product price itself. This factor is a basis for what is called prestige pricing. **Prestige pricing** is setting a high price to convey the image of high quality or uniqueness. The influence of prestige pricing varies from market to market and product to product. Higher-income-level markets are less sensitive to price variations than lower-income groups. Therefore, prestige pricing typically works better in these markets. Also, products sold to markets with low levels of product knowledge are candidates for prestige pricing. When customers know very little about product characteristics, they will often use price as an indicator of quality.

A company selling windshield-washer fluid found that it could use prestige pricing for its product. The product cost pennies to manufacture and, there-

prestige pricing
setting a high price
to convey the image
of high quality or
uniqueness

fore, sold at an extremely low price even with a large markup. The firm recognized an opportunity and raised its price repeatedly until it was selling at a price several times greater than it had been originally. Sales made the product extremely profitable.

Another small business, G.O.D., Inc., an overnight freight business, also experienced the benefits of prestige pricing. Walter Riley, the president of G.O.D., had kept prices competitive from the time the company first began operations. "We were toe to toe with them," he says, "and we still weren't getting any new business." Later the company increased its prices to a 5 percent to 7 percent premium. "Raising our prices startled purchasing agents into seeing that we weren't just like our competitors. And they were willing to pay extra for overnight delivery."[2]

Elasticity of Demand. The effect that a change in price has on the quantity demanded is called **elasticity of demand.** A product is said to have **elastic demand** if an increase in its price lowers total revenue or a decrease in price raises total revenue. A product is said to have **inelastic demand** if an increase in its price raises total revenue or a decrease in price lowers total revenue.

In some industries, the demand for products is very elastic—when prices are lower, the amount purchased increases considerably, thus providing higher revenues. An example of this can be found in the personal computer industry. For other products, such as salt, the industry demand is very inelastic. Regardless of its price, the quantity purchased will not change significantly because consumers use a fixed amount of salt.

The concept of elasticity of demand is important to a small firm because it suggests that inelastic demand is the optimum situation for a firm's products. Regardless of industry demand, the small firm should seek to distinguish its product or service in such a way that small price increases will result in increasing total revenues.

> **elasticity of demand**
> the effect of a change in price on the quantity demanded
>
> **elastic demand**
> a change in the price of a product produces a significant change in the quantity demanded
>
> **inelastic demand**
> a change in the price of a product does not produce a significant change in the quantity demanded

Break-Even Analysis in Pricing

Break-even analysis entails a formal comparison of cost and demand for the purpose of determining the acceptability of alternative prices. There are two stages of a comprehensive break-even analysis: cost break-even and cost-adjusted break-even. Break-even analysis can be explained via formulas or graphs. We will use the graphic presentation in this chapter.

Cost Break-Even Stage. The objective of the cost break-even stage is to determine the quantity at which the product, with an assumed price, will generate enough revenue to start earning a profit. Figure 13-4(a) presents a simple cost break-even chart. Total fixed costs are portrayed as a horizontal section in view of the fact that they do not change with the volume of production.

The variable-cost section slants upward, however, because of the direct relationship of total variable costs to output. The area between the slanting total cost line and the horizontal base line thus represents the combination of fixed and variable costs. The area between the revenue and total cost lines reveals the profit or loss position of the company at any level of sales. The intersection of these two lines is called the break-even point because sales revenue equals total cost at this point.

Additional revenue lines at other prices can be charted on the break-even graph to evaluate new break-even points. This gives a flexible break-even chart as shown in Figure 13-4(b). The assumed higher price of $18.00 in Figure

Figure 13-4
Break-Even Charts
for Pricing

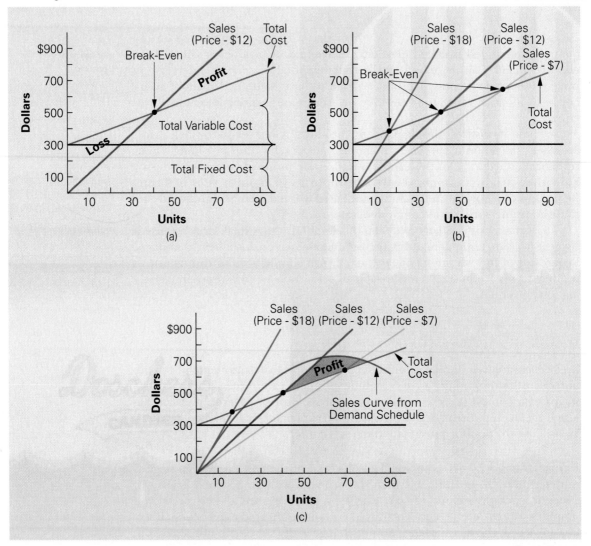

13-4(b) plots a more steeply sloped revenue line, resulting in an earlier break-even point. Similarly, the lower price of $7.00 produces a "flatter" revenue line, increasing the break-even point. Additional sales revenue lines could be plotted to evaluate other proposed prices.

The cost break-even chart implies that quantity sold can increase continually (as shown by the larger and larger profit area to the right). This is misleading and can be clarified by adjusting the cost break-even analysis with demand data.

Cost-Adjusted Break-Even Stage. The indirect impact of price on quantity sold is a confounding problem for pricing decisions. Typically, less of a product is demanded as price increases. In exceptional cases, as mentioned earlier, price may influence demand in the opposite direction, resulting in more demand for a product at higher prices. The estimated demand for a product at various prices needs to be incorporated into the break-even analysis. Marketing research can be used to estimate demand at various prices.

The usefulness of break-even analysis can be greatly increased by incorporating the estimated demand. A cost-adjusted break-even chart is developed by using the cost break-even data and adding a demand curve. A demand schedule showing the estimated number of units demanded and total revenue at various prices is listed in Table 13-1 and is used to plot the demand curve in Figure 13-4(c).

When this demand schedule is plotted on a flexible break-even chart, a more realistic profit area is identified, as shown in Figure 13-4(c). The break-even point in Figure 13-4(c) for an $18.00 unit price corresponds to sales quantities that cannot be reached at the assumed price. Therefore, the optimum of the three prices used in Figure 13-4(c) is $12.00. The potential at this price is indicated by the profit area in Figure 13-4(c).

Setting the Selling Price

After careful consideration of cost and demand data with break-even analysis, the small firm should have a better understanding of which prices are feasible. However, the seemingly precise nature of break-even analysis should not mislead the small-business manager. Break-even analysis is only one tool of pricing

Table 13-1
Demand Schedule

Price	Demand (Units)	Revenue ($)
$ 7	90	$630
12	60	720
18	15	270

and does not in itself determine the "right" price. In other words, price should never be determined in isolation from characteristics of the market niche and the current marketing strategy. Several examples of pricing strategies that reflect market considerations are discussed in the following sections.[3]

penetration pricing
setting lower than normal prices to hasten market acceptance or to increase existing market share

Penetration Pricing. The strategy called **penetration pricing** involves pricing products or services lower than a normal, long-range market price in order to gain more rapid market acceptance or to increase existing market share. This strategy can sometimes discourage new competitors from entering the market niche if they view the penetration price as a long-range price. Obviously, this strategy sacrifices some profit margins to achieve other marketing goals.

skimming-price strategy
setting very high prices for a limited period before reducing them to more competitive levels

Skimming Pricing. A **skimming-price strategy** sets prices for products or services at very high levels for a limited period before reducing the price to a lower, more competitive level. This strategy assumes that certain customers will pay the higher price because they view the product or service as a prestige item. This strategy is most practical when there is little threat of short-term competition or when startup costs must be recovered rapidly.

Follow-the-Leader Pricing. The probable reaction of competitors is a critical factor in determining whether to cut prices below a prevailing level. A small business in competition with larger firms seldom is in a position to consider itself the price leader. If competitors view the small firm's pricing as relatively unimportant, they may permit a price differential. This may well be the reaction if the price-cutting firm is sufficiently small. On the other hand, established firms may view a smaller price-cutter as a direct threat and counter with reductions of their own. In such a case, the smaller price-cutter accomplishes very little.

Variable Pricing. In some lines of business, the selling firm makes price concessions to individual customers even though it advertises a uniform price. Concessions are made for various reasons, one of which is the customer's knowledge and bargaining strength. In some fields of business, therefore, pricing decisions involve two parts: a stipulated "list price" and a range of price concessions to particular buyers.

Flexible Pricing. Although many firms use total cost as a point of resistance, most of them take into consideration special market conditions and practices of competitors in arriving at their prices. The following cases illustrate this point:

1. *Contractor A* estimates the full cost of building a house, but he modifies the price to meet market conditions. His concept of cost reflects variable estimates of the opportunity costs of his time. His time is less valuable in the

SMALL BUSINESS IN ACTION

Pricing for the Season

Products that are subject to seasonal sales fluctuations present a special production and pricing
challenge. This is the situation faced by Alan
Trusler, president of Aladdin Steel Products, in
Colville, Washington. Sales of his wood-burning
stove would predictably cool off toward the end of
winter's snowstorms. Trusler extended his selling
season by offering his 350 dealers:

> . . . discounts for the entire year if they stock
> stoves in the off-peak months—March through
> July.
> . . . [cash discounts] for buying early—8%
> off each invoice in March, 7% in April, 6% in
> May, on down.

Aladdin's company grew over 400 percent
from 1987 to 1991. Production now runs year-
round.

Source: Susan Greco, "Rx For a Short Sales Season," *Inc.*, Vol. 14, No. 10, p. 29. Reprinted with permission, *Inc.* magazine (October 1992). Copyright 1992 by Goldhirsh Group, Inc, 38 Commercial Wharf, Boston, MA 02110.

winter, when business is slack; he adjusts his estimates of cost accordingly.
He also shaves price on a cash sale of a house, recognizing the avoidance of
a risk as compared with sales involving complicated financing. Thus, the
emphasis on full cost does not mean inattention to demand.

2. *Printing Company B* also pays considerable attention to full-cost estimates.
   While the management insists that prices should be kept on a full-cost basis,
   actual practice is more flexible. The managers are critical of "rate cutters,"
   who, they claim, are responsible for the low industry profits. However, they
   themselves show some willingness to adjust to market conditions when the
   necessity arises.

3. *Furniture Company C* starts with a cost estimate, including an allocation of indirect labor and factory overhead. The management modifies the target return to meet market conditions.

There is an old anecdote about a business that lost money on each item it
sold but planned to make it up on volume. However, in certain circumstances it

may be logical to price at less than total cost. For example, if the facilities of a business are idle, some costs may be continuing. In any case, the price should cover all marginal or incremental costs—that is, those costs specifically incurred to get the added business. In the long run, however, all overhead costs must be covered as well.

price line
a range of several distinct merchandise price levels

Price Lining. A **price line** is a range of several distinct prices at which merchandise is offered for sale. For example, men's suits might be sold at $250, $300, and $600. The general level of the different lines would depend on the income level and buying desires of a store's customers. Price lining has the advantage of simplifying choice for the customer and reducing the necessary minimum inventory.

What the Traffic Will Bear. The policy of pricing on the basis of what the traffic will bear can be used only when the seller has little or no competition. Obviously, this policy will work only for nonstandardized products. For example, a food store might offer egg roll wrappers that the competitors do not carry. Busy consumers who want to fix egg rolls but who have neither the time nor the knowledge to prepare the wrappers will buy them at any reasonable price.

Calculating Markups in Retailing

Up to this point in our discussion of pricing, we have made no distinction between pricing by manufacturers and pricing by intermediaries. Such a distinction was not necessary since the concepts apply to all small businesses, regardless of their position in the distribution channel. Now, however, we will discuss some of the pricing arithmetic that is used in the retail trade. Since retail businesses often carry many products, a system of markup pricing has emerged as a manageable framework for pricing.

With this cost-plus system of pricing, retailers are able to price hundreds of products much more quickly than they could with a system involving individual break-even analyses. In calculating the selling price for a particular item, the retailer must add a markup percentage to cover the following:

1. Operating expenses.
2. Subsequent price reductions—for example, markdowns and employee discounts.
3. Profit.

Markups may be expressed as a percentage of either the *selling price* or the *cost*. For example, if an item costs $6.00 and is selling at $10.00, the markup of $4.00 would be 40 percent of the selling price ($4.00 ÷ $10.00 × 100) or 66⅔ percent of the cost ($4.00 ÷ $6.00 × 100). Although either method is correct, consistency demands that the same method be used in considering the components entering into the markup. If operating expenses amount to 35 percent of sales and a profit of 5 percent of sales is desired, the markup (assuming no markdown) must be 40 percent of selling price. This is clearly different from 40 percent markup based on cost. In fact, an incorrect application of the 40 percent figure to cost would produce a markup amounting to less than 29 percent of sales, which is not enough to cover operating expenses. Figure 13-5 presents simple formulas for markup calculations.

Additional Considerations in Pricing

In some situations local, state, and federal laws must also be considered in setting prices. For example, the federal Sherman Antitrust Act provides a general prohibition of price fixing. Most federal pricing legislation is intended to benefit small firms as well as consumers by keeping large businesses from conspiring to set prices that stifle competition.

If a small business markets a line of products—some of which may compete with each other—pricing decisions must also examine the effects of a single product price on the rest of the line. Pricing becomes extremely complex in these situations.

Constantly adjusting a price to meet changing marketing conditions can be both costly to the seller and confusing to buyers. An alternative approach is to make adjustments to the stated price—to arrive at the actual price offered to prospective buyers—by special price quotes. This is achieved with a system of discounting designed to reflect a variety of needs. For example, a seller may offer a trade discount to a buyer (such as a wholesaler) because the buyer per-

---

Figure 13-5
Formulas for
Markup Calculations

Cost + Markup = Selling Price
Cost   = Selling Price − Markup
Markup   = Selling price − Cost

$$\frac{Markup}{Selling\ Price} \times 100 = \text{Markup expressed as a percentage of selling price}$$

$$\frac{Markup}{Cost} \times 100 = \text{Markup expressed as a percentage of cost}$$

If a seller wishes to translate markup as a percentage of selling price into a percentage of cost, or vice versa, the two formulas below are useful:

$$\frac{Markup\ as\ a\ percentage\ of\ selling\ price}{100\% - Markup\ as\ a\ percentage\ of\ selling\ price} \times 100 = \text{Markup as a percentage of cost}$$

$$\frac{Markup\ as\ a\ percentage\ of\ cost}{100\% + Markup\ as\ a\ percentage\ of\ cost} \times 100 = \text{Markup as a percentage of selling price}$$

forms a certain marketing function, such as distribution. The stated price or list price is unchanged, but the seller offers a lower actual price via the discount.

A final word about pricing. Pricing mistakes are not the exclusive domain of small business. Large firms make pricing errors also. Remember that pricing is not an exact science. If the initial pricing decision appears off target, make the necessary adjustments and keep going!

CREDIT IN SMALL BUSINESS

In a credit sale, the seller conveys goods or services to the buyer in return for the buyer's promise to pay. The major objective in granting credit is an expansion of sales by attracting new customers and by an increase in volume and regularity of purchases by existing customers. Some retail firms—furniture stores, for example—cater to newcomers in the city, newly married couples, and others by inviting the credit business of individuals who have established credit ratings. In addition, credit records may be used for purposes of sales promotion by direct-mail appeals to credit customers. Adjustments and exchanges of goods are also facilitated through credit operations.

Benefits of Credit to Buyers and Sellers

If credit buying and selling did not benefit both parties to the transaction, its use would cease. Buyers obviously enjoy the availability of credit, and small firms, in particular, benefit from the judicious extension of credit by suppliers. Credit supplies the small firm with working capital, often permitting continuation of marginal businesses that might otherwise expire. Additional benefits of credit to buyers are:

1. It gives customers the ability to satisfy immediate needs while paying later.
2. It provides better records of purchases with credit billing statements.
3. It provides better service and ease of exchanging purchased items.
4. It offers greater convenience.
5. It builds a credit history.

Sellers extend credit to customers because they can obtain increased sales volume in this way. They expect the increased revenue to more than offset credit costs so that profits will increase. Other benefits of credit to the seller are:

1. It creates a closer association with customers because of implied trust.
2. It provides a marketing tool for easier selling through telephone and mail-order systems.
3. It tends to smooth out sales peaks and valleys since purchasing power is available throughout the month.
4. It provides a tool to stay competitive.

Kinds of Credit

There are two broad classes of credit: consumer credit and trade credit. **Consumer credit** is granted by retailers to final consumers who purchase for personal or family use. However, a small-business owner can use consumer credit to purchase certain supplies and equipment for use in the business. **Trade credit** is extended by nonfinancial firms, such as manufacturers or wholesalers, to customers that are other business firms.

Consumer credit and trade credit differ as to types of credit instruments used and sources for financing receivables. Another important distinction is the availability of credit insurance for trade credit only. Consumer and trade credit also differ markedly as to terms of sale.

Consumer Credit. The three major kinds of consumer-credit accounts are: open charge accounts, installment accounts, and revolving charge accounts. Many variations of these are also used.

Open Charge Accounts.   Under the **open charge account,** the customer obtains possession of goods (or services) when purchased, with payment due when billed. Stated terms typically call for payment at the end of the month, but customary practice allows a longer period for payment than that stated. There is no finance charge for this kind of credit if the balance of the account is paid in full at the end of the period. Customers are not generally required to make a down payment or make a pledge of collateral. Small accounts at department stores are a good example of such use.

Installment Accounts. The **installment account** is the vehicle of long-term consumer credit. A down payment is normally required, and annual finance charges can be 20 percent or more of the purchase price. The most common payment periods are from 12 to 36 months, although automobile dealers often offer extended payment periods of 60 months. An installment account is useful for large purchases such as automobiles, washing machines, and television sets.

Revolving Charge Accounts. The **revolving charge account** is another variation of the installment account. The seller may grant a line of credit, and the customer may then charge purchases at any time if purchases do not exceed this credit limit. A specified percentage of the outstanding balance must be paid monthly, which forces the customer to budget and limits the amount of debt that can be carried. Finance charges are computed on the unpaid balance at the end of the month. Credit cards use this type of credit. Because of their significance, credit cards are discussed in a separate section following trade credit.

Trade Credit. Business firms may sell goods subject to specified terms of sale, such as 2/10, n/30. This means that a 2 percent discount is given by the seller if the buyer pays within 10 days of the invoice date. Failure to take this

consumer credit
credit granted by retailers to consumers who purchase for personal or family use

trade credit
credit extended by nonfinancial firms to customers that are also business firms

open charge account
the customer obtains a product when purchased, with payment due when billed

installment account
credit that requires a down payment with the balance paid over a specified period of time

revolving charge account
a line of credit on which the customer may charge purchases at any time up to an established limit

discount makes the full amount of the invoice due in 30 days. Other discount arrangements in common use are shown in Figure 13-6.

Sales terms in trade credit depend on the kind of product sold and the buyer's and seller's circumstances. The credit period often varies directly with the length of the buyer's turnover period, which obviously depends on the type of product sold. The larger the order and the higher the credit rating of the buyer, the better the sales terms that can be granted if individual sales terms are fixed for each customer. The greater the financial strength and the more adequate and liquid the working capital of the seller, the more generous the seller's sales terms can be. Of course, no business can afford to allow competitors to outdo it in reasonable generosity of sales terms. In many lines of business, credit terms are so firmly set by tradition that a unique policy is difficult, if not impossible for a small firm to implement.

Credit Cards. Credit cards, sometimes referred to as "plastic money," have become a major source of retail credit. As mentioned earlier, credit cards are usually based on a revolving credit system. There are basically three types of credit cards, as distinguished by their sponsor—bank credit cards, entertainment credit cards, and retailer credit cards.

Bank Credit Cards. The best known bank credit cards are MasterCard and VISA. Figure 13-7 shows a credit agreement for a credit card issued by a credit union through a bank. Bank credit card systems are widely used by retailers who want to offer credit but do not feel they can offer their own cards. Most small-business retailers would fit into this category. In return for paying the bank a set fee (usually 5 to 6 percent of the purchase price), the bank takes the responsibility for making collections. Some banks charge annual membership fees to cardholders. Cardholders are frequently able to receive cash up to the

Figure 13-6
Examples of Trade Credit Terms

Sales Term	Explanation
3/10, n/60	Three percent discount if payment is made within the first 10 days; net (full amount) due by 60th day.
E.O.M.	Billing at end of month, covering all credit purchases of that month.
C.O.D.	Amount of bill will be collected upon delivery of the goods.
2/10, n/30, R.O.G.	Two percent discount if payment is made within 10 days; net due by 30th day-- but both discount period and 30 days start from the date of receipt of the goods.
2/10, n/30, E.O.M.	The percent discount if payment is made within 30th day—but both periods start from the end of the month in which the sale was made.

Figure 13-7
Credit Card
Agreement

LINE OF CREDIT (CREDIT CARD) AGREEMENT

_____ Credit Union

Address_____ , Texas
          Street   City   Zip   County

BORROWER(S) _____ Account Number: _____

TERMS USED IN THIS AGREEMENT: "You" and "your" mean any person who signs this Agreement or uses the card. "The card" means any credit card issued to you or those designated by you under the terms of this Agreement. "Use of the card" means any procedure used by you, or someone authorized by you, to make a purchase or obtain a cash advance whether or not the purchase or advance is evidenced by a signed written document. "Unauthorized use of the card" means the use of the card by someone other than you who does not have actual, implied, or apparent authority for such use, and from which you receive no benefit.

EXTENSIONS OF CREDIT: If your application is approved, the Credit Union may, at its discretion, establish a MasterCard and/or VISA Card account in your name and cause one or more cards to be issued to you or those designated by you. In such an event, you authorize the Credit Union to pay for your account, all items reflecting credit purchases and cash advances obtained through use of the card.

CREDIT LIMITS: You promise that payments made for your account resulting from use of the card will, at no time, cause the outstanding balance in your account to exceed your credit limit as disclosed to you at the time you receive your card or as adjusted from time to time at the discretion of the credit union.

PROMISE TO PAY: You promise to repay the Credit Union all payments made for your account resulting from use of the card plus a **FINANCE CHARGE** on the unpaid balance. At the end of each monthly billing cycle, you will be furnished with a periodic statement showing (i) the "previous balance" (the outstanding balance in the account at the beginning of the billing cycle), (ii) the amount of all cash advances, purchases and **FINANCE CHARGES** posted to your account during the billing cycle, (iii) the amount of all payments and credits posted to your account during the billing cycle, and (iv) the "new balance" which is the sum of (i) and (ii) less (iii).

You agree to pay on or before the "payment due date" shown on the periodic statment either the entire "new balance" or a minimum payment equal to 5% of the "new balance", or $18.00, whichever is greater. If the "new balance" is $18.00 or less, you will pay in full.

COST OF CREDIT: You will pay a **FINANCE CHARGE** for all advances made against your account at the periodic rate of .049315% per day, which has a corresponding **ANNUAL PERCENTAGE RATE** of 18%. Cash advances incur a **FINANCE CHARGE** from the date they are posted to the account. New purchases will not incur a **FINANCE CHARGE** on the date they are posted to the account if you have paid the account in full by the due date shown on your previous

(Continued)

Figure 13-7
(*Continued*)

monthly statement or if there was no previous balance. No additional **FINANCE CHARGE** will be incurred whenever you pay the account in full by the due date. The **FINANCE CHARGE** is figured by applying the periodic rate to the Balance Subject to **FINANCE CHARGE** which is the "average daily balance" of your account, including certain current transactions. The "average daily balance" is arrived at by taking the beginning balance of your account each day and adding any new cash advances, and, unless you pay your account in full by the due date shown on your previous monthly statement or there is no previous balance, adding in new purchases, and subtracting any payments or credits and unpaid **FINANCE CHARGES.** The daily balances for the billing cycle are then added together and divided by the number of days in the billing cycle. The result is the "average daily balance." Each **FINANCE CHARGE** is determined by multiplying the "average daily balance" by the number of days in the billing cycle and applying the periodic rates to the product. You may pay any amounts outstanding at any time without penalty for early payment.

CREDIT INSURANCE: If available, credit insurance is not required for any extension of credit under this agreement. However, you may purchase any credit insurance available through the credit union and have the premium added to the outstanding balance in your account. If you elect to do so, you will be given the necessary disclosures and documents separately.

LIABILITY FOR UNAUTHORIZED USE: You may be liable for the unauthorized use of your card. You will not be liable for unauthorized use that occurs after you notify the Credit Union (or Credit Union's designee) orally or in writing, of the loss, theft, or possible unauthorized use. In any case, your liability will not exceed $50.00.

credit limits of their cards. Although some entrepreneurs have used this source of credit for financing their business startups, it is a risky type of financing for this purpose.

Entertainment Credit Cards. Well-known examples of this form of credit are American Express and Diner's Club cards. These cards have traditionally charged an annual fee. Although originally used for charging services, these cards are now widely accepted for sales of merchandise. Just like bank credit cards, the collection of credit charges is the responsibility of the sponsoring agency.

Retail Credit Cards. Many companies issue their own credit cards for use in their stores or for purchasing their products in other outlets. Department stores, oil companies, and telephone companies are typical examples. Customers are usually not charged any annual fees or any finance charges if balances are paid each month.

The Decision to Sell on Credit

Nearly all small businesses can sell on credit if they wish, and so the entrepreneur must decide whether to sell for cash only or on credit. In some cases this is reduced to the question, "Can the granting of credit to customers be avoided?" Credit selling is standard trade practice in many lines of business, and in other businesses credit-selling competitors will always outsell the cash-selling firm.

Factors That Affect the Credit Decision. Numerous factors bear on the decision concerning credit extension. The seller always hopes to increase profits by credit sales, but each firm must also consider its own particular circumstances and environment.

Type of Business. Retailers of durable goods, for example, typically grant credit more freely than small grocers who sell perishables. Indeed, most consumers find it necessary to buy big-ticket items on an installment basis, and the product's life makes installment selling possible.

Credit Policy of Competitors. Unless a firm offers some compensating advantage, it is expected to be as generous as its competitors in extending credit. Wholesale hardware companies and retail furniture stores are businesses that face stiff competition from credit sellers.

Income Level of Customers. The income level of customers is a significant factor in determining a retailer's credit policy. Consider, for example, a corner drugstore adjacent to a city high school. High school students are typically unsatisfactory credit customers because of their lack of maturity and income.

Availability of Adequate Working Capital. There is no denying the fact that credit sales increase the amount of working capital needed by the business. Money that the business has tied up in open-credit and installment accounts cannot be used to pay business expenses.

The Four Credit Questions. In evaluating the credit standing of applicants, the entrepreneur must answer the following questions:

1.   Can the buyer pay as promised?
2.   Will the buyer pay?
3.   If so, when will the buyer pay?
4.   If not, can the buyer be forced to pay?

Before credit is approved, the answers to questions 1, 2, and 4 must be "yes"; to question 3, "on schedule." The answers depend in part on the amount of credit requested and in part on the seller's estimate of the buyer's ability and willingness to pay. Such an estimate constitutes a judgment of the buyer's in-herent credit worth.

Every credit applicant possesses credit worth in some degree, so that ex-tended credit is not necessarily a gift to the applicant. Instead, a decision to grant credit merely recognizes the buyer's credit standing. But the seller faces a possible inability or unwillingness to pay on the buyer's part. In making credit decisions, therefore, the seller decides the degree of risk of nonpayment that must be assumed.

Willingness to pay is evaluated in terms of the four C's of credit: character, capital, capacity, and conditions.[4] *Character* refers to the fundamental integrity and honesty that should underlie all human and business relationships. In the case of a business customer, it takes shape in the business policies and ethical practices of the firm. Individual customers who apply for credit must also be known to be morally responsible persons. *Capital* consists of the cash and other assets owned by the business or individual customer. In the case of a business customer, this means capital sufficient to underwrite planned operations, in-cluding adequate owner capital. *Capacity* refers to the business customer's abil-ity to conserve assets and faithfully and efficiently follow financial plans. The business customer with capacity utilizes the invested capital of the business firm wisely and capitalizes to the fullest extent on business opportunities. *Conditions* refer to such factors as business cycles and changes in price levels, which may be either favorable or unfavorable to the payment of debts. The economic re-cession of the early 1990s placed a strong burden on consumer's ability to pay their debts. Other adverse factors that might limit a customer's ability to pay in-clude fires and other natural disasters, new legislation, strong new competition, or labor problems.

Figure 13-8
Retail Furniture Stores Must Extend Credit to Customers in Order to Compete

Managing the Credit Activity

Unfortunately, most small businesses pay little attention to their credit management system until bad debts become a problem. Often this is too late. Credit management should begin prior to the first credit sale with a thorough screening process and continue throughout the credit cycle. The major issues in a comprehensive credit management program for a small business are discussed in the following sections and in Chapter 21.

Credit Investigation of Applicants. In most retail stores, the first step in credit investigation is the completion of an application form. The information obtained on this form is used as the basis for examining the applicant's financial responsibility.

Nonretailing firms should similarly investigate credit applicants. One small clothing manufacturer has every sales order reviewed by a Dun & Bradstreet-trained credit manager who maintains a complete file of D&B credit reports on thousands of customers. Recent financial statements of dealer-customers are filed also. These, together with the dealer's accounts-receivable card, are the basis for decisions on credit sales, with major emphasis on the D&B credit reports.

Credit Limits. Perhaps the most important factor in determining a customer's credit limits is the customer's ability to pay the obligation when it becomes due. This in turn requires an evaluation of the customer's financial resources, debt position, and income level.

The amount of credit requested by the customer is the second factor that requires consideration. Customers of a drugstore need only small amounts of credit. On the other hand, business customers of wholesalers and manufacturers typically expect larger amounts of credit. In the special case of installment selling, the amount of credit should not exceed the repossession value of the goods sold. Automobile dealers follow this rule as a general practice.

Sources of Credit Information. One of the most important and frequently neglected sources of credit information is found in the seller's accounts-receivable records. Properly analyzed, these records show whether the customer regularly takes cash discounts and, if not, whether the customer's account is typically slow.

Manufacturers and wholesalers frequently can use the financial statements submitted by firms applying for credit as an additional source of information. Obtaining maximum value from financial statements requires a careful ratio analysis, which will reveal a firm's working-capital position, profit-making potential, and general financial health. See Chapter 20 for an in-depth treatment of using financial statements and ratios to understand a firm's financial position.

Pertinent data may also be obtained from outsiders. For example, arrangements may be made with other suppliers to exchange credit data. Such credit interchange reports are quite useful in learning about the sales and payment experiences of others with one's own credit customers or applicants.

Another source of credit data, on commercial accounts particularly, is the customer's banker. Some bankers are glad to supply credit information about their depositors, considering this a service in helping them obtain credit in amounts they can successfully handle. Other bankers feel that credit information is confidential and should not be disclosed in this way.

trade-credit agencies
privately owned organizations that collect credit information on business firms

Organizations that may be consulted with reference to credit standings are trade-credit agencies and local credit bureaus. **Trade-credit agencies** are privately owned and operated organizations that collect credit information on business firms. After they analyze and evaluate the data, they make credit ratings available to client companies for a fee. These agencies are concerned with trade-credit ratings only, having nothing to do with consumer credit. Dun & Bradstreet, Inc., is a general trade-credit agency serving the nation. Figure 13-9 is a credit summary provided by D&B's Small Business Services. Manufacturers and wholesalers are especially interested in Dun & Bradstreet's reference book and credit reports. The reference book covers all U.S. businesses and shows credit rating, financial strength, and other key credit information. It is available to subscribers only.

credit bureau
an organization that summarizes firms' credit experience with particular individuals

A **credit bureau** serves its members—retailers and other firms in a given community—by summarizing their credit experience with particular individuals. A local bureau can also broaden its service by affiliation with either the National Retail Credit Association or the Associated Credit Bureaus of America. This makes possible the exchange of credit information on persons who move from one city to another. A business firm need not be a member of some bureaus in order to get a credit report. The fee charged to nonmembers, however, is considerably higher than that charged to members.

There are well over 1,000 automated credit bureaus, many of which are owned by either a private independent party or a merchant association. Most credit bureaus operate on one of the three on-line data processing systems—TRW, Inc.; Equifax, Inc.; and Trans Union Credit Information Co.[5] "The mission of the consumer reporting industry is to serve as an objective third-party provider of information to the companies and consumers involved in credit transactions," notes Walter R. Kurth, President of Associated Credit Bureaus.[6]

Billing Procedures. Timely notification of customers regarding the status of their accounts is one of the most effective methods of keeping credit accounts current. Most credit customers will pay their bills on time if the creditor provides them with the necessary information to verify the credit balance. Failure to send the correct number of invoices or other billing errors will only delay timely payments.

"The cornerstone of collecting accounts receivable on time is making sure you invoice your customers or send them their periodic billing statements promptly," says Robert M. Littman, a partner in the accounting firm of Saltz, Shamis & Goldfarb, Inc., in Akron, Ohio. "Keep a good pulse on the billing activity—the sooner you mail your invoice, the sooner the check will be in the mail," says Littman.[7]

Figure 13-9   Dun & Bradstreet's Credit Recommendation Summary

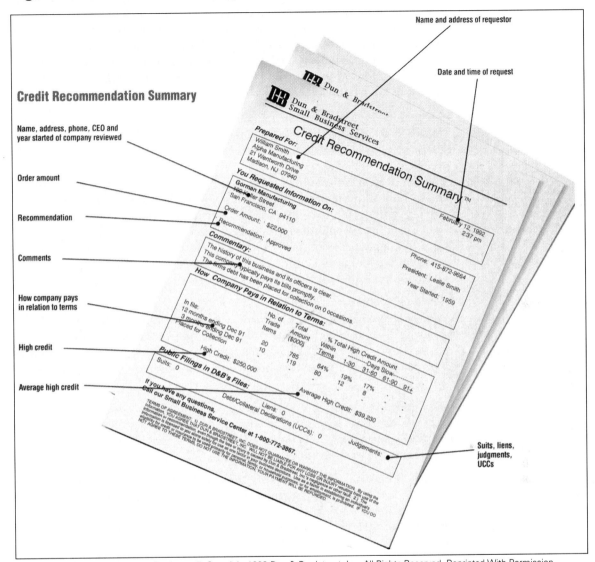

Cash discounts can also be offered as an incentive for quick payment. Discounts reduce the invoice amount by a stated percentage if payment is made within a specified time period.

Collection of Past-Due Accounts. Slow credit accounts are a problem because they tie up the seller's working capital, prevent further sales to the slow-paying customer, and lead to losses from bad debts. Even if the slow-paying customer is not lost, relations with this customer are strained for a time at least.

Inadequate records and collection procedures often fail to alert the small firm in time to permit prompt collections. Also, the personal acquaintance of seller and customer sometimes tempts the seller to be less than businesslike in extending further credit and collecting overdue accounts. Conceding the seriousness of the problem, the small firm must know what steps to take and how far to go in collecting past-due accounts. It must decide whether to undertake the job directly or to turn it over to an attorney or a collection agency.

Collection Procedures. Perhaps the most effective weapon in collecting past-due accounts is the debtors' knowledge of possible impairment of their credit standing. This impairment is certain if an account is turned over to a collection agency. Delinquent customers who foresee continued solvency will typically attempt to avoid damage to their credit standing, particularly when it would be known to the business community generally. It is this knowledge that lies behind and strengthens the various collection efforts of the business.

The small firm should deal with delinquent customers kindly and with compassion. A collection technique which is too threatening may not only fail to work but also could lose a customer or invite legal action. Consider the variety of collection philosophies and tactics shown in the following examples:

"I absolutely guarantee that I can outcollect the goons by being nice," declares Linda Russell, chief executive officer of CollectionCenter, Inc., of Rawlins, Wyoming. The 55-year-old grandmother of five says courtesy has always worked better. . . . The No. 1 rule: Never lose your cool. If a debtor launches into an X-rated rage . . . let him "vent" his frustrations and then say, "I understand how you feel. Let's talk about how we can solve the problem." [8]

Richard Ackerman, president of Credit Resolution Corp. of New York, deals mostly with commercial debtors . . . most are "honorable," . . . [but he] doesn't hesitate to turn the screws on those who aren't. . . . He pays 18 "operatives"—most of them beefy former security guards or policemen—to deliver notices. [9]

At Decoma Industries . . . the Vernon, California architectural firm . . . a red dot goes up next to the names of late-paying customers . . . says president Steve Notara. Notara mails or faxes the customer a copy of the invoice with a note saying work has stopped. Each day he personally calls the two most delinquent customers. Decoma . . . has never had a bad debt. [10]

Many business firms have found that the most effective collection procedure consists of a series of steps, each of which is somewhat more forceful than the preceding one. Although these typically begin with a gentle written reminder, they may include additional letters, telephone calls, registered letters, personal contacts, and referrals to collection agencies or attorneys.[11] The timing of these steps may be carefully standardized so that step two automatically follows step one in a specified number of days, with subsequent steps similarly spaced.

aging schedule
a categorization of accounts receivable based on the length of time they have been outstanding

Aging Accounts Receivable. Many small businesses can benefit from an **aging schedule,** which divides accounts receivable into age categories based on the length of time they have been outstanding. Usually, some accounts are current and others are past due. Various collection actions can be used for different-aged accounts. With successive scheduling, troublesome trends can be spotted and appropriate action taken. With experience, the probabilities of collecting accounts of various ages can be estimated and used to forecast cash conversion rates.

Table 13-2 shows a hypothetical aging of accounts receivable. It shows that four customers have overdue payments totaling $200,000. Only customer 005 is current. Customer 003 has the largest amount ($80,000) of overdue credit. In fact, the schedule shows that customer 003 is overdue on all charges and has a past record of slow payment (a credit rating of "C"). Immediate attention to collecting from this customer is necessary. Customer 002 should be contacted also. The status of this customer is critical because, among overdue accounts, customer 002 has the largest amount ($110,000) in the "Not Due" classifications. This customer could quickly have the largest amount overdue.

Customers 004 and 001 need a special kind of analysis. Customer 004 has $10,000 less overdue than customer 001. However, customer 004's overdue credit of $40,000, which is 60 days past due, may well have a serious impact on the $100,000 not yet due ($10,000 in the beyond-discount period plus $90,000 still in the discount period). On the other hand, even though customer 001 has $50,000 of overdue credit, he or she is overdue only 15 days. Also, customer 001 has only $50,000 not yet due ($30,000 in the beyond-discount period plus

Table 13-2
Hypothetical Aging of Accounts Receivable

Account Status	Customer Account Numbers					
	001	002	003	004	005	Total
Days Past Due						
120 days	—	—	$50,000	—	—	$ 50,000
90 days	—	$10,000	—	—	—	10,000
60 days	—	—	—	$40,000	—	40,000
30 days	—	20,000	20,000	—	—	40,000
15 days	$50,000	—	10,000	—	—	60,000
Total Overdue	$50,000	$30,000	$80,000	$40,000	$ 0	$200,000
Not Due (beyond-discount period)	$30,000	$ 10,000	$ 0	$10,000	$130,000	$180,000
Not Due (still in discount period)	$20,000	$100,000	$ 0	$90,000	$220,000	$430,000
Credit Rating	A	B	C	A	A	

SMALL BUSINESS IN ACTION

Bad Debt Not All Bad

Credit is a powerful sales tool. However, extending credit to maximize sales without regard to credit risk can lead to trouble. Nevertheless, zero credit risk may not be the wisest of goals either!

Consider the credit philosophy of James K. Ullery, who is credit manager for the small firm of Albany Ladder in Albany, New York. Ullery does not believe his only job responsibility is to keep bad-debt totals low. Lester J. Heath, III, president of the building supplies company, agrees. He contends that "sales and market share . . . are the key things you should look at, not bad debt. If your bad debt isn't high enough, you aren't taking enough risk." Albany Ladder's bad-debt ratio is nearly twice the industry average!

Heath began implementing his liberal credit policy when he grew tired of losing potential customers who did not have the ability to get loans to purchase building supplies from his company. "If you extend credit to a person who couldn't get it elsewhere, he'll remember that gesture forever and could be a customer for life."

Despite Albany Ladder's liberal credit policy, its collection policy is aggressive, beginning the first day that an account is overdue. "We make mistakes, no question about it," says Ullery. However, Albany Ladder is based on treating customers as human beings and recognizing that a few bad debts are only human.

Source: Paul B. Brown, "Bad Debt Can Be Good for Business." Reprinted with permission, *Inc.* magazine (March 1988). Copyright © 1988 Goldhirsh Group, Inc., 38 Commercial Wharf, Boston, MA 02110.

$20,000 still in the discount period) as compared to $100,000 not yet due from customer 004. Both customers have a credit rating of "A."

In conclusion, customer 001 is a better potential source of cash; so, collection efforts need to begin with customer 004 rather than with customer 001. Customer 001 may simply need a reminder that he or she has an overdue account of $50,000.

The Bad-Debt Ratio. In controlling expenses associated with credit sales, it is possible to use various expense ratios. The best known and most widely used ratio is the **bad-debt ratio,** which is computed by dividing the amount of bad debts by the total credit sales.

bad-debt ratio

a ratio of bad debts to total credit sales

The bad-debt ratio reflects the efficiency of credit policies and procedures. A small firm may thus compare the effectiveness of its credit management with that of other firms. There is a relationship between the bad-debt ratio on the one hand and the type of business, profitability, and size of firm on the other. Small profitable retailers have a much higher loss ratio than large profitable retailers. The bad-debt losses of all small-business firms, however, range from a fraction of 1 percent of net sales to percentages large enough to put them out of business!

Credit Regulation

The granting of credit is regulated by a variety of federal and state laws. Prior to the passage of legislation, credit customers were often confused by credit agreements and were sometimes victims of credit abuse. As is usually the case, legislation covering credit practices varies considerably from state to state. Further discussion can be found in Chapter 26, Working Within The Law.

By far the most significant piece of credit legislation is the federal Consumer Credit Protection Act, part of which is known as the 1968 Truth-in-Lending Act. Its two primary purposes are to inform consumers about terms of a credit agreement and to require creditors to specify how finance charges are computed. The law requires that the finance charge be stated as an annual percentage rate. The law also requires creditors to specify the procedures for correcting billing mistakes.

Other legislation related to credit management includes:

1. *The Fair Credit Billing Act*—This law provides protection to credit customers for cases involving incorrect billing. A reasonable time period is allowed for corrections.
2. *The Fair Credit Reporting Act*—This act gives certain rights to credit applicants regarding credit reports prepared by credit bureaus.
3. *The Equal Credit Opportunity Act*—This act protects widowed and divorced women against credit denial because of a lack of credit history.
4. *The Fair Debt Collection Practices Act*—This law bans intimidation and deception in collection.

1. Cost considerations in pricing involve an understanding of the components of total variable costs and of total fixed costs. Demand considerations involve such factors as product appeal, marketing effort, and product price, all of which exert an influence on demand. An understanding of elastic demand and inelastic demand is also important.
2. Break-even analysis in pricing entails a formal comparison of cost and demand for purposes of determining the acceptability of alternative prices. Fixed and variable costs are used to construct a cost break-even chart. Demand factors can be incorporated to construct a cost-adjusted break-even chart.
3. In setting the actual price for a product or service, a firm should also consider specific marketing objectives. Penetration pricing, skimming pricing, follow-the-leader pricing, flexible pricing, price lining, and what-the-traffic-will-bear pricing all reflect different objectives. Markup calculations should be understood by all businesses—especially retailers.
4. Consumer credit is credit granted by retailers to final consumers and includes open charge accounts, installment accounts, and revolving charge accounts. Trade credit is credit extended by nonfinancial firms to customers who are other business firms. Credit cards are a major source of retail credit.
5. Credit management should begin prior to the first credit sale and continue throughout the credit cycle. Collection of past-due accounts first involves an aging of accounts receivable and then a series of collection steps.

DISCUSSION QUESTIONS

1. Explain why both pricing and credit decisions are so vital to a small business.
2. How can average-cost pricing sometimes result in a bad pricing decision?
3. Explain the importance of fixed and variable costs to the pricing decision.
4. How does the concept of elasticity of demand relate to prestige pricing? Give an example.
5. Contrast the cost-break-even stage of break-even analysis with the cost-adjusted stage. Which is better? Why?
6. What is the difference between a penetration and a skimming-price strategy? Under what circumstances would each be used?
7. What is the psychology behind price lining?
8. If a small business has conducted its break-even analysis properly and finds break-even volume at a price of $10.00 to be 10,000 units, should it price its product at $10.00? Discuss.
9. What percentage markup on cost is a 70 percent markup on selling price? What percentage markup on selling price is a 40 percent markup on cost?
10. What is the difference between consumer credit and trade credit?
11. What are the major benefits of credit to buyers? What are the major benefits to sellers?

12. How does an open charge account differ from a revolving charge account?
13. What is meant by the terms 2/10, n/30? Does it pay to take discounts?
14. What is the major purpose of aging accounts receivable? At what point in credit management should this activity be performed? Why?
15. What impact has the Truth-in-Lending Act had on credit policies? What information in Figure 13-7, page 341, is a direct result of this legislation?

YOU MAKE THE CALL

Situation 1

Steve Jones is a 35-year-old owner of a highly competitive small business supplying temporary office help. Like most businesspeople, he is always looking for ways to increase profits. However, the nature of competition makes it very difficult to raise prices for the temps' services, and reducing their wages makes recruiting difficult. Jones has, nevertheless, found an area where improvement should increase profits—bad debts.

A friend and business consultant met with Jones to advise him on improved credit-management policies. Jones was extremely pleased to have help since bad debts were costing him about 2 percent of sales. Currently, Jones has no system of managing credit.

Questions

1. What advice would you give Jones regarding screening of new credit customers?
2. What action should Jones take to encourage current credit customers to pay their debts? Be specific.
3. Jones has considered eliminating credit sales. What are the possible consequences of this decision?

Situation 2

Mom's Monogram is a small firm manufacturing and imprinting monogramming designs for jackets, caps, T-shirts, and other articles of clothing. The business has been in operation for two years. In the first year, sales reached $50,000. The next year, sales raced up to $300,000. Pricing of the firm's service has been a straight, cost-plus approach.

Success has spawned plans to double plant and equipment. The owners have never spent money advertising and figure that the expansion will double sales within the next three years. The owners plan to continue pricing their services using a cost-plus formula.

Questions

1. What problems may be encountered by the business if it continues to use cost-plus pricing?
2. How should the firm's total costs be analyzed to ascertain its pricing strategy?

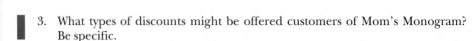

3. What types of discounts might be offered customers of Mom's Monogram? Be specific.

EXPERIENTIAL EXERCISES

1. Interview a small-business owner regarding his or her pricing strategies. Try to ascertain whether the pricing policy used reflects fixed and variable costs in the business. Prepare a report of your findings.
2. Interview a small-business owner regarding his or her policies for evaluating the credit risks of credit applicants. Summarize your findings in a report.
3. Invite a credit manager from a retail store to speak to the class on the benefits and problems of credit to buyers and sellers.
4. Interview a sample of small-business owners in your community who extend credit. Ask each owner to describe what credit management policies he or she uses to collect bad debts. Report your findings to the class.

REFERENCES TO SMALL-BUSINESS PRACTICES

Barrier, Michael. "Kemmons Wilson Changes His Mind," *Nation's Business,* Vol. 77, No. 3 (March 1989), pp. 77–78.

> An older and successful entrepreneur describes his new motel venture, including his pricing plan.

Brown, Paul B. "How to Compete on Price," *Inc.,* Vol. 12, No. 5 (May 1990), pp. 105–107.

> The small manufacturing firm described in this article uses a low pricing strategy to gain sales for its jewelry products.

Brown, Paul B. "You Get What You Pay For," *Inc.,* Vol. 12, No. 10 (October 1990), pp. 155–156.

> The young couple featured in this article use a multiple pricing strategy to properly reflect different levels of service offered to their supermarket customers.

Fraser, Jill Andresky. "Getting Paid," *Inc.,* Vol. 12, No. 6 (June 1990), pp. 58–69.

> How to make collecting bills easier is discussed in this article.

Gilbert, Nathaniel. "Coming To Terms," *Entrepreneur,* Vol. 19, No. 10 (October 1991), pp. 164–167.

> This article explores how credit terms can make or break a business.

Jereski, Laura. "Hearts, Minds and Market Share," *Forbes,* Vol. 143, No. 7 (April 3, 1989), pp. 80–82.

> The pricing strategy of husband and wife entrepreneurs is described in this article. Their company's all-natural toothpaste is priced higher than its competition.

ENDNOTES

1. Perfectly inelastic demand is assumed to emphasize the point.
2. "Higher Price, Higher Sales," *Inc.,* Vol. 10, No. 10 (October 1988), p. 112.
3. For an excellent discussion of price setting, see Charles W. Lamb, Jr., Joseph F. Hair, Jr., and Carl McDaniel, *Principles of Marketing* (Cincinnati, OH: South-Western Publishing Co., 1992), Chapter 17.

4. Gerald Pintel and Jay Diamond, *Retailing,* 4th ed. (Englewood Cliffs, NJ: Prentice-Hall, Inc., 1987), p. 428.

5. Daniel B. Klein and Jason Richner, "What You Should Know About Credit Ratings," *Consumers' Research,* Vol. 75, No. 9 (September 1992), p. 11.

6. *Ibid.*

7. Richard J. Maturi, "Collection Dues and Don'ts," *Entrepreneur,* Vol. 20, No. 1 (January 1992), p. 326.

8. Brent Bowers, "Bill Collectors Thrive Using Kinder, Gentler Approach," *The Wall Street Journal* (March 2, 1992), p. B2.

9. *Ibid.*

10. "Red Alert," *Inc.,* Vol. 12, No. 12 (December 1990), p. 148.

11. For an example of a well-written collection letter, see "The Ideal Collection Letter," *Inc.,* Vol. 13, No. 2 (February 1991), pp. 60–61.

CHAPTER 14

Promotion: Personal Selling, Advertising, and Sales Promotion

SPOTLIGHT ON SMALL BUSINESS

Brian Rekow

Sponsorship of events like the Olympics or the Super Bowl costs giant corporations millions of dollars; however, it greatly enhances the visibility of their products. Sponsorship of smaller events such as the local high school yearbook or a community clean-up day costs much less and likewise greatly benefits a small firm's image.

Local event sponsorship is an opportunity for a small business to say "thank you" to its customers. "At the very least, sponsoring an event allows you to show your company's best features to a highly qualified audience," says Linda Surbeck, president of a special event planning firm in Lexington, Kentucky. "Along the way, you can achieve market awareness, favorable name recognition and positive publicity . . .," she says.

Consider the educational toy retailer, Thinker Toys, in Bellevue, Washington. Its owner, Brian Rekow, is helping underwrite a children's film festival at the local Children's Museum.

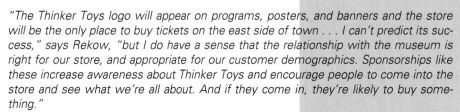

"The Thinker Toys logo will appear on programs, posters, and banners and the store will be the only place to buy tickets on the east side of town . . . I can't predict its success," says Rekow, "but I do have a sense that the relationship with the museum is right for our store, and appropriate for our customer demographics. Sponsorships like these increase awareness about Thinker Toys and encourage people to come into the store and see what we're all about. And if they come in, they're likely to buy something."

Rekow's testimony suggests that sponsorship is a viable strategy for small companies to enable them to break through the clutter of traditional promotions and target their market niches.

Source: Alison Davis, "Big Events for Small Businesses," *Independent Business*, Vol. 3, No. 5 (May–June 1992), pp. 56–57.

After studying this chapter, you should be able to:
1. Discuss considerations in developing a promotional mix.
2. List and explain four methods of determining promotional expenditures.
3. Prepare and make a sales presentation.
4. Identify advertising options for the small business.
5. Describe three types of sales promotional tools.

LOOKING BACK

NEW TERMS AND CONCEPTS

promotion
promotional mix
personal selling

prospecting
advertising
product advertising

institutional advertising
sales promotion
publicity

The old adage, "Build a better mousetrap and the world will beat a path to your door," suggests the value of innovation but does not eliminate the need for promotion. Why? Because potential customers must be informed of the new, improved "mousetrap" and how to get to the door! They may even need to be persuaded that the mousetrap is better. This process of informing and persuading is essentially promotion. **Promotion** is the marketing activity concerned with persuasive communications that facilitate the exchange of a firm's bundle of satisfaction.

promotion
persuasive communication between a business and its target market

Small businesses use promotion in varying degrees. Any given firm can use some or all of many promotional tools. Four promotional activities discussed in this chapter are promotional planning, personal selling, advertising, and sales promotion.

PROMOTIONAL PLANNING

Promotion is a complex area, and most entrepreneurs are not "turned" in that direction. However, you can begin to understand promotion by realizing that promotion is largely communication. In fact, promotion is worthless unless it communicates. Therefore, let's briefly look at the communication process and see how promotion needs to be built on a correct understanding of this process.

The Communication Process

All of us communicate each day. However, we may not realize that communication is a process with identifiable components. Every communication involves a source, a channel, and a receiver. Figure 14-1 depicts the components of communication.

Part A in the figure represents a nonbusiness communication. Part B represents a small-business communication. As you can see, the differences between

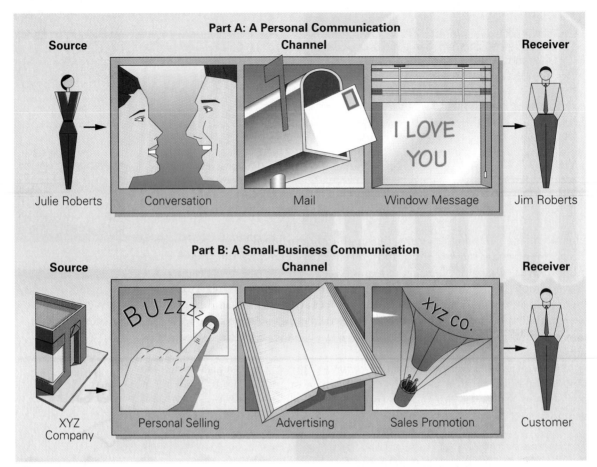

Figure 14-1
Analogy of Personal
and Small-Business
Communication

parts A and B are in form, not in basic structure. The receiver for Julie Robert's communication is Jim Roberts. She has used three different channels for her message: personal conversation, mail, and a special window message. The receiver for the small-business communications from the XYZ Company is the customer. The XYZ Company has used three message channels: personal selling, advertising, and sales promotion. The conversation and personal selling are both personal one-on-one communications. Likewise, the mail and the Yellow Pages are both forms of written, nonpersonal communication. Finally, the window message and the hot air balloon are both special promotional channels.

A strong promotional plan builds on the effective use of the communication process. A good promotional plan must consider three major topics: which promotional tools to mix together, how much to spend, and how to create the messages.

Promotional Mixes

A **promotional mix** involves a blend of personal and nonpersonal selling by marketers. The mixture of the various promotional methods—personal selling, advertising, and sales promotion—is influenced by three major factors. First is the geographical nature of the market to be reached. A widely dispersed market tends to favor mass coverage by advertising, in contrast to the more costly individual contacts of personal selling. On the other hand, if the market is local, with a relatively small number of customers, personal selling is more feasible.

promotional mix
the blend of promotional methods for a target market

Second, a small business must identify its customers. It is expensive to use shotgun promotion which "hits" potential customers and nonpotential customers alike. This error can be minimized by analyzing media audiences. The media are extremely helpful in profiling their audiences. But remember, a small business cannot obtain a media *match* until it has specified its target market carefully.

The third factor that influences the promotional mix is the product's own characteristics. If a product is of high unit value, personal selling will be a vital ingredient in the mix. Personal selling is also an effective method for promoting highly technical products. On the other hand, sales promotion will more likely be used with an impulse good than with a shopping good.

There are, of course, other considerations that must ultimately be considered when developing the promotional mix. For example, the high total cost of the optimum mix may necessitate substitution of a less expensive, and a less than optimum, alternative. Nevertheless, your promotional planning should determine the optimum combination of methods. You can then make cost-saving adjustments if absolutely necessary.

Techniques of Determining Promotional Expenditures

Unfortunately, there are no mathematical formulas to answer the question, "How much should a small business spend on promotion?" There are, however, some helpful approaches to solving the problem. The most common methods of budgeting funds for small business promotion are:

1. A percentage of sales (APS).
2. What can be spared (WCS).
3. As much as competition spends (ACS).
4. What it takes to do the job (WTDJ).

A Percentage of Sales (APS). Earmarking promotional dollars based on a percentage of sales is a simple method for a small business to use. A company's own past experiences are evaluated to establish a promotion/sales ratio.

SMALL BUSINESS IN ACTION

Creative Promotion Helps Firm Get Second Wind

How can a tiny firm promote a new product when it lacks the huge advertising resources of large corporations? One answer is to adopt promotional strategies that are creative without being too costly. Gus Blythe and his Paso Robles, California, firm used this approach to promote "Second-Wind," a product for cleaning sneakers.

Blythe first tried advertising in running magazines, but his budget was too small to be effective. He then conceived the idea of collaborating with running-shoe manufacturers. Blythe argued that his product was good and that promoting its use would also help the sneaker manufacturer.

At first, shoe manufacturers were reluctant to endorse SecondWind, feeling that clean shoes would deter repeat purchases. However, Blythe had an answer to this concern: "If you have two pairs of shoes in your closet, one clean and one dirty, which are you likely to wear?" asked Blythe. "The clean ones, right? If you wear them more,

they wear out faster, which means you have to buy new ones," he added.

He eventually convinced nine of the top ten sneaker manufacturers to recommend Second-Wind as a cleaner for their shoes. In return, Blythe agreed to include pictures of their shoes on the product's package.

Source: "Creative Promotion Helps Firm Get Second Wind." Reprinted with permission, *Inc.* magazine (July 1989). Copyright © 1989 by Goldhirsh Group, Inc., 38 Commercial Wharf, Boston, MA 02110.

If 2 percent of sales, for example, has historically been spent on promotion, the business will budget 2 percent of forecasted sales for promotion. Secondary data can be checked to locate industry averages for comparison.

The major shortcoming of this method is its inherent tendency to spend more dollars when sales are increasing and less when they are declining. If promotion stimulates sales, the reverse would seem desirable.

What Can Be Spared (WCS). A widely used piecemeal approach to promotional budgeting is to spend what is left over when all other activities have been funded. Sometimes a budget may be nonexistent and spending determined only when a media representative sells the entrepreneur on a special deal. Such an approach to promotional spending should be avoided because it neglects analysis of promotional needs.

As Much as Competition Spends (ACS). This technique builds a budget based on competition. If the small business can duplicate the promotional mix of close competitors, it will at least be spending as much as the competition. If a competitor is a large business, this approach is not feasible. However, this method can be used to react to short-run promotional tactics by small competitors. Unfortunately, it results in copying mistakes as well as successes, even though it may enable a firm to remain competitive.

What It Takes to Do the Job (WTDJ). The preferred approach to estimating promotional expenditures is to decide what it takes to do the job. This method requires a comprehensive analysis of the market and promotional alternatives. Assuming reasonably accurate estimates, this approach determines the amount that truly needs to be spent.

Our recommendation to a small business for estimating promotional expenditures incorporates all four approaches. This idea is represented by the flow chart in Figure 14-2. Start with an estimate of what it takes to do the job (WTDJ). If this estimate is equal to or smaller than any of the other three estimates, proceed to invest that amount in promotion. If the WTDJ estimate is larger than any of the others, compute the average of the four estimates [(WTDJ + APS + WCS + ACS)/4]. Then compare the what can be spared (WCS) estimate with this average. If WCS equals or exceeds the average estimate, proceed to develop the promotion at the average estimate. On the other hand, if the WCS is less than the average, additional funds for promotion should be sought.

Creating the Message

Most small businesses must rely on others' expertise in creating promotional messages. Therefore, this chapter does not pursue this topic.[1] Fortunately, there are several sources for this specialized assistance: advertising agencies, suppliers, trade associations, and the advertising media.

Some of the services that advertising agencies provide are:

1. Furnishing design, artwork, and copy for specific advertisements and/or commercials.
2. Evaluating and recommending the advertising media with the greatest "pulling power."
3. Evaluating the effectiveness of different advertising appeals.
4. Advising on sales promotions and merchandise displays.
5. Making market-sampling studies for evaluating product acceptance or area sales potentials and furnishing mailing lists.

Since an advertising agency may charge a fee for its services, the advertiser must make sure that the return from those services will be greater than the fees paid. Only a competent agency can be of real assistance to the advertiser.[2]

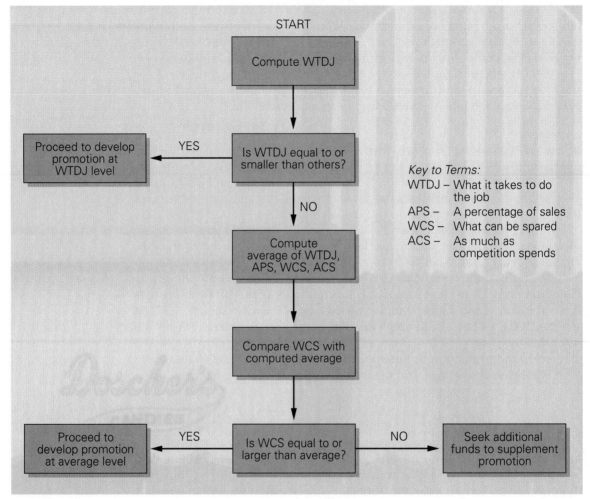

Figure 14-2
Flowchart for Comparing Alternative Promotion Expense Estimates

Other outside sources may also provide assistance in formulating and carrying out promotional programs. Suppliers often furnish display aids and even entire advertising programs to their dealers. Trade associations also are active in this area. Finally, the advertising media can provide some of the same services offered by an ad agency.

PERSONAL SELLING

personal selling
promotion delivered in a personal, one-on-one manner

Many products require personal selling. **Personal selling** is promotion delivered in a one-on-one environment. It includes the activities of both the inside salespersons of retail, wholesale, and service establishments and the outside sales representatives who call on business establishments and ultimate consumers.

Importance of Product Knowledge

Effective selling must be built upon a foundation of product knowledge. If a salesperson knows the product's advantages, uses, and limitations, she or he can educate the customers and successfully meet their objections. Most customers look to the salesperson for such information—whether the product is a camera, a suit of clothes, an automobile, paint, a machine tool, or an office machine. Customers seldom are specialists in the products they buy; however, they immediately sense the salesperson's knowledge or ignorance. The significance of product knowledge is revealed by the fact that personal selling degenerates into mere order taking when such knowledge is not possessed by the salesperson.

The Sales Presentation

The heart of personal selling is the sales presentation to the prospective customer. At this crucial point the order is either secured or lost. A preliminary step leading to an effective sales presentation is **prospecting,** a systematic process of continually looking for new customers.[3]

prospecting
a systematic process of continually looking for new customers

Techniques of Prospecting. One of the most efficient techniques of prospecting is through *personal* referrals. Such referrals come from friends, customers, and other businesses. The initial contact with a potential customer is greatly facilitated by the ability to mention that, "You were referred to me by. . . ."

Another technique of prospecting is through *impersonal* referrals. Examples of impersonal referrals are media publications, public records, and directories. Newspapers and magazines, particularly trade magazines, also help identify

Figure 14-3
Customers Depend on the Salesperson to Be Knowledgeable About a Product's Characteristics

prospects. These publications report on new companies entering the market, as well as on new products. Prospects can be derived from this information. For example, wedding announcements in the newspaper are impersonal referrals for a local bridal shop.

Public records of property transactions and building permits can also provide prospects. For example, a garbage pick-up service might find prospective customers from those who are planning to build houses or apartments.

Prospects can be identified without referrals through *marketer-initiated contacts.* Telephone calls or mail surveys, for example, isolate prospects. A market survey conducted for a small business by an author of this text used a mail questionnaire to identify prospects. The questionnaire, which asked technical questions about a service, concluded with the following statement: "If you would be interested in a service of this nature, please check the appropriate space below and your name will be added to the mailing list."

Finally, prospects can also be identified by recording *customer-initiated contacts.* Inquiries by a potential customer that do not conclude in a sale would classify that person as a "hot" prospect. Small furniture stores will often require their salespeople to create a card for each person visiting the retail store. These prospects are then systematically contacted over the telephone. Records of these contacts are updated periodically.

Practicing the Sales Presentation. The old saying that "practice makes perfect" applies to the salesperson prior to making the sales presentation. If you are a salesperson, make the presentation to your spouse, a mirror, or a tape recorder. You may want to use a camcorder to make a "practice video." You may feel a little silly the first few times you practice, but practicing will improve your success rate.

The salesperson should also be aware of possible objections and be prepared to handle them. Although there is no substitute for actual selling experience, there are certain ideas that have proven helpful to deal with objections.[4] Some of these are listed and briefly discussed below.

1. *Comparing the products.* When the prospect is mentally comparing a product being used now or a competing product with the salesperson's product, the salesperson may make a complete comparison of the two. The salesperson lists the advantages and disadvantages of each product.
2. *Relating a case history.* The salesperson describes the experiences of another prospect similar to the prospect to whom he or she is talking.
3. *Demonstrating the product.* A product demonstration gives a quite convincing answer to a product objection because the salesperson lets the product itself overcome the opposition.
4. *Giving guarantees.* Often a guarantee will remove resistance from the prospect's mind. Guarantees assure prospects that they cannot lose by purchasing. The caution, of course, is that guarantees must be meaningful and must provide for some recourse on the part of the prospect if the product does not live up to the guarantee.

5. *Asking questions.* The "why" question is of value in separating excuses from genuine objections and in probing for hidden resistance. The same question is useful in disposing of objections. Probing or exploratory questions are excellent in handling silent resistance. They can be worded and asked in a manner that appeals to the prospect's ego. In making the prospect do some thinking to convince the salesperson, questions of a probing nature get the prospect's full attention.

6. *Showing what delay costs.* A common experience of salespeople is to obtain seemingly sincere agreements to the buying decisions concerning need, product, source, and price, only to find that the prospect wants to wait some time before buying it. In such cases, the salesperson can sometimes take pencil and paper to show conclusively that delay of the purchase is expensive.

7. *Admitting and counterbalancing.* Sometimes the prospect's objection is completely valid because of some limitation in the salesperson's product. The only course of action in this case is for the salesperson to agree that the product does have the disadvantage to which the prospect is obviously objecting. Immediately after the acknowledgment, however, the salesperson should direct the prospect's attention to the advantages that overshadow the limitation of the product.

8. *Hearing the prospect out.* Some prospects object mainly for the opportunity to describe how they were once victimized. The technique recommended for this type of resistance is that of empathetic listening.

9. *Making the objection boomerang.* Once in a while the salesperson can take a prospect's reason for not buying and convert it into a reason for buying. This takes expert handling. Suppose the prospect says, "I'm too busy to see you." The salesperson might reply, "That's why you should see me—I can save you time."

10. *Using the "Yes, but" technique.* The best technique for handling most resistance is the indirect answer known as the "Yes, but" method. Here are two examples of what salespeople might say when using this technique: (1) "Yes, I can understand that attitude, but there is another angle for you to consider." (2) "Yes, you have a point there, but in your particular circumstances, other points are involved, too." The "Yes, but" method avoids argument and friction. It respects the prospect's opinions, attitudes, and thinking, and operates well where the prospect's point does not apply in a particular case.

Making the Sales Presentation. Salespersons must adapt their sales approach to the customer's needs. A "canned" sales talk will not succeed with most buyers. For example, the person selling personal computers must demonstrate the capacity of the equipment to fill a customer's particular word processing needs. Similarly, a boat salesperson must understand the special interests of particular individuals in boating and speak the customer's language. Every sales objection must be answered explicitly and adequately.

There is considerable psychology in successful selling. The salesperson, as a psychologist, must know that some degree of personal enthusiasm, friendliness, and persistence is required. Perhaps 20 percent of all salespersons secure as much as 80 percent of all sales made. This is because they are the 20 percent who persist and who bring enthusiasm and friendliness to the task of selling.

Some salespersons have special sales techniques that they use with success. One automobile salesperson, for example, offered free driving lessons to people who had never taken a driver's training course or who needed a few more lessons before they felt confident enough to take the required driving tests. When such customers were ready to take the driving tests, this salesperson accompanied them to the driver examination grounds for moral support. Needless to say, these special efforts could hardly be turned down by new drivers who were in the market for cars.

Cost Control in Personal Selling

There are both economical and wasteful methods of achieving the same volume of sales. For example, routing traveling salespersons economically and making appointments prior to arrival can conserve time and transportation expense. The cost of an outside sales call on a customer may be considerable— perhaps hundreds of dollars. This emphasizes the need for efficient, intelligent scheduling. Moreover, the salesperson for a manufacturing firm can contribute to cost economy by stressing products that most need selling in order to give the factory a balanced run of production.

Profitability is increased to the extent that sales are made on the basis of quality and service rather than price cutting. All products do not have the same margin of profit, however, and the salesperson can maximize profits by emphasizing high-margin lines.

Compensating Salespeople

Salespeople are compensated in two ways for their efforts: financially and non-financially. A good compensation program will allow its participants to work for both forms of rewards. However, an effective compensation program must begin by recognizing that salespeople's goals may be different from the entrepreneur's goals. For example, the entrepreneur may be seeking nonfinancial goals, but the salespeople may not.

Nonfinancial Rewards. Personal recognition and the satisfaction of reaching a sales quota are examples of nonfinancial rewards. Many small retail businesses will post the photograph of the top salesperson of the week on the bulletin board for all to see. Plaques are also used for a more permanent record of sales achievements.

Financial Rewards. Nonfinancial compensation is important to sales-people, but it doesn't put bread on the table. Financial compensation is typically the more critical issue. There are two basic plans of financial compensation: commissions and straight salary. Each has specific advantages and limitations.

Most small businesses would prefer to use a commission plan of compensation, which is simple and directly related to productivity. Typically a certain percentage of the sales generated by the salesperson is the salesperson's commission. A commission plan incorporates a strong incentive into the selling activities—no sale, no commission! With this type of plan, there is no drain on the firm's cash flow until there is a sale.

With the straight salary form of compensation, salespeople have more security because their level of compensation is assured regardless of personal sales made. However, this method can reduce a salesperson's motivation.

A combination of the two forms of compensation can give the small business the "best of two worlds." It is a common practice to structure combination plans so that salary represents the larger part for new salespeople. As the salesperson gains experience, the ratio is adjusted to provide a greater share from commissions and less from salary.

Building Customer Goodwill

The salesperson must look beyond the immediate sale to build customer goodwill and to create satisfied customers who will patronize the company in the future. One way to accomplish this is to preserve a good appearance, display a pleasant personality, and demonstrate good habits in all contacts with the customer. One can also help build goodwill by understanding the customer's point of view. Courtesy, attention to details, and genuine friendliness will help to gain acceptance with the customer.

Of course, high ethical standards are of primary importance in creating customer goodwill. This rules out misrepresentation, and it requires confidential treatment of a customer's plans.

ADVERTISING

Advertising is the impersonal presentation of an idea that is identified with a business sponsor and is projected through mass media. Common media include television, radio, magazines, newspapers, and billboards. Advertising is a vital part of the vast majority of small-business operations.

advertising
the impersonal presentation of a business idea through mass media

Table 14-1 reports the usage rates of various advertising media from a random survey of 130 small businesses in the state of Iowa.[5] As shown by this study, small firms rely on a number of advertising media. As would be expected, television was used less frequently than the other media. If cable is available, it may

Advertising Media	Type of Firm					
	Retail (n = 52)		Service (n = 50)		Other (n = 30)	
	First Year (percent)	Current Year (percent)	First Year (percent)	Current Year (percent)	First Year (percent)	Current Year (percent)
Referrals	34.9	31.8	19.7	20.5	34.1	32.6
Newspaper	33.3	28.0	15.9	14.4	31.5	21.2
Telephone Directory	23.4	21.9	15.2	15.2	25.0	22.0
Radio	23.5	19.7	7.6	10.6	16.7	11.4
Flyers	15.2	11.4	8.3	10.6	12.9	11.4
Community Events	14.4	14.4	12.9	12.9	11.4	13.6
Television	3.8	6.8	1.5	3.0	1.5	2.3

Source: Howard E. Van Auken, B. Michael Doran, and Terri L. Rittenburg, "An Emperical Analysis of Small Business Advertising," *Journal of Small Business Management,* Vol. 30, No. 2 (April 1992), p. 90.

Table 14-1
Percentage of Firms Using Each Advertising Media, First and Most Current Year of Operation

offer a channel for local advertising that would be an affordable and properly focused medium for small businesses.

It is interesting to note that referrals (word-of-mouth advertising) are used by a large percentage of the sample. Word-of-mouth is possibly the most effective form of promotion because of its inherent credibility and its low cost—it's free. This evidently is the view of Brooks O'Kane, president of Clear Vue Products in Lawrence, Massachusetts. He has decided to rely completely on word-of-mouth to increase sales for his firm's window cleaner product, Clear Vue. "I'm convinced that those customers who try it once will become repeat customers without the benefit of advertising. . . . Plus, for every one customer, I'm counting on bringing in three more of their friends."[6]

Objectives of Advertising

As a primary goal, advertising draws attention to the existence or superiority of a firm's product or service. To be successful, advertising must rest upon a foundation of product quality and efficient service. Advertising can bring no more than temporary success to an inferior product. Advertising must always be viewed as a complement to a good product and never as a replacement for a bad product.

The entrepreneur should not create false expectations with advertising. This can reduce customer satisfaction. Advertising may also accentuate a trend

SMALL BUSINESS IN ACTION

Successful Professional Selling

All salespeople need the attitude that meeting the client's need is the number-one priority. Consider the thoughts of Carroll Fadal, a highly successful life insurance salesman living in Waco, Texas.

My sales career has been spent in life insurance. I need not tell you the typical image of the life insurance salesperson—a loud, pushy boor in bad clothes who will try to sell you a policy, any policy, whether you need it or not.

Actually, there are some life insurance agents like that, but not nearly as many as some would have you believe. Upon entering the industry after a thirteen year career in journalism, I was determined to be "set apart" from that caricature. My faith made that easier than I had imagined.

Armed with very little knowledge, a lot of desire and a servant's attitude, I set about trying to sell life insurance professionally. My main goal in every client interview was to find out what he or she needed, then determine if I had a product that would fulfill that need. On

more than one occasion, I had to tell the prospect that he didn't need any more life insurance. Imagine his surprise!

Other factors such as education, diligence, honesty and perseverance are also important.

Temptation abounds. If one works on commission, the pressure to make a sale never goes away. At almost every juncture in the sales process, opportunities arise to shade the truth or to omit a seemingly insignificant detail. "Oh well, it's just a little thing, and if I bring it up, it might squirrel the deal," the thought goes.

For every temptation to make the sale without full disclosure, for every desire to "massage the numbers" on a sales proposal, there is the small, still voice reminding us that we are to deal with people with integrity. It is my firm belief, borne out in experience, that in the long run, integrity wins.

Clients want to know that they can count on what they've been told. It takes a lifetime to build a reputation for honesty and integrity; it takes only a moment's slip-up to ruin it.

Source: *Sales Leader,* Vol. 1, No. 2, The Center for Professional Selling, Baylor University, 1993.

in the sale of an item or product line, but it seldom has the power to reverse such a trend. It must, consequently, be closely related to change in customer needs and preferences.

Used superficially, advertising may appear to be a waste of money. It seems expensive, while adding little utility to the product. Nevertheless, the major alternative is personal selling, which is often more expensive and time-consuming.

Types of Advertising

There are two basic types of advertising—product advertising and institutional advertising. **Product advertising** is designed to make potential customers aware of a particular product or service and of their need for it. **Institutional advertising,** on the other hand, conveys an idea regarding the business establishment.

product advertising
advertising designed to make potential customers aware of a product or service and their need for it

institutional advertising
advertising intended to raise public awareness of a business establishment

It is intended to keep the public conscious of the company and of its good reputation. Figure 14-4 illustrates the differences between product advertising and institutional advertising for a small retail clothing store.

No doubt the majority of small-business advertising is of the product type. Retailers' advertisements, for example, stress products almost exclusively, whether those of a supermarket featuring weekend specials or a women's shop focusing upon sportswear. At times the same advertisement carries both product and institutional themes. Furthermore, the same firm may stress product advertising in newspapers and, at the same time, use institutional appeals in the Yellow Pages of the telephone book. Decisions regarding the type of advertising used should be based upon the nature of the business, industry practice, media used, and objectives of the firm.

How Often to Advertise

Frequency of advertising is an important question for the small business. Advertising should be done regularly. Attempts to stimulate interest in a company's products or services should be part of a continuous advertising program. One-shot advertisements that are not part of a well-planned advertising effort lose much of their effectiveness in a short period.

Some noncontinuous advertising, of course, may be justified. This is true, for example, of advertising to prepare consumers for acceptance of a new product. Similarly, special advertising may be employed to suggest to customers new uses for established products. This is also true in advertising special sales.

Where to Advertise

Most small firms have advertising restrictions—either geographic or by class of customer. Advertising media should reach—but not overreach—the present or desired market. From among the many media available, the small-business entrepreneur must choose those that will provide the greatest return for the advertising dollar.

The selection of the right combination of advertising media depends upon the type of business and its governing circumstances. A real estate sales firm, for example, may rely almost exclusively upon classified advertisements in a local newspaper, supplementing these with listings in the Yellow Pages of the telephone book. A transfer and storage firm may use a combination of radio, billboards, and telephone directory advertising to reach individuals planning to move household furniture. A small toy manufacturer may place greatest emphasis on television advertisements and participation in trade fairs. A local retail store may concentrate upon display advertisements in a local newspaper. The selection should be made not only on the basis of tradition but also upon an evaluation of the various ways to cover the particular market.

Figure 14-4

Two Types of Advertising: Product (*left*) and Institutional (*right*)

Figure 14-5
Billboards Are an
Effective Advertis-
ing Medium for
Some Businesses

A good way to build a media mix is to talk with representatives from each medium. The small-business manager will usually find these representatives willing to recommend an assortment of media, not just the ones they represent. Before you meet with these representatives, study as much as possible about advertising so you will know both the weaknesses and the strengths of each medium. Figure 14-6 on pages 374 and 375 gives a summary of several important facts about media.[7] Study this information carefully. Note particularly the advantages and disadvantages of each medium.

SALES PROMOTION

sales promotion
all promotional techniques that are neither personal selling nor advertising

Sales promotion serves as an inducement to perform a certain act while also offering value to recipients. Generally, the term sales promotion includes all promotional techniques that are neither personal selling nor advertising.

When to Use Sales Promotion

The small firm can use sales promotion to accomplish varied objectives. For example, small-business manufacturers can use sales promotion to stimulate commitments among channel intermediaries to market their product. Wholesalers can use sales promotion to induce retailers to buy inventories earlier than normally needed. Finally, with varied sales promotional tools, retailers may be able to induce final consumers to make a purchase.

Sales Promotional Tools

Sales promotion should seldom comprise the entire promotional effort of a small business. Typically, it should be interlaced with advertising and personal selling. A partial list of sales promotional tools follows:

1. Specialties.
2. Publicity.
3. Trade show exhibits.
4. Sampling.
5. Coupons.
6. Premiums.
7. Contests.
8. Point-of-purchase displays.
9. Cooperative advertising.
10. Free merchandise.

The scope of this book does not allow us to comment on each of the sales promotional tools listed. However, we will examine the first three on the list—specialties, publicity, and trade show exhibits.

Specialties. The most widely used specialty item is the calendar. Other examples are pens, key chains, and shirts. Actually, almost anything can be used as a specialty promotion. Every specialty item will be imprinted with the firm's name or other identifying slogan.

The most distinguishing characteristic of specialties is their enduring nature and tangible value. Specialties are referred to as the "lasting medium." As functional products they are also worth something to recipients.

Specialties can be used to promote a product directly or to create company goodwill. Specialties also are excellent reminder promotions. For example, Carpenter Reserve Printing Co., in Cleveland, Ohio, uses poster-calendars to create a lasting image among its customers:

The company's identity is tied to the image of an apple, obliquely suggesting that because of its distinctive qualities, the firm cannot be compared with any other, just as apples cannot be compared with oranges. Each limited-edition poster plays with that theme.

The posters are "eagerly anticipated" by customers each quarter, and many clients collect them, says Lynn Brewton, sales manager at Carpenter Reserve Printing. "It's been a great tool for us."[8]

Finally, specialties are personal. They are distributed directly to the consumer in a personal way; they are items that can be used personally; and they have a personal message. Since the small business needs to retain its personal image, entrepreneurs can use specialties to achieve this objective. Figure 14-7 on page 376 shows a photograph and ad copy of an award-winning specialty ad campaign.

Medium	Market Coverage	Type of Audience
Daily Newspaper	Single community or entire metro area; zoned editions sometimes available.	General; tends more toward men, older age group, slightly higher income and education.
Weekly Newspaper	Single community usually; sometimes a metro area.	General; usually residents of a smaller community.
Shopper	Most households in a single community; chain shoppers can cover a metro area.	Consumer households.
Telephone Directory	Geographic area or occupational field served by the directory.	Active shoppers for goods or services.
Direct Mail	Controlled by the advertiser.	Controlled by the advertiser through use of demographic lists.
Radio	Definable market area surrounding the station's location.	Selected audiences provided by stations with distinct programming formats.
Television	Definable market area surrounding the station's location.	Varies with the time of day; tends toward younger age group, less print-oriented.
Transit	Urban or metro community served by transit system; may be limited to a few transit routes.	Transit riders, especially wage earners and shoppers; pedestrians.
Outdoor	Entire metro area or single neighborhood.	General; especially auto drivers.
Local Magazine	Entire metro area or region; zoned editions sometimes available.	General; tends toward better educated, more affluent.

Figure 14-6   Media Summary

publicity
information about a firm, its products, or services appearing as a news item

Publicity. Of particular importance to retailers because of its high visibility is the type of promotion called **publicity.** Publicity can be used to promote both a product and a firm's image and is a vital part of good public relations for the small business. A good publicity program must maintain regular contacts with the news media.

Particular Suitability	Major Advantage	Major Disadvantage
All general retailers.	Wide circulation.	Nonselective audience.
Retailers who service a strictly local market.	Local identification.	Limited readership.
Neighborhood retailers and service businesses.	Consumer orientation.	A giveaway and not always read.
Services, retailers of brand-name items, highly specialized retailers.	Users are in the market for goods or services.	Limited to active shoppers.
New and expanding businesses; those using coupon returns or catalogs.	Personalized approach to an audience of good prospects.	High CPM.
Businesses catering to identifiable groups; teens, commuters, housewives.	Market selectivity, wide market coverage.	Must be bought consistently to be of value.
Sellers of products or services with wide appeal.	Dramatic impact, wide market coverage.	High cost of time and production.
Businesses along transit routes, especially those appealing to wage earners.	Repetition and length of exposure.	Limited audience.
Amusements, tourist businesses, brand-name retailers.	Dominant size, frequency of exposure.	Clutter of many signs reduces effectiveness of each one.
Restaurants, entertainments, specialty shops, mail-order businesses.	Delivery of a loyal, special-interest audience.	Limited audience.

Figure 14-6
(*Continued*)

Although publicity is considered to be "free" advertising, this is not always an accurate profile of this type of promotion. A cost is associated with this effort. Examples of publicity efforts that entail some expense are involvements with school yearbooks or youth athletic programs. While the benefits are difficult to measure, publicity is nevertheless important to a small business and should be exploited.

Figure 14-7
Award-Winning
Specialty
Advertising Effort

Objective: To create awareness and initiate sales of a new product line.

Strategy & Execution: This exclusive banana importer was expanding into the distribution of a variety of fresh fruits, and wanted to promote this to its existing accounts. Targeting 150 wholesaler customers, the advertiser's specialty advertising counselor developed a program involving the hand distribution of a magnetic spin-a-clip. The advertiser had new 800 numbers which spelled 'bananas' and 'fruit,' and illustrated these on both sides of the magnetic roller with colorful fruit graphics. The sales force also hand-delivered a unique candy jar filled with fruit-shaped candies in fruit colors. A colorful brochure complemented the items.

Results: It was reported reactions were excellent. The increased demand for the new fresh fruit product line and reorders for the spin-a-clip made the promotion a success.

Source: Specialty Advertising Association International.

As an example, Pet Cards, Inc., in Baltimore, Maryland, creates cards designed for pet-lovers to send to their favorite animals. These unique greeting cards are designed by the owners at their in-home business and feature special pet occasions such as Valentine's Day and congratulations on the birth of a new litter. These entrepreneurs found that advertising agencies were quoting a minimum of $200,000 for a startup campaign. Therefore, they decided to do the promotion themselves and began making phone calls to newspapers.

Our phone calls . . . produced several interviews and we are hoping for more. The publicity seems to be working. One retailer put the cards away but then had to display them again because of customer requests generated by a newspaper article.[9]

Trade Show Exhibits. The use of exhibits permits product demonstrations, or "hands-on" experience with a product. The customer's place of business is not always the best environment for product demonstrations in normal personal selling efforts. And advertising cannot always substitute for trial experiences with a product.

Exhibits are of particular value to manufacturers. The greatest benefit of exhibits is their potential cost savings over personal selling. Trade-show groups claim that the cost of exhibits is less than one-fourth the cost of a sales call.[10] Small manufacturers also view exhibits as offering a savings over advertising. For example, Neil Terk, president of Terk Technologies Corporation, located in New Rochelle, New York, manufactures FM radio antennas. He was pleased with his strategy to exhibit at a large Chicago trade show. "It was absolutely the right decision," he says. "My sales now are spectacular."[11]

LOOKING BACK

1. The promotional mix includes personal selling, advertising, and sales promotion. The exact mixture is influenced by the nature of the market and the nature of the product. The optimum promotional mix may be modified because of cost limitations.

2. The four techniques used to estimate promotional funding needs are (1) a percentage of sales, (2) what can be spared, (3) as much as competition spends, and (4) what it takes to do the job.

3. The two major steps in preparing for a sales presentation are prospecting and practicing. In making the sales presentation, salespersons must adapt their sales approach to the customer's needs and must show some degree of enthusiasm, friendliness, and persistence.

4. The two general types of advertising are product advertising and institutional advertising. Each available form of advertising has certain advantages and disadvantages. The majority of small-business advertising is product advertising.

5. Sales promotion can be used (1) by the manufacturer to stimulate commitments among channel intermediaries to market its product, (2) by the wholesaler to induce retailers to buy inventories earlier than normally needed, and (3) by the retailer to induce final consumers to make a purchase. Some sales promotional tools are specialties, publicity, and exhibits.

DISCUSSION QUESTIONS

1. Discuss the relationship between a small-business communication and a personal communication.

2. Outline a promotional mix that you believe would be appropriate to help market this textbook to college bookstores. Which promotional element do you feel is the most essential to your mix?

3. Discuss the advantages and the disadvantages of each of the methods of earmarking funds for promotion.

4. Which of the four methods of determining promotional expenditures is probably most widely used by small firms? Why?

5. Explain the method for estimating promotional expenditures recommended in the chapter.

6. Outline a system of prospecting that could be used by a small camera store. Incorporate all the techniques presented in the chapter.
7. Why are the salesperson's techniques for handling objections so important to a successful sales presentation?
8. Assume you are going to "sell" your instructor in this course on the idea of eliminating examinations. Make a list of objections you expect to hear and how you would handle each objection.
9. What are some nonfinancial rewards you could offer salespeople?
10. What are the advantages and disadvantages of compensating salespeople by salary? By commission? What is an acceptable compromise?
11. What problems, if any, do you see in selecting television to promote dental laboratory services to dentists? Be specific.
12. Refer to Figure 14-6 on page 374 and list five media that would give the small business the most precise selectivity. Be prepared to substantiate your list.
13. How does sales promotion differ from advertising and personal selling?
14. How do specialties differ from other sales promotional tools? Be specific.
15. Comment on the statement that "publicity is free advertising."

YOU MAKE THE CALL

Situation 1

The driving force behind Cannon Arp's new business was several unpleasant experiences with his car. In fact, there were six experiences—two speeding tickets and four minor "fender-benders." His insurance rates more than doubled, which set Arp to thinking. The result was an idea to design and sell a bumper sticker that read, "To Report Bad Driving, Call My Parents at . . . ."

With a $200 investment, Arp printed 15,000 of the stickers, which contained a space to write in the appropriate telephone number. Arp is now planning his promotion to support his strategy of distribution through auto parts stores.

Questions

1. What role, if any, should personal selling have in Arp's total promotional plan?
2. Arp is considering advertising in magazines. What do you think about this medium for his product?
3. What value might publicity have to selling his stickers? Be specific.

Situation 2

Cheree Moore owns and operates a small business that supplies delicatessens with bulk containers of ready-made salads. When served on salad bars, the salads appear to have been freshly prepared from scratch at the delicatessen. Moore wants additional promotional exposure for her products and is considering using her fleet of trucks as rolling billboards. If successful, she may even attempt to lease space on other trucks.

Moore is concerned about the cost-effectiveness of the idea and also whether the public will even notice the advertisements. She also wonders whether the image of her salad products might be hurt by this advertising medium.

Questions

1. What suggestions can you provide Moore that would help her make this decision?
2. How could she go about determining the cost effectiveness of this strategy?
3. What additional considerations should she evaluate before advertising on trucks?

EXPERIENTIAL EXERCISES

1. Interview the owner or manager of one or more small businesses and determine how he or she develops a promotional budget. Classify the owner's methods into one or more of the four categories (ACS, WCS, ACS, WTDJ) described in the textbook. Report your findings to the class.
2. Select another student in your class and plan a sales presentation. One member of each team should role-play a potential buyer. Make the presentations in class, and ask the remaining students for a critique.
3. Collect an example of a sales promotional item. Analyze the promotion and record your thoughts. Report your analysis in class.
4. Interview a media representative about advertising options for small businesses. Summarize your findings for the class.

REFERENCES TO SMALL-BUSINESS PRACTICES

Forbes, Christine. "Selling Points," *Entrepreneur,* Vol. 18, No. 7 (July 1990), pp. 96–100.
    The importance of a professional demeanor among salespeople is addressed by this article. Preparation of the sales presentation is the best way to demonstrate professionalism, according to the experiences of several entrepreneurs featured in the article.
Greco, Susan. "Do-it-Yourself Marketing," *Inc.,* Vol. 13, No. 11 (November 1991), pp. 52–67.
    This article discusses how small companies are doing more of their advertising and promotions. Event marketing and word-of-mouth advertising are examined extensively.
Lammers, Teri. "Commissions That Smooth Out Sales," *Inc.,* Vol. 13, No. 7 (July 1991), pp. 69–70.
    A vice-president of sales for a small software firm describes the consequence of his company's sales-commission plan—one that was revised to change sales behavior.
Sulski, Jim. "Don't Be a Trade Show Dud," *Independent Business* (July–August 1992), pp. 48–50.
    This article provides a strategy for using trade shows. Several examples of how firms have applied certain tactics are included.
Whittemore, Meg. "PR On a Shoestring," *Nation's Business,* Vol. 79, No. 1 (January 1991), pp. 31–32.
    The public relations experiences of several firms are enumerated by this article.

ENDNOTES

1. A well-written and easy-to-follow discussion of message creation can be found in James S. Norris, *Advertising* (Englewood Cliffs, NJ: Prentice-Hall, 1990).

2. A good article that outlines a step-by-step approach for selecting an advertising agency is Tibor Taraba, "Ad Agencies: 10 Steps to Making a Match," *Small Business Reports* (August 1991), pp. 46–50.

3. For a more detailed discussion of prospecting, see Lawrence B. Chonko and Ben M. Enis, *Professional Selling* (Boston: Allyn and Bacon, 1993), Chapter 9.

4. Joseph Hair, Francis Notturno, and Frederick A. Russ, *Effective Selling*, 8th ed. (Cincinnati, Ohio: South-Western Publishing Co., 1991), pp. 254–355.

5. Howard E. Van Auken, B. Michael Doran, and Terri L. Rittenburg, "An Empirical Analysis of Small Business Advertising," *Journal of Small Business Management*, Vol. 30, No. 2 (April 1992), p. 90.

6. Suzanne Alexander, "For Cleaner Maker, Madison Avenue Is Just a Street," *The Wall Street Journal* (October 5, 1990), p. B2.

7. Reprinted with permission from Bank of America, NT&SA, "Advertising Small Business," *Small Business Reporter,* Vol. 15, No. 2, Copyright 1981.

8. "How to Keep Your Name on the Minds of Clients," *Nation's Business,* Vol. 80, No. 9 (September 1992), p. 10.

9. Mary Jane Brand and Bitten Norman, "Greetings With a Playful Purpose," *Nation's Business,* Vol. 78, No. 7 (July 1990), p. 6.

10. Leslie Bloom, "Trade Show Selling Tactics," *In Business,* Vol. 10, No. 4 (July–August 1988), p. 43.

11. Jeffrey A. Tannenbaum, "Trade Shows Can Pay Off for New Firms," *The Wall Street Journal* (January 11, 1989), pp. B1–B2.

CHAPTER 15

Distribution Channels and International Markets

Lawrence Chan

SPOTLIGHT ON SMALL BUSINESS

Global markets often attract new firms that lack international experience. One option for these small firms is to hire people with international experience. This is the strategy adopted by Stratus, a Massachusetts-based computer manufacturer.

Stratus started from scratch in 1982 serving customer needs in several industries such as financial services, telecommunications, and travel. When Stratus decided to move into the Far East in 1985, it hired Lawrence Chan, a Hong Kong native with 23 years of computer experience. Chan said of Stratus, "I was really impressed with the whole operation there. . . . They were still very young, but they already had a global vision. So I decided to join."

Chan was given responsibility for setting up Stratus Far East, which he began in "his apartment with a telephone and a PC." Six years later, Stratus had gone from no systems in all of Asia to more than 150 systems. The company's strategy has paid off. The Asia/Pacific region is now the fastest growing market for the firm's products.

Source: Bryan Batson, "The Road Less Traveled," *Sales & Marketing Management*, Vol. 144, No. 15 (December 1992), pp. 46–51.

After studying this chapter, you should be able to:
1. Identify alternative channels of distribution.
2. Explain the functions of marketing intermediaries in a channel of distribution.
3. Recognize the need to study the cultural, political, and economic forces affecting foreign markets.
4. Describe various sales and distribution channels for exporting.
5. Discuss types of exporting assistance and trade agreements.

NEW TERMS AND CONCEPTS

distribution
physical distribution (logistics)
channel of distribution
direct channel
indirect channel
dual distribution
breaking bulk

assorting
merchant middlemen
agents and brokers
common carriers
contract carriers
private carriers
licensing
forfaiting

letter of credit
Free Trade Agreement (FTA)
North American Free Trade Agreement (NAFTA)

At some point every product or service must be delivered to a customer. Until this exchange is consummated, purchasers cannot derive the benefits they seek. Therefore, the small business requires a distribution strategy to ensure that products arrive at the proper place at the correct moment for maximum customer satisfaction.

Given today's global marketplace, a small business may find opportunities in international marketing. Therefore, this chapter examines several aspects of international distribution as well as distribution in the U.S. market.

DISTRIBUTION ACTIVITIES

distribution
physically moving products and establishing intermediary channels

physical distribution (logistics)
the physical movement activities of distribution

channel of distribution
the system of intermediaries that distribute a product

Distribution activities are frequently considered less glamorous than other marketing activities such as product design, packaging, name selection, and promotional decisions. Nevertheless, an effective distribution system is just as important to the small firm as is a clever promotional campaign.

Prior to formalizing a distribution plan, a small-business manager should understand and appreciate certain underlying principles of distribution. These principles apply to both domestic and international distribution.

Distribution Defined

The term **distribution** in marketing includes both the physical movement of products and the establishment of intermediary (middleman) relationships to guide and support the movement of the product. The physical movement activities form a special field called **physical distribution** or **logistics.** The intermediary system is called a **channel of distribution.**

Distribution is essential for both tangible and intangible goods (services).

Figure 15-1
Distribution Involves Establishing Intermediaries Such as This Dairy Products Distribution Center

Since distribution activities are more visible for tangible goods, our discussion will concentrate on them. Most intangible goods are delivered directly to the user. An income tax preparer and barber, for example, serve clients directly. But even a person's labor can involve channel intermediaries as when, for example, an employment agency for temporary employees is used to find an employer.

Channels of Distribution

A channel of distribution can be either direct or indirect. In a **direct channel,** there are no intermediaries. The product goes directly from producer to user. In an **indirect channel,** there may be one or more intermediaries between the producer and the user.

Figure 15-2 depicts the basic options available for structuring a channel of distribution. Channel A has no intermediaries; it is a direct channel. Door-to-door retailing and mail-order marketing are familiar forms of this channel system for consumer goods.

Channels of the type B incorporate one intermediary and are frequently used for both consumer and industrial goods. As final consumers, we are all familiar with retailers. Industrial purchasers are equally familiar with industrial distributors. Channel C, with two stages of intermediaries, is probably the most typical channel for small businesses that have a large geographic market. Channel D represents the further extension of Channel C. For example, there may be three or more separate intermediaries in the channel. It should be noted that a small business may use more than one channel of distribution—a practice called **dual distribution.**

Firms that successfully employ a single distribution channel may move to

direct channel
a distribution channel without intermediaries

indirect channel
a distribution channel with one or more intermediaries

dual distribution
distribution that involves more than one channel

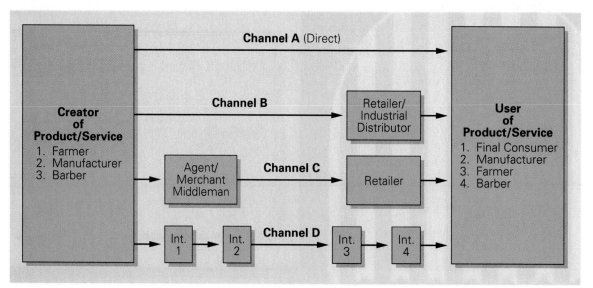

Figure 15-2
Alternative
Channels of
Distribution

dual distribution if an additional channel will improve overall profitability. For example, Avon, now a relatively large firm, is famous for its "Avon calling" theme, which symbolizes its traditional door-to-door product distribution. Recently, however, Avon has announced a toll-free telephone number for customers to place orders. This distribution strategy reflects cultural change— fewer women at home to answer the "Avon calling" message.[1]

Justifying Channels of Distribution

A manager may be puzzled over the use of intermediaries in a channel of distribution. Are they really necessary? What kinds of small businesses need them? Intermediaries exist to carry out necessary marketing functions. Often intermediaries can perform these functions better than the producer or the user of a product.

As an example of the need for intermediaries, consider small producers. The small producer can perform distribution functions if the geographic market is extremely small, if customers' needs are highly specialized, and if risk levels are low. Otherwise, intermediaries may be a more efficient means of performing distribution activities. Of course, many types of small firms also function as intermediaries—for example, retail stores. Four main functions of channel intermediaries are breaking bulk, assorting, providing information, and shifting risks.

breaking bulk
intermediary process that makes large quantities of product available in smaller amounts

Breaking Bulk. Few individual customers demand quantities that are equal to the amounts produced. Therefore, there must be channel activities that will take the larger quantities produced and prepare them for individual customers. **Breaking bulk** is the distribution term used to denote these activi-

SMALL BUSINESS IN ACTION

Dual Distribution Covers Market

Alternative channels of distribution in the marketplace make it possible to select the channel that best fits a given marketing strategy. But what if two channels seem feasible for the same basic product? Consider the response of Ken Dafoe to this problem.

Dafoe's company, named Dafoe & Dafoe, Inc., in Brantford, Ontario, was positioned to introduce a new disposable diaper into the U.S. market. His decision to use two distinct distribution channels came after he evaluated both alternatives and liked each one equally well. Using a distributor in

Arizona, Dafoe sells the product through mail-order, specialty, and natural food stores under the name Tender Care Biodegradable. The distributor promotes the diaper by emphasizing the environmental problems associated with disposal of conventional disposables.

Dafoe's company also distributes through a Massachusetts broker, under the name Nappies, to major grocery chains. The retail price of Nappies is lower than that of Tender Care.

Some observers have asked Dafoe whether he worries about the competition between Tender Care and Nappies. His reply: "I'd rather compete against myself than someone else."

Source: Reprinted with permission, *Inc.* magazine (April 1989). Copyright © 1989 by Goldhirsh Group, Inc., 38 Commercial Wharf, Boston, MA 02110.

ties. Wholesalers and retailers purchase large quantities from manufacturers, store these inventories, and sell them to customers in the quantities they desire.

Assorting. Customers' needs are diverse, requiring many different products to obtain satisfaction. Intermediaries facilitate shopping for a wide assortment of goods through the assorting process. **Assorting** consists of bringing together homogeneous lines of goods into a heterogeneous assortment. For example, a small business producing a special golf club can benefit from an intermediary who carries many other golf-related products and sells to retail pro shops. It is much more convenient for a pro shop manager to buy from one supplier than from all the producers.

assorting
bringing together homogeneous lines of goods into a heterogeneous assortment

Providing Information. One of the major benefits of using an intermediary is information. Intermediaries can provide the producer with extremely helpful data on market size and pricing considerations.

merchant middlemen
intermediaries who take title to the goods they distribute

Shifting Risks. By using intermediaries, the small business can often share or totally shift business risks. This is possible by using **merchant middlemen,** who take title to the goods they distribute. Other intermediaries, such as **agents** and **brokers,** do not take title to the goods.

agents and brokers
distribution intermediaries who do not take title to the goods they distribute

SMALL BUSINESS IN ACTION

Distribution Channel Smells Sweet

The simplest form of distribution channel involves no intermediaries. A product is sold directly by a producer to a final user. Entrepreneurs employing this type of distribution system typically incur high costs, but they also gain more direct control over the marketing of their products.

As an example of this simple channel, consider the distribution of fresh garlic by entrepreneur Carolyn Tognetti, of Gilroy, California. The Tognetti family farms garlic in a community that, since 1979, has held yearly garlic festivals attracting over 100,000 people. Carolyn Tognetti started selling garlic in 1971 through a roadside stand. In March, 1986, she and her husband opened a 10,000-square-foot store costing $750,000. In 1987, Garlic World, as it is called, sold over $300,000 worth of fresh garlic! The store sells garlic-flavored food items and also Garlic World sweatshirts and napkins.

Tognetti is now developing a mail-order business—another example of direct distribution from producer to consumer. Its first catalog mailing of 6,000 copies was made in 1987. (No Scratch-n-Sniff required!) The Tognettis are also "strongly" considering starting a restaurant with, of course, a garlic-flavored menu. This would also constitute direct distribution.

Source: Adapted from Michael Barrier, "Out of This World," *Nation's Business*, Vol. 77, No. 8 (August 1989), p. 13. Reprinted by permission, *Nation's Business*, August 1989. Copyright 1989, U.S. Chamber of Commerce.

Choosing a Distribution System

One source of ideas for the small-business producer in structuring a distribution system is competing businesses. Their distribution systems can at least be used as a starting point to see what system seems practical.

Basically there are three main considerations in structuring a channel of distribution. We will call these the "three C's" of channel choice: costs, coverage, and control.

Costs. We should not think that a direct channel is inherently less expensive than an indirect channel. This is not necessarily true. A small business may well be in a situation in which the less expensive channel is indirect. Small businesses should look at distribution costs as an investment: spending money in order to make money. They should ask themselves whether the money they would invest in intermediaries would get the job done if they used direct distribution.[2]

Coverage. Small businesses use indirect channels of distribution to increase market coverage. To illustrate this point, consider a small-business manufacturer whose sales force can make 10 contacts a week. This direct channel provides 10 contacts a week with the final users of the product. Now consider an indirect channel involving 10 industrial distributors who (for convenience of illustration) each make 10 contacts a week with the final users of the product. With this indirect channel, and no increase in the sales force, the small-business manufacturer is now able to expose the product to 100 final users a week.

Control. A third consideration in choosing a distribution channel is control. There is more control in a direct channel of distribution. With indirect channels, products may not be marketed as intended. The small business must select intermediaries that provide the desired support.

Control is the main reason Robin Rose, of Robin Rose Ice Cream in Los Angeles, distributes her products directly to customers. The reputation of her ice cream depends on the freshness and quality of the product; therefore, she "has purposely remained small in order to control both the production and distribution of her ice cream and chocolates."[3]

The Scope of Physical Distribution

The main component of physical distribution is transportation. Additional components are storage, materials handling, delivery terms, and inventory management. The following sections briefly examine all of these topics except inventory management, which is discussed in Chapter 19.

Transportation. The major decision regarding transportation concerns what mode to use. Alternative modes are traditionally classified as airplanes, trucks, railroads, pipelines, and waterways. Each mode has its unique advantages and disadvantages.[4]

Transportation intermediaries are of three types: common carriers, contract carriers, and private carriers. These are legal classifications that subject the first two types to regulations by federal and/or state agencies. **Common carriers** are available for hire to the general public, while **contract carriers** engage in individual contracts with shippers. Shippers who own their means of transport are called **private carriers.**

Storage. Lack of space is a common problem for a small business. When the channel system uses merchant middlemen or wholesalers, for example, title to

common carriers
transportation intermediaries available for hire to the general public

contract carriers
transportation intermediaries that contract with individual shippers

private carriers
shippers who own their means of transport

the goods is transferred, as is the storage function. On other occasions, the small business must plan for its own warehousing. If a business is too small to own a private warehouse, it can rent space in public warehouses. If storage requirements are simple and involve little special handling equipment, a public warehouse can provide an economical storage function.

Materials Handling. A product is worth little if it is in the right place at the right time but is damaged. Therefore, a physical distribution plan must arrange for materials-handling methods and equipment. Forklifts and special containers and packages are part of a materials-handling system.

Delivery Terms. A small but important part of a physical distribution plan is the terms of delivery. Delivery terms specify the following:

1. Who pays the freight costs.
2. Who selects carriers.
3. Who bears the risk of damage in transit.
4. Who selects the modes of transport.

The simplest delivery term and the one most advantageous to a small-business seller is F.O.B. (free on board) origin, freight collect. These terms shift all the responsibility for freight costs to the buyer. Title to the goods and the risk of loss also pass to the buyer at the F.O.B. point.

INTERNATIONAL MARKETS

International marketing for small firms is not just the wave of the future; it is present reality. Certain opportunities abroad are more profitable than those at home.

A small firm's potential role in international marketing can be clarified by considering the following six topics: the international challenge, understanding other cultures, researching foreign markets, sales and distribution channels, exporting assistance, and trade agreements. The following sections briefly examine each of these topics.

The International Challenge

It is a basic human characteristic that people shy away from the complex and shun the unfamiliar. Entrepreneurs are no different. They have traditionally held this same attitude regarding foreign markets. Unfortunately, "foreign" market has meant "extraneous" market to many businesses, as indicated by these facts:

- Only about 100,000 U.S. firms are now actively exporting.
- Nearly twice that many—some 175,000—U.S. firms are capable of exporting, but are not doing so.

SMALL BUSINESS IN ACTION

Distribution Fails Venture

Ultimately, the worth of a channel of distribution is determined by its ability to deliver a product to the right place at the right time. Sometimes, especially in the international marketplace, timely delivery can be a problem. Just ask Joe Reagan, owner of Reagan's Coffees, a coffee-supply company based in Springfield, Virginia, who decided to import bottled water from Ireland.

Mr. Reagan admits that he failed to properly investigate the distribution system that was to bring the bottled water to the U.S. market.

"What a mess," recalls Mr. Reagan. "The ship didn't come directly to the United States. They would fill it halfway up in Ireland with bottled

water. Then it would go to one of the Scandinavian countries where they loaded up the rest of the boat with drugs." At every port of call, suspicious customs officers searched all of the ship's cargo for drugs. While rummaging through the crates containing . . . bottled water, officials often broke bottles or left them on the dock, where they froze and cracked before being reloaded.

Initially, Reagan could not figure out why Customs found his shipment so intriguing. For three years, he kept trying different ports before he found out that the boat wasn't coming directly from Ireland. Finally, Reagan understood the problem and abandoned the bottled-water venture.

Source: Timothy L. O'Brien, *The Wall Street Journal* (October 16, 1992), p. R4. Reprinted by permission of *The Wall Street Journal*, © 1992 Dow Jones & Company, Inc. All Rights Reserved Worldwide.

• About 2,000 firms account for 70 percent of U.S. exported manufactured goods.[5]

Why have small firms historically shunned international trade? One survey of more than 5,000 independent U.S. businesses asked what prevented their firms from exploring or expanding exports. The major obstacles were:

• Obtaining adequate, initial knowledge about exporting (72 percent).
• Identifying viable sales prospects abroad (61 percent).
• Understanding business protocols in other countries (57 percent).
• Selecting suitable target markets on the basis of the available information (57 percent).[6]

More and more small firms are accepting the international challenge. This is good news for those most involved with U.S. trade problems. One trade representative says, "The growth in these smaller companies is where the growth in our country is."[7]

Following are three examples of small firms whose international involvement has been financially successful:

Six years ago, the management of Ohsman & Sons Company, Inc., of Cedar Rapids, Iowa, decided to make a commitment to find and develop more overseas markets for its products (hides, fur, and wool). In a deliberate and orderly way, the 12-employee firm tackled such problems as export financing; tough competition; arranging timely shipping; and finding new employees who have at least a basic knowledge of the languages of foreign trading partners, including Japanese, Korean, Spanish, and Russian. In a three-year period, Ohsman's exports grew from 30 percent of total shipments to more than 50 percent.[8]

Forest Lumber Company of Meridian, Miss., which has only 15 employees, won business from the Japanese by being patient and building up confidence through personal relationships. Clyde Brooks, export sales manager for the foreign products broker and export management company, said that keeping your word "is particularly important in doing business with the Japanese, because they value personal relationships. I have done business with a Japanese trading company for 25 years, and I've never had a problem." In the beginning, Brooks doubted business with the Japanese would ever develop, because it took nearly a year to nail down a deal. However, perseverance paid off, and the company's "best response" is from Japan.[9]

Three years ago, Rust Evader Corporation of Altoona, PA, made a calculation that its rust-prevention devices for motor vehicles might have better potential abroad than here. Dan Emanuelson, president of the 37-employee firm, explained, "Overseas, automobiles are more expensive. People keep them longer. There are many backyard mechanics who like to tinker with their cars. They are more apt to keep their cars for 10 years. Overseas, there is less of the planned obsolescence that we have in this country." Rust Evader now sells most of its products overseas.[10]

Many small firms can be just as successful as large businesses in international markets. The idea that international markets are for big business only is extremely damaging to small firms' efforts to market abroad. Data regarding big- versus small-business involvement in international markets is at best inconclusive.[11] However, when looking at exporting only, some writers conclude that more small firms export than do large firms.[12]

Understanding Other Cultures

A foreign market becomes less foreign as a person learns more about it. An entrepreneur needs to study the cultural, political, and economic forces in the foreign market in order to understand why adjustments to domestic marketing strategies are required. When crossing cultural lines, something as simple as a daily "good morning" greeting with a handshake may be misunderstood. The entrepreneur must evaluate proper use of names and titles and be aware of different styles of doing business. Figure 15-3 describes Japanese business negotiation practices—valuable information for a small business entering this international market. When a foreign market is not studied carefully, costly mistakes may be made. The following firms, for example, did not properly analyze their foreign markets:

Figure 15-3
Business Customs
and Practices in the
Japanese Market

The following are typical Japanese negotiating tactics:

- The Japanese usually respond to the other party's proposal rather than taking the initiative.

- The Japanese tend to single out specific elements and negotiate one element at a time rather than packaging a deal.

- The Japanese tend to maintain a relatively quiet response mode at meetings after stating their official position. They usually allow the other party enough maneuverability in order for the other party to keep giving bit by bit.

- Once a concession is made, it becomes the new baseline (without a counter-concession on their part) and they move on to the next item. Their strategy usually is to keep whittling away one concession at a time.

- The Japanese use time and patience to wear down their opponent—consciously planning on long, drawn out periods of successive meetings.

- The Japanese negotiating team never has the authority to commit in a "give and take" type approach. They are usually only authorized to receive offers and communicate prior authorized consensus positions.

- The Japanese tend to use the "bad guy" ploy extensively, that is, constantly referring to other organizations such as government agencies/authorities concerning requirements or required concessions.

How to respond:

- Do not expect rapid progress.

- Learn to be quiet and accept long pauses in discussions. Outwait the Japanese until they respond constructively to your last proposal.

- Do not make successive individual concessions—insist on a package deal.

- Do not make a follow-on proposal with further concessions until the Japanese respond to the current proposal with concessions on their part. Set an agenda for the next meeting accordingly.

- Do not fall for the "cultural differences" ploy. Be polite but direct. You can expect the Japanese to understand Western business practices and culture. They should be prepared to compromise and accommodate on those issues which you identify as vital and absolutely essential. However, you should likewise show an appreciation of Japanese culture. This will help facilitate negotiations.

- Keep records on concessions by both parties.

- Have a fluent Japanese speaker present at negotiations to preclude private discussions during meetings and to insure the translations are accurate.

- Negotiate from a position of strength and confidence. The Japanese do not respond positively to real or perceived weakness, nor do they respond to idle threats and intimidation.

Source: Adapted from *Destination Japan*, U.S. Department of Commerce (Washington, DC: U.S. Government Printing Office, 1991).

A mail-order concern offering American products to the Japanese didn't realize that the American custom of asking customers for a credit-card number before taking their order would insult the Japanese. Later, a Japanese consultant told the company that people in Japan think such an approach shows a lack of trust.[13]

A U.S. soft-drink firm marketed its product in Indonesia, but the drink did not sell. It was learned that the market for carbonated American soft-drinks consisted mainly of tourists and that most Indonesians preferred coconut-based drinks.

An hour before an American company was to sign a contract with a Middle-Eastern nation, the American executive met for tea with the responsible government official. The American propped his feet on a table with the soles facing his Arab host. The official became angry and left the room. Such an act is a grave insult in the Arab's culture. The contract was signed one year later.[14]

Researching a Foreign Market

Foreign market research should begin by exhausting as many secondary sources of information as possible. The U.S. government offers an array of publications on methods of reaching foreign markets. The Commerce Department's International Trade Administration (ITA) is the primary U.S. government agency responsible for assisting exporters. Figure 15-5 describes a number of ITA services.

One excellent publication prepared by the federal government is *A Basic Guide to Exporting,* which is available from the Superintendent of Documents, U.S. Government Printing Office. Also available is the *Exporter's Guide to Federal Resources for Small Business,* which provides the reader with an overview of major federal export programs and contact points for further information and exper-

Figure 15-4
The Japanese Prefer to Establish Trusting Relationships Before Conducting Business

Figure 15-5
Export Services of
the Commerce
Department's ITA

Export Counseling. Trade specialists are available at ITA district and branch offices for individualized export counseling.

Market Research. Analysts in foreign posts provide [the United States & Foreign Commercial Service] with timely, accurate, and in-depth marketing data on industrial sectors with high export potential in the most promising countries.

Agent/Distributor Service. A customized search for interested and qualified foreign representatives will identify up to six foreign prospects who have examined the U.S. firm's literature and expressed interest in representing it.

Commercial News USA. A monthly magazine that promotes the products or services of U.S. firms to more than 110,000 overseas agents, distributors, government officials, and purchasers. Exporters may submit a black-and-white photo and brief description of their product or service.

Comparison Shopping. A custom-tailored service that provides firms with key marketing and foreign representation information about their specific products. Commerce Department staff conduct on-the-spot interviews to determine nine key marketing facts about the product, such as sales potential in the market, comparable products, distribution channels, going price, competitive factors, and qualified purchasers.

Foreign Buyer Program. Exporters can meet qualified foreign purchasers for their product or service at trade shows in the United States. The Commerce Department promotes the shows worldwide to attract foreign buyer delegations, manages an international business center, counsels participating firms, and brings together buyer and seller.

Gold Key Service. A custom-tailored service for U.S. firms planning to visit a country. Offered by many overseas posts, it combines several services, such as market orientation briefings, market research, introductions to potential partners, an interpreter for meetings, and assistance in developing a sound market strategy and an effective followup plan.

Trade Opportunities Program. Provides companies with current sales leads from overseas firms seeking to buy or represent their product or service. These leads are available electronically from the Commerce Department and are redistributed by the private sector in printed or electronic form.

World Traders Data Report. Custom reports that evaluate potential trading partners. Includes background information, standing in the local business community, credit-worthiness, and overall reliability and suitability.

Overseas Catalog and Video-Catalog Shows. Companies can gain market exposure for their product or service without the cost of traveling overseas by participating in a catalog or video-catalog show sponsored by the Commerce Department. Provided with the firm's product literature or promotional video, an industry will display the material to select foreign audiences in several countries.

Overseas Trade Missions. Officials of U.S. firms can participate in a trade mission which will give them an opportunity to confer with influential foreign

(Continued)

Figure 15-5
(*Continued*)

business and government representatives. Commerce Department staff will identify and arrange a full schedule of appointments in each country.

Overseas Trade Fairs. U.S. exporters may participate in overseas trade fairs which will enable them to meet customers face-to-face and also to assess the competition. The Commerce Department creates a U.S. presence at international trade fairs, making it easier for U.S. firms to exhibit and gain international recognition. The Department selects international trade fairs for special endorsement, called certification. This cooperation with the private show organizers enables U.S. exhibitors to receive special services designed to enhance their market promotion efforts. There is a service charge.

Matchmaker Events. Matchmaker Trade Delegations offer introductions to new markets through short, inexpensive overseas visits with a limited objective: to match the U.S. firm with a representative or prospective joint-venture/licensee partner who shares a common product or service interest. Firms learn key aspects of doing business in the new country and meet in one-on-one interviews the people who can help them be successful there.

Trade Information Center. A one-stop source for information on all federal government export assistance programs. Call 1-800-USA-TRADE.

Source: U.S. Department of Commerce, *Business America,* Vol. 113, No. 9 (Washington, DC: U.S. Government Printing Office, 1992).

tise in utilizing these programs. The *Export Yellow Pages* is a useful directory of export trading companies and over 12,000 U.S. firms involved in foreign trade.

Banks, universities, and other private organizations also provide information on exporting. A good example is The Export Hotline started in February 1992 by International Strategies of Boston. Essentially a fax-retrieval service, it offers export profiles on 68 countries and 50 industries. One company says it was able to use the hotline information to make a $100,000 sale overseas. According to an International Strategies representative, over 15,000 companies have called the 800 USA-XPORT number.[15]

Talking with a citizen of a foreign country or even someone who has visited a potential foreign market can be a valuable way to learn about it. Most universities enroll international students who can be contacted through faculty members who teach courses in the international disciplines.

One of the best ways to study a foreign market is to visit that market personally. Representatives of small firms can do this either individually or in organized groups. Entrepreneur Peter Johns is a good example of how a small-business owner can research a foreign market on his own. His firm, Choices Unlimited, had obtained rights from over 20 U.S. companies to distribute their catalogs in Mexico City, but he could not find a good marketing study to determine the feasibility of the venture. Therefore, he went to Mexico City and toured more affluent neighborhoods and shopping areas to evaluate market potential.

SMALL BUSINESS IN ACTION

Government Helps Promote Go-Carts

From October 1990 through September 1991, the United States federal government spent $2.7 billion for export promotion, approved $12.8 billion in export loans and loan guarantees, and extended about $8.6 billion in export insurance. Clearly, the federal government supports exporting, but many small firms do not take advantage of this expertise and research help. Former Secretary of Commerce Robert A. Mosbacher said, "You pay taxes for us to gather this [trade] information. You ought to get it and use it."

This is exactly what Fred Schweser, president of Bird Corporation in Elkhorn, Nebraska, did when he decided to distribute his company's gasoline-powered go-carts internationally. He contacted a trade specialist at the Omaha District Office of the U.S. Commerce Department. This trade specialist suggested that Schweser place an advertisement in *Commercial News USA,* a magazine distributed to about 100,000 business readers.

The ad attracted more than 1,000 responses, which enabled Schweser to establish a dozen distributorships—from Japan to the United Kingdom. The distributors proved so effective that international customers now account for 10 to 15 percent of Bird's sales.

Source: Adapted from Albert G. Holzinger, "Paving the Way for Small Exporters," *Nation's Business,* Vol. 80, No. 6 (June 1992), pp. 42–43. Reprinted by permission, *Nation's Business,* June 1992. Copyright 1992, U.S. Chamber of Commerce.

What he saw brightened his spirits: satellite dishes, imported sports cars, and women carrying Louis Vuitton handbags around. Drawing on those impressions, and other information he gathered on his own, he came to his own conclusion: His target market is about 300,000 families. . . . "That's called grass-roots marketing intelligence," says Mr. Johns.[16]

A Department of Commerce-sponsored trade mission is another means of evaluating a foreign market. A trade mission is a planned visit to a potential foreign market to introduce U.S. firms to appropriate foreign buyers and to establish exporting relationships. These missions are usually composed of from five to ten business executives. They are organized and planned to achieve maximum results in expanding exports. Mission members typically pay their own expenses and share in the operating costs of the mission.

Sometimes foreign governments also sponsor trade missions for U.S. firms considering their markets. Japan, for example, has sponsored this kind of trade mission. Several small firms returning to the United States from a recent Tokyo-sponsored trip have made successful deals.

Richard Russell went a skeptic and came back a believer. His Tech Spray, Inc. of Amarillo, Texas, a maker of chemicals for the electronics industry, had tried to break into the Japanese market a decade earlier and "couldn't even get the products through customs,"... Mr. Russell says he only accepted the invitation from the Japan External Organization to fly to Tokyo last August because the trip was free. To his surprise he found the Japanese receptive . . . The New York-born entrepreneur found a Japanese distributor, and it already has placed two test orders worth several thousand dollars.

Another company, Ford Motor Box, Inc., a Wabash, IN maker of fittings for underground water lines, says an Osaka company is at the point of placing an initial order in the "thousands of dollars." . . . To do business in Japan, you've got to go over and meet the people, Mr. Doran says.[17]

Sales and Distribution Channels

licensing
legal agreement allowing a product to be produced in return for royalties

Exporting is not the only way to be involved in international markets. In fact, licensing is the simplest strategy for conducting international business. With a small investment, a firm can penetrate a foreign market. **Licensing** is an arrangement allowing a foreign manufacturer to use the designs, patents, or trademarks of the licenser. The practice of licensing helps overcome trade barriers surrounding exporting, because the product is produced in the foreign country. Michael Koss, CEO of Koss Corporation in Milwaukee, used licensing to diversify his stereo-headphone manufacturing company because "this seemed a good way to generate royalty income in the short run and cement a strategic partnership that could lead, over the long run, to joint ventures . . . ." His foreign licensee is the Dutch trading company Hagemeyer, which pays royalites to use Koss's brand name and logo. To ensure quality, Koss has "veto power over all product drawings, engineering specifications, first-product samples, and final products."[18]

A small firm can also participate in foreign-market sales via joint ventures and wholly owned subsidiaries in foreign markets. International joint ventures offer a greater presence abroad with less expense than establishing a firm's own operation or office in the foreign market. Some host countries may actually require that a certain percentage of manufacturing facilities be owned by nationals of that country, thereby forcing U.S. firms to operate through joint ventures. Other channel options for foreign distribution are identified in figure 15-6.

Figure 15-6
Foreign Market
Channels of
Distribution

Sales Representatives or Agents—A sales representative is the equivalent of a manufacturer's representative here in the United States. Product literature and samples are used to present the product to the potential buyer. The representative usually works on a commission basis, assumes no risk or responsibility, and is under contract for a definite period of time (renewable by mutual agreement). This contract defines territory, terms of sale, method of compensation, and other details. The sales representative may operate on either an exclusive or nonexclusive basis.

Distributor—The foreign distributor is a merchant who purchases merchandise from a U.S. manufacturer at the greatest possible discount and resells it for a profit. This would be the preferred arrangement if the product being sold requires periodic servicing. The prospective distributor should be willing to carry a sufficient supply of spare parts and maintain adequate facilities and personnel to perform all normal servicing operations. Since distributors buy in their names, it is easier for the U.S. manufacturer to establish a credit pattern so that more flexible or convenient payment terms can be offered. As with a sales representative, the length of association is established by contract, which is renewable if the arrangement proves satisfactory.

Foreign Retailer—Generally limited to the consumer line, this method relies mainly on direct contact by traveling sales representatives. Depending on the product, it can also be accomplished by the mailing of catalogs, brochures, or other literature. However, even though direct mail would eliminate commissions and traveling expenses, the U.S. manufacturer's direct mail proposal may not receive proper consideration.

Selling Direct to the End User—This is quite limited and again depends on the product. Opportunities often arise from advertisements in magazines receiving overseas distribution. Many times this can create difficulties because casual inquirers may not be fully cognizant of their country's foreign trade regulations. For several reasons they may not be able to receive the merchandise upon arrival, thus causing it to be impounded and possibly sold at public auction, or returned on a freight-collect basis that could prove costly.

State-Controlled Trading Companies—This term applies to countries that have state trading monopolies, where business is conducted by a few government-sanctioned and controlled trading entities. Because of worldwide changes in foreign policy and their effect on trade between countries, these areas can become important future markets. For the time being, however, most opportunities will be limited to such items as raw materials, agricultural machinery, manufacturing equipment, and technical instruments, rather than consumer or household goods. This is due to the shortage of foreign exchange and the emphasis on self-sufficiency.

New Product Information Service (NPIS)—This special service, offered by the Department of Commerce, can facilitate your direct selling effort to potential overseas customers. It enables U.S. companies interested in selling a new product overseas to submit appropriate data through Commerce Department District

(Continued)

Figure 15-6
(*Continued*)

Offices for placement in the Department's publication, *Commercial News USA*, which is distributed exclusively abroad through 240 U.S. Foreign Service posts. The new product data are extracted and reprinted in individual post newsletters that are tailored to local markets. Selected product information also is broadcast abroad by the International Communication Agency's (formerly the U.S. Information Agency) Voice of America.

Commission Agents—Commission or buying agents are "finders" for foreign firms wanting to purchase U.S. products. These purchasing agents obtain the desired equipment at the lowest possible price. A commission is paid to them by their foreign clients.

Country-Controlled Buying Agents—These are foreign government agencies or quasi-governmental firms empowered to locate and purchase desired goods.

Export Management Companies—EMCs, as they are called, act as the export department for several manufacturers of noncompetitive products. They solicit and transact business in the name of the manufacturers they represent for a commission, salary, or retainer plus commission. Many EMCs also will carry the financing for export sales, assuring immediate payment for the manufacturer's products.

This can be an exceptionally fine arrangement for small firms that do not have the time, personnel, or money to develop foreign markets, but wish to establish a corporate and product identity internationally.

Export Merchants—Export merchants purchase products direct from the manufacturer and have them packed and marked to their specifications. They then sell overseas through their contacts, in their own names, and assume all risks for their accounts.

Export Agents—Export agents operate in the same manner as manufacturer's representatives, but the risk of loss remains with the manufacturer.

In transactions with export merchants and export agents the seller is faced with the possible disadvantage of giving up control over the marketing and promotion of the product. This could have an adverse effect on future success.

Source: Adapted from U.S. Department of Commerce, *A Basic Guide to Exporting* (Washington, DC: U.S. Government Printing Office, 1992).

Many firms find that foreign distributors offer a low-cost way to market products overseas. A foreign distributor buys the product and finds the customers. However, some foreign distributors are not strongly committed to selling an individual manufacturer's products. If a small firm mistakenly picks one of these distributors, sales may not grow as they should. When B.D. Baggies, a New York men's shirt maker, first began its international marketing, it contracted with the first foreign distributor that offered to sell its shirts in Europe. "Later, we found that the distributor wasn't right. They were selling our shirts to women's stores as a unisex product," explains Charles M.

McConnell, B.D. Baggies' president. Subsequently, the firm carefully screened all distributors, and it is now doing good business in more than 40 countries.[19]

Exporting Assistance

Difficulty in getting trade information and arranging financing are often mentioned as the biggest barriers to small-business exporting. In reality, there are a number of direct and indirect sources of trade and financing information that help the small firm view foreign markets more favorably.

Private Banks. Commercial banks typically have a loan officer responsible for handling foreign transactions. In large banks there may be a separate international department. Banks also participate in a system called forfaiting. **Forfaiting** is used when a U.S. exporter makes a sale abroad and receives promissory notes. A bank will then purchase the notes from the exporter at a discount. Collection of a note becomes the responsibility of the bank. Exporters also use banks to issue commercial letters of credit and perform other financial activities associated with exporting.

A **letter of credit** is an agreement to honor drafts or other demands for payment when specified conditions are met. It helps assure a seller of prompt payment. A letter of credit may be revocable or irrevocable. An irrevocable letter of credit cannot be changed unless both the buyer and the seller agree to make the change. The typical procedure when payment is made by an irrevocable letter of credit confirmed by a U.S. bank is as follows:

1. After the exporter and customer agree on the terms of a sale, the customer arranges for its bank to open a letter of credit. (Delays may be encountered if, for example, the buyer has insufficient funds.)
2. The buyer's bank prepares an irrevocable letter of credit, including all instructions to the seller concerning the shipment.
3. The buyer's bank sends the irrevocable letter of credit to a U.S. bank, requesting confirmation. The exporter may request that a particular U.S. bank be the confirming bank, or the foreign bank selects one of its U.S. correspondent banks.
4. The U.S. bank prepares a letter of confirmation to forward to the exporter along with the irrevocable letter of credit.
5. The exporter reviews carefully all conditions in the letter of credit. The exporter's freight forwarder should be contacted to make sure that the shipping date can be met. If the exporter cannot comply with one or more of the conditions, the customer should be alerted at once.
6. The exporter arranges with the freight forwarder to deliver the goods to the appropriate port or airport.
7. When the goods are loaded, the forwarder completes the necessary documents.

forfaiting
discounted purchase of a promissory note received by an exporter

letter of credit
agreement that assures a seller of prompt payment

8. The exporter (or the forwarder) presents to the U.S. bank documents indicating full compliance.

9. The bank reviews the documents. If they are in order, the documents are airmailed to the buyer's bank for review and transmitted to the buyer.

10. The buyer (or agent) gets the documents that may be needed to claim the goods.

11. A draft, which may accompany the letter of credit, is paid by the exporter's bank at the time specified or may be discounted at an earlier date.[20]

However, a letter of credit, as important as it is, is not an absolute guarantee of payment. Consider seafood exporter Michael Graham and his experience with the Russian Republic. Graham's firm, Ocean Traders of North America, obtained a letter of credit to back an export order for 16,000 tons of fish. The foreign trade bank canceled the irrevocable letter of credit, admitting to a "technical error." In a letter of explanation, the Russian bank chairman says the deal was all a mistake.[21]

Factoring Houses. A factoring house buys clients' accounts receivable and advances money to these clients. The factor assumes the risk of collection of the accounts. The Factors Chain International is an association representing factors from more than 25 countries.[22] Its efforts have helped make factoring available on an international basis.

State Programs. More and more states each year are developing and implementing their own programs to help small companies finance exports.[23] For example, California guarantees 85 percent repayment on loans used to finance receivables related to exports. C. M. Magnetics, of Santa Fe Springs, California, was a beneficiary of state assistance when the company needed capital to fill an order for its videotapes from China. "Without their help . . . we probably wouldn't be in business today," says President J. Carlos Maciel.[24]

Export Trading Companies. In 1982, President Reagan signed into law the Export Trading Company Act for the stated purpose of increasing U.S. exports of goods and services.[25] The two areas covered by the Act relate to restrictions on trade financing and uncertainty about U.S. antitrust laws. Under the Act, an Export Trading Company (ETC) can be organized to facilitate the exporting of goods and services produced in the United States. Through a small firm's affiliation with the ETC, it could employ the resources of an ongoing organization that has exporting expertise. As of this writing, there had been only 125 certificates issued for ETCs. Their value to small firms is still in doubt. One recent study asking users of export trading companies to evaluate the performance of ETCs concluded that there is "a lack of congruence between what services small businesses desire from exporting intermediaries and the services ETCs perform well."[26]

The Export-Import Bank. To encourage businesses to sell overseas, the federal government created the Export-Import Bank (Eximbank). Although historically of greatest use to large firms, in recent years Eximbank has overhauled its programs to benefit small firms. The following programs are particularly helpful to small-business exporters:

1. *Export Credit Insurance.* An exporter may reduce its financing risks by purchasing export credit insurance. This insurance is available from Eximbank's agent, the Foreign Credit Insurance Association (FCIA). Policies available include insurance for financing or operating leases, medium-term insurance, the new-to-export policy, insurance for the service industry, the umbrella policy, and multibuyer and single-buyer policies.

2. *Working Capital Guarantee.* The Working Capital Loan Guarantee Program assists small businesses in obtaining crucial working capital to fund their export sales. The program guarantees working capital loans extended by banks to eligible U.S. exporters with exportable inventory or export receivables as collateral.

3. *Direct and Intermediary Loans.* Eximbank provides two types of loans: direct loans to foreign buyers of U.S. exports, and intermediary loans to fund responsible parties that extend loans to foreign buyers of U.S. capital and quasi-capital goods and related services. Both the local and guarantee programs cover up to 85 percent of the U.S. export value, with repayment terms of one year or more.

4. *Guarantees.* Eximbank's guarantee provides repayment protection for private sector loans to creditworthy buyers of U.S. capital equipment and related services. The guarantee is available alone or with an intermediary loan. Most guarantees provide comprehensive coverage of both political and commercial risks, but political-risks-only coverage is also available.

5. *Small-Business Advisory Service.* To encourage small business to sell overseas, Eximbank maintains a special office to provide information on the availability and use of export credit insurance, guarantees, and direct and intermediary loans to finance the sale of U.S. goods and services abroad.

Eximbank programs have been a victim of recent budget cuts. One recent study found only 2 percent of all U.S. export transactions had Eximbank financing.[27]

Small Business Administration. The Small Business Administration (SBA) serves U.S. small businesses primarily through its 107 regional, district, and branch offices. Small businesses that are either already exporting or interested in doing so can receive information through conferences and seminars, instructional publications, export counseling, and financial assistance. A few of the programs offered by the SBA to small firms are:[28]

- *Export Counseling*—International Trade Officers in SBA regional and district offices provide advice and counseling on exporting. These professionals help small businesses locate and utilize various government programs and guide them through the export process.

- *SCORE Program*—One-on-one assistance is provided by members of the Service Corps of Retired Executives (SCORE), many with years of practical experience in international trade. Specialists assist small firms in evaluating export potential and strengthening domestic operations by identifying financial, managerial, or technical problems.
- *SBDC/SBI Programs*—Basic business counseling and assistance are offered through Small Business Development Centers (SBDCs), some of which are located at colleges and universities. Through Small Business Institutes (SBIs), business students from more than 450 colleges and universities provide in-depth, long-term counseling under faculty supervision to small businesses.
- *Legal Advice*—Export Legal Assistance Network (ELAN) provides free, initial consultations to small companies on the legal aspects of exporting through an arrangement with the Federal Bar Association (FBA). Advice is provided by qualified attorneys from the International Law Council of the FBA.
- *Financial Assistance*—The SBA offers direct loan and loan guarantee programs to assist small-business exporters. To be eligible for a loan, a businessperson must first attempt to secure a loan from a private bank, invest a reasonable amount of capital in the business, and demonstrate that the loan can be paid back. The SBA provides guarantees of up to 85 percent of a private lending institution's loan to an eligible small business if the total SBA-guaranteed portion does not exceed the SBA's $750,000 statutory loan guarantee limit. However, the SBA can provide a maximum guarantee of 90 percent for loans less than $155,000.
- *Regular Business Loan Program*—Covers loans for fixed-asset acquisition or expansion and other working capital purposes up to $750,000 and having a maximum maturity of 25 years. Guarantees for general-purpose working capital loans are usually limited to a maximum term of seven years.
- *Export Revolving Line of Credit Program (ERLC)*—The SBA has established this program to encourage more small businesses to export their products and services abroad. Any number of withdrawals and repayments can be made as long as the dollar limit of the credit is not exceeded, and the disbursements are made within the stated maturity period. Proceeds can only finance labor and materials needed for manufacturing or wholesaling for export, or to penetrate or develop foreign markets. The maximum maturity of an ERLC guarantee is 18 months, including all extensions.
- *Small-Business Investment Company (SBIC) Financing*—For an export company requiring more than $750,000, an SBIC-approved loan is a financial option.

Trade Agreements

The differences in trading systems and import requirements of each country make international trade difficult. To appreciate the problems these differences create, consider the situation of Mentor O & O, Inc., a small manufacturer in Norwell, Massachusetts. This company produces diagnostic and surgical equipment used in eye care. Mentor markets internationally and is regularly modifying its products to meet rigid design specifications that vary from country to country. For example, an alarm bell on Mentor's testing device has an on/off switch that must be removed before it is acceptable in Germany.[29] This is typical of trade barriers throughout the world.

However, we appear to be in a period of positive change regarding trade barriers. In 1989 Canada and the United States signed the **Free Trade Agreement** (**FTA**), which calls for the elimination of most tariffs and other trade restrictions by January 1, 1998. The result should be an environment more conducive to trade between these two countries.[30]

In 1993, the United States and Mexico signed the **North American Free Trade Agreement** (**NAFTA**) conditional on approval by Congress.[31] Under NAFTA, all Mexican tariffs on U.S.-made products will be phased out over a period of 15 years; almost half of these tariffs being removed on the agreement's effective date of January 1, 1994.[32]

Also, January 1, 1993, marked the official beginning of the 12-nation European Community (EC). For the last decade, businesses of all sizes have watched preparations for a unified European Community. However, the fall of the Iron Curtain has created a more complex world and certain pressures on the EC to admit Eastern European nations. There is little certainty as to the exact impact this unification will have on small exporters.[33]

FTA
the Free Trade Agreement, which eases trade restrictions between the U.S. and Canada

NAFTA
the North American Free Trade Agreement, which removes Mexican tariffs on U.S.-made products

LOOKING BACK

1. A channel of distribution can be either direct—involving no intermediaries—or indirect—incorporating one or more intermediaries. Dual distribution exists when the same product is distributed through two different channels at the same time.

2. Intermediaries in a channel of distribution exist to carry out marketing functions. Small firms cannot always perform these functions or carry them out as efficiently as the intermediary. Channels of distribution perform four main functions: breaking bulk, assorting, providing information, and shifting risks.

3. An entrepreneur must study the cultural, political, and economic forces in foreign markets in order to develop appropriate marketing strategies. Sometimes a firm can transfer its product to a foreign market without major product-design changes. On other occasions, extensive product changes may be in order. The concept of a market niche also applies to international markets.

4. A tremendous amount of exporting information and assistance is available from states and the federal government. Private banks, factoring houses, export-trading companies, and Eximbank also provide exporting assistance to small firms. Trade agreements among nations are helping to reduce trade barriers.

DISCUSSION QUESTIONS

1. How does physical distribution differ from channels of distribution?
2. Why do small firms need to consider indirect channels of distribution for their products? Why involve intermediaries in distribution at all?
3. Discuss the major considerations in structuring a channel of distribution.
4. What are the major components of a physical distribution system?
5. Comment on the statement, "Channel intermediaries are not necessary and only increase the final price of products."
6. Discuss the importance of a careful cultural analysis before entering an international market.
7. What changes in a firm's marketing plan, if any, may be required when selling to foreign markets? Be specific.
8. Does the concept of a market niche apply to international markets? Explain with examples.
9. What is the position of the U.S. federal government regarding the potential for exporting among small U.S. firms? Do you agree or disagree? Why?
10. What are alternatives to exporting that provide small-business involvement with international markets? Which one(s) do you find most consistent with a small firm's situation? Why?
11. What is forfaiting? How does it work?
12. Explain how state governments are involved in assisting small firms with exporting.
13. What is an export trading company? How did they come about? What success have they had?
14. Explain the exporting assistance programs of Eximbank.
15. How have trade agreements helped reduce trade barriers? Do you believe these efforts will continue?

YOU MAKE THE CALL

Situation 1

Berney and Pat Anderson own and operate a manufacturing operation named the Great Out-of-Doors Company, in Coleman, Colorado. Their principal product is a rifle sling.

Berney conceived the product idea in 1986, and one year later he and his wife took in two investors and began manufacturing. Currently, the plant has six employees producing the rifle sling and a few minor complementary products. Pat takes care of the accounting, and Berney supervises the plant operations.

Their rifle sling product is patented and has been well received by those who have tried it. The nylon sling is produced in 1-inch and $1\frac{1}{2}$-inch straps and is available in 25 different colors.

The firm has manufactured the sling for other brand-name sporting goods manufacturers and has also sold it under its own name—Sports Sling—in sporting goods stores.

Questions
1. What do you see as the strong and weak points of the distribution channels the company is currently using?

2. What additional channels would you recommend for consideration?
3. Do you think exporting is a feasible alternative for the Andersons at this time? Why or why not?

Situation 2

John Adams is a veterinarian specializing in small-animal care in Jackson, Florida. For several years he has supplemented his professional income by exporting products he has invented and patented. His best seller is a dog leash that he originally sold to other veterinarians in the United States. However, after placing a product release in a Department of Commerce publication, he received inquiries from foreign importers who wanted the product, and his exporting began.

Based on his personal experiences with exporting, Adams is currently contemplating leaving his veterinary practice and becoming a full-time exporting distributor. He believes there is a growing number of U.S. businesses that do not want to get involved with the problems of the export business but would like the revenue from the overseas markets. His services as a distributor should be attractive to these firms.

Questions

1. Would you recommend that Adams leave his successful veterinary practice to pursue a business as an export distributor? Why or why not?
2. What would you anticipate Adams's biggest problems to be if he makes the move he is considering?
3. What private sources of assistance might he use?

EXPERIENTIAL EXERCISES

1. Contact a local banker to discuss that firm's involvement with international marketing. Report your findings.
2. Interview two different types of local retail merchants to determine how the merchandise in their stores was distributed to them. Contrast the channels of distribution and report your findings.
3. Review recent issues of *Entrepreneur, Inc.*, or *Nation's Business,* and report on articles discussing international marketing.
4. Interview a local distributor concerning how it stores and handles the merchandise it distributes. Report your findings.

REFERENCES TO SMALL-BUSINESS PRACTICE

Hyatt, Joshua. "Exporting the Risk," *Inc.*, Vol. 12, No. 11 (November 1990) pp. 163–164.
   A small firm manufacturing engineering software has been exporting since 1985. This article describes its distribution strategy, beginning with foreign distributors and evolving into direct distribution.
Hyatt, Joshua. "The G Factor," *Inc.*, Vol. 14, No. 1 (January 1992), pp. 68–73.
   This article describes the exporting experiences of a U.S. maker of laboratory equipment. The owner also discusses the nonsales benefits of exporting.

Mangelsdorf, Martha E. "Unfair Trade," *Inc.*, Vol. 13, No. 4 (April 1991), pp. 28–36.

>In this article an entrepreneur shares why he is not particularly excited about exporting. Several barriers to exporting are discussed.

Rondel, Stephen A. "On the Front Lines in the Trade War," *Nation's Business*, Vol. 77, No. 6 (June 1989), p. 10.

>This article describes how an entrepreneur, who began manufacturing in a horse stall in his barn, has entered exporting. His financial difficulties resulting from direct competition with foreign manufacturers are developed.

Thompson, Roger. "A Fresh Start After 40," *Nation's Business*, Vol. 77, No. 4 (April 1989), pp. 62–64.

>The entrepreneur featured in this article started a repair- and maintenance-parts company to supply businesses with repair parts for their equipment. His creative distribution idea has made his company one of the largest independent companies in this market.

ENDNOTES

1. Jeffrey A. Trachtenberg, "Avon's New TV Campaign Says, " 'Call Us,' " *The Wall Street Journal* (December 28, 1992), p. B1.

2. The reduction in product price given an intermediary is the investment cost to which we refer.

3. *Something Ventured: An Entrepreneurial Approach to Small Business Management*, Episode 115 of a telecourse produced by IN-TELE-COM (formerly the Southern California Consortium), Telephone (818) 796-7300.

4. A good discussion of modes of transportation is found in William M. Pride and O.C. Ferrell, *Marketing Concepts and Strategies* (Boston: Houghton Mifflin Company, 1993), Chapter 14.

5. Roger E. Axtell, "International Trade: A Small Business Primer," *Small Business Forum*, Vol. 10, No. 1 (Spring 1992), p. 47.

6. *Ibid.*, p. 49.

7. William J. Holstein and Brian Bremmer, "The Little Guys Are Making It Big Overseas," *Business Week* (February 27, 1989), p. 94.

8. U.S. Department of Commerce, "The ABCs of Exporting," *Business America*, Vol. 113, No. 9 (Washington, D.C.: U.S. Government Printing Office, 1992), p. 4.

9. *Ibid.*, p. 7.

10. *Ibid.*, p. 4.

11. An interesting analysis of firm size and exporting behavior is found in Abbas Ali and Paul M. Swiercz, "Firm Size and Export Behavior: Lessons from the Midwest," *Journal of Small Business Management*, Vol. 29, No. 2 (April 1991), pp. 71–78.

12. David L. Birch, "Trading Places," *Inc.*, Vol. 10, No. 4 (April 1988), p. 42.

13. Julie Amparano Lopez, "Going Global," *The Wall Street Journal* (October 16, 1992), p. R 20.

14. Charles F. Valentine, "Blunders Abroad," *Nation's Business*, Vol. 44, No. 3 (March 1989), p. 54.

15. Bill Holstein, "An Export Service of Great Import," *Business Week* (September 28, 1992), p. 138.

16. Dianna Solis, "Grass-Roots Marketing Yields Clients in Mexico City," *The Wall Street Journal* (October 24, 1991), p. B2.

17. Brent Bowers, "To Sell to the Japanese, Meet With Them Face to Face," *The Wall Street Journal* (March 12, 1992), p. B2.

18. Jill Andresky Fraser, "Structuring a Global Licensing Deal," *Inc.*, Vol. 14, No. 11 (November 1992), p. 45.

19. Julie Amparano Lopez, *op. cit.*

20. U.S. Department of Commerce, *A Basic Guide to Exporting* (Washington, D.C.: U.S. Government Printing Office, 1992), p. 13–2.

21. Eugene Carlson, "Entrepreneurs Risk Stumbling as They Rush Into Russia," *The Wall Street Journal* (May 15, 1992), p. B2.

22.   For more discussion of factoring, see R. Michael Rice, "Four Ways to Finance Your Exports," *The Journal of Business Strategy* (July–August 1988), pp. 30–31.

23.   For addresses and telephone numbers of state offices providing export assistance, see U.S. Department of Commerce, "The ABCs of Exporting," *Business America,* Vol. 113, No. 9 (Washington, D.C.: U.S. Government Printing Office, 1992), pp. 28–29.

24.   *Ibid.*

25.   For a complete description of the Act, see, U.S. Department of Commerce, *The Export Trading Company Guidebook* (Washington: U.S. Government Printing Office, 1987).

26.   Alex F. DeNoble, Richard M. Castaldi, and Donald M. Moliver, "Export Intermediaries: Small Business Perceptions of Services and Performance," *Journal of Small Business Management,* Vol. 27, No. 2 (April 1989), pp. 33–41.

27.   Martha E. Mangelsdorf, "Unfair Trade," *Inc.,* Vol. 13, No. 4 (April 1991), p. 33.

28.   U.S. Department of Commerce, "A Directory of Export Services," *Business America,* Vol. 113, No. 9 (Washington: U.S. Government Printing Office, 1992), pp. 10–11.

29. Roger Thompson, "EC92," *Nation's Business,* Vol. 77, No. 6 (June 1989), p. 18.

30.   A more detailed analysis of the FTA is found in "The Canada-United States Free Trade Agreement and Its Implication for Small Business," *Journal of Small Business Management,* Vol. 28, No. 2 (April 1990), pp. 64–69.

31. A comprehensive analysis of NAFTA is presented in the U.S. Chamber of Commerce publication *A Guide To the North American Free Trade Agreement: Implications for U.S. Business.*

32.   At the time of this writing, the U.S. Congress has not voted on NAFTA, although the Clinton administration supports the Agreement.

33. One interesting analysis is Saeed Samiee, "Strategic Considerations of The EC 1992 Plan for Small Exporters," *Business Horizons,* Vol. 33, No. 2 (April 1990), pp. 48–52.

PART 5

Managing Small Business Operations

Professional Management in the Growing Firm

David Usher

SPOTLIGHT ON SMALL BUSINESS

Tension between entrepreneurial and professional management often occurs as small firms grow. An entrepreneur's free-wheeling management style must give way to a more systematic, professional approach.

An example of the dilemma is found in the experience of the Marine Pollution Control Company of Detroit. Under the leadership of its founder, David Usher, it had grown to more than $10 million in revenues. Rapid growth and participation in a gigantic cleanup project—the *Exxon Valdez* oil tanker disaster in Alaska—created managerial tensions between the founder and the next generation, including son Charlie.

The sons contend they are hamstrung by an arbitrary-seeming, "Dave-centered" management structure in which virtually every decision must be cleared with Dave. Big jobs like the Valdez *one stretch this kind of structure to its limits and underline its weaknesses. Charlie and the others want Dave to delegate more authority so the company has the depth of management needed for the future.*

Dave, for his part, says he recognizes the need to delegate. He believes, however, in the loosely organized system that brought the company success, and he worries about losing touch with day-to-day operations. The same entrepreneurial personality that drove him to build the company won't allow him to let go of any part of it.

Source: Robert Charm, "Masters of Disasters," *Family Business* (premier issue, 1989), pp. 18–25.

After studying this chapter, you should be able to:
1. Identify prevalent weaknesses in small-firm management.
2. Discuss constraints faced by managers in small firms.
3. Explain how management is affected by the growth cycle of a small business.
4. Summarize how managers plan, lead, organize, and control business operations.
5. Discuss how a small-business manager can make effective use of time.
6. Identify sources of management assistance.

professional manager
management functions
long-range plans (strategic plans)
short-range plans
budget
business policies
procedures
standard operating procedures

line organization
chain of command
line-and-staff organization
line activities
staff activities
unity of command
delegation of authority
span of control

Small Business Institute (SBI)
Service Corps of Retired Executives (SCORE)
Small Business Development Centers (SBDCs)
networking

Both large and small firms require a management process to direct and coordinate work activities. If this process of directing and coordinating is carried out well, it contributes to productivity and profitability, whatever the size of the business. As a small firm grows, its management task becomes more complex, and its management methods must become more sophisticated. This chapter examines the unique aspects of managing the smaller enterprise and its transition to a more professional kind of management.

DISTINCTIVE FEATURES OF SMALL-FIRM MANAGEMENT

Even though managers in both large and small companies perform similar management functions, their jobs as managers are somewhat different. This is readily recognized by a manager who moves from a large corporation to a small firm. He or she encounters an entirely different business atmosphere. Furthermore, the small firm experiences constant change in its organizational and managerial needs as it moves from point zero, its launching, to the point where it can employ a full staff of **professional managers.** In this section we shall examine a number of these special features that serve to challenge managers of small firms.

professional manager
one who uses systematic, analytical methods of management

Prevalent Weaknesses in Small Firms

Although some large corporations experience poor management, small business seems particularly vulnerable to this weakness. Managerial inefficiency exists in tens (or even hundreds) of thousands of small firms. Many small firms are marginal or unprofitable businesses, struggling to survive from day to day and month to month. At best, they earn only a pittance for their owners. The reason for their condition is at once apparent to one who examines their operations. They "run," but it is an exaggeration to say that they are "managed."

One successful entrepreneur who started several businesses candidly admitted his own inadequacies as a manager.

You name the mistake, and I made it during those years. I didn't pay enough attention to detail. I wasn't clear about responsibilities. I didn't hold people accountable. I was terrible at hiring. We had three chief financial officers in 10 years. We didn't start tracking cash flow until we were up to about $12 million in sales, and we went all the way to $25 million without developing an inventory system that worked. As a company, we lacked focus. Once I brought in a consultant who asked our eight key people about the company's goals, and everyone give a different answer.[1]

Weaknesses of this nature are all too typical of small firms. The good news, however, is that poor management is neither universal nor inevitable.

Constraints on Management in Small Firms

Managers of small firms, particularly new and growing companies, are constrained by conditions that do not trouble the average corporate executive. Small firms have neither enough money nor enough talented people. They must face the grim reality of small bank accounts and limited managerial staff. These limitations are readily apparent to large-firm managers who move into management positions in small firms. As one writer says:

You cannot realize how lavish big business is until you try making the transition to small business. For example, a marketing man moving from a big company to a small one usually discovers, to his horror, that his new employer has no market surveys, and the sum of his research is a two-year-old article clipped from a trade magazine. Making bad matters worse, the little company desperately needs a four-color brochure for the salesmen. You can't sell without sales literature, now can you?

In big business there is no question about it; you get these tools, and a major skill the new employee brings with him is knowledge of how to use the tools. In small business the new employee will likely be told by the company president, "We can't afford research. We can't afford surveys and probably don't need them anyway. As far as that brochure is concerned, if we really need one, there is always Jiffy Printing across the street. They can whip something out for $600. Nothing fancy, mind you. And ask 'em not to bill us 'til September."[2]

In a small firm, the entrepreneur typically lacks adequate specialized staff. Most managers are generalists, and they lack the support of experienced staff in market research, financial analysis, advertising, human resources management, and other areas. The entrepreneur must make decisions involving these areas without the advice and guidance that is available in a larger business. Later in this chapter, we see that this limitation may be partially overcome by use of outside management assistance. Nevertheless, the shortage of immediately available talent is a part of the reality of the entrepreneurial firm.

Stages of Growth and Implications for Management

As a newly formed business becomes established and grows, its organization and pattern of management change. To some extent, management must adapt to growth and change in any organization. However, the changes involved as a business moves through periods of "childhood" and "adolescence" are much more extensive than those that occur with the growth of a relatively mature business.

As shown in Figure 16-1, a new firm passes through four stages of growth. Subordinates are employed and layers of management are added as it moves from Stage 1 to Stage 4.

In Stage 1, the firm is simply a one-person operation. Of course, not all firms begin at this level, but this situation is by no means rare. In Stage 2, the

Figure 16-1
Organizational Impact of Small-Business Growth

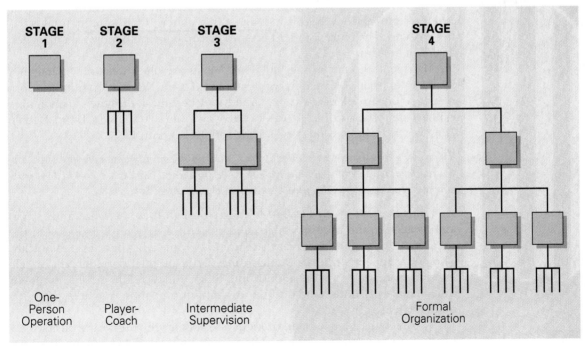

STAGE 1	STAGE 2	STAGE 3	STAGE 4
One-Person Operation	Player-Coach	Intermediate Supervision	Formal Organization

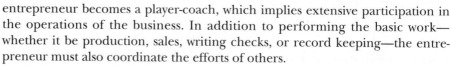

entrepreneur becomes a player-coach, which implies extensive participation in the operations of the business. In addition to performing the basic work—whether it be production, sales, writing checks, or record keeping—the entrepreneur must also coordinate the efforts of others.

In Stage 3, a major milestone is reached when an intermediate level of supervision is added. In many ways this is a difficult, dangerous point for the small firm, because the entrepreneur must rise above direct, hands-on management and work through an intermediate level of management.

Stage 4, the stage of formal organization, involves more than increased size and multilayered organization. The formalization of management involves the adoption of written policies, preparation of plans and budgets, standardization of personnel practices, computerization of records, preparation of organization charts and job descriptions, scheduling of training conferences, institution of control procedures, and so on.

Some formal management practices may be adopted prior to Stage 4 of the firm's growth. Nevertheless, the stages of management growth describe a typical pattern of development for successful firms. Flexibility and informality may be helpful at the beginning, but growth necessitates greater formality in planning and control. Tension often develops as the traditional easygoing patterns of management become dysfunctional. Great managerial skill is required to preserve the "family" atmosphere while introducing professional management.

Changing Skill Requirements

As a firm moves from Stage 1 to Stage 4, the pattern of entrepreneurial activities changes. The entrepreneur becomes less of a doer and more of a manager, as shown in Figure 16-2.

Managers who are strong on "doing" skills are often weak on "managing" skills. As an example, a family wholesale business in New York ran into serious management problems as it expanded and became a designer jeans maker called Gitano Group Inc. It was headed by a family member, Haim Dabah. However, the company outgrew Dabah's ability to control it.

There was no business plan, no budgeting, and no system to monitor the purchase and management of inventory. Admits Dabah: "The one thing I don't know how to do is make sure our systems, financial controls, and all that stuff work."[3]

Firms that are overly hesitant to move through these organizational stages and to acquire the necessary management limit their rate of growth. On the other hand, a small business may attempt to become a big business too quickly. The entrepreneur's primary strength may lie in product development or selling, for example, and a quick push into Stage 4 may saddle the entrepreneur with managerial duties and rob the organization of those valuable entrepreneurial talents.

The need for effective management becomes more acute as the business expands. Very small firms often survive in spite of weak management. To some

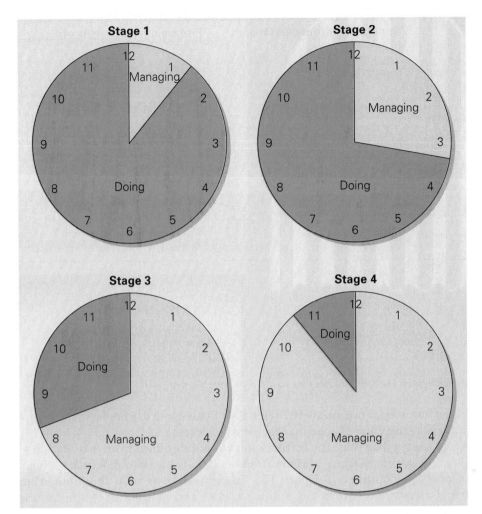

Figure 16-2
Managerial Time and
Stages of Business
Growth

extent, the quality of their products or services may offset deficiencies in their management. In the early days of business life, therefore, the firm may survive and grow even though its management is less than professional. Even in very small businesses, however, defects in management place strains on the business and retard its development.

Founders as Managers

Founders of new firms are not always good organization members. As Chapter 1 explained, they are creative, innovative, risk-taking individuals who have the courage to strike out on their own. Indeed, they are often propelled into entrepreneurship by precipitating events, some of which involve difficulty in fitting

Figure 16-3
How Do
Founder/Owners
Differ from
"Professional
Managers"?

	Entrepreneurs/founders/owners are	Professional managers are
Motivation and Emotional Orientation	Oriented toward creating, building.	Oriented toward consolidating, surviving, growing.
	Achievement-oriented.	Power- and influence-oriented.
	Self-oriented, worried about own image; need for "glory" high.	Organization-oriented, worried about company image.
	Jealous of own prerogatives, need for autonomy high.	Interested in developing the organization and subordinates.
	Loyal to own company, "local."	Loyal to profession of management, "cosmopolitan."
	Willing and able to take moderate risks on own authority.	Able to take risks, but more cautious and in need of support.
Analytical Orientation	Primarily intuitive, trusting of own intuitions.	Primarily analytical, more cautious about intuitions.
	Long-range time horizon.	Short-range time horizon.
	Holistic; able to see total picture, patterns.	Specific; able to see details and their consequences.

Source: Reprinted, by permission of the publisher, from ORGANIZATIONAL DYNAMICS, Summer 1983.
© 1983 American Management Association, New York. All rights reserved.

into conventional organizational roles. As a consequence, founders may fail to appreciate the value of good management practices.

In many subtle ways, the orientation of founders differs from that of professional managers. Edgar H. Schein has identified many such differences, some of which are outlined in Figure 16-3. These variations show the founder as being more self-oriented and willing to take risks, in contrast to the professional manager's greater organizational concern.

It is important to avoid stereotyping. Some entrepreneurs are professional in their approach to management, and some corporate managers are entrepreneurial in the sense of being innovative and willing to take risks. Nevertheless, a founder's less-than-professional management style often acts as a drag on business growth. Ideally, the founder adds a measure of professional management without sacrificing the entrepreneurial spirit and the basic values that gave the business a successful start.

THE NATURE OF MANAGERIAL WORK

management functions
the activities of planning, leading, organizing, and control-

The chapter thus far has treated the management process in a general way. Now it is time to look more closely at what managers do—how they plan, how they exercise leadership, how they organize, and how they control operations. These activities are sometimes called **management functions.**

S M A L L   B U S I N E S S   I N   A C T I O N

A Plan That Actually Guides Business Operations

In 1987, Western Windshields, Inc., a distributor of automobile replacement glass, needed to retrench, having lost money on one venture and having neglected its core business. Western's president, Neil Smith, with the help of management consultant Raymond Leon and Western's own management team, put together a comprehensive plan designed to turn strategies into action.

The plan was distinctive in that it was constructed for use as a management tool—to be followed during the year rather than being placed on a shelf and forgotten. Each department had a one-page summary of the plan that laid out its activities by calendar periods.

For instance, by last July Smith was to have hired a credit manager. And in the first two weeks of September he was to have analyzed the status of collection of receivables. "That's the beauty of this thing," says Smith. "At any given point we know exactly where we are on the plan."

Smith and other managers hold monthly meetings to monitor progress, and they update the plan annually. Western's plan was credited with helping the business to more than double its 1984 sales in the plan's first two years of use.

Source: Jeffrey Lener, "A Business Plan That Grows with You." Reprinted from the December 1988 issue of *VENTURE, For Entrepreneurial Business Owners & Investors,* © 1988.

Planning

Chapter 7 considered the preparation of a business plan for a new business. Such initial planning is only the first phase of an ongoing process of planning that guides production, marketing, and other activities on a month-to-month and year-to-year basis. This section focuses on this ongoing planning process.

Need for Formal Planning. Most small-business owners and managers plan to some degree. However, the amount of planning is typically much less than the ideal. Also, what little planning there is tends to be spotty and unsystematic—dealing with how much inventory to purchase, whether to buy a new piece of equipment, and other questions of this type. Specific circumstances affect the degree to which formal planning is needed, but most businesses could function more profitably by increasing their planning and making it more systematic.

The payoff from planning comes in a number of ways. First, the very process of thinking through the issues confronting a firm and developing a plan can improve its productivity. Second, during the year (in the case of an annual plan), decisions can be guided by the plan, and managers can work consistently toward the same goal. In addition, the existence of a plan provides credibility with bankers, suppliers, and other outsiders.

long-range plans (strategic plans)
a firm's basic plans for the long-term future

short-range plans
plans that govern a firm's operations for a specific time period

budget
a document that expresses future plans in monetary terms

business policies
guides to management practice

procedures
specific methods followed in business activities

standard operating procedures
established methods of conducting business

Kinds of Plans. A firm's path to the future is spelled out in its **long-range plans** or **strategic plans.** As Chapter 3 noted, strategy decisions are concerned with such issues as market niche and/or features that differentiate the firm from its competitors.

Short-range plans, in contrast, are action plans that govern activities in production, marketing, and other areas in a specific month, quarter, or other time period. An important part of short-range operating plans is the **budget**—a document that expresses future plans in monetary terms. A budget is usually prepared one year in advance, with a breakdown by quarters or months.

Other plans are less connected to the calendar and more concerned with the way things are done. **Business policies,** for example, are fundamental statements that serve as guides to management practice. They may be financial policies, personnel policies, or any of many other types of policies. A policy may state, for example, that no employee will accept a gift from a supplier unless it is of nominal value.

Procedures are more specific and deal primarily with methodology—how something is to be done. In a furniture store, for example, a procedure might require the sale of furniture on credit to be approved by a credit manager prior to delivery to the customer. Once a method of work is established, it may be standardized and referred to as a **standard operating procedure.**

Making Time for Planning. Small-business managers may easily succumb to the "tyranny of the urgent." Because they are so busy "putting out fires," they may never get around to planning. Planning is easy to postpone, and that makes it easy for managers to ignore it while concentrating on more urgent issues of production and sales. And, like quarterbacks blindsided by blitzing linebackers, such entrepreneurs may be bowled over by unsuspected competitors.

Some discipline is necessary to find time for planning and to gain its benefits. Time must be set aside and a degree of seclusion provided if significant progress is to be made. Planning is primarily a mental process. It is seldom done effectively in an atmosphere of ringing telephones, rush orders, and urgent demands for decision.

Employee Participation in Planning. A small-business owner is directly responsible for planning and, consequently, must personally spend time in planning. Nevertheless, this responsibility may be delegated to some extent, because some planning is required of all members of the enterprise. If the organization is of any size at all, the owner can hardly specify in detail the program for each department.

The concept that the boss does the thinking and the employee does the work is misleading. Progressive managers have discovered that employees' ideas are often helpful in developing solutions to company problems. The salesperson, for example, is closer to the customer and usually better able to evaluate the customer's reactions.

Leading and Motivating

As with any endeavor involving people, a small firm needs an atmosphere of co-operation and teamwork among all participants. Fortunately, employees in small firms can collaborate effectively. In fact, the potential for good teamwork is enhanced in some ways by the smallness of the enterprise.

Personal Involvement and Influence of the Entrepreneur.

In most small firms, employees get to know the owner-manager personally within a short period of time. This person is not a faceless "unknown" but an individual whom employees see and relate to in the course of their normal work schedules. This situation is entirely different from that of large corporations, in which most employees may never even see the chief executive. If the employer-employee relationship is good, employees in small firms naturally develop strong feelings of personal loyalty to the employer.

In very small firms—those of 20 or fewer employees—extensive interaction is typical. As a firm grows, the amount of personal contact naturally declines. Nevertheless, a significant personal relationship is characteristic of most small businesses.

In a large corporation, the values of top-level managers must be filtered through many layers of management before they come to those who produce and sell the products. As a result, the influence of those at the top may be diluted by the very process of going through channels. In contrast, personnel in a firm receive the leader's messages directly. This face-to-face contact facilitates their understanding of the leader's stand on integrity, customer service, and other important issues.

Leadership That Builds Enthusiasm.

Leadership that maximizes the contributions of personnel in a small firm will enable the firm to compete more effectively in the marketplace. Although larger competitors may have an advantage because of the economic resources at their disposal, they do not necessarily have an advantage in their methods of leadership. By creating an environment that inspires enthusiasm, the leader of a small firm can get the best from present company personnel and also offer a strong inducement to prospective employees. For example, most professional personnel prefer an organizational setting that minimizes "politics" as a factor in getting ahead. By creating a friendly atmosphere that avoids the intrigue common in some organizations, an entrepreneur can build an environment that is much more attractive to most employees.

Leadership that emphasizes positive, noncoercive approaches is increasingly replacing the more autocratic methods of earlier years. Positive leadership rests upon a respect for individual members of the organization and a basic fairness in decisions affecting them. Such leadership makes extensive use of communication, as noted in the next section.

S M A L L   B U S I N E S S   I N   A C T I O N

Upward Communication Gets Results

Upward communication is typically difficult, and in some companies it just doesn't happen. Robert Davies, founder and president of SBT Corporation in Sausalito, California, developed a special E-mail suggestion system that allowed employees to pass along new ideas or make direct requests to the CEO. A number of suggestions commented on the company's formal dress code. In this case, the boss explained that he actually listened.

Because I had always worked in places with a strict dress code, I didn't want to change it. But as suggestions for a more relaxed code kept making their way to me, I started to think that if it motivated my employees, why not?

So last October, I reluctantly agreed to experiment with suspending the old dress code in favor of more casual attire. At the end of the year, we made it permanent.

Interestingly, after trying the new system, I no longer feel comfortable in a suit and tie. Unless I'm giving a seminar or hosting an important guest, I usually wear a sweater and an open shirt.

Best of all, the employees now find me more approachable because I feel more comfortable and don't look as intimidating. And that makes it easier, I think, for me to be receptive to their ideas, too. And when you have 80 people contributing, you have a veritable "idea factory." From the receptionist to the programmer, I never know who will give us the next great suggestion.

Source: Robert Davies, "Entrepreneur's Notebook: Managing By Listening," *Nation's Business,* Vol. 80, No. 9 (September 1992), p. 6. Reprinted by permission, *Nation's Business,* September 1992. Copyright 1992, U.S. Chamber of Commerce.

Effective Communication. The key to healthy interpersonal relationships lies in effective communication. To be sure, much communication flows in the form of orders and instructions to employees. But communication is a two-way process, and it is difficult for employees to be either intelligent or enthusiastic teamworkers if they do not know the reasons for such orders and instructions. Furthermore, the opportunity to contribute ideas and opinions *before* the manager decides an issue adds dignity to the job in the eyes of most employees.

Other effective communication practices include telling employees where they stand, how the business is doing, and what the company's plans are for the future. Negative feedback to employees may be necessary at times, but positive feedback is the primary tool for establishing good human relations. Perhaps the most fundamental concept to keep in mind is that employees are people. They quickly detect insincerity, but they respond to honest efforts to treat them as mature, responsible individuals.

To go beyond good intentions in communicating, a small-firm manager may adopt some practical techniques of stimulating two-way communication. A few examples, by no means exhaustive, are the following:

Figure 16-4
Effective
Communication
Creates Enthusiasm
in Employees

1. Periodic performance review sessions as a time for discussing the employee's ideas, questions, complaints, and job expectations.
2. Bulletin boards to keep employees informed about developments affecting them and/or the company.
3. Suggestion boxes as a means of soliciting employee ideas.
4. Staff meetings for the discussion of problems and matters of general concern.

These methods can be used to supplement the most basic of all channels for communication—the day-to-day interaction between each employee and his or her supervisor.

Organizing

While an entrepreneur may give direction through personal leadership, he or she must also define the relationships among the firm's activities and among the individuals on the company payroll. Without some kind of organization structure, the situation eventually becomes chaotic, and morale suffers.

The Unplanned Structure. In small companies, the organization structure tends to evolve with little conscious planning. Certain employees begin performing particular functions when the firm is new and retain those functions as the company matures. Other functions remain diffused in a number of positions, even though they have gained importance as a result of company growth.

This natural evolution is not all bad. Generally, a strong element of practicality exists in organizational arrangements that evolve in this way. The structure is forged in the process of working and growing, not derived from a textbook. Unplanned structures are seldom perfect, however, and growth typically creates a need for organizational change. Periodically, therefore, the entrepreneur should examine structural relationships and make adjustments as needed for effective teamwork.

line organization
a small, simple structure in which each person in a firm reports to one supervisor

chain of command
superior-subordinate relationships in an organization structure

Establishing a Chain of Command. In a **line organization** each person has one supervisor to whom he or she reports and looks for instructions. Thus, a single, specific chain of command exists. All employees are engaged directly in getting out the work—producing, selling, or arranging financial resources. Most very small firms—for example, those with fewer than 10 employees—use this form of organization. A line organization is illustrated in Figure 16-5.

The term **chain of command** implies a superior-subordinate relationship with a downward flow of orders, but it involves much more. The chain of command is also a channel for two-way communication, although this does not mean that communication among employees at the same level is forbidden. Informal discussion among employees is inevitable. However, the chain is the official, vertical channel of communication.

An organizational problem occurs when managers or employees ignore organization lines. In small firms, the climate of informality and flexibility makes it easy to short-circuit the formal chain. The president and founder of the business, for example, may get in a hurry and give instructions to salespersons or plant employees instead of going through the sales manager or the production manager. Similarly, an employee who has been with the entrepreneur from the beginning tends to maintain that direct person-to-person relationship rather than observe newly instituted channels of communication.

Figure 16-5
Line Organization

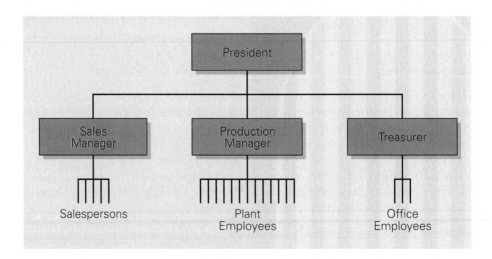

As a practical matter, adherence to the chain of command can never be complete. An organization in which the chain of command is rigid would be bureaucratic and inefficient. Nevertheless, frequent and flagrant disregard of the chain of command quickly undermines the position of the bypassed manager.

The **line-and-staff organization** is similar to a line organization in that each person reports to a single supervisor. However, in a line-and-staff structure there are also staff specialists who perform specialized services or act as management advisers in special areas. Examples of staff specialists include a human resources manager, a production control technician, a quality control specialist, or an assistant to the president. Small firms ordinarily grow quickly to a size requiring some staff specialists. Consequently, this is a widely used type of organization in small business. Figure 16-6 shows a line-and-staff organization.

Line activities are those that contribute directly to the primary objectives of the small firm. Typically, these are production and sales activities. **Staff activities,** on the other hand, are the supporting or helping activities. Although both types of activities are important, the focus must be kept on line activities—those which earn the customer's dollar. The owner-manager must insist that staff specialists function primarily as helpers and facilitators. Otherwise, the firm will experience confusion as employees receive directions from a variety of supervisors and staff specialists. **Unity of command**—that is, receiving direction from only one boss—would be destroyed.

Informal Organization. The types of organization structure previously discussed are concerned with formal relationships among members of an orga-

line-and-staff organization
an organization structure that includes staff specialists who assist line management

line activities
activities contributing directly to the primary objectives of a small firm

staff activities
activities that support line activities

unity of command
making sure that instructions come directly from only one immediate supervisor

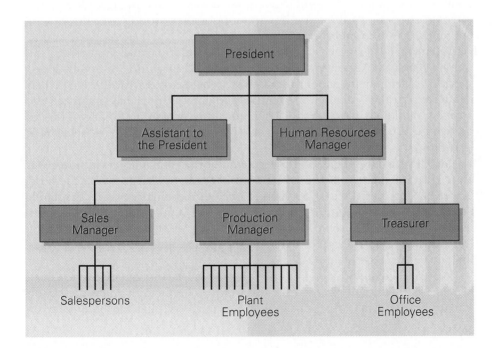

Figure 16-6
Line-and-Staff Organization

nization. In any organization, however, there are also informal groups that have something in common such as jobs, hobbies, carpools, age, or affiliations with civic associations.

Although informal groups are not a structural part of the formal organization, the manager should observe them and evaluate their effect on the functioning of the total organization. An informal group, for example, may foster an attitude of working hard until the very end of the working day or doing the opposite—easing up and coasting the last half hour. Ordinarily, no serious conflict arises between informal groups and the formal organization. It is probable that an informal leader or leaders will emerge who will influence employee behavior. The wise manager understands the potentially positive contribution of informal groups and the inevitability of informal leadership. Of course, if a leader were to persist in influencing other employees to behave contrary to the wishes of management, it might become necessary to discharge that individual.

Informal interaction among subordinates and managers can facilitate work performance and also can make life in the workplace more enjoyable for everyone. The value of compatible work groups to the individual became painfully clear to one college student who worked on a summer job:

I was employed as a forklift driver for one long, frustrating summer. Soon after being introduced to my work group, I knew I was in trouble. A clique had formed and, for some reason, resented college students. During lunch breaks and work breaks, I spent the whole time by myself. Each morning I dreaded going to work. The job paid well, but I was miserable.

delegation of authority
granting to subordinates the right to act or make decisions

Delegating Authority. Through **delegation of authority,** a manager grants to subordinates the right to act or to decide. By delegating authority, the superior can perform the more important tasks after turning over the less important functions to subordinates.

Failure to delegate may well be the weakest point in small-business organizations generally. Although the problem is found in all organizations, it is a special problem for the independent entrepreneur, whose background usually contributes to this situation. Frequently, the entrepreneur has organized the business and knows more about it than any other person in the firm. Thus, to protect the business, the owner is inclined to keep a firm hold on the reins of leadership.

Inability or unwillingness to delegate authority is manifested in numerous ways. For example, employees may find it necessary to "clear it with the boss" before making even a minor decision. A line of subordinates may be constantly trying to get the attention of the owner to resolve some issue that the subordinates lack authority to settle. This keeps the owner exceptionally busy, rushing from assisting a salesperson to helping iron out a production bottleneck to setting up a new filing system.

Delegation of authority is important for the satisfactory operation of a small firm and is an absolute prerequisite for growth. This factor alone is the reason why many firms can never grow beyond the small size that can be directly supervised in detail by the owner. One owner of a small restaurant operated it with excellent profits. As a result of this success, the owner acquired a lease on another restaurant in the same area and proceeded to operate it for one year. During this time, the owner experienced constant "headaches" with the second restaurant. Working long hours and trying to supervise both restaurants finally led the owner to give up the job. This person had never learned to delegate authority.

Deciding How Many to Supervise. The optimum **span of control** is the number of subordinates who can be effectively supervised by a manager. Although some authorities have stated that six to eight people are all that one individual can supervise effectively, the proper span of control actually is a variable depending upon a number of factors. Among these are the nature of the work and the superior's knowledge, energy, personality, and abilities. In addition, if the abilities of subordinates are greater than average, the span of control may be enlarged accordingly.

span of control
the number of subordinates who can be effectively supervised by one manager

As a very small firm grows and adds employees, the entrepreneur's span of control is extended. There is a tendency to stretch the span too far—to supervise not only the first 5 or 6 employees but later all 10 or 12 as they are needed. Eventually a point is reached at which the attempted span exceeds the entrepreneur's reach—the time and ability he or she can devote to the business. It is at this point that the entrepreneur must establish intermediate levels of supervision, devoting more time to management and moving beyond the role of player-coach.

Controlling

Controlling involves the appraisal of operating results, followed by remedial action when results deviate from the plan. Controlling activity is necessary to keep the business "on course" and to make sure that plans are followed.

The cornerstone of financial control is the budget, in which cost and performance standards are incorporated. Some very small businesses attempt to operate without a budget. However, even in these cases the owner may have a rough idea of what cost and performance should be, keep track of results, and investigate when results seem out of line.

TIME MANAGEMENT

Much of an owner-manager's time during the working day is spent on the firing line—meeting customers, solving problems, listening to employee complaints, talking with suppliers, and the like. The manager of a small firm tackles management problems with the assistance of only a small staff. All of this means that the manager's energies and activities are diffused more than those of managers in large firms. It also means that time is often the manager's scarcest resource.

Figure 16-7
Hours Per Week
Worked by New-
Business Owners

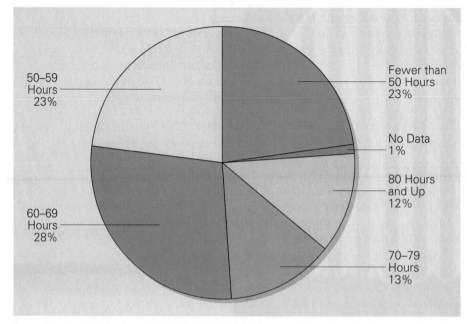

Source: Data developed and provided by The NFIB Foundation and sponsored by the American Express Travel
Related Services Company, Inc.

Problem of Time Pressure

Many entrepreneurs and key managers in small firms work from 60 to 80 hours
per week. The hours worked by most new-business owners are particularly long,
as shown in Figure 16-7. A frequent and unfortunate result of such a schedule
is their inefficient work performance. They are too busy to see sales representatives who can supply market information on new products and processes. They
are too busy to read technical or trade literature in order to discover what others are doing and what improvements might be adapted to their own use. They
are too busy to listen carefully to employees' opinions and grievances. They are
too busy to give instructions properly and to teach employees how to do their
jobs correctly.

Time-Savers for Busy Managers

One important solution to the problem of lack of time is good organization of
work. This means delegating duties to subordinates, who are permitted to discharge those duties without close supervision. Of course, this requires proper
selection and training of individuals to assume responsibility for the delegated
functions.

Perhaps the greatest time-saver is the effective use of time. If an individual
flits from one task to another and back again, it is likely that little will be ac-

complished. The first step in planning one's use of time should be a survey of time normally spent on various activities. Relying on general impressions is unscientific and is likely to involve error. For a period of several days, or preferably several weeks, the manager should record the time spent on various types of activities during the day. An analysis of these figures will reveal the pattern of activities, those projects and tasks involving the greatest time expenditure, and factors responsible for waste of time. It will reveal chronic waste of time caused by excessive socializing, work on trivial matters, coffee breaks, and so on.

After eliminating practices that waste time, a manager can carefully plan the use of available time. A planned approach to a day's work or week's work is much more effective than a haphazard do-whatever-comes-up-first approach. This is true even for small-firm managers whose schedules are interrupted in unanticipated ways.

Many specialists in time management recommend the use of a daily written plan of work activities. This may simply be an informal listing of activities on a note pad, but it should include an establishment of priorities. By classifying duties as first-, second-, and third-level of priority, the manager can identify and focus attention on the most crucial tasks.

Effective time management requires self-discipline. It is easy to begin with good intentions and later lapse into habitual practices of devoting time to whatever one finds to do at the moment. Procrastination is a frequent thief of time. Most of us delay unpleasant and difficult tasks. We often retreat to trivial or less threatening activities by rationalizing that we are getting those items out of the way in order to concentrate later on the important tasks.

Some managers devote much time to meetings with subordinates. Often these meetings just happen and drag on without any serious attempt to control them. The manager should prepare an agenda for such meetings, set starting and ending times, limit discussion to key issues, and assign the necessary follow-through to specific individuals. In this way the effectiveness of business conferences may be maximized and the manager's own time conserved, along with that of other staff members.

OUTSIDE MANAGEMENT ASSISTANCE

In view of the managerial deficiencies discussed earlier in this chapter, the entrepreneur should give careful consideration to the use of outside management assistance. Such outside assistance can supplement the busy owner-manager's personal knowledge and the expertise of the few staff specialists on the company's payroll.

The Need for Outside Assistance

The typical entrepreneur is not only deficient in managerial skills, but also lacks the opportunity to share ideas with managerial colleagues. Although entrepreneurs can confide, to some extent, in subordinates, many of them experience loneliness. A survey of 210 owners revealed that 52 percent of them "frequently felt a sense of loneliness."[4] Moreover, this same group reported a much higher incidence of stress symptoms than those who said they did not feel lonely.

By using consultants, entrepreneurs can overcome some of the management deficiencies and reduce the sense of isolation they experience. Furthermore, an "insider" directly involved in a business problem often "cannot see the forest for the trees." To offset this limitation, the consultant brings an objective point of view and new ideas, supported by a broad knowledge of proven, successful, cost-saving methods. The consultant also can help the manager improve decision making through better organization of fact gathering and the introduction of scientific techniques of analysis. Ideally the consultant should have an "on call" relationship with the small business so that improved methods may be put into use as the need arises.

Sources of Management Assistance

The sources of management assistance given here are by no means exhaustive. There are numerous, less obvious sources of management knowledge and approaches to seeking needed help. For example, owner-managers may increase their own skills by consulting public and university libraries, attending evening college, or considering suggestions of friends and customers.

New-Business Incubators. As discussed in Chapter 9, a new-business incubator is an organization and facility that offers both space and management services to new businesses. Chapter 9 referred to business incubators as one building-and-facilities option for startup businesses. This chapter directs attention to the more important aspect of incubator operation—the management counsel and administrative services they provide.

Although some new-business incubators existed prior to 1980, their rapid growth began in the 1980s. There are now several hundred incubators in the United States, and the number is growing rapidly. Most of them involve the participation of governmental and/or university agencies, although some have been launched as purely private endeavors. The primary motivation in establishing them has been a desire to encourage entrepreneurship and thereby contribute to economic development.

Incubators provide a supportive atmosphere for a business during the early months of its existence when it is most fragile and vulnerable to external dangers and internal errors. If the incubator system works as it should, the fledgling business gains strength quickly and, within a year or so, graduates from the incubator setting.

As one example of how an incubator business can help, Derrick Johnson saw his sales nearly triple in 1991 when he moved his bulk-mail firm, Coastal Mail Service, from his home into the West Charlotte (North Carolina) Business Incubator.[5] His rent of $1.60 per square foot was far below the local market rate of $7 to $15, and incubator banking connections helped him secure an equipment loan for the business.

Incubators offer new entrepreneurs on-site business expertise. Often, individuals who wish to start businesses are deficient in business knowledge and lacking in business experience. In many cases, they need practical guidance in marketing, record keeping, management, and preparation of business plans. These and other services, as portrayed in Figure 16-9, are available in a business incubator.

Small Business Institute (SBI) Programs. In 1972, the Small Business Administration implemented the **Small Business Institute (SBI)** program to make the consulting resources of universities available to small-business firms. SBI teams of upper-division and graduate students, under the direction of a faculty member, work with owners of small firms in analyzing their business problems and devising solutions. The primary users of such SBI consulting assistance are applicants for SBA loans, although the services are not restricted to such firms.

The program has been one of mutual benefit in providing students with a practical view of business management and in finding answers to the problems of

Small Business Institute (SBI)
a program making student consulting services available to small businesses

Figure 16-8
West Charlotte, North Carolina, Business Incubator Helps Entrepreneurs Such as Derrick Johnson Succeed

Figure 16-9
Contributions of
Incubators to
Tenant Firms

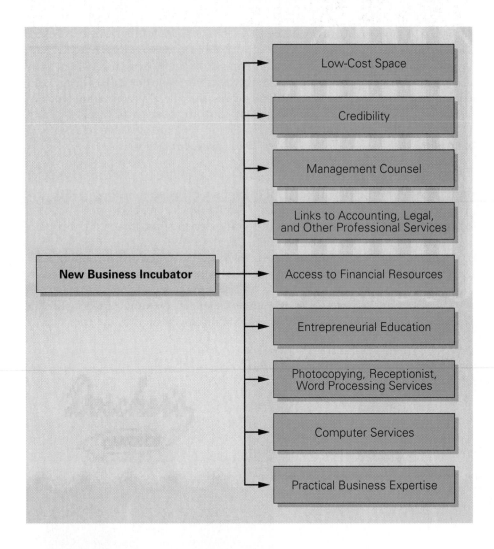

small firms. Students from small-business, business-policy, or similar courses are typically combined in teams that provide a diversity of academic backgrounds. Individual teams, for example, may have different members specializing in management, marketing, accounting, and finance. There has been an evident enthusiasm on the part of those participating in the program, and many feel it has been one of the most successful consulting programs for small business.

Service Corps of Retired Executives (SCORE). Small-business managers can obtain free management advice from a group called the **Service Corps of Retired Executives (SCORE)** by appealing to any Small Business Administration field office. SCORE is an organization of retired business executives who will consult on current problems with small-business managers. Functioning under the sponsorship of the Small Business Administration, this

**Service Corps of
Retired Executives
(SCORE)**
retired executives
who give free advice
to small businesses

group provides an opportunity for retired executives to be useful to society, and it helps small-business managers solve their problems. Hence, the relationship is mutually beneficial. It may also encourage entrepreneurs to utilize paid consultants as their firms grow, by demonstrating the worth of consulting services.

There are numerous stories of successful SCORE assistance to small firms. A race car driver, for example, went into the tire business but experienced problems with poor records and inadequate credit control. The SCORE counselor, a retired tire manufacturer and district sales manager, provided suggestions that led to an immediate increase in profits. Another firm, a small manufacturer, established a cost reduction/profit improvement program with the aid of a SCORE counselor. The enthusiastic owner reported increased sales volume, higher-than-industry profits, and improved financial standing.

Small Business Development Centers (SBDCs). **Small Business Development Centers,** which are patterned after the Agricultural Extension Service, were started in 1977 and now operate in most states. They are affiliated with colleges or universities as a part of the U.S. Small Business Administration's overall program of assistance to small business.

Small Business Development Centers provide direct consultation to small firms, continuing education, small-business research, export services, and minority support. Their staff typically includes faculty members, SCORE counselors, professional staff, and graduate student assistants.

Management Consultants. General management consultants serve small-business firms as well as large corporations. The entrepreneur should regard the service of a competent management consultant as an investment in improved decision making or cost reduction. Many small firms could save as much as 10 to 20 percent of annual operating costs. The inherent advantage in the use of able consultants is suggested by the existence of thousands of consulting firms. They range from large, long-established firms to small one- or two-person operations. Two broad areas of service rendered by management consultants are:

1. To help improve productivity and/or prevent trouble by anticipating and eliminating its causes.
2. To help a client get out of trouble.

Business firms have traditionally used consultants to help solve problems they could not handle alone. A consultant may be used, for example, to aid in the design of a new computer-based management information system. An even greater service that management consultants provide is their periodic observation and analysis, which keeps small problems from becoming big. This view of the role of consultants greatly enlarges their service potential.

Networks of Entrepreneurs. Entrepreneurs also gain informal management assistance through **networking**—the process of developing and engaging in mutually beneficial relationships with peers. As business owners meet

Small Business Development Centers (SBDCs) university-affiliated centers offering consulting, education, and support to small businesses

networking developing and engaging in mutually beneficial relationships with peers

SMALL BUSINESS IN ACTION

Developing a Network

Pamela Barefoot admitted to being scared and not knowing much about business when she started Blue Crab Bay Co., a specialty foods and gift company in Onancock, Virginia. As a result, she began networking by reaching out for advice to business friends and others.

> From the start, I joined as many trade and business associations as I could and relied heavily on help from sources such as SBA's Service Corps of Retired Executives (SCORE) and the Virginia Department of Economic Development.
>
> Networking within the specialty-foods business in Virginia led to the formation of a trade group that gives me insights on working in this industry and gives my firm low-cost exposure through trade shows and group-sponsored advertising.
>
> Generally, I take new proposals to the members of my personal network. Armed with their experience and my knowledge of the direction I want for the company, I can make the kind of calculated, educated decisions that have fueled our growth; Blue Crab Bay Co. expects sales of about $680,000 this year.

Source: Pamela Barefoot, "Entrepreneur's Notebook: Developing A Network," *Nation's Business,* Vol. 80, No. 10 (October 1992), p. 6. Reprinted by permission, *Nation's Business,* October 1992. Copyright 1992, U.S. Chamber of Commerce.

other business owners, they discover a commonality of interests that leads to an exchange of ideas and experiences. The setting for such relationships may be a trade association, civic club, fraternal organization, or some other situation that brings the parties into contact with one another. Of course, the personal network of an entrepreneur is not limited to other entrepreneurs, but those individuals are typically a significant part of that network.

One example of a formally structured networking system is called "The Alternative Board," started by businessman Allen Fishman. Fishman's company sets up advisory boards of about a dozen chief executives. Usually these people are the owners of small, noncompeting companies.

They meet one morning a month, with a paid "facilitator," most often a semiretired entre-preneur, as guide. The cost is $2,000 a year for small companies and $3,000 for midsized ones. Tom Epstein, president of Continental Research, St. Louis, says that in his six months as a TAB member, "I've made my money back 10 times over." [6]

Networks of entrepreneurs involve a variety of ties—instrumental, affective, and moral. An *instrumental* tie means that the parties find the relationship mu-tually rewarding—for example, exchanging useful ideas about certain business problems. An *affective* tie relates to emotional sentiments—for example, the sharing of a joint vision about the role of small business in doing battle with giant competitors or with the government. A *moral* tie involves some type of obligation—for example, a mutual commitment to the principle of private en-terprise or the importance of integrity in business transactions.

In personal networks of entrepreneurs, affective and moral commitments are believed to dominate those which are instrumental.[7] This suggests that a sense of identity and self-respect may be a significant product of the entrepre-neur's network.

Networking has been particularly helpful to some women entrepreneurs. In the New York area, a group of 10 women business owners meet monthly to help one another with business problems. They own and operate companies with an-nual sales of between $1 million and $10 million. One participant was quoted as saying, "The roundtable gives me the opportunity to hear what someone else has to say. They are much more capable of analyzing a problem sometimes be-cause I am too close to it."[8]

Other Business and Professional Services. A variety of business and professional groups provide management assistance. In many cases, the ex-tension of such service is part of a business relationship. Getting advice from a banker is one example. Sources of management counsel include not only bankers but also certified public accountants (CPAs), attorneys, insurance agents, suppliers, trade associations, and Chambers of Commerce. One study of small-business firms found that accountants or CPAs, lawyers, and bankers were the most extensively used sources of outside management assistance.[9]

It takes initiative to draw upon the management assistance available from such groups. For example, it is easy to confine relationships with a CPA to audits and financial statements, but the CPA can advise on a broader range of subjects.

Besides offering advice on tax matters, a good accountant can help in a variety of situa-tions. When you hire or fire, what benefits or severance package should you offer? When you're planning to open a new branch, will your cash flow support it? When you embark on a new sideline, will the margins be adequate? When you reduce insurance, what's the risk? When you factor receivables, how will it affect the balance sheet? When you take on a big account, what's the downside if you lose the account? Or when you cut expenses, how will the cuts affect the bottom line? [10]

1. A large part of small-business community is characterized by weak management. Small-firm managers are constrained by limitations in financial resources and lack of adequate professional staff.
2. Founders typically differ in a number of ways from professional managers, and they experience difficulties as a firm grows. As it grows, its founder becomes more a manager and less a doer and moves in the direction of becoming a professional manager or bringing in professional management.
3. The work of managers involves such activities or functions as planning, leading and motivating, organizing, and controlling.
4. Small-business managers who have difficulty finding time to perform managerial tasks efficiently should learn to delegate some duties to subordinates and to organize their use of time by careful planning.
5. Outside management assistance is provided by many types of consultants, including new business incubators, SBI student consultants, SCORE (retired executives), Small Business Development Centers, CPA firms, general management consultants, and various others, as well as by networking. The use of management consultants may be thought of as an investment in cost reduction.

DISCUSSION QUESTIONS

1. Is it likely that the quality of management is relatively uniform throughout the many types of small businesses? What might account for differences?
2. What are the four stages of small-business growth outlined in this chapter? How do managerial requirements change as the firm moves through these stages?
3. Evaluate founders as managers. Why is there a tendency toward managerial weakness in those who create new firms?
4. As noted in Figure 16-3, on page 416, entrepreneurs are thought to be primarily intuitive, whereas professional managers are thought to be primarily analytical. If this is true, how will collegiate education for business affect the development of entrepreneurs?
5. Some professional football coaches hold written game plans in their hands that they consult from time to time during games. If coaches need formal plans for this kind of competition, does it follow that small-business firms need them for their type of competition? Why?
6. Do you believe that most employees of small firms would welcome or resist a leadership approach that sought their ideas and involved them in meetings to let them know what was going on? Why might some resist such an approach?
7. According to one saying, "What you do speaks so loudly I can't hear what you say." What does this mean, and how does it apply to communication in small firms?
8. What type of small firm might properly use the line type of organization? When would its structure require change? To what type? Why?
9. What are the two most likely causes of failure to delegate authority properly? Is delegation important? Why?
10. What practices can a small-business manager utilize to conserve time?

11. Is it reasonable to believe that an outsider coming into a business could propose procedures or policies superior to those of the manager who is intimately acquainted with operations? Why?
12. What would be the advantages and drawbacks of a business-incubator location for a startup retail firm?
13. Explain the nature of the SBI student consulting program. Is this program of primary benefit to the client firm or to the students?
14. What might account for the fact that accountants and CPAs are among the most widely used sources of outside management assistance?
15. What is networking, and how can an entrepreneur use it to improve management within a small firm?

YOU MAKE THE CALL

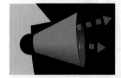

Situation 1

In one small firm, the owner-manager and his management team use various methods to push decision making onto employees at the operating level. New employees are trained thoroughly when they begin, but no supervisor monitors their work closely once they have learned their duties. Of course, help is available as needed, but no one is there on an hour-to-hour basis to make sure they are producing as needed and that they are avoiding mistakes.

Occasionally, all managers and supervisors leave for a day-long meeting and allow the operating employees to run the business by themselves. Job assignments are defined rather loosely. Management expects employees to assume responsibility and to take necessary action whenever they see that something needs to be done. When employees ask for direction, they are sometimes simply told to solve the problem in whatever way they think best.

Questions:
1. Is such a loosely organized firm likely to be as effective as a firm that defines jobs more precisely and monitors performance more closely? What are the limitations of the management style described above?
2. What do you think would be the morale effects of such management methods?
3. Would you like to work for this company? Why or why not?

Situation 2

A few years after successfully launching a new business, an entrepreneur found himself spending 16-hour days running from one appointment to another, negotiating with customers, drumming up new business, signing checks, and checking up as much as possible on his six employees. The founder realized that his own strength was in selling, but general management responsibilities were very time consuming and interfered with his selling efforts. He even slept in the office two nights a week.

No matter how hard he worked, however, he knew that his people weren't organized and that many problems existed. There was no time to set personnel policies or to draw up job descriptions for his six employees. One employee even took advantage of the laxity and sometimes skipped work. Invoices were sent to customers late, and delivery schedules were sometimes missed. Fortunately, the business was profitable in spite of the numerous problems.

Questions
1. Is this founder's problem one of time management or general management? Would it be logical to engage a management consultant to help solve the firm's problems?
2. If this founder asked you to recommend some type of outside management assistance, would you recommend a SCORE counselor, an SBI team, a CPA firm, a management consultant, or some other kind? Why?
3. If you were asked to improve this firm's management system, what would be your first steps and your initial goal?

EXPERIENTIAL EXERCISES

1. Interview a management consultant, SCORE member, SBI project director, or representative of a CPA firm to discuss small-business management weaknesses and the willingness or reluctance of small firms to use consultants. Prepare a report on your findings.
2. Select a small-business firm and diagram the organizational relationships in that firm. In your report, note any organizational problems that are apparent to you or that are recognized by the manager or others in the firm.
3. Most students have also been employees at some time or other. Prepare a report on your personal experience as an employee in responding to the leadership and delegation of authority by your supervisor. Include references to the type of leadership exercised and to the adequacy of delegation, its clarity, and problems involved.
4. Select an unstructured block of one to four hours in your schedule—that is, hours that are not regularly devoted to class attendance, sleeping, and so on. Carefully record your use of that time period for several days. Prepare a report showing your use of the time and a plan for its more effective use.

REFERENCES TO SMALL-BUSINESS PRACTICES

Bodenstab, Charles J. "Directional Signals: Why Your Company Should Have an Annual Business Plan," *Inc.,* Vol. 11, No. 3 (March 1989), pp. 139–141.
> The owner manager of an independent business tells how his business benefits from planning and shows a table of contents from the firm's annual plan.

Gutner, Toddi. "Father Doesn't Know Best," *Forbes,* Vol. 150, No. 4 (August 17, 1992), pp. 78–80.
> The founder of a meat processing business ran the business by instinct and intuition, but his son found it necessary to introduce professional management in order to maximize the value of the business.

Poole, Claire. "Risk Not Thy Whole Wad,' " *Forbes,* Vol. 148, No. 10 (October 28, 1991), pp. 94–98.
> A new firm, QMS, Inc., grew so rapidly that it began to get out of control. The story relates how management corrected the control problem.

Riggle, David. "Great Places to Grow a Business," *In Business*, Vol. 12, No. 5 (September–October 1990), pp. 20–22.

The article describes several incubators and the types of new businesses they have helped get started.

Welles, Edward O. "Bad News," *Inc.*, Vol. 13, No. 4 (April 1991), pp. 45–49.

A number of small firms shared bad news about their businesses with employees as a way of being fair and retaining credibility.

ENDNOTES

1. Jim Schell, "In Defense of the Entrepreneur," *Inc.*, Vol. 13, No. 5 (May 1991), p. 30. Reprinted with permission, *Inc.* magazine, May, 1991. Copyright 1991 by Goldhirsh Group, Inc., 38 Commerical Wharf, Boston, MA 02110.

2. Thomas P. Murphy, "From Eagles to Turkeys," *Forbes*, Vol. 134, No. 4 (August 13, 1984), p. 136. Excerpted from FORBES magazine by permission. © Forbes Inc. 1984.

3. "Is This Any Way To Run the Family Business?" *Business Week*, No. 3280 (August 24, 1992), pp. 48–49.

4. David E. Gumpert and David P. Boyd, "The Loneliness of the Small Business Owner," *Harvard Business Review*, Vol. 62, No. 6 (November–December 1984), p. 19.

5. Bradford McKee, "A Boost for Start-Ups," *Nation's Business*, Vol. 80, No. 8 (August 1992), pp. 40–42.

6. "Small Firms Get Help from Advisory Boards," *The Wall Street Journal*, September 23, 1991, p. B1.

7. Bengt Johannisson and Rein Peterson, *The Personal Networks of Entrepreneurs*. Paper appearing in conference proceedings, Third Canadian Conference, International Council for Small Business—Canada, Toronto, Canada, May 23–25, 1984.

8. "Women Chief Executives Help Each Other with Frank Advice," *The Wall Street Journal* (July 2, 1984), p. 19.

9. Robert A. Peterson, "Small Business Management Assistance," *American Journal of Small Business*, Vol. 9, No. 2 (Fall 1984), pp. 35–45.

10. Howard Scott, "Getting Help from Your Accountant," *IB Magazine*, Vol. 3, No. 3 (May–June 1992), p. 38. Reprinted from the May/June 1992 issue of *IB—America's Small Business Magazine*. © *IB Magazine*. All rights reserved. Small business owners can receive an upcoming issue. To reserve your issue, send your business card or letterhead to *IB* Free Issue, 875 S. Westlake Blvd., #211, Westlake Village, CA 91361.

CHAPTER 17

Managing Human Resources

Ideally, a compensation program motivates employees to perform well. Jon W. Wehrenberg, founder of Jamestown Advanced Products, Inc., a metal-fabricating business in Jamestown, New York, designed a bonus program to encourage the serious effort of the firm's 10 or 11 production workers. It was a simple system—one that paid employees any savings in targeted labor costs—and it succeeded in stimulating superior performance. Wehrenberg evaluated the plan as follows:

As time went on I could see the change in employees' attitudes. Before we were making bonus payments, workers didn't seem to care if we spent money on overtime because of a production snag. It was the company's nickel, not theirs. But once they crossed into bonus territory, they saw that production problems were costing them money, and they became very diligent about finding ways to improve.

Jon W. Wehrenberg and employees

Source: Jon W. Wehrenberg, "How My Company Learned to Run Itself," *Inc.*, Vol. 13, No. 1 (January 1991), pp. 54–60. Reprinted with permission, *Inc.* magazine (January 1991). Copyright 1991 by Goldhirsh Group, Inc., 38 Commercial Wharf, Boston, MA 02110.

After studying this chapter, you should be able to:
1. Explain the importance of recruitment and the sources that can be used in finding suitable applicants.
2. Identify the steps in evaluating job applicants.
3. Describe the types of training appropriate for both managerial and nonmanagerial employees.
4. Explain the various kinds of compensation and the differences between daywork and incentive plans.
5. Summarize the laws relating to human resources and the steps involved in formalizing human resource systems.

LOOKING AHEAD

headhunter
leasing employees
Job Instruction Training
daywork
fringe benefits
employee stock ownership plans (ESOPs)
Civil Rights Act of 1964

Age Discrimination in Employment Act of 1967
Americans with Disabilities Act
Occupational Safety and Health Act (OSHA)

Workers' Compensation Laws
National Labor Relations Act
Immigration Reform Act
Family and Medical Leave Act of 1993

NEW TERMS AND CONCEPTS

Smallness of business size creates a unique situation in the management of human resources. For example, the owner of a small retail store cannot adopt the human resources program of Wal-Mart stores, which has 375,000 employees, by merely scaling it down. The atmosphere of a small firm also creates distinctive opportunities to develop strong relationships among its members. In view of the special employment characteristics associated with smallness, the entrepreneur needs to develop a human resources program that is directly applicable to a small firm.

RECRUITING AND SELECTING PERSONNEL

The initial step in a sound human resources program is the recruitment of capable employees. In recruiting, the small firm competes with both large and small businesses. It cannot afford to let competitors take the cream of the crop. Aggressive recruitment requires the employer to take the initiative in locating applicants and to search until enough applicants are available to permit a good choice.

Importance of People

Hiring the right people and eliciting their enthusiastic performance are essential factors in reaching the potential of any business. "With every person you hire," as one writer suggested, "you determine how great your potential successes may be—or how awful your failures."[1] In many small firms, for example, the attitudes of salespeople and their ability to serve customer needs directly affect sales volume. Payroll expense is also one of the largest expense categories for most businesses, having a direct impact on the bottom line. Recruitment and selection of employees establish the foundation for a firm's ongoing human relationships. If talented, ambitious recruits can be obtained, the business will be able to build a strong human organization through effective management.

Attracting Applicants to Small Firms

There is competition in recruiting well-qualified business talent. Small firms, therefore, must identify their distinctive advantages in making an appeal to outstanding prospects for managerial and professional positions. Fortunately, small-firm recruiters can advance some good arguments in favor of small-business careers.

The opportunity for general management experience at a decision-making level is attractive to many prospects. Rather than toiling in obscure, low-level, specialized positions during their early years, capable newcomers can quickly move into positions of responsibility in well-managed small businesses. In such positions, they can see that their work makes a difference in the success of the company.

Small firms can structure the work environment to offer professional, managerial, and technical personnel greater freedom than they would normally have in big business. One example of a small company that created an atmosphere of this type is Stone Construction Equipment, Inc., of Honeoye, New York. This firm restructured the job of Stan Gerhart, who made metal engine covers for light machinery.

Figure 17-1
Improving the Work Environment for People Such as Stan Gerhart of Stone Construction Equipment Makes Recruitment Easier

Recognizing Importance of Employees

The enthusiastic effort of employees can make an important contribution to the success of a small firm. Hal Rosenbluth, the fourth-generation head of a family travel agency, recognized the importance of the firm's personnel and made employee relations a part of his strategy for greatly expanding the operations of Rosenbluth Travel.

Whether consciously or not, by allying himself with the troops at the bottom, Hal tapped into a resource overlooked by most businesses: legions of bright, young people hungry and grateful for an opportunity in a tight labor market. He used symbolism to make them feel part of the team, too, calling them "associates" instead of "employees." The label "employee," he explains, "has connotations of subservience. Once someone feels subservient, you're in deep trouble. I felt we all worked together."

Source: Dan Rottenberg, "The Young Maverick," *Family Business*, Vol. 2, No. 1 (January–February, 1991), p. 32.

For 16 years his job was to crank 'em out, put 'em on the shelf, punch out, and go home. Then Stone's new managers asked Gerhart to redesign his job from the ground up—and to run his one-man department as its own little business, dealing on his own with "vendors" and "customers" elsewhere in the shop. Today Gerhart can point to a dozen timesaving or quality-assuring ideas he has come up with. "It makes my job a whole lot easier because I control my own destiny."[2]

Individual contributions can be recognized rather than hidden under the numerous layers of a bureaucratic organization. It is also possible to structure compensation arrangements so that they provide a powerful incentive. The value of these policies as recruiting advantages depends to some degree on the circumstances of the particular firm. Ideally, the firm should be growing and profitable. It should also have a degree of professionalism in its management that can be readily recognized by prospective employees.

Sources of Employees

To recruit effectively, it is necessary to know where and how to obtain qualified applicants. The sources are numerous, and it is impossible to generalize about the best source in view of the variations in personnel requirements and quality of sources from one locality to another.

Walk-Ins. A firm may receive unsolicited applications from individuals who walk into the place of business to seek employment. This is an inexpensive source for lower-skilled jobs, but the quality of applicants may be mixed. If

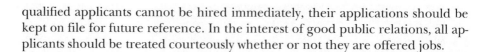

qualified applicants cannot be hired immediately, their applications should be kept on file for future reference. In the interest of good public relations, all applicants should be treated courteously whether or not they are offered jobs.

Schools. Secondary schools, trade schools, colleges, and universities are desirable sources for certain classes of employees, particularly those who need no specific work experience. Some schools and colleges have internship programs involving periods of work in business firms. These programs enable students to gain a measure of practical experience. Secondary and trade schools provide applicants with a limited but useful educational background. Colleges and universities can supply candidates for positions in management and in various technical and scientific fields. In addition, many colleges are excellent sources of part-time employees.

Public Employment Offices. State employment offices, which are affiliated with the United States Employment Service, offer without cost a supply of applicants who are actively seeking employment. These offices, located in all major cities, are for the most part a source for clerical workers, unskilled laborers, production workers, and technicians.

Private Employment Agencies. Numerous private agencies offer their services as employment offices. In some cases an employer receives their services without cost because the applicant pays a fee to the agency. However, most firms pay the fee if the applicant is highly qualified. Such agencies tend to specialize in people with specific skills such as accountants, computer operators, or managers.

Employee Referrals. If current employees are good employees, their recommendations may provide excellent prospects. Ordinarily, current employees will hesitate to recommend applicants thought to be inferior in ability. Many small-business owners say that this source provides more of their employees than any other source.

Help-Wanted Advertising. The "Help Wanted" sign in the window is one form of recruiting used by small firms. More aggressive recruitment takes the form of advertisements in the classified pages of local newspapers. Although the effectiveness of this source has been questioned by some, the fact remains that many well-managed organizations recruit in this way.

One small firm, North American Tool and Die, Inc., exercises great care in preparing such advertisements, avoiding standard clichés and focusing attention on the company and its achievements.[3] They point out, for example, that their rejects from customers average only 0.1 percent—a very high quality level—and that NATD is a "fun place" to work. Their purpose is to attract people who care about the company they work for and who are looking for such opportunities.

Temporary Help Agencies. The temporary help industry, which is growing rapidly, supplies temporary employees (or "temps") such as word processors, clerks, accountants, engineers, nurses, and sales clerks for short periods of time. By using agencies such as Kelly Services or Manpower, small firms can deal with seasonal fluctuations and absences caused by vacation or illness. It is a less useful source when extensive training is required or continuity is important.

Selection Guidelines

The small-business manager should analyze the activities or work to be performed and determine the number and kinds of jobs to be filled. Knowing the job requirements and the capacities and characteristics of the individual applicants permits a more intelligent selection of persons for specific jobs. In particular, the small business should attempt to obtain individuals whose capacities and skills complement those of the owner-manager.

Certainly the owner-manager should not select personnel simply to fit a rigid specification of education, experience, or personal background. Rather, the employer must concentrate upon the ability of an individual to fill a particular position in the business.

Recruiting Managerial and Professional Personnel

Personnel filling managerial and professional positions are obviously important in any business, especially in one that is small. Their recruitment, therefore, deserves special attention and also involves some special considerations.

Technical competence is necessary in small firms as it is in a large business, but versatility may be even more important. Engineers may occasionally need to make sales calls, and marketing people may need to pinch-hit in production. Versatility and flexibility are needed.

In filling key positions, small firms sometimes turn to executive search firms (**headhunters**) to locate qualified candidates. Plasticolors, Inc., a small Ohio manufacturer of colorants for fiberglass plastics, successfully used an executive recruiter to fill a position of company CEO, replacing the company founder.[4] In an unusual beginning, the recruiter spent about 45 hours interviewing directors and key employees, thereby developing a good relationship with the company and acquaintance with its managerial needs. Headhunters of this type can make a wide-ranging search for individuals who possess the right combination of talents.

headhunter
firm that locates qualified candidates for executive positions

Evaluating Applicants

Many techniques for evaluating applicants are available to the small business. An uninformed, blind gamble on new employees may be avoided by following the series of steps described in the following paragraphs.

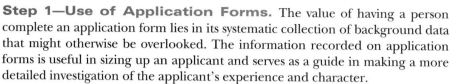

Step 1—Use of Application Forms. The value of having a person complete an application form lies in its systematic collection of background data that might otherwise be overlooked. The information recorded on application forms is useful in sizing up an applicant and serves as a guide in making a more detailed investigation of the applicant's experience and character.

An application form need not be elaborate or lengthy. However, care must be taken to avoid questions that may conflict with laws concerning unfair job discrimination. State and federal legislation, which has been changing frequently, limits the use of many questions formerly found on application blanks. Questions about race, color, national origin, religion, age, marital status, disabilities, or arrests are either prohibited or considered unwise unless the employer can prove their job relatedness.

Step 2—Interviewing the Applicant. An employment interview permits the employer to get some idea of the applicant's appearance, job knowledge, intelligence, and personality. Any of these factors may be significant in the job to be filled. Although the interview is an important step in the process of selection, it should not be the only step. Some individuals have the mistaken idea that they are infallible judges of human nature on the basis of interviews alone.

The value of the interview depends upon the interviewer's skill and methods. Any interviewer can improve the quality of interviewing by following these generally accepted principles:

1. Determine the questions you want to ask before beginning the interview.
2. Conduct the interview in a quiet atmosphere.
3. Give your entire attention to the applicant.
4. Put the applicant at ease.
5. Never argue.
6. Keep the conversation at a level suited to the applicant.
7. Listen attentively.
8. Observe closely the applicant's speech, mannerisms, and attire if these characteristics are important to the job.
9. Try to avoid being unduly influenced by the applicant's trivial mannerisms or superficial resemblance to other people you know.

To avoid the possibility of running into legal problems with the Equal Employment Opportunity Commission (EEOC), the interviewer should refrain from:

1. Direct or indirect inquiries that will reveal the applicant's national, ethnic, or racial origin.
2. Questions to female applicants on marital status, number and age of children, pregnancy, or future child-bearing plans.
3. Inquiries about arrest or conviction records, unless such information is demonstrably job-related.

Step 3—Checking References and Further Investigation.

When contacted, most references listed on application forms give a rose-colored picture of the applicant's character and ability. Nevertheless, careful checking with former employers, school authorities, and other references can be most constructive. A written letter of inquiry to these references is probably the weakest form of checking because people hesitate to put damaging statements in writing. However, individuals who provide little useful information in response to a written request often speak more frankly when approached by telephone or in person.

For a fee, an applicant's history (financial, criminal, employment, and so on) may be supplied by personal investigation agencies or local credit bureaus. If an employer needs an investigative consumer report to establish the applicant's eligibility for employment, the Fair Credit Reporting Act requires that the applicant be notified in writing prior to the request for such a report.

Step 4—Testing the Applicant.

Many kinds of jobs lend themselves to performance testing. For example, an applicant may be given a data-entry test to verify speed and accuracy. With a little ingenuity, employers may improvise practical tests pertinent to many positions.

Psychological examinations may also be used by small-business firms, but the results can easily be misleading because of difficulty in interpretation or in adapting the tests to a particular business. In addition, the United States Supreme Court has approved the EEOC's requirement that *any* test used in making employment decisions must be job-related.

Step 5—Physical Examinations.

Although the law permits drug screening of applicants, regular physical examinations must be delayed until a job offer has been made. Few small firms have staff physicians, but arrangements can be made with a local doctor to administer the examinations. In a few occupations, physical examinations are required by law. Even when they are not legally required, it is wise to discover physical limitations that may affect job performance.

Leasing Employees

Leasing equipment or property has long been an accepted alternative to buying it. **Leasing employees,** as surprising as it may seem, is also an alternative to hiring one's own employees!

An estimated 1,300 leasing companies have emerged in recent years to lease personnel to thousands of small businesses. For a fee of from 1 to 5 percent of payroll, the leasing company writes paychecks, pays the taxes, and files necessary reports with government agencies. Although small firms using this service escape certain paperwork, they do not usually escape the tasks of recruitment and selection. Typically, the employees of a small firm are simply

leasing employees
leasing personnel from an organization that cares for paperwork and benefits administration

An Example of Employee Leasing

David Hinds' Van Tone Company in Dallas, Texas, employed only 24 employees in the production of flavoring extracts. Faced with a drastic increase in workers' compensation and health-insurance costs, Hinds turned to employee leasing.

Once he decided to pursue the leasing option, Hinds settled on Employers Resource Management Co., an employee-leasing company based in Boise, Idaho. The leasing company lowered his health premiums because it has access to

cheaper, pooled rates not available to small employers. And it cut Hinds' workers' compensation costs because the leasing company's pool of workers had a better safety record—and therefore lower rates—than Hinds' own firm.

Even as he cut costs, the leasing arrangement made it possible for Hinds to expand the benefits offered to his workers. The leasing company's health plan added dental and vision care as well as yearly physicals, and it offered a lower deductible and out-of-pocket annual maximum. In addition, Hinds' workers now have access to a credit union through the leasing firm.

Source: Rosalind Resnick, "Leasing Workers," *Nation's Business,* Vol. 80, No. 11 (November 1992), pp. 20–28. Reprinted by permission, *Nation's Business,* November 1992. Copyright 1992, U.S. Chamber of Commerce.

shifted to the leasing company's payroll at some specified date. In most cases, the small firm still determines who works, who gets promoted, and who gets time off.

Many employees like the leasing arrangement. Small employers are often able to provide better benefit packages in this way since leasing companies employ hundreds or thousands of employees and thus qualify for better rates. The small business must bear the cost of the insurance and other benefits obtained through a leasing company, of course, in addition to the service fee mentioned above.

Some caution is necessary in selecting a leasing company. As leasing companies have proliferated in recent years, a number of them have run into financial trouble and left employers liable for unpaid claims. Some states have enacted legislation to protect employer-clients, and more regulation is likely.

Another note of caution pertains to the application of government regulations to small business. Very small employers are often excluded from specific regulations. For example, companies with fewer than 15 employees are exempt from the Americans with Disabilities Act. When these employees officially become part of a large leasing organization, however, the small firm using the leased employees becomes subject to the law.

TRAINING AND DEVELOPMENT

Once an employee has been recruited and added to the payroll, the process of training and development must begin. The new recruit is the "raw material," and the well-trained technician, salesperson, manager, or other employee is the "finished product."

Purposes of Training and Development

One obvious purpose of training is to prepare the new recruit to perform the duties for which he or she has been employed. There are very few positions in industry for which no training is required. It is a rare individual who has an adequate background when applying for employment. If the employer fails to provide training, the new employee must proceed by trial and error, frequently wasting time, materials, and money.

Training to improve skills and knowledge is not limited to newcomers. The performance of current employees can often be improved through additional training. In view of the constant change in products, technology, policies, and procedures in the world of business—even in a small business—training is necessary to update knowledge and skills. Only in this way can personnel become capable of meeting the changing demands placed upon them.

Both employers and employees have a stake in the advancement of personnel to higher-level positions. Preparation for advancement usually involves developmental efforts—possibly of a different type than those needed to sharpen skills for current duties.

In view of the fact that personal development and advancement are prime concerns of able employees, the small business can profit from careful attention to this phase of the personnel program. If the opportunity to grow and move up in an organization exists, it not only improves the morale of current employees, but also offers an inducement for outsiders to accept employment.

Orientation for New Personnel

The developmental process begins with the employee's first two or three days on the job. It is at this point that a new person tends to feel "lost." Much is confusing—a new physical layout, different job title, unknown fellow employees, different type of supervision, changed hours or work schedule, and a unique set of personnel policies and procedures. Any surprises that conflict with the newcomer's expectations are interpreted in the light of his or her previous work experience, and these interpretations can foster a strong commitment to the new employer or lead to feelings of alienation.

At this point of great sensitivity of the new employee, the employer can contribute to a positive outcome by proper orientation. Initial steps can be taken to help the newcomer adjust and to minimize feelings of uneasiness in the new setting.

In addition to explaining specific job duties, supervisors can outline the firm's policies and procedures in as much detail as possible. The new employee should be encouraged to ask questions, and time should be taken to provide careful answers. The employer may facilitate the orientation process by giving the recruit a written list of company procedures. These may include information about work hours, paydays, breaks, lunch hours, absences, holidays, names of supervisors, employee benefits, and so on. Since new employees are faced with "information overload" at first, it is good to schedule a followup orientation after a week or two.

Training Nonmanagerial Employees

Job descriptions or job specifications, if they exist, may identify abilities or skills needed for particular jobs. To a large extent, such requirements regulate the type of training that is appropriate.

Job Instruction Training
system to increase effectiveness of on-the-job training

For all classes of employees, more training is accomplished on the job than through any other method. The weakness of on-the-job training results from depending on haphazard learning in contrast to establishing planned, controlled training programs. A system designed to make on-the-job training more effective is known as **Job Instruction Training.** The steps of this program, listed below, are intended to help the manager who is not a professional educator "get through" to nonmanagerial employees.

Figure 17-2
The Success of On-the-Job Training for This Metal Worker Depends on Careful Planning of Instruction

1. *Prepare employees.* Put employees at ease. Find out what they already know about the job. Get them interested in learning the job. Place them in appropriate jobs.

2. *Present the operations.* Tell, show, illustrate, and question carefully and patiently. Stress key points. Instruct clearly and completely, taking up one point at a time—but no more than the employees can master.

3. *Try out performance.* Test the employees by having them perform the jobs. Have the employees tell, show, and explain key points. Ask questions and correct errors. Continue until the employees know that they know how to do the job.

4. *Follow up.* Check frequently. Designate the persons to whom the employees should go for help. Encourage questions. Get the employees to look for the key points as they progress. Taper off extra coaching and close follow-up.

Developing Managerial and Professional Employees

The small business faces a particularly serious need for developing managerial and professional employees. Depending on the size of the firm, there may be few or many key positions. Regardless of the number, to function most effectively the business must develop individuals in or for these key positions. Incumbents should be developed to the point that they can adequately carry out the responsibilities assigned to them. Ideally, potential replacements should also be available for key individuals who retire or leave for other reasons. The entrepreneur often postpones grooming a personal replacement, but this step is likewise important in assuring a smooth transition in the management of a small firm.

In accomplishing management training, the manager should give serious consideration to the following factors:

1. *Determine the need for training.* What vacancies are expected? Who needs to be trained? What type of training and how much training are needed to meet the demands of the job description?

2. *Develop the plan for training.* How can the individuals be trained? Do they currently have enough responsibility to permit them to learn? Can they be assigned additional duties? Should they be given temporary assignments in other areas—for example, should they be shifted from production to sales? Would additional schooling be of benefit?

3. *Establish a timetable.* When should training be started? How much can be accomplished in the next six months or one year?

4. *Counsel with employees.* Do the individuals understand their need for training? Are they aware of the prospects for them in the firm? Has an understanding been reached as to the nature of training? Have the employees been consulted regularly about progress in their work and problems con-

fronting them? Have they been given the benefit of the owner's experience and insights without having decisions made for them?

COMPENSATION AND INCENTIVES FOR SMALL-BUSINESS EMPLOYEES

Compensation and financial incentives are important to all employees, and the small firm must acknowledge the central role of the paycheck and any "extras" in attracting and motivating personnel. In addition, small firms can also offer several nonfinancial incentives that appeal to both managerial and nonmanagerial employees.

Wage or Salary Levels

In general, small firms find that they must be roughly competitive in wage or salary levels in order to attract well-qualified personnel. Wages or salaries paid to employees either are based on increments of time—such as an hour, a day, a month—or vary directly with their output. Compensation based on increments of time is commonly referred to as **daywork.** The daywork system is most appropriate for types of work in which performance is not easily measurable. It is the most common compensation system and is easy to understand and administer.

daywork
compensation based on increments of time

Financial Incentives

In order to motivate nonmanagerial employees to increase their productivity, incentive systems have been devised. Incentive wages may constitute an employee's entire earnings or may supplement regular daywork wages. The commission plan often used to compensate salespeople is one type of incentive plan. In manufacturing, employees are sometimes paid according to the number of units they produce.

More general bonus or profit-sharing systems are especially important for managerial or other key personnel, although such plans may also include lower-level personnel. These are plans that give personnel a "piece of the action." They may or may not involve giving them shares of stock. A given plan may simply entail a distribution of a specified share of the profits or a share of profits that exceed a target amount. The Spotlight on Small Business at the beginning of this chapter gives an example of such a plan.

Profit sharing provides a more direct work incentive in small companies than in large companies, because the connection between individual performance and company success can be more easily understood. Any such plans should be devised with care, however, usually with the aid of a consultant and/or public accounting firm.

SMALL BUSINESS IN ACTION

A Small-Firm Flexible Benefit Plan

Even very small firms can offer employees a choice of fringe benefits through the use of well-designed flexible benefit plans. An employee suggestion led to such a plan in a small Montana firm.

Susan Herman gave her boss a suggestion he couldn't ignore: Offer employees new health and child-care benefits and, by doing so, save the company money.

"He thought it sounded too good to be true," Herman recalls. But it wasn't.

Since last October, ChromatoChem, Inc., a biotechnology firm in Missoula, Mont., has enabled employees to set aside a portion of their salaries in untaxed reimbursement accounts to pay for certain health-care and day-care ex-

penses. Every dollar that goes into an employee's reimbursement account lowers both the employee's and the company's tax bills. Four of ChromatoChem's six employees are taking part, and everybody is happy, says Herman, the firm's controller.

Source: Roger Thompson, "Switching to Flexible Benefits," *Nation's Business*, Vol. 79, No. 7 (July 1991), p. 16. Reprinted by permission, *Nation's Business*, July 1991. Copyright 1991, U.S. Chamber of Commerce.

Fringe Benefits

Fringe benefits (which include payments for such items as social security, vacations, holidays, health insurance, and workers' compensation) are expensive. In 1991, the cost of fringe benefits was estimated to be just under 40 percent of the cost of direct compensation.[5] If health-care reforms proposed by the Clinton administration are adopted, they will undoubtedly increase these costs still further.

Even though fringes are expensive, a small firm cannot ignore them if it is to compete effectively for good employees. A small but growing number of small firms now use flexible benefits programs (or "cafeteria plans") that allow employees to choose the type of benefits they wish to receive.[6] All employees may receive a core level of coverage, such as basic health insurance, and then be allowed to choose among additional options. For example, employees might decide how some amount specified by the employer is to be divided between child care reimbursement, dental care, pension fund contributions, or additional insurance.

fringe benefits
supplements to monetary compensation of employees

Outside help in administering cafeteria plans is available to small firms that wish to avoid the detailed paperwork associated with them. Many small companies—including some with fewer than 25 employees—turn over flex plan administration to outside consulting, payroll accounting, or insurance companies that provide such services for a monthly fee. In view of the increasing popularity of these plans and the availability of administrative services, it seems only a matter of time until many small firms will also be offering flexible benefits.

Employee Stock Ownership Plans

employee stock ownership plans (ESOPs)
agreements that give employees a share of ownership in the business

Some small firms have created **employee stock ownership plans (ESOPs),** by which they give employees a share of ownership in the business.[7] These may be structured in a variety of ways. For example, a share of annual profits may be designated for the benefit of employees and used to buy company stock, which is then placed in a trust for the employees.

ESOPs also provide a way for owners to "cash out" and withdraw from a business without selling the firm to outsiders. The owner might sell equity to the firm's employees, who can borrow funds at attractive rates for this purpose. In fact, there are many tax advantages to both owners and employees that make ESOPs an increasingly popular ownership plan.

SPECIAL ISSUES IN HUMAN RESOURCE MANAGEMENT

Thus far in the chapter, we have dealt with recruitment, selection, training, and compensation of employees. In addition to managing these primary activities, the entrepreneur, as human resource manager, must deal with a number of other general issues. These issues—legal constraints, union relationships, formalizing personnel management, and using a human resource manager—are the focus of this concluding section.

The Law and Management of Human Resources

Employer-employee relationships, even in small firms, are affected by a variety of both federal and state laws. Although some laws limit their application to employers having a minimum of 15 to 20 employees, others are more broadly applicable. The legislation, therefore, applies to most small-business concerns. Because of its complexity, it is important to have competent legal counsel in dealing with specific issues. Some of the more significant types of regulation are identified here.

Equal Employment Opportunity Legislation. The **Civil Rights Act of 1964** and related amendments and executive orders prohibit discrimination on the basis of race, color, religion, sex, or national origin. This legislation and many state laws apply to all employment practices, including hiring, firing, promotion, compensation, and other conditions of employment. A separate act (**Age Discrimination in Employment Act of 1967** and amendments) requires employers to treat applicants and employees equally, regardless of age. Sexual harassment in the workplace has also become a highly sensitive issue in recent years, requiring employers to maintain a proper work environment.

Civil Rights Act of 1964
legislation prohibiting discrimination based on race, color, religion, sex, or national origin

Age Discrimination in Employment Act of 1967
legislation prohibiting discrimination based on age

Protection of People with Disabilities. The **Americans with Disabilities Act,** enacted in 1990, specifies that employers with more than 15 employees cannot refuse to hire a qualified disabled applicant if the individual can perform with "reasonable accommodations." Such accommodations might include making the workplace accessible, changing schedules, and, in some cases, providing helpers. This Act is discussed more fully in Chapter 26.

Americans with Disabilities Act
legislation guaranteeing equal access to employment for disabled people

Wage and Hour Laws. Federal legislation requires most employers to pay a specified minimum hourly wage and, usually, time-and-a-half for hours exceeding 40 per week. Employers must also comply with child labor regulations. Pay differentials between employees cannot be based on gender.

Safety Regulations. According to the **Occupational Safety and Health Act (OSHA),** employers must provide a workplace that is free from hazards that are likely to cause death or serious physical harm. Employers must also comply with various safety and health standards promulgated in accordance with the Act. Small-firm owners and managers have been charged in some states with criminal liability for allowing workplace hazards that resulted in the death of employees.[8]

Occupational Safety and Health Act (OSHA)
legislation requiring a workplace that protects the health and safety of employees

Workers' Compensation Laws. All states have enacted laws requiring employers to pay medical costs and wage losses arising from workplace accidents or illnesses. Such laws provide for this type of compensation through a system of private and public insurance. The increasing cost of medical care and broadening of the types of compensable injuries have made this a major cost burden for many small employers.

Workers' Compensation Laws
state laws guaranteeing compensation for work-related illness and injuries

Plant-Closing Law. The federal plant-closing law, enacted in 1988, requires employers to give employees 60 days' advance notice of plant closings or mass layoffs. The effect on small firms is minimal, because the law applies only to employers with 100 or more employees and to reductions affecting 50 or more full-time jobs.

Employee Unions Legislation. The **National Labor Relations Act** requires employers to avoid discrimination based on union affiliation and to bargain with a union if desired by a majority of employees in the bargaining unit.

National Labor Relations Act
legislation prohibiting discrimination based on union affiliation

Immigration Reform Act
legislation requiring that employees are either U.S. citizens or aliens authorized to work in the U.S.

Family and Medical Leave Act of 1993
legislation requiring unpaid leave for maternity or other specified emergency leaves

Immigration Reform. The **Immigration Reform Act**, which became effective in 1987, requires employers to check job applicants' papers to be sure they are either U.S. citizens or aliens authorized to work in the United States.

Family-Leave Law. The **Family and Medical Leave Act of 1993** requires businesses with 50 or more employees to provide up to 12 weeks of unpaid leave per year upon the birth of an employee's child or for other specified emergency needs, such as the serious illness of a parent or child.[9]

Wrongful Discharge Litigation. At one time, employment was assumed to involve an "at-will" contract, and the employer's right to fire was virtually unchallenged. Courts are increasingly coming to hold, however, that such contracts contain implied promises to deal fairly and in good faith. This means that employers must act carefully and avoid unfairness in discharge actions if they are to avoid lawsuits. By establishing a standard disciplinary procedure that contains protection against capricious firings or firings based on prohibited bases (such as age or race), an employer can help to assure fairness and avoid legal conflict.

Labor Unions and Small Business

Most entrepreneurs prefer to operate independently and to avoid unionization. Indeed, most small businesses are not unionized. To some extent, this results from the predominance of small business in such areas as services, where unionization is less common than in manufacturing. Also, unions typically concentrate their primary attention on large companies.

This does not mean that labor unions are unknown in small firms. Many types of firms—building and electrical contractors, for example—negotiate labor contracts and employ unionized personnel. The need to work with a union formalizes and, to some extent, complicates the relationship between the small firm and its employees.

If employees wish to bargain collectively, the law requires the employer to participate in such bargaining. The demand for labor union representation may arise from labor dissatisfaction with the work environment and employment relationships. By following enlightened human resource policies, the small firm can minimize the likelihood of labor organization and/or contribute to healthy management–union relationships.

Formalizing Employer–Employee Relationships

As explained earlier in the chapter, the management system of small firms is typically less formal than that of larger companies. A degree of informality can, in fact, constitute a virtue in small organizations. As personnel are added, however, the benefits of informality decline, and its costs increase. The situation has been portrayed in terms of family relationships as follows: "House rules are hardly necessary where only two people are living. But add several children, and before long Mom starts sounding like a government regulatory agency.[10] Large numbers of employees cannot be managed effectively without some system for regulating personnel relationships.

Growth, then, produces pressures toward formalizing personnel policies and procedures. The primary question is how much formality and how soon—a question that involves judgment. Probably some matters should be formalized from the very beginning. On the other hand, excessive regulation becomes paralyzing.

One way to increase the formality is to prepare a personnel policy manual or employee handbook. Although such an act may seem a bit dictatorial, it can meet a communication need by letting employees know the basic ground rules of the firm. It can also provide a basis for fairness and consistency in decisions affecting employees.

The content of a policy manual may be as broad or narrow as desired. It may include an expression of company philosophy—what the company considers important, such as standards of excellence or quality considerations. More specifically, personnel policies usually cover such topics as recruitment, selection, training, compensation, vacations, grievances, and discipline. Policies should be written carefully, however, to avoid misunderstandings. In some states, an employee handbook is considered part of the employment contract.

Procedures relating to management of personnel may also be standardized. For example, a performance review system may be established and a timetable set up for reviews, such as an initial review after six months and subsequent reviews on an annual basis.

Use of a Human Resource Manager

A firm with only a few employees cannot afford a full-time specialist to deal with personnel problems. Some of the more involved human resource tools and techniques that are required in large businesses may be unnecessarily complicated for the small business. As it grows in size, however, its personnel problems will increase in both number and complexity.

The point at which it becomes logical to hire a human resource manager cannot be specified precisely. Each entrepreneur must decide whether the type and size of the business would make it profitable to employ a personnel specialist. Hiring a part-time human resource manager might be a logical first step in some instances.

Some conditions that encourage the appointment of a human resource manager in a small business are:

1. When there is a substantial number of employees. (What is "substantial" varies with the business, but 100 employees is suggested as a guide.)
2. When employees are represented by a union.
3. When the labor turnover rate is high.

4. When the need for skilled or professional personnel creates problems in recruitment or selection.
5. When supervisors or operative employees require considerable training.
6. When employee morale is unsatisfactory.
7. When competition for personnel is keen.

Until the time when a human resource manager is employed, however, the owner-manager typically functions in that capacity. His or her decisions regarding selection, compensation, and other personnel issues will have a direct impact on the operating success of the firm.

1. To obtain capable employees, the small firm must take the initiative in seeking applicants. Sources include walk-ins, schools, public and private employment agencies, employee referrals, advertising, and temporary-help agencies. The selection process must conform to legislation applying to the hiring of minorities and other special employment groups. Leasing employees is an alternative to hiring that is used by some firms.
2. Steps in the evaluation of applicants include the use of an application form, applicant interviewing, checking references and background investigation, testing, and physical examinations.
3. Both managerial and nonmanagerial employees of small firms require training to develop skill and knowledge in their jobs and to prepare them for promotion. The need for developing personnel at the managerial and professional levels is particularly acute.
4. Small firms must be competitive in wage and salary levels and fringe benefits. They can use various types of incentive, profit-sharing, and stock-ownership systems to provide motivation for personnel, especially for those in key positions.
5. Special legislation such as that pertaining to wages, hours, safety, and discrimination regulate the management of human resources. As a firm grows, the need for formal methods of human resource management increases. This includes adoption of personnel policies, establishment of personnel procedures, and, at some point, employment of a human resource manager.

DISCUSSION QUESTIONS

1. As a customer of small-business firms, you can appreciate the importance of employees to their success. On the basis of your experience, cite one case in which the employee's contribution was positive and one in which it was negative.
2. What factor or factors would make you personally most cautious about going to work for a small business? Could these reasons for hesitation be overcome by a really good small firm? How?
3. Suppose you were trying to recruit a well-qualified graduate of your school to

work in a firm of fewer than 100 employees. What arguments would you use to persuade the student to join your firm? (You may state your assumptions as you develop these arguments.)

4. Under what conditions might walk-ins be most useful as a source of employees?

5. Assuming you have worked for a small firm for five years, what would be your attitude toward recommending an acquaintance for employment? What are the implications of your attitude for employee referrals as a source of employees?

6. How might the manager of a small business be aggressive in recruiting new employees? Explain.

7. Based on your own experience as an interviewee, what do you think is the most serious weakness in interviewing? How could this be remedied?

8. How does employee leasing differ from use of a temporary-help agency? What are the greatest values to be realized by employee leasing?

9. What steps and/or topics would you recommend for the orientation program of a printing firm with 65 employees?

10. Consider the small business with which you are best acquainted. Have adequate provisions been made to replace key management personnel? Is the firm using any form of executive development?

11. What problems are involved in using incentive wage systems in a small firm? How would the nature of the work affect management's decision concerning use or nonuse of wage incentives?

12. Is the use of a profit-sharing system desirable in a small business? What major difficulties might be associated with its effectiveness in providing greater employee motivation?

13. Which type of legislation cited in the chapter seems potentially most troublesome for small firms? Why?

14. It has been said that labor unions have been more successful in organizing small manufacturing firms than in organizing small merchandising firms. Why might this be true?

15. List the factors in small-business operation that encourage the appointment of a human resource manager. Should a human resource manager always be hired on a full-time basis? Why or why not?

YOU MAKE THE CALL

Situation 1

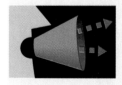

Following is an account of an employee's introduction to a new job:

It was my first job out of high school. They gave me a physical exam and a pamphlet on benefits, and they told me how dangerous a steel mill could be. But it was from the old-timers on the floor that I learned what was really expected of me.

The company management never told me about the corporate culture or the unspoken rules. The old-timers let me know where to sleep on what shift and which foreman to avoid. They told me how much work I was supposed to do and which shop steward I was to speak with if I had a problem.

Source: Gene Geromel, "A Good Start for New Hires," *Nation's Business,* Vol. 77, No. 1 (January 1989), p. 21. Copyright 1989, U.S. Chamber of Commerce.

Questions
1. To what extent should a small firm use old-timers to help introduce new employees to the workplace? Is it inevitable that newcomers will always look to old-timers to find out how things really work?
2. How would you rate this firm's orientation efforts? What are its strengths and weaknesses?
3. Assuming that this firm has fewer than 75 employees and no human resource manager, can it possibly provide any more extensive orientation than that described here? How? What low-cost improvements, if any, can you recommend?

Situation 2

Technical Products, Inc., distributes 15 percent of its profits quarterly to its eight employees. This money is invested for their benefit in a retirement plan and is fully vested after five years. An employee, therefore, has a claim to the retirement fund even if he or she leaves the company after five years service.

The employees range in age from 25 to 59 and have worked for the company from 3 to 27 years. They seem to have recognized the value of the program. However, younger members sometimes express a stronger preference for cash than for retirement benefits.

Questions
1. What are the most important reasons for structuring the profit-sharing plan as a retirement program?
2. What is the probable motivational impact of this compensation system?
3. How will age affect the appeal of this plan? What other factors are likely to strengthen or lessen its motivational value? Should it be changed in any way?

EXPERIENTIAL EXERCISES

1. Interview the director of the placement office for your college or university to discover the extent to which small firms use its services and to obtain the director's recommendations for improving college recruiting by small firms. Prepare a one-page summary of your findings.
2. Examine and evaluate the "help wanted" classified section of a local newspaper. Summarize your findings and formulate some generalizations about small-business advertising for personnel.
3. Join with another student to form an interviewer-interviewee team. Take turns interviewing each other as job applicants for a selected type of job vacancy. Critique each performance by using the interviewing principles outlined in this chapter.
4. Join with another student, taking turns role-playing job instruction training as outlined in this chapter. Each student-trainer should select a simple task and teach it to the other student-trainee. Jointly critique the teaching performance after each episode.

REFERENCES TO SMALL-BUSINESS PRACTICES

Bahls, Jane Easter. "Employees for Rent," *Nation's Business,* Vol. 79, No. 6 (June 1991), pp. 36–38.

> A small manufacturer simplified and improved its management of personnel by using an employee-leasing company.

Case, John. "Collective Effort," *Inc.,* Vol. 14, No. 1 (January 1992), pp. 32–43.

> This article describes the way in which an ESOP (employee stock ownership plan) was used to buy out the original owners and enable a highly successful firm to continue its growth.

Case, John. "The Best Small Companies to Work for in America," *Inc.,* Vol. 14, No. 11 (November 1992), pp. 89–113.

> The attractive employee-relations practices and environments provided by a number of small companies are described.

Machan, Dyan. "The Mommy and Daddy Track," *Forbes,* Vol. 145, No. 8 (April 16, 1990), pp. 162–164.

> The efforts of several small firms to provide day care for children of employees are described.

Szabo, Joan C. "Learning and Working—Together," *Nation's Business,* Vol. 80, No. 5 (June 1992), pp. 34–35.

> A group of small firms in Williamsport, Pennsylvania, join together to develop metalworkers through an apprenticeship training program.

ENDNOTES

1. Ellyn E. Spragins, "Hiring Without the Guesswork," *Inc.,* Vol. 14, No. 2 (February 1992), p. 81.

2. John Case, "The Best Small Companies to Work for in America," *Inc.,* Vol. 14, No. 11 (November 1992), p. 93. Reprinted with permission, *Inc.* magazine (November 1992). Copyright 1992 by Goldhirsh Group, Inc., 38 Commercial Wharf, Boston, MA 02110.

3. Thomas Melohn, "Screening for the Best Employees," *Inc.,* Vol. 9, No. 1 (January 1987), pp. 104–106.

4. Barbara Rudolph, "Make Me a Match," *Inc.,* Vol. 13, No. 4 (April 1991), pp. 116–117.

5. Roger Thompson, "Benefit Costs Surge Again," *Nation's Business,* Vol. 81, No. 2 (February 1993), pp. 38–39.

6. Roger Thompson, "Switching to Flexible Benefits," *Nation's Business,* Vol. 79, No. 7 (July 1991), pp. 16–23.

7. Joan C. Szabo, "Using ESOPs to Sell Your Firm," *Nation's Business,* Vol. 79, No. 1 (January 1991), pp. 59–60.

8. Joseph P. Kahn, "When Bad Management Becomes Criminal," *Inc.,* Vol. 9, No. 3 (March 1987), pp. 46–50.

9. Some firms are reportedly limiting expansion or using temporary workers to keep their payroll under 50 in order to escape the cost of compliance. See "Small Firms Try to Curb Impact of Leave Law," *The Wall Street Journal* (August 5, 1993), pp. B1 and B3.

10. "Do You Need an Employee Policy Manual?" *In Business,* Vol. 10, No. 4 (July–August 1988), p. 48.

Quality Management and the Operations Process

Larry Denny

SPOTLIGHT ON SMALL BUSINESS

Small firms can successfully implement quality-management programs and reap benefits in the marketplace. This fact was demonstrated by Larry Denny's stress on quality in Den-Con, his Oklahoma City firm that makes oil-drilling equipment. Denny drew up a quality-management program in 1983 when the company had only three or four employees. The firm's attention to quality permitted it to survive and even thrive despite the drop in world oil prices and the resulting drop in drilling.

Den-Con continued to focus on quality as the firm grew to 13 employees, and Denny used the firm's quality-management program to get a toehold in the market where he was competing against a well-established big business.

When he entered the international marketplace, he recalls, he was trying to sell to multinational drilling contractors, in competition with a much larger company. Better delivery and lower prices alone wouldn't be enough; he had to find some way to make Den-Con credible despite its size. Den-Con's quality program "allowed us to go out to the industry and show people, when they questioned our credibility, that we knew what we were doing," he says.

Source: Michael Barrier, "Doing Well What Comes Naturally," *Nation's Business*, Vol. 80, No. 9, pp. 25–26. Reprinted by permission, *Nation's Business*, September 1992. Copyright 1992, U.S. Chamber of Commerce.

After studying this chapter, you should be able to:

1. Explain how operations are carried out in both manufacturing and service businesses, and point out differences in manufacturing and service operations management.
2. Summarize the ways in which quality is created and controlled in both manufacturing and service operations.
3. Describe the role of maintenance and the differences between corrective and preventive maintenance.
4. Explain how work improvement helps increase productivity and profits, and identify methods of work study and measurement.

LOOKING AHEAD

NEW TERMS AND CONCEPTS

operations process (production process)
quality
operations management
job shops
repetitive manufacturing
batch manufacturing
total quality management (TQM)

quality circle
inspection
inspection standard
statistical quality control
attributes sampling plan
variables sampling plan
corrective maintenance
preventive maintenance
methods improvement

productivity
laws of motion economy
motion study
time study
micromotion study
work sampling
statistical inference

Product quality and service quality are keys to success and survival in today's competitive world. Customers expect quality, and a business can offer its customers only the quality that is created by its operations process. A small firm's long-term survival depends, therefore, upon an operations process that enables it to satisfy the quality demands of customers in a cost-effective manner.

This chapter examines the operations process with a special emphasis on the achievement of quality. Sometimes called *production,* the operations process includes the functions needed to transform a firm's inputs into outputs.

THE OPERATIONS PROCESS AND QUALITY

The **operations process** or **production process** consists of those activities necessary for "getting the job done," that is, for performing the work the firm was created to perform. To a great extent, a firm's profitability as well as its customer acceptance reflects the way it manages its basic operations.

operations process (production process)
the activities that accomplish a firm's work

The Quality Goal in Operations Management

Although the word **quality** is used in many ways, it is defined by the American Society for Quality Control as "the totality of features and characteristics of a product or service that bear on its ability to satisfy stated or implied needs."

quality
features of a product or service that enable it to satisfy needs

Quality has many different aspects. The way that restaurant customers perceive quality, for example, depends on the taste of the food, attractiveness of the decor, friendliness of the server, cleanliness of silverware, promptness of service, type of background music, and numerous other factors. The operations process establishes the level of quality as a product is produced or a service is provided. Although cost and other considerations cannot be ignored, quality must constitute a primary focus of a firm's operations.

International competition has increasingly turned on quality differences. Domestic automobile manufacturers, for example, in recent years have placed great emphasis on quality in their attempts to compete effectively with foreign-made cars. However, quality is not solely a concern of big business. The operations process of small firms deserves the same type of scrutiny that large corporations are beginning to give to the achievement of high quality. Many small firms have been slow to give adequate attention to this factor. An editorial in a leading business periodical holds that "many smaller companies have yet to achieve even a rudimentary understanding of how to achieve higher quality."[1] In examining the operations process, therefore, special attention must be directed to the achievement of superior quality.

Nature of the Operations Process

An operations process is required whether a firm produces a tangible product such as clothing or bread or an intangible service such as dry cleaning or entertainment. It includes the production process in clothing manufacturing, the baking process in a bakery, the cleaning process in dry cleaning, and the performance process in entertainment. Production systems differ for products and services, and they also differ from one type of product or service to another.

Despite their differences, operations processes are alike in that they all change inputs into outputs. These outputs are the products and/or services that a business provides to its customers. Thus, the operations process may be described as a conversion or transformation process. As Figure 18-1 shows, the operations process converts inputs of various kinds into products such as baked goods and services such as window cleaning.

Inputs include money, raw materials, labor, equipment, information, and energy—all of which are combined in varying proportions depending on the nature of the finished product or service. Printing plants and toy manufacturers, for example, use inputs such as paper, ink, wood products, the work of employees, printing presses, lathes, product designs, and electric power to produce printed material and toys. Car-wash facilities and motor freight firms, which are service businesses, also use operating systems to transform inputs into car-cleaning and freight-transporting services.

operations management
planning and control of the production process

Operations management involves the planning and control of the conversion process. It includes the acquisition of inputs and overseeing their trans-

Figure 18-1
The Operations
Process

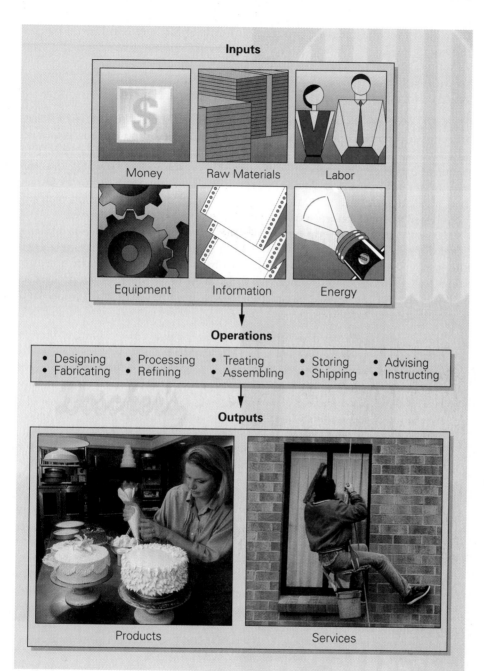

formation into the tangible products and intangible services desired by customers.

Manufacturing and Service Operations

Manufacturing results in a tangible physical product such as furniture or boats. In contrast, a service operation produces an intangible output such as grass cutting by a lawn-care company or advice by a management consulting firm. The distinction between the two types of operations is somewhat fuzzy, because the two areas tend to overlap. A manufacturer of a tangible product, for example, may also extend credit and provide repair service. And a restaurant, typically considered a service business, processes the food products that it serves.

Nevertheless, the operations of product-producing and service-producing firms differ in a number of ways. One of the most obvious differences relates to the greater customer contact typically involved in a service firm. In a beauty shop, for example, the customer is a participant in the operations process as well as a user of the service. James B. Dilworth has identified and summarized these differences as follows:

1. *Productivity generally is more easily measured in manufacturing operations than in service operations because the former provides tangible products, whereas the products of service operations are generally intangible. A factory that produces automobile tires can readily count the number of tires produced in a day. Repair service operations may repair or replace portions of a tangible product, but their major service is the application of knowledge and skilled labor. Advisory services may provide only spoken words, an entirely intangible product and one very difficult to measure.*
2. *Quality standards are more difficult to establish and product quality is more difficult to evaluate in service operations. This difference is directly related to the previous one. Intangible products are more difficult to evaluate because they cannot be held, weighed, or measured. We can evaluate a repair to a tangible product by comparing the product's performance after the repair with its performance before the repair. It is more difficult to know the worth of such a service or legal defense. No one knows for certain how the judge would have ruled had the attorney performed in some different manner.*
3. *Persons who provide services generally have contact with customers, whereas persons who perform manufacturing operations seldom see the consumer of the product. The marketing and customer relations aspects of a service often overlap the operations function. The doctor-patient relationship, for example, is often considered to be a very important component of the physician's services. In the service of hair care, the hairdresser-patron contact is necessary. The impact of discourteous salespersons or restaurant employees is of great concern in many establishments.*
4. *Manufacturing operations can accumulate or decrease inventory of finished products, particularly in standard product, repetitive production operations. A barber, in contrast, cannot store up haircuts during slack times so that he or she can provide service at an extremely high rate during peak demand time. Providers of services often try to overcome this limitation by leveling out the demand process. Telephone systems,*

for example, offer discount rates during certain hours to encourage a shift in the tim-ing of calls that can be delayed.[2]

Types of Manufacturing Operations

Manufacturing operations differ in the degree to which they are repetitive. Some factories produce the same product day after day and week after week. Other production facilities have great flexibility and often change the products they produce.

Job Shops.
Job shops involve short production runs with only one or a few products being produced before shifting to a different production setup. Job shops use general-purpose machines. Machine shops exemplify this type of operation. Each job may be unique, requiring a special set of production steps to complete the finished item.

job shops
manufacturing operations where many small, unique, short-run jobs are performed

Repetitive Manufacturing.
Firms that produce a standardized product or a relatively few standardized products use **repetitive manufacturing** that involves long production runs. This is thought of as mass production. It is associated with the assembly-line production of automobiles and other high-volume products. Highly specialized equipment can be employed, because it is used over and over again in manufacturing the same item. A few small-business firms engage in repetitive manufacturing. For example, a soft-drink bottling plant falls into this category.

repetitive manufacturing
production of a large quantity of a standardized product during long production runs

Batch Manufacturing.
An intermediate type of production is called **batch manufacturing.** This involves more variety (and less volume) than repetitive manufacturing but less variety (and more volume) than job shops. A production run may produce a hundred standardized units, for example, and then be changed to accommodate a production run for another type of standardized product. The different products may all belong to the same "family" and use a similar production process.

batch manufacturing
production that falls between the volume and variety ranges of job shops and repetitive manufacturing

Scheduling and Controlling Manufacturing

Production control procedures have been developed most extensively in manufacturing. They consist of steps designed to achieve the orderly sequential flow of products through the plant at a rate commensurate with scheduled deliveries to customers. To attain this objective, it is essential to avoid work stoppages, to eliminate production bottlenecks when they occur, and to utilize machines and personnel efficiently.

Simple, informal control procedures are frequently used in small plants. If a procedure is simple and the output small, the manager can keep things mov-

Figure 18-2
Management of
Operations
Requires
Acquisition and
Scheduling of
Materials Such as
High-Quality Copper
Wire

ing smoothly with a minimum of paperwork. Personal observation might even suffice. However, there comes a time in the growth of any manufacturing organization when formal procedures must be established to attain production efficiency.

Planning and Routing. Planning involves the determination of the basic manufacturing data needed. Among the most important data needed are:

1. Kinds of raw materials and fabricated parts required.
2. Number of fabricated parts and amounts of material of each kind required per unit of finished product.
3. Best sequence of processing operations for making each product.
4. Number of machines and operators needed on each processing operation.
5. Number and kinds of tooling items needed to set up each machine.
6. Standard output rate of each machine.
7. Number of units of finished product that the plant can produce daily or yearly.

Once the manufacturing data are determined, two forms can be prepared: (1) a bill of materials listing the raw materials, consumption standards, and other related information, and (2) a route list showing the sequence of processing operations and who will perform them.

In job shops, machines are shut down frequently and retooled to produce a different product. Therefore, the basic manufacturing data are needed well in advance of the start of production. This allows management sufficient time to make any necessary changes in plant layout, to buy new tooling items required, and to train workers.

In repetitive manufacturing, most or all of the machines run without stopping for long periods of time. Advance planning is even more essential, for once the machinery is set up and operations have begun, changes are both difficult and costly.

Scheduling and Dispatching. After a given process is planned and set up, timetables for each department and work center are established to control the flow of work. In repetitive manufacturing, which involves large-scale production and which is found in very few small factories, flow control is fairly simple and involves little paperwork. This is the case because repetitive operations assure a steady flow of finished products off the final assembly line. The dispatcher must keep all lines (subassembly and final assembly) operating all the time. If delays occur, rescheduling or other adjustment is required.

In job shops and batch manufacturing, which involve small- to medium-volume production where lots are produced one at a time, there are different flow-control techniques. Where a lot is in process for several days, or is slow-moving, it is possible to use visual control boards to reflect both work assignments and the progress of work toward completion. For fast-moving processes where a lot clears each machine quickly, the block control technique clears the oldest blocks first on each processing operation.

Supervising and Performance Follow-Up. Keeping the work moving on schedule is the major responsibility of the shop supervisor. Performance reports and necessary follow-up routines are established. After an order is completed, the schedules are terminated, and the work records are filed for future use.

Scheduling and Controlling Service Operations

Since service firms are tied closely to their customers, they are limited in their ability to produce services and hold them in inventory for customers. An automobile repair shop must wait until the auto arrives, and a beauty shop cannot function until a customer is available. A retail store can perform some of its services, such as transportation and storage, but it must wait until the customer arrives to perform other services.

A number of scheduling strategies are available to service firms. Appointment systems are used by many automobile repair shops and beauty shops, for example. Other service firms, such as dry cleaners and plumbers, take requests for service and delay delivery until the work can be scheduled. Still other firms, such as movie theaters, maintain a fixed schedule of services and tolerate some idle capacity. Some businesses attempt to spread out demand by offering incentives for using services at off-peak hours—an "early-bird" special at a restaurant, for example.

TOTAL QUALITY MANAGEMENT

Terms such as "total quality management" and "zero defects" indicate the emphasis given to quality by many modern managers. They understand that quality is more than a peripheral issue and that the quest for quality demands attention in all aspects of operations management.

Quality-Focused Management

total quality management (TQM)
an all-encompassing, quality-focused management approach

Total quality management (TQM) refers to an all-encompassing, quality-focused approach to managing a firm's operations. A small business that adopts a total quality management philosophy commits itself to the pursuit of excellence in all aspects of its activities. Such a dedication to quality is sometimes described as a cultural phenomenon—an adoption of basic values related to quality. Time and training are required, therefore, in building a TQM program that elicits the best efforts of everyone in the organization in producing a superior-quality product or service.

Total quality management involves a goal higher than merely meeting existing standards. Its objective is continuous quality improvement. If a process improves to the point that there is only one defect in 100 products, the process must then be shifted to the next level, with a goal of no more than one defect in 200 or 500 products. The ultimate goal is zero defects—a goal that has been popularized by many quality-improvement programs.

The general manager of any small firm must become personally involved in its quest for quality if that effort is to be meaningful.

Leadership is the key to excellence. The aim of management must be to help people to perform and improve their job. Leaders focus on improving the process, inform their management of potential problems, and act to correct problems. Leadership eliminates the need for production quotas which, by their very nature, focus attention away from quality. Leadership also means that fundamental changes in culture and actions occur first at the top of the organization.[3]

Building Quality into the Product

One company advertises, "The quality goes in before the name goes on." This slogan implies that quality does not originate with the inspection process that checks the finished product, but with the earlier production process. Quality of a product begins, in fact, with its design and the design of the manufacturing process.

S M A L L   B U S I N E S S   I N   A C T I O N

Maintaining Quality Through Careful Management

Quality cannot be "inspected" into a product. It must be built in, and this requires careful work. Careful work, in turn, depends on proper training and supervision of the operations process. Increasing production volume brings with it a threat to high quality standards. Chalif Mustard, a small Pennsylvania business operated by Nick and Liz Thomas, faced such a threat as mustard sales grew rapidly. The superior quality of their product was the key to their success, and they could tolerate no compromise with quality. Therefore, the owners trained employees thoroughly and kept a tight rein on production methods as they expanded output.

To ease that process, the Thomases developed a step-by-step checklist so that ingredients are added in the right order and in the right quantity. "In addition, we always have at least two people making the products so there is someone checking while the other is adding and mixing," [Liz Thomas] says. Nothing is ever done by eye or taste. "Every ingredient is measured to the hundredth of a pound by using a very sensitive scale," adds Thomas.

Through painstaking management, Nick and Liz Thomas succeeded in preserving the high quality of their product even in this stressful situation.

Source: Nora Goldstein, "Quest for Quality," *In Business*, Vol. 8, No. 4 (July–August 1986), pp. 50–51.

Another factor that contributes to product quality is the quality of the raw materials used. Generally the finished product is better if a superior grade of raw material is used. A building contractor who uses lumber of inferior grade produces a low-quality house.

In many types of businesses, an even more critical variable is found in the performance of employees. Employees who are careful in their work produce products of a better quality than those produced by careless employees. You have probably heard the admonition, "Never buy a car that was produced on Friday or Monday!" The central role of personnel in producing a high-quality product suggests the importance of human resources management—properly selecting, training, and motivating production personnel.

Quality Circles

Quality circles, a Japanese innovation, are used in small business as well as big business. A **quality circle** consists of a group of employees, usually a dozen or fewer. They meet periodically, typically about once a week, to identify, analyze, and solve work-related problems, particularly those involving product or service quality.

quality circle
group of employees who meet to discuss quality problems

The contribution of quality circles to quality improvement has been demonstrated by the performance of Globe Metallurgical, Inc., a small business located in Beverly, Ohio. This firm was one of three U.S. companies selected to receive the Malcolm Baldrige National Quality Award in 1988. Globe's use of employee participation in achieving this distinction is explained as follows:

Communication is a key. Every level of the company has a quality committee. Workers hash out issues in their own weekly "quality circles." Finally, in each of the company's two plants, still another committee, made up of the plant manager and department heads, assembles each morning to review the previous day's performance.[4]

For quality circles to function effectively, participating employees must be given appropriate training. Quality circles can help tap the often unused potential for enthusiastic contributions by employees.

Employers must be careful to structure quality circles properly and to place the emphasis on quality or other aspects of productivity improvement. Employee-participation programs dealing with compensation, working conditions, or labor relations could run afoul of the National Labor Relations Act. This act prohibits employer domination or support of an employee labor organization.[5]

Inspection: The Traditional Technique

inspection
scrutinizing a product to determine whether it meets quality standards

Inspection consists of scrutinizing a part or a product to determine whether it is good or bad. An inspector typically uses gauges to evaluate the important quality variables. For effective quality control, the inspector must be honest, objective, and capable of resisting pressure from shop personnel to pass borderline cases.

inspection standard
specification of desired quality level and allowable tolerances

Inspection Standards. In manufacturing, **inspection standards** consist of design tolerances that are set for every important quality variable. These tolerances show the limits of variation allowable above and below the desired dimension of the given quality variable. Tolerances must satisfy the requirements that customers will look for in finished products.

Points of Inspection. Traditionally, inspection occurs in the receiving room to check the condition and quantity of materials received from suppliers. Inspection is also customary at critical processing points—for example, *before* any operation that would conceal existing defects, or *after* any operation that produces an excessive amount of defective products or components. Of course, the final inspection of finished products is of utmost importance.

Reduction of Inspection Costs. To reduce costs, the manufacturer must be alert to possibilities for mechanization or automation of inspection. Automated inspection requires only first-piece inspection and periodic rechecks. So long as the setups remain satisfactory, the production run continues without other inspection.

SMALL BUSINESS IN ACTION

Keys to Quality Improvement

Marlow Industries, a Dallas, Texas, producer of customized thermoelectric coolers, was the small-company winner of the coveted Malcolm Baldrige National Quality Award in 1991. Raymond Marlow, the firm's president and CEO, has emphasized the importance of people in a small-business quality program.

According to Marlow, a small business can achieve quality improvement through what he calls the three P's: persistence, patience, and pizza. He explained that implementing quality is a long-term process and that any company needs the persistence to stick with it and lead the way. For the same reason, patience is critical. "It has to evolve," said Marlow. "It's a culture change and it takes time to do it." Pizza is the reward for employees. Marlow stressed the importance of paying attention to employees, be it through pizza parties or other reward systems.

Marlow throws a lot of pizza parties for his employees, but that is only one of the 25 ways that the company rewards individuals and employee teams.

Source: "Small Wonders," *Quality Progress,* Vol. 25, No. 11 (November 1992), pp. 31–32.

One Hundred Percent Inspection. When each item in every lot processed is inspected, this is called 100 percent inspection. Supposedly it assures the elimination of all bad materials in process and all defective products prior to shipment to customers. Such goals are seldom reached, however. This method of inspection is not only time-consuming, but also costly. Furthermore, inspectors often make honest errors in judgment. A reinspection of lots that have been 100 percent inspected, for example, will show that inspectors err by rejecting good items and accepting bad items. Also, some types of inspection—for example, opening a can of vegetables—destroy the product, making 100 percent inspection impractical.

Statistical Quality Control

To avoid the cost and time of 100 percent inspection, small firms can use statistical methods to devise sampling procedures for quality control. **Statistical quality control** enables the firm to inspect a small number of items in a group and make an inductive decision about the quality level of the entire group.

statistical quality control using statistical methods to make decisions regarding quality

Attributes Sampling Plans. Some products are judged to be either acceptable or unacceptable, good or bad. For example, a light bulb either lights up or it doesn't. Likewise, a product may be scratched or not scratched,

**attributes
sampling plan**
system that checks
sample items on a
pass/fail basis to de-
termine the accept-
ability of an entire
lot

dented or not dented. In these cases, control of quality involves a measurement of attributes. An **attributes sampling plan** is a plan that samples a production lot to determine whether the items do or do not work or whether they are or are not acceptable.

Suppose a small firm receives a shipment of 1,000 parts from a supplier. Rather than evaluating all 1,000 parts, the purchaser can check the acceptability of a small sample of parts and decide about the acceptability of the entire order. The size of the sample—for instance, a sample of 25 of the 1,000 parts—affects the discriminating power of an attributes sampling plan. The smaller the sample, the greater the danger of either accepting a defective lot or rejecting a good lot due to sampling error. A larger sample reduces this danger but increases the inspection cost. An attributes sampling plan must strike a balance—avoiding excessive inspection costs and simultaneously avoiding an unreasonable risk of accepting a bad lot or rejecting a good lot.

**variables
sampling plan**
system that com-
pares actual mea-
surements with tar-
get measurements

Variables Sampling Plans. A **variables sampling plan** measures the degree of a particular characteristic of a product (such as legth or weight), rather than simply judging the item as acceptable or unacceptable. If the characteristic being inspected is measured on a continuous basis, a variables sampling plan may be used. For example, the weight of a box of candy—which is being manufactured continuously throughout the day and week—may be measured in pounds and ounces. The process can be monitored to be sure it stays "in control." Periodic random samples are taken and plotted on a chart to discover whether the process is out of control, thus requiring corrective action.

The variables control chart used for this purpose has lines denoting the upper and lower control limits. For example, a shop might produce wooden pieces averaging 42 inches in length. The upper control limit might be 43 inches and the lower control limit 41 inches. A signal of a lack of control would be given by a measurement falling outside either control limit, by a trend run of measurements upward or downward, or by various other indicators.

To establish a specific variables or attributes sampling plan, the small-business manager may consult more specialized publications in production/operations management or statistical quality control. One example is William Messina, *Statistical Quality Control for Manufacturing Managers* (New York: John Wiley and Sons, 1987). Or, more likely, the manager may consult a specialist in quantitative methods, such as a university professor of operations management or management science, for assistance in devising a sound sampling plan. The savings made possible by using an efficient quality control method can easily justify the consulting fees required in devising a sound quality control plan.

Quality Management in Service Businesses

The discussion of quality typically centers on a manufacturing process involving a tangible product that can be inspected or measured in some way. However,

Adopting Statistical Quality Control

Small firms can sometimes improve their quality management by introducing statistical quality controls. Robert Slass, president and owner of Rotor Clip Company in Somerset, New York, realized a few years ago that his company needed to update its quality procedures in producing metal-stamped fasteners.

The area that needed the most updating was quality control. By this time, Japanese manufacturers' success with such techniques as statistical process control—or SPC—was well-docu-

mented. SPC is a statistical approach to monitoring a process with the use of graphs so that subtle changes can be detected and adjustments can be made before an unsatisfactory part is produced. This is in contrast to the former concept of quality control, which relied on inspection of parts after they were produced— when it was too late to make any meaningful adjustment to the process.

Adopting statistical quality control calls for an investment in time, training, and equipment. Slass elected to make that commitment, and the benefits have been described as "enormous."

Source: Robert Slass, "The Hard Road Is the Best Road," *Nation's Business,* Vol. 78, No. 4, p. 6. Reprinted by permission, *Nation's Business,* April 1990. Copyright 1992, U.S. Chamber of Commerce.

the need for quality management is not limited to producers of physical products. Service businesses such as motels, dry cleaners, accounting firms, and automobile repair shops also need to maintain and improve quality. In fact, many firms offer a combination of a tangible product and intangible services and, ideally, manage quality in both areas.

Service to customers may be effective or deficient in a number of ways. Following are six factors that positively influence customers' perception of service quality:

1. Being on target. *Set and meet the customer's expectations. Do what was promised, when and where it was promised. Heighten the customer's awareness of the service provider's actions.*
2. Care and concern. *Be empathetic. Tune in to the customer's situation, frame of mind, and needs. Be attentive and willing to help.*
3. Spontaneity. *Empower service providers to think and respond quickly. Allow them to use their discretion and bend, rather than quote, procedures.*
4. Problem solving. *Train and encourage service providers to be problem solvers. Service providers have the customer's undivided attention when that person is experiencing a problem. A positive response to a problem will stick in the customer's mind. Capitalize on this opportunity to show the organization's capabilities.*

Figure 18-3
Business Services
Such as This
Computer Repair
Shop Must Also
Manage Quality

5. Follow-up. *Follow-up captures customers' attention and is often sincerely appreciated. It is associated with caring and professionalism, so follow up with flair and create a reputation for legendary service quality.*

6. Recovery. *Customers experiencing problems often have low expectations for their resolution; thus, they are exceedingly mindful and appreciative of speedy solutions. Making things right quickly is a powerful factor in creating an enduring image of high-quality service.*[6]

Measurement problems exist in assessing the quality of a service. It is easier to measure the length of a piece of wood than the quality level of motel accommodations. Nevertheless, methods can be devised for measuring the quality of services. Customers of an automobile repair shop, for example, may be sampled to determine their view of the service they received. A motel can maintain a record of the number of "foul-ups" in travelers' reservations, complaints about cleanliness of rooms, and so on.

For many types of service firms, control of quality constitutes the single most important managerial responsibility. All that such firms sell is service, and the future of their businesses rests upon the quality of their service as perceived by customers.

PLANT MAINTENANCE

According to Murphy's Law, if anything can go wrong, it will. In operating systems that make extensive use of tools and equipment, there is indeed much that can go wrong. The maintenance function is intended to correct malfunctions of equipment and, as far as possible, to prevent such breakdowns from occurring.

Role of Maintenance in Small Firms

Effective maintenance contributes directly to product/service quality and thus to customer satisfaction. Poor maintenance often creates problems for customers. A faulty shower or reading lamp that doesn't work, for example, makes a traveler's motel stay less enjoyable.

Equipment malfunctions and breakdowns not only cause problems for customers but also increase costs for the producing firm. Employees may be unproductive while repairs are being made, and expensive equipment may stand idle when it should be producing. Furthermore, improperly maintained equipment wears out more rapidly and requires early replacement, thus adding to the overall cost of operation.

The nature of maintenance work obviously depends upon the type of operations and the nature of the equipment being used. In an office, for example, the machines that require maintenance may simply include computers, fax machines, typewriters, copiers, and related office machines. Maintenance services are usually obtained on a contract basis—either by calling for repair personnel when a breakdown occurs or by contracting for periodic servicing.

In manufacturing firms that use more complex and specialized equipment, the maintenance function is much more difficult. For all types of firms, maintenance of the plant includes housekeeping as well as equipment repair. Plant housekeeping contributes to effective performance, even in those operations that use simple facilities.

In small plants, maintenance work often is performed by regular production employees. As a firm expands its facilities, it may add specialized maintenance personnel and eventually create a maintenance department.

Types of Maintenance

Plant maintenance activities fall into two categories. One is **corrective maintenance,** which includes both the major and minor repairs necessary to restore a facility to good condition. The other is **preventive maintenance,** which includes inspections and other activities intended to prevent machine breakdowns and damage to people and buildings.

Corrective Maintenance. Major repairs are unpredictable as to time of occurrence, repair time required, loss of output, and cost of downtime. Because of these characteristics, some small manufacturers find it desirable to contract with other service firms for major repair work. In contrast, the regular occurrence of minor breakdowns makes the volume of minor repair work reasonably predictable. Minor repairs are completed easily, quickly, and economi-

corrective maintenance
repairs necessary to restore equipment to good condition

preventive maintenance
activities intended to prevent machine breakdowns

cally. Therefore, many small plants use one or two of their own employees to perform such work.

Preventive Maintenance. A small plant can ill afford to neglect preventive maintenance. If a machine is highly critical to the overall operation, it should be inspected and serviced regularly to preclude costly breakdowns. Frequent checking of equipment reduces industrial accidents, and installation of smoke alarms and/or automatic sprinkler systems minimizes the danger of fire damage.

Preventive maintenance of equipment need not involve elaborate controls. Some cleaning and lubricating is usually done as a matter of routine. But for preventive maintenance to work well, more systematic procedures are needed. A record card showing cost, acquisition date, periods of use and storage, and frequency of preventive maintenance inspections should be kept on each major piece of equipment. On any given day, the machinist is handed the set of cards covering that day's required inspections. The machinist inspects each piece of equipment, makes necessary notations on the cards, and replaces worn parts.

Good Housekeeping and Plant Safety

Good housekeeping facilitates production control, saves time in looking for tools, and keeps floor areas safe and free for production work. Disregard for good housekeeping practices is reflected in a plant's production record, for good workmanship and high output are hard to achieve in an ill-kept plant.

The Occupational Safety and Health Act of 1970 (OSHA) requires employers to provide a place of employment free from hazards that are likely to cause death or serious physical harm. This means that the building and equipment must be maintained in a way that minimizes safety and health hazards. Although very small firms have been relieved of some of OSHA's record-keeping requirements, they are still subject to the requirements of the law.

As far as safety of the premises is concerned, not all small manufacturers require a sophisticated security system. However, all should be aware of the security problems and of available security devices. Such devices include fences to deter intruders, security guards, burglar-alarm systems, and gates or doors equipped with access controls that are activated only by identification cards or keys given to authorized personnel.

PRODUCTIVITY AND METHODS IMPROVEMENT

methods improvement
finding methods that reduce physical effort, shorten execution time, and/or lower cost

Methods improvement is designed to find work methods that demand the least physical effort and the shortest execution time at the lowest possible cost. Efforts to improve methods might begin with a broad view of operations within an office, service center, or manufacturing facility and later examine the design of individual jobs.

SMALL BUSINESS IN ACTION

Improving Productivity in Floor Tile Manufacturing

A small firm can quickly increase profits by finding a way to become more productive. Vinyl Plastics Inc. (VPI), a small floor tile and plastic sheet products manufacturer in Sheboygan, Wisconsin, used a variety of approaches to improve its productivity and profitability. As an example, one improvement eliminated delays in changing from one color to another in the production process. VPI's president explained it as follows:

We have $250,000 in equipment that used to sit idle for three to four hours every time we

needed to change color to run a different job. With a $10,000 investment in some new conveyors, some procedural changes, and input from employees, we reduced color change time to zero. Now one job can flow right into the next without contamination.

VPI also boosted efficiency by reducing work-in-progress inventory—inventory that is stored in the warehouse between manufacturing stages. The goal is to reduce it to zero—to take raw material and put it through the entire manufacturing process without interruption.

Source: Wirt M. Cook, "Productive Reasoning," *Entrepreneur*, Vol. 19, No. 12 (December 1991), pp. 54–57.

Improving Productivity

The standard of living of any society depends, to some extent, upon its **productivity**—the efficiency with which inputs are transformed into outputs. In recent years—between 1985 and 1990, for example—productivity growth in the United States lagged behind that of Japan and Great Britain.[7] For individual firms, improving productivity provides a key to competing more vigorously and increasing profits.

productivity
the efficiency with which inputs are transformed into outputs

We may visualize a business firm's productivity as follows:

$$\text{productivity} = \frac{\text{outputs}}{\text{inputs}} = \frac{\text{goods and/or services}}{\text{labor} + \text{energy} + \text{money} + \text{tools} + \text{materials}}$$

A firm improves its productivity by doing more with less. This can be accomplished in many different ways. As one writer has pointed out, Mom's apple pie baking may be improved by sending Mom to cooking school, buying better apples, getting a better oven, or redesigning the kitchen.[8]

At one time, productivity and quality were viewed as competitive, if not conflicting. However, production at a high quality level reduces scrap and rework. Therefore, quality improvement, automation, and better methods are all routes to better productivity.

Improving productivity in the service sector has been especially difficult. Since it is a labor-intensive area, managers have less opportunity for improvement by using automation.

Nature of Work Study

When conducted for an overall operation, methods improvement involves an analysis of work flow, equipment, tooling, layout, working conditions, and individual jobs. For a manufacturing process, it means finding answers to such questions as:

1. Is the right machine being used?
2. Can one employee operate two or more machines?
3. Can automatic feeders or ejectors be utilized?
4. Can power tools replace hand tools?
5. Can the jigs and fixtures be improved?
6. Is the workplace properly arranged?
7. Is the operator's motion sequence effective?

Work methods can be analyzed for service or merchanding firms as well as for manufacturing businesses. For example, a small plumbing company serving residential customers might examine its service vehicles to see whether the best possible assortment and arrangement of parts, tools, and supplies have been achieved. In addition, the company could analyze the planning and routing of repair assignments to minimize unnecessary backtracking and waste of time.

To be successful, work improvement and measurement require the collaboration of employees and management. The assistance of employees is important both in the search for more efficient methods and in the adoption of improved work procedures.

The competitive pressures on today's small-business firms provide the incentive for work improvement. Small firms can improve their productivity and stay competitive. To the extent that methods can actually be improved, there will be increased output from the same effort (or even reduced effort) on the part of employees.

Laws of Motion Economy

laws of motion economy
guidelines for increasing the efficiency of human movement and tool design

The **laws of motion economy** underlie any work improvement program—whether it be for the overall operations of a plant or for a single task. These laws concern work arrangement, the use of the human hands and body, and the design and use of tools. Some of these laws are:

1. If both hands start and stop their motion at the same time and are never idle during a work cycle, maximum performance is approached.

2. If motions are made simultaneously in opposite directions over similar paths, automaticity and rhythm develop naturally, and less fatigue is experienced.
3. The method requiring the fewest motions generally is the best for performance of a given task.
4. When motions are confined to the lowest practical classification, maximum performance and minimum fatigue are approached. Lowest classification means motions involving the fingers, hands, forearms, and trunk.

A knowledge of the laws of motion economy will suggest various ways to improve work. For example, materials and tools should be placed so as to minimize movement of the trunk and the extended arms.

Methods of Work Measurement

There are several ways to measure work in the interest of establishing a performance standard. **Motion study** consists of a detailed observation of all the actual motions that the observed worker makes to complete a job under a given set of physical conditions. From this study the skilled observer should be able to detect any wasted movements that can be corrected or eliminated. **Time study,** which normally follows motion study, involves timing and recording each elemental motion of a job on an observation sheet. **Micromotion study** is a refinement of the time study in that a video camera, rather than a stopwatch, is used to record the elemental motions, as well as the times.

The methods of work measurement mentioned above require trained observers or analysts. Most small plants would find it impractical to utilize the costly methods of time study and micromotion study. A more practical method of work measurement, which provides little operating detail but estimates the ratio of actual working time and downtime, is **work sampling.** This method was originated in England by L.H.C. Tippett in 1934. Work sampling involves random observations in which the observer simply determines whether the observed worker is working or idle. The numbers of observations are tallied in "working" and "idle" classifications; the percentages of the tallies are estimates of the actual percentage of time that the worker was working and idle.

motion study
measurement of all the motions a worker makes to complete a job

time study
measurement of the time taken by a worker to complete a task

micromotion study
time study in which a worker's motions are videotaped

work sampling
method of work measurement that estimates the ratio of working time to idle time

Quantitative Tools in Operations Management

Many decisions in small firms can be improved by adopting quantitative decision-making techniques. Small-business owners may lack an awareness of the power of such techniques. Much of their decision making reflects personal experience—what they have learned through trial and error—and they fail to realize that such decisions can be made more rational. Reliance on intuitive approaches can be reduced by the analytical processes that are a part of management science.

As a practical matter, few managers of small firms have sufficient knowledge of advanced mathematics and statistics to apply these tools personally. A consideration of these tools is pertinent, however, for at least two reasons. First, the small-business owner should know that such tools exist and that assistance can be obtained from individuals qualified in the use of quantitative methods. Second, the growing use of these techniques points up the need for increased training in quantitative methods on the part of small-business managers. Even though an individual lacks the necessary technical knowledge for using the tools, it is desirable that he or she appreciate their possibilities, advantages, and limitations.

By means of statistical analysis, one can use quantitative data to arrive at conclusions that are useful in managing a small business. Suppose, for example, that you wish to judge the quality of a large production run without inspecting each item or that you wish to understand your market without surveying each individual customer. You may accomplish these objectives by sampling the population and then applying **statistical inference,** that is, inferring something about a large group on the basis of facts known about a smaller group.

statistical inference
using information about a small group to infer something about a larger group

Although sampling is not the only tool that uses statistical inference, it illustrates its practical application in small business. In sampling, the manager wishes to obtain a sample that is truly representative of the underlying population. A sample is representative when it is like the population in all important respects. To assure this condition, the researcher will often use a random sample in which every item in the population has a known chance of being included. The sample should also be adequate, that is, large enough to yield a dependable answer.

Sampling is essential for the simple reason that the entire population of data can seldom be investigated. Cost and time pressures make this prohibitive.

Limitations of Quantitative Tools

Quantitative tools do not preclude the exercise of managerial judgment, which is definitely required because of the human factor in any problem situation. The tools are a means to an end, not the end itself. The manager's judgment remains the decisive factor in planning.

Neither does the use of quantitative tools preclude the requirement of feedback. Any information about operating results must be fed back to the planner so that plans, programs, and instructions may be modified when necessary. For example, when feedback reports describe deviations from an existing budget, the budget may have to be modified as a means of corrective action.

It must be emphasized that quantitative tools are just that—they are tools, and no more. When used properly, they tend to improve managerial decision making. These decision-making tools do not eliminate business risk totally. Risk is inherent in the use of present resources and production facilities for the creation of new goods. It is inherent also in the purchase of merchandise for resale. Decision-making tools are designed merely to minimize risk by providing a rational approach to the solution of business problems.

LOOKING BACK

1. Both manufacturing and service organizations use an operations process that converts inputs into products or services. Three basic types of processes are job shops, repetitive manufacturing, and batch manufacturing. Proper scheduling and controlling of work flow are needed in both manufacturing and service organizations.

2. Total quality management is a quality-focused approach to managing operations. Quality is built into a product during the operations process, not at the inspection stage. The quality of a product is influenced by its design, the quality of raw materials, and the performance of employees. Quality circles draw upon the thinking of employees by bringing them together periodically to identify and solve problems. Inspection is the method traditionally used to maintain control of quality. Modern quality control involves the use of two statistical techniques: attributes sampling and variables sampling plans. Quality management is important in service businesses as well as in manufacturing.

3. The maintenance function is critical for firms that use complex and highly specialized equipment. Plant maintenance includes corrective maintenance to restore a facility to good condition and preventive maintenance to minimize breakdowns. Plant housekeeping and safety management are also part of the maintenance function.

4. Productivity improvement can contribute to the standard of living of our society and to the profits of individual firms. It is accomplished by an analysis of operations and jobs and uses tools and techniques of work measurement. Various quantitative methods may also be used in the analysis of small-firm operations.

DISCUSSION QUESTIONS

1. Describe the operations process for the following types of service firms: (a) management consultant, (b) barber shop, (c) advertising agency.

2. What is the difference between job shops and repetitive manufacturing?

3. Why might a small manufacturing or service firm prefer a versatile work force in its operations even though such employees might be paid more than less-versatile employees?

4. How do operations processes differ for manufacturing firms and service firms?

5. Customer demand for services is not uniform during the day, week, or other time period. What approaches or strategies can be used by service firms to relate customer demand for services to the firm's capacity to perform services?

6. Explain what is meant by "total quality management."

7. What is meant by the saying, "You can't inspect quality into a product"?

8. It is said that the major problems of manufacturing inspection are where to inspect, how much to inspect, and the cost of inspection. Explain each of these inspection problems concisely.

9. A small manufacturer does not believe that using statistical quality control charts and sampling plans would be useful. Can traditional methods suffice? Can 100 percent inspection by final inspectors eliminate all defective products? Why?

10. How can a service business, such as a dry cleaner, use the concept of quality control?
11. Explain the difference between preventive and corrective maintenance. Explain the relative importance of each of these types of maintenance when (a) one or more major breakdowns have occurred in a small plant, and (b) shop operations are running smoothly and maintenance does not face any major repair jobs.
12. The breakdown of machines during their use is a result of failure to exercise preventive maintenance. Why should these breakdowns always be investigated promptly? What should be the outcome of such investigations? Are cost considerations or lost production of paramount importance in such situations? Why?
13. How could improved housekeeping help raise productivity?
14. Doing something rapidly and doing it well are often incompatible. How could quality improvement possibly contribute to productivity improvement?
15. What is meant by the "laws of motion economy"?

YOU MAKE THE CALL

Situation 1

Broom making is a centuries-old craft. In the early 1980s Thurman Scheumack started a small broom-making business in the Ozark foothills. Although the workshop has only seven employees, including Scheumack and his wife, Rhonda, its output has grown to 20,000 brooms per year. Seventy-five percent of production is in standard kitchen models, and the rest have hand-carved faces in their handles. Some brooms are sold through art galleries, and some are sold at tourist attractions such as Disneyland and Colonial Williamsburg for prices up to $50 each.

The brooms are fashioned from broomcorn, a plant imported from Mexico. Most of the production equipment, initially built by Scheumack, is far from high tech. Developed in the 1700s, the machinery runs on a system of hand- and foot-operated weights and levers. One concession to technology is a single electric motor that operates a pulley for a broom-winding machine.

Source: Adapted from "Ozark Enterprise Handcrafts Brooms," *In Business*, Vol. 11, No. 1 (January–February 1989), p. 16.

Questions
1. In view of its antiquated technology, should this firm attempt to modernize its equipment and update its manufacturing methods? Would motion study be relevant and useful?
2. How would quality be defined for this type of product? How could quality be measured?

Situation 2

A college professor opened a furniture shop in Maine and saw it grow to $5 million in annual sales volume and 85 employees. The firm produces high-quality chairs, tables, and other items for the contract furniture market. Each piece is sanded and polished, sealed with linseed oil, and finished with paste wax. No stain, color, or varnish is added, and the furniture never needs refinishing.

As the firm grew larger, it began the equivalent of mass production. Many of the original craftspeople dropped out and were replaced with production workers. The founder is seeking to maintain quality through employee participation at all levels. He believes that quality can be maintained indefinitely if the company doesn't "get too greedy." He has expressed his philosophy as follows:

We're still not driven by profit but by meaningful relationships between employees and between the producer and the user. It's a way of life. We throw out a lot of good stuff. If we had to produce something just to make a buck, I'd go back to teaching school.

Source: Christopher Hyde, "The Evolution of Thomas Moser," *In Business*, Vol. 10, No. 4 (July–August 1988), pp. 34–37.

Questions

1. How does this firm's growth make quality management easier or more difficult?
2. The founder recognizes that people and people relationships have a bearing on quality. What can he do to persuade or enable production employees to have the right attitude toward quality?
3. The founder's comment suggests that profits and quality may be incompatible. When does "making a buck" lead to lower quality? Can or should this type of firm use financial incentives?

EXPERIENTIAL EXERCISES

1. Visit a small manufacturing plant or service organization. Ask the manager to describe the production/operations process, the way operations are controlled, and the nature of maintenance operations. Prepare a brief report on your findings.
2. Outline the operations process involved in your present educational program, identifying inputs, operations, and outputs.
3. Assume that you are responsible for quality control in the publication of this textbook. Prepare a report outlining the quality standards you would use and the points of inspection you would recommend.
4. Outline, in as much detail as possible, your customary practices in studying for a specific course. Evaluate the methods you use and specify changes that should improve your productivity.

REFERENCES TO SMALL-BUSINESS PRACTICES

Galagan, Patricia A. "How to Get Your TQM Training on Track," *Nation's Business*, Vol. 80, No. 10 (October 1992), pp. 24–28.

Small companies experience difficulties and challenges in training employees in total quality management.

Goldstein, Nora. "Production Strategies When Business Booms," *In Business,* Vol. 10, No. 2 (March–April 1988), pp. 32–34.

   This article describes the steps taken by a small manufacturing firm to expand output— changes in production processes, modifications of equipment, and new methods to maintain control of quality.

"Industrial Policy," *Business Week,* No. 3260 (April 6, 1992), pp. 70–75.

   This article discusses general issues of productivity improvement and includes an account of a technical assistance program in Pennsylvania that helped a small manufacturer quickly increase its productivity.

Logsdon, Gene. "Partners in Pasta," *In Business,* Vol. 9, No. 3 (May–June 1987), pp. 28–31.

   This article describes the production methods used by a small business in Marietta, Ohio, to produce pasta of exceptional quality.

ENDNOTES

1. "How to Spread the Gospel of Quality," *Business Week,* No. 3295 (November 30, 1992), p. 122.

2. James B. Dilworth, *Operations Management: Design, Planning, and Control for Manufacturing and Services* (New York: McGraw-Hill, Inc., 1992), pp. 13–14. Reproduced with permission of McGraw-Hill.

3. Kenneth E. Ebel, *Achieving Excellence in Business* (Milwaukee: American Society for Quality Control, 1991), pp. 12–13.

4. Donald C. Bacon, "How the Baldrige Winners Did It," *Nation's Business,* Vol. 77, No. 1 (January 1989), p. 32.

5. David S. Fortney and Sophia L. Ranalli, "How *Electromation* Affects Employers," *The National Law Journal* (February 15, 1993), pp. 19–20.

6. Ken Myers and Jim Buckman, "Beyond the Smile: Improving Service Quality at the Roots," *Quality Progress,* Vol. 25, No. 12 (December 1992), p. 57.

7. "Annual Indexes of Manufacturing Productivity and Related Measures, 12 Countries," *Monthly Labor Review* (November 1992), p. 101.

8. Michael LeBoeuf, *The Productivity Challenge: How to Make It Work for America and You* (New York: McGraw-Hill Book Company, 1982), p. 9.

CHAPTER 19

Purchasing and Managing Inventory

SPOTLIGHT ON SMALL BUSINESS

Although a very large inventory enables a firm to serve its customers quickly, the cost of carrying such an inventory is usually prohibitive. Therefore, a business must typically compromise between a "bare-bones" inventory that loses sales and an excessive inventory that loses money.

There are exceptions to every rule. A large inventory, even though costly to maintain, can occasionally be used as a sales tool. As one example, Joe Sugar's, a men's clothing store in St. Pauls, North Carolina, maintains a huge inventory, including 11,000 pairs of pants, in order to attract customers. Joe Sugar explained his store's reputation for being able to fit everyone:

That reputation helps us draw customers from distant markets. It's business we must have to survive because St. Pauls alone isn't big enough to support a store like ours.

We advertise in about a dozen regional papers and routinely draw customers more than an hour's drive away; if we didn't have the big inventory in all of those sizes, people wouldn't keep coming back.

Joe Sugar

Source: Joe Sugar, "A Strategy That Cuts Against the Grain," *Nation's Business,* Vol. 80, No. 6 p. 8. Reprinted by permission, *Nation's Business,* June 1992. Copyright 1992, U.S. Chamber of Commerce.

After studying this chapter, you should be able to:
1. List the steps involved in the purchasing cycle.
2. Explain key policies related to purchasing.
3. Explain the importance of good relations with suppliers and the factors to be considered in choosing suppliers.
4. Identify the objectives of inventory control.
5. Summarize the types of inventory costs and explain how they can be minimized.
6. Compare the major methods used in accounting for inventory.

NEW TERMS AND CONCEPTS

purchasing
purchase requisition
purchase order
reciprocal buying
make-or-buy decision
ABC method

reorder point
safety stock
two-bin method
just-in-time inventory system
economic order quantity

physical inventory system
perpetual inventory system
retail inventory valuation method

Many small businesses spend more money for materials or merchandise than for any other purpose. Many firms must also carry sizable inventories that are crucial for their operation. This chapter discusses how small firms should deal with these important areas of purchasing and inventory management.

PURCHASING

purchasing
process of obtaining materials, equipment, and services needed to meet business goals

The objective of **purchasing** is to obtain materials, merchandise, equipment, and services needed to meet production and/or marketing goals. Through effective purchasing, a firm secures all production factors except labor in the required quantity and quality, at the best price, and at the time needed. The purchasing function is necessary in merchandising and service organizations as well as in production organizations, but the following discussion gives primary attention to purchasing as it relates to the production process.

Importance of Effective Purchasing

There is a direct correlation between the quality of finished products and the quality of the raw materials placed in process. For example, if tight tolerances are imposed on a manufacturer's product by design requirements, this in turn requires the acquisition of high-quality materials and component parts. Then, given an excellent process, excellent products can be produced. Similarly, the acquisition of high-quality merchandise makes a retailer's sales to customers easier and reduces the number of markdowns required.

Delivery of goods should be timed to meet the exact needs of the buyer. In a small factory, failure to receive materials, parts, or equipment on schedule is likely to cause costly interruptions in production operations. Machines and personnel are idled until the items on order are finally received. And in a retail business, failure to receive merchandise on schedule may mean the loss of one or more sales and, possibly, the permanent loss of the customers who were disappointed. Effective purchasing can also affect the "bottom line" directly by securing the best price for a given product or raw material.

Changing economic conditions make purchasing and inventory management important. Such factors as shortages of materials, inflation, and fluctuating interest rates make it logical for the small business to emphasize purchasing and inventory activities.

The Purchasing Cycle

Purchasing involves a number of steps, as described in the following paragraphs.

Receipt of a Purchase Request. A **purchase requisition** originates within the firm. It is a formal, documented request from an employee or department for something to be bought—raw materials for production or other types of products such as office supplies or computers. In a small business, a purchase request is not always documented. However, financial control is improved by purchasing only on the basis of purchase requests.

purchase requisition
formal request for something to be bought for a business

Location of a Source of Supply. The firm can locate suitable suppliers through sales representatives, advertisements, trade associations, word of mouth, and company records of past supplier performance. The firm obtains price quotations and, for major purchases, solicits bids from a number of potential sources. The importance of good relationships with suppliers is discussed later in this chapter.

Issuance of a Purchase Order. The next step in purchasing is the issuance of a **purchase order**. A standard form, such as that shown in Figure 19-1, should be used in all buying operations. When the signed order is accepted by a vendor (supplier), it becomes a binding contract. In the event of a serious violation, the written purchase order serves as the basis for adjustment.

purchase order
written order issued to a supplier to buy something

Follow-Up of a Purchase Order. It may be necessary to follow up purchase orders to ensure delivery on schedule. This is particularly important in the case of orders involving large dollar amounts, long lead times, and/or items that are critical in the production process. Troublesome orders may require repeated checking to ensure that materials or merchandise will be available when needed.

PURCHASE ORDER
THE RED WING COMPANY, INC.
Fredonia, NY 14063-4925

No. 05282
SHOW THIS NUMBER
ON INVOICE

June 27, 19 - -

DATE OF ORDER

Byron Jackson & Company
4998 Michigan Avenue
Chicago, IL 60615-2218

SHIPPING INSTRUCTIONS:
Mark purchase order number
on each piece in shipment

DELIVERY REQUIRED	F.O.B.	ROUTING	TERMS
July 24	Chicago	via NYC-Buffalo	2/10 net 30

ITEM	QUANTITY & UNIT	DESCRIPTION	PRICE & UNIT
622	35 each	Spring assembly	14.35 ea
230	200 each	Bearings	3.35 ea
272	70 each	Heavy duty relay 50V	7.50 ea
478	490 each	Screw set	.03 ea

ORIGINAL BILL OF LADING MUST ACCOMPANY ALL INVOICES FOR GOODS SHIPPED BY FREIGHT.
2% DISCOUNT FOR PAYMENT IN 10 DAYS WILL BE DEDUCTED FROM FACE OF INVOICE UNLESS OTHERWISE SPECIFIED.

INVOICE IN DUPLICATE

BY _____ *Y Yromboski* _____
Purchasing Agent

Figure 19-1
A Purchase Order

Verification of Receipt of Goods. The receiving clerk takes physical custody of incoming materials and merchandise, checks their general condition, and signs the carrier's release. Goods should be inspected to assure an accurate count and the proper quality and kind of items. Figure 19-2 shows a weekly or quarterly summary analysis of the quality of a given material.

Purchasing Policies and Practices

A small firm can make its purchasing systematic by adopting purchasing policies and practices. These can help control purchasing costs and also contribute to good relationships with suppliers. Such policies are discussed next.

reciprocal buying
a firm's policy of
selling to businesses
from which it buys

Reciprocal Buying. Some firms try to sell to others from whom they also purchase. This policy of **reciprocal buying** is based on the premise that one company can secure additional orders by using its own purchasing requests as a

Figure 19-2
Materials Yield
Summary

Materials Yield Summary
The Iowa Manufacturing Company

Store Item _____   Week Ending _____

Store Item Number _____   Quarter Ending _____

Supplier	Units of Product Put in Process	Allowance per Unit of Finished Product	Total Units Allowed	Actual Units Used	Usage as % of Units Allowed
1	2	3	4 = 3•2	5	$6 = \frac{5}{4}$ (100) (Quotient) = %

bargaining weapon. Although the typical order of most small companies is not large enough to make this a potent weapon, there is a tendency for purchasers to grant some recognition to this factor. Of course, this policy would be damaging if it were allowed to obscure quality and price variations.

Making or Buying. Many firms face **make-or-buy decisions**. This choice is especially important for small manufacturing firms that have the option of making or buying component parts for the products they make. A less conspicuous make-or-buy choice occurs with respect to certain services—for example, purchasing janitorial or auto rental services instead of providing for those needs internally. Some reasons for *making* component parts, rather than buying them, are as follows:

make-or-buy decision
a firm's choice between making or buying component parts for the products it makes

Figure 19-3
La Petite Day-Care
Centers Lease Vans
to Control Costs

1. Uses otherwise idle capacity, thus permitting more economical production.
2. Gives the buyer greater assurance of supply with fewer delays and interruptions caused by difficulties with suppliers.
3. Protects a secret design.
4. Reduces expenses by saving an amount equivalent to transportation costs and the supplier's selling expense and profit.
5. Permits closer coordination and control of total production operations, thus facilitating operations scheduling and control.
6. Provides higher quality products than may be available from suppliers.

Some arguments for *buying* are as follows:

1. May be cheaper, due to the supplier's concentration on production of the given part, which makes possible specialized facilities and greater efficiency.
2. Avoids need for additional space, equipment, personnel skills, and working capital.
3. Requires less diversified managerial experience and skills.
4. Offers greater flexibility; for example, seasonal production of a given item makes manufacturing it risky.
5. Frees "in-plant" operations for concentration on the firm's specialty—finished products and services.
6. Reduces the risk of equipment obsolescence by transferring this risk to outsiders.

The decision to make or buy may be expensive to reverse. It should certainly be based on long-run cost and profit optimization. The underlying cost differences need to be analyzed very carefully, since small savings in buying or making may greatly affect profit margins.

Substituting Materials or Merchandise. New types of materials and merchandise are constantly being developed. Some of them may be both cheaper and better than older products. Nevertheless, the purchasing decision by a manufacturer must take into consideration not only the impact on the product and its cost but also the effect upon the process. A change in materials may alter the sequence of operations or may even cause the deletion or addition of one or more operations.

Purchasing policy should be sufficiently flexible to permit ready consideration of new or different materials or merchandise. Of course, a change must be based upon the possibility of producing or selling a better, cheaper product.

Taking Purchase Discounts. Cash discounts are granted by most sellers of industrial goods, although discount terms vary from one industry to another. The purpose of the seller's offering the discount is to obtain prompt payment. The purchaser can also benefit financially by taking advantage of such discounts. Terms of 2/10, net 30, for example, mean that the purchaser is entitled to a 2 percent discount if payment is made no later than the 10th day from date of invoice. After the 10-day discount period, the full amount is required, even if payment is delayed until the 30th day from date of invoice.

The effective annualized cost of not taking the discount can be significant. After all, with terms of 2/10, net 30, the purchaser is paying 2 percent to use the money for only 20 additional days. (The method for calculating the annual cost is explained in Chapter 21.) From an economic standpoint, therefore, prompt payment is desirable in order to avoid this cost. However, remember that payment of a purchase invoice also affects cash flow. If funds are extremely short, a firm may have no alternative. It may need to wait and pay on the last possible day in order to avoid an overdraft at the bank.

Diversifying Sources of Supply. In purchasing a given item, there is a question of whether it is desirable to use more than one supplier. The somewhat frustrating answer is, "It all depends." For example, the answer might be different with regard to buying a few rolls of transparent tape as opposed to buying a component part to be used in hundreds of products.

Some of the reasons a small firm might prefer to concentrate purchases with one supplier are these:

1. A particular supplier may be outstanding in product quality.
2. Concentrating purchases may lead to quantity discounts or other favorable terms of purchase.
3. Orders may be so small that it is simply impractical to divide them.
4. The purchasing firm may, as a good customer, qualify for prompt treatment of rush orders.

5. As a good customer, the purchaser may receive management advice, market information, and financial leniency in times of emergency.
6. A small firm may be linked to a specific supplier by the very nature of the business—a franchisee, for example.

Other reasons favor diversifying rather than concentrating sources of supply:

1. Shopping among suppliers enables the buying firm to locate the best source in terms of price, quality, and service.
2. A supplier, knowing that competitors are getting some of the business, may be more alert in providing good prices and service.
3. Diversifying supply sources for key products provides insurance against interruptions caused by strikes, fires, or similar problems with sole suppliers.

Some firms follow a compromise policy by which they concentrate enough purchases to justify special treatment. At the same time, they diversify purchases sufficiently to provide alternative sources of supply.

Forward Buying. Forward buying involves purchasing in quantities greater than needed for normal usage or sales. It may be motivated by a number of considerations. A purchasing firm may, for example, seek to protect itself from outages or delays caused by strikes or materials shortages. Another reason for forward buying is to avoid anticipated price increases.

Purchasing excessive quantities to avoid anticipated higher prices creates a speculative risk. Price appreciation after such a purchase would naturally produce inventory cost savings. However, price declines would create excessive inventory costs. Unless a firm is very stable financially or a forthcoming price increase is virtually assured, the firm should avoid speculative buying. Forward buying also adds to operating costs by increasing inventory size and thereby raising inventory carrying costs.

Forward buying runs counter to the concept of just-in-time inventory, a practice discussed later in this chapter. According to the just-in-time inventory philosophy, inventory levels should, ideally, fall to zero.

Scheduled Budget Buying. Buying to meet anticipated requirements is planned buying, or scheduled budget buying. This policy involves the adjustment of purchase quantities to estimated production or sales needs. Budget buying in suitable quantities will assure the maintenance of planned inventories and the meeting of product schedule requirements without delays in production due to delayed deliveries. It strikes the middle ground between just-in-time buying—with its planned minimal stocking of materials and its occasional delays due to late deliveries—and speculative buying, with its deliberate overstocking, which entails risk as it seeks speculative profits. It represents the best type of buying for the conservative small firm.

SMALL BUSINESS IN ACTION

Aggressive Purchasing Saves Money

A self-described "former hippie," Barry Schacht started in business when he lost a university lawn-mowing job. He mowed a big peace symbol in a lawn, and campus authorities thought it was less clever than he did!

Barry Schacht and his brother, Dan, then started Schacht's Spindle Company in Boulder, Colorado, to manufacture looms for hand weaving. They have found that astute buying of components can save thousands of dollars and that there is wide variation in prices quoted by vendors. Their ability to save money by shopping around is evidenced in Barry Schacht's description of his search for a spherical bearing:

The first place I called had spherical bearings that cost $20 apiece, real bad news for us. But that company made bearings for rockets. All we needed was one for a tool that had been state of the art five centuries ago. The next place had spherical bearings that cost $10, for airplanes. Hmmm. After about $100 in phone calls I found a little company that made all kinds of spherical bearings, and had exactly what we needed. He asked, ``How many do you want?" I said 500. He sighed. "Well if you only want a few, they are kind of expensive— 54¢ each."

Source: Gene Logsdon, "Factory Crafting," *In Business,* Vol. 10, No. 2 (March–April, 1988), pp. 35–37.

Selection of and Relations with Suppliers

Before making a choice of suppliers, the purchaser must know the materials or merchandise to be purchased, including details of construction, quality and grade, intended use, maintenance or care required, and the importance of style features. The purchaser must also know how different grades and qualities of raw materials affect various manufacturing processes.

Selection of Suppliers. A number of considerations are relevant in deciding which suppliers to use on a continuing basis. Perhaps the most obvious of these are price and quality. Price differences are clearly significant if not offset by quality or other factors.

Quality differences are sometimes difficult to detect. For some types of materials, statistical controls can be used to evaluate shipments from specific vendors. In this way, the purchaser obtains an overall quality rating for various suppliers. In some cases, the purchaser can work with a supplier to upgrade quality. If satisfactory quality cannot be achieved, the purchaser then has a rational basis for dropping the supplier.

Location becomes an especially important factor as a firm tries to reduce inventory levels and to make possible speedy delivery of purchased items. A supplier's general reliability in supplying goods and services is also significant. For example, can the purchaser depend upon the supplier to meet delivery schedules or to respond promptly to emergency situations?

Services provided by the supplier must also be considered. The extension of credit by suppliers provides a major portion of the working-capital requirements of many small firms. Some suppliers provide merchandising aids, plan sales promotions, and furnish management advice. In times of recession, some small retailers have even received direct financial assistance from major suppliers of long standing. Another useful service for some types of products is the provision of repair work by the supplier. A small industrial firm, for example, may select a vendor for a truck or diesel engine on the basis of the vendor's service department.

Importance of Good Relations with Suppliers. Good relations with suppliers are essential for firms of any size, but they are particularly important to small businesses. Perhaps the cornerstone of good supplier relationships is the buyer's realization that the supplier is usually more important to the buyer than the buyer (as a customer) is to the supplier. The buyer is only one among dozens, hundreds, or perhaps thousands buying from that supplier. Moreover, the buyer's volume of purchases over a year and the size of the individual orders are often so small that the business could be eliminated without great loss to the supplier.

To implement the policy of fair play and to cultivate good relations, the small buying firm should try to observe the following practices:

1. Pay all bills promptly.
2. See all sales representatives promptly, according them a full, courteous hearing.
3. Do not summarily cancel orders merely to gain a temporary advantage.
4. Do not argue over prices, attempting to browbeat the supplier into special concessions and unusual discounts.
5. Cooperate with the supplier by making suggestions for product improvement and/or cost reduction whenever possible.
6. Give courteous, reasonable explanations when rejecting bids, and make fair adjustments in case of disputes.

Small buyers must remember that it takes a long time to build good relationships with a supplier but that good relations can be destroyed by one ill-timed, tactless act.

INVENTORY CONTROL

Inventory control is not glamorous, but it can make the difference between success and failure. The larger the inventory investment, the more vital is its proper use and control. The importance of inventory control, particularly in small retail or wholesale firms, is attested to by the fact that inventory typically represents these firms' major dollar investment.

Objectives of Inventory Control

Both purchasing and inventory control have the same general objective: to have the right goods in the right quantities at the right time and place. This general objective requires other, more specific subgoals of inventory control.

Assured Continuous Operations. Efficient manufacturing requires work-in-process to be moved on schedule. A delay caused by lack of materials or parts can cause the shutdown of a production line, a department, or even the whole plant. Such interruptions of scheduled operations are both serious and costly. Costs jump when skilled workers and machines stand idle. Also, given a long delay, fulfillment of delivery promises to customers may become impossible.

Maximum Sales. Assuming adequate demand, sales are greater if goods are always available for display and/or delivery to the customer. Most customers want to choose from an assortment of merchandise. Customers who are forced by a narrow range of choice and/or stockouts to look elsewhere may be lost permanently. On the other hand, the small store might unwisely go to the other extreme and carry too large an inventory. Management must walk the line between overstocking and understocking in order to retain customers and maximize sales.

Protection of Assets. One of the essential functions of inventory control is to protect inventories against theft, shrinkage, or deterioration. The efficiency or wastefulness of storekeeping, manufacturing, and handling processes affects the quantity and quality of usable inventory. For example, the more often an article is picked up and handled, the more chance there is for physical damage. Inventory items that need special treatment can also spoil or deteriorate if improperly stored.

Minimum Inventory Investment. Effective inventory control permits smaller inventories without causing disservice to customers or to processing. This means that the inventory investment is lower. It also means lower costs for storage space, taxes, and insurance. And inventory deterioration or obsolescence is less extensive as well.

Controlling Inventory Costs

It is easy to understand that effective control of inventory contributes to the "bottom line," that is, to the profitability of a firm. It is more difficult, however, to understand how to make effective inventory decisions that will minimize costs.

Types of Inventory-Related Costs. Minimizing inventory costs requires attention to many different types of costs. Order costs include the preparation of a purchase order, follow-up, and related bookkeeping expenses. Quantity discounts must also be included in such calculations. Inventory carrying costs include interest costs on money tied up in inventory, insurance, storage, obsolescence, and pilferage costs. These are costs of carrying items in inventory. There is also a cost of not having items in inventory, because of lost sales or disrupted production resulting from the stockouts. Although stockout costs cannot be calculated as easily as other inventory costs, they are nonetheless real.

ABC Inventory Analysis. Some inventory items are more valuable or otherwise more critical in the operations process than others. Therefore, they are more crucial in their effect on costs and profits. For this reason, managers should give most careful attention to those items entailing the largest investment.

ABC method
method of classifying inventory by value

One widely used approach, the **ABC method,** classifies inventory items into three categories—*A, B,* and *C.* The few high-value items in the *A* category account for the largest percentage of total dollars or are otherwise critical in the production process and, therefore, deserve close control. These items might be monitored, for example, by an inventory system that keeps a running record of receipts, withdrawals, and balances of each such item. In this way, a firm avoids an unnecessarily heavy investment in costly inventory items. Category *B* items are less costly but deserve a moderate amount of attention because they make up a lesser but still significant share of the total inventory. Items in category *C* contain low-cost or noncritical items such as paperclips in an office or nuts and bolts in a repair shop. Their carrying costs are not large enough to justify close control. These items might simply be checked periodically to be sure that a sufficient supply is available.

The purpose of the ABC method is to focus managerial attention where it will do the most good. There is nothing sacred, of course, about the three classes. Four classes could be created if that seemed more appropriate.

reorder point
the level at which additional quantities of merchandise should be ordered

Reorder Point and Safety Stock. In maintaining inventory levels, a manager must decide the point at which additional quantities will be ordered. Calculating the **reorder point** requires consideration of the time necessary to obtain a new supply, which, in turn, depends on location of suppliers, transportation schedules, and so on.

Because of difficulty in getting new inventory at the exact time it is desired and because of irregularities in withdrawals from inventory, firms also typically maintain a **safety stock.** The safety stock provides a measure of protection against stockouts caused by emergencies of one type or another.

The **two-bin method** is a simple technique for implementing these concepts. Inventories are divided into two portions or two bins. When the first bin is exhausted, an order is placed to replenish the supply. The remaining portion should cover needs until a new supply arrives, and it includes a safety stock as well.

safety stock
stock maintained to protect against stockouts

two-bin method
a simple visual technique for showing the reorder point

Just-in-Time Inventory. Reducing inventory levels has been a goal of operations managers around the world. The **just-in-time inventory system** attempts to cut inventory carrying costs by reducing inventory to an absolute minimum. Popularized as the *Kanban system* in Japan, it has led to cost reductions there and in other countries. New inventory is received, presumably, just as the last item from the existing inventory is placed into service. Many large U.S. firms have adopted some form of just-in-time inventory and production, and small business likewise can benefit from its use.

just-in-time inventory system
system of reducing inventory levels to an absolute minimum

Adoption of a just-in-time system necessitates close cooperation with suppliers. That, in turn, involves considerations of supplier location, supplier production schedules, and transportation schedules. All of these affect the firm's ability to obtain materials quickly and in a predictable manner—a necessary condition for using just-in-time inventory.

There is some danger of possible failures in the system. Production may be interrupted or customers may be unhappy because of out-of-stock situations when delays or mistakes occur. If inventory levels are held too low, a firm can suffer because of breakdowns in the operations process or loss of sales resulting from disgruntled customers.

Most firms maintain some safety stock to minimize difficulties of this type. This represents a compromise of the just-in-time inventory philosophy but protects a firm against large or unexpected withdrawals from inventory and delays in delivery of replacement items.

Economic Order Quantity. If a firm could order and carry inventory with no expense other than the cost of the merchandise or material itself, it would be unconcerned about what quantity to order at one time. However, inventory costs are affected by both the cost of purchasing and the cost of carrying inventory. Thus,

$$\left(\begin{array}{c}\text{total}\\\text{inventory costs}\end{array}\right)=\left(\begin{array}{c}\text{total}\\\text{carrying costs}\end{array}\right)+\left(\begin{array}{c}\text{total}\\\text{ordering costs}\end{array}\right)$$

As noted earlier, carrying costs include warehouse space costs, insurance expense, cost of money tied up in inventory, spoilage or obsolescence, and other expenses of this type. Carrying costs increase as inventories increase in size. Ordering costs, on the other hand, include expenses associated with preparation and processing of purchase orders and related expenses of receiving and inspecting the purchased items. The cost of placing an order is a fixed

SMALL BUSINESS IN ACTION

The Impact of Just-in-Time on Small Distributors

As large manufacturing firms have adopted just-in-time production and inventory systems, they have forced changes on the more than 300,000 distributors in the United States. Most distributors are small businesses with less than $5 million in sales and fewer than 30 employees. Under the just-in-time or Kanban system, distributors must work closely with manufacturers to help them meet their inventory needs.

As an example, Continental Glass and Plastic, Inc., is a Chicago distributor supplying containers to Walgreen Laboratories to package health and beauty aids for the drugstore chain. When Walgreen decided to reduce inventory levels by one-third, it gave suppliers a choice of participating in a modified just-in-time delivery program or discontinuing the relationship. Continental chose to stay and now works closely with Walgreen, projecting container needs six months in advance and locking in delivery dates four weeks prior to delivery. In this case, the manufacturer has reduced its inventory by shifting a part of it to the small distributor.

Source: Steven P. Galante, "Distributors Bow to Demands of 'Just-in-Time' Delivery," *The Wall Street Journal* (June 30, 1986), p. 23. Reprinted by permission of *The Wall Street Journal,* © 1986 Dow Jones & Company, Inc. All Rights Reserved Worldwide.

---

economic order quantity
the quantity to be purchased that minimizes total inventory costs

cost, and total ordering costs increase, therefore, as a firm purchases smaller quantities more frequently. Also, quantity discounts, to the extent they are available, favor the placement of larger orders.

The **economic order quantity** is the quantity to be purchased that minimizes total costs; it is the point labeled "EOQ" in Figure 19-4. Notice that it is the lowest point on the total-costs curve and that it coincides with the intersection of the carrying-costs and order-costs curves. In those cases, where sufficient information on costs is available, this point can be calculated with some precision.[1] In all cases, even when the economic order quantity cannot be calculated with precision, the goal is still to avoid both high ordering costs and high carrying costs.

Inventory Accounting Systems

A small business needs a system for keeping tabs on its inventory. The larger the business, the greater is the need. Also, since manufacturers are concerned with three broad categories of inventory (raw materials and supplies, work-in-process, and finished goods), their accounting for inventory is more complex than that for wholesalers and retailers.

Although some record keeping is unavoidable, small firms should emphasize simplicity of control methods. Too much control is as wasteful as it is unnecessary.

physical inventory system
a system for periodic counting of inventory items

Physical Inventory Method. A **physical inventory system** involves an actual count of inventory items. Counting is done in physical units such as

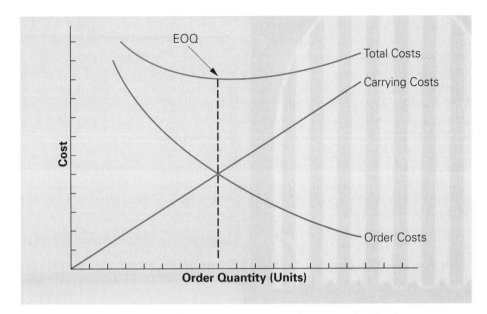

Figure 19-4
Determination of
Economic Order
Quantity

pieces, gallons, boxes, and so on. By using this method, the firm supposedly has an accurate record of its inventory at a given point in time. Some businesses have an annual shutdown to count everything—a complete physical inventory.

In some businesses, the process of taking a physical inventory has been simplified by using computers and bar-code systems. Bar codes are the printed patterns of lines, spaces, and numerals that appear on certain products. The codes can be read with a hand-held wand that transmits data to a computer.

Figure 19-5
Using a Bar-Code
Scanner to Take a
Physical Inventory

An example of its use for inventory purposes is found in the experience of a metal fabricating firm. Before bar coding was instituted at Tate Andale, a Baltimore-based manufacturing firm, recording inventory each year "required 24 people working two days," says Milt Thacker, the company's data-processing manager. "Then it would take 30 to 40 hours in the office to key in the data. With hand-held bar-code scanners, it takes four people eight hours in the warehouse, and manual data entry is eliminated. Not only do we save a tremendous amount of time, but the accuracy of our data is way up."[2]

perpetual inventory system

a system of maintaining a current record of inventory items

Perpetual Inventory Method. A **perpetual inventory system** provides a current record of inventory items. It does not require a physical count of inventory. Periodically, a physical count can be made to assure the accuracy of the perpetual system and to make adjustments for such factors as theft.

Records for a perpetual inventory system can be kept by computer (see Figure 19-6) or by a card system. If the business keeps accurate records of receipt and usage of goods, the firm will always know the number of units on hand. If each receipt and issue is costed, the dollar value of these units is also known.

Use of a perpetual inventory system may be justified in the small factory or the wholesale warehouse. In particular, this is desirable for expensive and critical items—for example, those which could cause significant losses through theft or serious production delays.

Figure 19-6   Computer Printout for Perpetual Inventory System

SHAFER SHOE COMPANY

Item: **Metal Eyelets**							**Maximum No. of Pairs**	**60,000**
							Reorder Point No. of Pairs	**24,000**
							Minimum No. of Pairs	**12,000**

	Receipts			Issue			Balance on Hand		
Date	Pairs	Price per Pair	Cost	Pairs	Price per Pair	Cost	Pairs	Price per Pair	Cost*
Jan.1							14,000	$.00400	$ 56.00
2				2,500	$.00400	$10.00	11,500	.00400	46.00
3	48,000	$.00420	$201.60				59,500	.00416	247.60
3				2,000	.00416	8.32	57,500	.00416	239.28
4				2,100	.00416	8.74	55,400	.00416	230.54
7				2,000	.00416	8.32	53,400	.00416	222.22

*Minor discrepancies in this column are due to 5-place rounding in the preceding column. The records are used by routing and planning clerks to assure an adequate supply of materials and parts to complete any given factory order.

Retail Inventory Valuation Method. The **retail inventory valuation method** was developed primarily for retail stores as a basis for dollar control of merchandise involving a wide variety of items. Such inventory conditions, together with a high volume of sales, preclude the use of perpetual inventory records for each item and also make the use of physical inventory methods time-consuming and unsatisfactory for control.

By using data on inventory cost, retail value, sales volume, purchases, markdowns, and so on, a manager is able to estimate the cost of inventory at the end of an accounting period. Use of this method facilitates the preparation of monthly financial statements. However, the system has weaknesses such as the arduous record keeping for frequent markups and markdowns. Thus, its use should be based on careful analysis and professional advice.

retail inventory valuation method
an inventory control system by which retailers estimate inventory cost from marked selling prices

1. The purchasing cycle includes the receipt and evaluation of a purchase request, location of a source of supply, issuance of the purchase order, follow-up of purchase orders, and verification of purchased items.
2. Policies and practices related to purchasing include reciprocal buying, making or buying parts, substituting materials or merchandise, taking purchase discounts, diversifying sources of supply, forward buying, and scheduled budget buying.
3. Choice of a supplier entails considerations of the supplier's price, quality rating, ability to meet delivery schedules, quality of service, and general reputation. Good relations with suppliers are particularly valuable to small firms.
4. The objectives of inventory control include assured continuous operations, maximum sales, protection of assets, and minimum inventory investment.
5. Maintaining inventory involves a variety of costs, including order costs, carrying costs, and stockout costs. The minimum amount that can be carried depends on the time required to replenish the supply and on the necessary safety stock. Carrying costs are minimized by holding inventory to a minimum, the objective of the just-in-time system. Total costs are minimized by calculating the economic order quantity, the purchase amount that most economically balances large-order costs and small-order costs.
6. A physical inventory system consists of taking an actual count of items on hand and recording the information. A perpetual inventory system does not require an actual count but provides a current record by recording additions and withdrawals. In retail businesses, the cost of inventories may be calculated by using the retail inventory valuation method.

DISCUSSION QUESTIONS

1. Suppose that you, as purchasing agent for a small firm, have read the story about Barry Schacht's purchasing experience in this chapter's Small Business in Action, "Aggressive Purchasing Saves Money," on page 493, and that you have

vowed to find similar savings for your business. Would you shop for the best price on all purchases? How would you decide which ones to shop for most aggressively? Explain.

2. What conditions make purchasing a particularly vital function in any given business? If it is important, can the owner-manager of a small firm safely delegate the authority to buy to a subordinate? Explain.

3. Explain the concept of reciprocal buying.

4. Under what conditions should the small manufacturer make component parts or buy them from others?

5. Compare the arguments for and against concentrating purchases with only one or two suppliers.

6. Compare the potential rewards and dangers of speculative buying. Is it more dangerous for a small firm or a large firm? Why?

7. State the factors governing a small manufacturer's selection of a supplier of a vitally important raw material.

8. In what ways is location a significant factor in the choice of suppliers? Is the closest supplier normally the best choice?

9. Does the maximization of inventory turnover also result in the maximization of sales? Explain.

10. Suppose that a small firm has excess warehouse space. What types of inventory carrying costs would apply to an inventory decision? How would such costs differ for a firm that does not have excessive storage space?

11. Explain and justify the use of the ABC method of inventory analysis. How would it work in an automobile repair shop?

12. What is just-in-time inventory? What are the advantages and dangers of using it in a small firm?

13. Inventory systems are sometimes described as "push" systems or "pull" systems. In which category does just-in-time belong? Explain.

14. What is safety stock and what determines the proper level of safety stock?

15. Explain the basic idea involved in calculating the economic order quantity.

YOU MAKE THE CALL

Situation 1

In a very general sense, a temporary-help employment agency maintains an inventory of service in the form of personnel awaiting assignment. Excel, a temporary-help agency, found that its inventory tended to disappear early each day. If assignments were not readily available, its "temps" would accept offers from other temporary-help agencies.

Excel wanted to have personnel available the moment they were requested by an employer. Much of the time, calls came early the same day that help was desired. The firm faced a dilemma in trying to match this unpredictable demand with its own inventory of temps. If an employer's request came at 10:00 A.M., for example, Excel often found that its best "temps" had already accepted assignments through other agencies. If Excel were to guarantee work, on the other hand, there was a probability that costs would be incurred for unused personnel on days when demand failed to materialize.

Questions

1. How does Excel's present system compare with a just-in-time system?
2. Can the firm solve its problem by smoothing out demand in some way? How?
3. Should temps be guaranteed work? How could this be arranged?
4. If you were a consultant for this firm, how would you recommend they solve this problem?

Situation 2

The owner of a small food products company was confronted with an inventory control dilemma involving differences of opinion among his subordinates. His accountant, with the concurrence of his general manager, had decided to "put some teeth" into the inventory control system by deducting inventory shortages from the pay of route drivers who distributed the products to stores in their respective territories. Each driver was considered responsible for the inventory on his or her truck.

When the first "short" paychecks arrived, drivers were angry. Sharing their concern, their regional manager went first to the general manager and, getting no satisfaction there, then appealed to the owner. The regional manager—the immediate supervisor of the drivers—argued that (a) there was no question that the drivers were honest; (b) he had personally created the inventory control system that was being used; (c) the system was admittedly time-consuming, difficult, and susceptible to clerical mistakes by the driver and also by the office; (d) the system had never been studied by the general manager or the accountant; and (e) it was ethically wrong to make deductions from the small salaries of honest drivers for simple record-keeping errors.

Questions

1. What is wrong, if anything, with the general manager's approach to making sure that drivers do not steal or act carelessly? Is some method of enforcement necessary to be sure the system is followed carefully?
2. Is it wrong to deduct shortages from drivers' paychecks when the records actually show the shortages?
3. How should the owner resolve this dispute?

EXPERIENTIAL EXERCISES

1. Interview an owner-manager regarding purchasing procedures used in her or his business. In your report, compare these procedures with the steps in the purchasing cycle outlined in this chapter.
2. Outline carefully the steps involved in an important purchase you have made personally—a purchase of more than $100, if possible. Compare those steps

with the steps identified in this chapter as part of the purchasing cycle, and explain any differences.

3. Using the ABC inventory system, classify your own personal possessions into these categories. Include at least two items in each category.

4. Interview the manager of your college bookstore (or some other bookstore) regarding the type of inventory control system being used. In your report, include an explanation of methods used to avoid buildup of excessive inventory and any use made of inventory turnover ratios.

REFERENCES TO SMALL-BUSINESS PRACTICES

Bodenstab, Charles J. "Surprise! Surprise!," *Inc.*, Vol. 10, No. 9 (September 1988), p. 135.
    The chief executive officer of Battery and Tire Warehouse, St. Paul, Minnesota, describes the "glitches" in the firm's inventory-control system and efforts over a four-year period to make the system more effective.

Davis, Leila. "Instant Orders," *Nation's Business,* Vol. 78, No. 4 (April 1990), pp. 34–36.
    A number of small firms are turning to a computer technology known as electronic data interchange to place merchandise orders quickly with few or no mistakes.

Marsh, Barbara. "Quick Success for Start-Ups Breeds Special Problems," *The Wall Street Journal* (August 30, 1991), p. B2.
    The special inventory problems of some rapidly growing firms are described.

"President and Chief Operating Officer," *Inc.*, Vol. 10, No. 12 (December 1988), pp. 120–121.
    When Frederick E. Zucker became president of Adept, San Jose, California, he found that inventory had gotten out of hand and that inventory turnover was much lower than the turnover rate in other companies. His efforts to bring inventory under control are described.

Rauen, Christopher. "Buying Groups Deliver Discounts," *Nation's Business,* Vol. 80, No. 5 (May 1992), pp. 41–42.
    Retailers of appliances, furniture, and other products join buying groups to increase their buying clout.

ENDNOTES

1. See an operations management text for formulas and calculations related to the economic order quantity. One example is James B. Dilworth, *Operations Management* (New York: McGraw-Hill, Inc., 1992), pp. 375–379.

2. Leila Davis, "Wider Uses for Bar Codes," *Nation's Business,* Vol. 77, No. 3 (March 1989), p. 34.

PART 6

Financial and Administrative Controls

CHAPTER 20

Understanding Financial Statements and Accounting Systems

SPOTLIGHT ON SMALL BUSINESS

Accounting requirements can place a burden on a small firm. The load is particularly heavy when the small business is inadequately staffed for the accounting function. Frequently, small firms find relief by using outside accounting services.

Thomas Golisano has developed a service to assist these small firms with one specific function—payroll accounting. His company, Paychex, Inc., based in Rochester, New York, has been extremely successful and was ranked 69th on *Forbes* magazine's recent *200 Best Small Companies in America* list. When Golisano started Paychex in 1971, he "just wanted to get 300 payrolls in Rochester and live happily ever after." Currently, Paychex has over 100,000 clients!

Paychex has received strong competition in the accounting service market, but Golisano believes there will continue to be strong demand. He estimates that 80 percent of small businesses still prepare their own payrolls.

Thomas Golisano

Source: Fleming Meeks, "Tom Golisano and the Red Tape Factory," *Forbes,* May 15, 1989. Adapted by permission of FORBES magazine. © Forbes Inc., 1989.

After studying this chapter, you should be able to:
1. Identify important considerations in establishing an accounting system.
2. Name two alternative accounting options.
3. Describe the purpose and procedures related to internal control.
4. Tell what the main financial statements used by businesses—the balance sheet, the income statement, and the cash flow statement—contain.
5. Distinguish between income and cash flow.
6. Use financial ratios to evaluate a company's financial position.

cash method of
  accounting
accrual method of
  accounting
single-entry system
double-entry system
internal control
income statement
operating income
  (earnings before
  interest and taxes)
interest expense
profits before tax
income tax expense

net profits after taxes
balance sheet
equity (net worth)
cash flow statement
cash flows from
  operations
cash flows from
  investment activities
cash flows from financing
  activities
net change in cash flows
direct method
indirect method
liquidity

current ratio
acid-test (quick) ratio
average collection period
accounts receivable
  turnover
inventory turnover
operating income return
  on investment
operating profit margin
total asset turnover
fixed asset turnover
debt ratio
times interest earned ratio
return on equity

Managers must have accurate, meaningful, and timely information if they are to have any hope of making good decisions. This is particularly true when it comes to the need for financial information about the firm's operations. Financial information comes from the company's accounting system.

Experience suggests that ineptness in the accounting system is a primary factor in failure among small enterprises. Many small firms that encounter financial distress have inadequate accounting records. The managers and owners of these companies seem to think they have less need for financial information because of their being intimately involved in all phases of the day-to-day operations. Such a conviction is not only incorrect but also dangerously deceptive. With few exceptions, proprietors of small businesses need to have an understanding of the accounting system within their firms. This chapter, therefore, examines the use of financial statements, in terms of both how they are constructed and how to interpret the information for decision making.

ACCOUNTING ACTIVITIES IN SMALL FIRMS

Very few small-business managers can expect to be expert accountants. But every entrepreneur should know enough about the accounting process, including the financial statements, to recognize which accounting methods will work to the advantage of the business.

Basic Requirements for Accounting Systems

An accounting system structures the flow of financial information from the initial transaction to the points necessary to develop a financial picture of business activity. Exactly where these points are depends on the firm and its financial reporting goals. Conceivably, a few very small firms may not even require formal financial statements. Most small firms, however, need at least monthly financial statements and they ought to be computer-generated.

Fulfillment of Objectives of Accounting Systems. Regardless of the level of sophistication, any accounting system for a small business should accomplish the following objectives:

1. The system should yield an accurate, thorough picture of operating results.
2. The records should permit a quick comparison of current data with prior years' operating results and with budgetary goals.
3. The records should provide financial statements for use by management, bankers, and prospective creditors.
4. The system should facilitate prompt filing of reports and tax returns to regulatory and tax-collecting agencies of the government.
5. The system should reveal employee fraud, theft, waste, and record-keeping errors.

Observance of Accounting Principles. In seeking to develop and interpret financial statements, a manager must remember that certain principles govern the preparation of accounting statements. For example, conservatism is a principle that guides accountants, and the most conservative method available is the one an accountant will typically choose. For instance, inventories are reported at the lower of cost or current market value. Another principle governing the preparation of statements is consistency. This means that a given item on a statement will be handled in the same way every month and every year so that comparability of the data will be assured. Also, the principle of full disclosure compels the accountant to insist that all liabilities be shown and all material facts be presented. This is intended to prevent misleading any investor who might read the firm's statements.

Availability and Quality of Accounting Records. An accounting system provides the framework for managerial control of the firm. The effectiveness of the system rests basically on a well-designed and managed record-keeping system. In addition to the financial statements intended for external use with bankers and investors (the balance sheet, the income statement, and the cash flow statement), the major types of internal accounting records and the financial decisions to which they are related are briefly described in the following list:

1. *Accounts-receivable records.* Records of receivables are vital not only to decisions on credit extension but also for accurate billing and maintenance of good customer relations. An analysis of these records reveals the degree of effectiveness of the firm's credit and collection policies.
2. *Accounts-payable records.* Records of liabilities show what the firm owes, facilitate the taking of cash discounts, and allow payments to be made when due.
3. *Inventory records.* Adequate records are essential to the control and security of inventory items. In addition, they supply information for use in purchasing, maintenance of adequate stock levels, and computation of turnover ratios.
4. *Payroll records.* The payroll records show the total salaries paid to employees and provide the base for computing and paying payroll taxes.
5. *Cash records.* Carefully maintained records showing all receipts and disbursements are necessary to safeguard cash. They provide essential information about cash inflows and outflows and about the cash balances on hand.
6. *Fixed-asset records.* These records show the purchase and the depreciation taken to date, along with other information such as the condition of the asset.
7. *Other records.* Among other accounting records that are vital to the efficient operation of the small business are the insurance register, which shows all policies in force; records of leaseholds; and records covering the firm's investments outside of its business.

Computer software packages are now available that can be used on personal computers. Most of the software packages include the following features:

1. A checkbook that automatically calculates the firm's cash balance, prints checks, and reconciles the account with the bank statement at month end.
2. A cash budget that compares actual expenditures with budgeted expenditures.
3. Automatic preparation of income statements and balance sheets.

Additionally, there are numerous software packages for specialized accounting needs such as graphs, cash-flow analysis, and tax preparation. The small company owner has a wide variety of hardware and software choices. Care should be taken in making buying decisions: The chance of making a mistake is significant. (Computer applications are discussed more fully in Chapter 23.)

As an alternative to account keeping by an employee or a member of the owner's family, a firm may have its financial records kept by a certified public accountant or by a bookkeeping or computer service agency that caters to small businesses. Very small businesses often find it convenient to have the same firm keep the books and prepare the financial statements and tax returns.

Numerous small public accounting firms offer complete accounting services to small businesses. These accounting firms frequently have a great deal to offer the smaller business needing accounting services, and their services have usually been offered at a lower cost than those of the larger accounting firms. However, larger accounting firms are now paying closer attention to the accounting needs of small businesses. The fees charged by these national accounting firms are usually higher than those of the accountant down the street, but discounts are available. While fees are an important consideration in selecting an accountant, there are other major factors in this decision.[1]

Mobile bookkeepers also serve small firms in some areas. They bring a mobile office, including computer equipment, to the premises of the small firm, where they obtain the necessary data and prepare the financial statements. Mobile bookkeeping thereby provides some firms with a fast, inexpensive, and convenient approach to obtaining certain accounting services. "We go after the small companies because they usually can't afford in-house accountants," says Jack Dunn, chairman of one such firm, Kansas City-based Debit One.[2]

Alternative Accounting Options

Accounting records can be kept in just about any form as long as they provide users with the data needed and are legally proper. The small business usually has certain options in selecting accounting systems and accounting methods.

Two such accounting options—cash versus accrual accounting, and single-entry versus double-entry systems—are examined in the following sections. These two alternatives represent only the most basic issues in developing an accounting system.

It is important to note that the accounting options chosen for financial reporting are not always required to be the same as those used for tax account-

Figure 20-1
A Mobile Bookkeeper Works on Site to Prepare Financial Statements for a Small Business

SMALL BUSINESS IN ACTION

Two Sets of Books?

Small-business owners logically use accounting practices that are legal and that minimize tax liabilities. However, good tax strategy is not automatically good business strategy.

David A. Towneson, a small-business accounting specialist in Wakefield, Massachusetts, feels that many of his clients want to deduct too many expenses against revenue when sometimes capitalization is a wiser alternative. "Small startup companies would be wiser to capitalize such costs . . . this boosts reported income, [but] it boosts their asset base, permitting them to borrow more and sell their concern for more."

Towneson recounts the circumstances of one client company that exemplifies his point. This company

lost a chance for a $1-million contract because it had used accelerated depreciation for its equipment. Using straight-line depreciation, the equipment would have been valued on the books at $525,000, or enough to collateralize a $420,000 loan from a bank. But after accelerated depreciation, the books only showed the equipment at $300,000, so the bank would supply only a $240,000 loan. The company needed $400,000 to gear up for the new order. It lost the sale.

Small-business owners should remember that it is acceptable to use different accounting methods for financial reporting and tax reporting. Regarding keeping two sets of books, Mr. Towneson says, "It's well worth it."

Source: Lee Berton, "Dos and Don'ts," *The Wall Street Journal,* June 10, 1988, p. 41R. Reprinted by permission of *The Wall Street Journal,* © Dow Jones & Company, Inc. 1988. All Rights Reserved Worldwide.

ing. This fact is emphasized by the Small Business in Action entitled "Two Sets of Books?"

Cash vs. Accrual Accounting. The major distinction between cash and accrual accounting is the point at which a firm "recognizes" revenue and expenses. The **cash method of accounting** is easier to use and reports revenue and expenses only when cash is received or payment is made. Under the **accrual method of accounting**, revenue and expenses are reported when they are incurred regardless of when the cash is received or payment is made.

The cash method of accounting is sometimes selected by the very small business, as well as those businesses whose receivables move slowly and who want to help their cash flow by avoiding the payment of taxes on income not yet received. However, the cash method does not provide an accurate matching of revenue and expenses.

On the other hand, the accrual method of accounting matches revenues when they are earned against the expenses associated with those revenues. The accrual method involves more record keeping is preferable because it provides a more realistic measure of profitability within an accounting period.

cash method of accounting
transactions are recognized only when cash is received or payment is made

accrual method of accounting
matches revenues when they are earned against the expenses associated with those revenues

Single-Entry vs. Double-Entry Systems. In the very small business, a single-entry record-keeping system is occasionally still found. It is not, however, a system to be recommended to businesses that are striving to grow and become efficient in financial planning. A single-entry system neither incorporates a balance sheet nor directly generates an income statement. A **single-entry system** is basically a checkbook system of receipts and disbursements supported by sales tickets and disbursement receipts.

A **double-entry system** of accounting incorporates journals and ledgers and requires that each transaction be recorded twice in the accounts—hence the name double-entry. There are two major advantages of the double-entry system. First, it has a built-in, self-balancing characteristic. If no math errors have been made, the debits recorded will always equal the credits recorded. Second, transactions are recorded in such a way as to provide a natural flow into finished financial statements.

Introductory accounting textbooks provide considerable information on setting up a double-entry system.[3] Office supply retail stores can provide most of the actual record-keeping journals and ledgers needed. However, relatively simple computerized systems are available that are appropriate for most small firms.

single-entry system

a checkbook system of accounting reflecting only receipts and disbursements

double-entry system

self-balancing accounting system that uses journals and ledgers

Internal Control

As already noted, an effective accounting system is vital to the success of the business. Without the information provided by the accounting system, a manager cannot make informed decisions. However, the quality of a firm's accounting system is dependent on the effectiveness of the internal controls that exist within the company. **Internal control** is a system of checks and balances that plays a key role in safeguarding a firm's assets and enhancing the accuracy and reliability of the financial statements.

Internal control has long been recognized as important in large corporations. However, some owners of smaller companies believe they cannot afford a system of internal controls or that internal controls are not applicable for a firm of their size. Nothing could be further from the truth.

Building internal controls within a small business is difficult, but no less important than for a large company. The absence of internal controls significantly increases the chances of fraud and theft, not to mention bad decisions that can come from inaccurate and untimely accounting information. Effective internal controls are also required if the owners ever need an audit by independent accountants. Certified public accountants are unwilling to express an opinion about a firm's financial statements if adequate internal controls are not present within the company.

Although a complete description of an internal control system is beyond the scope of this chapter, it is important to understand the concept. For instance, one dimension of internal control is to separate employees' duties so that the individual who maintains control over an asset is not the same person

internal control

system of checks and balances that enhances the accuracy and reliability of financial statements

How Internal Controls Helped Solve Cash Flow Problems

Bob Martin owned and managed Martin Distribution, a rapidly growing sports novelty company in its third year of operation, with 25 employees and total assets of over $3 million. Sales forecasts for the future indicated continued growth, but the company was currently experiencing cash flow problems.

Martin hired a local CPA to study the situation. The accountant discovered the following problems:

- In the last three years, the average collection time on the firm's accounts receivable had increased from 30 days to 48 days, and the percentage of accounts receivable that were actually collected had decreased.
- Accounts-receivable write-offs also increased during the same period by 67 percent.
- From the company's bank statements and deposit slips, it was determined that numerous deposits had been made by the company's office manager with a "less cash" notation. In

addition, deposits were not being made on a regular basis.

A significant factor in the problem was the lack of internal control. Credit policies were relaxed. Cash handling was sloppy. Daily deposits were not made. To cover daily expenditures, cash was extracted from bank deposits.

The solution to the problem was relatively simple. Procedures suggested by the CPA included:

- A thorough investigation of the creditworthiness of prospective customers before credit was extended to them.
- Controls that help ensure that sales orders will not be filled without prior credit approval.
- Periodic reviews of credit limits for existing customers.
- Cash deposited intact on a daily basis.

After approximately three months, the percentage of accounts receivable collected increased significantly. Bad debts and sales returns decreased, and profit margins increased. In addition, a strict accountability was established for cash collections and miscellaneous daily cash expenditures.

Source: Jack D. Baker and John A. Marts, "Internal Control for Protection and Profits," *Small Business Forum*, Vol. 8, No. 2 (Fall 1990), p. 32. Reprinted with permission.

recording the transactions in the accounting ledgers. For example, the employee who collects the cash from customers should not be the one who reconciles the bank statement. Other examples of internal control procedures include:

1. Identifying the types of transactions that require the authorization of the owners.
2. Establishing a procedure to ensure that checks presented for signature are accompanied by complete supporting documentation.
3. Limiting access to the accounting records.
4. Sending bank statements directly to the owner.
5. Safeguarding blank checks.

6. Establishing a policy of regular vacations.
7. Controlling access to the computer facilities.[4]

The importance of developing an effective system of internal controls cannot be overemphasized. Special efforts may be needed to implement internal controls in a small company where business procedures are informal and the segregation of duties is difficult because of the limited number of employees. Even so, every effort should be made to develop such controls wherever possible. It is wise to seek the assistance of an accountant to minimize the chance of any problems resulting from the absence of internal controls.[5]

TYPICAL FINANCIAL STATEMENTS

Financial statements consist of certain pieces of important information about the firm's operations that are reported in the form of (a) an income statement, (b) a balance sheet, and (c) a cash flow statement. We will look at each of these statements in turn.

The Income Statement

income statement
financial statement showing the profit or loss from a firm's operations over a period of time

operating income (earnings before interest and taxes)
profits before interest and taxes are paid

interest expense
the interest amounts owed to lenders on borrowed money

profits before tax
the amount of a firm's profits before paying taxes.

income tax expense
a firm's tax liability

net profits after taxes
income that may be distributed to the owners or reinvested in the company

The main elements of an **income statement** or *profit and loss statement* are shown in Figure 20-2. The top part of the income statement, beginning with sales and continuing down through **operating income** or **earnings before interest and taxes,** is affected solely by the firm's operating decisions. These decisions involve such matters as sales, cost of goods sold, marketing expenses, and general and administrative expenses. However, no financing costs are included to this point.

Below operating income, the results of the firm's financing decisions are shown along with the taxes that are due on the company's income. Here the company's **interest expense** is shown, which is the direct result of the amount of debt incurred and the interest rates charged by the lenders. The resulting **profits before tax** and the tax rates imposed on the company then determine the amount of the tax liability, or the **income tax expense.** The final number, the **net profits after taxes,** is the income that may be distributed to the company's owners or reinvested in the company, provided there is cash available to do so. (As we shall see later, merely because there are profits does not necessarily mean there is any cash.)

An example of an income statement for the LM Manufacturing Company is provided in Table 20-1 (page 516). The firm had sales of $830,200 for the 12-month period ending December 31, 1993. The cost of manufacturing their product was $539,750, resulting in a gross profit of $290,450. The firm had $190,750 in operating expenses, which involved selling expenses, general and administrative expenses, and depreciation expenses. After deducting the operating expenses, the firm's operating income (earnings before interest and taxes) amounted to $99,700. To this point, we have calculated the profits resulting only from operating activities, as opposed to financing decisions, such as

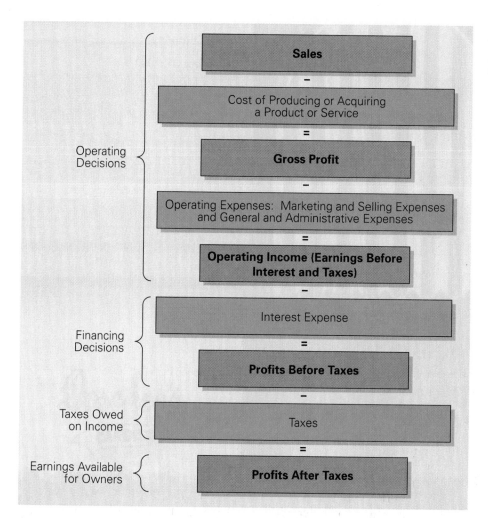

Figure 20-2
The Income
Statement: An
Overview

how much debt or equity is used to finance the company's operations. This amount represents the income generated as if LM Manufacturing were an all-equity company.

We next deduct LM's interest expense (the amount paid for using debt financing) of $20,000 to arrive at the company's profit before tax of $79,700. Lastly, we deduct the income taxes of $17,390 to leave the net profit after tax of $62,310. At the bottom of the income statement, we see the common dividends paid by the firm to its owners in the amount of $15,000, leaving $47,310, which eventually increases LM Manufacturing's retained earnings in the balance sheet.

The Balance Sheet

While the income statement reports the results from operating the business for a period of time, such as a year, the **balance sheet** provides a snapshot of the

balance sheet
financial statement that shows a firm's assets and liabilities at a specific point in time

Table 20-1
Income Statement
for LM
Manufacturing

The LM Manufacturing Company
Income Statement
for the Year Ending December 31, 1993

Sales		$830,200
Cost of goods sold		539,750
Gross profit		$290,450
Operating expenses:		
Marketing expenses	$90,750	
General and administrative expenses	71,800	
Depreciation	28,200	
Total operating expenses		$190,750
Operating income		$99,700
Interest expense		20,000
Profit before tax		$79,700
Income tax		17,390
Profit after tax		$62,310
Dividends paid		15,000
Change in retained earnings in the balance sheet		$47,310

firm's financial position at a specific point in time. Thus, a balance sheet captures the cumulative effect of prior decisions down to a single point in time.

The difference between the timing of an income statement and a balance sheet may be represented graphically as shown in Figure 20-3. Here we see five periods of operations, 1989 through 1993. There would be an income statement for the period of January 1 through December 31 for each year's operations and a balance sheet reporting the company's financial position as of December 31 of each year. Thus, the balance sheet on December 31, 1993, is a statement of the company's financial position at that particular date, which is the result of all financial transactions since the company began its operations.

Figure 20-4 (page 518) shows us the basic ingredients of a balance sheet. The assets fall into three categories:

1. Current assets, such as cash, accounts receivable, and inventories.
2. Fixed or long-term assets, such as equipment, buildings, and land.
3. Any other assets used by the company.

In reporting the dollar amounts of these various assets, the conventional practice is to report the value of the assets and liabilities on a historical cost basis.

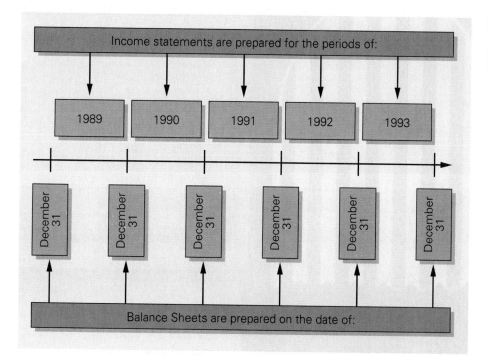

Figure 20-3
Timing of Income
Statement Vs.
Balance Sheet

There are some exceptions, such as inventory being shown at the lower of cost or current market value. Thus, the balance sheet is, for the most part, not intended to represent the current market value of the company; it merely reports the historical transactions at cost. Determining a fair value of the business is a more complicated matter.

The remaining part of the balance sheet, headed "Liabilities and Equity," indicates how the firm has financed its investments in assets. That is, assets must be financed either with debt (liabilities) or equity capital. The debt consists of such sources as credit extended from suppliers or a loan from a bank. If the firm is a sole proprietorship, the **equity** is the owner's personal investment in the company and also the profits that have been retained within the business from all prior periods. The terms *equity* and **net worth** are frequently used interchangeably. In a partnership, the equity represents the partners' contributions to the business and the cumulative retained profits. For a corporation, equity includes funds received from the purchase of the company's stock by investors and the retained profits to that point in time.

Balance sheets for the LM Manufacturing Company are presented in Table 20-2 (page 519) for both December 31, 1992, and December 31, 1993. By referring to the two balance sheets, we can see the financial position of the firm at both the beginning and end of 1993. By examining these two balance sheets, along with the income statement for 1993, we will have a more complete picture of the firm's operations as reflected in its financial statements.

equity (net worth)
all owner's investments in a company, and the profits retained in the firm

Figure 20-4
The Balance Sheet:
An Overview

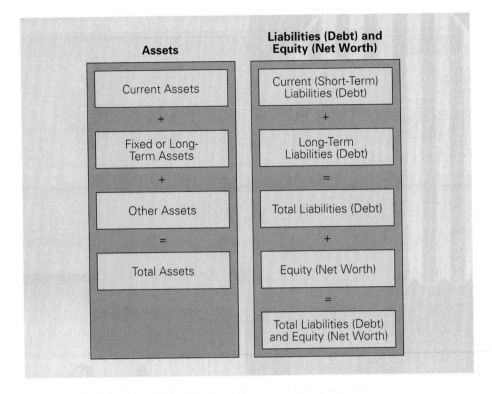

We are then able to see what the firm looked like at the beginning of 1993 (balance sheet on December 31, 1992), what happened during the year (income statement for 1993), and the final outcome at the end of the year (balance sheet on December 31, 1993). The perspective of 1993 is shown graphically in Figure 20-5 (page 520).

The balance sheet data for the LM Manufacturing Company shows that the firm began 1993 (December 31, 1992) with $804,000 in total assets and concluded the year (December 31, 1993) with total assets of $927,000. Most of the assets are invested in plant and equipment, amounting to $404,000 in 1992 and $454,800 in 1993. The investments in inventories were $177,000 and $211,400 at the end of 1992 and 1993, respectively. It was in these two accounts that most of the growth in the firm's assets occurred. The financing of the growth in assets came mostly from increased borrowing (long-term notes payable) and from the company's 1993 profits, as reflected in the increase in retained earnings.

cash flow statement
financial statement
that shows changes
in a firm's cash
position over a given
period of time

The Cash Flow Statement

The third key financial statement used in business is the **cash flow statement**. We could limit our study to interpreting the statement and not get into the computations. However, experience suggests that our understanding of cash

Table 20-2
Balance Sheets for
LM Manufacturing

The LM Manufacturing Company
Balance Sheets
December 31, 1992 and 1993

ASSETS

	1992	1993
Current assets:		
Cash	$39,000	$44,000
Accounts receivable	70,500	78,000
Inventories	177,000	211,400
Other current assets	13,500	13,800
Total current assets	$300,000	$347,200
Fixed assets;		
Land	$70,000	$70,000
Gross plant and equipment	759,000 838,000	
Accumulated depreciation	(355,000) (383,200)	
Net plant and equipment	$404,000	$454,800
Total fixed assets	$474,000	$524,800
Patents	30,000	55,000
TOTAL ASSETS	$804,000	$927,000

LIABILITIES AND EQUITY

	1992	1993
Current liabilities:		
Accounts payable	$60,810	$76,110
Income tax payable	12,000	17,390
Accrued wages and salaries	3,400	3,900
Interest payable	2,000	2,500
Total current liabilities	$78,210	$99,900
Long-term notes payable	146,000	200,000
Total liabilities	$224,210	$299,900
Common stock	$300,000	$300,000
Retained earnings	279,790	327,100
Total stockholders' equity	$579,790	$627,100
TOTAL LIABILITIES AND EQUITY	$804,000	$927,000

Figure 20-5
Relationship
Between Balance
Sheet and Income
Statement

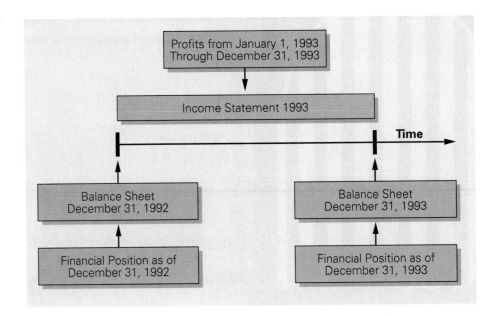

flows is limited if we do not know what drives the numbers. Also, without the computations, we will not be able to grasp the relationship between a firm's profits and its cash flows—a relationship of considerable importance.

Types of Cash Flow Activities. The primary cash flow categories are presented in Figure 20-6. The cash flows generated are divided into three main areas: (1) cash flows from operations, (2) investments made by the firm, and (3) financing transactions, such as issuing stock, or borrowing or repaying debt.

Table 20-3 (page 522) shows a cash flow statement for the LM Manufacturing Company. The data needed to construct a cash flow statement comes from two sources: (1) the two balance sheets for the firm, both at the beginning of 1993 (actually December 31, 1992) and at the end of 1993, and (2) the income statement for 1993. Let's look at the computations required in determining the cash flow for the LM Manufacturing Company. To do so, we will need to make frequent use of the company's income statement (Table 20-1) and the balance sheets (Table-20-2).

cash flows from operations
collections from customers and payments related to operations, interest, and taxes

Cash Flows from Operations. As already noted, a firm's **cash flows from operations** consist of (1) collections from customers; (2) payments to suppliers for the purchase of materials; (3) other operating cash outflows, such as marketing expenses, administrative expenses, and interest payments; and (4) cash tax payments.

Figure 20-6
The Cash Flow
Statement: An
Overview

Cash Flow from Operations, Which Includes:
Cash Collected from Customers
– Cash Paid to Suppliers
– Operating Cash Outflows
(Marketing and Administrative Expenses)
– Cash Tax Payments

minus or plus
Investments Made or Reduced
plus or minus

Financing Receipts or Payments, Which Include:
+ Receipts from New Stock Issue
+ Increased Borrowing
– Repayment of Debt Principal
– Interest Payments
– Dividend Payments

equals
Change in Cash Balances

---

1. *Collections from customers.* Our beginning point is to determine how much the firm has collected from its customers. We know how much they sold, but we want to know what was actually collected in cash. To find this number, we simply take the sales and subtract the change in accounts receivable. For example, if a firm had $200,000 in sales during a year, but its accounts receivable increased from $50,000 to $70,000, or by $20,000, that means that $20,000 of the sales were not collected. Thus, the firm's collections were only $180,000. For LM Manufacturing, sales were $830,200, but accounts receivable increased $7,500, from $70,500 to $78,000. (See the change in receivables in Table 20-2.)   Thus, actual collections were $822,700 ($830,200 – $7,500).

2. *Payments to suppliers.* When a firm purchases products from suppliers, the firm's inventories are increased. When the product is sold, the inventory decreases and cost of goods sold in the income statement increases. Thus, total purchases of products from suppliers are reflected in the cost of goods sold plus any increase in inventories. Then the firm will either pay for the products or rely on additional credit from suppliers, which is shown in accounts payable in the balance sheet. The actual payment to suppliers may therefore be calculated as follows:

$$\begin{pmatrix} \text{Payment} \\ \text{to suppliers} \end{pmatrix} = \begin{pmatrix} \text{Cost of} \\ \text{goods sold} \end{pmatrix} + \begin{pmatrix} \text{Change in} \\ \text{inventories} \end{pmatrix} - \begin{pmatrix} \text{Change in} \\ \text{accounts} \\ \text{payable} \end{pmatrix}$$

Table 20-3
Cash Flow
Statement for LM
Manufacturing

**The LM Manufacturing Company
Cash Flow Statement
for the Year Ending December 31, 1993**

CASH FLOWS FROM OPERATIONS

Cash inflows received from customers:

Net sales	$830,200
Less change in accounts receivable	−7,500
Cash inflows from customers	$822,700

Cash paid to suppliers:

Cost of goods sold	($539,750)
Plus change in inventory	(34,400)
Less change in accounts payable	15,300
Cash paid to suppliers	($558,850)

Other operating cash outflows:

Marketing expenses	($90,750)
General and administrative expenses	(71,800)
Less change in accrued expenses	500
Interest expense	(20,000)
Less change in interest payable	500
Total other operating cash outflows and interest payments	($181,550)

Cash tax payments:

Provision for taxes	($17,390)
Less change in accrued taxes	5,390
Cash tax payments	($12,000)
NET CASH FLOW FROM OPERATIONS	$70,300

CASH FLOWS—INVESTMENT ACTIVITIES

Purchase of fixed assets	($79,000)
Purchase of other current assets	(300)
Purchase of patents	(25,000)
NET CASH USED FOR INVESTMENTS	($104,300)

CASH FLOWS—FINANCING ACTIVITIES

Proceeds from long-term debt	$54,000
Common stock dividends	(15,000)
NET CASH PROVIDED (USED) BY FINANCING ACTIVITIES	**$39,000**
NET CHANGE IN CASH	$5,000

For the LM Manufacturing Company, cost of goods sold for 1993 were $539,750; inventories increased from $177,000 to $211,400, or by $34,400; and accounts payable increased $15,300, from $60,810 to $76,110. Thus, payments to suppliers were $558,850, computed as follows:

$$\left(\begin{array}{c}\text{Payment}\\\text{to Suppliers}\end{array}\right)=\left(\begin{array}{c}\text{Cost of}\\\text{goods sold}\end{array}\right)+\left(\begin{array}{c}\text{Change in}\\\text{inventories}\end{array}\right)-\left(\begin{array}{c}\text{Change in}\\\text{accounts}\\\text{payable}\end{array}\right)$$

$$= \$539,750 + \$34,400 - \$15,300$$
$$= \$558,850$$

3. *Other operating cash outflows.* We next calculate the actual cash outflows for operating expenses and any interest expense shown in the income statement. We only include those expenses that are cash outflows, and not such items as depreciation expense. We also adjust for any change in accrued expenses, an indication that some of the reported expenses were not really paid, but accrued as a liability. We see in Table 20-3 that the "other" operating cash outflows and interest payments come to $181,550, the combination of marketing expenses, general and administrative expenses (without any depreciation expense), and interest expenses. These amounts are adjusted for the $500 change in accrued expenses and the $500 change in interest payable to account for additional expenses recognized but not yet paid.

4. *Cash tax payments.* The tax expense shown in a firm's income statement is often not the actual amount paid at that time. The provision for taxes in the income statement is the amount attributable to income reported, but the company may be permitted to defer the payment. Thus, the cash payment would equal the provision for taxes reported in the income statement less (plus) any increase (decrease) in accrued or deferred taxes in the balance sheet. For LM Manufacturing, the cash tax payment is $12,000, the $17,390 in the provision for taxes less the $5,390 increase in deferred taxes, as reflected in a comparison of the two balance sheets in Table 20-2.

The net cash flow from operations is shown to be $70,300, the sum of these four cash flows.

Cash Flows from Investment Activities. Now that we have calculated the cash flows that were generated from the day-to-day operations, we next want to determine **cash flows from investment activities**—the amount of cash used for investments by the LM Manufacturing Company. As shown in Table 20-3, $104,300 was expended for investments during 1993, including $300 for other current assets (an increase from $13,500 to $13,800). In addition, $79,000 was spent for fixed assets (an increase from $759,000 to $838,000

cash flows from investment activities cash used for investments

in the *gross* fixed assets) and $25,000 for patents (increasing from $30,000 to $55,000 in the balance sheet).

Cash Flows from Financing Activities.

cash flows from financing activities
cash flows to or from a firm's creditors and investors, excluding interest payments

The last area of cash flows deals with **cash flows from financing activities**, including any cash inflows or outflows to or from the firm's investors, excluding interest payments. For the LM Manufacturing Company, the firm received a net positive cash flow from financing activities in the amount of $39,000. (The company borrowed $54,000 in long-term debt, but paid out $15,000 in common stock dividends.)

Summary of Cash Flows.

net change in cash flows
the net change in cash flows resulting from operations, investment, and financing activities

We can now combine the cash flows from operations, investments, and financing to obtain the **net change in cash flow**. We may summarize the cash flows for the LM Manufacturing Company as follows:

Cash flows from operations:	
Collections from customers	$822,700
Payments to suppliers	(558,850)
Other operating cash flows	(181,550)
Cash tax payments	(12,000)
Total cash flows from operations	70,300
Cash flows from investment activities	(104,300)
Cash flows from financing activities	39,000
NET CHANGE IN CASH FLOWS	$5,000

Measuring Cash Flows from Operations: An Alternative Approach.

direct method
a measurement of cash flows from operations that starts at the top of the income statement

indirect method
a measurement of cash flows from operations that starts at the bottom of the income statement

The format used in Table 20-3 to measure cash flow from operations is called the **direct method**. It begins with the cash flows collected from the firm's customers and then subtracts the different cash outflows occurring in regular operations of the business, such as the money paid to suppliers and for employee wages, just to mention two examples. We could also measure cash flows from operations by the **indirect method**. This approach, which gives us the same answer as the direct method, is shown in Table 20-4. Here, we see that the indirect method begins with net income and then adds back expenses that did not result in a cash outflow for the period such as depreciation. Also, it adjusts for changes in the current assets and current liabilities that relate to a firm's operations. So, in a sense, the two methods for arriving at cash flow from operations differ in terms of whether we start at the top (direct method) or the bottom (indirect method) of the income statement. Both methods simply convert the firm's statement of net income to its cash flow equivalent.

Cash Flows and Profits.

As a final thought about measuring cash flows, there is a popular belief that income plus depreciation is a reasonable measure of a company's cash flows. For instance, taking net profit after tax for LM Manufacturing Company of $62,310 and adding back depreciation of $28,200 gives us $90,510. Given conventional thought, someone might be tempted to use this amount as an estimate of the firm's cash flows. However, from the cash flow statement, we can see that the net cash flow was only $5,000. Thus, we can conclude that a firm's cash flows are more complicated than merely taking income and adding back depreciation. The changes in asset balances resulting from growth are just as important in determining the firm's cash flows as are profits, sometimes even more important. Hence, the owner-manager of a small growth company is well advised to think about both profits and cash flows.

FINANCIAL RATIO ANALYSIS

Having looked at the three primary financial statements, we next want to restate the data in relative terms (ratios) so that we may better understand the significance of the data. Ratios permit us to identify the financial strengths and

The LM Manufacturing Company **The Indirect Method for Measuring Cash Flow from Operations** **for the Year Ending December 31, 1993**	
Net income available to common stockholders (from the income statement)	$62,310
Add (deduct) to reconcile net income to net cash flow Depreciation expense	28,200
Less:	
Increase in accounts receivable	(7,500)
Increase in inventories	(34,400)
Plus:	
Increase in accounts payable	15,300
Increase in accrued wages	500
Increase in accrued taxes	5,390
Increase in interest payable	500
NET CASH FLOW FROM OPERATIONS	$70,300

Table 20-4
Indirect Method for Measuring Cash Flow for LM Manufacturing

weaknesses of the company by making comparisons to industry norms and by looking at changes in the ratios over time. Typically, we use industry norms published by firms such as Dun & Bradstreet or Robert Morris Associates.[6]

Using Ratios to Answer Questions About Operations

In learning about ratios, we could simply study the different types or categories of ratios, or we could use ratios to answer important questions about a firm's operations. We prefer the latter approach, and choose the following four questions as a map in using financial ratios:

1. How liquid is the firm?
2. Is management generating adequate operating profits on the firm's assets?
3. How is the firm financing its assets?
4. Are the owners (stockholders) receiving adequate return on their investment?

liquidity
the ability of a firm to meet maturing debt obligations

How Liquid Is the Firm? The **liquidity** of a business is defined as its ability to meet maturing debt obligations. That is, does or will the firm have the resources to pay creditors when debts come due?

There are two ways to answer the question. First, we can look at the firm's assets that are relatively liquid in nature and compare them to the amount of the debt coming due in the near term. Second, we can look at the timeliness with which such liquid assets are being converted into cash.

Measuring Liquidity: Approach 1. The first approach compares (a) cash and the assets that should be converted into cash within the year against (b) the debt (liabilities) that is coming due and payable within the year. The assets here are the current assets, and the debt is the current liabilities in the balance sheet. Thus, we can use the following measure, called the **current ratio**, to estimate a company's relative liquidity:

current ratio
the measure of a company's relative liquidity

$$\text{Current ratio} = \frac{\text{Current assets}}{\text{Current liabilities}}$$

Furthermore, remembering that the three primary current assets include cash, accounts receivable, and inventories, we can make our measure of liquidity more restrictive by excluding inventories, the least liquid of the current assets, in the numerator. This revised ratio is called the **acid-test (quick) ratio,** and is calculated as follows:

acid-test (quick) ratio
a measure of liquidity that excludes inventories

$$\text{Acid-test ratio} = \frac{\text{Current assets} - \text{Inventories}}{\text{Current liabilities}}$$

We can demonstrate the computations of the current ratio and the acid-test ratio by using the LM Manufacturing Company's 1993 balance sheet (Table 20-

2). These calculations and the industry norms or averages shown in the boxes, as reported by Robert Morris Associates, are as follows:[7]

	LM Manufacturing	**Industry Average**

$$\text{Current ratio} = \frac{\text{Current assets}}{\text{Current liabilities}}$$

$$= \frac{\$347,200}{\$99,900} = 3.48 \qquad \boxed{2.70}$$

$$\text{Acid-test ratio} = \frac{\text{Current assets} - \text{Inventories}}{\text{Current liabilities}}$$

$$= \frac{\$347,200 - \$211,400}{\$99,900} = 1.36 \qquad \boxed{1.25}$$

Thus, in terms of the current ratio and the acid-test ratio, LM Manufacturing is more liquid than the average firm in its industry. LM Manufacturing has $3.48 in current assets relative to every $1 in current liabilities (debt), compared to $2.70 for a "typical" firm in the industry. The firm has $1.36 in current assets less inventories per $1 of current debt, compared to $1.25 for the industry norm. While both ratios suggest that the firm is more liquid, the current ratio appears to suggest more liquidity than the acid-test ratio. Why might this be the case? Simply put, LM has more inventories relative to current debt than do most other firms. Which ratio should be given greater weight depends on our confidence in the liquidity of the inventories. We shall return to this question shortly.

Measuring Liquidity: Approach 2. The second view of liquidity examines the firm's ability to convert accounts receivable and inventory into cash on a timely basis. The conversion of accounts receivable into cash may be measured by computing how long it takes on average to collect the firm's receivables. That is, how many days of sales are outstanding in the form of accounts receivable? We may answer this question by computing the **average collection period**:

average collection period
the average time taken to collect acounts receivable

$$\text{Average collection period} = \frac{\text{Accounts receivable}}{\text{Daily credit sales}}$$

For LM Manufacturing, the average collection period, if we assume that all sales are credit sales, as opposed to some cash sales, is 34.3 days, compared to an industry norm of 35 days:

	LM Manufacturing	**Industry Average**

$$\text{Average collection period} = \frac{\text{Accounts receivable}}{\text{Daily credit sales}}$$

$$= \frac{\$78,000}{\$830,200 \div 365} = 34.30 \qquad \boxed{35}$$

Thus, the company collects its receivables in about the same number of days as the average firm in the industry. Accounts receivable it would appear are of reasonable liquidity when viewed from the perspective of the length of time required to convert receivables into cash.

We could have reached the same conclusion by measuring how many times accounts receivable are "rolled over" during a year, that being the **accounts receivable turnover.** For instance, LM Manufacturing turns its receivables over 10.64 times a year, that being:

accounts receivable turnover
the number of times accounts receivable "roll over" during a year

	LM Manufacturing	**Industry Average**

$$\text{Accounts receivable turnover} = \frac{\text{Credit sales}}{\text{Accounts receivable}}$$

$$= \frac{\$830,200}{\$78,000} = 10.64 \qquad \boxed{10.43}$$

(We could also measure the accounts receivable turnover by dividing 365 days by the average collection period: $365/34.30 = 10.64$.)

Whether we use average collection period or the accounts receivable turnover, the conclusion is the same: LM Manufacturing is comparable to the average firm in the industry when it comes to the collection of receivables.

We now want to know the same thing for inventories that we just determined for accounts receivable: How many times are we turning over inventories during the year? In this manner, we gain some insight about the liquidity of the inventories. The **inventory turnover** ratio is calculated as follows:

inventory turnover
the number of times inventories "roll over" during a year

$$\text{Inventory turnover} = \frac{\text{Cost of goods sold}}{\text{Inventory}}$$

Note that sales in this ratio are being measured at the firm's cost, as opposed to the full market value when sold. From the standpoint of logic, since the inventory (the denominator) is at cost, we want to measure sales (the numerator) also on a cost basis. Otherwise, our answer would be biased. (As a practical matter, however, we may at times need to use sales instead of cost of goods sold. Most suppliers of industry norm data use sales in the numerator. Thus, for consistency in our comparisons, we too may need to use sales.)

The inventory turnover for LM Manufacturing, along with the industry norm, is as follows:

	LM Manufacturing	**Industry Average**

$$\text{Inventory turnover} = \frac{\text{Cost of goods sold}}{\text{Inventory}}$$

$$= \frac{\$539,750}{\$211,400} = 2.55 \qquad \boxed{4.00}$$

We may have just discovered a significant problem for LM Manufacturing. It appears that the firm carries excessive inventory. That is, LM generates only $2.55 in sales (at cost) for every $1 of inventory, compared to $4 in sales for the average firm. Going back to the current ratio and the acid-test ratio, we remember that the current ratio made the firm look better than did the acid-test ratio, which means that LM Manufacturing's inventory is a larger component of the current ratio than it is for other firms. Now we see that we are carrying excessive inventory, maybe even some obsolete inventory.

Is Management Generating Adequate Operating Profits on the Firm's Assets?

A second relevant question is: Are profits sufficient relative to the assets being invested? The question is similar to a question one might ask about the interest being earned on a savings account at the bank. When you invest $1,000 in a savings account and receive $60 in interest during the year, you are earning a 6 percent return on your investment ($60 ÷ $1,000 = 6%). With respect to LM Manufacturing, we want to know something similar: the rate of return management is earning on the firm's assets.

In answering this question, we have several choices as to how we measure profits: gross profits, operating profits, or net profits after tax. The gross profits measure is not an acceptable choice because it does not include some important information, such as the cost of marketing and distributing the firm's product. Thus, we should choose between operating profits and net profits. For our purposes, we prefer to use the operating profits as our measure because it is independent of the company's financing policies. Since financing is explicitly considered in the next question, we want to isolate only the operating aspects of the company's profits at this point. In this way, we are able to compare the profitability of firms with different debt-to-equity mixes. Therefore, to examine the level of operating profits relative to the assets, we like to use the **operating income return on investment (OIROI):**

operating income return on investment (OIROI) a measure of operating profits relative to assets

$$\text{Operating income return on investment} = \frac{\text{Operating income}}{\text{Total assets}}$$

The operating return on investment for LM Manufacturing, and the corresponding industry norm, is as follows:

	LM Manufacturing	**Industry Average**
$\text{Operating income return on investment} = \dfrac{\text{Operating income}}{\text{Total assets}}$		
$= \dfrac{\$99,700}{\$927,000} = 10.76\%$		13.2%

Thus, we see that LM Manufacturing is not earning a return on investment equivalent to the average firm in the industry. For some reason, LM Manufacturing's managers are not generating as much income on each dollar of assets as are their competitors.

If we were the managers of LM Manufacturing, we would not be satisfied with merely knowing that we are not earning a competitive return on the firm's assets. We would also want to know *why we are below average*. For more understanding, we could separate the operating income return on investment, OIROI, into two important pieces, the operating profit margin and the total asset turnover. The **operating profit margin** is determined by dividing operating income by sales. The **total asset turnover** is found by dividing sales by total assets. The firm's OIROI is a multiple of these two ratios, and it may be shown algebraically as follows:

operating profit margin
profits derived from operations, divided by sales

total asset turnover
a measure of the efficiency with which a firm's assets are used to generate sales

$$OIROI = \left(\begin{array}{c} \text{Operating} \\ \text{profit margin} \end{array} \right) \times \left(\begin{array}{c} \text{Total asset} \\ \text{turnover} \end{array} \right)$$

or more completely,

$$OIROI = \left(\frac{\text{Operating income}}{\text{Sales}} \right) \times \left(\frac{\text{Sales}}{\text{Total assets}} \right)$$

Five factors or "driving forces" affect the operating profit margin and thus the OIROI. These driving forces are:

1. The number of units of product sold.
2. The average selling price for each product unit.
3. The cost of manufacturing or acquiring the firm's product.
4. The ability to control general and administrative expenses.
5. The ability to control the expenses in marketing and distributing the firm's product.

These influences should become apparent if we look at the income statement and think about what is involved in determining the firm's operating profits or income.

Total asset turnover is a function of how efficiently management is using the firm's assets to generate sales. If Company *A* can generate $3 in sales with $1 in assets compared to $2 in sales per asset dollar by Company *B*, we can say that Company *A* is using its assets more efficiently in generating sales. This is a major determinant in the return on investment.

We can compute LM Manufacturing's operating profit margin and total asset turnover as follows:

	LM Manufacturing	**Industry Average**

$$\text{Operating profit margin} = \frac{\text{Operating income}}{\text{Sales}}$$

$$= \frac{\$99,700}{\$830,200} = 12.01\% \qquad \boxed{11\%}$$

$$\text{Total asset turnover} = \frac{\text{Sales}}{\text{Total assets}}$$

$$= \frac{\$830,200}{\$927,000} = 0.90 \qquad \boxed{1.20}$$

Recalling that:

$$\text{OIROI} = \left(\begin{array}{c} \text{Operating} \\ \text{Profit margin} \end{array} \right) \times \left(\begin{array}{c} \text{Total asset} \\ \text{turnover} \end{array} \right),$$

we see that for LM Manufacturing,

$$\text{OIROI} = 12.01\% \times 0.896 = 10.76\%$$

and for the industry,

$$\text{OIROI} = 11\% \times 1.20 = \boxed{13.2\%}$$

Clearly, LM Manufacturing is competitive when it comes to keeping costs and expenses in line relative to sales. as reflected by the operating profit margin. In other words, its managers are performing satisfactorily in managing the five "driving forces" of the operating profit margin listed earlier. However, when we look at the total asset turnover, we can see why the firm's managers are less than competitive in terms of its operating income return on investment. The firm is not using its assets efficiently. LM Manufacturing generates slightly less than $.90 in sales per dollar of assets, while the competition produces $1.20 in sales from every dollar in assets. Here is the company's problem.

We should not stop here with our analysis. We now know the basic problem, but we should dig deeper. We have concluded that the assets are not being used efficiently, but now we should try to determine which assets are the problem. Are we overinvested in all assets, or more so in accounts receivable or inventory or fixed assets? To answer this question, we merely examine the turnover ratios for each respective asset. We have already illustrated the first two ratios—accounts receivable turnover and inventory turnover. The third ratio—**fixed asset turnover**—is found by dividing sales by fixed assets. Thus, these three ratios are as follows:

fixed asset turnover
the ratio of sales to fixed assets

	LM Manufacturing	**Industry Average**

Accounts receivable:

$$\frac{\text{Credit sales}}{\text{Accounts receivable}} \qquad \frac{\$830,200}{\$78,000} = 10.64 \qquad \boxed{10.43}$$

Inventories:

$$\frac{\text{Cost of goods sold}}{\text{Inventory}} \qquad \frac{\$539,750}{\$211,400} = 2.55 \qquad \boxed{4.00}$$

Fixed assets:

$$\frac{\text{Sales}}{\text{Fixed assets}} \qquad \frac{\$830,200}{\$524,800} = 1.58 \qquad \boxed{2.50}$$

LM Manufacturing's problems are now even clearer. The company has excessive inventories, which we had known from our earlier discussions. Also, there is too large an investment in fixed assets for the sales being produced. It appears that these two asset categories are not being managed well. The consequence is a lower operating income return on investment.

How Is the Firm Financing its Assets? We shall return to the firm's profitability shortly. For now, however, we turn our attention to the matter of how the firm is financed. The basic issue is the use of debt versus equity. Are the firm's assets financed more by debt or by equity? In answering this question, we will use two ratios (many more could be used). First, we will simply ask what percentage of the firm's assets are financed by debt, including both short-term and long-term debt. The remaining percentage must be financed by equity. We compute the **debt ratio** as follows:

debt ratio

the percentage of a firm's assets that are financed by debt

$$\text{Debt ratio} = \frac{\text{Total debt}}{\text{Total assets}}$$

The relationship may be stated in terms of debt to equity, rather than debt to total assets. We come to the same conclusion with either ratio.

For LM Manufacturing, debt as a percentage of total assets is 32 percent, compared to an industry norm of 40 percent. The computation is as follows:

LM Manufacturing	**Industry Average**

$$\text{Debt ratio} = \frac{\text{Total debt}}{\text{Total assets}}$$

$$= \frac{\$299,900}{\$927,000} = 32\% \qquad \boxed{40\%}$$

Thus, LM Manufacturing uses somewhat less debt than the average firm in the industry.

Our second perspective regarding the firm's financing decisions comes by looking at the income statement. When we borrow money, there is a minimum requirement that the firm pay the interest on the debt. Thus, it is informative to compare the amount of operating income that is available to pay the interest with the amount of interest that must be paid. Stated as a ratio, we compute the number of times we are earning our interest. Thus, a **times interest earned** ratio is commonly used when examining the firm's debt position. This ratio is computed in the following manner:

$$\text{Times interest earned} = \frac{\text{Operating income}}{\text{Interest}}$$

times interest earned
the ratio of operating income to interest charges

For LM Manufacturing,

LM Manufacturing	Industry Average

$$\text{Times interest earned} = \frac{\text{Operating income}}{\text{Interest}}$$

$$= \frac{\$99,700}{\$20,000} = 4.99$$ $\boxed{4.00}$

LM Manufacturing is better able to service its interest expense than most firms. We should remember, however, that interest is not paid with income but with cash. Also, the firm may be required to repay some of the debt principal as well as the interest. Thus, the times interest earned is only a crude measure of the firm's capacity to service its debt. Nevertheless, it does give us a general indication of a company's debt capacity.

Are the Owners (Stockholders) Receiving an Adequate Return on Their Investment? Our last remaining question looks at the accounting return on the equity investment. That is, we want to know if the earnings available to the firm's owners (or stockholders) are attractive when compared to the returns of owners of similar companies in the same industry. We measure the return to the owners as follows:

$$\textbf{Return on equity} = \frac{\text{Profit after tax}}{\text{Owners' equity}}$$

return on equity (return in net worth)
the rate of return the owners earn on their investment

The returns on equity for LM Manufacturing and the industry are 9.94 percent and 12.5 percent, respectively:

LM Manufacturing	Industry Average

$$\text{Return on equity} = \frac{\text{Profit after tax}}{\text{Owners' equity}}$$

$$= \frac{\$62,310}{\$627,100} = 9.94\%$$ $\boxed{12.5\%}$

It would appear that the owners of LM Manufacturing are not receiving a return on their investment equivalent to that of owners involved with competing businesses. Why not? In this case, the answer is twofold: First, LM Manufacturing is not as profitable in its operation as its competitors. (Remember the operating income return on investment of 10.76 percent for LM Manufacturing, compared to 13.2 percent for the industry.) Second, the average firm in the industry uses more debt, which causes the return on equity to be higher, provided, of course, that the company is earning a return on its investments that exceeds the cost of debt (the interest rate). However, the use of debt does increase the firm's risk. An example will clarify this point.

Assume that there are two companies, Firm A and Firm B. These two firms are identical in size. Both have $1,000 in total assets, and both have an operating income return on investment of 14 percent. However, they are different in one respect: Firm A uses no debt, while Firm B finances 50 percent of its investments with debt at an interest cost of 10 percent. Assuming there are no taxes for the sake of simplicity, the financial statements for the two companies are as follows:

	Firm A	Firm B
Total assets	$1,000	$1,000
Debt	$0	$500
Equity	1,000	500
TOTAL	$1,000	$1,000
Operating income (14% × $1,000)	$140	$140
Interest expense (10% × debt)	0	50
NET PROFIT	$140	$ 90

Computing the return on equity for both companies, we see that Firm B has a much more attractive return to its owners, 18 percent compared to Firm A's 14 percent:

$$\frac{\text{Return}}{\text{on equity}} = \frac{\text{Net profit}}{\text{Owners' equity}}$$

$$\text{Firm } A: \quad \frac{\$140}{\$1,000} = 14\% \qquad \text{Firm } B: \quad \frac{\$90}{\$500} = 18\%$$

Why the difference? Firm B is earning 14 percent on its investments but is having to pay only 10 percent for its borrowed money. The difference between the return on assets and the interest rate (14% − 10% = 4%) flows to the owners. This illustrates financial leverage at work: We borrow at a low rate of return and invest at a high rate of return. The result is magnified returns to the owners.

If debt is so attractive in terms of its ability to enhance the owners' returns, why not use lots of it all the time? Continuing our example will help us find the answer. Assume now that the economy falls into a deep recession, business declines sharply, and Firms *A* and *B* earn only 6 percent operating income return on investment. Let's recompute the return on common equity now.

	Firm **A**	Firm **B**
Operating income (6% × $1,000)	$60	$60
Interest expense (10% × debt)	0	50
NET PROFIT	$60	$ 10

$$\text{Firm } A: \quad \frac{\$60}{\$1,000} = 6\% \qquad \text{Firm } B: \quad \frac{\$10}{\$500} = 2\%$$

Now the use of leverage is negative in its influence, with Firm *B* earning less than Firm *A* for its owners. The problem comes from Firm *B*'s earning less than the interest rate of 10 percent and the owners having to make up the difference. Thus, financial leverage is a two-edged sword: When times are good, financial leverage can make them very, very good; but when times are bad, financial leverage makes them very, very bad. The use of financial leverage can potentially enhance the returns of the owners, but it also increases the uncertainty or risk for the owners.

In conclusion, the return on equity is a function of two variables:

1. The difference between the operating income return on investment and the interest rate.
2. The amount of debt used in the capital structure relative to the firm size.

Returning to the LM Manufacturing Company, remember that the operating return on investment is less than that of competing firms. Therefore, if the competing firms are paying comparable interest rates, the return on equity for LM Manufacturing will by necessity be less. Also, remember that the average firm in the industry uses more debt, which magnifies the return on equity but also exposes the owners to additional risk. So the return on equity for LM Manufacturing is less than that of competing firms for two reasons: (1) it has lower operating profits, and (2) it uses less debt. The first reason needs to be corrected by improved management of the firm's assets. The second reason may be a conscious decision of the managers not to assume as much risk as other firms do. This is a matter of tastes and preferences.

Summary of Financial Ratio Analysis

To review what we have learned about the use of financial ratios in evaluating a company's financial position, we present all the ratios for the LM Manufacturing Company for 1993 in Table 20-5. The ratios are grouped by the issue being addressed: liquidity, operating profitability, financing, and profits for the owners. As before, we use some ratios for more than one purpose, namely the turnover ratios for accounts receivable and inventories. These ratios have implications both for the firm's liquidity and its profitability; thus, they

Table 20-5 Financial Ratio Analysis

LM Manufacturing Company
Financial Ratio Analysis

Financial Ratios	LM Manufacturing		Industry Average
1. FIRM LIQUIDITY			
Current ratio	$\dfrac{\text{Current assets}}{\text{Current liabilities}}$	$\dfrac{\$347{,}200}{\$99{,}900} = 3.48$	2.70
Acid-test ratio	$\dfrac{\text{Current assets} - \text{Inventories}}{\text{Current liabilities}}$	$\dfrac{\$347{,}200 - \$211{,}400}{\$99{,}900} = 1.36$	1.25
Average collection period	$\dfrac{\text{Accounts receivable}}{\text{Daily credit sales}}$	$\dfrac{\$78{,}000}{\$830{,}200 \div 365} = 34.30$	35
Accounts receivable turnover	$\dfrac{\text{Credit sales}}{\text{Accounts receivable}}$	$\dfrac{\$830{,}200}{\$78{,}000} = 10.64$	10.43
Inventory turnover	$\dfrac{\text{Cost of goods sold}}{\text{Inventory}}$	$\dfrac{\$539{,}750}{211{,}400} = 2.55$	4.00
2. OPERATING PROFITABILITY			
Operating income return on investment	$\dfrac{\text{Operating income}}{\text{Total assets}}$	$\dfrac{\$99{,}700}{\$927{,}000} = 10.76\%$	13.2%
Operating profit margin	$\dfrac{\text{Operating income}}{\text{Sales}}$	$\dfrac{\$99{,}700}{\$830{,}200} = 12.01\%$	11%
Total asset turnover	$\dfrac{\text{Sales}}{\text{Total assets}}$	$\dfrac{\$830{,}200}{\$927{,}000} = 0.896$	1.20
Accounts receivable turnover	$\dfrac{\text{Credit sales}}{\text{Accounts receivable}}$	$\dfrac{\$830{,}200}{\$78{,}000} = 10.64$	10.43
Inventory turnover	$\dfrac{\text{Cost of goods sold}}{\text{Inventory}}$	$\dfrac{\$539{,}750}{\$211{,}400} = 2.55$	4.00
Fixed assets turnover	$\dfrac{\text{Sales}}{\text{Fixed assets}}$	$\dfrac{\$830{,}200}{\$524{,}800} = 1.58$	2.50
3. FINANCING DECISIONS			
Debt ratio	$\dfrac{\text{Total debt}}{\text{Total assets}}$	$\dfrac{\$299{,}900}{\$927{,}000} = 32\%$	40%

(Continued)

Figure 20-5   *(Continued)*

Financial Ratios	LM Manufacturing		Industry Average
Times interest earned	$\dfrac{\text{Operating income}}{\text{Interest}}$	$\dfrac{\$99,700}{\$20,000} = 4.99$	4.00
	4. RETURN ON EQUITY		
Return on equity	$\dfrac{\text{Profit after tax}}{\text{Owners' equity}}$	$\dfrac{\$62,310}{\$627,100} = 9.94\%$	12.5%

are listed in both areas. Also, we have shown both average collection period and accounts receivable turnover. Typically, we would only use one in our analysis, since they are just different ways to measure the same thing. Hopefully, presenting the ratios together will provide a helpful overview of what we have done.

LOOKING BACK

1. The owner of a small firm can ill afford to function without a sound accounting system. It need not be complicated, but it must provide timely and accurate information by which to evaluate the firm's performance and make decisions.
2. Three accounting statements most typically prepared by a small business are the income statement, the balance sheet, and the statement of cash flow. The income statement shows the results of a firm's operations over a period of time, usually one year. The balance sheet shows a firm's financial position at a specific date. The statement of cash flow accounts for changes in a firm's cash position over a given time period.
3. An understanding of the difference between profits and cash is essential for the entrepreneur. Cash is king. A company may be profitable, but still be out of cash.
4. Financial statements serve as the basis for computing financial ratios. These ratios can be used to answer important questions about the firm's financial performance.

DISCUSSION QUESTIONS

1. Explain the accounting convention that income is realized when earned, whether or not it has been received in cash.
2. Should entrepreneurs have someone else set up an accounting system for their proposed small firms or do it themselves? Why?

3. What are the major types of accounting records required in a sound accounting system?
4. What is the relationship between the income statement and the balance sheet?
5. What are the major advantages of a double-entry accounting system over a single-entry system?
6. Explain the purpose of the three major financial statements.
7. Define (a) current assets, (b) fixed assets, (c) current liabilities, (d) long-term debt, (e) equity, and (f) retained earnings.
8. Distinguish between (a) gross profits, (b) operating profits (earnings before interest and taxes), and (c) net profits.
9. What is liquidity? Differentiate between the two approaches given in the chapter to measure it.
10. How do we interpret the following ratios?
    a. Operating profit margin
    b. Asset turnover
    c. Times interest earned
11. What is the relationship among the operating return on investment, operating profit margin, and total asset turnover?
12. What would be the difference between using operating profit and using net profit when calculating a firm's return on investment?
13. What is the difference between the debt ratio and the debt-to-equity ratio?
14. What is financial leverage? When is it good and when is it bad? Why?
15. What determines a firm's return on equity?

YOU MAKE THE CALL

Situation 1

Mary and Matt Townsel are in their early retirement years after having worked for several different businesses over the last 30 years. Now, to supplement their Social Security income, Matt operates a newspaper delivery service. He has more than 600 customers in the retirement/vacation village where they live. Mary's major contribution to the business partnership, in addition to rolling papers early in the mornings, is bookkeeping.

Mary has recently purchased a computer to assist her with the accounting function. She has no software and is therefore looking for someone to write her programs.

Questions
1. What types of accounting records do you believe Mary should maintain? Why?
2. Does it appear that a computer will benefit Mary's record keeping task? How?

Situation 2

In 1991, J. T. Rose purchased a small business, the Baugh Company. The firm has been profitable, but J. T. has been disappointed by the lack of cash flows provided by the business. He had hoped to have about $10,000 a year available from the business that could be used for personal needs. However, there never seemed to be much cash available for purposes other than business needs. In a recent visit with J. T., he asked you to look at some recent financial statements, which are presented here, to see whether you could explain why he could be making profits but not have any discretionary cash for personal needs. During your visit, he observed, "I thought that you could take the profits and add back depreciation and it would tell you how much cash flow you were generating. However, that never seems to be the case. What is happening?"

1. From the information provided by the financial statements what would you tell him? (As part of your answer, develop a cash flow statement.)
2. Also, given the financial ratios for the industry, which are provided here, evaluate the Baugh Company's financial performance.

Table 20-1-1

The Baugh Company
Financial Statements
1992–1993

Balance Sheet	1992	1993
Cash	$8	$10
Accounts receivable	15	20
Inventory	22	25
Current assets	$45	$55
Gross fixed assets	$50	$55
Accumulated depreciation	15	20
Net fixed assets	$35	$35
Other assets	$12	$10
TOTAL ASSETS	$92	$100
Accounts payable	$10	$12
Accruals	7	8
Short-term notes	5	5
Total short-term debt	$22	$25
Long-term debt	15	15
Total debt	$37	$40
Equity	55	60
TOTAL DEBT AND EQUITY	$92	$100

(Continued)

Table 20-1-1   (*Continued*)

Income Statement

Sales	$175
Cost of goods sold	105
Gross profit	$70
Depreciation	5
Administrative expenses	20
Selling expenses	26
Total operating expenses	$51
Operating income (Earnings Before Interest and Tax)	$19
Interest expense	3
Earnings before taxes	$16
Taxes	8
NET PROFIT	$8

Table 20-1-2

Financial Ratios: Industry Averages

Current ratio	2.50
Quick ratio	1.50
Average collection period	30.00
Inventory turnover	6.00
Operating income (Return on Investment)	16.0%
Operating profit margin	8.0%
Total asset turnover	2.00
Fixed asset turnover	7.00
Debt/equity ratio	1.00
Times interest earned	5.00
Return on owners' equity	14.0%

EXPERIENTIAL EXERCISES

1. Interview a local CPA who consults with small firms and determine his or her experiences with small-business accounting systems. Report to the class on what levels of accounting knowledge the CPA's clients appear to possess.

2. Contact several very small businesses and explain your interest in their accounting systems. Report to the class on their level of sophistication—such things as whether they use a single-entry system, a computer, or an outside professional.

3. Go to your public or university library to see whether it subscribes to a financial service that provides industry financial ratios. Ask for Robert Morris Associates or Dun & Bradstreet. If the library does not subscribe to these two services, ask whether it subscribes to another financial service that does provide industry norms. When you find a source, select an industry and bring a copy of the ratios to class and share the nature of the information with the class.

4. Try to find a small company in your community that will allow you to use its financial statements to perform a financial ratio analysis. You will need to decide the industry that best represents the firm's business for comparison data and then find the norms in the library. Also, you may need to promise confidentiality to the company's owners by changing all the names on the statements.

REFERENCES TO SMALL-BUSINESS PRACTICES

American Institute of Certified Public Accountants, "Audit Problems Encountered in Small Business Engagements," *Auditing Research Monograph No. 5* (New York: 1982).

> The monograph describes problems in developing internal controls within a small company.

Baker, Jack D. and John A. Marts, "Internal Control for Protection and Profits," *Small Business Forum,* Vol. 8, No. 2 (Fall 1990), pp. 28–35.

> The authors present the need for internal control within the small company; they also give suggestions on how it is to be achieved.

Pearlstein, Steven, "Accounting Critic Robert Kaplan," *Inc.,* Vol. 10, No. 4 (April 1988), pp. 55–67.

> Harvard Business School professor Robert Kaplan is interviewed regarding current accounting practices, some having relevance for the small company.

Stevenson, Howard, and William Sahlman, "How Small Companies Should Handle Advisors," *Harvard Business Review,* Vol. 66, No. 2 (March–April 1988), pp. 28–35.

> The authors offer suggestions for using advisors, including accountants, effectively.

ENDNOTES

1. See Jill Andresky Fraser, "Accounting Search," *Inc.* (October 1992), p. 11.

2. Frank Mixson, "Accountants on the Move," *Entrepreneur,* Vol. 17, No. 4 (April 1989), p. 88.

3. An even simpler example of using journals and ledgers can be found in John A. Welsh and Jerry F. White, *The Entrepreneur's Master Planning Guide* (Englewood Cliffs, NJ: Prentice-Hall, Inc., 1983), pp. 265–269.

4. Jack D. Baker and John A. Marts, "Internal Control for Protection and Profits," *Small Business Forum,* Vol. 8, No. 2 (Fall 1990), p. 29.

5. See Baker and Marts, *ibid.,* for suggestions on developing internal controls appropriate for the small company.

6. Dun & Bradstreet annually publishes a set of 14 key ratios for each of 125 lines of business. Robert Morris Associates, the association of bank loan and credit officers, publishes a set of 16 key ratios for over 350 lines of business. In both cases the ratios are classified by industry and by firm size to provide the basis for more meaningful comparisons.

7. The industry averages have been taken from a Dun & Bradstreet publication.

CHAPTER 21

Working-Capital Management

SPOTLIGHT ON SMALL BUSINESS

Rapid growth can create enormous financial problems for small businesses. Donald Weck's company, Love At First Bite, Inc., is a classic example of a firm that expanded too swiftly without careful working-capital management. Weck and a partner launched the San Mateo, California, company in 1981 to make patés and quiches. When sales grew, the partners borrowed money to finance the expansion.

"We spent way too much money on things we had no business spending money on," says Weck. *"We took out a $15,000 loan for a computer that we didn't need. We hired a controller for $30,000 when we were only grossing $400,000 a year. We were acting like a much bigger company."*

Donald Weck

Failure to manage its finances properly led this business to the brink of bankruptcy. Fortunately, Weck, after buying out his partner, was able to slash expenses, restructure loans, and pay off debt, thereby salvaging a profitable business.

Source: Jeannie Ralston, "Specialty Food with All the Trimmings." Reprinted from the February 1989 issue of *VENTURE, For Entrepreneurial Business Owners & Investors,* © 1989.

After studying this chapter, you should be able to:
1. Describe the working-capital cycle within a small business.
2. Identify the important issues in managing a firm's cash flows.
3. Differentiate between profits and cash flows.
4. Explain what is involved in managing accounts receivable, inventory, and accounts payable.

working-capital
  management
working capital
working-capital cycle

cash conversion period
growth trap
cash budget

pledged accounts
  receivable
factoring

Ask the owner of a small company about financial management and you will hear about the joys and tribulations of managing cash, accounts receivable, inventories, and accounts payable. Effectively managing *short-term* assets (current assets) and *short-term* sources of financing (current liabilities), is a matter of great importance to most small-firm owners. A perfectly good business opportunity can literally be destroyed by ineffectively managing the firm's short-term assets and liabilities. No single financial matter is more important to the small company than **working-capital management**—the management of the firm's short-term assets and short-term sources of financing. This chapter focuses on how to manage a small company's working capital.

working-capital management
management of current assets and current liabilities

THE WORKING-CAPITAL CYCLE

Working capital consists primarily of three assets—cash, accounts receivable, and inventories—and two sources of short-term debt—accounts payable and accruals. (Accruals are not considered in terms of managing working capital. Accrued expenses, while shown as a short-term liability, primarily result from the accountant's efforts to match revenues and expenses. There is little that could be done to "manage accruals.") A firm's **working-capital cycle** refers to the flow of resources through these accounts as part of the company's day-to-day operations. For instance, businesses purchase or produce inventories; sell these inventories, either for cash or on credit; collect the accounts receivables resulting from the credit sales; and then begin the process again. Figure 21-1 shows this cycle graphically. The steps are as follows:

working capital
the sum of a firm's current assets, (cash accounts receivable, and inventories) and current liabilities (accounts payable and short-term notes)

working-capital cycle
the day-to-day flow of resources through a firm's working-capital accounts

Purchase or produce inventory for sale, which

Step 1
• increases accounts payable, $\boxed{A}$, assuming the business purchases the product on credit, and
• increases inventories on hand, $\boxed{B}$.

Step 2a Sell the inventory for cash, which increases cash, $\boxed{D1}$,

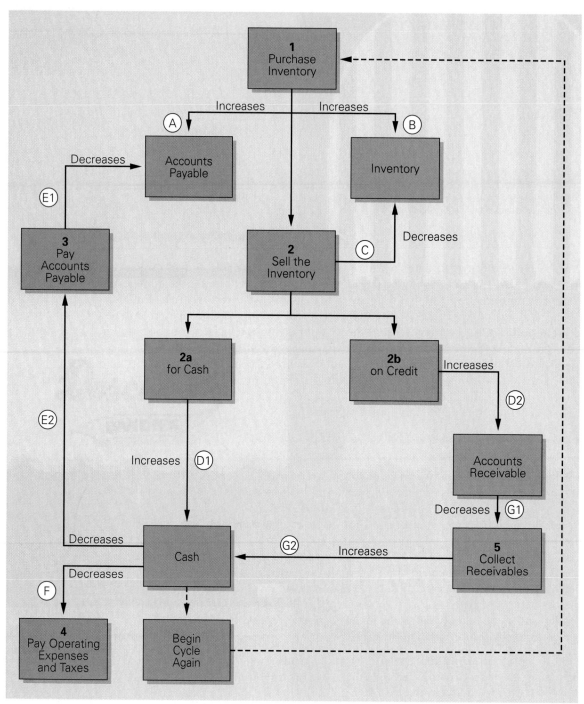

Figure 21-1   Working-Capital Cycle

or

Step 2b Sell the inventory on credit, which increases accounts receivable, D2.

Step 3 Pay on the accounts payable, which
- decreases accounts payable, E1, and
- decreases cash, E2.

Step 4 Pay operating expenses and taxes, which decreases cash, F.

Step 5 Collect the accounts receivable when due, which
- decreases accounts receivable, G1, and
- increases cash, G2.

The cycle is then repeated, quickly in the grocery business and more slowly for an automobile dealer.

It is imperative that owners of small companies understand the working-capital cycle, in terms of both the timing of these investments and the amount of the investment required, such as the size of the investment in inventories and accounts receivable. Failure to understand these relationships underlies many of the financial problems of small companies.

With respect to the first issue, that of timing, Figure 21-3 helps us visualize the chronological sequence of a hypothetical working-capital cycle. Using a time line, we can show the events as they unfold, beginning with the investments in inventories and ending with the collection of the accounts receivable. The key dates in the exhibit are as follows:

- *Day a:* Inventory is ordered in anticipation of future sales.
- *Day b:* Inventory is received.
- *Day c:* Inventory is sold on credit

Figure 21-2
The Working-Capital Cycle Moves Slowly for an Automobile Dealership, Quickly for a Grocery Store

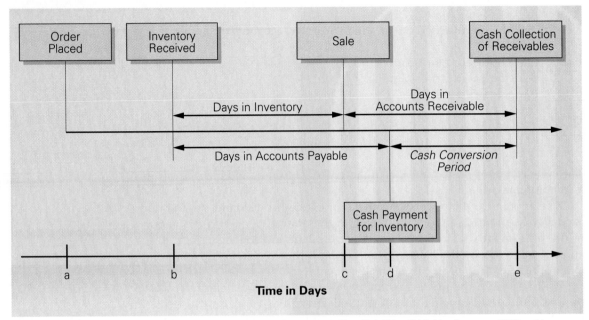

Source: Terry S. Maness and John T. Zietlow, *Short-Term Financial Management* (New York: West Publishing Company, 1993), p. 14.

Figure 21-3
Working-Capital
Time Line

- *Day d:* Accounts payable come due and are paid.
- *Day e:* Accounts receivable are collected.

The investing and financing implications of the working-capital cycle, as reflected in Figure 21-3, are as follows:

1. We invest money in inventory from day *b* until day *c*.
2. The supplier provides us with financing for the inventories from day *b* until day *d*.
3. We invest money in accounts receivable from day *c* until day *e*.
4. We must find a way to finance the firm's investment in accounts receivable from day *d* until day *e*. This time period is called the **cash conversion period**. It represents the number of days required for us to complete the working-capital cycle, ending with the conversion of accounts receivable into cash. During this period, the firm no longer has the benefit of the financing (accounts payable) provided by the supplier. The longer this period, the greater the potential cash flow problems for the firm.

cash conversion period
time required to convert paid-for inventories and accounts receivable into cash

We can clarify Figure 21-3 with two examples. In Figure 21-4, we have pictured two companies with different working-capital cycles: Pokey, Inc., and Quick Turn Company. Both companies buy inventory on August 15 and then receive it on August 31. The similarity ends at that point. Pokey, Inc., must pay for the product on September 30 before the firm eventually resells it on October 15. It collects from its customers on November 30. That is, the firm is having to pay for the product two months prior to collecting from its own customers (paying on September 30 and collecting on November 30). The firm's cash conversion period—the time required to convert the paid-for inventories and accounts receivable into cash—is 60 days. The company's managers will need to find a way to finance this investment in working capital (inventories and accounts receivable) or else the firm will have cash flow problems. Furthermore, the more the company sells, the greater the problem will be, even though the increasing sales should result in higher profits.

Now consider Quick Turn Company's working-capital cycle in the bottom portion of Figure 21-4. Compared to Pokey, Inc., Quick Turn Company has an enviable working-capital position. By the time Quick Turn must pay for its inventory purchases (October 31), it has sold (September 30) and collected from its customers (October 31). Thus, the cash conversion period is nonexistent, because the supplier is essentially financing Quick Turn's working-capital needs.

To gain an even better understanding of the working-capital cycle, look again at Pokey, Inc. In addition to the working-capital cycle as shown for Pokey in Figure 21-4, consider the following information about the firm:

1. Pokey is a new company, having started operations in July. The beginning assets and sources of financing at the outset were as follows:

Cash	$400
Fixed assets	600
TOTAL ASSETS	$1,000
Debt	$300
Common stock	700
TOTAL DEBT AND EQUITY	$1,000

2. On August 15, the firm's managers ordered $500 in inventories, which were received on August 31. (Follow along the time line in Figure 21-3.) The supplier allowed Pokey, Inc., terms of 30 days from the time the inventory was received to pay for the purchase; thus, inventories and accounts payable both increased by $500 when the inventory was received.
3. On September 30, Pokey paid for the inventory; both cash and accounts payable decreased by $500.
4. On October 15, the merchandise was sold on credit for $900; sales and accounts receivable increased by that amount.
5. During the month of October, the firm incurred operating expenses (selling and administrative expenses) in the amount of $250, to be paid in early November; thus, operating expenses and accrued expenses increased by $250. (An additional $25 in accrued expenses resulted from taxes, as explained later.)

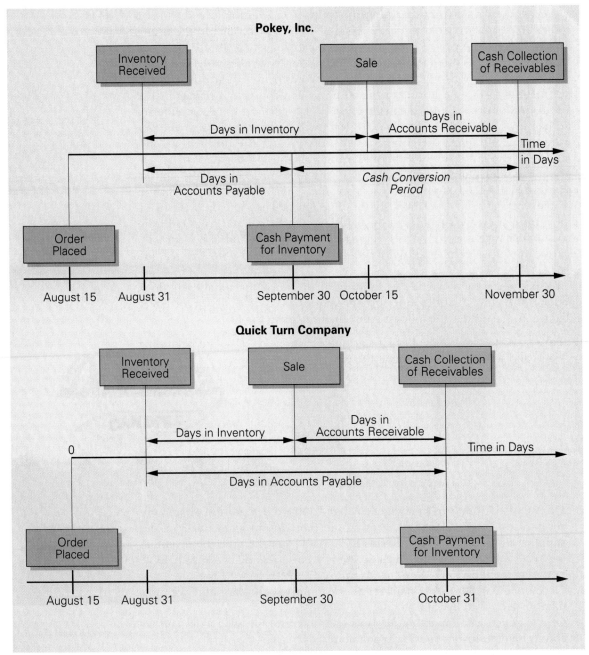

Figure 21-4   Examples of the Working-Capital Time Line

6. Also in October, the firm's accountants recorded $50 in depreciation expense, which means that accumulated depreciation on the balance sheet increased to $50.
7. During early November, the accrued expenses were paid, which resulted in a decrease of cash by $250, along with an equal decrease of accrued expenses. At the end of November, the accounts receivable were collected, whereby cash increased by $900 and accounts receivable decreased by a like amount.

Figure 21-5 shows the consequences of the foregoing events on Pokey's balance sheet month by month. All the changes in each balance sheet can be traced directly to the events that transpired, except for retained earnings and taxes payable. As a result of the firm's activities, Pokey, Inc., reported $75 in profits for the period. Disregarding any interest expense that was incurred on the outstanding debt and assuming that the income tax rate is 25 percent, the income statement for the period ending November 30 would appear as follows:

Sales		$900
Cost of goods sold		500
Gross profits		$400
Operating expenses	$250	
Depreciation expense	50	
Total operating expenses		$300
Operating income		$100
Taxes (25%)		25
EARNINGS AFTER TAX		$75

The $75 in profits is therefore reflected as retained earnings in the balance sheet to make everything balance. Also, the $25 in taxes shown in the income statement results in taxes payable of $25 in the balance sheet in October and November.

Looking at Table 21-1, we can quickly see a big problem—the negative effect of the transactions on Pokey's cash balances. While the business is profitable, Pokey runs out of cash in September and October (−$100) and does not recover until November, when the sales are collected. This 60-day cash-conversion period represents the critical time when the company must find another source of financing if it is to survive.

The examples of Pokey and Quick Turn, which may seem a bit contrived, make an important point. The owner of a small company must understand the working-capital cycle of his or her firm. Otherwise, some real cash flow problems can develop for the company—problems that can be fatal to even a profitable firm.

With a general understanding of the working-capital cycle, we can now examine the primary components that comprise working capital: cash, accounts receivable, inventories, and accounts payable.

ASSETS	July	Balance Sheets Pokey, Inc. August	September	October	November
Cash	$400	$400	($100)	($100)	$550
Accounts receivable	0	0	0	900	0
Inventory	0	500	500	0	0
Fixed assets	600	600	600	600	600
Accumulated depreciation	0	0	0	-50	-50
TOTAL ASSETS	$1000	$1500	$1000	$1350	$1100
LIABILITIES AND EQUITY					
Accounts payable	$0	$500	$0	$0	$0
Accruals	0	0	0	250	0
Taxes payable	0	0	0	25	25
Debt	300	300	300	300	300
Common stock	700	700	700	700	700
Retained earnings	0	0	0	75	75
TOTAL DEBT AND EQUITY	$1000	$1500	$1000	$1350	$1100

Table 21-1
Balance Sheets,
Pokey, Inc.

MANAGING CASH FLOW

As should be clear by now, at the core of working-capital management is the monitoring of cash flow. Cash is constantly pumping through a healthy business. It flows in, for example, as customers pay for products or services, and it flows out as payments are made to suppliers. The typically uneven nature of inward and outward flows makes it imperative that they be properly understood and regulated.

The Nature of Cash Flows

A firm's net cash flow may be determined quite simply by examining its bank account. Cash deposits during a month less checks written during the same period equal its net cash flow. If deposits for a month add up to $100,000 and checks total $80,000, the firm has a net positive cash flow of $20,000. The cash balance at the end of the month is $20,000 higher than it was at the beginning of the month. Figure 21-5 portrays the total flow of cash through a business. This figure represents not only the cash flows that arise as part of the firm's working-capital cycle, which were presented earlier in Figure 21-1, but other

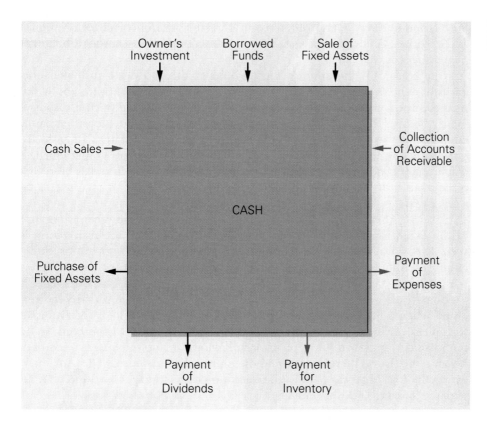

Figure 21-5
Flow of Cash
Through a Business

flows as well, such as the purchase of fixed assets and issuing stock. More specifically, the shaded arrows in Figure 21-5 reflect the inflows and outflows of cash that relate to the working-capital cycle, while the unshaded arrows represent other longer-term cash flows.

In calculating net cash flows, it is necessary to distinguish between revenues and cash receipts. They are seldom the same. Revenues are recorded at the time a sale is made, but they do not affect cash at that time unless the sale is a cash sale. Cash receipts, on the other hand, are recorded when the money actually flows into the firm, often a month or two after the sale. Similarly, we must distinguish between expenses and disbursements. Expenses occur when the material, labor, or other item is used; payments (disbursements) for these expense items may be made later, at the time that checks are issued.

Net Cash Flow and Profit Are Different

In view of the differences just noted, it should come as no surprise that net cash flow and net profit are different. Net cash flow is the difference between cash inflows and outflows. Net profit, in contrast, is the difference between revenues and expenses. Failure to understand this distinction can play havoc with a small firm's financial well-being.

One reason for the difference is the uneven timing of cash disbursements and the expensing of those disbursements. As an example, think about the merchandise purchased by a retail store. It may be paid for (a cash disbursement) before it is sold (when it becomes an expense). On the other hand, labor may be used (an expense) before the paycheck is written (a cash disbursement). In the case of a major cash outlay for a building or equipment, the disbursement will show up immediately as a cash outflow, but it will be recognized as an expense only as the building or equipment is depreciated over a period of years.

Likewise, there is uneven timing of sales revenue and cash receipts because of the extension of credit. A sale is made, at which time the transaction is recorded as revenue, and the cash receipt is recorded when payment for the account receivable is received 30 or 60 days later. We observed this fact earlier as part of the working-capital cycle.

Some cash receipts, furthermore, are not revenue and never become revenue. When a firm borrows money from a bank, for example, it receives cash without receiving revenue. When the principal is repaid to the bank some months later, a cash disbursement occurs. However, no expense is recorded, because the firm is merely returning the money that was borrowed. (Any interest on the loan that was paid to the bank would, of course, constitute both an expense and a cash disbursement.)

Because of the important differences between net cash flow and profit, it is imperative that small firms manage cash flows as carefully as they manage revenues, expenses, and profits. Otherwise, they may find themselves insolvent while showing handsome paper profits.

The Growth Trap

Some firms experience rapid growth of sales volume. The firm's income statement may simultaneously reflect growing profits. However, rapid growth in sales and even profits may be hazardous to the firm's cash. This happens because growth tends to soak up additional cash more rapidly than such cash can be generated in the form of additional profits.

Inventory, for example, must be expanded as sales volume increases. This means that additional dollars must be expended for merchandise or raw materials to accommodate the higher level of sales. Similarly, accounts receivable must be expanded proportionally to the increased sales volume. It should be evident, then, that a growing, profitable business can quickly find itself in a financial bind. As Welsh and White point out, "It is perfectly normal to find that a business is growing profitably while going broke down at the bank."[1]

The distinctive characteristics of small firms make the growth problem particularly acute for them:

Profits But No Cash

A manager needs to monitor both profits and cash flow. Otherwise, the company's checking account may "run dry" at the same time that its income statement shows profits.

The president of a small Midwestern manufacturing company made the mistake of concentrating exclusively on the firm's monthly profit-and-loss statements—statements that showed profits of $5,000 on sales of $100,000. He assumed that cash balances would not be a problem. However, one day the president received a call from an irate creditor who had not been paid. When the president looked into the situation, he found that his company had, indeed, held up payment on a number of bills because of a cash shortage. Concentration on the income statement alone had led to neglect of cash-flow analysis and to the embarrassing surprise that the company's sales dollars had not made it to the bank in time to pay the bills.

Source: Ron D. Richardson, "Managing Your Company's Cash," *Nation's Business,* Vol. 74, No. 11 (November 1986), pp. 52–54. Copyright 1986, U.S. Chamber of Commerce.

Larger businesses usually grow at slower rates than smaller businesses. It is possible to double sales in one year if what is being doubled is small. It is nearly impossible to double sales in one year if annual sales are already a billion dollars. Because of this, smaller businesses are more likely to have a continuous and urgent need for proportionally more money to overcome negative cash flow than their larger counterparts.[2]

In view of the small firm's characteristic difficulty in obtaining funds externally, it is apparent that the **growth trap** can be lethal for small businesses unless cash is managed carefully.

growth trap
a cash shortage resulting from rapid growth

To show the danger of the growth trap, consider the Martin Corporation. The firm's most recent balance sheet is shown in Table 21-2. Martin's annual sales for the past several years have been $500,000, but it now has the opportunity to expand into a new geographical area. The expansion could result in a 50 percent increase in sales for the next two years; that is, sales would increase from $500,000 to $750,000 in the first year and from $750,000 to $1,125,000 in the second year. The company's after-tax net-profits-to-sales ratio (net profit margin) is expected to be about 15 percent for the next several years.

As explained in Chapter 10, a sales increase typically causes an increase in assets at about the same rate. That is, if sales increased by 50 percent, the firm's needs for cash, accounts receivable, inventories, and fixed assets would also increase by 50 percent. Furthermore, if inventories increased by 50 percent, accounts payable would probably increase by 50 percent. Thus, the increase in accounts payable would help finance some of the firm's growth. The firm's

Table 21-2
Martin
Corporation—
Balance Sheet

Cash	$50,000
Accounts receivable	100,000
Inventories	75,000
Fixed assets	175,000
TOTAL ASSETS	$400,000
Accounts payable	$50,000
Debt	120,000
Common equity	40,000
Retained earnings	190,000
TOTAL DEBT AND EQUITY	$400,000

profits could be retained to finance some of the growth, but even that might not be enough for a high-growth company. The managers might still need to borrow more money or raise new equity to avoid decreasing cash balances below the desired amount.

The requirement for additional financing is shown in Table 21-3. An explanation of the pro forma balance sheets is in order:

1. Martin's assets are assumed to increase by the same percentage that sales are increasing (50 percent), which implicitly means that each asset is a constant percentage of sales. For example, each year cash remains at 10 percent of sales, and accounts receivable are 20 percent of sales. (A constant asset-to-sales relationship is typically true to life.)
2. Accounts payable likewise increase 50 percent each year along with sales. That is, accounts payable remain at 10 percent of sales.
3. Debt and common stock remain constant. These two sources will not increase unless the firm actively seeks out new sources.
4. Retained earnings increase as the firm's profits are retained within the business. The computations are as follows:

Current retained earnings	$190,000
Profits for Year 1 (15% of $750,000 sales)	112,500
Retained earnings at end of Year 1	$302,500
Profits for Year 2 (15% of $1,125,000 sales)	168,750
Retained earnings at end of Year 2	$471,250

5. The sources of financing are insufficient for the projected growth. As shown in Table 21-3, the total assets amount to $600,000 in Year 1 and $900,000 in Year 2. Assets exceed the total sources of financing in those years by $62,500 and $156,250, respectively.

Table 21-3
Pro Forma Balance
Sheet for Martin
Corporation Sales

Martin Corporation Sales Projections and Pro Forma Balance Sheets Years 1 and 2

		Projections	
	Current	Year 1	Year 2
Sales	**$500000**	**$750,000**	**$1,125,000**
Cash	$ 50,000	$ 75,000	$112,500
Accounts receivable	100,000	150,000	225,000
Inventories	75,000	112,500	168,750
Fixed assets	175,000	262,500	393,750
TOTAL ASSETS	$400,000	$600,000	$900,000
Accounts payable	$50,000	$75,000	$112,500
Debt	120,000	120,000	120,000
Common equity	40,000	40,000	40,000
Retained earnings	190,000	302,500	471,250
TOTAL DEBT AND EQUITY WITHOUT NEW FINANCING	$400,000	$537,500	$743,750
Additional financing needed		62,500	156,250
TOTAL DEBT AND EQUITY WITH NEW FINANCING		$600,000	$900,000

The conclusion provided by the example may be summarized as follows: The need for additional financing of a high-growth company may exceed the firm's available resources, even though the company is profitable. Without the additional resources, the firm's cash balances may well decline sharply, leaving the company in a precarious financial position. In this example, the Martin Corporation could be just another small company that fell prey to the growth trap.

The Process of Cash Budgeting

Cash budgets are tools for managing cash flow. They differ in a number of ways from income statements. Income statements take items into consideration before they affect cash—for example, expenses that are incurred but not yet paid

cash budgets
budgets strictly concerned with the receipt and payment of dollars

and income earned but not yet received. Cash budgets, in contrast, are concerned specifically with dollars as they are received and paid out.

By using a cash budget, the entrepreneur can predict and plan the cash flow of a business. No single planning document is more important in the life of a small company, either for avoiding cash flow problems when cash runs short or for anticipating short-term investment opportunities if excess cash becomes available.

The process of preparing a cash budget can be explained by use of an example. Consider the Carriles Corporation, a manufacturer of cartons. The firm wishes to develop a monthly cash budget for the next quarter (July–September), and the owner, Catalina Carriles, has made the following forecasts:

1. Historical and predicted sales:

Historical		**Predicted**	
April	$80,000	July	$130,000
May	100,000	August	130,000
June	120,000	September	120,000
		October	100,000

2. Of the firm's sales, 40 percent is collected in the month of sale, 30 percent one month after sale, and the remaining 30 percent two months after sale.
3. Inventory is purchased one month before the sales month and is paid for in the month it is sold. Purchases equal 80 percent of projected sales for the next month.
4. Carriles has estimated cash expenses for wages and salaries, rent, utilities, and tax payments, which are reflected in the cash budget.
5. The firm's beginning cash balance for the budget period is $5,000, and Carriles would like to maintain at least this amount as a minimum cash balance.
6. The firm has an $80,000 line of credit with its bank at an interest rate of 12 percent annually (a one percent monthly rate). The interest owed is to be paid monthly.
7. Interest on a $40,000 bank note (principal due in December) is payable at an 8 percent annual rate for the three-month period ending in September.

Based on the information above, Carriles has used a computer spreadsheet to prepare a monthly cash budget for the three-month period ending September 30. The results of her computations are shown in Table 21-4. The calculations involve the following steps:

1. Determine the amount of collections each month, based on the projected collection patterns.
2. Estimate the amount and timing of the following cash disbursements:

Carriles Corporation
Three-Month Cash Budget
July–September

	May	June	July	August	September
Monthly sales	$100,000	$120,000	$130,000	$130,000	$120,000
Cash receipts					
Cash sales			$52,000	$52,000	$48,000
1 month			36,000	39,000	39,000
2 months			30,000	36,000	39,000
Total collections			$118,000	$127,000	$126,000
Purchases (80% of next month's projected sales)		$104,000	$104,000	$96,000	$80,000
Cash disbursements					
Payments on purchases			$104,000	$104,000	$96,000
Rent			3,000	3,000	3,000
Wages and salaries			18,000	18,000	16,000
Tax prepayment			1,000		
Utilities (2% of sales)			2,600	2,600	2,400
Interest on long-term note					800
Short-term interest (1% of short-term debt)				106	113
Total cash disbursements			$128,600	$127,706	$118,313
Net change in cash			(10,600)	(706)	7,687
Beginning cash balance			5,000	5,000	5,000
Cash balance before borrowing			($5,600)	$4,294	$12,687
Short-term borrowing (payments)			10,600	706	(7,687)
ENDING CASH BALANCE			$5,000	$5,000	$5,000
CUMULATIVE SHORT-TERM BORROWING			$10,600	$11,306	$3,619

Table 21-4
Cash Budget for
Carriles Corporation

a. Inventory purchases and payments. (The amount of the purchases is shown in the boxed area of the table, with payments being made one month later.)

b. Rent, wages, taxes, utilities, and interest on the long-term note.

c. The interest to be paid on any outstanding short-term borrowing. For example, the bottom of the table for the month of July shows that Carriles would need to borrow $10,600 to prevent the firm's cash balance from falling below the $5,000 minimum acceptable cash balance. Assume that the money will be borrowed at the end of July and the interest will be due and payable at the end of August. The amount of the interest in August equals $106, or one percent of the $10,600 cumulative short-term debt outstanding at the end of July.

3. Calculate the *net change in cash* (cash receipts less the cash disbursements).

4. Determine the *beginning cash balance* (ending cash balance from the prior month).

5. Compute the *cash balance before short-term borrowing* (net change in cash for the month plus the cash balance at the beginning of the month).

6. Calculate the *short-term borrowing (payment)*—the amount borrowed if there is a cash shortfall for the month or the amount repaid on any short-term debt outstanding.

7. Compute the cumulative amount of short-term debt outstanding, which also determines the amount of interest to be paid in the following month.

As you can see, the company does not achieve a positive cash flow until September. Short-term borrowing must be arranged, therefore, in each of the two months. By preparing a cash budget, Carriles can anticipate these needs and avoid the nasty surprises that might otherwise occur.

On those occasions when a small business has idle funds, the cash should be invested. The cash forecast is a basis for anticipating these occasions. If unexpected excess funds are generated, they can be invested also. Many short-term investment opportunities are available. Certificates of deposit and money market certificates are just two of the many vehicles for putting excess cash to work for the firm.

MANAGING ACCOUNTS RECEIVABLE

Chapter 13 discussed the extension of credit by small firms and their practices in managing and collecting accounts receivable. This section considers the impact of credit decisions on working capital and particularly on cash flow.

How Accounts Receivable Affect Cash

Granting credit to customers is a marketing decision that directly affects a firm's cash account. By selling on credit, the selling firm delays the inflow of cash by allowing customers to delay payment.

The total of customer credit balances is carried on the balance sheet as accounts receivable—one of the current assets of the business. Of all noncash assets, accounts receivable is closest to becoming cash. Sometimes called "near cash," accounts receivable are typically paid and become cash within 30 to 60 days.

The Life Cycle of Receivables

The receivables cycle begins with a credit sale. In many businesses, an invoice is then prepared and mailed to the purchaser. When the invoice is received, the purchaser processes it, prepares a check, and mails the check in payment to the seller.

Under ideal circumstances, each of these steps is taken in a timely manner. It is obvious, however, that delays can occur at any stage of this process. Some, indeed, may result from inefficiencies within the selling firm. One small-business owner found that the shipping clerk was "batching" invoices before sending them to the office for processing. This naturally delayed the preparation and mailing of invoices to customers. Of course, this practice also postponed the day on which the customer's money was received and deposited in the bank so that it could be used to pay bills.

Credit management policies, practices, and procedures, as explained in Chapter 13, affect the life cycle of receivables and the flow of cash from them. It is important that, in establishing credit policies, small-business owners consider cash flow requirements as well as the need to stimulate sales. Following are some examples of credit-management practices that can have a positive effect on a company's cash flow:

1. Minimizing the time between shipping, invoicing, and sending notices on billings.
2. Reviewing credit experience to determine impediments to cash flow, such as continued extension of credit to slow-paying or delinquent customers.
3. Providing incentives for prompt payment by granting cash discounts or charging interest on delinquent accounts.
4. Aging accounts receivable on a monthly or even weekly basis to identify quickly any delinquent account.
5. Using the most effective methods for collecting overdue accounts.

Accounts-Receivable Financing

Some small businesses can speed up the cash flow from receivables by borrowing against them. By financing receivables, they can often secure the use of their money 30 to 60 days earlier than would be possible otherwise. Although at one time this practice was concentrated largely in the apparel trades, it has expanded to many other types of small business such as manufacturers, food processors, distributors, home building suppliers, and temporary employment

SMALL BUSINESS IN ACTION

Factoring: A Way to Finance Growth

In the late 1980s and early 1990s, banks became far more restrictive in making loans. A firm that had a long-standing relationship with its bank might be told that the bank would not be renewing its loan or was unwilling to extend additional credit to finance the firm's growth.

John Yatsko, the owner of MPG Inc., a commercial printing company, had such an experience. His firm's sales increased from $1.3 million to $3.3 million in one year, which meant increased financing needs. But the bank refused to increase his lending limits, which left him with no choice but to seek other funding. His choice: selling (factoring) his receivables to Allstate Financial Corporation at a discount. By selling accounts receivable, a company can dramatically shorten the time it takes to turn inventory into cash, thus enhancing the firm's capacity to grow.

For Yatsko, selling the firm's accounts receivable provided cash at a crucial time. "We had gotten behind in taxes and also with some suppliers. It was a continual uphill struggle," he recalls.

There is, however, some bad news about factoring: It costs significantly more than borrowing from a bank. It is not meant to be a long-term solution to financing needs. Rather, it should be used only until growth levels off and you can find another financing source.

Source: Ellyn E. Spragins, "Quick Cash," *Inc.*, Vol. 13, No. 3, pp. 95–96. Adapted with permission, *Inc.* magazine, March 1991. Copyright 1991 by Goldhirsh Group, Inc., 38 Commercial Wharf, Boston, MA 02110.

agencies. Financing of this type is provided by commercial finance companies and by some banks.

Two types of financing are possible. In one, a firm's **pledged accounts receivable** serve as collateral for a loan. When payments are received from customers, the payments are forwarded to the lending institution to pay off the loan. In the second type of financing, a business sells its accounts receivable to a finance company, a practice known as **factoring.** The finance company assumes the bad-debt risk associated with receivables it buys.

The obvious advantage of accounts-receivable financing is the immediate cash flow it provides for firms that have limited working capital. As a secondary benefit, the volume of borrowing can quickly be expanded proportionally to a firm's growth in sales and accounts receivable.

pledged accounts receivable
accounts receivable used as collateral for a loan

factoring
selling accounts receivable to a finance

A drawback to this practice is the high finance cost. Interest rates typically run several points above the prime interest rate, and factors also charge a fee that compensates them for their credit-investigation activities and for the risk they take that customers may default in payment. However, a borrower may escape the expense of conducting a credit investigation of customers by turning this function over to the factor. Another weakness is that pledging accounts receivable may limit a firm's ability to borrow from a bank by removing a prime asset from its available collateral.

MANAGING INVENTORY

Inventory is a "necessary evil" to the financial management system. It is necessary because supply and demand cannot be manipulated to coincide precisely in day-to-day operations. It is an evil because inventory ties up funds that are not actively productive.

Freeing Cash by Reducing Inventory

Inventory is a bigger problem to some small businesses than to others. The inventory of many service firms, for example, consists of only a few supplies. A manufacturer, on the other hand, has several inventories—raw materials, finished goods, and supplies. Also, retailers and wholesalers, especially those with high inventory turnover rates (such as those in grocery distribution), are continually involved in inventory-management problems.

Chapter 19 discussed several ideas related to purchasing and inventory management that were designed to minimize inventory carrying costs and processing costs. The emphasis here is on practices that will minimize average inventory levels, thereby releasing funds for other applications. A correct minimum of inventory is the level needed to maintain desired production schedules or a required level of customer service. A concerted effort to manage inventory can trim inventory fat and pay handsome dividends. For example, the Boston-based Superior Pet Products Company tightened its inventory policies and freed up about $400,000 in capital. This released capital also meant a savings of $80,000 in interest expense, which was being paid to finance the inventory.[3]

Staying on Top of Inventory

One of the first tactics of managing inventory to reduce capital investment is to discover what is in inventory and how long it has been there. Too often, items are purchased, warehoused, and essentially lost! A yearly inventory for accounting purposes is inadequate for good inventory control. Items that are slow movers may sit in a retailer's inventory beyond the time when markdowns should have been applied.

Computers can provide assistance in inventory identification and control. The use of physical inventories may still be required, but only as a supplement to the computer system.

Holding the Reins on Stockpiling

Some small-business managers tend to overbuy inventory. There are several possible reasons for this behavior. First, the entrepreneur's enthusiasm may forecast greater demand than is realistic. Second, the personalization of the business-customer relationship may motivate the manager to stock everything customers want. Third, the price-conscious entrepreneur may overly subscribe to vendor appeal—"buy now, prices are going up."

Stockpiling is not bad per se. Improperly managed and uncontrolled stockpiling may, however, greatly increase inventory carrying costs and place a heavy drain on the funds of a small business. Managers must exercise restraint.

MANAGING ACCOUNTS PAYABLE

Cash-flow management and accounts-payable management are intertwined. As long as a payable is outstanding, the buying firm can keep cash equal to that amount in its own checking account. When payment is made, however, the company's cash account is reduced accordingly.

Even though payables are legal obligations, they can be paid at various times or even renegotiated in some cases. Therefore, financial management of accounts payable hinges on negotiation and timing.

Negotiation

Any business is subject to emergencies, which may lead to a request for the postponement of its payable obligations. If a firm finds itself in this situation, it should so inform its creditors. Usually creditors will cooperate in working out a solution because they are interested in the firm and want it to succeed.

Timing

It would not be surprising to find the motto "Buy Now, Pay Later, Later, Later . . ." over all enterpreneurs' desks. By buying on credit, a small business is using creditors' funds to supply short-term cash needs. The longer the creditors' funds can be "borrowed," the better. Payment, therefore, should seemingly be made as late as the agreement specifies.

Typically, trade credit will include payment terms that contain a cash discount. With trade-discount terms, the entrepreneur's motto of "Buy Now, Pay

Table 21-5
An Accounts-
Payable Timetable

Timetable (Days after invoice date)	Account Settlement Costs for a $100,000 Purchase (Terms: 3/10, net 30)
Day 1 through Day 10	$97,000
Day 11 through Day 30	$100,000
Day 31 and thereafter	$100,000 + possible late penalty + deterioration in credit standing

Later" may be inappropriate. For example, terms of 3/10, net 30 offer a 3 percent potential discount. Table 21-5 shows the possible settlement costs over the credit period of 30 days. For a $100,000 purchase, a settlement of only $97,000 is required if payment is made within the first 10 days ($100,000 minus the 3 percent discount of $3,000). During the interim between Day 11 and Day 31, a settlement of $100,000 is required. After 30 days, the settlement cost may exceed the original amount, as late-payment fees are added.

The timing question is as follows: Should the account be paid on Day 10 or Day 30? There is little reason for paying $97,000 on Day 1 through Day 9, when the same amount will settle the account on Day 10. Likewise, if payment is to be made after Day 10, why not wait until Day 30 to pay $100,000?

By paying on the last day of the discount period, the buyer saves the amount of the discount that is offered. The other alternative, payment on Day 30, allows the buyer to use the seller's money for an additional 20 days by foregoing the discount. In the example shown in Figure 21-10, the buyer can use the seller's $97,000 for 20 days at a cost of $3,000. The annualized interest rate that is involved can be calculated as follows:

$$\text{Annualized rate} = \frac{\text{Days in year}}{\text{Net period} - \text{Cash disc. period}} \times \frac{\text{Cash discount \%}}{100 - \text{Cash disc. \%}}$$

$$= \frac{365}{30-10} \times \frac{3}{100-3}$$

$$= 18.25 \times .030928$$

$$= 56.4\%$$

By failing to take a discount, a business typically pays a high rate for use of a supplier's money—56.4 percent in this case. Payment on Day 10 appears entirely logical. Recall, however, that the payment also affects cash flow. If funds are extremely short, the small firm may simply have to pay on the last possible day in order to avoid an overdraft at the bank.

1. The working-capital cycle begins with the purchase of inventory and ends with the collection of accounts receivable. The relative timing of events within the cycle can be represented graphically by a time line. The cash conversion period is the most critical period of the working-capital cycle, because it is in this time period that a firm can become illiquid.

2. The cash flow system consists of cash flowing into a business (through sales revenue, borrowing, and so on) and cash flowing out of the business (through purchases, operating expenses, loan repayments, and so on). These inflows and outflows are reconciled in the cash budget, which involves forecasts of receipts and expenditures on a month-to-month basis. If projections indicate a negative cash flow from operations, arrangements must be made to secure additional funds through borrowing or investment.

3. Profits and cash flows are different. Many small companies are profitable, but they develop cash flow problems, either from failing to understand the nature of the working-capital cycle or from failing to anticipate the negative consequences of growth on the company's cash flows.

4. Management of working capital requires attention not only to cash flow but also to accounts receivable, inventory, and accounts payable. A firm can improve its cash flow by speeding up collections from customers, minimizing inventories, and using the maximum allowable time in paying suppliers.

DISCUSSION QUESTIONS

1. Describe the working-capital cycle by listing the events that directly affect cash and those that do not.

2. What are the key dates within the working-capital cycle?

3. What information would you have from a company's financial statements to calculate the average days in inventories and in accounts payable?

4. What determines the length of a firm's cash conversion period?

5. What are some examples of cash receipts that are not sales revenue?

6. Explain how expenses and cash disbursements during a month may be different.

7. Explain how a firm may be unable to pay its bills when its income statement shows a profit.

8. Assume that a small firm is growing rapidly. What kind of pressures or problems does this create in its working-capital management?

9. If a small business has a reasonably accurate projected income statement, does it need a cash budget? Why?

10. In a typical small business, what is the source of most cash receipts shown in the cash budget?

11. Suppose you are a banker and are considering loan requests from two small firms. One of them has a cash budget. How does this fact affect your evaluation of the two requests? Explain.

12. How may a seller speed up the collection of receivables? Give examples that may apply to various stages in the life cycle of receivables.
13. Explain the difference between borrowing by pledging accounts receivable and factoring. What are the principal drawbacks to accounts-receivable financing?
14. Suppose that a small firm could successfully shift to a just-in-time inventory system. How would this affect its working-capital management?
15. Do you think a business has an obligation to pay its accounts payable before the net due date if it has the funds? Why or why not?

YOU MAKE THE CALL

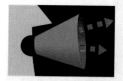

Situation 1

A small firm specializing in the sale and installation of swimming pools was profitable but devoted very little attention to management of working capital. It had, for example, never prepared or used a cash budget.

To be sure that money was available for payments as needed, the firm kept a minimum of $25,000 in a checking account. At times, this account grew larger, and it totaled $43,000 at one time. The owner felt that this practice of cash management worked well for a small company because it eliminated all of the paperwork associated with cash budgeting. Moreover, it had enabled the firm to pay its bills in a timely manner.

Questions
1. What are the advantages and weaknesses of the minimum-cash-balance practice?
2. There is a saying, "If it's not broke, don't fix it." In view of the firm's present success in paying bills promptly, should it be encouraged to use a cash budget? Defend your answer.

Situation 2

Ruston Manufacturing Company is a small firm selling entirely on a credit basis. It has experienced successful operation and earned modest profits.

Sales are made on the basis of net payment in 30 days. Collections from customers run approximately 70 percent in 30 days, 20 percent in 60 days, 7 percent in 90 days, and approximately 3 percent bad debts.

The owner has considered the possibility of offering a cash discount for early payment. However, the practice seems costly and possibly unnecessary. As the owner has put it, "Why should I bribe customers to pay what they legally owe?"

Questions
1. Is a cash discount the equivalent of a bribe?
2. How would a cash discount policy relate to bad debts?
3. What cash discount policy, if any, would you recommend?
4. What other approaches might be used to improve cash flow from receivables?

EXPERIENTIAL EXERCISES

1. Interview the owner of a small company to determine the nature of the firm's working capital time line. Try to estimate the cash conversion period.
2. Prepare a cash budget projecting your personal cash receipts and cash expenditures month by month for the next three months. Include an explanation of any unusual features.
3. Interview a small-business owner or credit manager regarding the extension of credit and/or the collection of receivables in that firm. Summarize your findings in a report.
4. Interview a banker or CPA concerning weaknesses of small firms in managing cash flow. Include in your report one or more examples cited by your interviewee.

REFERENCES TO SMALL BUSINESS PRACTICES

Borden, Karl, "Managing Collection," *Small Business Forum,* Vol. 9, No. 2 (Fall 1991), pp. 35–45.

Borden, Karl, "Managing Inventory," *Small Business Forum,* Vol. 9, No. 3 (Winter 1991/1992), pp. 38–51.

Borden, Karl, "Managing Accounts Payable," *Small Business Forum,* Vol. 10, No. 1 (Spring 1992), pp. 32–46.

> The foregoing three articles comprise a series providing practical ideas on how to manage a small company's accounts receivable, inventory, and accounts payable.

"Convince Us You Can Solve Your Cash Flow Problems: A Case Study," with responses by Herbert E. Kierulff, Dean Treptow, Aaron Caillouet, Alvin J. Williams, Steven K. Lacy, Susan G. Macy and Donald T. Nicholaisen, *Small Business Forum,* Vol. 8, No. 3 (Winter 1990/1991), pp. 6–32.

> The article provides a case of a small company having cash flow problems. The case was reviewed by a number of people with expertise in the area, who then offered suggestions to the owner on how to resolve the problems.

McKeown, Kate, "Go with the Cash Flow." *D&B Reports,* Vol. 36, No. 5 (September–October, 1988), pp. 30–35.

> This article describes the frustrations of a small-business owner in trying to exercise financial control without adequate information on cash flow. The improvement achieved through better analysis of cash aspects of the business is explained.

ENDNOTES

1. John A. Welsh and Jerry F. White, Administering the *Closely Held Company* (Englewood Cliffs, NJ: Prentice-Hall, Inc., 1980), p. 50.

2. *Ibid.,* p. 51.

3. "How to Unlock Your Company's Hidden Cash," *Inc.,* Vol. 2, No. 7 (July 1980), p. 64.

CHAPTER 22

Capital Budgeting

SPOTLIGHT ON SMALL BUSINESS

A small company often uses very simple methods for evaluating new investment opportunities. As it grows, it tends to adopt more sophisticated analytical methods. This progression is evident in the Visador Corporation, a building materials manufacturing company. As explained by Stuart Hall, grandson of the founder:

In the early years of Visador, my grandfather and company founder, J. D. Hall, Jr., developed a simple set of rules for managers under his supervision.

Stuart Hall

- *If an asset purchase would result in a payback period of more than three years, he wanted to discuss the project but would probably not approve it.*

- *If the payback period was one to three years, he still wanted to discuss the project before its probable approval.*

- *If the project would yield a payback of between six months and one year, he expected the manager to purchase the asset (assuming funds were available) and then discuss the project with him.*

- *If the asset purchase was projected to yield a payback of less than six months, the manager was expected to make the purchase and not even discuss the project with him.*

- *In later years, our approval rules changed somewhat to mirror the overall corporate goal for return on assets used in Visador's Bonus Program. If a project would yield an internal rate of return in excess of 14 percent, we generally approved the project.*

LOOKING AHEAD

After studying this chapter, you should be able to:
1. Apply the techniques commonly used in making capital budgeting decisions.
2. Determine the firm's cost of capital or the discount rate to be used in discounted cash flow techniques, and understand the mistake in using the firm's cost of debt as the discount rate in capital budgeting.
3. Explain the small firm's need for liquidity in long-term investments.
4. Describe capital budgeting practices of small firms.
5. Evaluate expansion opportunities by considering such factors as growth philosophy, constraints on expansion, and the nature of search activity.

NEW TERMS AND CONCEPTS

accounting return on investment	net present value (NPV)	weighted cost of capital
payback period	internal rate of return (IRR)	favorable financial leverage
discounted cash flow techniques	cost of capital	discounted payback method
	opportunity cost	

Capital budgeting analysis helps managers make decisions about long-term investments. In developing a new product line, for instance, a firm needs to expand its manufacturing capabilities and buy inventory required to make the product. That is, it makes investments today with the expectation of receiving profits or cash flows in the future, possibly over 10 or 20 years. This chapter explains how a firm's managers can carefully analyze capital expenditure questions and best make such crucial decisions.

Examples of capital budgeting decisions made by a small company include the following:

1. Development and introduction of a new product that shows promise but requires additional study and improvement.
2. Replacement of the company's delivery trucks with newer models.
3. Expansion of sales activity into a new territory.
4. Construction of a new building.
5. Employment of several additional salespersons for more intensive selling in the existing market.

Although the owner of a small business does not make long-term investment decisions on a frequent basis, capital budgeting is still important. Correct investment decisions will add value to the firm. A wrong capital budgeting decision, on the other hand, may prove fatal to a small firm.

This chapter: (a) describes the basic capital budgeting techniques, especially as they relate to the small company, (b) looks at how the managers and owners of small firms evaluate capital investments, and (c) looks briefly at growth philosophy and other considerations important to the small firm in long-term expansion decisions.

CAPITAL BUDGETING TECHNIQUES: AN OVERVIEW

Three techniques for making capital budgeting decisions are considered here. They all attempt to answer one general question: Do the future benefits from an investment exceed the cost of making the investment? However, each of the three techniques has its own specific question to answer. The techniques and the specific question each addresses can be stated as follows:

1. *Accounting return on investment.* How many dollars in average profits are generated per dollar of average investment?
2. *Payback period.* How long will it take to recover the original investment outlay?
3. *Discounted cash flow technique.* How does the present value of future benefits from the investment compare to the investment outlay?

There are three simple rules to be used in judging the merits of an investment. While they may seem trite, they state in simple terms the best thinking about the attractiveness of an investment. They are:

1. Businesses prefer more cash rather than less.
2. Businesses prefer cash sooner rather than later.
3. Businesses prefer less risk rather than more.

Figure 22-1
A Long-Term Investment in a New Fleet of Cement Trucks Should Be Based on Careful Analysis Using Capital Budgeting Techniques

Accounting Return on Investment: A Profit Criterion

accounting return on investment
ratio of average annual profits to the average book value of an investment

A small firm invests because it intends to earn profits. The **accounting return on investment** technique compares the average annual after-tax profits it expects to receive with the dollars it expects to invest. That is,

$$\text{Accounting return on investment} = \frac{\text{Average annual profits}}{\text{Average book value of the investment}}$$

The average annual profits can be estimated by adding the after-tax profits expected over the life of the project and dividing by the number of years. The average book investment equals the average of the initial outlay and the estimated ending project salvage value.

To make an accept-reject decision, the calculated return is compared with a minimum acceptable return. The minimum acceptable rate of return is usually based on past experience.

To illustrate the use of the accounting return on investment, assume that you are contemplating buying a piece of equipment for $10,000 and depreciating it over four years to a book value of zero (it will have no salvage value). Further assume that you expect the investment to generate after-tax profits each year as follows:

Year	After-tax Profits
1	$1,000
2	2,000
3	2,500
4	3,000

The accounting return on the proposed investment is calculated as follows:

$$\text{Accounting return on investment} = \frac{(\$1,000+\$2,000+\$2,500+\$3,000)\div 4}{(\$10,000+\$0)\div 2}$$

$$= \frac{\$2,125}{\$5,000} = .425 = 42.5\%$$

For most people, a 42.5 percent profit rate would seem outstanding! Assuming the calculated accounting return on investment of 42.5 percent exceeds your minimum acceptable return, you will accept the project. If not, you will reject the investment, provided of course that you have confidence in the technique.

While the accounting return on investment is simple to calculate, it has two major shortcomings. First, it is based on accounting profits rather than actual cash flows received. As an investor, you should be more interested in the future cash produced by the investment than by the reported profits. Second, the return measurement ignores the time value of money. Thus, while it is a popular technique, the accounting return on investment fails to satisfy any of the three criteria given earlier about preference for more cash received sooner and with less risk.

Payback Period:
A Nondiscounted Cash Flow Criterion

The **payback period** technique, as the name suggests, measures how long it will take to recover the initial cash outlay of the investment. As such, it deals with cash flows as opposed to accounting profits. The merits of any project are judged on whether it recovers the initial investment outlay in less time than some maximum acceptable payback period. For example, an owner may not want to invest in any project that requires more than five years to recoup the investment.

payback period
the length of time before a cash investment is recovered

To illustrate, assume that we are studying an investment in equipment with an expected life of ten years. The investment outlay will be $15,000, and we will depreciate the cost of the equipment on a straight-line basis, or $1,500 per year. If we make the investment, we estimate the after-tax profits will be as follows:

Years	Annual After-tax Profits
1–2	$1,000
3–6	2,000
7–10	2,500

To determine the after-tax cash flows from the investment, we would merely add back the depreciation of $1,500 each year to the profit. The reason for adding the depreciation to the profit is that it was deducted in calculating the profits (as an accounting entry) even though it was not a cash outflow. The results, then, would be as follows:

Years	Annual After-tax Cash Flows
1–2	$2,500
3–6	3,500
7–10	4,000

By the end of the second year, we will have recovered $5,000 of our investment outlay ($2,500 per year). By the end of the fourth year, we will have recouped another $7,000, or $12,000 in total. We still need $3,000, which can be recovered in year five when $3,500 is expected. Thus, it will take 4.86 years (4 years plus $3,000 ÷ $3,500) to recover the investment. If our maximum acceptable payback is more than 4.86 years, we will accept the investment.

The popularity of the payback method is unquestioned. Many managers and owners of companies use the technique in evaluating investment decisions. However, it has some real deficiencies. Although it does use cash flows, rather than accounting profits, it contains two significant weaknesses. First, it does not consider the time value of money (prefer cash sooner rather than later). Second, it fails to consider the cash flows received after the payback period (prefer more cash rather than less), which may be significant. In contrast, discounted cash flow techniques allow managers to do the best job in making investment decisions.

Discounted Cash Flow Techniques

discounted cash flow techniques methods of comparing the present value of future cash flows with the value of the initial investment

Managers can avoid the deficiencies of the accounting return on investment and the payback period techniques by using discounted cash flow analysis. **Discounted cash flow techniques** take into consideration the fact that cash today is more valuable than cash received one year from now. One can earn interest, for example, on cash that one can invest immediately, which is not true for cash to be received later. (To use these techniques, you must understand the basic concept of the time value of money and how to compute the present value of a future dollar. If you have not studied present value computations or need a refresher, you may want to read Appendix C, "Time Value of Money," at the end of the text.)

The discounted cash flow techniques compare the present value of the future cash flows with the initial investment outlay. The analysis may take the form of (a) the net present value method or (b) the internal rate of return method.

net present value the present value of future cash flows, less the initial investment outlay

Net Present Value. To measure a project's **net present value**, we estimate *today's* value of the dollars flowing in from the project in the future and deduct the amount of the investment being made. That is, we discount the future after-tax cash flows back to their present value and then subtract the initial investment outlay. The computation may be represented as follows:

$$\text{Net present value} = \left(\begin{array}{c} \text{Present value of future} \\ \text{after-tax cash flows} \end{array} \right) - \left(\begin{array}{c} \text{Initial} \\ \text{investment outlay} \end{array} \right)$$

If the net present value of the investment is positive (that is, if the present value of future cash flows exceeds the initial outlay), we would accept the project. Otherwise, we would reject the investment.

The actual computation for finding the net present value is as follows:

$$NPV = \left(\frac{ACF_1}{(1+K)^1} + \frac{ACF_2}{(1+K)^2} + \frac{ACF_3}{(1+K)^3} + \ldots + \frac{ACF_n}{(1+K)^n} \right) - IO$$

where NPV = net present value of the project.

ACF_t = the after-tax cash flow in year t.

n = the life of the project in years.

K = the discount rate (required rate of return).

IO = the initial investment outlay.

To illustrate how to compute the net present value, assume that we are looking at an investment that will cost $12,000. We should be able to salvage the equipment for $2,000 at the end of the product's expected life of five years. The investment is expected to provide the following after-tax cash flows as a result of increased product sales.

Years	Annual After-tax Cash Flows
1	$1,500
2	2,500
3	4,000
4	4,000
5	3,000

These cash flows, plus the $2,000 in expected salvage value, could be represented graphically on a time line as follows. (Notice that the after-tax cash flow in the fifth year includes both the $3,000 cash flows from operating the project and the $2,000 expected salvage value.)

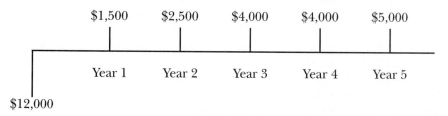

Further assume the firm's required rate of return, or cost of capital as it is often called, is 14 percent. As will be explained later in the chapter, a firm's cost of capital, which is used as the discount rate, is the rate the firm must earn to satisfy its investors. Given this information, we can compute the investment's net present value as follows:

$$NPV = \left(\frac{\$1,500}{(1+.14)^1} + \frac{\$2,500}{(1+.14)^2} + \frac{\$4,000}{(1+.14)^3} + \frac{\$4,000}{(1+.14)^4} + \frac{\$5,000}{(1+.14)^5} \right) - \$12,000$$

Using the Present Value Interest Factors $(PVIF_{k,n})$ for discount rate k and year n in Appendix A at the end of the text, we find the net present value of the investment to be −$1,099, calculated as follows:

$$NPV = [\$1,500(PVIF_{14\%,\ 1\ yr.}) + \$2,500(PVIF_{14\%,\ 2\ yr.})$$
$$+\$4,000(PVIF_{14\%,\ 3\ yr.}) + \$4,000(PVIF_{14\%,\ 4\ yr.})$$
$$+\$5,000(PVIF_{14\%,\ 5\ yr.})] - \$12,000$$

$$NPV = [\$1,500(.877) + \$2,500(.769) + \$4,000(.675) + \$4,000(.592)$$
$$+\$5,000(.519)] - \$12,000$$

$$= \$10,901 - \$12,000$$

$$= -\$1,099$$

Rather than using the present value tables, we could solve for the present value of the project by using a financial calculator. (Such computations are shown in Figure 22-2 for two Hewlett Packard calculators, models 10B and 17B II.)

Since the net present value of the proposed investment is negative (i.e., the present value of the future cash flows is less than the cost of the investment), we should not make the investment. The negative net present value shows that the investment would not satisfy the firm's required rate of return of 14 percent. Only if the present value of the future cash flows were greater than the $12,000 investment outlay would the firm's required rate of return be exceeded.

Internal Rate of Return. In the preceding example, we calculated the net present value and found it to be negative. Given the negative net present value, we concluded, and rightfully so, that the project does not earn the 14 percent required rate of return. It must be earning a rate less than 14 percent. But we did not take the next logical step and ask what rate would be earned, assuming our projections are on target. The **internal rate of return (IRR)** provides that answer by measuring the rate of return we expect to earn on the project.

internal rate of return (IRR)

the rate of return a firm expects to earn on the project

To calculate the internal rate of return, we must find the discount rate that gives us a zero net present value. At that rate, the present value of the future cash flows just equals the investment outlay. Using the previous example, we need to determine the discount rate that causes the future cash flows to equal $12,000, the cost of the investment. In other words, we need to find the discount rate or *IRR*, that satisfies the following condition:

$$\left(\begin{array}{c}\text{Present value of future}\\\text{after-tax cash flows}\end{array}\right) - \left(\begin{array}{c}\text{Initial}\\\text{investment outlay}\end{array}\right) = \$0$$

or

$$\left(\begin{array}{c}\text{Present value of future}\\\text{after-tax cash flows}\end{array}\right) = \left(\begin{array}{c}\text{Initial}\\\text{investment outlay}\end{array}\right)$$

Figure 22-2
Solving *NPV*
Problems Using
Hewlett Packard
10B and 17B II
Calculators

Problem:

Years	Annual After-tax Cash Flows
0	–$12,000
1	1,500
2	2,500
3	4,000
4	4,000
5	5,000

Solution:

Hewlett Packard 10B

1. Clear the memory.

2. Enter the investment outlay, CF_0, as follows: 12,000 $\boxed{+/-}$ $\boxed{CF_i}$.

3. Enter the first year after-tax cash flow, CF_1, as follows: 1,500 $\boxed{CF_i}$. (If the $1,500 was expected for three years consecutively, we could have pressed '3' and $\boxed{}$ $\boxed{N_i}$ to indicate three years of cash flows.)

4. Repeat the process to enter the other cash flows.

5. Enter 14 $\boxed{I/YR}$ to indicate the discount rate.

6. Press $\boxed{}$ $\boxed{NPV}$ to find the project net present value of –$1,095.49.

Hewlett Packard 17B II

1. Select the FIN menu and then the CFLO menu; clear memory if FLOW(0) = ? does not appear.

2. Enter the investment outlay, CF_0, as follows: 12,000 $\boxed{+/-}$ $\boxed{INPUT}$.

3. Enter the first-year after-tax cash flow, CF_1, as follows: 1,500 $\boxed{INPUT}$.

4. Now the calculator will inquire if the $1,500 is for period 1 only. Press $\boxed{INPUT}$ to indicate the cash flow is for one year only. If the $1,500 was expected for three years consecutively, we could have pressed '3' and $\boxed{INPUT}$ to indicate three years of cash flows.

5. Enter the remaining CFs and $\boxed{INPUT}$, followed each time by another $\boxed{INPUT}$ to indicate that each cash flow is for one year only.

6. Press $\boxed{EXIT}$ and then $\boxed{CALC}$.

7. Enter 14 $\boxed{I\%}$ to indicate the discount rate.

8. Press $\boxed{NPV}$ to find the project net present value of –$1,095.49.

Remembering that ACF_t is the after-tax cash flow received in year t, IO is the amount of the investment outlay, and n is the life of the project in years, the internal rate of return, IRR, is the discount rate where:

$$\left(\frac{ACF_1}{(1+IRR)^1}+\frac{ACF_2}{(1+IRR)^2}+\frac{ACF_3}{(1+IRR)^3}+ \ldots +\frac{ACF_n}{(1+IRR)^n}\right)-IO=\$0$$

In the previous example, the IRR would be found as follows:

$$\left(\frac{\$1,500}{(1+IRR)^1}+\frac{\$2,500}{(1+IRR)^2}+\frac{\$4,000}{(1+IRR)^3}+\frac{\$4,000}{(1+IRR)^4}+\frac{\$5,000}{(1+IRR)^5}\right)-\$12,000=\$0$$

To compute the internal rate of return, we have a bit of a problem. We cannot solve for the answer directly. Either we must try different rates until we discover the rate that gives us a zero net present value, or we can use a financial calculator and let it derive the answer for us. Let's look at the first approach, which uses the present value table at the end of the text.

As already noted, finding the internal rate of return using the present value tables involves a trial-and-error process. We have to keep trying new rates until we find the discount rate that results in the present value of the future cash flows just equaling the initial investment outlay. If the internal rate of return is somewhere between rates in the present value tables, we then must use interpolation to estimate the exact rate.

In the example, we know that a 14 percent discount rate results in the present value of the future cash flows being less than the initial outlay. Thus, we would not earn 14 percent if we made the investment. We will therefore want to try a lower rate. Let's arbitrarily select 12 percent and see what happens:

$$NPV=\left(\frac{\$1,500}{(1+.12)^1}+\frac{\$2,500}{(1+.12)^2}+\frac{\$4,000}{(1+.12)^3}+\frac{\$4,000}{(1+.12)^4}+\frac{\$5,000}{(1+.12)^5}\right)-\$12,000$$

Using the Appendix A Present Value Interest Factors at the end of the text, we find the net present value at a discount rate of 12 percent to be $-\$441$.

$$NPV=[\$1,500(.893)+\$2,500(.797)+\$4,000(.712)+\$4,000(.636)$$
$$+\$5,000(.567)]-\$12,000$$
$$=\$11,559-\$12,000=-\$441$$

Since the net present value is still negative, we know that the rate is even less than 12 percent. So let's try 10 percent.

$$NPV=\left(\frac{\$1,500}{(1+.10)^1}+\frac{\$2,500}{(1+.10)^2}+\frac{\$4,000}{(1+.10)^3}+\frac{\$4,000}{(1+.10)^4}+\frac{\$5,000}{(1+.10)^5}\right)-\$12,000$$
$$=[\$1,500(.909)+\$2,500(.826)+\$4,000(.751)+\$4,000(.683)+\$5,000(.621)]$$
$$-\$12,000$$
$$=\$12,270-\$12,000=\$270$$

Given that we now have a positive net present value ($270), we know that the internal rate of return is between 10 percent and 12 percent.[1] Since the internal rate of return is less than the firm's required rate of return of 14 percent, we would reject the investment. (Note: Any time net present value is positive, the internal rate of return will be greater than the company's required rate of return. Conversely, any time the net present value is negative, the internal rate of return will be less than the company's required rate of return.)

Capital Budgeting: A Comprehensive Example

Let's consider one more example where we use the various capital budgeting techniques on a single project. Suppose it is the end of 1993, and we are thinking about making a capital expenditure of $25,000 to invest in a new product line. The cost of the investment includes $15,000 for equipment and $10,000 in working capital (additional accounts receivable and inventories). The investment would have a five-year life (1994–1998), after which the equipment would have a zero salvage value. The cost of the equipment would be depreciated over the five years on a straight-line basis. The working capital would need to be maintained for the five years, but could then be liquidated and the firm would recover the full $10,000 in 1998. That is, the accounts receivable would all be collected and the inventories would be liquidated. The projected income statements and after-tax cash flows for the next five years are given in Table 22-1. Relying on the data in Table 22-1, each of the evaluation techniques is calculated below:

1. *Accounting return on investment:*

$$\text{Accounting return on investment} = \frac{\sum_{t=1}^{n} (\text{Expected earnings after taxes in year } t) \div n}{(\text{Initial outlay} + \text{Expected salvage value}) \div 2}$$

$$= \frac{(\$3,000 + \$4,500 + \$6,000 + \$6,000 + \$6,000) \div 5}{(\$25,000 + \$10,000) \div 2}$$

$$= \frac{\$5,100}{\$17,500} = .2914 = 29.14\%$$

2. *Payback period:*

Year	After-tax Cash Flow	Cumulative Cash Flows
1	$6,000	$6,000
2	7,500	13,500
3	9,000	22,500
4	2,500	25,000
	$25,000	

Payback period $= 3 + (\$2,500 / \$9,000)$ years $= 3.28$ years

	1993	1994	1995	1996	1997	1998
Sales		$30,000	$35,000	$40,000	$40,000	$40,000
Cost of goods sold		18,000	21,000	24,000	24,000	24,000
Gross profit		$12,000	$14,000	$16,000	$16,000	$16,000
Operating expenses:						
Marketing expenses		5,000	5,000	5,000	5,000	5,000
Depreciation expense		3,000	3,000	3,000	3,000	3,000
Operating profits		$4,000	$6,000	$8,000	$8,000	$8,000
Taxes		1,000	1,500	2,000	2,000	2,000
Earnings after taxes		$3,000	$4,500	$6,000	$6,000	$6,000
Plus depreciation		3,000	3,000	3,000	3,000	3,000
Plus working capital						10,000
After-tax cash flows	($25,000)	$6,000	$7,500	$9,000	$9,000	$19,000
Book value of the investment						
Working capital	$10,000	$10,000	$10,000	$10,000	$10,000	$10,000
Equipment	15,000	12,000	9,000	6,000	3,000	0
Total book value	$25,000	$22,000	$19,000	$16,000	$13,000	$10,000

Table 22-1
Profits and Cash Flows— Comprehensive Example

3. *Net present value:*

$$NPV = \left(\frac{ACF_1}{(1+K)^1} + \frac{ACF_2}{(1+K)^2} + \frac{ACF_3}{(1+K)^3} + \frac{ACF_4}{(1+IRR)^4} + \frac{ACF_5}{(1+K)^5} \right) - IO$$

$$= \frac{\$6,000}{(1+.15)^1} + \frac{\$7,500}{(1+.15)^2} + \frac{\$9,000}{(1+.15)^3} + \frac{\$9,000}{(1+.15)^4} + \frac{\$10,000}{(1+.15)^5} - \$25,000$$

Using a financial calculator, we find the net present value to be $6,398. (The same answer could be found, subject to rounding differences, using Appendix A at the end of the text.)

4. *Internal rate of return:*

$$\left(\frac{ACF_1}{(1+IRR)^1} + \frac{ACF_2}{(1+IRR)^2} + \frac{ACF_3}{(1+IRR)^3} + \frac{ACF_4}{(1+IRR)^4} + \frac{ACF_5}{(1+IRR)^5} \right) - IO = \$0$$

$$\frac{\$6,000}{(1+IRR)^1} + \frac{\$7,500}{(1+IRR)^2} + \frac{\$9,000}{(1+IRR)^3}$$

$$+ \frac{\$9,000}{(1+IRR)^4} + \frac{\$19,000}{(1+IRR)^5} - \$25,000 = \$0$$

Again using a financial calculator, we find the internal rate of return to be 23.6 percent.

We have now presented several approaches that are available to the owner-manager of a small firm for evaluating investment opportunities. We have suggested that the greatest trust should be placed in the discounted cash flow techniques when wanting to reach good decisions. However, we have said nothing about how we determine the discount rate or required rate of return in our discounted cash flow analyses. The discount rate used has come to be called the *cost of capital,* or more precisely the *weighted cost of capital,* and it is an issue that deserves attention.

DETERMINING THE FIRM'S COST OF CAPITAL

The **cost of capital** is the rate of return a firm must earn on its investments in order to satisfy its debt holders and its owners. An investment with an internal rate of return below the cost of capital—a rate of return below what creditors and owners require—will decrease the value of the firm and the owner's equity value. An investment with an expected rate of return above the cost of capital, on the other hand, will increase the owner's value. Although the issue is extremely important for effective financial management, experience suggests that few owners of small firms are aware of the cost-of-capital concept, much less able to estimate their company's cost of capital.

cost of capital
the rate of return a firm must earn to satisfy owners and debt holders

Measuring a Firm's Cost of Capital

The firm's cost of capital is based on the opportunity-cost concept. An **opportunity cost** is the rate of return an owner could earn on another investment of similar risk. For example, an owner of a company contemplating an expansion would want to know what rate of return could be earned elsewhere for the same amount of risk. If the owner could earn 15 percent with the money by investing elsewhere, then the expansion investment should not be made unless it is expected to earn at least 15 percent on the owner's investment. The 15 percent is the opportunity cost of the money, and therefore should be the cost of capital for the firm's equity investors.

opportunity cost
the rate of return an owner could earn on a similar investment

The cost of capital should recognize all permanent sources of finance, both debt and ownership equity. That is, we need a **weighted cost of capital**. For instance, assume that a firm expects to finance future investments with 40 percent debt and 60 percent equity. Further assume that the opportunity cost of funds supplied by debt holders (that is, the current interest rate) is 10 percent. However, since the interest paid by the company is tax deductible and the firm's tax rate is 25 percent, the after-tax cost of the money for the company is only 7.5 percent $(10\% \times (1 - .25))$. Further assume that the opportunity cost of capital for the owners is thought to be 18 percent. From this information, the firm's weighted cost of capital would be 13.8 percent:

weighted cost of capital
the cost of capital adjusted to reflect the relative costs of debt and equity financing

	Weight	Cost	Weighted Cost
Debt	40%	7.5%	3.0%
Equity	60	18.0	10.8
	100%		13.8%

The 13.8 percent rate becomes the discount rate in present value analysis, assuming that future investments will be financed on average by 40 percent debt and 60 percent equity and that the riskiness of the future investments will be similar to the riskiness of the firm's existing assets.

The great difficulty in measuring a company's weighted cost of capital is estimating the cost of owners' equity. Debt holders receive their rate of return mostly through the interest paid to them by the company, and the cost estimation is relatively straightforward. The required return for the owners is another matter, however. Their expected returns are partially in the form of dividends received, but mostly are derived through the increase in the value of the firm—what is generally called capital gains.

In measuring the cost of equity for a large publicly traded company, an analyst uses market data to estimate the owners' required rate of return. However, a small firm is owned either by a family or a specific small group of investors. Consequently, we need not use market data but can inquire directly about these owners' required rates of return. We need only be assured that they are informed about competitive rates in the marketplace, and then allow them to set the required rate of return as the owners.

Using the Cost of Debt as an Investment Criterion

The weighted cost of capital may be fine in theory, but what if a company could borrow the entire amount needed for an investment in a new product line? Is it really necessary to use the weighted cost of capital, or would it be all right to base the decision simply on the cost of the debt providing the funding?

Consider the Poling Corporation. The firm's owners believe they could earn 14 percent from purchasing $50,000 in new equipment to expand the business. Although the firm tries to maintain a capital structure with equal amounts of debt and equity, it can borrow the entire $50,000 from the bank at an interest rate of 12 percent. Without even having to compute it, we know that a firm's net income will increase from using debt anytime the return on the investment is greater than the cost of the debt financing. In this case, the expected return on investment is 14 percent and the cost of debt financing is 12 percent. The increase in net income comes from the use of **favorable financial leverage,** investing at a rate of return that exceeds the interest rate on borrowed money.

favorable financial leverage
investing at a rate of return that exceeds the interest rate on borrowed money

The owners of the firm have also estimated the required rate of return for their funds to be 18 percent. However, since the firm can finance the purchase totally by debt, the owners have decided to make the investment and finance it by borrowing the money from the bank at 12 percent. The investment is made, and all seems well.

The following year, the firm's owners find another investment opportunity costing $50,000, but with an expected internal rate of return this time of 17 percent—better than the previous year's 14 percent. However, when Poling's owners approach the bank for financing, they find it unwilling to lend any more money . In the words of the banker, "Poling has used up all of its debt capacity." Before the bank will agree to fund any more loans, the owners either must contribute more of their own money in the form of common equity or find some new investors to invest in the business. However, since the investment does not meet the owners' required rate of return of 18 percent, they feel there is no other option than to reject the investment.

What is the moral of the story for Poling? Intuitively, we can see that Poling's owners have made a mistake. Making the investment in the first year has denied the firm the opportunity to make a better decision in the second year.

As a more general statement, we can conclude that a firm should never use a single cost of financing as the hurdle rate (discount rate) for making capital budgeting decisions. When a firm uses debt, it has implicitly used up some of its debt capacity for future investments, and only when it complements the use of debt with equity will it be able to continue to use more debt in the future. Thus, business owners should always use a weighted cost of capital that recognizes the need to blend equity with debt over time.

CAPITAL BUDGETING AND THE SMALL FIRM'S NEED FOR LIQUIDITY

Although the payback method has definite limitations for evaluating investment opportunities, it does provide an indication of how long funds are tied up in an investment. As such, it gives some measure of liquidity, which may be vitally important for the small firm. Also, while the payback approach ignores cash flows beyond the payback period, such a limitation may have less significance for the small firm. The reason is that long-run cash flows are more uncertain in a small firm. While it is not an ideal answer, a case may be made for the small firm to use a discounted payback period in evaluating a proposed investment. The **discounted payback method** simply calculates the present value of the cash flows before measuring the project's payback period. Thus, we find how many years it will take to recoup an investment when the cash flows are restated on a present-value basis. In this way, we address the liquidity issue and also recognize the time value of money.

To illustrate the use of the discounted payback period, we have estimated the cash flows for a project for the first five years of its life. The project is ex-

discounted payback method
a capital budgeting technique using the present value of future cash flows to determine the payback period

pected to cost $50,000, and the owners have a required rate of return of 15 percent. The expected cash flows for the first five years and their present values are as follows:

Years	Expected Cash Flows	Present Value of Expected Cash Flows
1	$12,000	$10,435
2	14,000	10,586
3	17,000	11,178
4	20,000	11,435
5	20,000	9,944
	Total present value	$53,578

Using the expected cash flows, the payback period for the investment would be 3.35 years ($43,000 received in three years and the remaining $7,000 recouped in .35 year ($7,000 ÷ $20,000 = .35). However, when we recognize the owner's required rate of return of 15 percent, we find the present value of the first five years' expected cash flows to be $53,578. Using these present values, we see that the owners recoup their investment in 4.64 years ($43,634 of the investment received in four years and the remaining $6,366 in .64 year ($6,366 ÷ $9,944 = .64). By comparing projects in this manner, we give consideration both to the present value criterion and the liquidity of the project. Given the importance of liquidity to the small firm, this approach may have some appeal to owners of a small business.

The discussion thus far has been prescriptive in nature (what owners ought to do); but we have not described how owners of smaller companies actually make decisions. The next section provides some insight into how owners of small businesses do make investment decisions.

CAPITAL BUDGETING PRACTICES OF SMALL FIRMS

In an early study (1963) of capital budgeting practices in small firms in Iowa, the owners were asked how they went about analyzing capital budgeting projects.[2] The findings were not encouraging. Fifty percent of the respondents said they used the payback technique. Even worse, 40 percent of the firms used no formal analysis at all. However, these results are extremely dated, going back 30 years. Even the large firms, for the most part, would not have been using discounted cash flow (DCF) techniques to any great extent so long ago.

In a 1983 study, 200 small companies with net worths between $500,000 and $1 million were surveyed.[3] An examination of their approaches for evaluating the merits of proposed capital investments revealed that only 14 percent of the firms used any form of a discounted cash flow technique; 70 percent indicated they used no DCF approach at all; and 9 percent used no formal analysis of any form. While we may be encouraged that the practice of not relying on any formal analysis has declined significantly, little use is made of any market-value rules afforded by present value analysis.

Why were so few small businesses using DCF? Have small-firm decision makers not been taught? Maybe, but we believe that the issue is bigger than training. Since the 1983 study dealt with firms having net worths under $1 million, there were probably a significant number of owners who had not been exposed to financial theory. However, the cause for such limited use of DCF tools probably rests more with the nature of the small firm itself. We would agree that several more important reasons exist, including the following:

1. For many owners of small firms, the business is an extension of their lives. What happens with the business affects them personally, and the same is true in reverse: What happens to the owners personally affects decisions about the firm. The firm and owner are inseparable. You cannot fully understand their decisions about the firm without being aware of the personal factors in their lives. As a consequence, nonfinancial variables may play a significant part in their decisions. For instance, the desire to be viewed as a respected part of the community may be more important to the owner than purely the present value of a decision.
2. The frequent undercapitalization and liquidity problems of the small firm

Figure 22-3
Many Small-Firm Decision Makers, Like This Hardware Store Owner, Are Influenced by Nonfinancial Variables

directly affect the decision-making process, and survival often becomes the top priority. Long-term planning is, therefore, not viewed as a high priority in the total scheme of things.

3. The greater uncertainty of cash flows within the small firm makes long-term forecasts and planning seem unappealing and even a waste of time. The owner simply has no confidence in his or her ability to predict cash flows beyond two or three years. Thus, calculating the cash flows for the entire life of a project is viewed as an effort in futility.

4. The value of a closely held firm is less observable than that of a publicly held firm whose securities are actively traded in the marketplace. Therefore, the owner of a small firm may consider the market-value rule of maximizing net present values irrelevant. In this environment, estimating the firm's cost of capital is also difficult. If computing the large firm's cost of capital is difficult at best, the measurement for the small firm becomes nearly impossible.

5. The smaller size of projects of a small firm may make net present value computations less feasible in a practical sense. Much of the time and expense required to analyze a capital investment is the same whether the project is large or small. Therefore, it is relatively more costly for a small firm to conduct such a study.

6. Management talent within a small firm is a scarce resource. Also, the training of the owner-managers is frequently of a technical nature, as opposed to a business or finance orientation. The perspective of these owners is influenced greatly by their backgrounds.

The foregoing characteristics of the small firm and its owners have a significant effect on the decision-making process within the firm. The result is often a short-term mind set, induced partly by necessity and partly by choice. To the extent possible, the owner of the small company should make every effort to use discounted cash flow techniques and to be certain that contemplated investments will in fact provide returns that exceed the firm's cost of capital.

OTHER CONSIDERATIONS IN EVALUATING EXPANSION OPPORTUNITIES

Having focused on capital budgeting methods for evaluating investment opportunities, let us now turn to other considerations that enter into expansion decisions. These considerations involve a firm's growth philosophy, constraints on expansion, and search activity.

Growth Philosophy

There are many entrepreneurs who prefer smallness. Some of them begin business with the expectation that their firms will remain small, while others come to this conclusion after experimenting with growth. As an example of the latter,

Dangers in Rapid Expansion

Spectacular success and rapid growth are sometimes matched by an equally spectacular demise. James Bildner opened his first upscale grocery store (J. Bildner & Sons, Inc.) in 1984. The store was an instant hit, and it was featured, within a month, in a *Newsweek* story on Yuppies. By 1987, the company had grown to 21 stores with 2,000 employees and $49 million in sales.

By 1988, however, the company had filed for protection under Chapter 11 of the federal Bankruptcy Code.

J. Bildner was a textbook example of the dangers of overexpansion. It grew too fast, too haphazardly. Its market research was flawed, its management ill-equipped to handle rapid growth. And it strayed from its original concept.

This failure revealed a management group that lacked extensive experience. Only one of its 10 officers, for example, was older than 35.

Source: Buck Brown, "James Bildner's Spectacular Rise and Fall," *The Wall Street Journal* (October 24, 1988), p. B1. Reprinted by permission of *The Wall Street Journal,* © Dow Jones & Company, Inc. 1988. All Rights Reserved Worldwide.

Skip Kelley converted his remodeling business into a franchise of Mr. Build International and grew quickly.[4] Sales climbed from $320,000 to $1.2 million in just three years, but Kelley found himself with a company he couldn't control. Problems eventually led to liquidation of the business. "This whole thing cost me a business. It cost me a sports car. It cost me a wife," he says now. "It cost me a lot of things."[5] After Kelley closed the business, he began operating a small building-inspection company out of his house in Byfield, Massachusetts. He values his less-hectic lifestyle and recognizes he was not "the right guy to run a multimillion-dollar company."

Many other small-business owners carry growth ambitions from the very early days of starting their businesses. Growth is a continuing goal for these entrepreneurs. For example, Carl Karcher, who founded Carl's Jr. Hamburgers in California in 1941, expresses his growth philosophy by saying, "If your company decides not to grow, that's the beginning of the end."[6]

But growth is not without its problems. Expansion can strain a firm's capital position and damage current operations. It can also spread managerial skills too thin.

Constraints on Expansion

How rapidly can a small business grow? There is obviously no simple answer to such a question. Even so, a small firm must often decide how rapidly it can grow as it is faced with opportunities for expansion. Such opportunities carry the incentive of increased profits, but they can also stretch a firm's resources to their limit and sometimes beyond. The depth and quality of a company's resources, therefore, impose limits on the rate of expansion.

As noted in earlier chapters, some constraints are financial in nature. Long-term investments in buildings, equipment, new products, or new territories, for example, require infusions of capital that may or may not be available. Also, as noted earlier, growth of sales volume requires a corresponding increase in working capital.

There are also nonfinancial constraints that limit the scope and rapidity of expansion. As explained in Chapter 16, more sophisticated management methods are needed as small firms become big businesses. Time is needed to develop or expand a management team to the point that it can successfully manage a much larger business. Unless a small firm's leadership is truly outstanding, its expansion can sometimes outrun the growth of its management team.

Search Activity

All growth opportunities must be scrutinized carefully. For too long, small business has been saddled with the reputation of making growth decisions without extensive investigation. Small-business managers have often considered growth opportunities on a one-at-a-time basis. They have been less concerned with ranking a number of growth possibilities than with trying to determine the merit of one particular proposal. Moreover, in the analysis of a single proposal, they have often jumped to a conclusion on the basis of sketchy information.

The apparent deficiencies in small-business search activities provide an opportunity for improvement in the quality of small-business investment decisions. By breaking out of the pattern of routine activity or by delegating such work to others, the small-business entrepreneur can make more time for the search activity that leads to more profitable expansion.

Friends and acquaintances who are in management positions with other firms are valuable sources of information about expansion opportunities. Many other professionals, such as lawyers and bankers, are also reliable sources of this type of information. Trade journals and publications, such as *The Wall Street Journal,* can also contain notifications of purchase opportunities that represent potential growth developments.

LOOKING BACK

1. Capital budgeting is the process of planning expenditures on which returns are expected to extend well into the future. The most popular capital budgeting techniques among small businesses are the payback period and return on investment methods. The net-present-value method and the internal-rate-of-return method are additional techniques that are considered to be theoretically correct.
2. Few small firms make exclusive use of the concept of cost of capital, which may result in bad economic decisions.
3. Liquidity continues to be a prime concern for the small firm, even in making long-term investment decisions.
4. The very nature of small firms may contribute to the fact that they seldom use the conceptually richer techniques for evaluating long-term investments.
5. Small-business owners have various expansion philosophies. Success in expansion is facilitated by proper search activity and an adequate base of financial and managerial resources.

DISCUSSION QUESTIONS

1. How do working-capital management and capital budgeting differ?
2. Contrast the approach of the different techniques that can be used in capital budgeting analysis.
3. Why are the discounted cash flow techniques preferred over the accounting return on investment and the payback period?
4. Could you conceive how a firm could make an investment that would increase its earnings or profits but cause the firm's value to be less?
5. a. Find the accounting return on investment for a project that costs $10,000, will not have any salvage value, and has expected annual after-tax profits of $1,000.
   b. Determine the payback period for a capital investment that costs $40,000 and has the following after-tax profits:

Year	Profits ($)
1	5,000
2	12,000
3	12,000
4	8,000
5	8,000
6	7,000
7	6,000

The project outlay of $40,000 would be depreciated on a straight-line basis to a zero salvage value.

6. Assuming a discount rate of 16 percent, compute the present value of the following cash flow streams:
   a. $15,000 per year for 20 years.
   b. $10,000 per year for 10 years.
   c. $20,000 annually for five years and $30,000 annually for a second five years.
   d. $25,000 each year for five years and $35,000 in the sixth year.
7. Compute the internal rate of return for the following projects, all of which cost $25,000:
   a. $10,000 per year for four years.
   b. $6,000 annually for six years.
   c. $8,000 each year for five years.
8. Calculate the net present value for a project that will cost $50,000. The owner expects to receive $15,000 annually in after-tax cash flows for the next five years, plus a salvage value of $10,000. The firm's cost of capital is 15 percent.
9. What is the net present value of an investment that would cost $32,000, where you expect to receive $14,000 annually for four years? The cost of capital is 17 percent. Also, compute the internal rate of return. Would you accept the project? Why?
10. Define the internal rate of return and explain the logic for computing the rate.
11. Define cost of capital. Why is it important?
12. Why do we compute a *weighted* cost of capital?
13. If you could buy equipment that would earn an internal rate of return of 16 percent, and the banker is willing to finance the purchase in total at an interest cost of 10 percent, should you make the investment? Explain.
14. Why might the discounted payback method be used by a small firm in evaluating capital investments?
15. Why do so few small firms use discounted cash flow techniques?

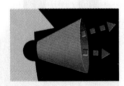

YOU MAKE THE CALL

Situation 1

Your firm is considering a major expansion of its product line and has estimated the following cash flows associated with such an expansion. The initial outlay associated with the expansion would be $250,000 and the project would generate incremental after-tax cash flows of $75,000 per year for six years. The company's cost of capital is 15 percent.

Question
Should the expansion be made?

Situation 2

The Wingo Corporation, a distributor of electronic components, is considering replacing a hand-operated machine used in the warehouse with a new, fully automated machine. Making the replacement would cost the firm $60,000, which would include the purchase price of the new machine less the after-tax selling price of the old machine of $12,000. The following facts apply:

Existing situation:

Two full-time machine operators—salaries $10,000 each per year.

Cost of maintenance—$5,000 per year.

Cost of defects—$5,000.

Expected life—10 years.

Age—five years old.

Expected salvage value—$0.

Depreciation method—straight-line over 10 years, $3,000 per year.

Marginal tax rate—34 percent.

Proposed situation:

Fully automated machine.

Cost of maintenance—$6,000 per year.

Cost of defects—$2,000 per year.

Expected life—five years.

Salvage value—$0.

Depreciation method—straight-line method over five years.

Question

Given the information as shown, would you recommend the replacement?

EXPERIENTIAL EXERCISES

1. Identify a small company in your community that has recently expanded. Try to interview the owner of the firm about the methods used in evaluating the expansion.
2. Talk to an accountant who consults with small companies and inquire about the practices of these clients when making capital budgeting decisions.
3. Either alone or with a fellow student, approach an owner of a small company about taking the data of a current problem or one the firm encountered at some time in the past to see whether you would reach the same decision as that made by the owners.
4. Interview a small-business owner to inquire about growth possibilities for the firm, factors that might limit growth, and the owner's personal feelings and attitudes concerning growth.

REFERENCES TO SMALL-BUSINESS PRACTICES

Bierman, Harold, Jr., *Implementing Capital Budgeting Techniques* (Cambridge, MA: Ballinger Publishing Company, 1988).

   A small book written for business people, explaining how to make capital budgeting decisions.

Bowlin, Oswald D., John D. Martin, and David F. Scott, *A Guide to Financial Analysis* (New York: McGraw Hill, 1990).

   A practical book on financial decision making, along with a clear explanation of capital budgeting techniques.

"Dell Computer Goes into the Shop, "*Business Week,* Vol. 3327 (July 12, 1993), pp. 138–140.

   Problems resulting from Dell's rapid expansion are identified, and contraints limiting future growth are discussed.

Schifrin, Matthew "Know Thy Customer," *Forbes,* Vol. 151, No. 10 (May 10, 1993), pp. 122–123.

   The very rapid expansion of a tiny business and the problems it experienced are described.

ENDNOTES

   1. To find the internal rate of return using either the Hewlett Packard 10B or the 17B II, repeat the steps taken in Figure 22-2. Then for 10B, press ⬜ IRR , and for the 17B II, press IRR . The answer will be 10.74 percent. Rather than having to enter the data again to compute the *IRR,* we could have solved for the *NPV* and the *IRR* while the data were still in the calculator. An even better approach is to use a computer spreadsheet, such as Lotus or Excel, to solve the problem.

   2. Robert M. Soldofsky, "Capital Budgeting Practices in Small Manufacturing Companies," in Studies in the *Factor Markets for Small Business Firms,* Dudley G. Luckett, ed. (Washington, DC: Small Business Administration, 1964).

   3. Reprinted by permission of the publisher from "Capital Expenditure Decision Making in Small Firms," by L.R. Runyon, *Journal of Business Research,* Vol. 11, No. 3 (September 1983), pp. 389–97. Copyright 1983 by Elsevier Science Publishing Co., Inc.

   4. "Big Dreams," *Inc.,* Vol. 9, No. 11 (November 1987), p. 14.

   5. *Ibid.*

   6. Doris A. Byron, "Carl's Jr.: 306-Unit Restaurant Chain Began as a Hot Dog Cart," *Los Angeles Times,* May 26, 1981, p. 1.

CHAPTER 23

Computer-Based Technology for Small Businesses

SPOTLIGHT ON SMALL BUSINESS

Many small businesses are using a new technology known as electronic data interchange (EDI) to place orders with vendors or suppliers by communicating through computers. The total time required to process an order is reduced by at least 25 percent with EDI systems. EDI also increases the accuracy of orders. Small businesses can hold smaller inventory levels and still maintain the same customer service level. A supplier can offer EDI as a competitive advantage to a small business. EDI was initially developed for use between large businesses, but now small businesses can afford the technology.

Independent retailers of Hallmark greeting cards use electronic data interchange to place orders with the headquarters in Kansas City, Missouri. Marian Robbins, manager of Lynn's Hallmark store in Pasadena, California, says the major incentive for using EDI "was being able to get our orders filled faster. We are out of stock less, and there is now no chance of our orders being lost in the mail." A physical inventory can be taken using a handheld terminal, and then orders can be placed by computer electronically across telephone lines.

Marian Robbins

Source: Leila Davis, "Instant Orders," *Nation's Business,* Vol. 78, No. 4 (April, 1990), pp. 34–36. Reprinted by permission, *Nation's Business,* April 1990. Copyright 1990, U.S Chamber of Commerce.

After studying this chapter, you should be able to:
1. Identify available technology.
2. Describe the hardware and software components of an information processing system.
3. Explain the role of computers in data communications.
4. Provide examples of office and production technology.
5. Identify decisions in the purchasing and management of technology.
6. Project the future application of computers in small business.

electronic data interchange (EDI)
local area network (LAN)
work group software
computer-aided design (CAD)
computer-aided manufacturing (CAM)
distributed processing
personal computer (microcomputer)
Windows
workstations
multitasking
minicomputer
throughput
mainframe
supercomputers
hardware
input device

magnetic disk drive
mouse
central processing unit (CPU)
microprocessor
random-access memory (RAM)
read-only memory (ROM)
output device
software
system software
operating system
application software
template
word processing
spreadsheet
cell
database program
customized software
telecommunications

modem
communications control program
terminal emulation
network card
file server
network control program
client/server model
telecommuting
electronic mail (E-mail)
voice mail
desktop publishing
WYSIWYG
facsimile machine (FAX)
fax modem
multimedia
material requirement planning (MRP)
geographic information systems (GIS)

In concept, a computer is a relatively simple device—a machine designed to follow instructions. In reality, a computer is a complex data processing machine, vastly outperforming human beings in tasks of recording, classifying, calculating, storing, and communicating information. The availability of inexpensive, powerful computer systems has revolutionized small-business access to automation. Advances in computer technology, coupled with lower prices, have made what was once available only to large businesses accessible to small businesses as well. This chapter discusses current computer-based technology for small businesses.

OVERVIEW OF AVAILABLE TECHNOLOGY

Computer-based functions for small businesses are not limited to routine record-keeping activities but include a number of diverse applications. Tasks such as desktop publishing, communicating electronically with vendors and customers, and electronic banking are but a few of the new applications helping small businesses contain costs and improve services. The accuracy and speed of acquiring data have increased substantially with the use of computer systems. Today, more often than not, a computer plays a vital role in a small business.[1]

Financial and Marketing Applications

Computer technology is applied heavily in small businesses for tracking financial transactions with systems such as order entry, accounts receivable, accounts payable, payroll, and inventory management. The more sophisticated systems are integrated so that duplication of data entry is minimized. Information is entered only once, and all the subsystems provide data to an accounting system that produces financial statements such as profit-and-loss statements and balance sheets. Many small businesses have access to an online, 24-hour-a-day information service capable of providing credit information about customers. Vendor stock availability can also be ascertained on a timely basis due to telecommunications. **Electronic data interchange (EDI)**, the exchange of data between businesses through computer links, is often available in place of the manual transmission of purchase orders and sales invoices.

electronic data interchange (EDI)
exchange of data between businesses through computer links

Computer Networks

Office automation has grown dramatically with the popularity of the local area network. A **local area network (LAN)** is a connected series of computer devices, mainly personal computers, that are capable of communicating and sharing information within a limited geographic area. A local area network is usually found within one building or plant. Other computer devices such as large magnetic disk drives and high-quality printers or plotters can be attached to the network. The capability of each personal computer on the network is enhanced by having access to more powerful storage and output devices than its own.

local area network (LAN)
an interconnected group of computers and related devices within a limited area

Applications such as electronic mail have become more commonplace with LANs. Office personnel are less intimidated by personal computer-based systems, which are more user-friendly than the larger computers. **Work group software** has become popular with LANs. Work group software facilitates the coordination of several employees working on a common project. Work group software is more than a simple messaging system; it allows for an efficient sharing of data and decisions among team members working toward a common goal.

work group software
computer programs that help coordinate the efforts of employees working on a common project

Operations Technology

The manufacturing process has benefited greatly from computer technology. Powerful workstation units (personal computers with increased memory, faster

computer-aided design (CAD)
using sophisticated computer systems to design new products

computer-aided manufacturing (CAM)
using computer-controlled machines to manufacture products

processors, and high-resolution display monitors) are used in **computer-aided design (CAD)** and **computer-aided manufacturing (CAM).** CAD programs are used in preparing engineering drawings of new products. CAM programs are used to control machines that cut, mold, and assemble products. These systems once required million-dollar investments, but now the CAD equipment and programs are within the reach of most small manufacturing businesses.

COMPUTER SYSTEMS: HARDWARE AND SOFTWARE

Various categories of computers exist for business applications. Computer systems range from small, single-user personal computers to large multi-user systems. Computer systems are composed of the equipment (hardware) and programs (software—the instructions that control the steps the computer follows).

Categories of Computers

Computers are classified into four broad categories:

1. Personal computers (microcomputers).
2. Minicomputers.
3. Mainframe computers.
4. Supercomputers.

Many factors are involved in choosing the appropriate type of computer for a particular task. No one type of computer is best suited for all applications. Many times, more than one type of computer could be used to accomplish the same result. Sometimes the best solution is to use a mixture of the different types of computers linked together. For instance, one might enter transaction data with a personal computer and then submit all of the data in a batch to a minicomputer or mainframe for processing. This is sometimes called **distributed processing** when more than one computer is used in combination to solve a problem.

distributed processing
using two or more computers in combination to process data

personal computer (microcomputer)
a small computer used by only one person at a time

Personal Computers. **Personal computers**, also known as **microcomputers,** are the least expensive and smallest in physical size (see Figure 23-1). The term *personal computer* comes from the fact that the computer's operating instructions typically allow only one person at a time to use it. Personal computers can function in a stand-alone mode to enhance the productivity of one person or in a network of other personal computers.

Commercially there are two broad categories of personal computers—IBM and Apple. Additionally, there are IBM-compatible personal computers referred to as clones that can use IBM specific software. In general, software that was created to be used on an IBM will not work on an Apple computer. However, many software producers are beginning to produce counterpart versions of their programs for both types of computers. The computer software company Microsoft has developed a user-friendly software known as **Windows** for IBMs and IBM compatibles that has minimized the differences between the IBM and Apple systems. Typical software applications for a personal computer are word processing for correspondence, spreadsheets for budgeting and graphs, and database programs to manage mailing lists. Tax planning/preparation and project management are other personal computer applications.

Workstations are the most powerful versions of personal computers. Workstations are used in applications that need the ability to carry out multitasking. **Multitasking** is the ability of a computer to carry out more than one function at a time. A personal computer on a secretary's desk might need the capability of simultaneously sorting a large mailing list by ZIP code for bulk mailing purposes and receiving an incoming facsimile (fax) transmission. A more powerful operating system software is what gives the workstation the multitasking quality.[2]

Minicomputers. A **minicomputer** affords multi-user capability to a common database. A small business with a high volume of credit sales requiring several clerks to enter data simultaneously in order to keep the billing/accounts receivable data current would be a candidate for a minicomputer. The hardware of a minicomputer system is not much different from that of a personal computer, except that the memory and storage capacities are usually much larger for a minicomputer. Each input device for a minicomputer may consist of only a keyboard and a monitor that are cabled to a common central processing unit. The operating system software for a minicomputer is more complex than the operating software for a personal computer. The operating system controlling the resources of a minicomputer must be capable of dividing processing time to simultaneous users.

Local area networks of personal computers have blurred the distinction somewhat between personal computers and minicomputers. Some of the same multi-user functionality of a minicomputer can be replicated by a network of personal computers. The **throughput,** the amount of work that can be done in a given amount of time, is usually higher for a correctly configured minicomputer than for a local area network. However, the overall price of the network may be lower. There is always a trade-off between speed and cost when choosing a computing solution.

Both minicomputer and LAN environments usually require an increased level of technical expertise of the person managing the system. This should be taken into consideration when evaluating the costs of competing computer solutions. More elaborate procedures will need to be implemented for such things as training and security.

A minicomputer or LAN system will need to have formal daily backup, (a copy of the data stored in another physical location) to guard against equipment malfunction or a natural disaster such as a fire. The disk storage of a personal computer should be backed up as well, but the process is simpler because

Windows
IBM-compatible software that creates an Apple-like operating environment

workstations
powerful personal computers able to carry out multitasking

multitasking
the ability of a computer to carry out more than one function at a time

minicomputer
a medium-sized computer capable of processing data input simultaneously from a number of sources

throughput
the amount of work that can be done by a computer in a given amount of time

Part 6   Financial and Administrative Controls

the volume of storage is usually much less for a stand-alone personal computer.

Mainframes and Supercomputers. A **mainframe** computer is a large multi-user computer that might be found in a large bank, hospital, or university. The processing speed, the amount of internal memory, and the amount of disk storage are much greater on a mainframe system than on a minicomputer. A mainframe can usually support more simultaneous users than a minicomputer. The throughput for a mainframe is substantially higher than for a minicomputer. The typical small business probably does not need an in-house mainframe.

Supercomputers are found in large government agencies and research organizations that require extremely fast calculations. For example, supercomputers are used for weather forecasting, where huge amounts of data must be manipulated. These computers cost many millions of dollars and, therefore, have no relevance for the smaller firm.

mainframe
a large, multi-user computer

supercomputers
the largest and fastest computers, which process huge amounts of data

Computer Hardware

No matter how large the computer system, the **hardware** or equipment components of a computer system can be categorized into four groups:

hardware
the equipment components of a computer system

1. Input.
2. Processing.
3. Output.
4. Storage.

Figure 23-1 depicts the basic relationship among these components, which are described below.

Input. An **input device** is any device that is used in entering data or information into the computer. At least initially, most data and commands to a computer system are entered through a keyboard device much like the keyboard of a typewriter. Some additional keys are added to a computer keyboard—for instance, directional arrow keys used in screen positioning and special function keys that can be programmed by different software. A **magnetic disk drive** could be considered an input device. Once data have been stored on a disk, the data can be recalled and transferred into the computer memory. A popular input device with Windows-based software is a hand-controlled pointing device known as a **mouse**. As the mouse is moved across a flat surface, signals are relayed to the computer that direct a pointer on the screen. This pointer is used to choose a command from a menu of choices by "clicking" the mouse button. The mouse is used to minimize the amount of typing necessary to invoke a command to the computer. A bar code reader is another example of an input device.

input device
any device used to enter data or commands into a computer

magnetic disk drive
a device that transfers data from magnetic disks to the computer's memory and vice versa

mouse
a hand-controlled device that directs an on-screen arrow

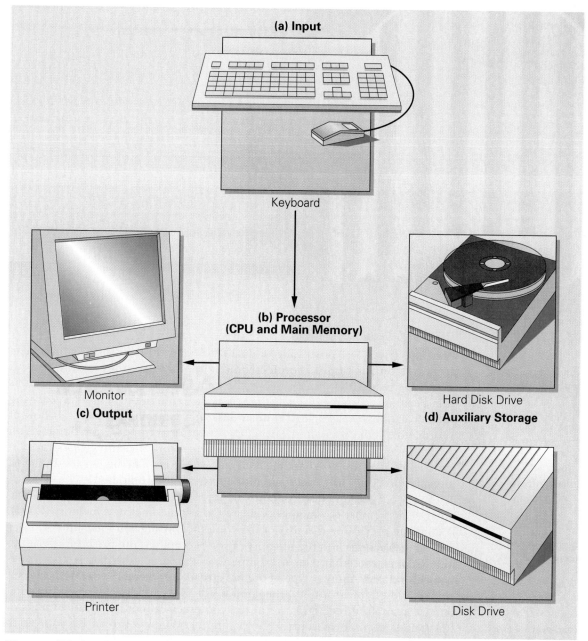

Figure 23-1   Basic Components of a Computer System

Figure 23-2
The Microprocessor
Contains the CPU of
a Personal
Computer

central processing unit (CPU)
the electronic components that perform calculations and control the flow of information in a computer

microprocessor
a miniaturized CPU mounted on a silicon chip

random-access memory (RAM)
the computer memory area where data are temporarily stored for processing

read-only memory (ROM)
the memory area that contains permanent operating instructions for the computer

Processing. The processing of data takes place in the processor unit. The processor unit includes the electronic components known as the **central processing unit (CPU)**, which allows the computer to handle literally millions of instructions per second. The CPU acts as the brain of the computer, carrying out calculations, making logical decisions, and controlling the overall flow of information in the computer. The CPU of a personal computer is contained on a silicon wafer-like chip known as a **microprocessor**. Microprocessors for personal computers are rated as 286, 386, and 486 levels. The higher the rating of the microprocessor, the faster and more powerful the computer.

The processor unit also contains the internal or main memory of the computer. This memory is sometimes referred to as **random-access memory (RAM)**. RAM is the processing memory of the computer. When you load a program or a set of instructions into the memory of your computer, the program is loading into RAM. As you enter data as prompted by a program, the data is stored temporarily in RAM. Another type of memory, **read-only memory (ROM)**, is also included in the processor unit. The contents of ROM are defined when the computer is manufactured. The user of the computer cannot alter the contents of ROM; ROM is used to control the computer. When you turn off your computer, the contents of RAM are erased. The contents of ROM are not erased when you power down the computer. With a personal computer, the microprocessor and memory, both RAM and ROM, are located on a single integrated circuit board known as the motherboard. The amount of RAM is much more important than ROM. The amount of RAM controls the level of sophistication of the software that the computer is capable of running. Additional RAM can be added to increase the capability of a computer. The amount of RAM a computer has is stated in megabytes; one megabyte is approximately one million memory locations. It is not uncommon for a personal computer to have between two and six megabytes of RAM, or even more.

Output. **Output devices** allow the viewing of processed data. The main output devices are monitors (screens) and printers. Monitors are classified as monochrome or color. Color monitors are further categorized based on clarity and resolution. Printers are classified as impact and nonimpact. A dot-matrix printer is an impact printer, because the printed characters are formed by a print element striking an inked ribbon against the paper. The characters are composed of different combinations of tiny dots. A laser printer is an example of a nonimpact printer. High-quality printing requires a laser printer.[3]

output device
a device that allows the processed data to be viewed or transmitted

Auxiliary Storage. Computer files are permanently stored on either magnetic tape or disks. Magnetic tape is used primarily for backup purposes. Magnetic disks are used for storing the results of input and processing. For example, a draft of a report can be stored on a magnetic disk. The draft of the report can be recalled from the disk for changes without retyping the entire document. On personal computers, both removable and fixed disks exist. The removable disk, known as a diskette, can be either a 5¼" or 3½" format. The typical 5¼" and 3½" diskette can store 1.2 megabytes and 1.44 megabytes of data, respectively. Fixed or hard disks are capable of storing hundreds of megabytes of data.[4]

Computer Software

The **software,** or operating instructions, of a computer system can be classified either as system software or application software.

software
programs that provide operating instructions to the computer

System Software. **System software** is the instructions that provide the overall control of the resources of the computer. The most common type of system software is the operating system. The **operating system** controls the resources of the computer and the flow of information in and out of the computer. The operating system provides a link between the hardware and a specific application program, such as a customer billing system. For personal computers, there are usually only one or two operating systems between which to choose. For an IBM or IBM-compatible personal computer, the choices are the Disk Operating System (DOS) or OS/2. An IBM or IBM-compatible using

system software
programs that control the internal functioning of the computer

operating system
the system that controls the flow of information in and out of the computer and links the hardware to application programs

Figure 23-3
Desktop Publishing
May Be Done on a
Personal Computer

multitasking would require OS/2. For minicomputers and especially main-frame computers, there are several choices of operating systems. The operating system is chosen based on the type of work expected of the system.[5]

application software
programs that perform specific tasks

Application Software. **Application software** are programs that perform specific business processing. Application software can be classified as productivity packages or customized packages.

Productivity Packages. Productivity packages include such programs as word processors, spreadsheets, and database programs. In productivity software, the user is not locked into specific predefined functions. The user is free within the bounds of the productivity package to create original applications. For example, with a spreadsheet program a small-business owner might create a projected income statement in order to apply for a loan. The software might provide a template that facilitates the creation of the income statement. A **template** is a previously defined form on the screen for which the user would simply have to fill in blanks with specific data.

template
a preprogrammed form on which the user fills in the blanks with specific data

word processing
creating and manipulating text and graphics on a computer

Word processing packages allow the user to create, edit, and print documents that include text, graphics, and scanned objects. Correspondence and office memorandums, for example, can be prepared by word processing in small businesses. Spelling checkers and thesauruses have greatly extended the capability of word processing programs. The mail-merge application, whereby a form letter is sent to a predefined list of customers on a regular basis, is a timesaving function of a word processing program. Some popular word processing packages are *WordPerfect, Microsoft Word, Microsoft Word for Windows,* Ashton-Tate's *MultiMate Advantage,* and MicroPro's *WordStar.*

Spreadsheet programs turn the computer screen into an electronic sheet of accounting paper divided into a grid of rows and columns. Applications involving calculations and graphs are best suited to a spreadsheet. By using the keyboard, entries can be made into a **cell,** an intersection of a row and column. These entries can be titles, numbers, or formulas. Through these entries, applications such as budgets and loan schedules showing the amount of principal and interest in each payment can be prepared easily. Most spreadsheet programs have a list of powerful key words, known as *functions,* that allow for statistical and financially related calculations such as the return on an investment. "What If" scenarios can be played out in a spreadsheet to check the effect of changing assumptions in a financial analysis. Popular spreadsheet programs include *Lotus 1-2-3, Microsoft Excel,* Borland's *Quattro,* and Computer Associates' *SuperCalc.* Figure 23-4 provides a spreadsheet example.

A **database program** is used to manage a file of related data. A customer list used for marketing purposes, containing a customer's name, address, date last contacted, and comments, could be managed with a database program. New customers could be added, and data for existing customers could be modified easily. Mailing labels could be printed for mass mailings of advertisements. Popular database programs are Ashton-Tate's *dBase,* Symatec's *Q&A,* Borland's *Paradox,* and Microrim's *R:Base.*[6]

Customized Software. The programs that allow the computer to process business functions such as billing, general ledger accounting, accounts receivable, and accounts payable are considered **customized software**. Customized software can either be purchased from another company or created in-house. Most small businesses would not need a full-time computer programmer but could engage one on a contract basis for special software customization needs. Customized software packages exist for most small businesses that have been tailored to the specific needs of these particular kinds of businesses. A general business system for an auto supply store, for example, would be quite different from a system for a dentist. In some cases, the software vendor can offer modifications to adapt an existing software package to meet special needs. When purchasing customized packages, the business owner should find out whether modifications are possible and who would make them.

Customized packages for small businesses are often a comprehensive system of programs that can be used individually or in combination. They are typically menu-driven systems whereby the user simply has to select a specific option from a series of choices. These systems are mainly concerned with tracking data

spreadsheet
an electronic worksheet divided into rows and columns

cell
the intersection of a row and a column on a spreadsheet

database program
a program used to manage a file of related data

customized software
programs designed or adapted for use by a particular company or type of business

	A	B	C	D	E	F	G
1		PRO FORMA INCOME STATEMENT					
2							
3							
4			YEAR				
5							
6		1	2	3	4	5	TOTAL
7							
8	SALES	$110,000	$121,000	$133,100	$146,410	$161,051	$671,561
9							
10	COST OF GOODS SOLD	82,500	90,750	99,825	109,808	120,788	503,671
11							
12	GROSS PROFIT	27,500	30,250	33,275	36,603	40,263	167,890
13							
14	G & A EXPENSES						
15	Salaries	14,000	14,000	15,500	15,500	17,000	76,000
16	Commissions	2,750	3,205	3,328	3,660	4,026	16,789
17	Utilities	1,375	1,513	1,664	1,830	2,013	8,395
18	Telephone	2,200	2,420	2,662	2,928	3,221	13,431
19	Depreciation	1,500	1,500	1,500	1,500	1,500	7,500
20	Travel	3,025	3,328	3,660	4,026	4,429	18,468
21	Ent./Prom.	1,375	1,513	1,664	1,830	2,013	8,395
22	Payroll Taxes	980	980	1,085	1,085	1,190	5,320
23							
24	TOTAL EXPENSES	27,205	28,278	31,062	32,360	35,392	154,297
25							
26	OPER. PROFIT BEFORE TAXES	295	1,973	2,213	4,243	4,870	13,593
27							
28	TAXES	89	592	664	1,273	1,461	4,078
29							
30	PROFIT AFTER TAXES	207	1,381	1,549	2,970	3,409	9,515

Figure 23-4   Electronic Spreadsheet

about customers, employees, and assets such as inventories. These systems contain modules for payroll, order entry, billing, accounts receivable, accounts payable, general ledger, and inventory management. Each of these modules is described below.

- The payroll function is often one of the first to be automated in a small business. A payroll program requires as input employee time records, wage rates, tax tables, and other information pertinent to calculating the salary of an employee. The output of a payroll system includes paychecks or electronic transfers to employee bank accounts, updated year-to-date records detailing earnings and withholdings, and entries to the general ledger accounting system. At the end of each year, W-2 tax forms are printed for each employee.

- Order-entry systems are used to enter initial data concerning an order for merchandise or service. The ability to check against existing inventory levels to determine whether an order can be filled or a backorder is necessary is part of the order-entry system. An invoice detailing the information about the order is the normal output of the order-entry system. A picking ticket specifying a list of merchandise to be selected from inventory is often prepared.

- Billing systems are used to collect data necessary to compile a periodic statement sent to customers. The statement lists the previous balance and any current charges or payments since the last statement. A document that the customer is to return with the payment might be included.

- An accounts receivable system maintains the current amount owed to a business by its customers. The amount owed may also be aged into categories of less than 30 days, 30 to 60 days, 60 to 90 days, and over 90 days. Printed reports can be generated to identify customers who are not paying on a timely basis. These reports are also used to determine whether a customer should be extended credit in the future.

- An accounts payable system is used to track the amounts owed to vendors or suppliers. An accounts payable program may actually write the checks to pay the bills. Some payable programs are sophisticated enough to question making an early payment at a discount in view of projected cash needs.

- A general ledger accounting system performs the bookkeeping function for a business and prepares income statements, balance sheets, and cash flow statements as required. For just a few hundred dollars, a small business can computerize its accounting system with a general ledger program.

- An inventory management system maintains the data about items in stock. These include items available for sale by a distributor or component parts to be used in manufacturing. As items are received or sold (used), the quantity-on-hand amounts are adjusted. Sophisticated inventory systems are integrated with the order entry and purchasing system to adjust the quantities on hand accordingly.[7]

SMALL BUSINESS IN ACTION

Automating Routine Tasks

Most small business managers understand the advantages of computerizing a process like payroll. However, they are often unaware of the way other routine tasks can be automated with inexpensive personal computers. Communication systems such as telephones and facsimiles can be enhanced through PC-based software.

Foreign Auto Parts, a Sharon, Mass., importer of parts for foreign cars, has implemented an automated phone system controlled by a personal computer. Bert Patkin, the assistant treasurer, has witnessed a dramatic increase in customer service. "No more lost or misplaced messages on lit-tle pink slips," Patkin says. The system can take and route messages 24 hours a day.

If a business prints computer documents and feeds them into a facsimile machine for transmission, it is a candidate for a fax modem. A fax modem is a circuit card that, when inserted in a personal computer, allows the personal computer to fax computer documents directly to a fax machine. Frank Anthony, office manager for Schlott Realty, in Morris Township, N. J., uses a fax modem to transmit copies of advertisements to the firm's advertising agency. Anthony estimates the fax modem saves one to two hours a week. The fax modem can function as a regular modem for normal computer communication across telephone lines.

Source: Albert G. Holzinger and Ripley Hotch, "Upgrade For Growth," *Nation's Business,* Vol. 79, No. 4, pp. 14–22. Reprinted by permission, *Nation's Business,* April 1991. Copyright 1991, U.S. Chamber of Commerce.

COMMUNICATIONS AMONG COMPUTERS

telecommunications
exchanging data
between remote
computers

Many of the newer computer applications involve data communications between computers. The process of communicating at a distance, which may be done between or among computers, is referred to as **telecommunications.** The improved timeliness of information due to computer telecommunications plays a crucial part in effective decision making. Speed and accuracy are increased when documents are transmitted electronically. Due to the increased need for data communications, computers are becoming more standardized. In the future, computers will rarely exist in an unconnected, stand-alone mode.

Hardware and Software Requirements

A computer system that is capable of communicating with another system has some additional hardware and software requirements. Data can be stored in a digital form in the computer memory, but in order to transmit the data across a standard telephone line, the data must be converted to a smooth, continuous

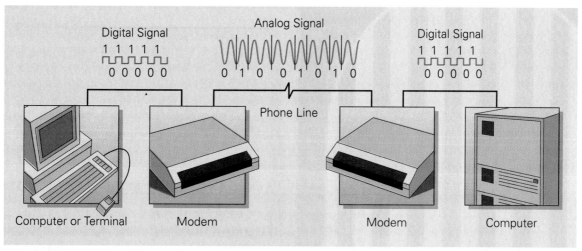

Figure 23-5
Computer
Communications
Hardware

signal, like a human's voice. This is known as an *analog* signal. The computer on the receiving end must convert the data from analog back to digital. A hardware device known as a **modem** (<u>mo</u>dulate, <u>dem</u>odulate) is required on both the sending and receiving computer to make these conversions (see Figure 23-5). A modem can be either an external device that connects to the system unit or an internal circuit card within the system.

A **communications control program** is necessary to connect a microcomputer through a telephone line to another microcomputer or to a larger host computer system such as a minicomputer or mainframe. The communications control program can allow access to public information service companies such as CompuServe and Prodigy. These programs offer such services as electronic mail, stock prices, and airline schedules with reservation options. Some of the services come with a monthly subscription fee; others are over and above the base fee. Most public information services offer electronic bulletin boards that allow a user to give and receive information about a specific subject. A communications control program will also allow a personal computer to emulate or act like a terminal for a larger system. This mode of communication is often referred to as **terminal emulation.** Small businesses often need to communicate to vendors with larger computer systems. This can be accomplished through terminal emulation. *Crosstalk* and Hayes *Smartcom II* are widely used communication control programs.[8]

The linking of personal computers in a local area network (LAN) requires additional hardware and software. Each personal computer requires a special circuit card known as a **network card** in order to communicate on a LAN. At least one of the personal computers in the network must be dedicated as a file server. The **file server** stores the programs and common database that are

modem
a device that converts digital data to analog and vice versa

communications control program
software that controls the flow of information between computers

terminal emulation
a communications mode that allows personal computers to telecommunicate with mainframes

network card
a circuit card required for computers on a local area network

file server
the computer that stores the programs and common data for a local area network

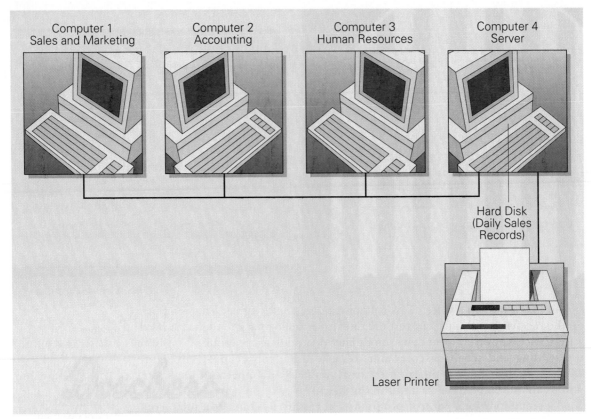

Figure 23-6
Local Area Network
(LAN)

shared by the different computers on the network (see Figure 23-6). The file server is usually a more powerful computer than the normal units in terms of processing speed, RAM memory, and disk storage capacity. A special program known as the **network control program** is also stored on the file server. The network control program provides security and access controls to the network. Two popular network control programs are Novell's *NetWare* and Microsoft *LAN Manager*.

network control program
software that controls access to a local area network

client/server model
a system whereby the client (the user's personal computer) obtains data from a central computer, but processing is done at the client level

Telecommunication Applications

The term **client/server model** has gained much popularity with the advent of local area networks. Local area networks are replacing former minicomputer systems in many small businesses. In the conventional minicomputer environment, the data and application programs are stored on a centralized system. Users log on to the minicomputer and run application programs from the centralized minicomputer. When many users are logged on, the performance of the minicomputer can be seriously degraded. The terminal used in communicating to the minicomputer adds nothing to the process but acts as a "dumb" communication device. No processing actually takes place in the terminal. In the client/server model, the user's personal computer (the client) runs or processes the application software locally. The client is not waiting on a host computer for major processing. The client makes data requests of the server (a file server in the LAN), but the actual processing takes place at the client (personal computer) level. Response time and throughput can improve dramatically because the resources of a single CPU are not being divided among several users.[9]

A primary use of telecommunication capability is electronic data interchange (EDI). EDI transmits business documents such as purchase orders electronically rather than through such conventional methods as mail or telephone. Orders are typically placed faster and data entry errors are reduced. Smaller inventories made possible by speedier orders can also help improve profitability.[10]

Another possibility, **telecommuting,** allows employees to work at home by using a computer link. Some jobs, such as computer programming or technical writing, are well suited to telecommuting. Reduced employee fatigue from long physical commutes and decreased costs from reduced office space are two of the benefits. Some jobs are obviously not well suited to telecommuting.

telecommuting
working at home by using a computer link to the business location

OFFICE AND PRODUCTION TECHNOLOGY

Many computer-based products have helped make office personnel more productive. Local area networks allowing for information sharing and other "smart" devices have changed significantly how office work gets done.

Computer-Based Office Technology

Local area networks have extended the technology of electronic mail to even the smallest businesses. **Electronic mail (E-mail)** allows users to send messages electronically from one computer to another. Messages can be sent to a specific person or a predefined group of people. For example, a small-business manager might want to send a message to only the supervisory personnel. Computer-stored documents can be attached with the message. Most E-mail systems have an interface that works much like a simple word processing program with a few special commands for receiving and transmitting messages.[11]

Voice mail is another type of technology used in office communication. Voice mail is a computerized system that captures telephone messages and stores the messages on a magnetic disk. Upon returning to the office, the user

electronic mail (E-mail)
text messages transmitted by computer

voice mail
a computerized system for storing telephone messages

can dial a number that will play back the calls. The voice mailbox can also be accessed from a remote telephone. For an office setting without a receptionist, voice mail is an attractive alternative.

desktop publishing
producing high-quality printed documents on a personal computer

Desktop publishing is a hardware/software, personal computer-based system used in producing brochures, advertisements, manuals, and newsletters. Predefined artwork, known as clip art, can be "pasted" electronically into the document. Existing diagrams can be scanned and then entered into the document. Desktop publishing systems can greatly reduce the need for the services of graphic artists and professional printers. Desktop publishing requires a more powerful personal computer than the typical system used for routine word processing. The monitor should be larger to accommodate full-page composition with a quality known as WYSIWYG. **WYSIWYG** stands for "What You See Is What You Get" and means that what you see on the monitor or screen is what the document will look like when it prints. A fast microprocessor is needed in order to refresh the display on the screen rapidly when changes are made. A larger than normal hard disk is required because documents that include artwork take up a huge amount of disk storage. A laser printer is required to produce a high level quality final printed copy. Laser printers provide many different font styles and sizes, allowing for near-typeset quality.[12]

WYSIWYG
what you see is what you get

facsimile machine (fax)
a device that transmits copies of documents through telephone lines

Few businesses operate today without the services of a **facsimile machine (fax).** A facsimile machine, commonly referred to as a fax machine, allows for transmitting copies of physical documents across a standard telephone line. Most fax machines print about one to four pages per minute. A recent innovation for a personal computer is a device known as a fax modem. A **fax modem** is a circuit board that is installed in a personal computer and allows the sender to transfer documents on a computer disk directly to a fax machine or to another personal computer having a fax modem. This eliminates printing the document and then feeding it into a fax machine. Incoming faxes can be stored on disk and printed later. The fax modem cannot completely replace the regular fax machine, because users may still need to transfer documents that are not stored on disk.

fax modem
a circuit board that permits sending a document from a computer to a fax machine

multimedia
a combination of text, graphics, audio, and video in a single presentation

Multimedia technology and presentation software merge text, graphics, audio, and video into a single presentation. The presentation can be viewed through a regular computer monitor or through a large-screen projection system. A device known as an LCD panel connected to a multimedia personal computer can be used in conjunction with a special overhead projector to display the presentation. Multimedia presentations are popular at trade shows for promoting products or services. The presentation can be made interactive, with the viewer selecting different paths through the presentation. Multimedia is useful in computer-assisted training materials. An employee can watch a video clip on a new process and then take a test to measure comprehension. Remedial training can be provided for the questions missed. All of this can be done with a single multimedia presentation.

Desktop Publishing

Small businesses can sometimes use desktop publishing as a substitute for professional typesetting for brochures, newsletters, and advertisements. When Wade Appelman, account manager for the 25-employee Synon Corporation in Framingham, Mass., reviewed the four brochures that Synon used to present the bank software it sold, he discovered out-of-date information. A trade show was only two weeks away, and time was too short to have an outside printer make the corrections.

Appleman purchased a copy of Spinnaker Software Corporation's PFS:Publisher, a desktop publishing program. He was able to produce four "pretty good-quality" brochures with the software. Using a laser printer, he printed 250 copies of each brochure before the trade show. The day was saved by desktop publishing software.

Source: Kimberly French, "Start the Presses," *Inc.*, Special Issue—The Office Technology Adviser (Fall 1992), pp. 56–58. Reprinted with permission, *Inc.* magazine (Fall 1992). Copyright 1992 by Goldhirsh Group, Inc., 38 Commercial Wharf, Boston, MA 02110.

Computer-Based Production Technology

Small manufacturing businesses have available computer-based systems known as computer-aided design (CAD) and computer-aided manufacturing (CAM). CAD uses a computer to automate the design process of new products. A CAD system involves a powerful workstation personal computer coupled with a drawing pad or a touch-sensitive monitor activated with a light pen. A designer or engineer can draw a model of the product on the screen. The computer model can then be rotated to see different views and even used to test the product by simulating real-world stresses and strains on the model.

In computer-aided manufacturing (CAM), computers are used in the actual manufacturing process. For instance, the computers might monitor temperatures and pressures with sensors and make adjustments automatically based on certain decision rules or control machines to cut and mold materials based on a model design. Robots are an example of computer-aided manufacturing used in processes such as painting and welding.

The computer is also used in the manufacturing process through **material requirement planning (MRP)** software. MRP systems produce a bill-of-materials document based on the production schedule. The bill-of-materials document specifies the quantity of each component needed and when it is needed. This information is coupled with an inventory and purchasing system to provide the necessary parts on a timely basis. MRP systems can place orders for inventory items and minimize wasted time waiting for critical parts to arrive.[13]

material requirement planning (MRP) controlling the timely ordering of production materials by using computer software

Figure 23-7
Computerizing
Operations Is Not
an Easy Process

"I don't want to talk to a middleman . . . put
me straight through to the computer!"

PURCHASING AND MANAGING TECHNOLOGY

If a small business is considering the use of a computer in a comprehensive, integrated fashion, it should analyze the potential benefits, estimate the costs, and work out an appropriate plan. There are no quick and easy procedures to follow in this decision process. Each business will have a unique set of problems.

The Feasibility Study

As a first step, the small business should make a feasibility study. This study should determine whether the firm has a sufficient workload or need for efficiency to justify the expense of a computer. The cost/benefit analysis is difficult to make, but it is the most important step in the decision-making process. This analysis can be performed by the business owner-manager or by an outside computer consultant. The feasibility should be assessed from a technical and a cost basis. The technical feasibility will determine whether current technology exists to solve the particular problem. The cost feasibility will ascertain whether the cost of the computer solution is justified based on the benefits received.

The feasibility study may indicate that the business should not adopt an integrated computer system. However, with the decreased costs of computers, it is hard to imagine a business that would not benefit from some level of automation.

Available Options

If the feasibility study justifies use of a computer system, a decision to use a service bureau, to use a time-sharing relationship, to lease a computer, or to buy a computer must be made.

Service Bureaus. Service bureaus are computer firms that receive data from business customers, perform the data processing, then return the processed information to the customers. The service bureaus charge a fixed fee for the use of their computers. For a small firm desiring a single application and lacking computer experience, the service bureau represents a logical first choice.

Using a service bureau has several advantages. The user avoids an investment in equipment that will soon become obsolete. The user also avoids the need for specialized computer personnel. Some service bureaus even provide guidance to make it easy for the user to start and expand computer usage.

The disadvantages of a service bureau include slow turnaround time in receiving processed information from the service bureau, divulgence of confidential information to outside parties, and difficulty in working with a group unfamiliar with the client company's procedures.

Time-Sharing. Time-sharing allows a business to have the capabilities of a powerful computer without buying or leasing one. The business pays a variable fee for the privilege of using a computer system. The user must have at least one terminal in order to input and receive data. The terminal is connected to the time-sharing computer via a telephone line with a modem.

Early time-sharing systems provided computer time for professionals who knew how to program a computer. Now time-sharing is used more to process data and information for a company by using existing programs. The time-sharing approach is often a good first or second step for small firms that decide to computerize.

The advantages of time-sharing include control of company records, more sophisticated applications of programs, and lower cost of installing a working system. Possible disadvantages include variable costs, waiting time when other customers are using the system, and the need for the user to have some computer ability.

Leasing a Computer. For most businesses, leasing a computer means possessing and using a computer without buying it. The most common leasing arrangement is the full payback lease. Usually the lease periods are fairly long term (around eight years). A shorter lease period may be more expensive, but it reduces the possibility of having to use outdated equipment. With the current rapid advances in computer technology, some computer users claim that computer equipment becomes outdated every two years!

Two advantages of leasing are the use of a complete computer system without a large initial investment and the availability of consulting help through the leasing company's computer specialists. The disadvantages relate to the length of the lease period and the possibility of having to use outdated equipment. In addition, leasing a computer requires the lessee to have skilled computer personnel.[14]

Buying a Computer. The advantages of buying a computer are that the owner has total control and ownership of the computer and that depreciation expense reduces the business owner's taxable income. The disadvantages are the large expense of the computer system, the need for trained computer personnel to operate the programs and maintain the hardware, and the possible obsolescence of the equipment.

For small firms choosing to purchase a computer, the key to creating a successful computer system is a carefully planned approach. It is important for the first-time computer user to look first at the programs, not at the hardware. The following ten steps set forth an orderly approach to computerization.

Step 1: Learn About Computers. Visit other firms that are already using computers for similar applications. Ask for a vendor demonstration. Be aware that the changeover will require much time and thought. If possible, hire a data processing manager with experience, or at least place someone in charge of the changeover. In summary, the computer is not an easy way out. If the business is in basic trouble, the computer system will not save it. The computer can help a successful business become more successful.

Step 2: Analyze the Present Manual System. Examine the transactions that involve routine actions. Restudy the routine manual actions to find a more efficient procedure if possible. Involve as many employees as possible because early participation by the users of the new system will improve its chances of success. Having established an efficient procedure, you are then ready to think about introducing a computer.

The detailed study of the business and the areas that might be computerized help to clarify computer needs. This is information that computer vendors need in order to propose ways to computerize a company efficiently.

Step 3: Clearly Define Your Expectations of the Computer System. Having reviewed your manual system, decide what you need in a computer system. Be specific in the functions you want the computer to perform. For example, you may decide to computerize mailing lists, payroll, inventory control, or sales analysis. These needs should be outlined for five years in the future. If you are unable to determine your exact needs, you may want to seek help. Possible sources are other small businesses, computer consultants, or an employee with computer experience.

Step 4: Compare Costs and Benefits. It is easy to estimate the costs of current manual systems, but it is difficult to estimate the cost of computerization. Estimates should be obtained from several vendors to help determine the cost of changeover. Also, there are hidden costs incurred. For example, the patience and endurance of employees are tested during the conversion.

Step 5: Establish a Timetable for Installing the System. A five-year schedule should be made to install the computer system. It is best to automate the simplest manual operations first. Each computerized operation should be working before going to the next. Be aware that the transition will be slow. If possible, run the manual system parallel with the automated system until the rough spots are smoothed out. Be willing to adjust the timetable from time to time as unexpected problems occur.

Step 6: Write a Tight Contract. Both the purchaser and the vendor should be willing to sign a formal agreement on the function the computer is expected to perform. The specifications should contain details rather than general summaries of expected performance. Obligations for servicing the equipment should also be clearly specified. The contract should specify what the vendor must do before each step in the payment schedule.

Is it usually unwise to agree to field-test new equipment. It is best to obtain established equipment and programs that have been working in other small businesses.

Step 7: Obtain Programs First, Then Obtain the Computer. There are several options for obtaining computer programs:

1. Obtain programs that are already working at other, similar small businesses.
2. Hire a programmer to write programs.
3. Hire a consultant who has programs that can serve most business functions.

The manager must make the decision about which alternative is best for the particular business. Once the needed programs are identified, the most economical hardware to run the programs can be obtained.

Step 8: Prepare Your Employees for Conversion. It is commonplace for employees to resist the move to computers. They may feel the computer is a threat to their jobs. Assure employees that the change will be beneficial to the business and consequently beneficial to them. People who are unwilling to become involved should be moved to other departments. A good attitude, with interest in the computerization, must prevail for a successful transition from manual power to computer power. Without the complete support of top management, a new system is likely to fail.

Step 9: Make the Conversion. First, assign the responsibilities carefully for the conversion process. The conversion period will require extra work because daily work must continue. Second, remember to convert operations one at a time. Again, if possible, keep the parallel manual system functioning as long as possible. Third, be patient, remembering that pitfalls will occur. Do not plan on using the system until it begins functioning.

Step 10: Reap the Benefits. The goal of the transition is to obtain the following benefits:

1. Earlier, more accurate, and more extensive information.
2. Better organization of information because of the discipline the computer requires.
3. Current information on costs and sales.
4. Current information on inventory levels.
5. Better cash control.

Evaluation and Maintenance

After a computer system has been installed and is in use, the process of evaluation and maintenance begins. Not until the system is in real use will some potential problems surface. Corrections to problems may be made with future updates of the software, or temporary fixes may be necessary. Either the software vendor or contract programmers can make changes to the computer programs to make corrections or modifications. Modifications are sometimes necessary due to new legislation or business reorganization.

THE FUTURE OF COMPUTERS

A recent survey found that of small businesses with 100 employees or fewer, 63 percent own computers and 29 percent plan to buy more. The category of software most often used was word processing (75 percent), followed by accounting software (70 percent) and spreadsheets (67 percent). Only 17 percent of those businesses having computers had local area networks. The number of businesses having LANs is sure to rise in the future as they become cheaper and easier to use. The increased application of telecommunications will no doubt dominate new computer applications for small businesses.[15]

Higher levels of software integration will allow computers and computer software systems to "speak" to one another more easily than can current systems. For example, a single data update, such as changing a customer's address, will change the address in all the necessary data files. The ability to "cut and paste" information from one application to another will make the computer more productive.

Computers may be used to conduct electronic meetings. In conventional meetings, some participants may feel intimidated and fail to participate. A computer network will allow the meeting to be conducted with the responses handled anonymously if so desired. Research is being conducted to see whether there is any loss in meeting effectiveness without having the visual cues and body language that a face-to-face meeting provides.

Business presentations and employee training will benefit from the increased merging of computer and television technology in the form of multimedia software. A presentation or training scenario will combine text, graphics, video, and audio through multimedia software. Computers will be used for more varied applications in the future due to multimedia capabilities.

Geographic information systems (GIS) will become widely used to create "smart" maps. A small business will be able to connect a physical map with a customer file database and carry out "what if" analysis with the output in map form. Decisions about optimal shipping routes and new store locations will be improved through GIS.

geographic information systems (GIS) programs that connect a physical map with a customer file database

To maintain a competitive edge in the future, small-business managers must be computer literate and be able to determine what computer technology will help their businesses in a cost-effective way.

1. Small-business computer systems consist of hardware and software components. The hardware is the equipment of the system and includes input, processing, output, and storage devices. The software consists of system and application programs that provide instructions to control the system.
2. Computers are categorized as personal computers, minicomputers, mainframe computers, and supercomputers. Small businesses normally use personal computers (microcomputers) as stand-alone units or as units in a local area network. Larger small businesses use minicomputers that have multi-user capability.

3. Application software is divided into customized packages or productivity packages. Customized software is used for such tasks as payroll, order entry, billing, accounts receivable, accounts payable, general ledger, and inventory management. Productivity software includes programs for word processing, spreadsheet analysis, and database management.

4. Through telecommunications, small businesses have the ability to use electronic data interchange (EDI) to place orders with vendors and to access information services for news, stock prices, and airline reservations, or to use electronic bulletin boards. Some additional hardware and software are required for telecommunications.

5. Office technology has improved through electronic mail, voice mail, desktop publishing, facsimile machines and modems, and multimedia capabilities. Small manufacturers have benefited from computer-aided design (CAD) and computer-aided manufacturing (CAM).

6. The small-business manager who decides a computer is feasible for business operations has several options: using a service bureau, time-sharing, leasing a computer, or buying a computer.

7. To maintain a competitive advantage, the small-business manager of the future needs to be computer and telecommunications literate. Computers and information will affect every aspect of business life.

DISCUSSION QUESTIONS

1. Computers are classified into what four categories?
2. Explain what is meant by the term "distributed processing."
3. Explain the advantage of a computer capable of multitasking.
4. What differentiates a mainframe computer from a minicomputer?
5. What are the four categories of hardware of a computer system?
6. Contrast the two types of internal memory of a computer, RAM versus ROM. Which one is more important when purchasing a computer? Why?
7. What is the primary purpose of magnetic tape as a storage medium in a modern computer system?
8. What are the two types of software?
9. Give an example where a spreadsheet program would be useful.
10. Explain the role that a modem plays in a computer system.
11. Give the advantages of connecting personal computers in a local area network (LAN).
12. What is EDI? How do small businesses use EDI?
13. What is meant by the acronym WYSIWYG?
14. Discuss the advantages and disadvantages of (a) service bureaus, (b) time-sharing systems, (c) leasing computers, and (d) buying computers.
15. List and discuss the 10 steps a business should take when obtaining a computer system for the first time.

YOU MAKE THE CALL

Situation 1

Rick's Hardware carries over 15,000 line items from over 200 vendors. A time-sharing arrangement for billing and accounts receivable is the only automation currently in use. The only way to tell whether a particular line item is in stock is for a clerk to physically search for the item. The owner/manager, Rick Johnson, believes too much inventory is not selling. Several clerks need access to current-stock-level and pricing information simultaneously for handling over-the-counter sales and sales called in from outside salespersons. Johnson is considering installing an in-house computer system for the company. Several departments of the company would need access to the computer information system throughout the work day.

Questions
1. What is the first step that Rick Johnson should take in exploring further automation of his company?
2. Give two types of computer systems that might be used to automate Rick's Hardware.
3. Which type of application software, customized or productivity, would be appropriate for Rick's Hardware?

Situation 2

Rather than having eight separate offices, a group of eight independent insurance agents have decided to share the overhead of a single office complex. They plan on sharing a receptionist and office equipment such as a copying machine and facsimile machine. Each agent has his or her own personal computer. The agents have expressed an interest in having access to a laser printer and some common insurance-related databases. The agents would like to have electronic mail, since they will work together with some clients.

Questions
1. Explain what can be done to tie the agents' individual personal computers together. What additional hardware and software will be required?
2. What is an alternative to a standard facsimile machine for transmitting computer-generated documents to clients?

EXPERIENTIAL EXERCISES

1. Conduct a personal interview with a local small-business manager who uses a computer system in his or her firm. Determine the types of hardware the manager purchased and why. Report your findings.
2. Locate a local small firm that does not yet use a computer. Interview the owner to determine whether she or he has ever considered computerizing the firm. Determine what reservations there are to purchasing a computer. Report your findings to the class.

3. Talk with a local computer store owner, or a salesperson representing a computer manufacturer, and ask him or her to demonstrate the hardware and software that small businesses might use. Obtain copies of literature from this individual and bring them to class.
4. Interview the manager of a local small firm to determine whether its computer applications are productivity packages, customized software, or both. Summarize your findings.

REFERENCES TO SMALL-BUSINESS PRACTICES

Case, John. "The Knowledge Factory," *Inc.*, Vol. 13, No. 10 (October 1991), pp. 54–59.
    A small-business manufacturer of metal springs uses state-of-the-art computerization to bring his family-owned business back to being competitive. More timely and accurate information about customers and products was the result of the increased automation. Employees have learned to work smarter due to more available information.
Kotite, Erika. "See How Small Business Can Put Equipment to Work—Behind the Scenes," *Entrepreneur,* Vol. 18, No. 5 (May 1990), pp. 89–92.
    This article reports interviews with several small-business owner/managers on how they select new office equipment.
Leidner, John and Joe Link. "Write Checks with Computers," *Progressive Farmer,* Vol. 108, No. 1 (January 1993), pp. 56–57.
    A simple and inexpensive computer program for writing checks and simple bookkeeping for a small business is explained.
Schuyler, Chet. "Off-the-Shelf Network Offers Solution to Rapid Growth," *PC Week,* (June 14, 1991), p. 58.
    Green Spring Mental Health Services (GSMHS) of Columbia, Maryland, provides mental health care review and case management for insurers such as Blue Cross and Blue Shield of Maryland. GSMHS had outgrown its computer system and needed more data communications capability. The installation of a Novell local area network is described.

ENDNOTES

1. Udayan Gupta, "Smoke and Mirrors," *The Wall Street Journal* (October 16, 1992), pp. R16–R17.
2. Jon Pepper, "Should You Do Windows? It Depends," *Nation's Business,* Vol. 78, No. 11 (November 1990), p. 44.
3. Paul W. Ross, et. al., *Understanding Computer Information Systems* (St. Paul, MN: West Publishing Company, 1992).
4. Alan Radding, "Disappearing Data—How to Avoid a Data Disaster with Computer Backup," *Independent Business,* Vol. 3, No. 6 (November/December 1992), pp. 60–62.
5. Ripley Hotch, "New Engines for Your Desktop," *Nation's Business,* Vol. 80, No. 4 (April 1992), pp. 54–57.
6. Ross, *op. cit.,* pp. 14–15.
7. Ripley Hotch, "The Most Desired, Troubling Categories of Programs," *Nation's Business,* Vol. 78, No. 9 (September 1990), pp. 50–53.
8. Jeanne Saddler, "Electronic Bulletin Boards Help Businesses Post Success," *The Wall Street Journal* (October 29, 1992), p. B2.
9. Patrick H. Corrigan, "The Well-Connected Office," *Inc.,* Vol. 14, No. 12 (Fall 1992), pp. 36–41.
10. James A. O'Brien, *Management Information Systems—A Managerial End User Perspective* (Homewood, IL: Richard D. Irwin, Inc., 1993), pp. 306–308.

11. Ron Mansfield, "Mailbox of the '90s," *Entrepreneurial Women* (July/August 1990), pp. 28–31.

12. O'Brien, *op. cit.*, pp. 280–282.

13. Erika Kotite, "Computer Revolution," *Entrepreneur,* Vol. 19, No. 11 (November 1991), pp. 76–82.

14. Nancy Nichols, "Lease or Buy," *Inc.,* Vol. 13, No. 10 (October 1991), pp. OG60–OG62.

15. Albert Holzinger and Ripley Hotch, "Upgrade for Growth," *Nation's Business,* Vol. 79, No. 4 (April 1991), p. 17.

CHAPTER 24

Risk and Insurance Management

SPOTLIGHT ON SMALL BUSINESS

A major risk associated with small-business retailing is shoplifting. This type of theft costs businesses of all sizes nationwide an estimated $26 billion per year.

Unfortunately, Tom Parr III, of Hillsboro, Texas, is all too familiar with this problem.

Parr, 44, says the thieves steal mainly small items—parts, nuts and bolts from his bins and, ironically, security items such as padlocks and deadbolts. Once he displayed 20 high-quality hammers. By the end of the day 16 were gone. None had been purchased. "If the shoplifters are good at it, they'll get you," says Parr, acknowledging that his prevention efforts came up short.

He estimates a yearly loss of $2,000 from shoplifting at his True Value Hardware store.

Tom Parr III

Source: Joe Dacy II, "They Come to Steal," *Independent Business,* Vol. 3, No. 5 (September–October 1992), pp. 24–29.

After studying this chapter, you should be able to:
1. Define concepts of risk and risk management.
2. Classify business risks by their asset-centered focus.
3. Discuss methods of coping with business risks.
4. Explain basic principles of insurance.
5. Identify types of insurance coverage.

risk
risk management
self-insurance
business interruption
  insurance
dishonesty insurance

coinsurance clause
surety bonds
credit insurance
general liability insurance
employer's liability
  insurance

workers' compensation
  insurance
key-person insurance
risk-retention group
purchasing group

It is said that "nothing is certain except death and taxes." Entrepreneurs would probably extend this adage to read, "Nothing is certain except death, taxes, and small-business risk." In Chapter 1, we noted the moderate risk-taking propensities of entrepreneurs and their preference for risky situations in which they can exert some control over the outcome. As a consequence, they seek to minimize business risk as much as possible. The first step toward reducing business risk is to understand the different types of business risks and alternatives for managing them.

DEFINING SMALL-BUSINESS RISKS

Simply stated, **risk** is "a condition in which there is a possibility of an adverse deviation from a desired outcome that is expected or hoped for."[1] Applied to the small-business situation, risk translates into losses associated with company assets and earning potential of the business. As used here, the term *asset* includes not only inventory and equipment but also such assets as the firm's employees and its reputation.

risk
the chance that a situation may end with loss or misfortune

Small-business risks can be classified in several ways. One simple approach is to group them by their causes. For example, fire, personal injury, theft, and fraud would be items on such a list. Another system identifies business risks by grouping them into those that are generally insurable and those that are largely uninsurable. A fire loss would typify the first category; product obsolescence the second category.

A third classification approach, one that is used in this chapter, emphasizes the asset-centered focus of the risk by categorizing business risks into four areas: market-centered risks, property-centered risks, personnel-centered risks, and customer-centered risks. A substantial loss in any one category could mean devastation for the small business. Figure 24-1 portrays these four risk cate-

Figure 24-1
The Wheel of
Misfortune

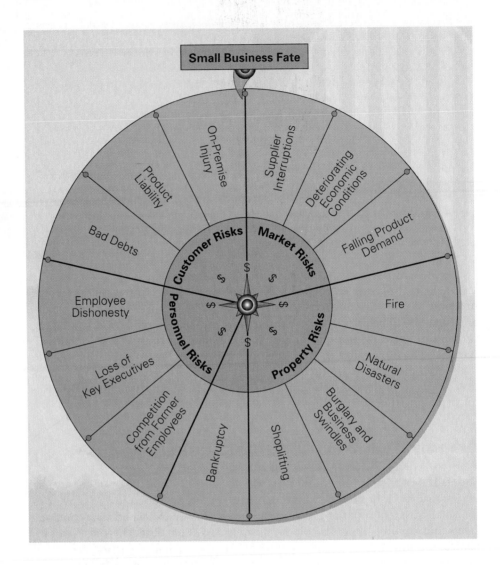

gories and their components, with bankruptcy as the ultimate small-business risk. This chapter will examine the forms of risk displayed in Figure 24-1, identifying possible alternatives for coping.

MARKET-CENTERED RISKS

Some crippling forms of business risks exist because of possible negative changes within a firm's target market and marketing efforts. Many of these factors directly affect the firm's competitive position and potential for long-term survival. Most, but not all, market-related risks develop slowly from day to day until they finally become destructive. Three examples of market-centered risks are supplier interruptions, deteriorating economic conditions, and falling product demand. These market-centered risks are generally uninsurable through standard insurance policies.

Supplier Interruptions

A small firm is dependent on suppliers of products and services to continue running smoothly. When major suppliers experience an interruption of their business operations, fallout from their hard times disrupts the operations of their customers. In 1990, for example, a power substation in New York City shut down, leaving Wall Street companies without electricity for over one week. Both small and large businesses in the service area were impacted. Estimates of lost business were set at $1 billion.[2]

Deteriorating Economic Conditions

Periods of high inflation, rising interest rates, declining discretionary income, and recessions are all symptoms of a deteriorating economy and are uncontrollable variables that have a major impact on the small firm's level of risk. Rapidly rising prices for materials and labor, for example, may catch the small firm in a vulnerable position, particularly if it is locked into a fixed price with customers. The increased cost of a bank loan might also be the straw that pushes a marginally profitable venture into bankruptcy.

Management of this form of risk is difficult. Entrepreneurs are extremely vulnerable because much discipline is required to save profits in times of prosperity to guard against a weak working-capital position.

Falling Demand for a Product

As noted in Chapter 12, all products go through a life cycle. Often, however, the downturn in sales occurs suddenly and with little warning. A small firm should make every possible effort to escape such surprises by keeping abreast of the market.

Product innovation is a key factor for the business that stays competitive. The risk of having to sell an obsolete product is increased when product innovation is lacking. A firm must adapt its product mix to survive! The strategy of the Bonne Bell Company is an excellent example of successful product mix adaptation by a firm. The company was started in 1927 when its founder, Jesse Grover Bell, began manufacturing cosmetic products in his basement. In 1936 Bell purchased the formula for a medicated skin wash and named it Ten-O-Six. This product became Bonne Bell's flagship product. However, the company continued to introduce new products to meet the needs of a changing market. Today, it remains one of the few family businesses in the cosmetics industry.[3]

The best way to avoid the risk of product mix neglect is to keep up with changes in the market. In this way, a firm can turn perceived threats into opportunities. An entrepreneur must maintain the entrepreneurial spirit and not neglect the product mix of the firm.

2. PROPERTY-CENTERED RISKS

In contrast to market-centered risks, property-centered risks involve tangible and highly visible assets. When these physical assets are lost or destroyed, they are quickly missed. Fortunately, many property-centered risks are insurable. Four examples of property-centered risks are fire, natural disasters, burglary and business swindles, and shoplifting.

Fire Hazards

Buildings, equipment, and inventory items can be totally or partially destroyed by fire. Of course, the degree of risk and the loss potential differ with the type of business. For example, industrial processes that are hazardous or that involve explosives, combustibles, or other flammable materials enlarge this risk.

Fire not only causes a direct property loss, but also interrupts business operations. During the period when business operations are interrupted, such fixed expenses as rent, supervisory salaries, and insurance charges continue. To minimize losses arising from business interruptions, a business might, for example, have alternative sources of electric power, such as its own generators, for use in times of emergency.

Natural Disasters

Floods, hurricanes, tornadoes, and hail are often described as "acts of God" because of human limitations in foreseeing and controlling them. As in the case of fire, natural disasters may also interrupt business operations. Although a business may take certain preventive measures—for example, locating in areas not subject to flood damage—little can be done to avoid natural disasters. Major reliance is placed upon insurance in coping with natural-disaster losses. In 1989, Hurricane Hugo hit the southeastern United States, resulting in approximately $10 billion in insurance claims.[4] In 1992, Hurricane Andrew caused even more devastating property damage.

Burglary and Business Swindles

The unauthorized entering of premises, with the intent to commit a crime, such as the removal of cash or merchandise, is called burglary. Although insur-

Figure 24-2
Damage from
Hurricane Andrew,
1992

ance should be carried against losses from burglary, it may prove helpful for a business to install burglar alarm systems and arrange for private security services.

Business swindles cost firms thousands of dollars a year. Small firms in particular are susceptible to swindles. Examples of these are bogus office-machine repairers, phony charity appeals, billings for listing in nonexistent directories, sale of advertising space in publications whose nature is misrepresented, and advanced-fee deals. Risks of this kind are avoidable only through the alertness of the business manager.

Shoplifting

Shoplifting jumped 35 percent in the four years from 1987 through 1990, according to FBI statistics, making it the fastest-growing larceny crime in the United States. Estimates of the cost to U.S. businesses vary dramatically, with figures ranging from $9 billion to $16 billion annually.[5] All such estimates are at best educated guesses, however, since in the majority of cases the crime of shoplifting goes undetected.

Shoplifting occurs primarily on the sales floors or at the checkout counters of retail stores. On the sales floor, nonprofessional shoplifters steal goods that can be quickly and easily hidden inside clothing, a backpack, or a handbag. Professional shoplifters—those for whom crime is a primary source of income—are much more skillful. Cleverly designed devices, such as clothing with large hidden pockets and shielded shopping bags for transporting merchandise with antitheft tags past detection gates, help the "pro" conceal items both small and large.

Various precautionary measures may be taken by small businesses to minimize shoplifting. One business publication has a "top ten" list of antishoplifting tactics.[6] They are:

1. *Training employees is crucial.* "Shoplifting is a constant problem for us," says Ed Sherman, owner of Sherman's Inc., a Tulsa, OK, variety store. "It costs us a lot of money." Sherman's solution is to train employees in customer service. "An attentive sales force is the best deterrent to shoplifting," says Sherman, "because the shoplifter's first requirement is privacy."
2. *Post signs around the store warning potential thieves that you will prosecute. Follow up on that threat.* Katy Culmo, owner of By George, a women's clothing store in Austin, TX, maintains that the best shoplifting defense is a strong offense. She cultivates a reputation for being hard on thieves. "An ambivalent approach makes you a target," Culmo says. Her clothes bear tags that sound an alarm if not removed at the cash register and she trains her staff to catch and detain shoplifters.
3. *Hang convex mirrors to eliminate blind aisles and install alarms on emergency exits.*
4. *Display expensive items in security cases.* Place "targeted" merchandise—items most at risk—near checkout stands. Howard Laves, owner of Benolds, a jewelry store in Austin, uses cameras and alarms to deter shoplifters. "We show expensive pieces one at a time," he says. And when a thief is caught, Laves prosecutes.
5. *Reduce clutter; arrange merchandise so that unexplained gaps on shelves can be easily detected.*
6. *Channel the flow of your customers past the cashier and block off unused checkout stands.*
7. *Attend to the needs of your customers. Be visible. Be available. Be attentive.*
8. *Monitor fitting rooms and employee-only areas.*
9. *Consider using uniformed or plain-clothed store detectives, two-way mirrors, electronic sales tags, and TV cameras.*
10. *Ask the police to do a "walk-through" of your store and tell you where you are vulnerable.*

Understanding the type of person who shoplifts can help a manager better understand the problem. The profile that follows was developed by the Council of Better Business Bureaus:

Most shoplifters are amateurs rather than professionals. Juvenile offenders, who, according to the Small Business Administration, account for about 50 percent of all shoplifting, may steal on a dare or simply for kicks. Impulse shoplifters include many "respectable" people who have not premeditated their thefts but instead succumb to the temptation of a sudden chance, such as an unattended dressing room or a blind aisle in a supermarket. Alcoholics, vagrants, and drug addicts are often clumsy and erratic in their behavior but may be violent as well—their apprehension is best left to the police. Kleptomaniacs, motivated by a compulsion to steal, usually have little or no actual use for the items they steal and in many cases could well afford to pay for them. All of these types of amateur shoplifters can be relatively easy to spot. The professional shoplifter, on the other hand, is usually highly skilled at the business of theft. Professionals generally steal items that can be resold quickly to an established fence, and they tend to concentrate on high-demand consumer goods such as televisions, stereos, and other small appliances. Even the professional, however, can be deterred from theft by a combination of alert personnel and effective store layout.[7]

PERSONNEL-CENTERED RISKS

Personnel-centered losses occur through actions of employees. For example, employee theft is an illegal and intentional act against the business and constitutes a major concern for many small businesses. A physically sick or injured employee also causes a business loss. Three types of various personnel-centered risks are dishonesty of current employees, former-employee competition, and loss of key executives. Most employee-centered risks are insurable.

Employee Dishonesty

One form of employee dishonesty is theft. Estimates of the magnitude of employee theft are difficult to make and tend to vary considerably. Small businesses are particularly vulnerable to theft because their antitheft controls are characteristically lax.

Thefts by employees may include not only cash but also inventory items, tools, scrap materials, postage stamps, and the like. Then there is the possibility of forgery, raising the amounts on checks, or other fraudulent practices. The trusted bookkeeper may collude with an outsider to have bogus invoices or invoices double or triple the correct amount presented for payment. The bookkeeper may approve such invoices for payment, write a check, and secure the manager's signature. Consider the following incidents. A company hired a person who had excellent academic credentials. The company didn't suspect any problems until the employee left town two years later. Although the employee had recorded accounts as paid, creditors began to claim the company owed thousands of dollars in past-due accounts. The company discovered that the employee had been drawing extra payroll checks by forging signatures. She had also altered amounts on her expense reimbursement checks. The company found that she had been keeping money intended for creditors, while sending the creditors only small amounts to buy time.[8]

In addition to bonding employees (insuring against dishonesty), the firm's major protection against employee fraud is a system of internal control.[9]

Competition from Former Employees

Good employees are always hard to get; they are even harder to keep. When a business has employee turnover—and it always will—there may be risks associated with former employees. Salespeople, beauticians, and other employees often take business with them when they leave. The risk is particularly acute with turnover of key executives. They are the more likely candidates to start a competing business or to leave with trade secrets.

Companies are very sensitive to the activities of former employees. Consider the following risk situation. Michael worked for a company that made equipment and supplies used in hot stamp decorating. Through this job, Michael met Robert, who owned a company that sold tools to Michael's employer. Michael began ordering patterns and models from a second company owned by Robert. In time, Michael and Robert formed their own corporation. Michael quit his job and began competing with his former employer. Michael's former employer sued Michael and Robert for misappropriating its manufacturing procedures manual and other alleged trade secrets. The court awarded Michael's former employer nearly $200,000 in damages.[10]

One common practice to help avoid this kind of employee-centered risk is to require employees to sign employment contracts clearly setting forth the employee's promise not to disclose certain information or use it in competition with the employer.

Loss of Key Executives

Every successful small business has one or more key executives. These employees could be lost to the firm by death or through attraction to other employment. If key personnel cannot be successfully replaced, the small firm suffers appreciably as the result of the loss of their services.

In addition to valuable experience and skill, the executive may have certain specialized knowledge that is vital to the successful operation of the firm. For example, a certain manufacturer was killed in an auto accident at the age of 53. His processing operations involved the use of a secret chemical formula that he had devised originally and divulged to no one because of the fear of losing the formula to competitors. He neither reduced it to writing nor placed it in a safety-deposit box. Not even his family knew the formula. As a result of his sudden death, the firm went out of business within six months. The expensive special-purpose equipment had to be sold as junk. All that his widow salvaged was about $60,000 worth of bonds and the Florida residence that had been the couple's winter home.

At least two solutions are available to the small firm faced with this contingency. The first of these is life insurance, which is discussed later in the chapter. The second involves the development of replacement personnel. A potential replacement should be groomed for every key position, including the position of the owner-manager.

CUSTOMER-CENTERED RISKS

Customers are the source of profit for small businesses, but they are also the center of an ever-increasing amount of business risk. Much of this risk is attributable to on-premise injury, product liability, and bad debts.

On-Premise Injury to Customers

Customers may initiate claims because of on-premise injuries. Because of high store traffic, the risk is particularly acute for small retailers. Personal injury liability of this type may occur, for example, when a customer breaks an arm by slipping on icy steps while entering or leaving the business. An employer is, of course, at risk with employees who suffer similar fates; but customers, by their sheer numbers, make this risk larger.

Another form of on-premise risk comes from inadequate security, which may result in robbery, assault, or other violent crimes. The number of so-called premises-liability cases involving violent crimes has "doubled during the past five years to about 1,000 annually," according to estimates by Liability Consultants, Inc., a security consulting firm in Framingham, Massachusetts.[11] Victims, often customers, look to the business to recover their losses. For example, in 1988, a freelance photographer was assaulted during her stay at a motel. Fortunately, the woman survived, but she later sued the business and the insurers paid $10 million to settle the suit.[12]

Good management of this kind of customer-centered risk demands that a regular check of the premises for hazards be conducted. The concept of preventive maintenance applies to management of this risk factor.

Product Liability

Recent product liability court decisions have broadened the scope of this form of risk. No reputable small business would intentionally produce a product that would potentially harm a customer, but good intentions are weak defenses in liability suits.

A product liability suit may be filed when a customer becomes ill or sustains physical or property damage in using a product made or sold by a company. Class-action suits, together with individual suits, are now widely used by consumers in product liability cases. Some types of businesses operate in higher-risk markets than others. For example, the insulation business has been targeted with numerous claims based on the effects of asbestos.

"Right now a small business can be wiped out by one punitive-damage award," says Victor Schwartz, counsel to the Product Liability Alliance, in Washington, DC. "The rules on punitive damage in most states are open-ended, the standards are vague, and there are no limits on the amounts of money for which a company can be sued."[13]

SMALL BUSINESS IN ACTION

Fighting Product Liability

A small business can never be completely shel-
tered from liability risks. Harry Featherstone, president of the Will-Burt Company in Orrville, Ohio,
can attest to that! One day, in 1980, Featherstone
was notified that he was being sued. An accident
had occurred at a construction site in Florida,
killing one worker and severely injuring another.
The scaffolding—the cause of the accident—was
produced by another company but included parts
manufactured by Will-Burt. The scaffolding company went bankrupt and Will-Burt was sued
"under the theory that all companies involved in
the production and sale of a defective product are
jointly liable . . ."

Eventually, Will-Burt's insurance company settled out of court even though Featherstone argues
that his parts were never defective. He further
contends that the suit might never have been filed
if there had been a federal product liability law to
clarify the legal questions surrounding conflicting
state laws. According to Featherstone, "A plaintiff
can win a suit in one state, lose in another, and be
prohibited even from filing in a third."

Faced with the settlement payment and loss of
liability coverage, Will-Burt laid off employees and
discontinued some of its product lines. Although it
was down, it was not knocked out. In spite of ad-
versity, this small firm is still in business.

Source: Adapted from Roger Thompson, "Deciding Who's to Blame," *Nation's Business*, Vol. 76, No. 5 (May 1988), pp. 26–27.
Reprinted by permission, *Nation's Business*, May 1988. Copyright 1988 U.S. Chamber of Commerce.

Even when a small firm is able to successfully defend itself against a product
liability suit, it must incur legal fees. H. E. Featherstone, who is featured in the
Small Business in Action "Fighting Product Liability," has not lost any suits but
has spent $600,000 in defending the business.[14]

Bad Debts

Bad debts are an unavoidable risk associated with credit selling. Most customers
will pay their obligations with no more than a friendly reminder. A few customers will intentionally try to avoid payment. These accounts should be
turned over to a lawyer quickly for litigation or be written off.

Customers who fall between the two groups of "quick pay" and "no pay" are the ones who cause the most trouble. These customers may be individuals who, for various reasons, temporarily experience difficulty and become slow payers. Every effort should be made in an aggressive but courteous manner to offer these customers options that encourage payment.

BANKRUPTCY

In one sense, the ultimate risk for a business is bankruptcy. It may, indeed, result from some of the risks described earlier. In recent years, hard economic times have fostered an increase in formal bankruptcy filings. According to the American Bankruptcy Institute, 972,490 businesses and individuals filed for bankruptcy between June 1991 and June 1992. This number represents a 10.5 percent increase over filings the previous year.[15] However, a bankruptcy filing can sometimes mean a fresh start and not the end of the road for a small firm.

The 1978 Bankruptcy Act established two types of legal bankruptcy status for businesses. The so-called Chapter 7 bankruptcy involves the appointment of a trustee to liquidate assets to pay off creditors. A Chapter 11 bankruptcy is basically a reorganization plan whereby the firm is permitted to continue operations subject to certain restrictions imposed by the court and the bankruptcy status. Confirmation of the reorganization plan by the courts has the following legal ramifications:[16]

- The plan has a binding effect on the business owner and the creditors.
- All property of the bankruptcy estate is vested in the reorganized debtor, free and clear of all liens and encumbrances unless otherwise stated in the plan.
- All prior debts of the business owner are discharged, except as may be provided in the plan.
- The debtor company commences its operations pursuant to the terms of the plan.

Unfortunately, bankruptcy courts often allow these cases to drag on for years. This time delay is one reason why up to 80 percent of Chapter 11 filers are eventually liquidated.[17] Chapter 11 "is too costly and takes too much time," says William Norton, III, a Nashville, Tennessee, bankruptcy lawyer. "Ultimately, the small business strangles under the weight of it."[18]

COPING WITH SMALL-BUSINESS RISKS

Risk management consists of all efforts designed to preserve the assets and earning power of the business. Risk management has grown out of insurance

risk management
efforts designed to preserve assets and the earning power of the firm

SMALL BUSINESS IN ACTION

A Failing Ski Resort Gets Passing Grade

One person's bankrupt business may be another person's golden opportunity. This was the situation involving entrepreneur Peter Pitcher when he became owner of Discovery Basin, a ski area in Montana's Deer Lodge National Forest. This account reflects the risk-management failures of the previous owner and also describes the positive steps taken by the new owner to avoid a recurrence of the bankruptcy.

Now, the previous owner had defaulted on his loans, and Discovery Basin was to be auctioned off.

"The area had changed hands three times in 10 years," Pitcher says. "The last owner had taken over what was already a 'white elephant,' and in two years, it was completely bankrupt. He had sold off most of the assets that weren't tied down, and hardly any maintenance had been done for two years."

That was 1984. At the time, Pitcher was managing a ski area near Santa Fe, New Mexico. "But I wasn't happy working within the confines of someone else's program. I wanted to be in charge and use my own ideas." That's when he saw a notice that the Small Business Administration (SBA) was auctioning off the Discovery Basin Ski Area.

"Mine was the only bid," Pitcher recalls. "I offered $500,000 for it, and had to put 10 per-

cent down." Pitcher's father helped him put a financing package together for the purchase and improvements, and the SBA agreed to give him a 15-year loan.

When he took over as new owner of Discovery, Pitcher faced a tremendous task. "I spend another $200,000 the first year just to get the area in reasonable condition. It was so run down it was hardly fit to be called a ski area."

The previous owner claimed he had an average of 20,000 "skier visits per year," but his cash flow didn't show it. The first two years, Pitcher had a negative cash flow, too. "Our first year, we had 25,000 skier visits, but the next year was a poor snow year and we dropped to 19,000." Pitcher said his staff persevered.

They painted the buildings, added a deck onto the ski lodge and cut new ski trails. Service was upgraded, top-of-the-line rental ski equipment was added, and quality food was served in the lodge.

"I knew we were on the right track," Pitcher says. "The third year, we put in another ski lift, and the first full season it was operating, we had one of our best years ever."

For the past three seasons, Discovery Basin Ski Area has averaged 40,000 skier visits, and 1990's sales figures were $581,000. Pitcher says, "My goal is to make Discovery a microcosm of what a top ski area should be—the best equipment, the best-maintained runs, and the best service."

Source: Gary F. Burchfield, "Ski Whiz," *Entrepreneur*, Vol. 19, No. 7 (April 1991), p. 164.

management. Therefore, the two terms are often used interchangeably. Actually, risk management has a much broader meaning, covering both those risks that are insurable and those that are not, and including noninsurance approaches to reducing all types of risks.

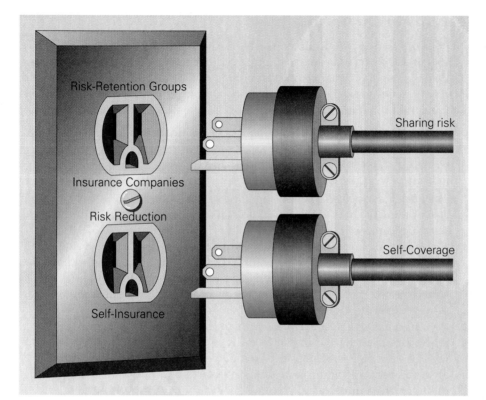

Figure 24-3
Power Sources
for Business Risk
Management

Risk management in a small firm differs from risk management in a large firm. In a large firm, the responsibilities of risk management are frequently assigned to a specialized staff manager. In contrast, the manager of a small business is usually the risk manager. Generally, small businesses have been slow to focus on managing risk. Ric Yocke, a consultant in risk management with the accounting firm of Ernst & Young, says, "I think it's easier for a small company not to address risk management because people wear so many hats. It's not something that requires immediate attention—until something happens."[19] In practicing risk management, the small-business manager needs to identify the different types of business risks and find ways to cope with them.

Once a manager is fully aware of the sources of risk, programs of risk management can be developed. Two basic alternatives of coping with risks can be pursued individually or in combination. These options are: (1) sharing the risk and (2) self-coverage. Figure 24-3 depicts these two risk-coping alternatives along with more specific methods of risk management. Many small businesses rely solely on sharing business risks via insurance when they should be using the options in combination.

Reducing Business Risks

Small-business risks of all kinds can be reduced with sound, common-sense management. Preventive maintenance applied to risk management means eliminating the circumstances and situations that create risk. For example, the small firm needs to take every possible precaution to prevent fires. Some possible precautions include the following:

1. *Use of safe construction.* The building should be made of fire-resistant materials, and electrical wiring should be adequate to carry the maximum load of electrical energy that will be imposed. Fire doors and insulation should be used where necessary.
2. *Provision of a completely automatic sprinkler system.* With an automatic sprinkler system available, fire insurance rates will be lower—and the fire hazard itself is definitely reduced.
3. *Provision of an adequate water supply.* Ordinarily this involves location in a city with water sources and water mains, together with a pumping system that will assure the delivery of any amount of water needed to fight fires. Of course, a company may hedge a bit by providing company-owned water storage tanks or private wells.
4. *Institution and operation of a fire-prevention program involving all employees.* Such a program must have top-management support, and the emphasis must always be on keeping employees fire-safety conscious. Regular fire drills for all employees, including both building-evacuation and actual fire-fighting efforts, may be undertaken.

Self-Insurance

Intelligent personal financial planning usually follows the practice of "saving for a rainy day." This concept should also be incorporated into small-business risk management. It is a difficult practice to follow in a business, but one that will pay dividends. This is a form of risk management frequently called self-insurance.

self-insurance
earmarking part of a firm's earnings as a contingency for possible future losses

Self-insurance can take a general or specific form. In its general form, a part of the firm's earnings is earmarked as a contingency fund for possible future losses regardless of the source. In its specific form, a self-insurance program designates funds to individual loss categories such as property, medical, or workers' compensation. Some firms have moved quite heavily into self-insurance.

Medical coverage is one area in particular where small firms are moving to self-insurance. In a 1991 survey by a benefits consulting firm, it was found that 22 percent of firms with between 100 and 500 employees were self-insured, compared with a 1988 study where 8 percent and 26 percent of firms with 500 employees were self-insured.[20]

Pepper . . . and Salt

Figure 24-4
Risk-Taking Begins
Early

THE WALL STREET JOURNAL

**"We're starting first-aid training, Dad. I need
$150,000 for malpractice insurance."**

Source: From *The Wall Street Journal*—Permission, Cartoon Features
Syndicate.

Obviously, self-insurance is not affordable for every small firm. One insurance specialist, Lori Raffel, director of the stop-loss division of Mutual Group, offers a general rule of thumb: Your company should have a net worth of at least $250,000 and at least 25 employees to be self-funded.[21]

Sharing Risks

The rapid increase in insurance premiums in the 1980s—particularly for general liability coverage—has resulted in an inability of many small businesses to obtain affordable insurance.[22] Small-business owners hope this trend will be reversed. Nevertheless, insurance still provides one of the most important means of sharing business risks. A sound insurance program is imperative for the proper protection of a business.

Regardless of the nature of the business, risk insurance is a serious issue. Too often in the past, the small firm has paid insufficient attention to insurance matters and has failed to acquire skill in analyzing risk problems. Today such a situation is unthinkable. The small-business manager *must* take an active role in structuring an insurance package.

INSURANCE FOR THE SMALL BUSINESS

Many small firms carry insufficient insurance protection. The entrepreneur often comes to such a realization only after a major loss. Careful risk management dictates a study of adequate insurance policies *in advance of a loss* rather than after the occurrence of the event.

Basic Principles of an Insurance Program

What kinds of risks can be covered by insurance? What kinds of coverage should be purchased? How much coverage is adequate? Unfortunately, there are no clear-cut answers to these questions. Probably the best advice to a small-business manager is to seek advice from a professional insurance agent. A reputable insurance agent can provide valuable assistance to small firms in evaluating risks and designing proper protection plans. However, the entrepreneur should enter this consultation as knowledgeable about insurance as possible. Some of the basic principles of insurance are discussed in the next paragraphs.

Identify the Business Risks to Be Covered. Although the common insurable risks were pointed out earlier, other, less obvious, risks may be revealed only by a careful investigation. The small firm must first obtain coverages required by law or contract, such as workers' compensation insurance and automobile liability insurance. As part of this risk-identification process, the plant and equipment should be reappraised periodically by competent appraisers in order to maintain adequate insurance coverage.

Obtain Coverage Only for Major Potential Losses. The small firm must determine the magnitude of loss that it could bear without serious financial difficulty. If the firm is sufficiently strong, it may cover only those losses exceeding a specified minimum amount to avoid unnecessary coverage. It is important, of course, to guard against the tendency to underestimate the severity of potential losses.

Relate Cost of Premiums to Probability of Loss. Because the insurance company must collect enough premiums to pay the actual losses of insured parties, the cost of insurance must be proportional to the probability of occurrence of the insured event. As the chance of loss becomes more and more certain, a firm finds that the premium cost becomes so high that insurance is simply not worth the cost. Thus, insurance is most applicable and practical for improbable losses.

Requirements for Obtaining Insurance

Before an insurance company is willing to underwrite possible losses, certain requirements about the risk or the insured must be met.

The Risk Must Be Calculable. The total overall loss arising from a large number of insured risks can be calculated by means of actuarial tables. For example, the number of buildings that will burn each year can be predicted with some accuracy. Only if the risks can be calculated will it be possible for the insurance company to determine appropriate insurance rates.

The Risk Must Exist in Large Numbers. The particular risk must occur in sufficiently large numbers to permit the law of averages to work and be spread over a wide geographical area. A fire insurance company, for example, cannot afford to insure only one building or even all the buildings in one town. It would have to insure buildings in many other towns and cities to get an adequate, safe distribution of risk.

The Insured Property Must Have Commercial Value. An item that possesses only sentimental value cannot be insured. For example, an old family picture that is of no value to the public may not be included among other tangible items whose value can be measured in monetary terms.

The Policyholder Must Have an Insurable Interest in the Property or Person Insured. The purpose of insurance is reimbursement of actual loss and not creation of profit for the insured. For example, a firm cannot insure a building for $500,000 if its true worth is only $70,000. Likewise, it cannot obtain life insurance on its customers or suppliers.

Types of Insurance

There are several classifications of insurance and a variety of coverages available from different insurance companies.[23] Each insurance purchaser should seek a balance between coverage, deductions, and premiums. Since the trend is toward higher and higher premiums for small businesses, the balancing act becomes even more critical.

Commercial Property Coverage. This class of insurance provides protection from losses associated with damage to or loss of property. Examples of property losses that can be covered are fire, explosion, vandalism, broken glass, business interruption, and employee dishonesty.

Most entrepreneurs will see the need for fire coverage and maybe a few other more traditional losses, but not enough small businesses realize the value of business interruption insurance. **Business interruption insurance** protects companies during the period necessary to restore property damaged by an insured peril. Coverage pays for lost income and certain other expenses of rebuilding the business. John Donahue, vice-president of the commercial insur-

business interruption insurance
coverage of lost income and certain expenses while rebuilding the business

Figure 24-5
Commercial
Property Coverage
Can Keep This Firm
in Business

ance division for The Hartford Insurance Company, says that the "biggest mistake" small companies make

is in not having sufficient . . . coverage that protects them against some catastrophe, such as a flood or fire, which would close down their business; while standard property insurance will pay to replace a building and its contents, it will not cover the payroll and other expenses that must be paid during the three or four months the factory is being rebuilt.[24]

Proving the extent of lost profits can be difficult. The process is difficult because you are trying to reconstruct what never was.

dishonesty insurance
coverage to protect
against employees'
dishonesty and their
other crimes

Dishonesty insurance covers such traditional areas as fidelity bonds and crime insurance. Employees occupying positions of trust in handling company funds are customarily bonded as a protection against their dishonesty. The informality and highly personal basis of employment in small firms make it difficult to realize the value of such insurance. On the other hand, the possible loss of money or other property through the dishonesty of persons other than employees is easy to accept. Crime insurance can cover such dangers as theft, robbery, and forgery.

coinsurance clause
requires the insured
to maintain a
specific level of
coverage or to
assume a portion of
any loss

Many commercial property policies contain a **coinsurance clause.** Under this clause, the insured agrees to maintain insurance equal to some specified percentage of the property value.[25] (Eighty percent is quite typical.) In return for this promise, the insured is given a reduced rate. If the insured fails to maintain the 80 percent coverage, only part of the loss will be reimbursed. To see how a coinsurance clause determines the amount paid by the insurer, assume that the physical property of a business is valued at $50,000. If the business insures it for $40,000 (or 80 percent of the property value) and incurs a fire loss of $20,000, the insurance company will pay the full amount of $20,000. However, if the business insures the property for only $30,000 (which is 75 percent of the specified minimum), the insurance company will pay only 75 percent of the loss, or $15,000.

Surety Bonds.

Surety bonds insure against the failure of another firm or individual to fulfill a contractual obligation. Surety bonds are frequently used in connection with construction contracts.

surety bonds
protection against another firm's failure to fulfill a contractual obligation

Credit Insurance.

Credit insurance protects businesses from abnormal bad-debt losses—for example, losses that result from a customer's insolvency due to tornado or flood losses, depressed industry conditions, business recession, or other factors. Credit insurance does not cover normal bad-debt losses that are predictable on the basis of business experience. Insurance companies compute the normal rate on the basis of industry experience and the loss record of the particular firm being insured.

credit insurance
protection against abnormal bad-debt losses

Credit insurance is available only to manufacturers and wholesalers. It is not available to a retailer. Thus, only trade credit may be insured. There are two reasons for this. The more important reason is found in the relative ease of analyzing business risks as compared with analyzing ultimate consumer risks. The other reason is that retailers have a much greater number of accounts receivable, which are smaller in dollar amount and provide greater risk diversification, so that credit insurance is less acutely required.

The collection service of the insurance company makes available legal talent and experience that may otherwise be unavailable to a small firm. Furthermore, collection efforts of insurance companies are generally conceded to be superior to those of regular collection agencies.

The credit standing of a small firm that uses credit insurance may be enhanced. The small firm can show the banker that steps have been taken to avoid unnecessary risks, and thus it might obtain more favorable consideration in securing bank credit.

Credit insurance policies typically provide for a collection service on bad accounts. Although collection provisions vary, a common provision requires the insured to notify the insurance company within 90 days of the past-due status of the account and to turn it in for collection after 90 days.

Although the vast majority of policies provide general coverage, policies may be secured to cover individual accounts. A 10 percent, or higher, coinsurance requirement is included to limit the coverage to approximately the replacement value of the merchandise. Higher percentages of coinsurance are required for inferior accounts in order to discourage reckless credit extension by insured firms. Accounts are classified according to ratings by Dun & Bradstreet or ratings by other recognized agencies. Premiums vary with account ratings.

Commercial Liability Insurance. There are two general classes of this form of insurance—general liability and employers' liability/workers' compensation. **General liability insurance** covers business liability to customers who might be injured on the premises or off-premises or who might be injured from the product sold to them. General liability insurance does not cover injury to a firm's own employees. However, employees using products such as machinery purchased from another manufacturer can bring suit under product liability laws against the equipment manufacturer.

general liability insurance
coverage against suits brought by customers

Employer's liability and workers' compensation insurance are required by most states to insure employees. As the titles imply, **employer's liability insurance** provides protection against suits brought by employees who suffer injury. **Workers' compensation insurance** obligates the insurer to pay eligible employees for injury or illness related to employment.

employer's liability insurance
coverage against suits brought by employees

workers' compensation insurance
obligates the insurer to pay employees for injury or illness related to employment

Key-Person Insurance. By carrying **key-person insurance**, protection for the small business can be provided against the death of key personnel of the firm. This insurance is purchased by the company with the company as sole beneficiary. It may be written on an individual or group basis.

Most small-business advisers suggest term insurance for key-person insurance policies, primarily because of lower premiums. How much to buy is more difficult to decide. Face values of key-person insurance policies usually begin around $50,000 and may go as high as several million dollars. Bayshore Metals of San Francisco, for example, has two $500,000 policies on its partners, while Reebok International has a $50 million policy to cover its key executives.

key-person insurance
coverage that protects against the death of key personnel of a firm

Insurance Cooperatives

Another option by which a small business can share its risk via insurance is to join with other, similar firms in a cooperative effort. This option was made possible with the passage of the federal Product Liability Risk Retention Act in 1981. This legislation allowed organizations to form special risk-retention groups or join together into a purchasing group.[27]

risk-retention group
an insurance company started by a homogeneous group of entrepreneurs or professionals to provide liability insurance for its members

A **risk-retention group** is an insurance company started by a homogeneous group of entrepreneurs or professionals. The group provides liability insurance for its members. A **purchasing group** is any unincorporated group of firms that has the purpose of purchasing liability insurance for the group. It is subject to less regulation than a risk-retention group. Prior to passage of the 1981 act, it was almost impossible for these cooperatives to function under state regulations of a nonlicensing state.

purchasing group
an unincorporated group of firms who purchase liability insurance for the group

The Risk Retention Amendments of 1986 broadened the scope of risk-retention and purchasing groups. The new law permits a group to provide any

commercial liability coverage to its members who all face a common risk. A co-operative effort to share risks with other small businesses is not necessarily a viable option for all small firms. It does, however, offer another alternative for coping with business risk.

1. Risk management is concerned with the protection of the assets and earning power of a business against risks of accidental loss. The three ways to manage business risks are: reduce the risk, save to cover possible future losses, and transfer the risk to someone else by carrying insurance. The best solution often is to combine all three approaches.
2. Business risks can be classified by the causes of accidental loss, by insurability, or by type of assets that are preserved with risk management. In using the last system, risks are classified as market-centered, property-centered, personnel-centered, or customer-centered.
3. The small firm should carry enough insurance to protect against major losses. Beyond this, the decision on coverage requires judgment that balances such factors as magnitude of possible loss, ability to minimize such losses, cost of the insurance, and financial strength of the firm.
4. To obtain insurance, several requirements must be met. The risk must be calculable in probabilistic terms, the risk must exist in large numbers, the insured property must have commercial value, and the policyholder must have an insurable interest in the property or person insured.
5. The basic types of insurance coverage that the small business might require are commercial property coverage, surety bonds, credit, commercial liability, and key-person insurance. Risk-retention and purchasing groups provide a mechanism for obtaining insurance coverage through nontraditional channels.

DISCUSSION QUESTIONS

1. Which of the different classifications of business risks is the most difficult for the small firm to control? Why? Which is the least difficult to control? Why?
2. Do you feel the product liability suit brought against the Will-Burt Company (Small Business in Action, page 630) was fair? Why or why not?
3. If you were shopping in a small retail store and somehow sustained an injury such as a broken arm, under what circumstances would you sue the firm? Explain.
4. Do you think some firms are hesitant to enter formal bankruptcy proceedings even though they could save the business? Why?
5. What are the basic ways to cope with risk in a small business?
6. Can a small firm safely assume that business risks will never turn into losses sufficient to bankrupt it? Why or why not?
7. How can a small business deal with the risk entailed in business recessions?

8. Could a small firm safely deal with such hazards as property loss from fire by precautionary measures in lieu of insurance?
9. When is it logical for a small business to utilize self-insurance?
10. Enumerate a number of approaches for combating the danger of theft or fraud by employees and also by outsiders.
11. Under what conditions would life insurance on a business executive constitute little protection to the business? When is such life insurance helpful?
12. Are any kinds of business risks basically human risks? Are the people involved always employees?
13. Is the increase in liability claims and court awards of special concern to small manufacturers? Why?
14. What types of insurance are required by law for most business firms?
15. Explain how risk-retention groups are an alternative way for small firms to cope with risk. Do you believe these groups will become popular? Why or why not?

YOU MAKE THE CALL

Situation 1

The Amigo Company manufactures motorized wheelchairs in its Bridgeport, Michigan, plant under the supervision of Alden Thieme. Alden is the brother of the firm's founder, Allen Thieme. The company has around 100 employees and does $10 million in sales a year.

Like many other firms, Amigo is faced with increased liability insurance costs. It is contemplating dropping all coverage. However, it realizes that the users of its product are individuals who have already suffered pain and trouble. Therefore, if an accident were to occur and there was a liability suit, there might be a strong temptation for juries to favor the plaintiffs. In fact, the company has already experienced litigation. A woman in an Amigo wheelchair was killed by a car on the street. The driver of the car had no insurance, so Amigo was sued.

Questions
1. Do you agree that the type of customer to whom the Amigo Company sells should influence its decision regarding insurance?
2. In what way, if any, should the outcome of the firm's current litigation impact Amigo's decision to renew its insurance coverage?
3. What options for going without insurance does Amigo have? What is your recommendation?

Situation 2

Pansy Ellen Essman is a 42-year-old grandmother who is chairman of a company based in Atlanta, Georgia, that does $5 million in sales each year. Her company, Pansy Ellen Products, Inc., grew out of a product idea Essman had as she bathed her squealing, squirming granddaughter in the bathroom tub. Her idea was to produce a sponge pillow to cradle a child in, thus freeing the mother's hands so she could easily clean her baby.

Since production of this initial product, the company has expanded its product line to include nursery lamps, baby food organizers, strollers, and hook-on baby seats. Essman has seemingly managed her product mix risk well. However, she is concerned that other sources of business risk may have been ignored or slighted.

Questions
1. What particular other types of business risk do you think Essman might be considering? Be specific.
2. Would a risk-retention group be a good possibility for this company? Why or why not?
3. What different types of insurance coverage should a company like this carry?

EXPERIENTIAL EXERCISES

1. Locate a recent issue of a business magazine wherein you can read about new small-business startups. Select one new firm that is marketing a product and another that is selling a service. Compare their situations relative to business risks. Report to the class on your analysis.
2. Contact a local small-business owner and obtain his or her permission to conduct a risk analysis of the business. Note the business's situation in regard to risk and what preventive or protective actions you suggest. Report your findings to the class.
3. Contact a local insurance company and arrange to conduct an interview. Determine in the interview the various types of coverage the company offers for small businesses. Write a report on your findings.
4. Assume that upon graduation you enter your family business or obtain employment with an independent business back in your home town. Further assume that after five years of employment you leave the business to start your own competing business. Make a list of the considerations you perceive you would face regarding leaving the business with trade secrets after just five years of experience.

REFERENCES TO SMALL-BUSINESS PRACTICES

Bowes, David. "Sudden Departures," *Nation's Business,* Vol. 79, No. 1 (January 1991), pp. 44–46.
     The negative consequences of the loss of a chief executive and 100 percent owner of a business are described in this article.
Brody, Michael. "When Products Turn into Liabilities," *Fortune,* Vol. 113, No. 5 (March 3, 1986), pp. 20–24.
     Some of the responses companies have taken to the increase in lawsuits are discussed in this article. Several lawsuits over product liability are described.
Fraser, Jill Andresky. "Business As Unusual," *Inc.,* Vol. 13, No. 8 (August 1991), pp. 39–43.

This article describes the experiences of a small firm committed to managing its comprehensive insurance plan. Much of the article is devoted to a yearly account of the firm's insurance management tactics.

Joseph, Eileen Z. "Managing Your Risks," *Nation's Business*, Vol. 74, No. 4 (April 1986), pp. 66–68.

A step-by-step approach for controlling risks and lowering insurance costs is included in this article. The need for risk-management plans is emphasized by the author.

Thompson, Roger. "States Take Lead in Health Reform," *Nation's Business*, Vol. 80, No. 4 (April 1992), pp. 18–23.

In this article several small firms are spotlighted regarding their efforts to join coalitions to reduce health-care costs.

ENDNOTES

1. Emmett J. Vaughan, *Fundamentals of Risk and Insurance*, 4th ed. (New York: John Wiley & Sons, 1986), p. 4.

2. "A Guide to Small-Company Disaster Planning & Recovery," *Inc.*, Vol. 14, No. 3 (March 1992), Special Ad Section.

3. Gayle Olinekova, "Bringing Up Bonne," *Entrepreneur*, Vol. 17, No. 10 (October 1989), pp. 44–51.

4. "A Guide to Small-Company Disaster Planning & Recovery," *Op. cit.*

5. *How To Protect Your Business*, Council of Better Business Bureaus, 1992, p. 116.

6. Joe Dacy II, "They Come to Steal," *Independent Business*, Vol. 3, No. 5 (September–October 1992), pp. 24–29.

7. *How to Protect Your Business, Op. cit.* Reprinted with permission of the Council of Better Business Bureaus, from *How to Protect Your Business*, copyright 1992. Council of Better Business Bureaus, Inc., 4200 Wilson Blvd., Arlington, VA 22203.

8. Dorothy Simonelli, "A Small Owner's Guide to Preventing Embezzlement," *Independent Business* (September–October 1992), pp. 30–31.

9. For a good discussion of these controls, see Neil H. Snyder and Karen E. Blair, "Dealing with Employee Theft," *Business Horizons*, Vol. 32, No. 3 (May–June 1989), pp. 27–34.

10. Fred S. Steingold, "Competing with Your Former Employer," *Inc.*, Vol. 5, No. 1 (January 1983), p. 91.

11. Barbara Marsh, "Small Businesses Face Problem From Crime Lawsuits," *The Wall Street Journal* (February, 1993), p. B2.

12. Terri Thompson, David Hage, and Robert F. Black, "Crime and the Bottom Line," *U.S. News & World Report* (April 13, 1992), p. 56.

13. Joan C. Szabo, "The Maze of Product Liability," *Nation's Business*, Vol. 78, No. 6 (June 1990), p. 62.

14. *Ibid.*

15. Meg Whittemore, "Managing Bankruptcy," *Nation's Business*, Vol. 81, No. 1 (January 1993), p. 69.

16. Bankruptcy and Its Alternatives," *D & B Reports* (March/April 1991), p. 8.

17. Howard Gleckman, "Why Chapter 11 Needs To Be Rewritten," *Business Week*, No. 3266 (May 18, 1992), p. 116.

18. Michael Selz, "For Many Small Firms, 'Chapter 11' Closes the Book," *The Wall Street Journal* (November 4, 1992), p. B2.

19. Jane Easter Bahls, "The Rewards of Risk Management," *Nation's Business*, Vol 78, No. 9 (September 1990), p. 61.

20. Edward Felsenthal, "Self-Insurance of Health Plans Benefits Firms," *The Wall Street Journal* (November 11, 1992), p. B1.

21. Dale Buss, "Can You Afford to Self-Insure?" *Independent Business*, Vol. 4, No. 1 (January–February 1993), p. 40.

22. See for example the discussion in Archer W. Huneycutt and Elizabeth A. Wibker, "Liability Crisis: Small Businesses at Risk," *Journal of Small Business Management,* Vol. 26, No. 1 (January 1988), pp. 25–30.

23. Much of the terminology used here to describe the different types of insurance is consistent with that used in the new Portfolio Program, suggested by the Insurance Services Office, which is a national rating bureau that publishes rates for property and liability insurance. This program introduced simplified policy terminology effective January 1, 1986.

24. Nancy McConnell, "Business Insurance Good News and Bad News," *Venture,* Vol. 10, No. 9 (September 1988), p. 64.

25. It should be remembered that this is value at time of the actual loss.

26. John S. DeMott, "Key People, Key Protection," *Nation's Business,* Vol. 81, No. 3 (March 1993), p. 43.

27. For an excellent discussion of the act, see John Harkavy, "The Risk Retention Act of 1986: The Options Increase," *Risk Management,* Vol. 34, No. 3 (March 1987), pp. 22–34.

CHAPTER 25

Social and Ethical Issues

SPOTLIGHT ON SMALL BUSINESS

Corporate codes of ethical conduct are often viewed with skepticism. To some, they seem to be ideals that are compromised when profits are threatened. Here is an observer's testimony about a small company in Minnesota that not only maintains a written code of ethics but also practices what it preaches:

I'm delighted to report that I've stumbled across a Twin Cities company that not only has committed itself in writing to ethical treatment of employees, customers and suppliers, but has spent 20 years demonstrating in rather dramatic fashion that it actually means what it says.

Allow me to introduce you to Reell Precision Manufacturing Co. (RPM), a privately held Vadnais Heights company that, among other odd notions, places the well-being of its 100 employees and their families above unfettered profit growth. RPM makes electromechanical motors, clutches, and other parts used in copiers, automatic addressing machines, and similar devices.

From left: Robert L. Wahlstedt, President; Lee Johnson, CEO; Dale Merrick (Retired)

This firm's code of ethics specifies that commitments to workers come before short-term profits and that conflicts between the job and the family are to be resolved in favor of the family. Because jobs come before profits, there has never been an economic layoff, and, according to RPM's president, they will take profits down to zero before there's a layoff. Because of the firm's commitment to the family, as a further example, it does not ask employees to travel on weekends to take advantage of lower airline fares.

Source: Dick Youngblood, "A Firm That Means What It Says," *Star Tribune* (December 28, 1992), p. 2D. Reprinted with permission of the *Star Tribune,* Minneapolis-St. Paul.

After studying this chapter, you should be able to:
1. Explain the nature of a small firm's social responsibilities.
2. Summarize the ways that small-firm managers view their social responsibilities.
3. Recognize the conflict between socially-responsible behavior and profits.
4. Illustrate the types of ethical problems in small business.
5. Explain how small firms can attain high ethical standards.

social responsibilities   ethical issues   code of ethics
environmentalism   underlying values   bait advertising
consumerism

Business owners obviously intend to earn a profit, and our society agrees with that right by granting freedom to operate as part of a private enterprise system. In addition, society expects business firms—including small ones—to operate in a responsible manner and to contribute positively to the welfare of the community and nation.

Some social expectations are incorporated in the law—for example, a prohibition against misleading advertising. The law, however, is not so detailed or explicit that it spells out answers to all of the social and ethical issues confronting small and growing firms. Therefore, small-business owners need a general understanding of the social context of business operations.

SOCIAL RESPONSIBILITIES OF SMALL BUSINESS

In recent years, public attention has been focused on the social obligations of business organizations. These feelings of concern are rooted in a new awareness of the role of business in modern society. In a sense, the public regards managers as trustees and expects them to act accordingly to protect the interests of suppliers, employees, customers, and the general public, along with making a profit.

How Small Firms View Their Social Obligations

Conservation, fair hiring practices, consumerism, environmental protection, and the public welfare are popular themes in the news media. One might wonder about the extent to which small businesses are responsive to these issues.

Intuitively, one would expect to find great variation in social sensitivity among business owners, and this is indeed the case. One study asked small-business owners and managers, "How do you see your responsibilities to society?"[1] In response, 88 percent mentioned at least one type of social obligation,

**social
responsibilities**
ethical obligations
to customers, em-
ployees, and the
community

whereas only 12 percent felt they had no specific responsibilities or did not know how to respond to the question.

The majority who recognized **social responsibilities** cited obligations to customers, to employees, and to the community, as well as a general responsibility to act ethically. On the basis of these responses, it is evident that most small-business owners are aware that their firms function within the context of the broader society.

A few entrepreneurs have been outspoken in their commitment to social responsibility. The Body Shop and Ben & Jerry's Homemade, Inc., provide two good examples.[2] These two firms—the first of which sells cosmetics, the second ice cream—have shown great concern for protection of the environment and other social objectives. They are two of the 55 companies that formed an organization called Businesses for Social Responsibility in 1992 to promote the idea that social responsibility is good for business and long-term profits.[3] However, entrepreneurs and businesses of this type are the exception in displaying such a high degree of social sensitivity.

Granted that small-business CEOs have some awareness of social obligations, how do they compare with big-business CEOs in their views of social responsibility? The evidence is limited, but entrepreneurs who head small, growth-oriented companies seem to be more narrowly focused on profits and therefore less socially sensitive than are large-corporation CEOs. A study that compared entrepreneurs with CEOs of large businesses concluded:

> *The entrepreneurial CEOs were found to be more economically driven and less socially oriented than their large-firm counterparts. Apparently, CSR [corporate social responsibility] is a luxury many small growth firms believe they cannot afford. Survival may be the first priority.*[4]

Nevertheless, these entrepreneurs were not totally self-centered. According to the study, they were still sensitive to social issues, but to a somewhat lesser degree than were CEOs of large corporations.

It is apparent, then, that small-business leaders differ in the importance they attach to social obligations. Most of them seem to accept some degree of social responsibility. Perhaps due to financial pressures, many of them also show concern about a possible trade-off between social responsibility and profits.

Social Obligations and Profit Making

Small firms, as well as large corporations, must reconcile their social responsibilities with their need to earn profits. Meeting the expectations of society can be expensive. Small firms must sometimes purchase new equipment or make costly changes in operations in order to protect the environment. Here are some examples of environmental costs facing some small businesses in the 1990s:[5]

SMALL BUSINESS IN ACTION

Social Objectives in an Entrepreneurial Firm

The Body Shop, a firm started by Anita Roddick in England in 1976, gives social responsibilities a high priority in its operation. Its principal business is the sale of skin and hair care products. From its beginning as one tiny shop, this firm has made customer and community service a major objective.

One example is The Body Shop's efforts to protect the environment by offering discounts to customers who return plastic bottles, using products that are biodegradable, recycling waste, using recycled paper, and providing biodegradable carrier bags. To serve its customers well, The Body Shop places greater emphasis on health and well-being than on beauty, avoids high-pressure selling, seeks to provide adequate product information, keeps packaging at a minimum so that customers pay only for the product, and uses a range of container sizes so that customers can buy only what they need.

Source: *What Is The Body Shop?*, a brochure distributed in The Body Shop stores.

1. Gas stations may need to install hydrocarbon devices on gas pumps.
2. Auto-body paint and repair shops and furniture makers may have to buy equipment to catch hydrocarbon emissions from spray paint.
3. Restaurants may need containment units to collect hydrocarbon emissions from charcoal grills.
4. Bakeries may require equipment to control the hydrocarbon ethanol that is produced by yeast while dough is fermenting and released during baking.
5. Printing shops may need costly emission control devices or other equipment changes to deal with chemicals that contribute to ozone formation.

From these examples, it is evident that acting in the public interest may require the expenditure of money, with a consequent reduction of profits. There are limits, therefore, to what particular businesses can afford.

Figure 25-1
The Cost of Controlling Hydrocarbon Ethanol Reduces a Bakery's Profits

Fortunately, some types of socially responsible action can be consistent with a firm's long-term profit objective. Indeed, some socially desirable practices—honesty in advertising, for example—entail no additional costs. Some firms actually thrive by making a special point of their dedication to certain social objectives. Walnut Acres, for example, is a Pennsylvania farm that specializes in production of organically grown foods. Organic farming avoids the use of pesticides and chemical fertilizers, thereby protecting the environment and the health of consumers. This farm has expanded to the point that it employs about 100 people and had 1992 revenues of about $7 million.[6] The success of Walnut Acres shows that environmental protection and profits are not always in conflict. In this case, indeed, the firm prospered as customers were attracted by its special farming methods.

There is also some degree of goodwill that is earned by socially acceptable behavior. A firm that consistently fulfills its obligations makes itself a desirable member of the community and may attract patronage because of that image. Conversely, a firm that scorns social responsibilities may find itself the object of restrictive legislation and discover its employees to be lacking in loyalty. To some extent, therefore, socially responsible practices can have a positive impact on profits.

Recognition of a social obligation does not change a profit-seeking business into a charitable organization. Earning a profit is absolutely essential. Without profits, a firm is in no position to recognize social responsibilities toward anyone. The point is that profits, although essential, are not the only factor of importance.

The Special Challenge of Environmentalism

In recent decades the deterioration of the environment has become a matter of widespread concern. One source of pollution has been business firms that discharge waste into streams, contaminants into the air, and noise into areas surrounding their operations. **Environmentalism**—the effort to preserve and redeem the environment—thus directly affects business organizations, including small-business firms.

environmentalism
concern with protecting the environment from damage

The interests of small-business owners and environmentalists are not necessarily or uniformly in conflict. Some business leaders, including those in small business, have worked and acted for the cause of conservation. For example, many small firms have taken steps to remove eyesores and to landscape and otherwise improve plant facilities. Others have modernized their equipment and changed their procedures to reduce air and water pollution. In a few cases, small business has been in a position to benefit from the emphasis on ecology. Those companies whose products are harmless to the environment gain an edge over competitive products that pollute. Also, small firms are involved in servicing pollution-control equipment. The auto repair shop, for example, services pollution-control devices on automobile engines.

Some small firms are adversely affected by efforts to protect the environment. Livestock feeding lots, cement plants, pet-food processors, and iron foundries are representative of industries that are especially vulnerable to extensive regulation. The cost impact on businesses of this type is often severe. Indeed, the required improvements can force the closure of some businesses.

The ability to pass higher costs on to customers is dependent upon the market situation and is ordinarily quite difficult for the small firm. Resulting economic hardships on small business must, therefore, be recognized as a cost of pollution control and evaluated accordingly. The controls are hard on the small, marginal firm with obsolete equipment. Environmental regulation may merely hasten the inevitable closing of such a firm.

The level of government regulation poses another potential problem for small business. Legislation, whether state or local, may prove discriminatory by forcing higher costs on a local firm than on competitive firms outside the regulated territory. The immediate self-interest of a small firm, therefore, is served by regulations that operate at the highest or most general level. A federal regulation, for example, applies to all U.S. firms and thereby avoids giving competitive advantages to low-cost polluters in other states.

The Special Challenge of Consumerism

At one time the accepted philosophy of business was expressed as "let the buyer beware." In contrast, today's philosophy says "let the seller beware." Today's sophisticated buyers feel that they should be able to purchase products that are safe, reliable, durable, and honestly advertised. This theme has influenced various types of consumer legislation. The Magnuson-Moss Warranty Act, for exam-

Environmental Concerns in Construction

South Mountain Company, a tiny Massachusetts construction company with only 16 employees, builds houses that feature durability, low maintenance, health, comfort, and environmental sustainability. The firm's emphasis on environmentalism is evident in the following explanation by its president, John Abrams:

> Some clients, for instance, want a house with air conditioning. "The houses we build don't have air conditioning," Abrams says. "In the area where we do most of our building, it is not necessary if the house is built properly. The area is relatively cool, and there are constant sea breezes."
>
> Clients are usually well versed in energy efficiency, but the life cycle impact of materials is a relatively new concept "and one that interests people greatly," he adds. For example, some people might request the use of mahogany, which comes from rain forests, or other old growth wood. "You can explain that there are substitutes that can do the same thing without the hidden costs," Abrams says. "You can use salvage timber, wood that is grown on a sustainable yield basis, or materials from wood by-products."

Source: "Long Range Planning for Business Success," *In Business*, Vol. 15, No. 1 (January–February 1993), pp. 26–27.

ple, imposes special restrictions on sellers, such as requiring that any written warranties be available for inspection rather than being hidden inside a package.

consumerism
a movement that stresses the needs of consumers and the importance of serving them honestly and well

Small firms are directly involved in the **consumerism** movement. To some extent, they stand to gain from it. Attention to customer needs and flexibility in meeting these needs have traditionally been strong assets of small firms. Their managers have been close to customers and thus able to know and respond easily to their needs. To the extent that these potential features have been realized in practice, the position of small business has been strengthened. And to the extent that small firms can continue to capitalize upon customer desires for excellent service, they can reap rewards from the consumerism movement.

Consumerism also carries threats to small business. It is hard to build a completely safe product and to avoid all errors in service. Moreover, the growing complexity of products makes their servicing more difficult. The mechanic or repairer must know a great deal more to render satisfactory service today than was needed two or three decades ago. Rising consumer expectations, therefore, provide a measure of danger as well as opportunity for small firms. The quality of management will determine the extent to which opportunities are realized and dangers avoided.

ETHICAL RESPONSIBILITIES OF SMALL BUSINESS

Stories in the news media concerning insider trading, fraud, and bribery have usually involved large corporations. Does that mean that ethical problems are confined to big business? Clearly not. In the less-publicized, day-to-day life of small business, decision makers also face ethical dilemmas and temptations to compromise principles for the sake of business or personal advantage. The topics of environmentalism and consumerism discussed earlier have an ethical dimension, but we move on in this section to more individual ethical issues.

Kinds of Ethical Issues in Small Firms

Ethical issues are those that involve questions of right and wrong. Such questions go far beyond what is legal or illegal. Many small-business relationships call for decisions about what is honest or dishonest, fair or unfair, respectful or disrespectful.

ethical issues
practices and policies involving questions of right and wrong

Only the naive would argue that small business is pure in terms of ethical conduct. In fact, there is widespread recognition of unethical and even illegal activity. There is no way of measuring the extent of unethical conduct, of course, but there is an obvious need for improvement in small, as well as big, businesses.

One glaring example of poor ethics practiced by many small businesses is fraudulent reporting of income and expenses for income-tax purposes. This conduct includes "skimming" of income (that is, keeping some income off the record) as well as improperly claiming certain business expenses. The following account illustrates the nature of these practices:

To countless small businesses, cheating Uncle Sam is as routine as making the payroll and marketing the product.

For a Georgia cafeteria owner, it involved skimming at least $100 a day from the cash register before recording his receipts on the ledger. On the docks in Massachusetts, seafood buyers carry briefcases full of cash so their suppliers don't have to account for checks. A fashion designer refurbished his suburban Philadelphia mansion as a tax-deductible corporate expense.

The government pressed charges in these cases, but most income-tax chiseling by small business goes undetected by overworked tax agents and accountants unable to probe deep enough to find it.[7]

The reference to income-tax cheating by small business does not imply that all or even most small firms engage in such practices. It simply tells us that tax evasion does occur within small firms and that the practice is sufficiently widespread as to be recognized as a general problem.

Cheating on taxes represents only one type of unethical business practice. Questions of right and wrong permeate all areas of business decision making,

SMALL BUSINESS IN ACTION

Herman Miller's Reputation for Integrity

One of the nation's best-known family businesses is Herman Miller, Inc., Zeeland, Michigan, manufacturer of fine office furniture. Founded in 1923 by D. J. DePree, the firm is now headed by his son, Max DePree. Its reputation as a well-managed company rests not only on its superb products—acclaimed by some as the highest-quality office furniture made anywhere—but also by its integrity in relationships with employees, customers, and others. Following is an outsider's assessment of the company and its present leader:

Herman Miller is a place with integrity. Max defines integrity as "a fine sense of one's obligations." That integrity exhibits itself in the company's dedication to superior design, to quality, to making a contribution to society—and in its manifest respect for its customers, investors, suppliers and employees.

Source: The statement is that of James O'Toole, University of Southern California, and appears in the foreword to Max DePree, *Leadership Is An Art* (East Lansing: Michigan State University Press, 1987), pp. xvii–xviii.

as they do all areas of life itself. It may be helpful to identify some common types of ethical issues confronting small-business managers in order to better understand the dimensions of this problem.

In *marketing decisions,* the entrepreneur is confronted with a variety of ethical questions. For example, the entrepreneur must devise advertising content that sells but also tells "the truth, the whole truth, and nothing but the truth." Salespeople must walk a fine line between persuasion and deception. In some types of small business, the seller can obtain sales contracts more successfully by offering improper inducements to buyers or by joining with competitors in rigging bids.

In *management decisions,* the entrepreneur affects the personal and family lives of employees. Issues of fairness, honesty, and impartiality easily surface in decisions and practices regarding hiring, promotion, salary increases, dismissals, layoffs, and work assignments. In communication with employees, the entrepreneur may be truthful, vague, misleading, or totally dishonest.

In *financial and accounting decisions,* the entrepreneur must decide the extent to which he or she will be honest and candid in reporting financial information. Even with a small firm, outsiders such as bankers and suppliers depend upon its financial reports to be accurate.

These examples are not meant to be exhaustive in outlining ethical issues in small business. Instead, they are intended to illustrate the existence of such issues in the various areas of small-business operation.

Vulnerability of Small Firms

Walking the "straight and narrow" may be more difficult and costly on Main Street than it is on Wall Street.[8] In other words, small firms—the Main Street type—may face greater temptations and pressures to act unethically because of their smallness.

As an example, a lack of resources may make it difficult for a small firm to resist extortion by public officials.

Prof. William Baxter of the Stanford Law School notes that for such owners, delayed building permits or failed sanitation inspections can be "life-threatening events" that make them cave in to bribe demands. By contrast, he adds, "the local manager of Burger King is in a much better position" to tell these people to get lost.[9]

The small firm may also be at a disadvantage in competing with larger competitors that have superior resources. As a result, the small-firm owner may be tempted to rationalize bribery as a way of offsetting what seems to be a competitive disadvantage and securing an even playing field.

While these pressures do not justify unethical behavior, they help explain the context for decisions involving ethical issues. Ethical decision making often calls for difficult choices by the entrepreneur.

The temptation for entrepreneurs to compromise ethical standards as they strive to earn a profit is evident in the results of a study of entrepreneurial ethics.[10] In this study, entrepreneurs were compared with other business managers and professionals in their views about various ethical issues. Respondents were presented with 16 vignettes, each involving a business decision having ethical overtones. They were asked to indicate the degree to which they found each action compatible with their own ethical views by checking a seven-point scale ranging from 1 (never acceptable) to 7 (always acceptable). Following is an example of one vignette:

An owner of a small firm obtained a free copy of a copyrighted computer software program from a business friend rather than spending $500 to obtain his own program from the software dealer.

On 5 of the 16 cases, entrepreneurs appeared significantly less moral (more approving of questionable conduct) than other respondents.[11] Each of these situations involved an opportunity to gain financially by taking a profit from someone else's pocket. For example, entrepreneurs were more willing to condone collusive bidding and the duplicating of copyrighted computer software without payment to the manufacturer for its use.

These choices reveal the special temptation for entrepreneurs who are strongly driven to earn profits. However, this issue must be kept in perspective. Even though entrepreneurs appeared less moral than other business respondents in their reaction to these five issues, the majority of entrepreneurs were significantly *more* moral in their responses to two other issues in which there was no immediate profit impact.[12] The evidence shows, then, that most entrepreneurs display a general ethical sensitivity but that some of them show vulnerability in issues that directly affect profits.

Underlying Values and Business Ethics

underlying values
unarticulated ethical beliefs that provide a foundation for ethical behavior

Business practices that the leaders or employees of a business view as right or wrong reflect the firm's **underlying values.** What a person believes affects what that person does on the job and how she or he acts toward customers and others. This is not to deny that people sometimes speak more ethically than they act. Whatever the verbal posturing, however, behavior provides clues to a person's underlying system of basic values. Behaviors may reflect either commitment or lack of commitment to honesty, respect, truthfulness—to integrity in all of its dimensions.

The values that serve as a foundation for ethical behavior in business grow out of one's view of the universe and the role of humankind in that universe. Values, therefore, are a part of the individual's basic philosophical and/or religious convictions. Traditionally in the United States, Judeo-Christian values have served as the most general body of religious beliefs underlying business behavior, although there are examples of ethical behavior based on principles derived from other religious systems. The point is that religious and/or philosophical values, or the lack thereof, are reflected in the conduct of business in firms of all sizes. Thus, a strong value system is important in determining the ethical climate established by the leader in a small firm.

As one example of the way a leader's basic values affect business practice, consider the company featured in this chapter's opening Spotlight on Small Business—Reell Precision Manufacturing Corporation.[13] The founders of this firm shared a religious belief that shaped their approach to conducting business. The leaders also involved the company's personnel in discussing ethical issues by forming a committee called "The Forum," a group of four management and nine rank-and-file representatives who meet weekly to discuss corporate policy. As a part of their deliberations, the members of this group examine basic religious teachings as they relate to practical business ethics. Within one period of a few weeks, for example, they invited a rabbi, a priest, and a Lutheran minister to address the group on the subject of applying religious values in the business arena.

One observer of the firm and its operations described the firm's religious foundations as follows:

Their original corporate directions statement talked unabashedly about "a personal commitment to God, revealed in Jesus Christ," and about following "the will of God" in business dealings. But that seemed a bit much to some employees who did not share their strong convictions, so the matter was tossed to The Forum.

The result: Most of the religious language was excised—although the founders insisted on keeping the thought that the business is based on "practical application of Judeo-Christian values." The reasoning was simple, Wahlstedt [the president and one of the partners] said: "I don't see how you can approach the subject of ethics without relating it to some base of values."[14]

Earlier, the way in which these values influenced business practices of this firm—reducing profits, for example, rather than laying off employees—was noted. It seems apparent that a deep commitment to certain basic values leads in the direction of behavior that is widely appreciated and admired. Without such a commitment on the part of small-business leadership, ethical standards can easily be compromised.

Ethical Leadership in Small Firms

Entrepreneurs who care about ethical performance in their firms can do something about it! They can use their powerful positions of leadership and ownership to insist that their firms display honesty and integrity in all of their operations. Ethical values are established by leaders in all organizations, and those at lower levels take their cues regarding proper behavior from the pronouncements and conduct of their leaders.

In a small organization, the ethical influence of a leader is more pronounced than it is in a large corporation. In a giant corporation, leadership becomes diffused, and the chief executive must exercise great care to make sure that his or her precepts are shared by those in the various divisions and subsidiaries. Some corporate CEOs have professed great shock to discover behavior at lower levels that conflicted sharply with their own espoused principles.

Leaders of large corporations are also responsible to stockholders, many of whom are more aware of and concerned with corporate profits than corporate ethics. The position of an entrepreneur is much simpler. Recall the Reell Precision Manufacturing Corporation, mentioned earlier, in which owner-managers were able to make difficult decisions based on their underlying ethical values. In effect, the founder or head of a small business can say, "This is my personal integrity on the line, and I want you to do it this way!" Such statements are easily understood. And such a leader becomes even more eloquent as he or she backs up such statements with appropriate behavior.

We can see, then, the potential for high ethical standards in small firms. An entrepreneur who believes strongly in honesty and truthfulness can insist that those principles be followed throughout the organization. Earlier in this chapter, we cited Herman Miller, Inc., the furniture manufacturer, as a family firm exhibiting high standards of integrity. This ethical stance reflects the values of the DePree family. The ethical values of the founder and his son, the present CEO, have obviously permeated and continue to characterize this firm's operation.

In summary, the personal integrity of the founder or owner—the top management of the small firm—is a key to ethical performance. It is obviously important in any organization, but the dominant role of this one person or leadership team in a small firm gives them a powerful voice in the ethical performance of that firm.

Developing a Code of Ethics

As a small firm grows, the personal influence of the entrepreneur inevitably declines. Personal interaction with the leader occurs less and less. The result is that the powerful, personal enunciation of ethical values is no longer quite as effective as it was earlier. The entrepreneur's basic principles simply cannot be expressed or reinforced as frequently or consistently as the business grows larger.

code of ethics
official standards of behavior for employees

At some point, therefore, the firm should formulate a **code of ethics,** as most large corporations have done. Such a code should express the principles to be followed by members of the firm and give examples of these principles in action. A code might, for example, prohibit acceptance of gifts or favors from suppliers and then point out the standard business courtesies, such as a free lunch, that might be accepted without violating the policy. (Sample codes can be obtained from Ethics Resource Center, Inc., 1025 Connecticut Avenue, N.W., Washington, DC 20036.)

If a code of ethics is to be effective, employees must be aware of its nature and convinced of its importance. As a minimum, they should read and sign it. As a firm grows larger and employees know less about the firm's commitments, however, training is necessary to be sure the code is well understood and taken seriously. It is also imperative, of course, that management operate in a manner that is consistent with its own principles and deal decisively with any infractions.

Better Business Bureaus

bait advertising
an insincere offer to sell in order to lure customers and switch them to more expensive products

In any sizable community, all shades of ethical and unethical business practices can be found. A few businesses are little more than rip-offs. Others use highly questionable practices—for example, **bait advertising,** which is an insincere offer to sell in order to lure customers and switch them to the purchase of more expensive products. Other firms are totally dishonest in the services they provide—for example, replacing auto parts that are perfectly good.

Figure 25-2
Better Business
Bureau Code of
Advertising

Bait Advertising and Selling

A "bait" offer is an alluring but insincere offer to sell a product or service which the advertiser does not intend to sell. Its purpose is to switch consumers from buying the advertised merchandise or service in order to sell something else, usually at a higher price or on a basis more advantageous to the advertiser.

a. No advertisement should be published unless it is a bona fide offer to sell the advertised merchandise or service.

b. The advertising should not create a false impression about the product or service being offered in order to lay the foundation for a later "switch" to other, more expensive products or services, or products of a lesser quality at the same price.

c. Subsequent full disclosure by the advertiser of all other facts about the advertised article does not preclude the existence of a bait scheme.

d. An advertiser should not use nor permit the use of the following scheme practices:

   • refusing to show or demonstrate the advertised merchandise or service;

   • disparaging the advertised merchandise or service, its warranty, availability, services and parts, credit terms, etc.;

   • selling the advertised merchandise or service and thereafter "unselling" the customer to make a switch to other merchandise or service;

   • refusing to take orders for the advertised merchandise or service or to deliver it within a reasonable time;

   • demonstrating or showing a defective sample of the advertised merchandise; or

   • having a sales compensation plan designed to penalize salespersons who sell the advertised merchandise or service.

e. An advertiser should have on hand a suffecent quantity of advertised merchandise to meet reasonably anticipated demands, unless the advertisement discloses the number of items available. If items are available only at certain branches, their specific locations should be disclosed. The use of "rainchecks" is no justification for inadequate estimates of reasonably anticipated demand.

f. Actual sales of the advertised merchandise or service may not preclude the existence of a bait scheme since this may be merely an attempt to create an aura of legitimacy. A key factor in determining the existence of "bait" is the number of times the merchandise or service was advertised compared to the number of actual sales of the merchandise or service.

Unethical operations reflect adversely on the honest members of the business community. As a result, privately owned business firms in many cities have banded together to form Better Business Bureaus. The purpose of such organizations is to promote ethical conduct on the part of all business firms in the community.

Specifically, a Better Business Bureau's function is twofold: (1) it provides free buying guidelines and information about a company that the consumer should know *prior* to completing a business transaction, and (2) it attempts to solve questions or disputes concerning purchases. As a result, business swindles often decline in a community served by a Better Business Bureau. Figure 25-2 presents a small section from a code of advertising ethics developed by the Better Business Bureaus.

LOOKING BACK

1. Society gives business firms the freedom to operate as part of a private enterprise system. In return, society expects these privately owned firms to contribute positively not only by providing goods and services but also by protecting the environment, treating customers fairly, and promoting the public welfare in various ways.

2. Most small-firm managers recognize some types of social responsibility in the operation of their businesses. However, they differ greatly in their emphasis on social objectives, and they show considerable sensitivity to the economic costs that are associated with such objectives.

3. Efforts to act in a socially responsible manner must be reconciled with a firm's long-term profit needs. Some types of socially responsible behavior are virtually cost free, while others are expensive. Costs, therefore, limit and regulate the extent and types of social programs that are possible.

4. Small firms encounter a wide variety of opportunities to act unethically. These include temptations such as cheating on income-tax returns, deceiving customers, treating employees unfairly, and lying to employees and outsiders. The smallness of these firms makes them especially vulnerable to pressures to act unethically.

5. Entrepreneurs, by virtue of their positions, can exert a powerful influence for moral virtue in small firms. Their underlying values are particularly significant in shaping the nature of their ethical leadership. As a business grows, their personal leadership can be supplemented by the adoption of codes of ethics and by support of local Better Business Bureaus.

DISCUSSION QUESTIONS

1. The chapter's opening Spotlight on Small Business referred to Reell Precision Manufacturing Corporation's intention to cut short-term profits rather than lay off employees. How can this be justified in a competitive enterprise system in which the goal of the business is profits?

2. To what extent do small-business owners recognize that they have a social responsibility? How, if at all, could you defend the position of those who say they have no social responsibility?

3. A small-business owner is asked to place an advertisement in the local high school yearbook. Is this part of a firm's social responsibility? What would be the effect on profits?

4. Why might small-business CEOs focus more attention on profit and less on social goals than large-business CEOs?

5. Is it necessary for an entrepreneur to be a philanthropist to some degree in order to recognize and fulfill the firm's social responsibilities?

6. What are some examples of expenditures required on the part of small-business firms to protect the environment?

7. Should all firms use biodegradable packaging? What is your answer if you know its use adds 25 percent to the price of the product?

8. What are some examples of small businesses that profit from the increased efforts to clean up and protect the environment? How do they profit?

9. What is "skimming"? How do you think owners of small firms might attempt to rationalize such a practice?

10. What are some examples of ethical issues in small-business marketing? In small-business management?

11. Give an example of an unethical business practice that you have personally encountered.

12. An auto salesman is willing to allow as much as $4,200 as a trade-in allowance. However, he tries to get the customer to settle for less by saying, "Four thousand dollars is as much as I can give." On a scale of 1 (extremely ethical) to 9 (extremely unethical), how would you rate the tactics of this salesman? Why?

13. Based on your experience as an employee, customer, or other observer of some particular small business, how would you rate its ethical performance? Upon what evidence or clues do you base your opinion?

14. Explain the connection between underlying values and ethical business behavior.

15. Give some examples of the practical application of a firm's basic commitment to supporting the family life of employees.

YOU MAKE THE CALL

Situation 1

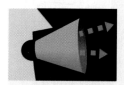

When Ben Cohen, founding partner of Ben & Jerry's Homemade, Inc. (purveyor of gourmet ice cream), considered selling his share of the business, he decided instead to keep the business and run it in a socially responsible way. This was different in his mind from operating as a traditional business, and it apparently gave him a greater sense of purpose as an entrepreneur.

Following is a description of action he took based on this motivation:

Because he felt strongly that "the community should prosper right along with the company," Cohen engineered an equity offering pitched first to Vermonters and, a year later, to fellow ice cream fanatics nationwide; $500,000 from the $5.1-million offering helped start a nonprofit foundation that, bolstered by 15% of Ben &

Jerry's pretax profits, supports local causes. Internally, Cohen also instituted a five-to-one salary-ratio cap, whereby the lowliest line employee cannot make any less than 20% of what top management makes.

Source: Reprinted with permission, *Inc.* magazine (May 1986). Copyright © 1986 by Goldhirsh Group, Inc., 38 Commercial Wharf, Boston MA 02110.

Questions
1. Is selling equity to Vermonters more socially responsible than selling equity to people in other states?
2. In what way is the salary cap a socially responsible policy?
3. Is a business that sells double fudge ice cream to overweight customers acting in a socially responsible way?

Situation 2

A software producer sells its product to retailers and dealers for resale to end users. It has been a slow year, and profits are running behind those of a year ago. One way to increase sales is to persuade dealers to stock more inventory. This is achievable by exaggerating total product demand a bit and presenting the dealers with an extremely optimistic picture of the size and effectiveness of the company's promotional program. This should encourage dealers to build larger inventories sooner than they would normally.

The software itself is regarded as a basically good product, and the producer merely wishes to build sales by putting its best foot forward in this way.

Questions
1. Is this firm acting ethically if it attempts to increase sales in this way?
2. If this approach is sound ethically, is it also good business?
3. What course of action do you recommend? Why?

EXPERIENTIAL EXERCISES

1. Visit or telephone the nearest Better Business Bureau office to discover the types of unethical business practices existing in your community and the ways in which the Better Business Bureau is attempting to raise ethical performance. Report briefly on your findings.
2. Employees sometimes take sick leave when they are merely tired, and students sometimes miss class when they are merely tired. Divide into groups of four or five and prepare a brief statement showing the nature of the ethical issue (if any) in both of these practices.
3. Examine a recent issue of *The Wall Street Journal* or another business periodical and report briefly on the nature of some ethical problem in the news. Could this type of ethical problem occur in a small business? Explain.
4. Interview a small-business manager to discover how (or whether) environmental protection affects the manager's business. Does the business face any special governmental restrictions? Are there costs involved?

REFERENCES TO SMALL-BUSINESS PRACTICES

Alexander, Suzanne. "Life's Just a Bowl of Cherry Garcia for Ben & Jerry's," *The Wall Street Journal* (July 15, 1992), p. B3.

An ice cream maker with an unusually strong interest in the firm's broader role in society prospers in the marketplace.

Kotite, Erika. "De-Beefing the Burger," *Entrepreneur,* Vol. 18, No. 5 (May 1990), p. 11.

The consumer demand for healthier food has provided a business opportunity for an entrepreneur to produce and successfully market vegetarian burgers and other meat substitutes.

Logsdon, Gene. "Canadian Company Solves Disposal Problem for Printers," *In Business,* Vol. 15, No. 1 (January–February 1993), pp. 44–45.

A new small business finds opportunity in environmentalism by developing a method of recycling ink for printers and ink manufacturers.

Meeks, Fleming. "'Upselling,'" *Forbes* (January 8, 1990), pp. 70–72.

A family business uses very hard selling that some find ethically repugnant to sell its product, adjustable beds, to customers.

"The Soft Path to a Home Business," *In Business,* Vol. 15, No. 1 (January–February 1993), p. 25.

A small business prospers by producing a nontoxic paint that is safe for children's furniture and toys.

ENDNOTES

1. Erika Wilson, "Social Responsibility of Business: What Are the Small Business Perspectives?" *Journal of Small Business Management*, Vol. 18, No. 3 (July 1980), pp. 17–24.

2. See, for example, Jean Sherman Chatzky, "Changing the World," *Forbes*, Vol. 149, No. 5 (March 2, 1992), pp. 83–87; and "Making Ice Cream with Solar and Rock," *In Business*, Vol. 12, No. 6 (September–October 1991), pp. 30–31.

3. Gary Strauss, "Businesses' Cry: Do the Right Thing," *USA Today* (June 10, 1992), p. B1.

4. Kenneth E. Aupperle, F. Bruce Simmons III, and William Acar, "An Empirical Investigation into How Entrepreneurs View Their Social Responsibilities," Paper presented at the Academy of Management Meetings, August, 1990.

5. These examples were among those cited in Bradford McKee, "Small Firms Pay for Clear Air," *Nation's Business*, Vol. 79, No. 3 (March 1991), p. 54.

6. Michael Barrier, "A Simple Life No Longer," *Nation's Business*, Vol. 81, No. 2 (February 1993), pp. 13–14.

7. Sanford L. Jacobs, "Hide and Sneak," *The Wall Street Journal* (May 20, 1985), p. 13C.

8. This possibility is advanced by Michael Allen in "Small-Business Jungle," *The Wall Street Journal* (June 10, 1988), p. 19R.

9. *Ibid.*

10. Justin G. Longenecker, Joseph A. McKinney, and Carlos W. Moore, "Egoism and Independence: Entrepreneurial Ethics," *Organizational Dynamics*, Vol. 16, No. 3 (Winter 1988), pp. 64–72.

11. These differences were significant at the .05 level.

12. These differences were also significant at the .05 level.

13. Dick Youngblood, "A Firm That Means What It Says About Ethical Conduct," *Star Tribune* (Minneapolis-St. Paul), (December 28, 1992), p. 2D.

14. *Ibid.* Reprinted with permission of the *Star Tribune*, Minneapolis-St. Paul.

CHAPTER 26

Working Within the Law

SPOTLIGHT ON SMALL BUSINESS

Legal aspects of the patent process are often perplexing to patent applicants. However, the potential benefits of a patent encourage entrepreneurs to work within the law and receive their just protection. One inspirational story of persistent effort is found in entrepreneur Barbara Stenger.

Barbara Stenger

Barbara Stenger, a home-based business owner in Brimfield, Illinois, was turned down when she first sought patent protection for a three-ring binder index for recipes.

The patent office "sent back copies of five old patents, saying, 'Yours isn't something new,' " she says.

Rather than accept that determination, she appealed the denial and succeeded in showing that her index was in fact the first of its kind. "I never give up easily," Stenger says.

Her experience demonstrates that an initial rejection to a patent application is not necessarily final. The U.S. Patent Office has a built-in mechanism for applicants wanting a second opinion—the Board of Patent Appeals.

The appeals process begins with the applicant's filing of a notice to appeal, which is followed by the filing of a brief setting forth the applicant's reasons for the appeal. In addition, a request for a formal hearing might be filed. For what the Patent Office terms "small entities"—individuals and unincorporated businesses—the fee for filing the notice of appeal is $135, and it's the same for filing the brief. The request for a formal hearing carries a fee of $115.

Source: "A First Refusal Isn't Necessarily Final," *Nation's Business*, Vol. 81, No. 2 (February 1993), p. 10. Reprinted by permission, *Nation's Business*, February 1993. Copyright 1993, U.S. Chamber of Commerce.

After studying this chapter, you should be able to:
1. Discuss the regulatory burden placed on small firms.
2. Identify how a small firm can benefit from regulation.
3. Describe how the legal system protects the marketplace.
4. Illustrate the importance of making sound legal agreements with other parties.
5. Point out certain issues related to federal income taxation.

Regulatory Flexibility Act	blue-sky laws	design patent
Paperwork Reduction Act	Clean Air Act	plant patent
Equal Access to	Americans with	copyright
Justice Act	Disabilities Act	trade dress
Women's Business	Civil Rights Act	contracts
Ownership Act	Family and Medical	statute of frauds
Telephone Consumer	Leave Act	agency
Protection Act	trademark	negotiable instruments
Nutrition Labeling and	patent	
Education Act	utility patent	

Chapter 25 presented several social and ethical issues confronting small firms and discussed how small businesses might deal with these challenges. However, observance of social responsibilities and ethical standards is not left entirely to the discretion of those in business. Federal laws, as well as state laws and local ordinances, regulate business activity in the public interest. Therefore, this chapter examines the legal framework within which business firms operate and also considers some examples of regulation and the burden regulation places on small firms.

REGULATION AND SMALL-BUSINESS OPPORTUNITY

Not all entrepreneurs can be or want to be lawyers. Nevertheless, they must have some knowledge of the law in order to appreciate how the legal system safeguards the marketplace and to help make wise business decisions.

The Burden of Regulation

The growth of government regulation has reached the point that it imposes a real hardship on small firms. To some extent, the problems arise from seemingly inevitable "red tape" and bureaucratic procedures of governments. But the sheer magnitude of regulation is the major problem.

Small-business owners complain openly that government regulation threatens their livelihoods. A 1992 survey by the National Federation of Independent Business supports this attitude. This study reports that government regulation ranked eighth in a list of 75 top concerns among small-business respondents.[1]

Another study, published in *Small Business Reports,* found that from 1989 to 1992 the government tax and regulatory burden per worker increased 34 percent while business profit per worker declined 22 percent. Authors of the report name four specific regulations that are the major contributors to the increased burden—the 1989 minimum-wage increase, the 1990 Americans with Disabilities Act, the 1990 amendments to the Clean Air Act, and the 1991 Civil Rights Act. The study concluded: "Federal government policies since 1989 amount to nothing less than economic crib death, suffocating jobs in the cradle of small business."[2] Other spokesmen for small business agree with this assessment. "The current level of regulation is so high, and so complicated, and so intrusive that it's strangling business and suppressing productivity," according to Brink Lindsey, director of regulatory studies for the Cato Institute in Washington, DC.[3]

Thomas D. Hopkins, of the Rochester Institute of Technology in Rochester, New York, estimates that in 1991 federal regulations cost over $400 billion— more than $4,200 per household.[4] Since regulation occurs at other levels also—state and local—the total cost of regulation is even greater than this figure suggests. Regulatory costs at the state and local levels are virtually impossible to estimate. Nevertheless, it is important to recognize that states are extremely active in establishing regulatory policies. For example, in the two-year period of 1987 and 1988, more than 215,000 regulatory bills were introduced in state legislatures nationwide.[5]

Another type of governmental burden is that of taxes. Taxes have a direct impact on small-business cash flow and, therefore, present a costly drain on the financial income of the firm. The federal income tax is the most publicized but certainly not the only tax facing small firms. States raise funds from their citizens and businesses with state income taxes, sales taxes, and other forms of revenue production.

A small firm must work within these state laws if it is to avoid legal problems. Major differences between state regulations compound the difficulty of this task. Consider the following state sales tax rules:

Tennessee imposes a sales tax on mandatory tips added to a customer's bill. Minnesota taxes the preparation of a floral arrangement by a florist or nursery.

Maryland now applies its sales tax to cellular telephones, telephone answering machines, pay-per-view television, newspapers, and prescribed cat and dog food; Missouri considers trophy fees charged to guests at a wild game ranch taxable, and North Carolina deems water-treatment equipment subject to sales tax.[6]

It is impossible for an entrepreneur to stay abreast of all state laws. Fortunately, state chambers of commerce are able to provide small firms with reg-

Regulations Apply Brakes to New Product

Entrepreneurs face rules and regulations that are designed to protect the public interest but can also serve to frustrate their efforts to operate a business. Entrepreneur Phillip Ramos, Jr., founder of Philatron International, Inc., in Santa Fe Springs, California, is a good example. Federal regulations recently halted efforts to market his new product.

Ramos invented a new coiled air-brake hose for attaching the braking system of a trailer to the back of heavy-duty trucks. Ramos maintains that his design is more durable than existing designs and provides superior performance. Introducing the product in 1991, Philatron sold more than 45,000 units within the first few months.

Customers obviously liked the new hose, but the product had a major problem: It did not meet federal safety requirements, which specified that a hose "withstand prolonged immersion in very hot oil." Philatron petitioned that this rule was an outdated requirement passed decades ago when tractor-trailer designs were different. Philatron's biggest critics, his competitors, disagreed with Philatron's argument.

However, with the assistance of several members of Congress and the U.S. Small Business Administration, the National Highway Traffic Safety Administration ruled in June 1992 that the critics complaints "aren't relevant to the real-world safety performance" of the hose. This ruling saved the company from an expensive product recall, but it did not allow Philatron to resume sales.

Philatron petitioned the Safety Adminstration to abolish the test standard. As of the printing of this text, agency officials had not yet decided the request.

Source: John R. Emshwiller, "Maker of Air-Brake Hoses is Seeking Regulatory Relief," *The Wall Street Journal* (February 10, 1993), p. B1. Adapted by permission of *The Wall Street Journal*, © 1993 Dow Jones & Company, Inc. All Rights Reserved Worldwide.

ulatory information. The U.S. Chamber of Commerce offers a publication titled *Staff Directory—State Chambers of Commerce and Associations of Commerce and Industry*, which provides addresses of all state chambers of commerce. Also, a newly formed National Resource Center for State Laws and Regulations has a 50-state network to help firms respond to proposed new taxes, laws, and regulations.

Benefits from Regulations

Regulation of small-business activity is not all bad. Imagine a business world without some degree of regulation. Sounds scary, right? Absolute zero regulation would surely be chaotic, and some degree of regulation is of general social value. Therefore, small firms should recognize the value of regulatory policies and show some willingness to shoulder the burden. Eugene Kimmelman, legislative director of the Consumer Federation of America, says, "It's hypocritical for small business to seek tax relief and loans from the government to boost their position in the marketplace and then to decry any costs imposed on them to protect the health, safety, and other needs of their employees and customers."[7]

Some entrepreneurs accept government regulation as occasionally creating profit-making opportunities. New regulations can sometimes spawn a market niche for a new product. When the Environmental Protection Agency announced standards for automobile replacement-market catalytic converters, for example, Perfection Automotive Products in Livonia, Michigan, saw an opportunity to expand its product mix. "The new legislation created a market for replacement models that could be made more cheaply because they wouldn't have to last as long in aging vehicles." Perfection says its sales have "significantly increased because of the catalytic-converter market."[8]

Still other entrepreneurs find profit opportunities in increasing of regulations by creating new services. One example is found in Counterpoint Publishing, Inc., of Cambridge, Massachusetts. Counterpoint sells an optical disk containing the *Federal Register*—a federal government publication containing newly proposed regulatory changes. Over 50,000 pages of these rules are published yearly. The optical disk provides easier access to the material. The firm describes itself as "a company whose only reason for being is to help people handle the sheer volume of regulation issued by federal government agencies."[9] Another example of a small firm profiting from regulation is Advantage Business Services in Auburn, Maine. This small firm offers a payroll service for clients whose companies need help in complying with complicated federal and state withholding regulations. Advantage has grown to over 30 outlets from its original single location in 1967. President David J. Friedrich admits, "We probably wouldn't be in business if it weren't for government. And the states make things as messy as the feds," he adds.[10]

Finally, consider the new service of Clean Duds franchisees. This franchise is actively pursuing new clients after a new rule from the Occupational Safety and Health Administration was issued requiring medical professionals to clean their uniforms more thoroughly. Under the rule, dental and medical offices, blood banks, ambulance services, mortuaries, and other similar businesses must clean apparel that could transmit blood-borne diseases. Philip Akin, CEO of Clean Duds, says the new business has been extremely profitable.[11]

Very small firms may find that they are exempt from some regulations, thereby creating a favorable competitive situation for them. However, size requirements to quality for exempt status vary from law to law.

Regulatory Flexibility Act protects small firms from excessive federal regulation by simplifying rules and reducing paperwork

Paperwork Reduction Act created OIRA to simplify regulatory rules for small businesses

Government Reaction to the Regulatory Burden

Recognition of the burdensome nature of small-business regulation at the federal level has led to a number of legislative attempts to alleviate the problem. The **Regulatory Flexibility Act** of 1980, for example, requires federal agencies to assess the impact of proposed regulations on small business. They are required to reduce paperwork requirements and to exempt small firms or simplify rules whenever possible. A somewhat similar law is the **Paperwork Reduction Act** of 1980. This act created the Office of Management and Bud-

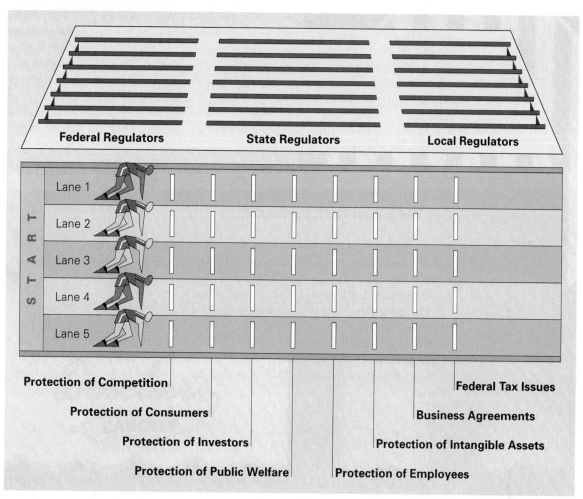

Figure 26-1
The Regulatory
Hurdle Race

get's Office of Information and Regulatory Affairs (OIRA). Unfortunately, in 1990, a U.S. Supreme Court decision drastically reduced the power of the act.

Another law recognizing the regulatory plight of small firms is the **Equal Access to Justice Act** of 1980. A strengthened version of the 1980 Act was passed in 1985. This law mandates the federal government to reimburse court costs for small firms that win cases against regulatory agencies. Incorporated and unincorporated businesses, partnerships, and organizations having a net worth of less than $7 million are eligible for recovery of attorneys' fees.

The immediate concern for small businesses is knowing what laws must be obeyed and how they can operate within these laws—not whether they should or should not be regulated. Therefore, the remaining sections of this chapter cover laws that influence small-business operations. In a single chapter only a

Equal Access to Justice Act mandates reimbursement of legal expenses in cases won by small firms against regulatory agencies

sampling of laws and legal issues is possible. We have, however, attempted to include both old and new legislation, all of which impact the small firm.

Figure 26-1 summarizes the legal issues selected for inclusion. The regulatory areas are represented symbolically as "hurdles" facing the five entrepreneurs as they run the business race. Also, note that three sources of governmental control—federal, state, and local regulatory agencies—are on the sidelines watching the race to be sure it is run legally. Regulatory agencies are not discussed specifically, but they are important in a small firm's efforts to function within the law.

REGULATION AND PROTECTION OF THE MARKETPLACE

The varieties of regulation are endless. They affect the ways in which small firms pay their employees, advertise, bid on contracts, dispose of waste, promote safety, and care for the public welfare. Of necessity, the discussion here will be limited to a few key areas of regulation.

The next four sections emphasize broad areas of governmental regulation of the marketplace. These are followed by sections describing protection of employees and a firm's intangible assets. The last two sections of the chapter look at business agreements and the issue of taxation. Remember, the subject of regulation is massive, and, therefore, all small firms should seek professional legal counsel.

Protection of Competition

A fully competitive economic system presumably benefits customers who can buy products and services from those firms which best satisfy their needs. Of the various laws intended to maintain a competitive economy, perhaps the best known are the federal antitrust laws, especially the Sherman Antitrust Act of 1890 and the Clayton Act of 1914. Both acts were designed to promote competition by eliminating artificial restraints on trade.

Although the purpose of federal and state antitrust laws is noble, the results leave much to be desired. One would be naive to think that small business need no longer fear the power of oligopolists which would control markets. Antitrust laws prevent some mergers and eliminate some unfair practices, but giant business firms continue to dominate many industries.

To some extent, at least, the antitrust laws offer protection to small firms. For example, a local distributor of petroleum products sued a major oil company and another dealer for $6 million, charging violation of antitrust laws. The suit alleged that the plaintiff was overcharged for gasoline, given unreasonably low allocations of petroleum products, and forced to make one station a nonbrand station. In another case, a small processor of waste material from slaughterhouses, stores, and restaurants sought treble damages of $300,000 and the prohibition of unfair practices by a larger competitor. The plaintiff claimed that the competitor had begun offering unreasonably high prices for waste products in the plaintiff's territory, far above the prices offered in the defendant's established territory. The suit alleged that the defendant's purpose was to establish a monopoly.

An amendment to the Clayton Act, the Robinson-Patman Act of 1936, prohibits price discrimination by manufacturers and wholesalers in dealing with other business firms. In particular, the law is designed to protect independent retailers and wholesalers in their fight against large chains. Quantity discounts may still be offered to large buyers, but the amount of the discounts must be justified economically by the seller on the basis of actual costs. Vendors are also forbidden to grant disproportionate advertising allowances to large retailers. The objective is to prevent unreasonable discounts and other concessions to large purchasers merely because of superior size and bargaining power.

The effectiveness of the Robinson-Patman Act and its benefits to small business have been debated. Some have argued that it discourages both large and small firms from cutting prices. Others say this act makes it harder to expand into new markets and to pass on to customers the cost savings on large orders.

Since women-owned business firms have become a growing part of the economy, the federal government has recognized the possibility of discriminatory barriers. Therefore, Congress has created legislation to encourage fair opportunities for women owners in the free enterprise system. The **Women's Business Ownership Act** of 1988 was passed for this reason. Programs initiated under the authority of this act are intended to promote the interests of women-owned small businesses and remove discriminatory barriers in obtaining capital.

Women's Business Ownership Act removes discriminatory barriers to women-owned firms

Protection of Consumers

Insofar as freedom of competition is provided by the laws discussed above, consumers benefit indirectly. In addition, consumers are given various forms of more direct protection by federal, state, and local legislation.

The Wheeler-Lea Act of 1938 gave the Federal Trade Commission (FTC) a broad mandate to attack unfair or deceptive acts or practices in commerce. The FTC's original focus on antitrust practices has been expanded through the years to cover a wide range of business activities: labeling, safety, packaging, and advertising of products; truth-in-lending; fair credit reporting; equal credit opportunity; and many others. States have also enacted laws and created consumer protection agencies to deal with unfair or deceptive practices. A few examples of the types of trade practices scrutinized by the Federal Trade Commission are: labeling goods as "free" or "handmade"; advertising that offers unreal "bargains" by pretended reduction of unused "regular" prices; and bait and switch advertising.

Figure 26-2
Standards Set by
the Consumer
Product Safety
Commission Ensure
That Babies' Toys
Are Safe

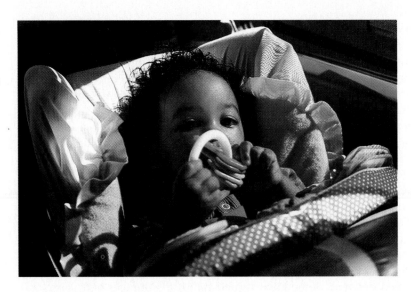

Telephone
Consumer
Protection Act
offers consumers
protection from
intrusive
telemarketing

Nutrition Labeling
and Education Act
requires producers
to carry labels dis-
closing nutritional
information on food
packaging

The passage of the **Telephone Consumer Protection Act** in 1991 is another effort to protect consumers. The problem addressed by the legislation is unrestricted telemarketing, which many individuals feel is an invasion of privacy. The act places restrictions on the use of automated telephone equipment in telemarketing.

The **Nutrition Labeling and Education Act** of 1990 is a recent example of federal labeling regulation. The law requires many food products to carry labels disclosing the amount of nutrients. Every food product covered by the law must have a uniform nutrition label listing the amount of calories, fat, salt, and nutrients. The law also addresses the issue of advertising claims such as "low salt" or "fiber prevents cancer." Some people criticize the law because of the labeling costs, which some experts estimate at thousands of dollars per product.

As still another measure to protect the public against unreasonable risk of injury, the federal government enacted the Consumer Product Safety Act of 1972. This act created the Consumer Product Safety Commission to set safety standards for toys and other consumer products and to ban those goods which are exceptionally hazardous.

Protection of Investors

To protect the investing public against fraudulent schemes and swindles in the sale of stocks and bonds, both federal and state laws regulate the issuance and public sale of securities. The federal laws involved are the Securities Act of 1933 and the Securities Exchange Act of 1934. The latter act established the powerful Securities and Exchange Commission to enforce the regulations implemented by both Acts.

Because of the small amounts involved and the private nature of much of their financing, most small businesses are excluded from extensive regulation under federal law. However, they are subject to state **blue-sky laws.** In general, these laws cover registration of new securities; licensing of dealers, brokers, and salespersons; and prosecution of individuals charged with fraud in connection with the sale of stocks and bonds.

blue-sky laws
state laws that protect investors from securities fraud

Promotion of Public Welfare

Other laws are designed to benefit the public welfare in various ways. Local ordinances, for example, establish minimum standards of sanitation for restaurants to protect the health of patrons. Zoning ordinances protect the community from unplanned development.

Environmental protection legislation—at the federal, state, and local levels—constitutes another example. The major laws of this type deal with air pollution, water pollution, solid-waste disposal, and toxic substances. As explained earlier in the chapter, environmental laws adversely affect some small firms, although they occasionally provide opportunities for others.

The decade of the 1990s is shaping up to be a period of strong emphasis on environmental protection. With the 1990 amendments to the federal **Clean Air Act** of 1970, for example, states are feeling the pressure to develop better systems for vehicle emissions testing. This in turn is requiring small service stations to make additional investments in testing equipment. This same act requires Freon—a contributor to the destruction of the earth's ozone layer—to be recycled from automobile and business air conditioning systems.

Clean Air Act
federal legislation regulating air pollutants

The **Americans with Disabilities Act** (ADA) was passed by Congress in 1990 to bar discrimination against people with disabilities. The act is enforced by the Equal Employment Opportunity Commission. Title I of the act provides for nondiscrimination in employment. Title III prohibits discrimination with regard to access to various services, programs, and activities that are available to the general public. Title I provisions apply to any business with 15 or more employees. It prohibits discrimination against disabled persons who, with or without reasonable accommodations by the employer, are qualified to perform the essential functions of the job. Title III applies to businesses with more than 10 employees and gross receipts of more than $500,000.[12] Some observers believe the ADA will generate numerous lawsuits.[13] Fortunately, there are certain tax deductions related to compliance with the public-accommodations provisions of the ADA.[14]

Americans with Disabilities Act
guarantees equal access to employment for disabled people

State governments restrict entry into numerous professions and types of businesses by establishing licensing procedures. For example, physicians, barbers, pharmacists, accountants, lawyers, and real estate salespersons are licensed. Insurance companies, banks, and public utilities must seek entry permits from state officials. Although licensing protects the public interest, it also tends to restrict the number of professionals and firms in such a way as to reduce competition and increase prices paid by consumers.

SMALL BUSINESS IN ACTION

Paperwork, Paperwork, Paperwork . . .

Environmental concerns in society place a huge responsibility on businesses. Unfortunately, complex environmental laws designed to protect the environment do not make this task easy. Paperwork requirements of these laws, for example, are frequently confusing and burdensome to the small firm. A firm that is not harming the environment may still be subject to fines. How can this be?

Consider the problem faced by manufacturer Peter Zahn, whose San Diego, California, electronic-components firm received a $34,000 fine from the U.S. Environmental Protection Agency (EPA) in December 1991. The EPA had conducted a random inspection of Zahn's 160-employee Autosplice, Inc., plant six months earlier and found no environmental violations. However, Form R—

the paperwork mandated by the Emergency Planning and Community Right-to-Know Act—had not been filed by Autosplice. This form is a nine-page report that "asks for a great deal of information; the most important consists of the purposes, types, and amounts of substances a company uses."

Autosplice has since filed Form R for 1988 through 1991 and is contesting the $34,000 fine, contending that the company recycles 100 percent of the waste brass from its manufacturing process. Companies are exempt from the information-reporting requirements if they have on site no more than a half-pound a year of waste material that contains a toxic substance. Autosplice's case is now before an EPA administrative law judge.

Some trade associations estimate the compliance costs for this law exceed $400 million a year!

There is a difference between licensing that involves a routine application and that which prescribes rigid entry standards and screening procedures. The fact that the impetus for much licensing comes from within the industry suggests the need for careful scrutiny of licensing proposals. Otherwise, we may be merely protecting a private interest and minimizing freedom to enter a field of business. In fact, a case can be made for the regulation of almost any business. However, failure to limit such regulation to the most essential cases erodes the freedom of opportunity to enter business and thereby provide an economic service to the community.

Protection of Employees

Business employees are citizens first and employees second. Therefore, employees are afforded protection from robbery, assault, and other crime at work just as they are at home. In addition, there are a few laws directed primarily to employees and potential employees. Four examples are the Age Discrimination

Act of 1967, the Occupational Safety and Health Act of 1970, the Civil Rights Act of 1991, and the Family and Medical Leave Act of 1993.

The **Civil Rights Act** of 1964, amended by the Civil Rights Act of 1991, prohibits employment discrimination based on race, color, sex, religion, or national origin. The 1991 Civil Rights Act allows employers to be tried by juries in employment discrimination cases. Workers may now recover punitive damages in sexual harassment cases involving intentional discrimination. Workers who win a civil rights suit can receive punitive awards from $50,000 (from employers with 100 or fewer employees) to $300,000 (for employers with over 500 employees).[15]

The act does exempt firms with fewer than 15 employees. Some entrepreneurs may limit their firms' growth to avoid the employment limit. In reference to this exemption, Thomas Van Cleave, president of Windmill City Travel in Chicago, Illinois, says just that, "I have to look at how much I want to expand; that's a real consideration on my part."[16]

The **Family and Medical Leave Act** of 1993 was passed and signed into law by President Clinton in February 1993. The new law applies to firms with 50 or more employees and requires such firms to allow workers as much as 12 weeks of unpaid leave after adoption or childbirth or other specified family needs. Furthermore, the employer must continue health-care coverage during the leave and guarantee that employees can return to the same or comparable jobs.

Civil Rights Act
prohibits discrimination based on race, color, sex, religion, or national origin

Family and Medical Leave Act
ensures unpaid leave for childbirth or medical emergencies

Protection of a Firm's Intangible Assets

In addition to managing and protecting physical assets, a business must protect its intangible assets. A brief examination of the regulatory issues surrounding the four intangible assets depicted in Figure 26-3 follows.

Trademarks. A **trademark** is a word, name, symbol, device, slogan, or any combination thereof that is used to distinguish a product sold by one manufacturer or merchant. In some cases, a color or scent has been found to be part of a trademark.[17] Small manufacturers, in particular, often find it desirable to adopt an identifying trademark and to feature it in advertising.

Since names that refer to products are trademarks, they should be investigated carefully to be sure they are not already in use. Joseph W. Alsop, president of Data Language Corporation of Billerica, Massachusetts, thought its name for a computer software program, *Progress,* was cleared for use. A trademark application was initially rejected because another company was using the name to sell educational materials. An agreement was worked out allowing both firms to use the name. But later a Houston, Texas, software company, not uncovered in the trademark search, was found to be using the *Progress* name. However, Data Language was able to work out still another agreement with the Houston firm.[18]

Trademark
an identifying feature used to distinguish a manufacturer's product

Figure 26-3
Trademarks,
Patents, Copyrights,
and Trade Dress

Trademarks   Trade Dress

Patents   Copyrights

Common law recognizes a property right in the ownership of trademarks. However, reliance on common-law rights is not always adequate. For example, Microsoft Corp., the major supplier of personal computer software, claims it has common-law rights to the trademark *Windows* due to the enormous industry recognition given the product. Nevertheless, Microsoft filed a trademark application in 1990 seeking to gain exclusive rights to the name *Windows*. The U.S. Patent & Trademark Office rejected the bid, claiming the word to be a generic term and therefore in the public domain.[19]

Registration of trademarks is permitted under the federal Lanham Trademark Act—a step that generally makes protection easier if infringement is attempted. Since revision of the act in November 1989, trademark rights can arise from just a bona fide intention to use a trademark, along with the filing of an application and payment of fees. Before this revision, a firm must have already used the mark on goods shipped or sold. A trademark registration lasts for 10 years and may be renewed for additional 10-year periods. Application for registration is made to the U.S. Patent and Trademark Office.

A small business must use a trademark properly in order to protect the trademark.[20] Two rules can help. One is to be sure the name is not carelessly used in place of the generic name. For example, the Xerox company never wants people to say that they are "xeroxing" something. Second, the business should inform the public that the trademark is a trademark by labeling it with the symbol ™. If the trademark is registered, the symbol ® or the phrase "Registered in U.S. Patent and Trademark Office" should be used.

Patents. A **patent** is the registered right of an inventor to make, use, and sell an invention. The two primary types of patents are utility patents and design patents. A **utility patent** covers a new process or protects the function of a product. A **design patent** covers the appearance of a product and covers everything that is an inseparable part of the product. Utility patents are granted for a period of 17 years, while design patents are given a 14-year protection. Patent law also provides for **plant patents**, which cover any distinct and new variety of plants.

Items that may be patented include machines and products, improvements on machines and products, and new and original designs. Some small manufacturers have patented items that constitute the major part of their product line. Indeed, some businesses such as Polaroid and IBM can trace their origins to a patented invention. A patent attorney is often retained to act for a small-business applicant preparing an application.

Figure 26-4 is a copy of a patent sheet appearing in the government publication *The Official Gazette of the U.S. Patent & Trademark Office*. As you can see, the advertising cap nameplate received its patent April 2, 1991. This is a very simple idea and not necessarily one that will be profitable for the inventor— but it might be.

Suits for patent infringements may be brought, but they are costly and should be avoided if possible. Finding the money and legal talent with which to enforce one's legal rights is one of the major problems of patent protection in small business. Monetary damages and injunctions are available, however, if an infringement can be proved.

For many years patent infringement decisions were appealed to 12 circuit courts. Each court often had its own interpretation of patent law, which resulted in much confusion about what was and was not legal. However, in 1982, the U.S. Court of Appeals for the Federal Circuit was formed. All patent appeals are now directed to this one court. This system is helping to make patent law more understandable.

Copyrights. A **copyright** is the exclusive right of a creator (author, composer, designer, or artist) to reproduce, publish, perform, display, and sell the work that is the product of the intelligence and skill of that person. According to the Copyright Act of 1976, the creator of an original work receives copyright protection for the duration of the creator's life plus 50 years. A "work made for hire" is protected for 100 years from its creation or 75 years from publication, whichever is shorter. Copyrights are registered in the Copyright Office of the Library of Congress.

Under the Copyright Act of 1976, copyrightable works are automatically protected from the instant of their creation. However, if a work is distributed to

patent
the registered right of an inventor to make, use, and sell an invention

utility patent
a patent that covers a new process or protects a product's function

design patent
a patent that covers the appearance of a product and its inseparable parts

plant patent
a patent that covers any distinct and new variety of plant

copyright
the exclusive right of a creator to reproduce, publish, and sell his or her own works

United States Patent [19]

Pizzacar

[54] **ADVERTISING CAP NAMEPLATE**

[76] Inventor: **Anthony Pizzacar,** 160 Greenway West, New Hyde Park, N.Y. 11040

[21] Appl. No.: **417,204**

[22] Filed: **Oct. 4, 1989**

[51] Int. Cl.^{5} **A42B 1/24**

[52] U.S. Cl. ....**2/199;** 2/197; 2/185 R; 2/DIG. 6

[58] **Field of Search** ....2/174.4–174.8, 2/181, 181.2, 181.4, 182.1–182.7, 183, 184.5, 197, 209.3, 209.4, 199, 195, 185 R, DIG. 6; 40/329

[56]   **References Cited**
U.S. PATENT DOCUMENTS

525,287	8/1894	Ruth	2/185 R
676,293	6/1901	Wright	2/185 R
1,294,595	2/1919	Allen	40/329
1,559,917	11/1925	Schnebel	2/183
1,808,966	6/1931	Morgan	2/181
2,181,446	11/1939	Ames	2/171.4

[11] **Patent Number:** **5,003,640**

[45] **Date of Patent:** **Apr. 2, 1991**

4,776,043	10/1988	Coleman	2/185 R
4,872,218	10/1989	Holt	2/197
4,905,406	3/1990	Warner	2/199

FOREIGN PATENT DOCUMENTS

444667	6/1936	United Kingdom	2/185 R

Primary Examiner—William A. Cuchlinski, Jr.
Assistant Examiner—Alvin Wirthlin
Attorney, Agent, or Firm—Michael I. Kroll

[57]   **ABSTRACT**

An advertising cap for a user has a back, a headband, a pair of straps disposed at the back of the conventional cap for adjustment of the size of the headband of the conventional cap, an advertising cap nameplate for concealing the pair of straps after the headband of the conventional cap is adjusted, and structure for removably mounting the advertising cap nameplate so that the advertising cap nameplate may be changed depending upon the preference of the user.

8 Claims, 2 Drawing Sheets

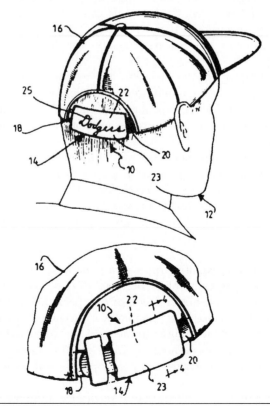

Figure 26-4 Patent Description

S M A L L · B U S I N E S S · I N · A C T I O N

Greetings, You Are Being Sued

Large companies sometimes add products that re-semble those of small firms. If the new product resembles the original too closely, the producer may be found guilty of infringing on the trademark or trade dress of the small business. Susan Polis Schutz and Stephen Schutz, creators of Blue Mountain cards, believed that Hallmark Cards Inc. had copied the Blue Mountain line of highly emo-tional nonoccasion cards.

The Schutzes contended that Hallmark had contacted them in 1985 about working for Hall-mark or selling Blue Mountain Cards. They de-clined. About one year after this meeting, Susan Schutz was in a California card shop and noticed a card design which appeared to be her own but carried the Hallmark name. Therefore, Blue Mountain filed a $276-million suit against Hallmark.

The suit was settled in 1988 with Hallmark agreeing to replace the card line and not to in-fringe on Blue Mountain's design. The financial terms were not disclosed.

Source: Several publications including Amy Dockser Marcus, "Greeting-Card Entrepreneur Finds Success in the Courts," *The Wall Street Journal* (March 9, 1990), p. B2.

the public, it should contain a copyright notice. The notice consists of three el-ements (see the page following the title page of this textbook):

1. The symbol ©.
2. The year when the work was published.
3. The copyright owner's name.

The law provides that copyrighted work cannot be reproduced by another person or persons without authorization. Even photocopying of such work is prohibited, although an individual may copy a limited amount of material for purposes such as research, criticism, comment, or scholarship. A copyright holder can sue a copyright violator for damages.

Trade Dress. A small business may also possess a valuable intangible asset called trade dress. **Trade dress** describes those elements of a firm's distinctive operating image not specifically covered as a trademark, patent, and so on. It is the "look" that a firm creates to provide its marketing advantage.

trade dress
elements of a firm's distinctive image not covered as a trade-mark or patent

Although there are currently no statutes covering trade dress, the courts are beginning to recognize a value to this asset. Consider the situation of Daniel and Monika Crotta, owners of NYPD (New York Pizza Department), based in San Diego. In 1983, they began a unique pizza franchise, which delivered pizza in cars that looked like police cars. Their employees wore actual police uniforms. In 1987, the Crottas learned there was an Iowa company delivering pizza in police cars using the name LAPD (Los Angeles Pizza Delivery). The Crottas sued LAPD's parent company, using the argument that NYPD's trade dress should be protected. In July 1988, an out-of-court settlement was reached whereby LAPD agreed to change its name and refrain from using a police theme.[21]

BUSINESS AGREEMENTS AND THE LAW

An entrepreneur should be careful in making agreements with individuals and businesses. Today's society seems to encourage lawsuits and legal action toward others. Therefore, it is important that entrepreneurs understand such basic elements of law as contracts, agency relationships, and negotiable instruments, just to name a few. (See Figure 26-5.)

Figure 26-5
Selected Legal Issues

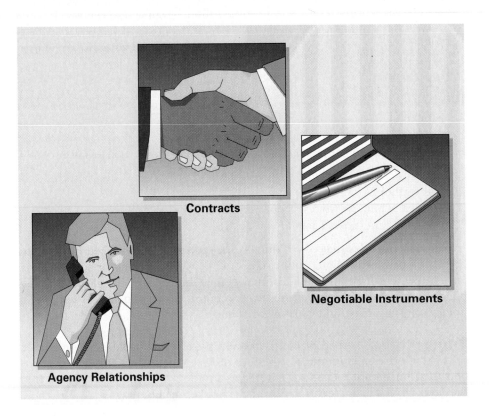

Contracts

Negotiable Instruments

Agency Relationships

Contracts

Managers of small firms frequently make agreements with employees, customers, suppliers, and others. If the agreements are legally enforceable, they are called **contracts.** For a valid contract to exist, the following requirements must be met:

1. *Voluntary agreement.* A genuine offer must be accepted unconditionally by the buyer.
2. *Competent contracting parties.* Contracts with parties who are under legal age, insane, seriously intoxicated, or otherwise unable to understand the nature of the transaction are typically voidable.
3. *Legal act.* The subject of the agreement must not be in conflict with public policy, such as a contract to sell an illegal product.
4. *Consideration.* The parties must exchange something of value, or consideration.
5. *Form of contract.* Contracts may be written or oral. Some contracts must be in written form to be enforceable. Under the **statute of frauds**, sales transactions of $500 or more, sales of real estate, and contracts that cannot be performed within one year after the contract is made must be in writing. The existence of an oral contract must be demonstrated in some way; otherwise it may prove difficult to establish.

If one party to a contract fails to perform in accordance with the contract, the injured party may have recourse to certain remedies. Occasionally, a court will require specific performance of a contract when money damages are not adequate. However, courts are generally reluctant to rule in this manner. In other cases, the injured party has the right to rescind, or cancel, the contract. The most frequently used remedy takes the form of money damages, which are intended to put the injured party in the same condition that he or she would have been in had the contract been performed.

Agency Relationships

An **agency** is a relationship whereby one party, the agent, represents another party, the principal, in contracting with a third person. Examples of agents are: the manager of a branch office who acts as the agent of the firm, a partner who acts as an agent for the partnership, and real estate agents who represent buyers or sellers.

Agents differ in the scope of their authority. The manager of a branch office is a general agent with broad authority. A real estate agent, however, is a special agent with authority to act only in a particular transaction.

The principal is liable to a third party for the performance of contracts made by the agent acting within the scope of the agent's authority. A principal is also liable for fraudulent, negligent, and other wrongful acts of an agent that are executed within the scope of the agency relationship.

contracts
agreements that are legally enforceable

statute of frauds
a law under which specific agreements must be made in writing

agency
a relationship whereby one party represents another party in dealing with a third party

Figure 26-6
Sharon Lee-Tucci,
President of Talent
Plus Agency in St.
Louis, Represents
This Aspiring Actor
with Hollywood
Studios.

An agent has certain obligations to the principal. In general, the agent must accept the orders and instructions of the principal, act in good faith, and use prudence and care in the discharge of agency duties. Moreover, the agent is liable if he or she exceeds stipulated authority and causes damage to the third party as a result. An exception occurs when the principal ratifies or approves the act, whereupon the principal becomes liable.

It is apparent that the powers of agents can make the agency relationship a potentially dangerous one. For this reason, small firms should exercise care in selecting agents and clearly stipulate their authority and responsibility.

Negotiable Instruments

negotiable instruments
credit instruments that are transferable from one party to another in place of money

Credit instruments that can be transferred from one party to another in place of money are known as **negotiable instruments.** Examples of negotiable instruments are promissory notes, drafts, trade acceptances, and ordinary checks. When a negotiable instrument is in the possession of an individual known as a holder in due course, it is not subject to many of the defenses possible in the case of ordinary contracts. For this reason, the small-business firm should secure instruments that are prepared in such a way as to make them negotiable. In general, the requirements for negotiable instruments are:

1. There must be a written, signed, unconditional promise or order to pay.
2. The amount to be paid in money must be specified.
3. The instrument must provide for payment on demand, at a definite time, or at a determinable time.
4. The instrument must be payable to the bearer or to the order of someone.

THE CHALLENGE OF TAXATION

"Nothing is for certain except death and taxes." This widely quoted phrase expresses the mood of most taxpayers, whether individuals or businesses. Yet the Internal Revenue Service (IRS) estimates that underpaid federal income taxes in 1992 amounted to over $120 billion.[22] Tax evasion is a big part of this shortfall, but some underpayment is unintentional and due to the complexity of the tax laws. Even an honest mistake can bring the IRS to your business. "Nothing strikes the fear of God in people like receiving a letter from the IRS," says Thomas Sherman, a tax partner in the Coopers & Lybrand firm.[23] Most audits are triggered by IRS computers using a special "score" based on relationships of various items on the tax return. Also, certain deductions may be scrutinized in some years due to related court decisions. For example, a 1993 Supreme Court decision restricted the types of business activity that can qualify as home-office deductions. This will likely call attention to these expenses in future audit analyses. Since small firms are often accused of being major tax offenders, they need professional tax advice to ensure that all taxes are paid properly.[24]

Many issues have arisen since passage of the Tax Reform Act of 1986. A complete presentation of tax issues involving small firms would fill several books. In fact, the federal government provides Publication 334 each year as a tax guide for small business, and the 1992 edition is 204 pages in length!

Figure 26-7 summarizes the different federal taxes for which a small firm may be liable. It also indicates what type of business organization is liable for each tax, the form numbers, and filing dates. All these filing requirements can certainly tend to depress and confuse the small-business manager.

Figure 26-8 summarizes selected tax regulations relating to small-firm issues. The particular issues selected for highlighting are those that are significantly impacted by the Tax Reform Act of 1986 and subsequent rulings.

Several personal computer tax-preparation software packages are available to assist entrepreneurs who choose to prepare their own tax returns. These programs can be a tremendous help in finding the way through the complicated IRS forms.[25] They also virtually eliminate the math errors commonly associated with tax preparation. Most of these programs will also allow the taxpayer to file returns electronically.

The emphasis here on the tax burden facing a small firm has been directed toward federal taxation. Of course, state, county, and local entities also have taxing authority. In many situations these taxes may be more troublesome than the federal income tax. When a small firm has no taxable income, it will most likely still have other taxes to pay. For example, each of the following kinds of taxes or fees involves a nonfederal agency:

- Sales taxes
- School property taxes
- Motor fuel taxes
- Incorporation fees
- Business license fees
- State income taxes

Figure 26-7   Federal Taxes and Tax Filing Requirements Facing Small Businesses

You may be liable for:	If you are:	Use Form:	Due on or before:
Income tax	Sole proprietor	Schedule C (Form 1040)	Same day as Form 1040
	Individual who is a partner or S corporation shareholder	1040	15th day of 4th month after end of tax year
	Corporation	1120 or 1120-A	15th day of 3rd month after end of tax year
	S corporation	1120S	15th day of 3rd month after end of tax year
Self-employment tax	Sole proprietor, or individual who is a partner	Schedule SE (Form 1040)	Same day as Form 1040
Estimated tax	Sole proprietor, or individual who is a partner or S corporation shareholder	1040-ES	15th day of 4th, 6th, and 9th months of tax year, and 15th day of 1st month after the end of tax year
	Corporation	1120-W	15th day of 4th, 6th, 9th and 12th months of tax year
Annual return of income	Partnership	1065	15th day of 4th month after end of tax year
Social security and Medicare taxes (FICA taxes) and the with-holding of income tax	Sole proprietor, corporation, S corp-oration, or partnership	941 8109 (to make deposits)	4-30, 7-31, 10-31, and 1-31
Providing information on social security and Medicare taxes (FICA taxes) and the with-holding of income tax	Sole proprietor, corporation, S corp-oration, or partnership	W-2 (to employee) W-2 and W-3 (to the Social Security Administration)	1-31 Last day of February
Federal unemployment (FUTA) tax	Sole proprietor, corporation, S corp-oration, or partnership	940-EZ or 940 8109 (to make deposits)	1-31 4-30, 7-31, 10-31,and 1-31, but only if the liability for unpaid tax is more than $100

Source: *1992 Tax Guide for Small Business,* Publication 334, Internal Revenue Service, Washington, DC, 1992.

Figure 26-8   Highlights of Federal Income Tax Regulations for Small Businesses

Accounting Period:

- A partnership is now required to conform its tax year to the tax year of either its majority partners, its principal partners, or a calendar year, in that order, unless it can establish a business purpose for using a different year.

- An S corporation must now use as its tax year a year that ends on December 31 (the calendar year), unless the corporation establishes a business purpose for using a different tax year or makes a section 444 election.

Accounting Methods:

- The cash method may not be used by corporations (other than S corporations), partnerships having a corporation (other than an S corporation) as a partner, or by tax shelters. An exception allows businesses with gross receipts of $5 million or less to continue using the cash method. This exception does not include tax shelters.

- IRS consent is required to change accounting methods.

Going into Business Costs:

- Costs such as conducting market surveys, travel to look over various business possibilities, and fees to have a lawyer organize a business or an accountant set up your recordkeeping system cannot be deducted as business expenses but rather must be amortized.

- If a business wishes to amortize startup expenditures, it must make an election to do so. Generally, these costs are deducted in equal amounts over a period of 60 months or more.

Depreciation:

- The maximum section 179 deduction for a trade or business property is $17,500.

- A new depreciation method applies to tangible property placed in service after 1986. This system, which is referred to as the modified accelerated cost recovery system (MACRS), has eight classes of property with depreciation periods ranging from 3 to 31.5 years.

Business Expenses:

- A small business may deduct advertising expenses if they are reasonable and related to the business activities. A business cannot deduct the cost of advertising if its purpose is to influence legislation. Expenses for public service advertising, such as encouraging people to contribute to the Red Cross, are deductible.

- If a business is located in the taxpayer's home, expenses associated with the part of the home used exclusively and regularly as the principal place of business can be deducted.

- Amounts paid to buy a franchise, trademark, or trade name where the transferor does not retain any significant power, right, or continuing interest (noncontingent payments) must be capitalized. Payments which are based on the productivity and use of the franchise, trademark, or trade name (contingent payments) are deductible as expenses.

Source: Excerpted from *Tax Guide for Small Business,* Publication 334, Internal Revenue Service, Washington, DC, 1992, and David R. Evanson, "A New Balancing Act," *Entrepreneur,* Vol. 21, No. 10 (October 1993), p. 29.

LOOKING BACK

1. Government regulation has become burdensome to small business because of its bureaucratic nature, the excessive paperwork required, and the small firm's lack of time and expertise in responding to regulation. Some legislative attempts have been made to reduce this burden by encouraging greater flexibility in regulation.

2. Government regulation is intended to protect customers, competitors, employees, and others from injurious acts of business firms. Today's regulations affecting small business deal with freedom and fairness of competition, consumer protection, and investor protection, as well as other areas of the public welfare.

3. Small firms may seek protection of their names and original work by registering their trademarks and applying for patents or copyrights. Registration of trademarks is permitted under the federal Lanham Trademark Act. A copyright is the exclusive right of a creator to reproduce, publish, and sell the work that is the product of the intelligence and skill of that person. Trade dress describes those elements of a firm's distinctive operating image not specifically covered by a trademark or patent.

4. Contracts are binding agreements for legal acts made by competent contracting parties, and they involve something of value for both parties. A small firm should exercise care in selecting its agents and clearly stipulate their authority and responsibility. Negotiable instruments facilitate the transfer of credit from one party to another.

5. Tax planning and reporting are important for the small firm and should draw upon the professional expertise of accounting and/or financial specialists either within the business or outside as members of a firm's public accounting firm.

DISCUSSION QUESTIONS

1. One business owner contends that competition protects the customer and that governmental regulation is simply unnecessary except for special situations such as insider trading on Wall Street. How would you argue for or against this point of view?

2. Do any of the regulatory requirements of government conflict with the interests of small business?

3. What evidence is there that indicates that small business has political power?

4. Why is governmental regulation burdensome to small firms?

5. Is it inherently unfair to accord special attention to small firms in formulating governmental regulations?

6. Give the legal requirements that must be fulfilled to make a contract valid and binding.

7. How will the Americans with Disabilities Act impact small firms? Be specific.

8. What is meant by "agency" relationships?

9. What are the requirements of negotiable instruments?

10. Discuss the legal protection afforded by trademarks. Does registration guarantee ownership?
11. List the various types of patents. What kinds of fees should a small firm expect to pay for a patent?
12. What is a copyright? How can copyright materials be protected?
13. What is trade dress? What is the legal status of trade dress?
14. Why were the situations of NYPD and Blue Mountain cards not covered by trademark or patent law? Be specific.
15. For what kinds of taxes, in addition to the income tax, may a small firm be liable?

YOU MAKE THE CALL

Situation 1

A manufacturer refused to buy back a dealer's unsold inventory, citing a written contract with the dealer. One clause of the contract did indeed make repurchase by the manufacturer optional. The dealer, however, argued that he had a prior oral agreement that the manufacturer would repurchase unsold inventory.

As a further complication, the manufacturer had neither signed nor dated the contract when the dealer signed it. Also, the dealer's minimum inventory requirements were left blank, and the contract failed to mention other details.

Questions
1. Does the dealer appear to have a strong legal case to force the manufacturer to repurchase the inventory?
2. How would an attorney be useful in this case?

Situation 2

Ann Landers is president of her own company, Nationwide Drinks, Inc., which she founded in 1980 to produce and market a natural soda that she formulated in her kitchen. The company had grown and prospered over its first 10 years of operation, but a major problem emerged when Ms. Landers saw a television commercial promoting a new natural soda that an industry giant was introducing at 20 cents below her soda's price.

Ms. Landers was obviously concerned that there was a competing brand to battle, but she was also distressed that the bottle design was almost identical to Nationwide's. Ms. Landers was a fighter; therefore, she sued the competitor, charging infringement of her design—even though she had no formal ownership of a copyright or trademark. A federal judge granted Nationwide Drinks a preliminary injunction.

Questions
1. What arguments should Nationwide Drinks present to the court?
2. Do you predict that the large competitor will eventually win by forcing Nationwide Drinks to face huge legal costs? Why or why not?
3. In your opinion, what course of action should Nationwide Drinks have taken to avoid this situation? Can a small firm afford to pursue your recommendation?

EXPERIENTIAL EXERCISES

1. Interview a local attorney regarding the attorney's patent or trademark work for small-business clients. Report on the problems this laywer has faced in this work.
2. Interview a local business owner—a manufacturer, if possible—and ask about his or her strategy to protect the intangible assets of the business.
3. Interview a local lawyer and determine what areas of law she or he considers most vital to small-firm managers. Report your findings to the class.
4. Interview a tax accountant and determine the major tax issues for her or his small-business clients. Report your findings to the class.

REFERENCES TO SMALL-BUSINESS PRACTICES

Bahls, Jane Easter. "Rights or Wrongs," *Entrepreneur,* Vol. 20, No. 2 (February 1992), pp. 95–100.
> A small-business owner discusses the potential impact on his business of the Civil Rights Act of 1991.

Buss, Dale. "Family Matters," *Independent Business,* Vol. 3, No. 6 (November–December 1992), pp. 26–28.
> This article describes how several small-business owners are accommodating their employees' family needs. The point is made that small businesses have a competitive edge over large firms in competing for employees with this issue.

Emshwiller, John R. "Don't Tell Mort Diamond You Can't Fight City Hall," *The Wall Street Journal* (March 12, 1991), p. B2.
> A small-business owner fights city hall when he is told he cannot store his hot-dog cart at home due to health regulations.

McKee, Bradford. "Disability Rules Target Job Bias," *Nation's Business,* Vol. 80, No. 6 (June 1992), pp. 29–33.
> Several entrepreneurs use this article to comment on the Americans with Disabilities Act. Making job accommodations to comply with the law is addressed.

Thompson, Roger. "The IRS Targets Small Pension Plans," *Nation's Business,* Vol. 79, No. 5 (May 1991), pp. 44–47.
> A small restaurant management company experiences the power of the Internal Revenue Service's audit program. The IRS contends that the firm is placing too much money into the pension plan.

ENDNOTES

1. Jeanne Saddler, "Small Businesses Complain that Jungle of Regulations Threatens Their Futures," *The Wall Street Journal* (June 11, 1992), p. B1.

2. Reported in "Crippling Regulations," *Small Business Reports,* Vol. 18, No. 4 (April 1993), p. 5.

3. David Warner, "Regulations' Staggering Costs," *Nation's Business,* Vol. 80, No. 6 (June 1992), p. 50.

4. David Warner, "How Do Federal Rules Affect You?" *Nation's Business,* Vol. 80, No. 5 (May 1992), p. 56.

5. David Warner, "Watch the States," *Nation's Business,* Vol. 78, No. 11 (November 1990), p. 15.

6. Timothy D. Schellhardt, "Tax Changes by States Vex Small Concerns," *The Wall Street Journal* (June 17, 1992), p. B1.

7. Saddler, *op. cit.,* p. B2.

8. Jeffrey A. Tannenbaum, "Government Red Tape Puts Entrepreneurs in the Black," *The Wall Street Journal* (June 12, 1992), p. B2.

9. *Ibid.*

10. *Ibid.*

11. Michael Selz, "Medical-Apparel Rule Is Boon for Laundries," *The Wall Street Journal* (August 14, 1992), p. B1.

12. The Title I exemption is effective July, 1994. The Title III exemption is effective January, 1993. For a comprehensive discussion of this act, see Bruce Elder and Karl Borden, "A Small Business Owner's Guide to the Americans with Disabilities Act," *Small Business Forum,* Vol. 10, No. 2 (Fall 1992), pp. 66–80.

13. For example, see Catherine Yang, "The Disabilities Act Is a Godsend—For Lawyers," *Business Week* (August 17, 1992), p. 29.

14. See Albert B. Ellentuck, "Tax Benefits for Complying with the Disabilities Law," *Nation's Business,* Vol. 81, No. 2 (February 1993), p. 60.

15. "Here Comes the Fallout," *Independent Business,* Vol. 3, No. 7 (January–February 1992), p. 44.

16. Jeanne Saddler, "Small Businesses Will Experience Very Big Impact," *The Wall Street Journal* (November 4, 1991), p. B2.

17. See Junda Woo, "Trademark Law Protects Colors, Court Rules," *The Wall Street Journal* (February 1993), p. B1.

18. Christine Quarembo, "Trademarking Your Name," *Venture,* Vol. 7, No. 6 (June 1985), p. 34.

19. G. Pascal Zachary, "Microsoft Loses Bid for a Trademark on the Word Windows for PC Software," *The Wall Street Journal* (February 25, 1993), p. B9.

20. For a comprehensive discussion of trademark strategy, see Dorothy Cohen, "Trademark Strategy Revisited," *Journal of Marketing,* Vol. 55, No. 7 (July 1991), pp. 46–59.

21. Sheryl Jean, "Beware of Copycats," *Venture,* Vol. 10, No. 10 (October 1988), p. 24.

22. Cary Henrie, "Notes From the Underground Economy," *Business Week* (February 15, 1993), p. 99.

23. Rick Wartzman, "Don't Wave a Red Flag at the IRS," *The Wall Street Journal* (February 24, 1993), p. C1.

24. Henrie, *op. cit.*

25. A good discussion of two of these software programs is found in Walter S. Mossberg, "These Two Programs Offer Some Relief in Taxing Situations," *The Wall Street Journal* (March 11, 1993), p. B1.

ROBERT MULDER, SOLE PROPRIETOR
Entrepreneurial Motivations and Attitudes

In the following account, small-business owner Robert Mulder reflects on the nature of his landscaping business in Raleigh, North Carolina. This firm is extremely small. Mulder's testimonial is noteworthy, however, because of its vivid portrayal of issues involved in small-business ownership. These issues, which exist in most independently owned businesses, include entrepreneurial motivations, customer relations, expansion decisions, attitudes toward risk, growth orientation, family concerns, social responsibility, and personal values.

I own a small landscaping business that operates out of my house in Raleigh, N.C. The business, Amsterdam Landscaping, grosses less than $50,000 annually. I have three part-time employees, a 1976 Ford pickup truck with 102,000 miles on it, a plant nursery in my backyard, and nine regular customers who contract for my services. If you divide my income by the hours I spend doing everything I do—laying brickwork, trimming hedges, filing entries in my maintenance log—I probably earn only slightly more than minimum wage. My "salary" last year—the money I took out of the business for food, rent, and other family expenses—came to just under $16,000. Cash out all my assets, and I doubt you'd find me worth more than $10,000, total.

As a very small-business man, I've had to face many of the same questions confronting owners of *Inc.*-type, fast-growth companies, yet the answers I've come up with don't always fit the conventional profile of corporate success.

I started my business seven years ago for two principal reasons: because I like working with plants and shrubs and because I don't particularly like working for other people. At various times since college—I'm 35 years old and graduated from North Carolina State University in 1975 with a degree in horticulture—I have done yard work for a Catholic diocese, run a small printing operation, been employed by a property-management firm, and driven a beer truck. Nothing has been as satisfying to me as running my own business. I'm doing what I like to do every day, looking after my accounts personally, and making sure my customers get the kind of service they've come to expect. I figure I turned away as much business as I took in last year.

Most of my accounts are residential ones, the kind of jobs where personal contact is high and the profit opportunities relatively low. Last year, however, I had the opportunity to expand my business substantially by picking up a major commercial account. By borrowing $30,000 or so in working capital (and coming up with $7,500 myself), I would have been in a position to get an exclusive landscaping contract with a Raleigh builder who was constructing houses in the $150,000-to-$200,000 range. More such contracts could have followed, and soon I would have been managing a fast-growing business.

Many friends and customers urged me to go this route. They said I'd make more money—and be that much more satisfied, I guess—if I started managing landscaping projects instead of doing them myself.

I couldn't live with that decision, though. Never having borrowed money to finance the business—I have a $1,500 line of credit on my checking account at Wachovia Bank & Trust Co. and good credit at the local plant nursery, but that's it—I suddenly found myself waking up in the middle of the night thinking, $30,000! How do I make payments if business starts drying up? Who'll I be working for, myself or the bank? After that, sleep was hopeless. I couldn't function at all.

One mentor—Bill Kopke, a client of mine who owns a very successful fruit-importing business in the New York City area—recognized this right away. Bill and I had dinner during the time I was thinking about expanding my business, and Bill told me in no uncertain terms that he thought it would be a mistake. I was tremendously relieved when he said this, because I knew in my gut he was right. In fact, as it turned out, not as many houses have been built in the project as had been anticipated. So if I'd become involved in the project, I'd probably be in Chapter 7 by now. Trusting my own instincts in this situation may well have saved my business.

Beyond keeping my own enterprise afloat, I also feel there's a subtle tendency in our society to belittle the very small-business person, to champion growth at the expense of other issues. In my view, there are people for whom growing bigger is a disaster, a promotion to incompetence, if you will. Plus there's the issue of losing touch with what I consider the fundamentals. I remember visiting my uncle in Ontario—he's a very successful car dealer up there, with a house on 70 to 80 acres—and asking him how a certain piece of equipment on one of his cars worked. He said he didn't know, that he managed the business and that wasn't his department, so he hadn't bothered to find out. That kind of attitude doesn't sit well with me. I like knowing what I'm working with, just as I like showing my employees how to do the job right the first time. I'd hate to have to go back and have them redo a project to my standards because I hadn't been around in the first place.

So I made a conscious decision to stay small. Not because I couldn't get the business, but because it would have changed me in ways I didn't really want to change. For one thing, I would have had to drop at least some of my residential customers, the ones who helped me get started in this business. Most landscapers are all too eager to go into commercial work—that's where the big money is—and abandon the residential stuff. I feel just the opposite: I've always said I'll continue to work for these people until they either die or buy a town house and don't need me anymore.

More importantly, if I had grown my business the way the "experts" say, I would have lost the time to do the little things that make work so enjoyable to me. Having lunch with my client, a retired army lieutenant colonel who tells me about his battle campaigns in World War II. Fixing somebody's leaky faucet as a favor or listening to a personal problem because I'm an "outsider" who can. There would be less time too for things like taking my wife and two children off to the mountains for long weekends. Or for projects like The Land Stewardship Council of North Carolina, a broadly ecumenical, Judeo-Christian group I work with that tries to promote intelligent land use, alternatives to chemical pesticides, and other environmental concerns.

Since 99% of my friends and customers had urged me to expand, a lot of them took my decision to mean that I simply wasn't ambitious as a businessman. That really griped me at first. I do have ambitions, and I do consider myself a successful businessman. My ambitions just don't lie in the area of making more money. Instead of mortgaging myself to the hilt and not having time for my family, I'd rather grow along with them and have a little less now, a little more later. We all hear about chief executives who wish they'd spent more time with their families and less with their businesses. I don't want to look back in 10 years and make the same complaint.

This isn't to say that I haven't already made my share of mistakes. Years ago I had no idea how to charge for my services. I underbid on a lot of jobs simply through lack of a sophisticated cost analysis. If a job that I figured would take 80 hours actually took 100—well, there went my profit. It's tough doing business with friends, which most of my clients have become. But I can't stay in business by undercharging them. Now I provide them with a complete cost analysis of all my work and a detailed letter of explanation whenever I feel it necessary to raise my rates. And they have stayed as loyal to me as I am to them.

Being an independent sole proprietor, I probably measure the business universe differently from, say, the average *Inc.* 500 company manager. My idea of a small company, for instance, is one with two or three employees and revenues of less than $100,000 a year. A midsize company would have maybe three or four full-time workers, an equal number of part-time workers, and no more than $500,000 in sales. Large companies? To me, that would be 20 to 25 employees and around $2 million in revenues.

Also, unlike many successful company builders, I don't consider myself to be a risk-taker. I'm actually fairly conservative by nature, although not always politically (and certainly not environmentally). As a businessman, I like to buy good equipment, but if I can't afford what I want, I'll do without it. Individually, given the opportunity to save money, I can probably save it better than anyone I know.

My 1985 federal tax return shows I paid $3,935 in wages last year, spent $8,383 on landscaping supplies, $2,676 on insurance, $2,512 on truck expenses, $53 on office supplies, and $0 on travel and entertainment (no three-martini lunches for me). My total tax liability, state and federal, came to about $5,000. I took nothing in oil-depreciation allowances and the only stock in

my investment portfolio, a fast-food restaurant chain out of Atlanta, went from $3.50 a share to Chapter 11.

I did win $1,329 in a local radio station cash-call contest. The money was nice, but I forgot to set some of it aside and that screwed up my tax situation. Right now I'm paying off the Internal Revenue Service $1,800 that I owe from last year. That's really the key to good business management, I feel. Setting aside money when you have it for the times when you really need it. Ideally, I'd have $10,000 in the bank at all times to cover emergencies. That's ideally, however. The closest I have gotten so far is $5,000, and my operating cushion is usually a lot less than that.

I know that businesses like my own aren't the sexiest part of the U.S. economy. We don't hire a lot of people or rent out five floors in an office building. We don't get recruited with tax incentives by governors who want to rebuild their local economies. I have often paged through the *Inc.* 500 issue, and I have wondered if there would be a way to measure my side of the equation. How do I fit in with the Bill McGowans (MCI Communications Corp.) and the Alvin McCall Jrs. (Ryan's Family Steak Houses Inc.) of the business world?

The effect of companies like mine is cumulative. Last year I pumped $22,910 into the local economy. Multiply that times the thousands of very small businesses in the Raleigh area, and it spells big bucks. We provide a stable and healthy local economy, one on which the McGowans and McCalls depend for growing their own companies. We can't afford to do without these people: men and women who see a small niche, a window of economic opportunity, and are determined to fill it.

If I were to measure success by the personal satisfaction I get in owning my own business, then I would consider myself as successful as the McGowans of the world. I may never make the *Inc.* 500, but I am making my fortune every day— when I nurture my young nursery plants or have

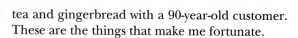

tea and gingerbread with a 90-year-old customer. These are the things that make me fortunate.

Questions

1. Is Mulder, the owner of this business, an entrepreneur? If so, is he a craftsman entrepreneur or an opportunistic entrepreneur?

2. To what extent can you support the no-growth or low-growth philosophy of Mulder?

3. Is Mulder correct in associating smallness with customer satisfaction? Would customer service inevitably deteriorate if he expanded?

4. What rewards is Mulder seeking and finding in this business? Would greater emphasis on profit interfere with attainment of the other rewards?

5. Is Mulder's attitude toward risk typical of the independent business owner? Is it commendable or totally unacceptable for someone in business? Why?

6. How can you explain Mulder's environmental concerns? Are they consistent with his role as a business owner?

MARTY'S LANDSCAPING, INC.
Danger of Business Failure

George J. Davis, a management consultant, received an urgent call from Wendell Martin, owner of Marty's Landscaping, Inc. This business was located on a county road a few miles from Atlanta. It had fallen on hard times, and the owner was seeking help that would enable it to survive and eventually prosper.

When Davis attempted to make his first visit, he experienced difficulty in finding the place of business. He passed it four times and made two inquiries before he was able to recognize it! Eventually, he saw a portable sign with the name of the business sitting back about 100 feet from the highway. It was also hard to see because a bulldozer and two pickup trucks were parked in front of the office building, making the business look more like a construction company than a landscaping company.

Upon entering the office building, Davis found a spacious outer office with several pieces of office furniture and equipment, all of which were dusty and ill-kept. There was no one in the reception area. Finally, a man (who later proved to be the landscape architect) appeared from an office at one side of the reception area. Upon asking to see the president of the company, Davis was escorted to an office at the opposite side of the reception area and introduced to Wendell Martin.

In the discussion that followed, Martin explained that the company's major problem arose from loss of two contracts. The company had been doing landscaping for two major builders of apartment complexes in the Atlanta area, and

both had stopped construction because of overbuilding in the area. Martin further explained that the company was continuing to do maintenance work at the various apartment complexes. The firm used 10 employees for this purpose in addition to the landscape architect and office personnel.

Martin believed they were losing money because of heavy payments on leased equipment they were no longer using. He felt that turning the leased equipment back might tend to destroy the company's credit. Also, the vehicles could be purchased at an attractive price at the end of the lease. Martin also mentioned that they were considering going into the nursery business as a move to turn the business around.

Davis received a copy of the balance sheet and income statement for the latest eight months. (See Figures C2-1 and C2-2.) In the letter accompanying the report, the CPA noted that management had failed to make all of the disclosures required by generally accepted accounting principles.

After reviewing the statement, Davis asked about the nature of two accounts receivable items, "Green Valley Ranch" and "Green Valley Youth Retreat." It was explained to him that these receivables related to a 75-acre piece of land about one-half mile from the landscaping business. Martin had purchased the property for $7,500 some time earlier with the intention of developing it into a retreat site. The property was estimated to have a current value of $75,000—

Source: This case was prepared by George J. Davis.

Figure C2-1   Balance Sheet

Marty's Landscaping, Inc.
Balance Sheet
August 31

ASSETS

Current assets:
Cash	$ 195	
Accounts receivable	46,188	
Accounts receivable, Green Valley Ranch	52,424	
Accounts receivable, Green Valley Youth Retreat	25,586	
Inventory	11,622	
Prepaid expenses	27,373	
Total current assets		$163,388

Fixed assets:
Transportation equipment	$ 89,024	
Machinery and equipment	20,108	
Other equipment and furniture	14,986	
	$124,118	
Less accumulated depreciation	97,922	
Total fixed assets		26,196
TOTAL ASSETS		$189,584

LIABILITIES AND EQUITY

Current liabilities:
Short-term debt	$282,437	
Current portion of long-term debt	13,606	
Accounts payable	23,779	
Accrued expenses	9,508	
Total current liabilities		$329,330
Long-term liabilities		23,841
Total liabilities		$353,171

Stockholder's equity:
Common stock	$ 100	
Retained earnings (deficit)	(163,687)	(163,587)
TOTAL LIABILITIES AND EQUITY		$189,584

the approximate amount of the mortgage on that property. However, the ranch and youth retreat were maintained as a venture completely separate from Marty's Landscaping.

Martin gave Davis a tour of the Green Valley Ranch. He explained his own religious interests and his intention to build the center as a site primarily, though not exclusively, for religious gatherings. The area appeared ideal for a retreat site, but little development had been done. There was no work currently in progress. A tractor stood in a field of high grass. There was one partially com-

Figure C2-2   Income Statement

Marty's Landscaping, Inc.
Income Statement
Eight Months Ending August 31

	Current Month	Eight Months
Sales..	$33,841	$341,517
Direct labor..	$ 8,634	$ 68,929
Plants, grass, materials	13,897	121,419
Contract labor..	783	88,264
Depreciation expense	1,722	13,777
Other expense	5,314	43,972
Cost of sales	$30,350	$336,361
Gross profit	$ 3,491	$ 5,156
General and administrative expense		
(See schedule below)...	12,243	90,440
Net income (loss)	$ (8,752)	$ (85,284)
Schedule of General and Administrative Expenses		
Executive salaries..	$ 3,151	$ 24,384
Office salaries	1,427	12,790
Interest..	4,399	24,452
Legal and accounting	350	7,233
Other...	2,916	21,581
TOTAL...	$12,243	$ 90,440

pleted barracks building, some stacks of lumber, one graded sports field, and a small lake. Davis quickly estimated that some $200,000 to $300,000 would be needed to complete the project even if equipment were available to clear and grade the area where buildings were to be built.

Even though business had turned sour, Martin wanted to take the steps necessary to rescue his firm and make it a winner. Additional funds were needed, but the firm had no additional collateral to pledge for a loan. "What can I do," he asked Davis, "to avoid bankruptcy and become profitable again?"

Questions

1. Evaluate the present condition of this business and its prospects for the future.
2. Evaluate Martin's idea of opening a nursery as a means of strengthening the business.
3. What steps can you, as a consultant, recommend to improve the business?
4. What appear to be the primary causes of the present dilemma? Were they avoidable?

THE FANTASTIC CATALOGUE CO.
Gaining a Competitive Advantage in the Mail-Order Market

It would be quite a wedding; the nuptials would take place in the stone chapel at the school from which the bride and groom had graduated. A reception for 400 guests would follow at the seaside home of the bride's parents. And from start to finish, the festivities would be imbued with Gatsby-esque elegance and style. Kathleen Mahoney, the bride herself, would see to that.

"I researched every aspect of it to the nth degree," she says, recalling the year of preparation. "I went haywire. I looked at 20 guest books, 20 bridesmaids' gifts, 20 different goblets, and so on. I wanted everything to be perfect."

Only the finest items would do, and finding them was frustrating. "There's a decentralized flow of information and goods in the wedding industry," Mahoney says. "There was no source for the upscale bride to find all the high-quality, tasteful wedding accessories she'd need." Her search took her to some 50 stores from Boston to San Francisco—gift shops, bridal boutiques, stationery stores.

All of which got her thinking. And by the time Mahoney and Ozzie Ayscue were married in June 1990, she had a new business on her hands. One-stop shopping for brides—the idea seemed irresistible. "It made intuitive sense to me, from my own experience," says Mahoney, 31. "I did some research with friends, and it made sense to everyone."

With 2.5 million weddings a year in the United States, a huge and lucrative market beckoned. The most promising targets, Mahoney reasoned, were career women, brides age 26 and up. They'd have the discetionary income to purchase topflight wedding goods but not the time to hunt for them.

How best to capitalize on the opportunity? She had dismissed a retail store as too limiting—hers was a national concept. A catalog, though, could put the products right at brides' fingertips. Mahoney was a catalog nut—she loved them. She didn't know the first thing about publishing one, she admits, but she figured she could learn.

The timing was fortunate. Mahoney was at American Express in Manhattan, in the direct-mail travel business. Ayscue was working for a travel-industry start-up in San Francisco, where the couple had decided to settle. In late 1989 Mahoney left American Express and moved west, itching to take a crack at the catalog game.

It's no cakewalk to start a consumer catalog from scratch. Typically, retailers branch into mail order to augment established store-based operations. Other merchants tiptoe into the field by first advertising a few items in magazines. That's a cost-effective way of learning what sells while building a buyer file. Gradually, their product lines expand to fill full-blown catalogs. That's how Land's End got started, for example.

One impediment to launching cold is capital. Catalogs inhale money. One might open a retail store for, say, $50,000, but that won't even get you off the ground in the catalog trade. It can easily cost $150,000 or more to get that first book in the mail, and follow-on editions are needed to

Source: Jay Finegan, "Made to Order," *Inc.,* Vol. 14, No. 5 (May 1993), pp. 74–84. Reprinted with permission, *Inc.* magazine (May 1993). Copyright 1993 by Goldhirsh Group, Inc., 38 Commercial Wharf, Boston, MA 02110.

build a buyer file. First come production costs for photography, copy writing, layout, and design—the "creative" end of the business. Then come costs for list rental, photographic color separation, printing, fulfillment, data processing, and postage. And even before that first order comes in, a start-up needs to stock most of the featured items.

Mind you, all that happens before you know if the phone will ever ring. What if all the recipients throw your catalog in the trash? By definition, a start-up has zero name recognition. And with an estimated 9,000 consumer catalogs in the country, mailing hundreds of millions of copies, it's easy to get lost in the clutter. Given that saturation, catalogs are creeping into ever smaller niches, staking out tiny franchises in hopes of survival.

Even so, most of them don't last long. Industry lore is replete with tales of first-timers who sank $1 million or more into a black hole before calling it quits. The market is ruthless in weeding out the glut. According to Leslie Mackenzie, publisher of *The Directory of Mail Order Catalogs,* between 1,000 and 1,500 of them fail or cease operations every year.

It is a business, analysts stress, in which you must get everything right. For instance, you might have terrific merchandise, a superb shipping operation, and a good mailing list. But you drop the ball on the creative—the product photos and the copy don't quite click. In that case, says consultant Bill Nicolai, "you are toast. It's a very tricky business, but it's one where sharp entrepreneurs can find their way in."

As Mahoney mapped her plans, however, she felt confident. A private investor had promised her $1 million, for 30% of the company, plus a $500,000 loan. That would sustain business for two years or more. The wedding niche, moreover, seemed solid. "I knew in my heart it was a good idea, so I didn't do much formal market research other than some demographics," she says.

She presented her concept to Jeff Haggin, chairman of the MoreNow Corp., a catalog-pro-

duction firm in Sausalito, Calif. Over the years, MoreNow had handled the creative work for many prominent catalogers—Smith & Hawken, Sierra Club, and dozens more. Haggin knew the industry cold, and he thought Mahoney's idea had real merit.

That's all she needed to hear. And thus was born, in February 1990, the Wedding Fantastic Inc.

With that start date, the earliest Mahoney could mail her first catalog would be July. That wasn't optimal. The big wedding season is spring and summer, and she would miss most of it. But impatient to get something into the market, she plunged in, headquartered in her San Francisco apartment.

Ayscue pitched in and joined the company in July as copresident. Two years as an analyst with Morgan Stanley had given him strong number-crunching skills. He'd handle strategic planning, statistical analysis, and financial management, while Mahoney concentrated on merchandising and marketing. Working with list brokers, she identified between 3.5 million and 10 million rentable names that met her demographic profile. Industry wisdom has it that you must mail at least 100,000 books to get a reasonable response. To reach her target market, she rented 100,000 names from Bloomindale's, Williams Sonoma, Victoria's Secret, Nieman-Marcus, and 16 other upscale catalogers. She also rented from bridal-magazine subscriber lists. "I wanted to reach not just brides but brides' mothers, aunts, and shower throwers," she says.

From each list she rented a "cell" of 5,000 names. As a rule, names rent for about a dime each for onetime use, with rates rising to 15¢ depending on the number of "selects." That is, a renter can request names based on such factors as the timing, frequency, and monetary value of the customers' catalog purchases. Mahoney shot for people who had ordered through the mail in the previous six months, a common select.

The use of competing cells is key. It allows a cataloger to see which lists work best, so that when more names are needed, one can mine deeper into good ones. Essentially, a cataloger cold calls people in their mailboxes, and on average only 1.66% of the prospects respond. In other words, for every 100 catalogs mailed to rented names, better than 98 yield no sales. And those who do respond place smaller orders than established buyers.

To succeed, a mail-order operator must build a buyer file so that repeat customers represent a substantial percentage of total circulation. That can take several years. In Mahoney's model, the critical mass would be reached in 1994, when, she calculated, 12% of the 7 million people receiving her catalog would be buyers. That's the point at which her business would turn profitable. Her plan projected net sales that year of $12.5 million, with purchases averaging $95. That translates to more than 131,500 orders, enough that the company could amortize its costs over a far larger business base. General operating expenses, for example, would shrink from 41% of net sales in 1991 to 8% in 1994. Publicity expenses—creative work, color separation, printing, list rental—would drop from 89.5% of sales to 30%. And net income would rise from a 1991 loss of $837,000 to a positive $484,000.

Economies of scale work their magic all over the place once catalogs grow large, but reaching the magic number of 236,000 was, and remains, an ambitious goal. By comparison, Gump's, an old-time San Francisco gift cataloger, has a buyer file of about 100,000 names.

Pressing on, Mahoney contracted with MoreNow for production and arranged to have the book printed by Alden Press, a catalog specialty house in Elk Grove Village, Ill. Fulfillment—everything from inventory storage to order taking to product packing—was farmed out to a small San Francisco company. United Parcel Service would handle deliveries.

Time was short. To get the catalog out in July, all the merchandise had to be selected and turned over to MoreNow by April 1, to start photography. It was a crash project, but Mahoney made it. Just three weeks after she and Ayscue exchanged vows, 100,000 copies of the inaugural edition of *The Wedding Fantastic* hit the mail.

It was very classy, a glossy, beautifully designed 32-pager featuring pretty much everything an upscale bride would need except a gown and a groom. Most items were the fruits of Mahoney's research for her own nuptials. There was a personalized Limoges porcelain ring box ($125), an heirloom-quality moiré hatbox ($298), a lace picture frame ($85), and even a sterling-silver service for the wedding cake (knife and server, $95 each).

The other half of the equation called for putting wedding gifts right in the catalog, to make it a complete wedding resource. They included some of Mahoney's personal favorites, among them a sterling ice-cream scoop ($95), a Zen rock garden ($48), and a birdhouse shaped like a Victorian manor ($145)—"mainstream products," she says, "but with a twist." In all, the catalog had 120 handpicked items.

Established catalogers know from experience how much inventory to carry. Start-ups don't know which items will be best-sellers and which will be dogs, and guessing wrong either way can be costly. "That's one of the hardest things we do," says Ayscue. "If you overstock, you are stuck with products. If you understock, you have to back-order and you might not make the sale." Going conservative, Mahoney went with a barebones inventory.

Competing not on price but on quality and uniqueness, she marked the products up 60% on average. On shipping and handling charges she aimed for break-even. The order form listed an 800 number and a fax number and allowed payment by check, money order, or credit card. On page three, a chatty "Dear brides" letter from Mahoney touted her commitment to top-quality goods and superb customer service, plus a full refund-exchange policy.

Getting that first book out was pricey. MoreNow's bill for the creative was $74,000—over

$2,300 per page. Color separation added another $30,000. Alden charged 22¢ each for the 112,000 copies printed (there were some extras), and postage totaled $24,640. The combined in-the-mail cost came to $153,000, excluding list rental.

So handsome was the book that it won second prize that year in a new-catalog competition. "Even the most cynical of readers cannot help but be charmed by the catalog's sentimental approach to weddings," gushed trade journal *Catalog Age*.

The problem, however, was meager response, well below the 1.66% industry average for prospects. Response fell further when Mahoney "dropped" the second batch, 88,000, in September 1990, and further still when 127,000 went out in November. On the up side, however, the average order was $90, against an industry average of $61.

The new, updated spring edition hit the mail in three volleys, in February, March, and May of 1991. With 40 pages, it featured new items as well as top sellers from the first book. A total of 501,000 copies went out, half of them in May. With timing on the edition's side, the response rates climbed across the board. The new mailings generated sales of $917 per 1,000 catalogs, versus $547 for the first edition. Still, the response rate remained discouragingly below the industry standard, and the average order dipped to $81. "The wedding books were very narrowly targeted," Mahoney says now, "but we were taking a shot-gun approach."

Needing something with broader appeal, she and Ayscue brought forth in September 1991 a brand-new catalog—*The Christmas Fantastic*. Weddings were seasonal, so why not launch a sister publication for the hottest shopping time of the year?

Working again with MoreNow, they developed a 32-page version known in the trade as a "slim jim." By virtue of its dimensions, 6 inches by 11 inches, it was cheaper to print and mail. To give the new catalog a better product mix, Mahoney and her employee sidekick, Georgina

Sanger, scoured gift shows all over the country and developed several exclusives with California artists.

As with the wedding catalog, the products in *The Christmas Fantastic* were eclectic and fairly expensive. The new book featured about 150 items, everything from personalized tree ornaments and stockings to a hand-painted "kitty privy" and a $795 "Grand Mr. President" desk set. There were books and CDs, festive party invitations, ever a beer-brewing kit. Some old favorites encored—the silver ice-cream scoop, the Victorian birdhouse, and the Zen rock garden.

The company sent out a test quantity of 112,000 catalogs in three mailings (early returns provide a "product read" that removes some inventory guesswork), and this time it hit pay dirt. The response rate topped the national norm, orders averaged $97, and sales per 1,000 catalogs mailed hit $1,584, beating the industry standard by $566.

So compelling were the overall economics that Mahoney and Ayscue retooled, shifting entirely away from the bridal market and into the gift business. There will be no new *Wedding Fantastic* this spring, although some of its products are featured in full-page ads in bridal magazines, and a leftover 10,000 copies are available for $3 each. Instead, they launched another new catalog—*The Celebration Fantastic*—and changed their name to the Fantastic Catalogue Co.

The newest book, a 32-page slim jim, is billed as a way to "celebrate life's special occasions with romance, whimsy and imagination!" While some core items remain—the birdhouse, for one—the new catalog is heavy on unusual gifts for Easter, Mother's Day, Father's Day, graduations, anniversaries, and new babies. Its 120 items include everything from a complete gourmet picnic hamper for six ($525) to donkey and elephant earrings for this election year ($34). Like Mahoney's other books, it strikes an upscale and upbeat tone.

"We think now we are sending the right message to the right people," she says. "Our targeting is getting more refined."

If *The Celebration Fantastic* yields results comparable with the Christmas edition's, as Mahoney expects, she will have a strengthening, nonseasonal business and a more secure foothold in the $2-billion mail-order consumer gift market.

But as they say, that's a big if. Having virtually abandoned the wedding niche, she is stepping into a gift sector already sated with some 630 catalog companies, many of them large and resource rich. The Fantastic Catalogue Co. has to establish itself fast. "We need to become the household name, the completely trusted brand name for this whole celebration segment," Mahoney says.

To do that she feels she has to expand quickly. She'd like to circulate a million copies of *The Christmas Fantastic* this fall to aggressively build her buyer file from its current 15,000 names. But with the initial financing of $1.5 million fast depleting, that hinges on raising $1.25 million or so by summer. And another $1 million will be needed in 1993 to move *The Celebration Fantastic* beyond the test phase.

As the company expands and Mahoney increasingly understands exactly who her customer is, she has begun to focus on servicing that customer better. Toward that end she brought the company's fulfillment operations in-house early this year, a move that will require more employees and might produce as-yet-unseen complications.

Then there are also problems looming for the whole catalog industry: the always worrisome possibility of postal-service and UPS price hikes and a U.S. Supreme Court case that could require catalogers to pay sales tax to states other than the one in which they are based. That would create a paperwork nightmare and chip away at catalog sales overall.

To try to raise the cash all these plans and contingencies will require, Ayscue is probing the venture-capital market. Meanwhile, central to the whole operation is the idea that there is an expanding, loyal, and non-price-sensitive market for innovative gift merchandise. That's a tall order in recessionary times, but one Mahoney is sure she can fill.

Questions

1. Do you think Mahoney has correctly assessed the basic nature of competition she faces? Why or why not?
2. What is the competitive advantage Mahoney is trying to create? Do you agree with this appeal? Why?
3. What market segmentation strategy is Fantastic Catalogue following?
4. How can this firm use customer service to gain a competitive advantage?

STITCH CRAFT
Buying a Small Business

Helen and Martha, recent graduates from the School of Fabric Design at Webster University, are interested in going into business in some field that will utilize their education. They both have been steady customers of Stitch Craft, a nationally franchised business, since it opened a year ago, and they both know Peggy and Susan, the owners. Helen and Martha have learned from Peggy that the store is doing quite well for having been in business only a year. Just the other day, while Martha was shopping in Stitch Craft, she was approached by Susan, who told her that she and Peggy were considering selling the business. Susan said the reason they wished to sell was that they had overextended themselves in terms of time availability and were having difficulties maintaining their homes, children, outside interests, and the business simultaneously. Since Helen and Martha had expressed an interest in the business and had experience in fabric design, Peggy and Susan thought they should be given first chance to buy the business.

Helen and Martha were quite excited about this prospect and made an appointment to meet with Peggy and Susan. At this meeting they were shown the whole business from inventory procedures to ringing out the cash register at night. They were quite impressed and eager to proceed with the takeover. When they discussed finances with Peggy and Susan, they were told that since the business was only one year old they were only asking Helen and Martha to assume the existing balance of the SBA loan and pay the invoice price of the inventory and $20,000 for the fixtures, leasehold improvements, and franchise fee. Helen and Martha don't know anything about finances, so they have come to you with a copy of last year's income statement and this month's income and balance sheets for you to review (Figures C4-1, C4-2, and C4-3).

Other points that have come up in your discussion with Helen and Martha are that they have contacted the Stitch Craft Corp., which granted Peggy and Susan the franchise, and were informed that they could indeed take over the remaining nine years of the franchise agreement. Peggy also explained that the Stitch Craft brand is nationally known for quality and style, which accounts for its rapid acceptance in the Webster City market. Helen and Martha have given a great deal of thought to the store's current location, which is in a strip mall on the south end of town. The south end is the "lower-rent" district, and the store's customers are mainly from the higher-income northwest section of town. Helen and Martha feel the store should be moved to a location that is closer to the market. If they buy the business, they plan to move the store at the end of the current lease, which expires in two years. However, they have options to extend the lease for six years after the current lease expires should they decide not to move. They have talked to the landlord, and she will convert Peggy and Susan's lease to Helen and Martha as is.

Source: This case was prepared by Professor Carl Schweser of the University of Iowa.

Figure C4-1   Income Statement

Stitch Craft
Income Statement
1989

	Stitch Craft	Industry Data % of Sales
Sales:		
Fabric	$144,376	82.0%
Patterns/books	16,871	10.0%
Sewing classes	6,932	7.0%
Other	1,621	1.0%
Total sales	$169,800	100.0%
Cost of goods sold	$ 79,300	51.0%
Gross profit	$ 90,500	49.0%
Expenses:		
Wages	$ 30,600	14.0%
Supplies	2,575	1.0%
Rent	15,000	7.5%
Utilities	2,880	1.5%
Advertising	9,572	5.5%
Displays	2,220	1.0%
Travel	375	1.0%
Phone	1,550	.5%
Services	1,875	.5%
Royalty fee (4.5% of sales)	7,436	4.5%
Depreciation and amortization	4,128	2.0%
Interest	7,185	1.0%
Other	5,654	5.0%
Total Expenses	$ 91,050	45.0%
Income before taxes & owner's draw	$ (550)	4.0%

Figure C4-2   Balance Sheet

Stitch Craft
Balance Sheet
January 31, 1990

Current Assets:	
Cash on hand	$ 400
Cash in the bank	(1,245)
Accounts receivable	0

(Continued)

Figure C4-2   (Continued)

Inventory:		
Fabrics	20,372	
Notions	3,900	
Patterns/books	2,190	
Sewing machines	1,345	
Prepaid rent:	1,250	
Total current assets		$28,212
Fixed Assets:		
Fixtures	$12,000	
Less: Accumulated depreciation	(1,300)	
	$10,700	
Leasehold improvements	11,760	
Less: Accumulated depreciation	(1,820)	
	$ 9,940	
Franchise	12,500	
Less: Amortization	(1,352)	
	$11,148	
Total fixed assets		31,788
TOTAL ASSETS		$60,000
Current Liabilities:		
Accounts payable—Trade	$21,873	
Withholdings payable	550	
Sales tax payable	202	
Total current liabilities		$22,625
Long-Term Liabilities:		
SBA Loan—Balance due		
($50,000 over 7 years @ 15%)		46,025
Equity:		
Capital—Peggy Ralson	$ (275)	
Add: Current income/loss	(1,550)	
Training expense draw	(2,500)	
Plus other withdrawals	0	
New balance	$(4,325)	
Capital—Susan Keightly	(275)	
Add: Current income/loss	(1,550)	
Training expense draw	(2,500)	
Plus other withdrawals	0	
New balance	$(4,325)	
Total equity		(8,650)
TOTAL LIABILITIES AND EQUITY		$60,000

Figure C4-3   Income Statement

Stitch Craft
Income Statement
Month of January 1990

Sales..	$6,750
Cost of goods.................................	3,649
Gross margin..................................	$3,101
Operating expense.........................	6,001
Net income.....................................	($2,900)

Note: January/February sales are lowest in year. October/November sales are highest.

Question

Your job is to review the current financial statements and all the data presented to you and make a recommendation on whether or not Helen and Martha should buy Stitch Craft. What counteroffer would you recommend they make if you feel the current asking price is not attractive?

THE MEDICINE SHOPPE
Selecting a Franchise

Kara has recently graduated from pharmacy school and registered as a pharmacist in her state. She recognizes the need for professional business guidance to allow her to successfully operate her own pharmacy. She realizes that her consumers would rely upon her professional skills and seek her help because she works in the health-care profession. She wants to be her own boss, to own her own store, and not be part of a large chain.

Kara's dream has always been to open her own pharmacy, yet in today's fast economy it is difficult for anyone to start a business and make it profitable. For her, it is even more difficult to buy an existing pharmacy because of the high sale price and the low return on investment. One of her best options is to become a franchisee of Medicine Shoppe International, Inc.

The Medicine Shoppe franchise offers her a way of maintaining a sound balance between professionalism and profit. It would help her find a prime location with approximately 800 to 1,000 square feet in a high-traffic area. In addition, she would receive help with interior decor, external signs, and internal fixtures, in an attempt to maximize the image exposure and efficiency of the location.

The Medicine Shoppe program enables the franchisee to purchase in volume and develop specific inventory-control guidelines. The parent company is involved in daily marketing needs, pharmacy supplies, generic and other ethical drugs, promotional materials, fixtures and equipment, store insurance, and promotional articles. The Medicine Shoppe also has its own private label, with over 100 items currently available.

An intensive one-week training seminar at the Medicine Shoppe's corporate headquarters helps train the franchisee in all aspects of business. Additionally, a six-week grand-opening program generates tremendous exposure of the business to consumers in the marketing area. Substantial assistance is given in site selection, lease negotiation, store layout, personnel selection and training, opening procedures, purchasing, inventory control, record keeping, budgeting, and management.

The initial capital required is approximately $60,000, which includes the original franchising fee of $16,000 plus fixtures, supplies and inventory, and opening promotions. In addition, a 5 percent royalty fee on all gross receipts is to be paid to the company.

Kara has little, if any, managerial background. She is very well aware that many pharmacists have failed because of poor managerial ability, and she knows that most businesses in general fail because the owners lack management experience and expertise. Because of her lack of knowledge in management, Kara is gravely concerned about opening a Medicine Shoppe franchise.

Source: Robert Justis and Richard Judd, *Franchising* (Cincinnati, OH: South-Western Publishing Co., 1989), p. 268.

Questions

1. Do you think Kara's professional background will be adequate to help her achieve success in the business, or does she need the assistance she has indicated?

2. What recommendations for evaluating the franchise would you give Kara?

3. What ongoing training should Kara seek from the franchisor?

4. What other alternatives does Kara have for starting her business?

CONSTRUCTION EQUIPMENT DEALERSHIP
Weighing a Career with IBM Against Running the Family Business

As Professor Alan Stone talked on the telephone, he watched his graduate assistant, Jerry Westin, shifting nervously in his chair. When Stone had completed his call, the following conversation with Jerry took place.

Professor: Sorry we were interrupted, Jerry! You said you have a problem. How can I help you?

Jerry: Dr. Stone, I'll be finishing my M.B.A. next month, and I still haven't been able to decide which job offer to accept. Two of the companies want answers next week, so I simply have to make some decisions.

Professor: Well, Jerry, you will have to make the final determination yourself, but we can certainly discuss the various alternatives. As a matter of curiosity, did any of the consulting work we did for IBM ever result in a job offer?

Jerry: Yes, sir! IBM has offered me a really intriguing project-planning job in their National Marketing Division in Atlanta at $47,800. I would have a lot of responsibility from the start, and I would be coordinating the efforts of personnel from several functional departments. If all went well, they have indicated I'd probably have a good chance to be the head of product development for the entire division. Of course, they would pay all moving expenses, and they really have a package of fringe benefits.

Professor: That sounds awfully good! What else do you have?

Jerry: Samsonite, Shell Development, and Boise Cascade. If my wife has her way, we'll go to San Francisco with Boise Cascade. My only question is, can two people live in San Francisco on $44,000 a year, particularly if one of them is my wife?

Professor: Say, what about the family business? Have you given up the idea of being the biggest construction equipment dealer in Billings, Montana?

Jerry: No, sir, not really! As a matter of fact, that's one of the complicating factors. I've been getting some pressure to go back to Billings.

Professor: How do you mean, Jerry?

Jerry: Well, I never really noticed how subtle Dad has been until I started thinking about it. As far as I can recall, he has never specifically said that he thought I should come into the business. But he always said that the opportunity was there if I wanted to take it. His classic statement is how good the business and Billings have been to the family, and I think it is fair to say he influenced me to go to Iowa State, his alma mater, and even to major in accounting. My uncle, who is the accountant in our company, is retiring this year, and I see now that I was probably being prepared all along for that position.

Professor: Does your mother voice an opinion?

Jerry: Yes, sir! She voices more than an opinion! To give you an idea, the last time I talked to her about some of the job offers, she burst into tears and said that it would break my father's heart if I didn't join the business. She said they built the business for me and that they hadn't worked all those years to turn it over to some stranger. Since

Source: This case was prepared by John E. Schoen.

my uncle has to retire because of his health, she accused me of turning my back on Dad just when he needs me the most. By the time she finished, she had me feeling confused, miserable, and mad!

Professor: Mad?

Jerry: Yeah! Mom made some statements about Carol, my wife. Mom thinks Carol is trying to persuade me not to go back to Billings because it's too small and I'd be too close to the family. I suppose I wouldn't have been so angry if it hadn't been partially the truth!

Professor: You mean your wife doesn't want to go to Billings?

Jerry: Oh, I'm sure she'll go if that's what I decide to do, but I think she'd greatly prefer San Francisco. She is from Seattle and likes all the bright lights and activity in big cities. In addition, she has a degree in interior design and the opportunities for employment and learning would be greater in San Francisco than any of the other places, particularly Billings. She has worked to help put me through school for the last two years, so I may owe this to her. She also believes it would be better for me to stand on my own two feet and asks why I went for an M.B.A. if all I was going to do was join the family business. She made me mad, too, last week when she said the worst thing she can imagine is being barefoot and pregnant and eating at my folks' house three times a week.

Professor: What about the Shell and the Samsonite offers?

Jerry: Oh, they're really just offers I've had. It is basically San Francisco, IBM, or home!

Professor: Well, Jerry, you do seem to have a problem. Can you compare the nature of the work in each job?

Jerry: Yes, sir! The IBM job looks very interesting, and the possibilities for advancement are good. Boise Cascade, on the other hand, has a typical cost accounting position. I suppose it would be all right for a couple of years while Carol does her thing and we see if we like San Francisco, but something else would have to come along eventually!

Professor: What about your work in the family business?

Jerry: That's the funny part of it! Everything about the IBM offer—the salary, fringes, authority, prestige, promotion possibilities, and so forth—appeals to me, but I like the family business, too. I mean I've grown up in the business; I know and like the employees, customers, and suppliers; and I really like Billings. Of course, I'd be working as an accountant for awhile; but I would eventually succeed my father, and I've always thought I'd like to run the business someday.

Professor: What about salary in the family business?

Jerry: That's a part I've forgotten to tell you! Last week, my uncle was in town, and even he was dropping broad hints about the family looking forward to our return to Billings and how he will give me a short orientation and then "get the heck outa Dodge." His parting comment was that he was certain Dad would match anything the big companies could do on starting salary.

Professor: Even $47,800?

Jerry: Apparently! Well, there it is, Dr. Stone! What do you think? I've got to let IBM know by the end of the month.

Professor: I don't know, Jerry. Could you go with IBM or Boise Cascade for a couple of years and then go back to the family business?

Jerry: I thought of that possibility, but I think that if I'm going to go with the family business, this is the right time. Uncle Phil is retiring, so there is a position; and I know Dad was a little hesitant about the M.B.A. versus getting experience in the family business. Dad is approaching 60, and the business is hitting all-time highs, so I believe he will try to sell it if I go somewhere else. No, I think it's now or never!

Professor: Well, you were right about one thing, Jerry. You do have a dilemma! This reminds me of the cases in management textbooks—no easy solution! Good luck, and let me know your decision.

Jerry: Thanks, Prof!

Questions

1. Does Jerry Weston have an obligation to the family to provide leadership for the family business?

2. What obligation does Jerry have to his wife in view of her background, education, and career interests?

3. Should Jerry simply do what he wants to do? Does he know what he wants to do?

4. In view of the conflict between Jerry's own interests and those of his wife, what should his career choice be?

ROBINSON ASSOCIATES, INC.
Business Plan for a New Venture

This case presents a business plan for a proposed man-agement-consulting firm. This plan was prepared by a graduate student in business as the basis for his own livelihood both during and after his period of graduate study. A few details, such as name and location, have been changed, but the situation is real.

Business Plan
for
David R. Robinson
Minneapolis, Minnesota

SCOPE OF THE BUSINESS

Personal

I plan to start a business-consulting service in conjunction with USA Consultants (a nationwide business-consulting firm).

History of USA Consultants

USA is over 30 years old. It originated in Boston and Atlanta. It started out as P. Miller Management Consultants. The named changed to USA in 1972. Paul Miller III is the current president of USA. They have over 160 consultants in more than 50 cities.

SPECIFIC AREAS OF ASSISTANCE

Company (Brochure Available on Request)

1. Analysis Phase
2. Implementation Phase (selected examples)
   a. Marketing programs
   b. Organization planning
   c. Personnel training programs
   d. Cost reduction programs
   e. Loan package preparation
   f. Inventory control systems
   g. Financial control and reporting
   h. Mergers and acquisitions
   i. Strategic business planning
   j. Business evaluation

Personal

With my accounting background (CPA—inactive) and current experience consulting with small businesses, I would concentrate on:

1. Analysis phase
2. Implementation phase—especially on:
   a. Organization planning
   b. Loan package preparation
   c. Strategic business planning
   d. Financial control and reporting systems
3. USA continuing education programs in various areas in which I could update my skills.

GOALS

Personal

1. I plan to begin the business July 1 and operate it part time for three months. I will cut back my hours to 32 per week. I will still be eligible for full-time benefits including health insurance and tuition remission. I will go into the business full time starting October 1.
2. I plan to continue pursuing a Ph.D. in business administration. This is entirely compatible with the consulting business. (See attached projected cash flow statements).

Financial

I plan to reach the following cumulative gross billing goals:

Six months ....$ 22,500
Twelve months...$ 86,500
Eighteen months $137,000
Twenty-four months $191,000

MANAGEMENT CAPABILITY

See attached résumé.

Strong Points

1. Four years' consulting experience with Small Business Development Centers.
2. Admitted to Ph.D. program at the university in business administration. Major: management; minor: international business, with current G.P.A. of 4.0 out of possible 4.0.
3. Accepted by USA. USA advertised in *The Wall Street Journal, Inc., USA Today*. To date, they have received over 3,000 applications but selected only 158.
4. Education will be continued through schooling and USA continuing education program.

MARKETING

Competition

External.

1. Review of the Minneapolis-St. Paul *Webb's Directory* on management consultants shows no direct competition.
2. Typically consultants specialize in one to three areas. No firm can offer the wide range of services that USA can.

Internal. There are two other USA consultants in the Minneapolis-St. Paul area. One started his business in December of last year, and the second is just starting. Both are on the Minneapolis side of the river. There appears to be plenty of room for a third USA consultant.

Customer Analysis

USA billing rates are $125/hour to $300/hour. These rates will preclude very small businesses from using our services in most cases. The firms that appear to be best suited for a USA consultant would be firms with 30 to 400 employees.

These firms can be identified through the use of *Webb's Directory* and various other publications.

Reaching the Customer

There are three primary methods to reach customers:

1. *Salesperson.* USA will assist consultant in hiring and training.
2. *MAS services to small accounting firms.* USA works with accounting firms that do not have an MAS department to provide them with consulting services.
3. *Personal contacts.* Extensive contacts have been developed on both sides of the river and will be used to assist in identifying potential customers.

Table C7-1   Projected Billable Hours for First Year

	Hours	Billings	Compensation (@ 50%)
July	10	$ 1,250	$ 625
August	15	$ 1,875	$ 938
September	25	$ 3,125	$ 1,563
October	40	$ 5,000	$ 2,500
November	50	$ 6,250	$ 3,125
December	40	$ 5,000	$ 2,500
January*	55	$ 8,250	$ 4,125
February	55	$ 8,250	$ 4,125
March	70	$10,500	$ 5,250
April	85	$12,750	$ 6,375
May	85	$12,750	$ 6,375
June	75	$11,250	$ 5,625
Totals		$86,250	$43,125

*Pay review is conducted every six months—expect increase to $150/hour.
After $50,000 in gross billings, consultant receives back $7,500 deposit. This should occur about the end of March.

Table C7-2   Cash Flow Projections for David R. Robinson Family

Item	July	Aug.	Sept.	Oct.	Nov.	Dec.
Husband	$1,396	$1,396	$1,396	$ 0	$ 0	$ 0
Wife	$ 783	$ 783	$ 783	$ 783	$ 783	$ 783
USA	$ 0	$ 625	$ 935	$1,560	$2,500	$3,125
Subtotal	$2,179	$2,804	$3,114	$2,343	$3,283	$3,908
Expenses	$3,300	$3,300	$3,400	$3,500	$3,600	$3,700
Overage (Shortage)	($1,121)	($ 496)	($ 286)	($1,157)	($ 317)	$ 208

	Jan.	Feb.	Mar.	Apr.	May	June
Husband	$ 0	$ 0	$ 0	$ 0	0	$ 0
Wife	$ 783	$ 783	$ 783	$ 0	$ 0	$ 0
USA	$2,500	$4,125	$4,125	$ 5,250	$6,375	$6,375
Other	$ 0	$ 0	$ 0	$ 7,500	0	$ 0
Subtotal	$3,283	$4,908	$4,908	$12,750	$6,375	$6,375
Expenses	$5,500	$3,800	$3,900	$ 4,000	$3,800	$3,900
Subtotal	($2,217)	$1,108	$1,008	$ 8,750	$2,575	$2,475

(Continued)

Table C7-2   *(Continued)*

Summary of Overages (Shortages):

July	($1,121)	
Aug.	($ 496)	
Sept.	($ 286)	
Oct.	($1,157)	
Nov.	($ 317)	
Dec.	$ 208	
Jan.	($2,217)	
Additional cash needed	($5,386)	

Figure C7-1   Personal Résumé—David R. Robinson

CAREER OBJECTIVE

To make optimal use of my organizational analysis and human relations abilities to become a skilled consultant to clients and/or management.

This will result in:
- More coordinated organizations
- Increased job satisfaction/productivity

QUALIFIED BY

Training and over 10 years' experience encompassing:

- Organizational skills
- Human relations
- Leadership skills
- Financial analysis
- Reporting

ACHIEVEMENTS

Organizational Skills

- Effectively worked with the Small Business Development Center (SBDC) director to present a highly rated conference on SBDCs for state and federal government personnel.

- Supervised and coordinated other staff accountants in the preparation of audited financial statements.

- Coordinated with volunteer personnel to achieve a very successful fund drive.

- Developed and coordinated with other area procurement specialists to present two highly rated seminars.

(Continued)

Figure C7-1   (*Continued*)

Human Relations

- Quickly developed an atmosphere of trust with established clients through careful consideration of their accounting and tax needs.

- Successfully assisted two business partners in planning, starting, and operating their own small business.

- Provided clear direction to several small businesses, which enabled them to successfully bid on government contracts.

Leadership Skills

- Effectively taught a government procurement seminar in a concise and clear manner to small-business persons.

- Successfully started and developed a Procurement Assistance Center in assisting local businesses obtain over $1,000,000 in government contracts in just over two years.

Financial Analysis

- Developed and successfully implemented annual budgets for the SBDC and Procurement Assistance Center for over two years.

- Thoroughly completed audits and prepared financial statements for corporations with assets up to $2,000,000.

- Developed an accounting system for the Chaplain Fund that provided more complete documentation and permitted audits to be completed in half the expected time.

Reporting

- Coordinated development of successful funding proposals for the local Small Business Development Center and Procurement Assistance Center.

- Thoroughly prepared two nominations for awards, one national and one state, which resulted in the nominees' receiving the rewards.

- Gathered information regarding a specific question by the Chaplain Fund council, then translated this information into a short, understandable format that permitted an immediate, well-informed decision.

EXPERIENCE

State University, Minnesota (June 1989–Present)
Procurement specialist/small business counselor/graduate assistant

Bellhaven Hospital (November 1987–May 1989)
Advanced staff auditor

Moore, Synder CPA, Inc. (December 1986–June 1987)
Staff accountant

Harry C. Reynolds & Co. (January 1985–November 1986)
Staff accountant

(*Continued*)

Figure C7-1   *(Continued)*

U.S. Army (1980–1984)
    Fund custodian, Chaplain Fund, Illinois
    Chapel activities specialist, Korea
    Funds clerk, Chaplain Fund, Texas

EDUCATION

B.S. in Accounting, State University, Ohio

M.A. in industrial/organizational psychology, State University, Minnesota
    (Thesis title: Comparative Psychological Characteristics of Entrepreneurs vs. Small-Business Owners)

OTHER

Licensed as a CPA (inactive) in Minnesota.

Market Trends

Many businesses today are downsizing. Typically the person businesses are outplacing is in middle management. Businesses still have the same problems as before. Businesses will then turn to a consultant to assist in solving these problems.

FINANCIAL

Amount Needed

$ 7,500   Initial deposit*
$ 1,000   Supplies**
$ 4,000   Working capital***
$12,500   Bank financing
$ 9,500   Personal collateral (certificate of deposit)
$22,000

*To be refunded when $50,000 in gross billings have been achieved.
**Supplies include *Webb's Dictionary*, file cabinet, office supplies, shelving, business subscriptions, business phone.
***See attached cash flow statement for details.

Questions

1. As a potential investor, which part of this business plan would impress you most favorably?
2. As a potential investor, what are the most serious concerns or questions you would have after reading this plan?
3. What additional information should be added to strengthen the plan?
4. What changes should be made in the format or wording of the plan to enhance its communication effectiveness?
5. As a banker, would you make a working-capital loan to this business? Why?

HOT Magazine
Researching Market Potential

Kate Johnson, director of public information for a social-service organization in Waco, TX, was scanning the newspaper at lunch with her friend Susan Baldwin, an advertising account representative for the *Waco Tribune-Herald*.

"Did you see this story about the city magazine the Waco Chamber of Commerce may start?" asked Kate.

"Yeah, sounds interesting. They'd probably have to hire an editor. Would you be interested? You've had a lot of experience with publications."

"I just don't know, Sue. I think Waco is ripe for a city magazine, but I just can't get excited about a Chamber of Commerce publication. They're all so boring."

"You're right about that. But what do you expect? The editors don't have much freedom, having to answer to the business establishment," Susan added.

"I really think Waco needs a city magazine. We've got a lot going on here, and we're virtually ignored by *Texas Monthly* and the special-interest magazines. They've all written us off as a small town," Kate said. "What we really need is a high-quality, independent city magazine like *D, the Magazine of Dallas* or *Philadelphia*."

"Do you really think a magazine like that would go in Waco?"

"I know it would, and I think we're the ones who could pull it off, Sue," Kate replied.

"There would be quite a risk involved, and we'd have to quit our jobs," Susan commented.

"Well, I don't want to be an employee and a public servant all my life. I'm ready for something new and challenging, something on my own," said Kate.

"A city magazine would certainly be a challenge, Kate."

BACKGROUND OF THE WOULD-BE ENTREPRENEURS

Kate, who was 35 years old, had worked in public affairs positions for local, regional, and state organizations during the past 13 years, editing a variety of organizational newsletters, magazines, and brochures. In addition, she had been editor of both a small-town newspaper and a special-interest publication about music. Kate's longest tenure in any of the jobs was less than three years. As soon as she mastered a job, she would begin looking around for a new challenge. Kate had lived in Waco a total of 11 years, including the time she spent studying journalism at Baylor University.

Although the Waco Chamber of Commerce eventually abandoned the idea of sponsoring a city magazine, Kate held tenaciously to her aspirations for an independent city magazine. She persuaded her 30-year-old sister, Debra Lunsford, and Susan Baldwin, who was 23 years old, to join her in the venture. Although Susan had been out of college for only two years, she had worked for the newspaper in her hometown

Source: This case was prepared by Minette E. Drumwright.

since she was 16 years old. Debra was the vice-president and business manager of a shipping company in Houston. The three women would form the full-time staff of the publication with Kate serving as editor. Susan would be the advertising sales director, and Debra would be the business manager. All the stories, photography, and graphics would be contracted on a freelance basis, providing local artists a showcase for their work.

THE *HOT* Idea

Kate proposed to call the publication *HOT*, which was a commonly used abbreviation for "Heart of Texas." *HOT* would include an entertainment guide; features on local personalities; and a variety of stories focusing on social, economic, and political trends of the locality. The target audience would be central Texans between the ages of 25 and 55 years with annual incomes ranging from $18,000 to $50,000.

The percentage of advertising in each issue is a key variable for any publication, representing the primary source of revenue. Susan projected that the initial advertising-to-editorial-contents ratio would be 60:40 and that eventually a 70:30 ratio would be attained.

Debra determined that an initial investment of $400,000 would need to be contributed by local investors to launch the magazine. The $400,000 would be used to sustain the magazine through the initial periods of loss, providing for salaries, freelance work, promotion, and production.

Together, the three entrepreneurs interested James Jenkins, a 32-year-old accountant, in the magazine idea. James, who was from an established Waco family, was president of Downtown Waco, Inc., a group of retail merchants with a vested interest in reviving the downtown area. His family owned and operated one of the city's highly successful specialty retail businesses.

Before approaching potential investors about the city magazine, James insisted that the entrepreneurs substantiate their feelings that the magazine would be a success. In an effort to get the necessary information, Kate called a professor specializing in marketing research at Baylor University's Hankamer School of Business. The professor referred the entrepreneurs to two graduate students in his seminar in marketing research.

THE RESEARCH

The graduate students set out to develop a profile of independent city magazines to determine the feasibility of initiating a successful venture in Waco. Using a structured, undisguised questionnaire, they surveyed city-magazine publishers throughout the nation. The sample included the publishers of all the city magazines with complete listings in Standard Rate and Data Service. Participants were asked to enclose a recent issue of their magazine along with the completed questionnaires. A $2 incentive was enclosed to defray the cost of the magazine and the mailing expense. Among the survey questions were those shown in Figure C8-1.

ANALYSIS OF THE QUESTIONNAIRE

The response rate to the survey was 63 percent. As the questionnaires were returned, the data were analyzed with a computer using a variety of procedures. The means for some of the quantitative variables are listed in Figure C8-2.

Readership Profile

Ninety percent of the participants responded to the open-ended questions asking them to describe their readerships with the word "affluent." Ninety-six percent of the readership had an an-

Figure C8-1   Survey Questions

General Information

1. How many employees do you have?
    In editorial   _____
    In advertising   _____
    Other   _____

2. On the average, what percentage of the stories are written by freelance writers?

3. What is your production cost per issue?
    _____ less than $25,000   _____ $40,001–$50,000
    _____ $25,000–$30,000   _____ more than $50,000
    _____ $30,001–$40,000

Advertising

4. What was the approximate ratio of advertising to editorial contents

	Advertising		Editorial
in the first issue?	_____	to	_____
after a year of issues?	_____	to	_____
currently?	_____	to	_____

5. What was the advertising revenue during the magazine's first year?
    _____ less than $100,000   _____ $500,001–$1,000,000
    _____ $100,000–$500,000   _____ more than $1,000,000

6. What was the advertising revenue last year? (Please omit this question if last year was your first year of publication.)
    _____ less than $100,000   _____ $500,001–$1,000,000
    _____ $100,000–$500,000   _____ more than $1,000,000

7. What business are your major advertisers in?
    _____
    _____
    _____

Subscriptions

8. At the time of the first issue, what was the total circulation of the magazine?
    _____ less than 5,000   _____ 10,001–15,000   _____ 25,001–40,000
    _____ 5,000–10,000   _____ 15,001–25,000   _____ more than 40,000

9. When the first issue was published, how many paid subscriptions did the magazine have?
    _____ less than 5,000   _____ 10,001–15,000   _____ 25,001–40,000
    _____ 5,000–10,000   _____ 15,001–25,000   _____ more than 40,000

10. What is the average income bracket of your readership?
    _____ less than $15,000   _____ $30,001–$50,000   _____ more than $75,000
    _____ $15,000–$30,000   _____ $50,001–$75,000   _____ don't know

11. What is the average age of your readership?
    _____ less than 25 years   _____ 36–45 years   _____ 56–65 years
    _____ 25–35 years   _____ 46–55 years   _____ more than 65 years

(*Continued*)

Figure C8-1   *(Continued)*

12. Please rank in priority order the subject matter your readers prefer. Let a "1" represent the most preferred topic and a "5" represent the least preferred topic.

_____ local politics   _____ local news analysis   _____ business news
_____ entertainment   _____ local personalities

13. What adjectives would you use to describe your readership?

_____

14. What advice would you give to someone interested in starting a city magazine?

_____
_____

Figure C8-2   Survey Tabulations

Percentage of stories written by freelance writers	59.4%	Promotion expenditure before publication	$29,000
Percentage of advertising in the first issue	40.3%	Promotion expenditure during the first year	$39,958
Percentage of advertising after one year of issues	45.5%	SMSA population*	671,924
		Circulation**	59,178
Percentage of advertising currently	49.5%	Newsstand price***	$1.80

*The population of the Standard Metropolitan Statistical Areas (SMSA) in which the magazines were located were taken from the *1980 Census of Population and Housing: United States Summary.*
**The circulations were listed in consumer magazines and farm publications published by Standard Rate and Data Service, Inc.
***The issue prices were taken from the covers of the sample issues submitted by participants.

nual income greater than $30,000, and more than 80 percent ranged from 36 to 45 years of age. Participants ranked the subjects their readers preferred in the following order: (1) feature stories on local personalities, (2) entertainment, (3) local news analysis, (4) local politics, and (5) business news.

Major Sources of Advertising

Participants were asked to list the businesses of their major advertisers to permit an analysis of the primary sources of advertising in city magazines. Eighty-eight percent of the respondents listed retail businesses, while 38 percent included restaurants and banks in their lists. Nineteen percent mentioned real estate companies.

National advertising appeared in the lists of only two respondents, and one of the two specified that the national ads were "occasional." The respondent who indicated that national advertising was a frequent source of revenue was the publisher of a magazine in an SMSA with a population exceeding 3,000,000.

Figure C8-3   Profile of Waco SMSA
(McLennan County)[1]

Population	172,800
Population ranking in the United States	194
Number of households	63,000
Total effective buying income (in thousands of dollars)	$1,189,402
Retail sales	$840,358,000
Retail sales per household	$13,381
Age groups:	
18–24	24,000
25–34	23,000
35–49	27,000
50–64	28,000
65 or older	23,000
Undetermined	1,000
Median age	44
Income distribution of adult population:	
Under $10,000	37,000
$10,000–$19,999	38,000
$20,000 or more	51,000
Median Income	$16,800

[1]This abbreviated profile was obtained from federal government
Census publications.

Questions

1. Do you see any flaws in the sample selection that would create a bias toward larger, metropolitan areas?
2. What other questions should have been included in the questionnaire?
3. Do the survey data support the entrepreneur's plans for the advertising-to-editorial ratio?
4. What additional information about the Waco market is needed by the entrepreneurs?
5. Given the research findings, do you recommend that a city-magazine venture be initiated in Waco? Why or why not?

FROST JEWELRY STORE
Can the Smallest Jewelry Store in a Large Shopping Mall Survive?

The Monday morning coffee break during football season is a popular time for college professors to gather in faculty lounges for "Monday morning quarterbacking." On one particular occasion, Professor Charles Morris, a long-time marketing professor, was visiting with Professor Mike Agee, who was recently employed to teach accounting. After Saturday's game had been replayed, Morris learned that Mike and his wife Jean operated a business. Charles was interested in the small-business area and began to inquire into their business experiences. The ensuing conversation ran as follows:

Mike: My wife Jean and I operate a very small jewelry store in Fort Collins, Colorado. It's located in the city's biggest mall. It occupies a very small space—only about 450 square feet.

Charles: How did you get into that particular business?

Mike: I saw a little ad in the newspaper one day. I was teaching accounting in Fort Collins at the time. I had been looking for something—kind of wanted to see if I could make a profit. The ad didn't name the business. After answering the ad, I learned where it was and recognized the store name—Frost Jewelry Store.

Charles: I don't believe I've heard of that name.

Mike: It started out as a franchise. It seems the franchisor-owners lost interest and got into some other things, but they still have the lease on the mall space. I have a sublease with them. However, I am not operating as a franchise, and my contract with them gives me control over renewing the lease.

Charles: How did you finally decide to make the purchase?

Mike: Let me give you a little background. The previous owner, who ran the ad, wanted to leave Fort Collins and go back home to Louisiana. Also, his wife was not in very good health. He was the sole owner. I knew his accountant and, with the owner's permission of course, got three years' sales figures on the business. Sales in the past year (1990) had dipped considerably from the previous years. The accountant was sure that the owner had been skimming (not reporting cash income). In fact, the owner had actually told us he was skimming. We figured about $22,500 in cash had been taken in the last part of the year. When we compared the last-quarter figures of 1990 with those for 1988 and 1989, it was pretty obvious.

Charles: Did this almost scare you away from the deal?

Mike: No, not really. We certainly planned to operate the business honestly, and other factors made the deal look good. David Jones, a friend of mine, and his wife decided to join Jean and me in buying the business as a partnership. The financing was no problem. We went to the bank that had the loan with the previous owner. We took over during the last week of March, 1991.

Charles: Tell me more about the store.

Mike: My wife's first impression of the store was that it had junk. She never went in there. It was

725

just sort of a cheapie earring-type place. She was a little bit surprised when we did go in and look at it and saw the amount of 14-karat gold stuff they had. We, of course, bought his inventory. We have changed the inventory mix and gotten much more costume jewelry and much lower-priced merchandise. Currently costume jewelry accounts for about 50 percent of our sales. We also sell gift items such as belt buckles, plastic trays, combs, hairbrushes, and mirrors. Most of these items can be personalized, which we send out to have done. Gift items probably account for 30 percent of our business. Most of our jewelry and gift items are relatively inexpensive. We do have some 14-karat gold items that run up to $90. These sell to customers who go to May D&F, a department store, and stop and shop with us. However, most of our customers tend to be of the lower middle class. Also, we still do ear piercing. In fact, it accounts for almost 20 percent of our business. It's the number-one place in the county for ear piercing. We've done as many as 40 on a Saturday.

Charles: Does your store have a good location in the mall?

Mike: The ad said this was the best location in the mall. And that's probably true. You go in the main entrance, then you go straight back; there's a fountain and a May D&F store, which is a fine department store. We are next to May D&F on the corner, with an entrance open from two sides. On the other corner is Flowerama, a shop that sells live plants.

Charles: How is the partnership working out?

Mike: I forgot to mention it's no longer a partnership. A partnership is just not like owning your own business. We were leaving Fort Collins to come here, and so we all decided to sell. Toward the end of 1991, we put the store up for sale. We had a number of people talk to us about it. One party seemed to be pretty serious about it and asked us to try to clarify the lease arrangement. This person wanted to be sure she wouldn't have any problems renewing the lease in three years when it expires. My partner sent a letter asking the property managers, located in Boston, to give us some encouragement. The reply was a little upsetting to us. (See Figure C9-1.)

Charles: What was in the letter?

Mike: It referred to a decrease in sales from 1990 to 1991 but overlooked the fact that we generated $120,000 in the 9 months and 1 week of 1991 that we were owners. If the previous owner had been up to par for the first two months and three weeks, we probably would have had an increase over 1990. Also, we had spent a considerable amount of money on the appearance of the store with new paint, carpet, and display cases. We had some new signs and different things made, and we got a lot of favorable comments from people, including the manager of the mall. I don't believe the property managers looked at anything but the computer printout showing sales and the square footage of the store. I've heard some of the mall people say they would like to see a franchise store selling nuts in my location. A store like that would probably make more revenue per square foot. I suspect that, at the end of the lease, people will be after that space. I'll show you a copy of the letter sometime.

Charles: How are lease payments arranged?

Mike: There is a minimum monthly rent paid to the mall, and I cannot remember exactly what it is. It's either the minimum or 8 percent of sales. Now, this means that we have to sell about $144,000 a year, or close to that, before we have to pay more than the minimum. There are some additional bills, such as utilities and taxes, which are prorated to tenants based on their square footage. Anyway, to make a long story short, Jean and I decided to keep the store. So, we made an offer to our partners and they accepted.

Charles: What are you going to do about the lease when the time comes for renewal?

Mike: A very good question!

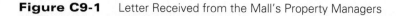

Figure C9-1   Letter Received from the Mall's Property Managers

March 4, 1992

Dear Mr. Agee:

We received your letter of February 23 asking for an extension of your lease for the purpose of making a sale of the business. This is a most unusual request at this time, but we do understand your concern.

We have, therefore, reviewed the sales performance of this store so that we can make some kind of sensible decision. In doing so, we have discovered that, for the calendar year of 1991, the store produced approximately $135,000 in volume, which was a decrease of 1.6% from the previous year. You should be aware that there was a general overall increase in the mall during that calendar year. Further, in the category of jewelry, you have the smallest store which has the lowest sales per square foot of all the stores in the category. Normally the smallest store would have the highest sales per square foot.

The general appearance of the store does not seem to fit the standard of better costume jewelry stores that we have seen in various parts of the country. Based on these assessments, there does not seem to be any reason for us to extend the lease as per your request. It seems to us that both Landlord and Tenant should seriously consider whether this is the proper use for this space.

Very truly yours,

Property Managers
Fort Collins Mall

Questions

1. Assess the bargaining position of Professor Mike Agee in dealing with the property-management firm. How does the smallness of the store affect its bargaining power?

2. How would you respond to the property managers' criticisms regarding decreased sales volume and low sales per square foot? Is it too early for Professor Agee to worry about the lease?

3. What alternatives are available to Professor Agee if he cannot obtain a lease extension? Evaluate the alternatives you have suggested.

4. Of what significance is the jewelry store's location next to the May D&F department store?

5. What is the nature of "skimming" as described by Professor Agee? What are its implications in assessing the health of this business and its prospects for the future?

WALKER MACHINE WORKS
Financing Arrangements for a New Venture

Jim Walker was a management consultant on a continuing but indefinite assignment with a medium-sized plastics company. He was also an M.B.A. candidate at a nearby university. He had thought that the consultant's position would be challenging and would add a dimension of practical experience to his academic background. But after several months Jim had become very disenchanted with his job. Although he seemed to have much freedom in his duties, he began to discover that his reports and suggestions could not be translated into meaningful results and solutions. He realized that the management was interested only in maintaining the status quo and that he was hired as a more or less token consultant. His efforts to help the company were largely ignored and overlooked. It seemed as if his job was quickly becoming nothing more than an exercise in futility.

Jim discussed the situation with a few friends, most of whom urged him to seek a more fulfilling position with another company. But he had another idea: Why not start a small company of his own? He had toyed with this idea for the past couple of years, and there was no better time than the present to give it a try. At least it would be a real test of his management abilities.

After a few days and considerable thought, Jim had several potential ventures in mind. The most promising idea involved the establishment of a machine shop. Before entering college, he had worked two years as a general machinist and acquired diversified experience operating a variety of lathes, milling machines, presses, drills, grinders, and more. And he really enjoyed this sort of work. He guessed that making things on machines satisfied some sort of creative urge he felt.

After a very comprehensive and systematic research of the local market, it appeared that there was a definite need for a high-quality machine-shop operation. Thus, Jim's mind was made up. He was sure that he had an adequate knowledge of machining processes (and enough ambition to find out what he didn't know), and his general business education was also a valuable asset. The problem was money. The necessary machinery for a small shop would cost about $12,000, yet he had only about $3,000 in savings. Surely he could borrow the money or find someone willing to invest in his venture.

A visit to one of the local banks was something less than productive. The vice-president in charge of business investments was quite clear. "You don't have a proven track record. It would be a big risk for us to lend so much money to someone with so little actual experience," the vice-president said. Jim was greatly disappointed but unwilling to give up yet. After all, there were six other banks in town, and one of them might be willing to lend him the money.

FINANCING PROPOSAL 1

One possibility lay in a suggestion the banker had given Jim. He was told to contact Russ

Source: This case was prepared by Richard L. Garman.

Williams, the president of a local hydraulics company. The banker felt that Russ might be interested in investing a little money in Jim's venture. It was certainly worth a try, so Jim called Russ and made an appointment to see him.

Russ had been involved in manufacturing for over 40 years. As a young man, he had begun his career as Jim had—in the machine shop. After several years of experience as a journeyman machinist, Russ was promoted to shop supervisor. Rising steadily through the ranks, Russ, now in his early sixties, had been promoted to president of the hydraulics company only two years ago.

Jim had never met Russ before and knew little about the man or his background. Nevertheless, Jim soon found Russ to be pleasant in nature and very easy to talk to. Jim spent about an hour presenting his business plan to Russ, who seemed impressed with the idea. Although Russ's time and energies were currently committed to an expansion project for the hydraulics company, he indicated that he might be interested in contributing both money and management. As Jim rose to leave, Russ proposed a 50-50 deal and asked Jim to think it over for a few days.

FINANCING PROPOSAL 2

A few days later, Stan Thomas came by to see Jim. They had been good friends for about a year and had even roomed together as undergraduates. Stan had talked with his father about Jim's idea and perhaps had even glorified the possibilities a little. Stan's father was intrigued with the plan and offered to meet with Jim to discuss the possibility of a partnership.

Phil Thomas, Stan's father, was a real estate investor who owned his own agency. Although he had been in business only a few years, he was very successful and was constantly looking for new investment prospects. He drove the 250 miles from his home to meet with Jim one Saturday. After looking over the business plan and some pro-forma financial statements that Jim had pre-

pared, he agreed that it might be a worthwhile venture. "I'll contribute all of the capital you need and give you a fair amount of freedom in running the business. I know that most investors would start out by giving you only 10 or 15 percent of the equity and then gradually increase your share, but I'll make you a better deal. I'll give you 40 percent right off the bat, and we'll let this be a sort of permanent arrangement," he said. Jim was a little unsure about that, so he said he'd think it over for a few days and then let him know.

Jim didn't know quite what to do. He had several options to choose from, and he wasn't sure which would be best. The sensible thing would be to talk to someone who could offer some good advice. So, he went to the business school to talk to a professor he knew fairly well.

FINANCING PROPOSAL 3

Jim found Professor Wesley Davis in his office and described the situation to him. The professor was an associate dean and a marketing specialist. Although he had no actual manufacturing experience, he had edited some semitechnical publications for the Society of Manufacturing Engineers. Thus, he had at least a general knowledge of the machining processes involved in Jim's proposed business.

The professor had been aware of Jim's interest in starting a business and frequently inquired about the progress Jim was making. At the end of this discussion, Jim was surprised to hear the professor offer to help by investing some of his own money. "It sounds like you have an excellent idea, and I'd like to see you give it a try. Besides, a little 'real-world' experience might be good for an old academic type like me," said the professor. "And I would suggest bringing in Joe Winsett from the accounting department. I know neither one of us relishes keeping the books. Besides, Joe is a CPA who could provide some valuable assistance. I'll talk to him if you like." The professor suggested that the equity be split into equal thirds, giving Jim the first option to increase his share of the equity.

Questions

1. Evaluate the backgrounds of the possible "partners" in terms of the business and management needs of the proposed firm.
2. Evaluate the three financing proposals from the standpoint of Jim Walker's control of the firm and the support or interference he may experience.
3. Compare Jim's equity position under each of the three proposals.
4. What are some important characteristics to look for in a prospective business partner?
5. Which option should Jim choose? What reasons can you give to defend your answer?

VMG PRODUCTS
Formation of a Limited Partnership

As a salesman of industrial adhesives, Timothy Wagner discovered a business opportunity in the disposable diaper marketplace. Although two companies (Procter and Gamble and Kimberly-Clark) dominated the market, Wagner believed that a low-cost producer located in the Pacific Northwest should be able to compete effectively in that area. He and two associates prepared a 60-page business plan and took it to William N. Prater, Jr., head of Weatherly Private Capital, an investment firm in Seattle. Prater helped them to establish a limited partnership.

The three founders would be one of two general partners in the venture. Weatherly would be the other—acting in an administrative role, just to assuage investors who might be nervous about the founders' youth and lack of experience, Prater had explained. Neither one would put any significant cash into the deal; that would come from the limited partners. In return, the limiteds would be first in line for a payback, getting nearly all the net income from the diaper line until they had recovered their original investment. Then their share would decline, stepwise, until they had earned seven times their
capital. At that point the founders would get 60% of the partnership's income, the limiteds 30%, and Weatherly 10%.

Right there, Prater had said, was the beauty of the partnership structure. If he had set up a corporation right away, the founders would have had to give up most of the equity just to attract capital. This way they could work themselves up from 1% to what amounted to 60% ownership.

The partnership agreement provided that the two general partners were supposed to agree before they took significant action. The limited partners had no day-to-day authority, but they had the power, if it came to that, to kick out either or both general partners.

Questions

1. What makes such an ownership arrangement attractive to limited partners?
2. What are the advantages for Wagner and his two associates?
3. What are the disadvantages for Wagner and his two associates?

CASE 12

THE EXPECTANT PARENT CENTER
Linking Consumer Behavior with a New Service Business

In February, 1991, Mrs. Ramona Caliban started a profit-oriented childbirth education center in Scranton, Pennsylvania. On the basis of eight years' hospital experience as a registered nurse in obstetrics, Ramona made the decision to establish herself as an entrepreneur in the fast-growing service area of childbirth education.

LOCATION AND FACILITIES

Ramona conducted her first prenatal classes in the fellowship hall of her church, charging $20 per couple. She stated:

At first my only clients were three ladies in the married's Sunday school class at church, so space and facilities were no problem. However, the popularity of my instruction and techniques soon grew to the point that I needed additional room and more professional facilities.

Ramona then rented a small office in a mini shopping center in May 1991, and began operating as The Expectant Parent Center (EPC). She subsequently moved into a slightly larger facility in the same shopping center.

NATURE AND GROWTH OF SERVICES

The Expectant Parent Center provided childbirth preparation and instruction to expectant parents through four separate classes, as follows:

1. Childbirth preparation at $45 per couple (six instructional sessions).
2. Prenatal hygienics and orientation at $20 per couple (two sessions).
3. C-section at $50 per couple (five sessions).
4. Prenatal and postpartum exercises at $25 per couple (five sessions).

Ramona shared instructional duties with two other registered nurses (RNs), who were compensated on the basis of number of teaching contact hours and class size.

The Center had experienced steady growth in enrollments despite lack of advertising. Ramona commented, "We doubled enrollment from May 1991, to January 1992. Between January and August of 1992, we doubled once again, peaking at 35 couples per month. Enrollment figures for the last quarter of 1992 averaged 33 couples per month."

POTENTIAL DEMAND

Ramona felt that the Center had only scratched the surface of demand for childbirth education in the Scranton area. She said:

For a city with more than 100,000 people, I know we could be doing a great deal more business than we are. I have been so busy over the last year with teaching and managerial duties that I really haven't had much time for growth planning. However, I feel that we offer a service very much in demand by enlightened couples. There's no reason why we can't continue to grow at a

Source: This case was prepared by Steve R. Hardy and Professor Philip M. Van Auken of Baylor University.

healthy pace. We'll need larger facilities and more teachers, but that will all come in time.

MARKETING ISSUES

Ramona characterized her marketing strategy as a "bewildering bundle of unanswered questions and unstated assumptions." In particular, she was confused about pricing and advertising. She claimed:

I just don't know what the market will bear in paying for prenatal education. I'm not even sure what the market is here in Scranton—to whom I should target my services.

Only two hospitals in town offer alternative childbirth education, and they do it for $25 for two sessions. However, their classes are typically overcrowded, poorly taught, and offered only sporadically. There is no doubt that most expectant couples are willing to pay for better instruction, but I just don't know how high they are willing to go. Right now I'm pricing pretty much at break-even, at least from the looks of my latest profit-and-loss statement. Now that the business has established itself locally, I want to start turning a decent profit. Prices will definitely have to go up, but I just don't know how far.

Neither am I sure how to best market my services. Obviously our clients are fairly well educated and somewhat affluent, or they wouldn't be interested in paying for first-class prenatal care. Beyond this reference point, however, my customer profile is fuzzy. If I had a better feel for which people are most interested in The Expectant Parent Center, I would know how to promote and diversify my services better.

PRODUCT LINE

In addition to its four areas of childbirth instruction, the Center sold a limited line of child-care books, equipment, and educational toys. Included in the products inventory was a back massager invented by Ramona to aid mothers during labor. She explained:

The massager helps the mother to relax during labor and minimizes muscle spasms in and around the back. The thing has a simple design consisting of a handle with two attached wooden doorknobs. When rolled up and down the back, the wooden wheels greatly counteract muscle tension.

I subcontract out the manufacturing at a cost of $2.40 a unit. I sell them at the Center for $7.00, and they go like hotcakes. I'm currently in the process of getting a manufacturer's rep to circulate them at medical trade shows. He thinks they have national potential if properly marketed.

COMPETITIVE STRENGTH

Ramona summed up her perceived competitive edge as follows:

The Expectant Parent Center offers the very finest in childbirth education, presented with tender loving care. We have good facilities, top-notch instructors, auxiliary products, and an affordable price. Given the right marketing, the Center's growth should really explode. To use a bad pun, we're really in a growth business!

Questions

1. Evaluate Ramona Caliban's pricing concerns and her firm's name in the light of consumers' perceptions of marketing stimuli. Recommend an appropriate pricing strategy.
2. What social and cultural influences may impact the demand for Ramona's services?
3. What types of social power can Ramona use if she begins to promote her services more actively? Be specific. Give an example.
4. How important do you think opinion leadership would be in "selling" Ramona's services? Why?
5. Would you recommend that Ramona continue to pursue the marketing of auxiliary products through the Center? Why or why not?

THE JORDAN CONSTRUCTION ACCOUNT
Extending Credit and Collecting Receivables

Bob McFarland was the president and principal stockholder of Iowa Tractor Supply Company, a farm and construction equipment distributor located in Marshalltown, Iowa. The firm employed 27 persons, and in 1991 sales and net profit after taxes reached all-time highs of $3.4 million and $81,500, respectively. The ending net worth for 1991 was slightly in excess of $478,000.

Bob was highly gratified by these figures as 1991 was the first full year since he had appointed Barry Stockton as general manager. Although the company had been in operation since 1957, it had prospered only from the time Bob had purchased it in 1969. Having been a territorial sales manager for the John Deere Company, he was able to obtain that account for Iowa Tractor, and it typically contributed two-thirds or more of the annual sales volume. After struggling successfully for 10 years to build Iowa Tractor into a profitable firm, he decided that it was time to take things a little easier. Accordingly, he promoted Barry and delegated many of his day-to-day duties to him. Fortunately, Barry seemed to do an outstanding job, and during the summer of 1992, Bob felt secure enough to spend six weeks in Europe with his wife.

One day shortly after Bob returned to work, he looked up from his desk and saw his accountant, Marvin Richter, approaching with several ledger cards in his hand. Marvin entered the office, carefully closed the door, and began to speak earnestly. Marvin said:

Mr. McFarland, I think you should look at these accounts receivable, particularly Jordan Construction.

I've been telling Barry to watch out for Jordan for two months, but he just says they're good for it eventually. I got the latest Dun & Bradstreet monthly report today, which didn't look very good, so I've called Standifer Equipment in Ames and the Caterpillar branch at Cedar Rapids. Jordan seems to have run up some pretty good bills with both of them, and Carter at Standifer said some of the contractors in Des Moines think that the two jobs Jordan got on Interstate 80 are just too big for them to handle. If Jordan can't finish those jobs, we are going to be in trouble! Carter says they're probably going to put them on C.O.D. and call in the rental equipment.

Bob examined the data for a few minutes, asked Marvin several questions before dismissing him, and then summoned Barry to his office. The following dialogue took place between Bob and Barry:

Bob: Barry, I've just been looking over the sheets on Jordan and the amount really scares me. Apparently they are over 90 days on nearly $21,000, between 30 and 90 days on another $17,000, and the total due is more than $45,000. Payments on their account have been dropping off since April, and last month they barely covered the interest on the amount outstanding.

Barry: I know, Bob, I've been over to talk to old man Jordan twice in the last three weeks. He admits they are having some trouble with those jobs on the Interstate, but he claims it is only temporary. I hate to push him too hard because he has bought a lot of equipment from us over the years.

Source: This case was prepared by John E. Schoen, Waco, Texas.

Bob: That's right, Barry, but we're talking about $45,000! At this rate, we'll soon have more money in Jordan's business than he does! I'm not so sure we shouldn't put Jordan on C.O.D. until he makes some substantial payments on their account.

Barry: I don't think so, Bob! Old man Jordan has a real mean streak, and the first time I went over there he really cussed me out for even questioning his account. He reminded me that he had been a good customer for more than 10 years, and he threatened to cut us off if we put any pressure on him.

Bob: Yes, but you've heard that before, Barry. Here we are contributing capital to his business involuntarily; we never get a share of his profits if he succeeds, but we sure get a share of the losses if he goes "belly-up." Barry, I don't want any $45,000 losses!

Barry: Well, I won't say that Jordan doesn't have some problems, but Harry thinks they'll be all right. It's just that if we put them on C.O.D. or pick up the rental equipment and they make it, I'm sure they'll never spend another dollar in here.

Bob: Harry thinks they'll be O.K.?

Barry: Yes, sir.

Bob: Get Harry in here!

In a few minutes Barry returned with Harry Reiser, the sales manager for Iowa Tractor. The following dialogue took place between Bob and Harry:

Harry: Barry says you wanted to talk to me?

Bob: That's right, Harry. We've just been discussing Jordan Construction, and I'd like to get any information you have on them.

Harry: Well, they're pretty good customers, of course. I rented them two tractor-backhoes last month. There are some rumors about their Interstate jobs, but I don't think there is much to it because Jordan was talking about buying a couple of crawler tractors last Friday. I think we have a good chance to get those crawlers if that joker over at Ames doesn't sell his below cost.

Bob: Just a minute. You rented them some back-hoes last month?

Harry: Yes, sir, two model 310-A's.

Bob: How much are we getting for those units?

Harry: $1,400 a month each, and I think we have a good chance to convert them to a sale if Jordan gets six months' rent into them.

Bob: Did you check with anybody before you put those units out with Jordan?

Harry: Well, I think I asked Barry. No, I think he was busy that day. I'm really not certain, but Jordan Construction is one of our best accounts, isn't it?

Bob: That's what we are trying to determine, Harry. Did you know that their accounts receivable is over $45,000?

Harry: No! That's great! I knew we'd really been selling them. I'm sure those rumors. . . .

Bob: And did you know that $38,000 of the $45,000 is past due and that $21,000 is over 90 days?

Harry: Oh!

Then Bob turned to Barry and said:

Barry, I think we've established what Harry knows about Jordan. Why don't we get Marvin in here and see what information he has. Then I think the four of us need to decide the best approach to getting as much of our money back as soon as possible.

Questions

1. Evaluate the quality of the information provided Bob McFarland by each of his subordinates.
2. Evaluate the alternatives in solving the Jordan situation.
3. What action should Bob take regarding the Jordan account?
4. How could Bob improve the credit and collections procedure of Iowa Tractor to minimize problems of this nature?
5. Evaluate the performance of Marvin Richter, Barry Stockton, and Harry Reiser in handling the Jordan account. Do the circumstances warrant any type of disciplinary action?

MITCHELL INTERIORS
Developing a Promotional Strategy

Joyce Mitchell, age 38 and married for 20 years, was a native Texan with two children. Her husband Joe, age 40, had recently taken a 20-year retirement from his firefighter's job in Dallas, Texas. Together, Joyce and Joe operated an interior decorating business located on North Main Street in Corsicana, Texas, a town of approximately 25,000 people.

JOYCE'S BACKGROUND

During her early years of marriage, Joyce tried several jobs but was mainly a housewife. She was not content at being a housewife because, as she said, "I have a tendency to get everything done. I'm usually a pretty good organizer, and I just didn't feel fulfilled." When her children were older, she went back to school to pursue a home economics degree. During this time, she accepted a kindergarten teaching job at a private school.

Joyce soon found out she was not cut out to be a teacher. In her words, "I cannot train people. You know how some people play piano by ear—well, I'm that way. I feel I know how to do something, so why shouldn't you? So, teaching was frustrating to me." About this time, Joe and Joyce decided to move south of Dallas into the country. Joyce happily gave up her teaching.

Joe and Joyce decided to personally build their house on the land they purchased in Navarro County about 12 miles west of Corsicana. Therefore, the first year after Joyce had left teaching, she was busy helping with the construction project. "If I wasn't busy with a hammer and nails, wallpaper, or helping the plumber, I was running back and forth to Corsicana picking out interior decorations."

WORKING FOR A LARGE CHAIN

Joyce began helping her friends with their decorating. A large chain store in Corsicana was a place Joyce would go for her decorating purchases. The store manager was always impressed by the well-organized clippings and folders that she would bring into the store. One day the manager offered Joyce an opportunity to work with the store in a newly created interior decorating job. This chain was just getting into this type of business activity. Joyce was not interested at that time because she had enrolled for 18 credit hours at a local college. The manager persisted, "I've been watching you for four months, and I know you are what I need." Finally, Joyce consented to work on Saturdays beginning in December after the semester concluded. The manager agreed, and Joyce continued for two months under this arrangement. Then, in February, she began working full time and set up the interior design department. During the next five years, she was highly successful and reached the point where she was earning more than $1,500 a month from salary and commissions. For the Corsicana area, this was a high income and an excellent supplement to Joe's salary.

One day Joyce realized she was "working around the clock for another company." She would get up at 5 A.M. to figure bids, report to the store at 8 A.M., oversee installations, and then come home to figure more bids at night. "I really had too many clients," she recalled. She was overloaded and uncomfortable with carrying heavy carpet samples and wallpaper samples in and out of clients' houses. The weight of these samples was also wearing on her personal car. Finally, she requested a company van to carry these samples. The request was received favorably, but the company never did buy the van.

Joyce was also being asked to train interior decorators from other stores in the chain organization. "I was also getting behind in my other work. It was a nice compliment from the store, but I got to looking at it and decided they would have to compensate me or get me some help. I decided to resign." Later, Joyce was told the company was about to promote her to regional supervisor. This would have meant she would be teaching even more, something she didn't enjoy. Joyce decided, "I like decorating because that's my talent. That's the talent God gave me, so I'm going to stay with it."

BEGINNING HER OWN BUSINESS

Since the lack of a van to transport decorating samples to clients' homes was a key issue in Joyce's departure from the chain store, Joe and Joyce decided to begin their own business with a used Dodge Motor Home—thus, Mitchell Interiors was born. The business began smoothly. All of Joyce's suppliers were eager to help because they had observed her success with the large chain store. She had no trouble opening accounts with them because they knew she could sell.

After nine months, the van became crowded. Joyce told Joe, "If we are going to do this, let's do it big." So they bought a 28-foot Winnebago and Joyce personally designed a plush interior. Joe

built the interior, and they had a decorating studio on wheels. "The type of clients I want need to see what you can do the minute they step into your place," Joyce commented. "I want them to think, `If she can do this to a van, she can do my home to please me.'"

OPENING THE MITCHELL INTERIORS STORE

The Mitchell Interiors store was located in Corsicana and occupied 2,000 square feet of store and warehouse space. The store allowed for increased display of many items that were also for sale to walk-in customers. The location was leased and had three neighbor tenants: Prestige Realty, Clint's Jewelers, and Pat Walker's (a reducing salon). All four businesses catered to the same type of clientele.

Joyce still used the Winnebago for travel to clients' homes. Business had been good. In fact, Joyce said, "I am so busy, I cannot take everything that comes in off the street. The first question I ask is: Have you been recommended? I cannot physically get to all the potential business. Therefore, I consider only those jobs I know I can get. I am really wasting time going out to bid on a job if they don't know whether they want me to do it or not."

Joyce was a strong believer in bringing the personal touch to a business. She always tried to bring this to her clients. Even Joe, who installed all drapes and supervised carpet installation, believed in the personal touch. Joyce said, "I hope our business never gets so big that we cannot personally oversee all our jobs."

THE PRODUCT/SERVICE MIX

Contract sales provided about 75 percent of the total business volume of Mitchell Interiors. Contract sales were those made to interior decorating clients—individual homeowners or business owners. Joyce occasionally contracted with builders for the decorating of new houses. Recently, however, because of high interest rates, there was little speculative building in the area. The main products that sold in contract jobs were carpet, vinyl floor covering, draperies, and wallpaper. Drapery sales constituted 60 percent of the contract sales, and Joyce was happy with this situation because of the higher markup associated with draperies. Since competition was much greater in carpeting and vinyls, these products produced a much lower markup. The remaining 25 percent of the business volume came from in-store sales of tables, lamps, ceiling fans, and other decorative accessories.

Joyce saw her customers as upper-middle class and upper class, 35 to 50 years old, both in Corsicana and in surrounding towns.

PROMOTIONAL PRACTICES

Most of Joyce's promotion had been accomplished through the recommendations of satisfied customers. Customers who had known Joyce when she worked for the chain store recommended her to their friends. When Mitchell Interiors was initially "garaged" at Joe and Joyce's home, few people who had a cursory interest would call because of the long-distance telephone charges. Joyce would advertise such things as a drapery sale in the newspaper or on some other special occasion such as Mother's Day. Joyce also used radio advertising on the local FM country-western radio station. Joyce had done all the design work for the firm's stationery and for print advertising.

Joyce used direct mail advertising, too. She felt very strongly that this was an effective medium for her business. These mail-outs were primarily a reminder that her store was there and that she was available. The mailing lists came mainly from an internal file of satisfied customers. This file was updated to remove customers who had not visited the store after about three mail-outs. Additional names were solicited from employees, the Corsicana telephone directory, new residents in the more elite parts of town, and listings of doctors and lawyers.

Yearly promotional expenditures were planned by Joyce at the beginning of the year when the master budget was finalized. Joyce forecasted the expenses and the sales needed to meet these expenses. Break-even sales were around $20,000 per month. In the master budget Joyce included an advertising budget because she believed that advertising was important. Last year, she allowed approximately $300 of the total budget per month for promotion on newspaper advertising, radio, direct mail, business gifts, and specialty advertising. Most of her promotion emphasized accessory items. Joyce reasoned, "I want people to come in and buy accessories. I want people to get used to having a store like this in Corsicana."

THE STORE EMPLOYEES

The business had only one full-time employee and four part-time helpers. According to Joyce, "Joe is the only person besides me who gets outside the business and works with clients." Joyce wanted to remain as the designer-buyer for the store but was willing to take on another designer. She was also looking for someone to manage the accessories area at the store. She wanted the manager to pre-interview other employees, but she wished to make the final hiring decisions.

Questions

1. What other types of promotion would "fit" Joyce Mitchell's customers?
2. Evaluate the promotional practices of Mitchell Interiors.
3. Should Joyce continue to advertise when she already has more business than she can handle? Why or why not?
4. How can Mitchell Interiors grow and also retain the personal touch that is so important to Joyce?

LITTER RIDDER
Finding the Best Distribution Channel for a New Product

It is often said that necessity is the mother of invention. Sometimes unpleasant household chores can be that necessity. Such was the case with Don and Marsha Hostetler. Don and Marsha liked cats, but they hated cleaning the cat litter box.

Don decided there must be a better way. In 1990, he developed "Litter Ridder," a disposable cat litter box. The cat owner need never see or smell cat litter again. He or she could merely throw out the old box and install a new one each week. The box was made of two cardboard pieces. The bottom piece held the cat litter, and the top piece popped up to form a covering over the litter. The cat could then easily go in and out of the enclosed litter box.

Don's architectural drafting background helped him not only to design the product but also to design and build a small assembly line to produce Litter Ridder. Marsha proved to be a hard-nosed negotiator with suppliers, and this helped to minimize materials costs.

Don and Marsha needed assistance in two primary areas: finance and marketing. They found three local investors to provide the initial financial support. One was an attorney. The other two (father and son) were owners of a professional services firm. Don said the investors were picked because they made the first offer to finance the business. None of the investors had marketing expertise. The financial support gave Don and Marsha the resources they needed to set up production facilities, begin production, and develop a marketing strategy.

Four major grocery chains operated in the St. Louis area: Schnucks, Dierbergs, National, and Shop 'N Save. Schnucks and Dierbergs stores were upscale stores patronized by affluent customers. Shop 'N Save was a discount grocer drawing lower-income customers. National was positioned in the middle in terms of customer appeal.

Litter Ridder was sold in the upscale Schnucks and Dierbergs stores throughout the greater St. Louis area. In order to get Litter Ridder into the stores, Don approached the respective buyers and showed them a sample of Litter Ridder. Both the Schnucks and Dierbergs buyers readily agreed to put Litter Ridder on their shelves. There were no wholesalers or food brokers involved in the process. For Schnucks, Don delivered Litter Ridder to a central warehouse, while for Dierbergs, he delivered to each store.

Marketing was not a high priority. A total of eight ads were placed with local newspapers. One was placed with the *St. Louis Post-Dispatch,* four with *The Riverfront Times* (a free weekly paper distributed throughout the metropolitan St. Louis area), and three were placed with the *Ladue News.* (Ladue is the wealthiest suburb in the St. Louis area.) The company was also featured in 13 public relations articles appearing in the *Post-Dispatch* and suburban newspapers.

Don, Marsha, and the other investors intended to advertise on television, but funds ran low before the television advertising could be de-

Source: This case was prepared by Philip R. Carpenter. He gratefully acknowledges the support of the St. Louis University Small Business Development Center and Don Kirchgessner of the St. Louis County Enterprise Center.

veloped. Radio advertising had not been developed. They believed that Litter Ridder was a product that could be advertised best by using visual media.

The retail price of Litter Ridder was $3.85 per box. Competition included national and generic brands of cat litter such as the following:

Brand	Bag Size	Price
Tidy Cat 3	25 pounds	$3.50
Fresh Step	16 pounds	$4.59
Generic	25 pounds	$1.79–2.29

A 25-pound bag would typically last three or four weeks (changing the litter once a week), while Litter Ridder would last one week. Customers who bought Litter Ridder were not minimizing their costs. Rather, they were buying convenience in changing litter and avoiding the unpleasant sights and odors related to ordinary litter.

In early 1992, in-store demonstrations were held. The stores decided which personnel would demonstrate the product; Don and Marsha had no say in this. However, they did send an instruction sheet on how to present Litter Ridder. The results from demonstrations were discouraging. Several customers made negative remarks regarding the product. Discount coupons were offered, but the response was low. As if these problems weren't enough, one of the product demonstrators was quite negative toward Litter Ridder during the demonstration.

Sales were increasing slowly. (See Table C15-1. No sales were recorded in May because the stores made large purchases in April in anticipation of increased sales after the in-store demonstrations.) Sales volume was still well below the break-even point. Don thought the price might be too high. He spent time redesigning the box and was able to reduce the cost of production significantly.

After current inventory was used up, Don planned to begin production of the new box. He would pass on the cost savings to the supermarkets. There was a positive response from the supermarket buyers. They said they would in turn pass on the savings by reducing Litter Ridder's price. Don started the lower pricing in June.

Don thought that by expanding their market they could increase sales. Visiting a large regional grocer in Indianapolis, he found himself unprepared for the detailed questions concerning pricing, delivery, food brokers, discounting, and couponing asked by the grocer's buyers.

By June 1993, the investors were becoming restless. While the father and son were willing to be patient and stick it out, the lawyer was not. He wanted out, and he persuaded the other two to join him. The investors had been supporting the business on a modified pay-as-you-go plan. They each made an equal initial investment. When this sum was gone, they paid the monthly expenses of the business. They stopped paying the monthly expenses at the end of June. Their total investment in the corporation was $52,000, which was split evenly among them. Don and Marsha had invested no cash in the business. The agreement was that their share would be 25 percent in event the business was sold.

Don and Marsha believed there was potential for a new investor. Don had been reviewing patent applications for products similar to Litter Ridder. One day he came across one in the local St. Louis area. He called the person, who expressed an interest in providing financial and marketing assistance for Litter Ridder. The discussion had remained at a preliminary stage.

Don and Marsha stopped production in June and planned to sell their three-month backlog. During this time, they planned to make some difficult decisions regarding Litter Ridder's future.

Questions

1. How might this firm's distribution channels be related to its failure to attain a larger sales volume?
2. What distribution channels would be most appropriate for this product?

Table C15-1   Litter Ridder Sales History

Sales	December 92 Dollars	Units	January 93 Dollars	Units	February 93 Dollars	Units	March 93 Dollars	Units	April 93 Dollars	Units	May 93 Dollars	Units	June 93 Dollars	Units
Schnucks	$423	144	$846	288	$1058	360	$1058	360	$2328	792	$0	0	$1332	720
Dierbergs	$133	43	$151	49	$231	75	$408	131	$478	73	$0	0	$204	105
Total	$556	187	$997	337	$1289	435	$1466	491	$2806	865	$0	0	$1536	825

3. What types of marketing research are needed by this firm? What questions need to be answered?

4. Evaluate their sales and promotional efforts.

Suggest types of advertising and advertising media that might be most appropriate.

5. What should the Hostetlers do next?

CENTRAL ENGINEERING
How the Entrepreneur's Managerial Practices Hampered Decision Making

Henry and Jami Wolfram, a husband-and-wife team, owned and operated Central Engineering, a heating and air-conditioning firm located in Huntsville, Alabama. The business prospered during the six years they owned it, and it served both residential and commercial accounts.

ORGANIZATION STRUCTURE

Henry served as general operations manager. (Figure C16-1 shows the simple organization structure of the firm.) As the business grew, more and more responsibility fell on Henry's shoulders. Although Jami assumed some of the burden by acting as treasurer and supervising the office work, Henry was personally involved in most of the key decisions. Henry's son, Jeff Wolfram, had started work on an installation crew. Later he moved into the position of estimator-salesman and acted as manager on those occasions when his father was away.

THE BOTTLENECK

An unfortunate consequence of Henry's growing work load was the creation of a bottleneck at the very top of the business. Since he was a key person, his judgment seemed indispensable in many actions. As a result, decisions were sometimes de-

Figure C16-1   Organization Structure of Central Engineering

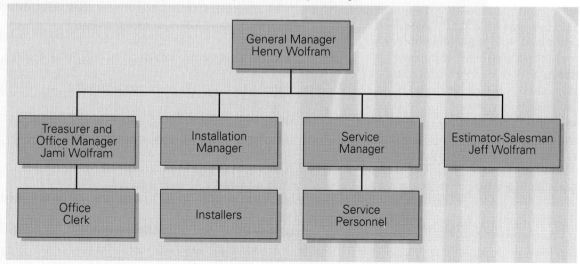

General Manager
Henry Wolfram

Treasurer and Office Manager Jami Wolfram

Installation Manager

Service Manager

Estimator-Salesman Jeff Wolfram

Office Clerk

Installers

Service Personnel

layed while waiting for his attention. Others in the organization sometimes found themselves waiting in line to get a chance to talk with him. And Henry found himself rushed, with insufficient time to think carefully about some aspects of the business. In addition, he would have liked to devote a little more time to family, church, and personal interests.

REVIEW OF CUSTOMER BILLING

One task that required Henry's attention was his personal review of bills before they were sent to customers. When a management consultant asked why this was necessary, the following dialogue took place:

Henry: I really need to take a last look before bills are sent out. For example, on construction jobs there may be additions or extras that were included after we had made the original bid.

Consultant: On regular service calls, is there a similar chance of an error?

Henry: That's right. For instance, maybe the worker has left something off the work order. The worker may say he has done this and this and this, but over here on the material list he has some items that don't match up or that are missing from what he said he's done.

Consultant: Can you tell me how many hours in a day or week are required for this?

Henry: Well, it cuts into a lot of time. This is part of another problem. The office is too open, with Jeff and his customers in the same office with me. I just don't have any place where I can concentrate on this type of work. I think that, when we get that physical arrangement changed, it will help some.

Consultant: So, how many hours a week does this take?

Henry: Sometimes we stay here at night or come in Saturday to do this. But I suppose it might run 8 or 10 hours a week.

Consultant: Is there anybody else who could do this?

Henry: Well, on service calls Jami can usually spot such discrepancies. She is getting enough experience that she can recognize them.

Consultant: What is Jeff's role? Could he do this?

Henry: He's an estimator and does sales work. He doesn't quite have the experience yet. Well, he might be close to being capable. But he's pretty busy. Also, I have a service manager who could catch a lot of this when the orders are turned in. But he does not manage that carefully. I have a more aggressive manager in installation who is better at catching things like this.

The general theme in Henry's discussion with the management consultant was the difficulty of resolving the time-management problem. Henry recognized the burden this placed on him personally and on the business, but there seemed to be no obvious answer at this stage in the life of the firm.

REVIEW OF ACCOUNTS PAYABLE

Henry also tried to look over all payments being made on trade accounts payable. His discussion with the management consultant regarding this function ran as follows:

Henry: These payments need to be checked over because we may be charged too much on some bills.

Consultant: How does this happen?

Henry: On particular jobs we may get special pricing. Say I'm working on a bid. I may pick up a phone and say to the supplier, "We need some special pricing. Here's what we're up against, and we need the special pricing to get this job." And if they give us the special pricing, we should pay accordingly.

Consultant: And you can't depend on them to bill you at that special price?

Henry: I don't think it is anything intentional. But they give it to their clerks to bill, and they may overlook the special pricing that was promised. So, if we don't catch it, we lose it.

HENRY'S DILEMMA

The responsibilities relative to accounts receivable and accounts payable were typical of the overall situation. In many aspects of the business, Henry felt compelled to give his personal attention to the issues and the decisions that needed to be made. In a sense he felt trapped by the very success and work that accompanied the operation of the business. He enjoyed the work, every minute of it, but occasionally he wondered why there was no obvious solution to his dilemma.

Questions

1. Is Henry Wolfram's personal involvement in the various specific aspects of the business necessary, or is it a matter of habit or of simply enjoying doing business that way?
2. What changes would be necessary to extricate Henry from the checking of customer bills before they are mailed?
3. If you were the consultant, what changes would you recommend?

GIBSON MORTUARY
Human Resource Problems in a Small Family Business

Gibson Mortuary was founded in 1929 and grew to become one of the best known funeral homes in Tacoma, Washington. One of its most persistent problems over the years had been the recruitment and retention of qualified personnel.

BACKGROUND OF THE BUSINESS

Gibson Mortuary was a family business headed by Ethel Gibson, who owned 51 percent of the stock. As an active executive in the business, Ethel had become recognized as a community leader. She had served in various civic endeavors, had been elected to the city council, and had served one term as mayor.

The mortuary had built a reputation as one of the finest funeral homes in the state. The quality of its service over the years had been such that it continued to serve families over several generations. While large corporations had bought up many mortuaries in recent years, Gibson Mortuary continued to remain competitive as an independent family firm—a "family serving families." Funeral homes in general had become the target of public criticism, and books such as *The American Way of Death* had reflected adversely on this type of business. Nevertheless, Gibson Mortuary had withstood this threat by its determined, consistent effort to provide the best possible customer service. In its most recent year it had conducted 375 funerals, which placed it in the top 9 percent of all funeral homes in the nation when measured in terms of volume of business.

Ethel's son, Max Gibson, had entered the business after completing military service and had become general manager of the firm. He was a licensed funeral director and embalmer. Both mother and son were active in the day-to-day management of the firm.

RECRUITMENT AND RETENTION PROBLEM

Perhaps the most difficult problem facing Gibson Mortuary was the recruitment and retention of qualified personnel. The image of the industry made it difficult to attract the right caliber of young people as employees. Many individuals were repelled by the idea of working for an organization in which they daily and personally faced the fact of death. In addition, the challenges raised by social critics reflected poorly on the industry and conveyed to many youth the impression that funeral homes were profiteering on the misery of those who suffered bereavement.

One source of employees was walk-in applicants. Also, Gibson Mortuary worked through sales representatives who sold throughout that geographical area. They often knew of people who might be considering a change in their careers.

As a small business, Gibson Mortuary also presented fewer total opportunities than a larger company or even a funeral home chain. The fact that it was a family business also suggested to prospective employees that top management would remain in the family. It was apparent to all that the two top management spots were family positions. However, Ethel and Max were the only family members employed, so there was some hope for the future for nonfamily employees. Max was 49 years old.

TRAINING PROBLEM

Gibson Mortuary used two licensed embalmers— Max and another individual. The pressure of other managerial work made it difficult for Max to devote sufficient time to this type of work. To become a licensed embalmer, one had to attend mortuary college and serve a two-year apprenticeship. (Mortuary science programs were part of some community-college programs.) The apprenticeship could be served either prior to or after the college training. Gibson Mortuary advised most individuals to take the apprenticeship prior to the college training so that they could evaluate their own aptitude for this type of career.

Gibson Mortuary preferred its personnel to be competent in all phases of the business. The work involved not only embalming, but also making funeral arrangements with families and conducting funerals and burials. However, some part-time employees assisted only in conducting funerals and did not perform preparatory work.

PERSONAL QUALIFICATIONS FOR EMPLOYMENT

All employees who met the public and had any part in the funeral service needed the ability to interact with others in a friendly and relaxed but dignified manner. The personalities of some individuals were much better suited to this than those of others. Ethel described one of the problem personalities she had encountered at Gibson Mortuary as follows:

In the first place, he didn't really look the part for our community here. He was short and stocky, too heavy for his height. His vest was too short, and he wore a big cowboy buckle! *Can't you see that going over big in a mortuary! He wanted to stand at the door and greet people as they came. We do furnish suits, so we tried to polish off some of the rough edges.*

But he was still too aggressive. He became upset with me because I wouldn't get him any business cards immediately. One day I had to send him to the printers, and he came back and said, "While I was there, I just told them to make some cards for me. I'll pay for them myself." I said to him, "Willis, you go right back there and cancel that order! When you are eligible for cards, I'll have them printed for you." We couldn't have him at that point scattering his cards with our name all over town.

Ethel also discussed a young applicant who made an impressive appearance but lacked polish. His grammar was so poor that he lacked the minimal skills necessary for any significant contact with the public.

Two characteristics of employment that discouraged some applicants were the irregular hours and the constant interruptions that were part of the life of a funeral director. A funeral director might start to do one thing and then find it necessary to switch over to another, more urgent matter. Then there was the requirement for some night and weekend duty in the work schedule.

SOLVING THE HUMAN RESOURCE PROBLEMS

Although Gibson Mortuary had not completely solved its need for qualified personnel, the business was working at it. While waiting for the right person to come along, Gibson Mortuary had started another apprentice prior to any college training. In addition, it was following up on a former apprentice who was attending mortuary college and working during summer vacations. The business also employed a part-time minister as an extra driver. In these ways Gibson Mortuary was getting along, but it was still seeking to do a better job in personnel staffing.

Questions

1. Evaluate the human resource problems facing this firm. Which of these appears most serious?
2. How can Gibson Mortuary be more aggressive in recruitment? How can it make such a career attractive to applicants?
3. Does the fact that Gibson Mortuary is a family firm create a significant problem in recruitment? How can the firm overcome any problems that may exist in this area?
4. Assuming you are the proper age to consider such employment, what is the biggest question or problem you would have in considering employment with Gibson Mortuary? What, if anything, might the Gibsons do to deal with that type of question or problem?

BURTON WALLS ELECTRIC
Expansion of an Electrical Contracting Business

"How big should we grow?" That was the question posed by Burton Walls of Burton Walls Electric, a small electrical contracting firm in Seattle. Walls had started the firm with one associate working out of the basement in his home. After 14 years, he had built the business to the $1-million annual revenue level, with 13 employees, projects throughout the metropolitan area and as far as 100 miles away, and $50,000 in profit (not including his own salary).

Since growth to this point had been successful, Walls naturally thought about further expansion. Should he try to make it a bigger small business by shooting for $3 million in revenue and 35 employees? "There's a 'no man's land' between 15 and 25 employees," he explained. "Adding four or five employees would stretch our present staff too far but still not give us enough volume to justify additional management personnel. If we want to grow, we should plan for somewhere between 25 and 50 employees."

Walls had completed a bachelor's degree in business administration before starting the business. However, both he and his associate performed the electrical work in the beginning stages. As the work expanded, Walls devoted more of his time to estimating and eventually devoted all of his time to management of the business. Because of this background, he understood the nature of the work and the concerns of electricians who worked for him. He operated on a nonunion basis and felt that he had developed a very loyal group of employees.

The company's electrical work was varied—60 percent on commercial buildings and 40 percent on residential dwellings. More than half of the residential work was obtained through property management companies rather than through individual homeowners. Typical projects were bid through a general contractor and ranged from a few thousand dollars to $100,000. Usually, these covered the electrical portion of remodeling or tenant upgrade projects. Recently, for example, they had rewired a building to be used as a radio station. The firm also provided repair and maintenance service as needed by individual and commercial customers.

The firm's most recent income statement and balance sheet are shown in Figures C18-1 and C18-2. Even though the business is currently successful, profits have fluctuated considerably. The financial results in some recent years have, in fact, been disappointing. This has raised questions about the effectiveness of the managerial control system. As one example, Walls and the firm's CPA discovered a weakness in the accounting for labor cost on specific projects—a weakness that had worked to hold down profits. By following some suggestions of the CPA, the firm was able to remedy that problem and thereby help improve profitability.

Growth should bring increased profits as well as an increase in salary for the owner. With $3 million in revenue, profits should hit the industry average of $90,000 to $110,000. It seemed possible, in fact, that he might do better than the industry average. Throughout the firm's entire existence, Walls had tried to provide excellent service to customers—for example, meeting the needs of contractors to have electricians available at just the time needed to facilitate overall progress on construction. As a result of such reli-

Figure C18-1   Income Statement

Burton Walls Electric
Annual Income Statement

Revenues		$954,801
Direct costs of revenues:		
Materials	$304,557	
Wages and salaries	220,857	
Other direct costs	108,857	634,271
Indirect costs of revenues		91,554
Gross profit		$228,976
General and administrative expenses		178,400
NET INCOME		$ 50,576

Figure C18-2   Balance Sheet

Burton Walls Electric
Balance Sheet

ASSETS

Current Assets:		
Cash	$ 33,629	
Receivables	190,954	
Inventory	20,000	
Job progress—unbilled	33,459	
Other current assets	3,844	$281,886
Fixed Assets:		
Total fixed assets	$169,809	
Less accumulated depreciation	116,743	53,066
TOTAL ASSETS		$334,952

LIABILITIES AND EQUITY

Current Liabilities:		
Trade accounts payable	$ 23,265	
Deferred income tax	34,450	
Other payables	17,737	$ 75,452
Long-term liabilities		21,752
Total liabilities		$ 97,204
Stockholder's equity		237,748
TOTAL LIABILITIES AND STOCKHOLDER'S EQUITY		$334,952

ability, the firm had established a good reputation with general contractors and occasionally obtained contracts on a negotiated bid basis.

Prospects for profitable growth, however, were not without difficulties and dangers. A substantial additional investment would be required. Although the firm used a small computer for accounting and job costing, a much larger computer system and more sophisticated software would be necessary. Also, additional working capital would be needed, because there is typically a 30- to 60-day lag in payment for work that is completed. The following investment requirements were estimated:

Computer system	$ 65,000
Additional trucks	22,000
Additional tools	10,000
Additional working capital	250,000

Overhead salary costs would increase with the addition of two supervisors (approximately $35,000 each), three estimators (approximately $45,000 each), and two clerical positions (approximately $20,000 each). Direct labor cost could be controlled in the event of a business downturn by laying off electricians. It would be difficult to cut overhead costs quickly, however, in the event of a downturn. Additional borrowing would also be required, and this would increase interest expense substantially. Even so, the expansion should generate additional profits if the firm could operate as well as the average firm in the industry.

Profit margins would be threatened somewhat as the firm started bidding on projects in the $100,000 to $300,000 range. Large contracts of this type attract more bidders and more aggressive competition. Furthermore, Burton Walls Electric would need to price very competitively since it had no "track record" on projects of this size. In the past, the firm had been most successful and earned the best profit margins on contracts between $2,000 and $10,000 and on maintenance work.

Effective control of work operations would also become more difficult. The firm had been reasonably successful in effectively supervising the work of nine electricians. In addition to Walls, who served as general manager, the firm employed one supervisor and one estimator who could also give some supervision of jobs in case of emergency. With a larger scale of operation, control would necessarily become less personal. To some extent, formal systems of control and computer printouts would be needed to replace some of the personal, face-to-face direction that was possible with a smaller group of employees. The question was whether the same efficiency could be realized with more supervisors and a larger administrative structure. Production efficiency required skill in shifting electricians from one project to another and back again according to the demands of each job.

An expanded scope of operation would entail increased risk. In the past, Walls had depended upon his personal investment in commercial rental property to provide stability in the electrical business. The rental property produced a steady income flow and enabled the business to function without difficulty even when the electrical business slackened, as happened occasionally. For example, his outside income enabled him to forego taking his own salary when money was tight and taking it when conditions improved. In all of its years of operation, Burton Walls Electric had never failed to meet a payroll on schedule.

Walls was also concerned with the implications of expansion for key employees, who over the years had become a closely knit group. The present congenial relationships would undoubtedly be altered as personnel were added and additional levels of supervision created. In general, Walls practiced a somewhat participative style of management that invited the input of key personnel. Once a month, for example, he held a breakfast meeting with all employees for open discussion of concerns and business conditions. He realized that these people had a stake in the business that deserved consideration and that their commitment to expansion would be necessary if it was to succeed.

A number of more personal questions were also involved in such a decision. Entrepreneurial motivations are complex, and Walls thought about the extent to which expansion might be merely an "ego trip" in which he sought community respect and recognition by his peers. An expansion would add emotional stress and perhaps take time away from highly valued family activities with his wife and two school-aged children.

Expansion offered opportunities but also entailed costs and risks—the ingredients of any entrepreneurial decision. As Walls pondered the future of Burton Walls Electric, he wanted to make an intelligent decision concerning the best size for the long-run best interests of the business, the employees, and his own family.

Questions

1. How would expansion impact the operations management process of this firm?
2. Do the firm's present managerial system and resources appear adequate as a foundation for changes necessitated by expansion? How difficult will it be to adapt the management system to an expanded level of operation?
3. Is Walls's concern for the welfare of employees consistent with the best interests of the business?
4. How should the owner treat the possibility of increased stress and disruption of family time in reaching a decision on expansion?
5. Can or should such an expansion be financed by borrowing? What advantages or risks would this entail?
6. Should this firm expand to the $3 million revenue level?

MATHER'S HEATING AND AIR CONDITIONING
Selecting and Dealing with Suppliers

Fred Mather operated a small heating and air-conditioning firm that sold and serviced heating and air-conditioning systems. Over the years the firm had changed from primary reliance on one manufacturer—Western Engineering—as the major supplier to a more balanced arrangement involving three suppliers. In the following discussion with a consultant, Fred described some points of friction in dealing with Western Engineering.

Fred: Western Engineering is so big that it can't be customer-oriented. Why, with my firm they've probably lost $600,000 or $700,000 worth of business just because of their inflexibility!

Consultant: They can't bend to take care of your needs?

Fred: Right. They're not flexible. And part of it, of course, is due to the sales reps they have. They just blew the Mather account. We sold Western equipment mostly until we just got disgusted with them.

Consultant: Did the situation just deteriorate over time?

Fred: True. Finally, after a good period of time, I started getting on them. I'm kind of temperamental. I finally just made up my mind—although I didn't tell them—that in the future our policy will be to sell other equipment also. In essence, what we've done since then is sell more Marshall Corporation and Solex equipment than we have Western.

Consultant: What bothered you about Western Engineering?

Fred: It is really a combination of things. The sales rep, for example. Instead of creating a feeling that he was going to try to take care of you and work with you and be for you, he was always on the opposite side of the fence. It was really strange. Western had certain items that were special quotes to help us be competitive. Well, he was always wanting to take different items off the special quote list every time there was a price change. But we needed every item we could get. This is a very competitive area.

Consultant: What other kinds of problems did he create?

Fred: On paperwork, he would not get it done. Let me give you an example about this sign in front of the business. We bought that sign when we bought the business, and we paid Western for it. About a year later, he came back and said, "Western has a new policy. The sign can no longer belong to the owner, so we will return the money you paid for the sign." I said, "Now that you have operated on my money for a year, the sign doesn't belong to me?" I went along with it, but it was the idea of the thing. They tell you one thing and then do something else.

Consultant: Were there other special incidents that occurred?

Fred: One time we got a job involving $30,000 or $40,000 worth of equipment. I told the rep it *appeared* that we had the job. We had a verbal contract, but that wasn't final. The next thing I knew, the equipment was sitting in Central Truck Lines out here. I hadn't ordered the equipment or anything. Fortunately, we did get the contract. But we weren't ready for the equipment for two more months and had no place to put it. And I ended up paying interest. It irritated me to no end.

Consultant: Was that what made you lean toward the other suppliers?

Fred: The final straw was the Park Lake project—a four-story renovation. I had designed the heating and air-conditioning system myself. I called the rep, intending to use Western equipment, and requested a price. So he called back and gave me a lump sum. There were lots of different items, and they were broken down into groups. I asked him to price the items by groups to provide various options to the purchaser. He replied, "We can't break it out." I said, "What do you mean, you can't break it out?" He said something about company policy. I really came unglued, but he never knew.

Consultant: What did you do about it?

Fred: As soon as I quit talking with him, I picked up the phone and called the Marshall Corporation rep. In just a few hours, we had prices that were broken down as I wanted them. The total price turned out to be $2,500 more, but I bought it! That was the end of Western Engineering as sole supplier.

Questions

1. What services did Fred Mather expect from the supplier? Were these unreasonable expectations?

2. Evaluate Fred's reaction when the Western Engineering rep declined to give him a breakdown on the price. Was Fred's decision to pay $2,500 more for the other equipment a rational decision?

3. Was Western Engineering at fault in shipping the large $30,000 or $40,000 order on the basis of an oral commitment and in the absence of an order? What should Fred have done about it?

4. Are the deficiencies that bother Fred caused by weaknesses of Western Engineering or merely the sales rep who sells for them?

5. Should Fred continue to use three separate suppliers or concentrate more purchases with one of them?

STYLE SHOP
A "Tough Guy" Uses Financial and Accounting Information for Decisions

A friend of mine recently said that 1990 is going to be the year of the tough guys, and that's right. It's for guys and gals who care enough to put everything they've got into what they're doing, and do their best. It's not the year for sitting around and letting everyone else do it for them. It's a good year for challenge and productivity because there is still money there, and there are still people who are ready to spend it. It's up to the tough guys, to the ones who merit being the ones with whom that money is spent!

Dorothy Barton, sitting at her desk in the small office just off the Style Shop sales floor, pondered this quotation which happened to catch her eye as she leafed through the latest edition of the *Dallas Fashion Retailer.*

In the women's ready-to-wear business, as in many other businesses, 1989 had been a rough year. It was particularly rough, however, for the attractive, energetic Style Shop owner. Wife and the mother of four teenage daughters, Mrs. Barton saw her sales fall 12.5 percent from 1988 to 1989; but, more significantly, her net profit plunged 62.5 percent over the same time period. She spent untold hours on the sales floor catering to her customers' eye for quality and fashion; in the office appealing to manufacturers to ship the next season's orders even though the current ones were yet to be paid; and at the Dallas Apparel Mart buying just the fashions she hoped would fit the needs and desires of her customers. At the same time, she was spending many hours each week in an effort to help her husband get his infant construction business off the ground.

She remembered hearing one "expert" say, "This is not a time for pessimism, nor a time for optimism. This is a time for realism." And an economic prognosticator had indicated that he saw a good future in the industry, despite the economic slowdown. Buyers, he noted, are working a little more cautiously right now. They are still buying, just looking at things a little more carefully.

"But what is 'realism' for me?" she asked herself. "Am I one of the tough guys who can stick it out and 'merit being the one with whom the money is spent!'?"

STYLE SHOP LOCATION AND BACKGROUND

The Style Shop opened its doors on February 12, 1969, in Lufkin, Texas, and in 1984 it moved to its location in the Angelina Mall. The mall contains a major discount chain store, two full-line department stores, and a number of specialty shops. Located nearby are a twin cinema, motel, and junior college. The mall serves as the hub of a trade area extending over a radius of more than 100 miles. The only centers comparable to the Angelina Mall at the time were as distant as Houston, 120 miles to the southwest, and Dallas, 166 miles to the northwest.

Dorothy Barton began with the Style Shop as a part-time accountant in March 1977. She became a 50-50 partner when the new shop opened

Source: This case was prepared by Janelle C. Ashley, Dean, School of Business, of Stephen F. Austin State University.

in 1984 and purchased the 50 percent belonging to the other partner in January 1989. She operates the business as a sole proprietorship.

THE STYLE SHOP UP TO 1989

Personnel

The Style Shop employed four full-time clerks, one alteration lady, and a maid. A former employee and the teenage daughter of Mrs. Barton were frequently called in for part-time work during peak seasons.

Mrs. Flo Gates had been with the shop for 10 years. She worked as a clerk and floor manager and accompanied Mrs. Barton to market. The other three clerks had been with the Style Shop from one to three years each. Personnel turnover and apathy had been problems in the past, but Mrs. Barton was quite pleased with her present work force.

Policies

The Style Shop operated with no formal, written policies. Personnel were paid wages and benefits comparable to other workers in similar capacities in the city. They enjoyed a great deal of freedom in their work, flexibility in hours of work, and a 20 percent discount on all merchandise purchased in the shop.

Competition

Lufkin had an average number of retail outlets carrying ladies' ready-to-wear for cities of its size. Several department stores and other specialty shops carried some of the same lines as did the Style Shop, but they were all comparable in price. The Style Shop did handle several exclusive lines in Lufkin, however, and enjoyed the reputation of being the most prestigious women's shop in town. Its major competition was a similar, but larger, specialty shop complete with a fashion shoe department in neighboring Nacogdoches, 19 miles away.

Inventory Control

The Style Shop used the services of Santoro Management Consultants, Inc., of Dallas, Texas, for inventory control. IBM inventory management reports were received each month, broken down into 23 departmental groupings. These reports showed beginning inventory, sales and purchases for the month and year to date, markdowns, ending inventory, and various other information. Cost for the services was $110 per month.

Financial Position

It is often quite difficult and sometimes next to impossible to evaluate the "true" financial position of a single proprietorship or a partnership due to the peculiarities that are either allowed or tolerated in accounting practices for these forms of ownership. This is evident in looking at the Style Shop's five-year Comparative Balance Sheets (Figure C20-1), the Comparative Statement of Financial Condition (Figure C20-2), plus a more detailed Statement of Income for 1989 (Figure C20-3) and 1989 Balance Sheet (Figure C20-4). Key business ratios (median) for women's ready-to-wear stores are also given for comparative purposes in Figure C20-5.

Two explanatory comments should be added to these statements. First, the jump in fixed assets between 1985 and 1986 (see Figure C20-2) and the subsequent changes were due in large part to the inclusion of personal real estate on the partnership books. Second, the long-term liability initiated in 1986 was an SBA loan. Caught in a period of declining sales (due in part to the controversy over styles) and rapidly rising expenses in the new mall location, the Style Shop owners found themselves in that proverbial

Figure C20-1 Comparative Statement of Income

Item	1985	1986	1987	1988	1989
Sales..............	$200,845.43	$213,368.15	$216,927.31	$217,969.59	$190,821.85
Cost of sales.........	132,838.30	133,527.91	131,900.84	138,427.14	121,689.74
Gross profit..........	$ 68,007.13	$ 79,840.24	$ 85,026.47	$ 79,542.45	$ 69,132.11
Expenses............	60,727.46	70,051.29	67,151.58	69,969.93	65,438.20
Net Profit............	$ 7,279.67	$ 9,788.95	$ 17,874.89	$ 9,845.52	$ 3,693.91

Figure C20-2 Comparative Balance Sheets

Item	1985	1986	1987	1988	1989
Current assets*...........	$38,524.93	$ 70,015.11	$ 66,749.78	$ 58,530.44	$ 68,458.34
Inventory................	23,039.00	37,971.00	33,803.00	36,923.00	35,228.00
Fixed assets	7,314.58	86,504.94	83,924.45	80,534.06	63,943.67
Total assets............	$45,839.51	$156,520.05	$150,674.23	$139,064.50	$132,402.01
Current liabilities.........	$35,892.81	$ 19,586.45	$ 20,161.93	$ 31,587.57	$ 55,552.70
Long-term liabilities........	0	39,042.90	33,680.07	26,841.76	20,003.45
Total liabilities............	$35,892.81	$ 58,629.35	$ 53,842.00	$ 58,429.33	$ 75,556.15
Net worth................	9,946.70	97,890.70	96,832.23	80,635.17	56,845.86
Total....................	$45,839.51	$156,520.05	$150,674.23	$139,064.50	$132,402.01

*Current-asset values include the amounts shown for inventory.

Figure C20-3   Statement of Income

Style Shop
Statement of Income
For Year Ended Dec. 31, 1989

Sales		$190,821.85
Cost of goods sold:		
Beginning inventory	$ 36,923.00	
Purchases	119,994.74	
	$156,917.74	
Ending inventory	35,228.00	121,689.74
Gross profit		$ 69,132.11
Expenses:		
Advertising	$ 3,034.63	
Auto expense	1,509.63	
Bad debts	(439.83)	
Depreciation	1,580.49	
Freight, express, delivery	2,545.90	
Heat, light, power, and water	1,847.96	
Insurance	1,431.80	
Interest expense	4,064.25	
Legal and accounting	2,034.74	
Rent	11,220.40	
Repairs	528.98	
Salary	26,227.69	
Suppliers	5,138.11	
Tax—Payroll	1,656.18	
Income tax	604.62	
Telephone	784.67	
Dues and subscriptions	601.89	
Travel	1,066.09	65,438.20
Net profit		$ 3,693.91

"financial bind" in late 1984 and 1985. They needed additional funds both for working capital and fixed investments. Since a big jump in sales was anticipated in the new location, additional working capital was necessary to purchase the required inventory. The new tenants also desired fixed-asset money to purchase display fixtures for their new store. They obtained this money through a local bank in the form of an SBA-insured loan.

THE STYLE SHOP, 1990

"Certainly there is no longer an arbiter of the length of a skirt or the acceptance of different styles," Mrs. Barton mused. "The economic picture is looking brighter. The experts tell us there will be more disposable personal income and a lower rate of inflation. Yet this is a time for 'realism.' Am I a 'tough guy'?"

Figure C20-4   Statement of Financial Condition

Style Shop
Balance Sheet
December 31, 1989

ASSETS

Current assets:		
Cash on hand and in banks		$ 4,923.92
Accounts receivable		21,306.42
Inventory		35,228.00
Cash value—Life insurance		7,000.00
Total current assets		$ 68,458.34
Fixed assets:		
Furniture and fixtures and leasehold improvements	$27,749.94	
Less: Allowance for depreciation	9,806.27	$ 17,943.67
Auto and truck		9,500.00
Real estate		20,000.00
Furniture		10,000.00
Boat and motor		2,000.00
Office equipment		2,500.00
Jewelry		2,000.00
Total fixed assets		$ 63,943.67
TOTAL ASSETS		$132,402.01

LIABILITIES AND NET WORTH

Current liabilities:	
Accounts payable	$ 30,413.12
Accrued payroll tax	825.64
Accrued sales tax	1,193.94
Note payable—Due in one year	9,420.00
Note payable—Lot	10,700.00
Note payable—Auto	3,000.00
Total current liabilities	$ 55,552.70
Note payable—Due after one year	20,003.45
Total liabilities	$ 75,556.15
Net worth	56,845.86
TOTAL LIABILITIES AND NET WORTH	$132,402.01

Figure C20-5   Key Business Ratios for Women's Ready-to-Wear Stores

Ratio	1989	1988	1987	1986	1985
Current assets ÷ Current liabilities...................	2.65X	2.81X	2.51X	2.38X	2.50X
Net profit ÷ Net sales	2.05%	2.30%	1.81%	1.86%	2.18%
Net profit ÷ Net worth	8.92%	8.53%	6.86%	7.14%	8.73%
Net sales ÷ Total assets	3.82X	3.96X	3.95X	3.76X	3.78X
Net sales ÷ Net working capital......................	4.61X	4.92X	4.73X	4.90X	4.49X
Net sales ÷ Inventory..	6.70X	6.70X	6.60X	6.70X	6.10X
Net sales ÷ Fixed assets.................................	12.0X	11.0X	12.5X	12.0X	11.5X
Current liabilities ÷ Net worth.........................	49.4%	49.2%	51.0%	54.5%	56.5%
Total liabilities ÷ Net worth.............................	98.50	100.10	104.00	124.10	125.80
Inventory ÷ Net working capital......................	73.0%	72.3%	76.7%	71.1%	78.3%

Note: Collection period not computed. Necessary information as to the division between cash sales and credit sales was available in too few cases to obtain an average collection period usable as a broad guide.

Questions

1. Using Style Shop's comparative financial statements for 1985–1989, evaluate:
   a. the firm's liquidity
   b. the company's profitability
   c. the firm's use of debt financing
   d. the return on equity

2. Why are we unable to use the "four-question" approach exactly as suggested in Chapter 20? What modifications were required?

3. Should Mrs. Barton have kept the business or sold it? What are the primary factors to be considered in reaching such a decision?

BARTON SALES AND SERVICE
Managing the Firm's Working Capital

Barton Sales and Service was located in Little Rock, Arkansas. Its owners were John and Joyce Barton. John served as general manager, and Joyce as office manager. The firm sold General Electric, Carrier, and York air-conditioning and heating systems and serviced these and other types of systems as well. It served both commercial and residential customers. Although the business had operated successfully since the Bartons purchased it five years earlier, it continued to experience working-capital problems.

BARTON'S FINANCIAL STRUCTURE

The firm had been profitable since the Bartons purchased it. Profits for 1989 were the highest for any year to date. Figure C21-1 shows the income statement for that year.

The balance sheet as of December 31, 1989, for Barton Sales and Service is shown in Figure C21-2. Note that the firm's equity was somewhat less than its total debt. However, $51,231 of the firm's liabilities was a long-term note carrying a modest rate of interest. This note was issued at the time the Bartons purchased the business, and the payments were made to the former owner.

BARTON'S CASH BALANCE

A minimum cash balance is necessary in any business because of the uneven nature of cash inflows and outflows. John explained that they needed a substantial amount in order to "feel comfortable." He felt that it might be possible to reduce the present balance by $5,000 to $10,000, but he stated that it gave them some "breathing room."

BARTON'S ACCOUNTS RECEIVABLE

The trade accounts receivable at the end of 1989 were $56,753, but at some times during the year the accounts receivable were twice this amount.

Figure C21-1   Barton Sales and Service Income Statement for the Year Ended December 31, 1989

Sales..	$727,679
Less: Cost of sales...	466,562
Gross profit	$261,177
Less: Selling, general & administrative expenses (including officers' salaries)...........	189,031
Income before taxes	$ 72,086
Provision for income taxes...	17,546
Net income...	$ 54,540

Figure C21-2   Barton Sales and Service Balance Sheet as of December 31, 1989

ASSETS

Current assets:

Cash	$ 28,789
Trade accounts receivable	56,753
Inventory	89,562
Prepaid expenses	4,415
Total current assets	$179,519
Loans to stockholders	41,832
Autos, trucks, and equipment, at cost, less accumulated depreciation of $36,841	24,985
Other assets—Goodwill	16,500
TOTAL ASSETS	$262,836

LIABILITIES AND STOCKHOLDERS' EQUITY

Current liabilities:

Current maturities of long-term notes payable (see Note 1)	$ 26,403
Trade accounts payable	38,585
Accrued payroll taxes	2,173
Accrued income taxes	13,818
Other accrued expenses	4,001
Total current liabilities	$ 84,980
Long-term notes payable (see Note 1)	51,231
Stockholders' equity	126,625
TOTAL LIABILITIES AND STOCKHOLDERS' EQUITY	$262,836

Note 1: Current and long-term portions of notes payable

		Current	Long-Term	Total
(1)	10% note payable, secured by pickup, due in monthly installments of $161 including interest	$ 1,827	$ 1,367	$ 3,194
(2)	10% note payable, secured by equipment, due in monthly installments of $180 including interest	584	0	584
(3)	6% note payable, secured by inventory and equipment, due in monthly installments of $678 including interest	6,392	39,127	45,519
(4)	9% notes payable to stockholders	0	10,737	10,737
(5)	12% note payable to bank in 30 days	17,600	0	17,600
		$26,231	$51,231	$77,634

These accounts were not aged, so the firm had no specific knowledge of the number of overdue accounts. However, the firm had never experienced any significant loss from bad debts. The accounts receivable were thought, therefore, to be good accounts of a relatively recent nature.

Customers were given 30 days from the date of the invoice to pay the net amount. No cash discounts were offered. If payment was not received during the first 30 days, a second statement was mailed to the customer and monthly carrying charges of one tenth of 1 percent were added. The state usury law prohibited higher carrying charges.

On small residential jobs, the firm tried to collect from customers when work was completed. When a service representative finished repairing an air-conditioning system, for example, the rep presented a bill to the owner and attempted to obtain payment at that time. However, this was not always possible. On major items such as unit changeouts—which often ran as high as $2,500—billing was practically always necessary.

On new construction projects, the firm sometimes received partial payments prior to completion of a project. This helped to minimize the amount tied up in receivables.

BARTON'S INVENTORY

Inventory accounted for a substantial portion of the firm's working capital. It consisted of the various heating and air-conditioning units, parts, and supplies used in the business.

The Bartons had no guidelines or industry standards to use in evaluating their overall inventory levels. They felt that there *might* be some excessive inventory, but, in the absence of a standard, this was basically an opinion. When pressed to estimate the amount that might be eliminated by careful control, John pegged it at 15 percent.

The firm used an annual physical inventory that coincided with the end of its fiscal year.

Since the inventory level was known for only one time in the year, the income statement could be prepared only on an annual basis. There was no way of knowing how much of the inventory was expended at other points and thus no way to calculate profits. As a result, the Bartons lacked quarterly or monthly income statements to assist them in managing the business.

Barton Sales and Service was considering changing from a physical inventory to a perpetual inventory system. This would enable John to know the inventory levels of all items at all times. An inventory total could easily be computed for use in preparing statements. Shifting to a perpetual inventory system would require the purchase of proper file equipment, but that cost was not large enough to constitute a major barrier. A greater expense would be involved in the maintenance of the system—entering all incoming materials and all withdrawals. The Bartons estimated that this task would necessitate the work of one person on a half-time or three-fourths time basis.

BARTON'S NOTE PAYABLE TO THE BANK

Bank borrowing was the most costly form of credit. Barton Sales and Service paid the going rate, slightly above prime, and owed $17,600. The note was a 90-day renewable note. Normally some was paid on the principal when the note was renewed. The total borrowing could probably be increased if necessary. There was no obvious pressure from the bank to reduce borrowing to zero. The amount borrowed during the year typically ranged from $10,000 to $25,000.

The Bartons had never explored the limits the bank might impose on borrowing, and there was no clearly specified line of credit. When additional funds were required, Joyce simply dropped by the bank, spoke with a bank officer, and signed a note for the appropriate amount.

BARTON'S TRADE ACCOUNTS PAYABLE

A significant amount of Barton's working capital came from its trade accounts payable. Although accounts payable at the end of 1989 were $38,585, the total payable varied over time and might be double this amount at another point in the year. Barton obtained from various dealers such supplies as expansion valves, copper tubing, sheet metal, electrical wire, electrical conduit, and so on. Some suppliers offered a discount for cash (2/10, n/30), but Joyce felt the credit was more important than the few dollars that could be saved by taking a cash discount. By giving up the cash discount, the firm obtained the use of the money for 30 days. Although the Bartons might wait a few days beyond the 30 days before paying, their suppliers quickly applied pressure. The Bartons could stretch the payment dates to 45 or even 60 days before being "put on C.O.D." However, they found it unpleasant to delay payment more than 45 days because suppliers would begin calling and applying pressure for payment.

The major manufacturers (Carrier, General Electric, and York) used different terms of payment. Some major products could be obtained from Carrier on an arrangement known as "floor planning." This meant that the manufacturer (Carrier) shipped the products without requiring immediate payment. The Bartons made payment only when the product was sold. If still unsold after 90 days, the product had to be returned or paid for. (It was shipped back on a company truck, so there was no expense in returning unsold items.) On items that were not floor-planned but were purchased from Carrier, Barton paid the net amount by the 10th of the month or was charged 18 percent interest on late payments.

Shipments from General Electric required payment at the bank soon after receipt of the products. If cash was not available at the time, this necessitated further borrowing from the bank.

Purchases from York required net payment without discount within 30 days. However, if payment was not made within 30 days, interest at 18 percent per annum was added.

CAN GOOD PROFITS BECOME BETTER?

Although Barton Sales and Service had earned a *good* profit in 1989, the Bartons wondered whether they were realizing the *most possible* profit. The slowness in construction was slowing their business somewhat. They wanted to be sure they were meeting the challenging times as prudently as possible.

Questions

1. Evaluate the overall performance and financial structure of Barton Sales and Service.
2. What are the strengths and weaknesses in this firm's management of accounts receivable and inventory?
3. Should the firm reduce or expand its bank borrowing?
4. Evaluate Barton's management of trade accounts payable.
5. Calculate Barton's "cash conversion period." Interpret your computation.
6. How can Barton Sales and Service improve its working-capital situation?

WILLINGHAM COURSES, INC.
Capital Budgeting: Basic Techniques

Willingham Courses, Inc., founded by Ron Willingham in 1972, has dealt primarily in personal and professional motivational courses, particularly for corporate employees. Most recently, the firm has focused on development material to be used to prepare a company's sales force to be more effective in their efforts.

At the present time, extensive thought and effort have been given to developing a new sales program. The course material, titled *Integrity Selling*, provides an approach to selling based on a clear identification of the customer's legitimate needs. Willingham has identified a strong potential market for such a course among the Fortune 500 firms to be used in training their sales personnel. In visiting with the sales executives of several of these companies, he has received commitments to purchase the course. However, he is reluctant to begin selling the program before investigating the merits of the two possible strategies. Specifically, questions still remain concerning the expected life of the instructional material and the marketing strategy.

In analyzing the prospects of the investment, Willingham considers the basic product to have an expected life of approximately five years (Strategy A). However, this estimate could be significantly lengthened by undertaking a major revision in the course package in the fifth year (Strategy B). The options under consideration may be summarized as follows:

- *Strategy A:* The first strategy requires an investment at the present time totaling $300,000. This amount would provide the necessary funds for course development and production equipment ($250,000) as well as working capital requirements of $50,000. The working capital portion of the investment may be liquidated upon the termination of the course. The expected life of the project is five years.

- *Strategy B:* The second strategy involves a two-phase investment in which the initial investment of $350,000 is committed ($250,000 in course development and equipment plus $100,000 of working capital), but $200,000 must also be expended on course development at the conclusion of the fifth year. This investment would result in substantive modifications and improvements in the program. While time is of the essence in going to the market, within the next few years several major improvements in educational equipment are expected. Such a two-phase investment would allow the firm to reap the benefits of these developments.

To sum up, the management is considering two basic approaches for promoting *Integrity Selling:* (1) a concentrated effort whose intent is to saturate the market during a five-year period (Strategy A); (2) an extended investment in *Integrity Selling* with the prolonged life being the result of a major revamping of the course structure in the fifth year (Strategy B).

The estimates of the annual receipts and operations expenses for the two strategies are given in Figure C22-1.

Additional information relevant to the situation is as follows:

Figure C22-1   Ron Willingham Courses, Inc. Estimated Annual Receipts and Operational Expense

	Sales	
Year	**Plan A**	**Plan B**
1	$100,000	$ 75,000
2	300,000	125,000
3	450,000	200,000
4	450,000	280,000
5	450,000	350,000
6		475,000
7		500,000
8		500,000
9		500,000
10		500,000

	Marketing Expenses per Year	
Year(s)	**Plan A**	**Plan B**
1–5	$ 35,000	$ 25,000
6–7		25,000
8–9		25,000
10		25,000

1. The production of the material will require the use of a portion of an existing plant not included in the cost of the investment. This part of the plant, which represents excess floor space, could be considered to have a book value of $150,000 and a corresponding annual depreciation of $10,000 per year. However, this segment of the plant is not used presently and could not be used otherwise, owing to the floor plan of the building.

2. Cost of goods sold of similar programs has generally been a variable cost approximating 60 percent of sales.

3. Administrative expenses for the company will be $10,000 annually, which has been the level of administrative expenses for the past year. However, only $4,000 of this amount will be allocated via the cost accounting system to the new program.

4. The bank has agreed to finance $100,000 of the investment at an interest rate of 10 per-

cent, with the interest being payable yearly and the principal coming due at the end of the project life.

5. The company's tax rate is 30 percent, and it uses straight-line depreciation (no salvage) for all expenditures. Assume that the cost of course development, equipment and plant expenditures will be depreciated over the life of the project, while the cost of the working capital is not depreciated, but any working capital will be recovered at the end of the project.

Questions

1. Compute the annual after-tax cash flows for the two plans.

2. Compute the net present value and the internal rate of return for each plan, assuming a cost of capital of 12 percent.

3. Which course of action should be taken by the firm? Explain.

FRANKLIN MOTORS
Selecting a Computer System

Franklin Motors, a new and used car dealer, currently uses a computer service bureau for limited data processing including payroll and general ledger accounting applications. The service bureau provides either payroll checks or electronic direct deposits for the employees of Franklin. At the end of the year, W-2 tax statements are provided for the employees. The software of the service bureau is programmed to produce a profit/loss statement and a balance sheet only once a quarter. All other data processing tasks are currently done manually.

Until now, the management of Franklin Motors did not think they could afford either the computer hardware, software, or personnel necessary to run their own in-house system. Several factors have caused the management to reconsider owning a computer system. First, Franklin's primary supplier has requested that Franklin obtain the necessary technology for placing orders and checking stock availability electronically. This would require at least one personal computer with a modem for communicating data to the manufacturer through a standard telephone line. Second, the accounting reports from the service bureau are often so late that they are useless in planning and budgeting decisions. Management feels that the timeliness and accuracy of important reports would be faster if the work were done in house. The cost of a multiuser system has dropped so substantially that even small businesses can afford them. The newer computer systems require fewer technical employees than the older systems.

The management of Franklin Motors decided that the controller, Bob Mathis, would head a team to conduct a feasibility study and to evaluate the alternative solutions. The feasibility study showed that the company had a desperate need for a new information system for management and clerical employees. Mathis's team narrowed the computer vendor choices to two firms. Each of the competing firms offered a "turnkey" system including installation, training, and an 800 telephone number for troubleshooting problems. A turnkey computer system is supposed to be like a new car in that you merely have to turn the key in order to use it. One of the systems is based on using a centralized minicomputer with multiple terminals. The terminals were simply input devices that rely upon the central processing unit (CPU) of the minicomputer. The other vendor configured a local area network (LAN) of personal computers. The personal computers in the network could be used either as input devices for the management information system of the car dealership or as stand-alone computers with their own processors. The LAN solution would allow the use of popular personal computer software such as word processors, spreadsheets, and desktop publishing.

The vendor proposing the minicomputer solution has several installations of the same system with excellent recommendations. The vendor proposing the LAN solution has only one installation, since it is based on newer technology. The LAN-based system did not receive as good a recommendation as the minicomputer vendor's system. The LAN vendor explained that the system was being tested and corrected in a live environment for the first time. Many of the problems with the LAN system had been corrected and should not pose a problem with the second installation. The costs of the two systems are practically the same.

Questions

1. Which alternative should Bob Mathis recommend to management and why?

2. What problems will occur as a result of acquiring an in-house computer system, and how can these problems be headed off or managed?

FOX MANUFACTURING
Responding to Disaster

The end of the workday on May 12, 1990, was like any other—or so Dale Fox thought when he closed up shop for the night. But 12 hours later, an electrical fire destroyed Fox Manufacturing Inc.'s only plant, in Albuquerque, N.M. The damage exceeded $1.5 million.

"It was the largest fire New Mexico had seen in years. About 37 fire trucks were at the scene trying to put out the fire. We made local and national news," recalls Fox, president of the family-owned manufacturer and retailer of southwestern-style and contemporary furniture. The fire was especially devastating since all orders from the company's three showrooms are sent to the plant. Normally, the furniture is built and delivered 10 to 12 weeks later.

Such a disaster could force many companies out of business. But just eight weeks after the fire, the first piece of furniture rolled off the Fox assembly line in a brand new plant in a new building. The company even managed to increase sales that horrible year. And now, just three years later, the company has emerged stronger than ever. Annual sales average between $3.5 million and $5 million.

How did Fox Manufacturing manage literally to rise from the ashes? By forging an aggressive recovery plan that focused not only on rebuilding the business, but also on using the untapped skills of employees and an intensive customer relations campaign. Indeed, with more than $1 million in unfilled orders at the time of the fire, Fox offered extra services to retain his customer base.

Dale Fox also took advantage of his unusually close relationships with his financial and legal experts to help him manage the thicket of legal and insurance problems that arose.

Painfully aware that another disaster could strike at any time, Fox now takes disaster preparation to a justified extreme. He doesn't leave anything to chance; he takes numerous safety precautions that should make it easier for the company to rebound should it be dealt a similar setback again.

Other companies would do well to follow his lead. After all, what happened to Fox Manufacturing can happen to any company. Witness the damage done to businesses by the violent hurricanes and tornadoes that recently ripped through parts of Florida, Louisiana, and Kansas, as well as the Hawaiian island of Kauai.

RISING FROM THE ASHES

Recovering from this disaster, and getting the company up and running again, was a particularly grueling experience. Having to complete the monumental task in just eight weeks added to the pressure. "We had no choice," says Fox. "Because we had more than $1 million in orders, we had to get back in production quickly so we wouldn't lose that business."

Fox found himself working up to 20 hours a day, seven days a week. One of his first tasks was finding a new building to house his manufactur-

Source: Don Nichols, "Back in Business," *Small Business Report,* Vol. 18, No. 3 (March 1993), pp. 55–60. Reprinted, by permission of publisher, from SMALL BUSINESS REPORT, March/1993 © 1993. American Management Association, New York. All rights reserved.

ing facility. Remodeling the old site—and the requisite tasks of clearing debris, rebuilding, and settling claims with the insurance companies—would take too long and hold up the production of new furniture. At the same time, however, he had to quickly replace all the manufacturing equipment lost in the fire. He decided to hit the road, attending auctions and other sales across the country in search of manufacturing equipment, including sanders, glue machines, molding machines, and table saws. Unfortunately, all the company's hand-drawn furniture designs and cushion patterns also perished in the fire and had to be redrawn because no backup copies existed.

To meet the challenge, here's what Fox did.

Tapped the Full Talent of All Employees

Although Fox initially laid off most of his hourly workers, he put the company's 15 supervisors to work building new work tables that would be needed once manufacturing resumed. They did the work at an empty facility loaned to Fox by a friend. At the same time, the company's draftsmen—working in a rented garage—started redrawing the furniture designs, this time using a computer. (It took nearly a year to redraw all the designs lost in the fire.) To check frame configurations and measurements, they had to tear apart showroom furniture. A handful of hourly employees also started tearing apart cushions to redraw the patterns.

When Fox found the new building—the former home of a beer distributor—two weeks after the fire, he started rehiring the 65-plus hourly employees to help with the remodeling. Fox knew what construction skills—such as carpentry, plumbing, metalworking and painting—they had to offer because the day he laid them off he had them fill out a form listing such skills.

His reasoning: "If I had gone through the process of having contractors bid on the work, we never would have reopened as fast as we did. Plus, our employees needed the work to feed their families," says Fox.

Within five weeks of the fire, Fox had rehired most employees. The employees, who were paid the same hourly rate they earned before the fire, proved to be competent and cooperative. Like Fox, they often worked up to 20 hours a day because they knew their boss's ambitious timetable for reopening.

Stayed in Close Contact with Customers

Fox's salespeople started calling customers the day of the fire to explain what had happened and assure them the company planned to bounce back quickly. Just days later, Fox's two sons called the same customers to reinforce that message and let them know that the Fox family appreciated their patience. In subsequent weeks, customers received three or four more calls or letters that updated them on the company's progress. Fox even rented billboard space in Albuquerque to advertise that the company planned to be manufacturing furniture again soon.

"If we hadn't kept in such close contact with our customers, we probably would have lost 50 percent of the orders," Fox says. But Fox's strategy paid off handsomely; the company lost less than 3 percent of its pre-fire orders. That's an amazingly low percentage, especially considering that some customers had to wait up to 36 weeks for delivery, instead of the usual 10 to 12 weeks.

Customers had good reason to be patient. When they place their orders, all customers are required to pay a 25 percent to 33 percent deposit. After the fire, as a goodwill gesture, the company agreed to pay them 1 percent per month on the deposited money until their orders were filled. To calculate his customers' interest, Fox started from the order date, not the fire date. And rather than simply deduct the interest from the final amount due, Fox wrote each customer a check, so they could see exactly how much money they had earned.

Because Fox also kept his suppliers informed, most of them continued filling the company's orders after the fire and told Fox not to worry about paying until his operation was in full swing again. "Factors were the only people we had any problem with," says Fox. "Once they found out about the fire, they wanted money that wasn't even due yet."

Relied Heavily on the Expertise of Professionals

During a normal year, Fox pays his CPA and lawyer to handle tasks such as tax planning and consulting on leases, insurance, and operations. Together, their bills run about $25,000 to $30,000. The year of the fire, however, Fox Manufacturing's accounting bill topped $50,000; the legal bill, $75,000. As far as Fox is concerned, it was money well spent: "Without their help, I couldn't have gotten back in business as quickly as I did."

Fox called his CPA and his lawyer as soon as he got news of the Saturday-morning fire. While the firemen battled the blaze, the three met with key management employees to develop a comeback plan. During subsequent weeks, his accountant and lawyer assumed so much responsibility for valuing lost assets and haggling with the insurance company that Fox felt comfortable leaving the city to travel around the country buying manufacturing equipment.

One decision that was made early on was to apply for a $1-million loan to buy the new building. The CPA put together all the paperwork necessary for the bank to approve it—such as a financial analysis, a cash flow statement and profit projections. He also played a key role in helping Fox's in-house accountant determine the value of the inventory, machinery, and work in progress destroyed in the fire, which totaled about $800,000.

His involvement lent credibility to the numbers that were generated, which quelled any concerns or doubts that the insurance companies

had. "It was very important to have an outside CPA firm verify the numbers. If we had tried to just throw some numbers together ourselves, we could have been in over our heads in arguments with insurance companies," Fox says.

Even so, settling insurance claims was difficult, and that's where Fox's lawyer earned his money. For example, what the insurance company thought it would cost to replace the old plant was less than half of what Fox claimed. One figure over which they disagreed was the cost of replacing the electrical wiring. The insurance company estimated that it would cost $30,000; Fox and his lawyer insisted it would cost $120,000. The lawyer had a local electrician familiar with the Fox plant verify that Fox's estimate was accurate. The insurance company finally settled the claim at Fox's value.

"Dealing with the insurance company was a constant battle. There are a lot of things they won't tell you unless you bring it up," Fox warns. Indeed, it was his lawyer, not the insurance company, who pointed out that Fox was entitled to $25,000 for the cost of cleaning away debris and $2,000 to replace shrubbery that was destroyed.

And even after they settled the claim on Fox's business-interruption insurance, it took much longer than expected to get the final $750,000 payment. Fox finally had to call his insurance company with an ultimatum: "If I didn't get the check, I told them my lawyer and I were going to Santa Fe the next day to a file a formal complaint with the insurance commissioner. I got the check."

Questions

1. Do you think Fox was wise in carrying a business-interruption policy? Why?
2. What specific fire-prevention tactics would have possibly helped Fox avoid some of its losses?
3. Do you believe the customer relations steps taken were necessary? Why or why not?
4. What other actions would you recommend Fox take to prepare for the possiblity of another fire?

JOHNSON UTILITY TRAILER, INC.
The Cost of Acting Ethically

It was a disappointingly damp spring afternoon. Instead of lifting, the fog was getting heavier. It was beginning to look like the kind of fog that Hollywood uses in scenes when bad news is at hand.

And bad news was at hand—but this was the outskirts of Des Moines, Iowa, not Hollywood—and it was happening to Steve Johnson, founder and owner of Johnson Utility Trailer, Inc. Here he was, on a Sunday afternoon, at his son's fifteenth birthday party, sitting in his avocado kitchen with his parents, his wife and his son. And he was looking at his worn-out corduroys, his wife's grey sweat suit, the cake and melting ice cream, wondering how he should break the news.

After his son opened the last present—a pair of tennis shoes that cost *how* much?—and left to join his friends, Steve knew that if he were a character in a B-movie, he would be able to hear the drum roll in the background. He said, "This is a bad time to talk shop, but there probably isn't going to be a better time to tell you about what happened last week."

Martha, his wife, stiffened and sat up perfectly straight. "I'm glad you're going to tell us. You've been pretty grouchy lately, and I knew there was something wrong."

Steve looked down at his coffee cup. "Last Wednesday, one of the trailers that we made in '86 came in for maintenance. One of the guys told me that the joint between the tongue and the trailer looked weak. He was right. It *was* weak."

The word *weak* settled into the quiet of the kitchen for several moments. Then Lars, Steve's father, asked, "But didn't you start using bigger bolts there a few years ago?"

"In '87, we started using three-eighths-inch bolts instead of quarter-inch bolts. We should have put them in from the start. It was stupid not to. I can't even remember why we didn't. They cost almost nothing more."

"But those first bolts met all the specs, didn't they?" Lars asked.

"Of course they did. Don't you remember the week I spent reading six volumes of SAE standards? I almost went blind. Before I hired anybody, I made sure everything met every standard."

Steve's mother, Barbara, said, "Let me see if I understand what you men are talking about. The joint between the trailer and the tongue is wearing out in one of your older models and you could have prevented it by using a bigger bolt, but you didn't. But everything wears out. What's the big deal? You have always been such a worrier, Stevie."

"What if it breaks while it's being pulled uphill? It could slam into the next car and kill someone. That's a big deal."

"But honey, don't you have safety chains?"

"The safety chains go in *front* of the joint, Mom. They keep the coupler from breaking off the hitch, but they don't keep the tongue from breaking off the trailer."

Steve stood up, walked over to the kitchen window and looked toward his shop. It was a big

Source: Catherine Stover, "How Ethical Can I Afford to Be?" *Small Business Forum*, Vol. 9, No. 1 (Spring 1991), pp. 6–10.

grey building that always shimmered in Steve's dreams. "How could I live with that?" He turned back toward the table. "One lawsuit could shut this place down."

"Would it be our fault?" Martha asked.

"We say in three different places that the trailer's limit is 1,000 pounds. I'm sure the joint would be okay if everyone did that. The reason we started using bigger bolts in '87 was because we saw that people were rough with the trailers or were overloading like idiots. You wouldn't believe what people put in trailers. And they drive like they're in the Indy 500."

Martha asked, "The trailer that you saw last Wednesday—had it been overloaded or something?"

"I told the owner that I thought his trailer looked heavily used. He said that he drives over railroad tracks twice every day on his route. He looks like the kind of guy who wouldn't slow down. This trailer wasn't designed to hit railroad tracks at 60 miles per hour twice every day."

"So is it ready to fall apart?" Martha asked. Martha always spoke quickly, and today it annoyed Steve.

"He has a good maintenance record. But when anyone brings a trailer in, we always check the components."

"Components?" Barbara asked.

"The chain, the coupler, and the joint between the tongue and the trailer. All high stress points."

"Are the other two components okay?" Martha asked.

"They're fine. The chains are tested to break at three times their rating. The coupler is at two times. Now the joint is at two, but it wasn't before."

Barbara said, "So the joint wasn't as strong as the rest. It was the weakest part."

"Right. And it didn't have to be stronger, to meet the standards. It just made sense to upgrade it after I saw that people didn't take the 1,000-pound limit seriously. It never said anywhere in the standards that all the components have to be equally upgraded. It just made sense

to me to strengthen the weakest one."

"You have insurance, don't you?" Lars asked.

"Of course I do. But I never told the insurance company that in 1987 I decided to improve the joint. What if they say, 'You used to make inferior trailers so we won't cover those.' What if they say, 'Your old trailers are not safe and it's your own damn fault'?"

Steve's father cleared his throat. "Everyone makes mistakes. In the 30 years that I ran my business, I learned a lot along the way by making my fair share of mistakes. Lay all your cards on the table and we'll look at your options. First of all, has anyone ever filed a complaint?"

"No."

"Anyone ever bring the joint in for repairs?"

"No. We spotted this one by ourselves."

"You don't think this will happen to the trailers you made since you started using the bigger bolt in '87?"

"I'm confident it won't."

"You opened in '86 right? How many trailers did you make before you improved the joint?"

"I looked it up. We made the change on November 13th, and we had manufactured 916 trailers before that."

"Do you have all those addresses?"

"Yeah. But probably a third or a fourth of the trailers have been resold. And some of the people have moved. It won't be easy to track them down."

"Tracking them down probably won't be the worst part or the most expensive part," Lars said. "The worst part will be disrupting your business so you can make the repairs. And you have to decide if you will cover the owner's cost of bringing the trailer in."

"We can't afford to do that," Martha said quickly. "Remember, we have twelve people on our payroll. Cash is tight. And if the recession hits Iowa the way they say it's hitting the coasts, our cash flow is going to only get tighter."

Barbara said, "Martha, honey, I know this business means a lot to you too. Men tend to think their wives—"

Figure C25-1   Profit and Loss Statements

Johnson Utility Trailer, Inc.[1]
Comparative Profit and Loss Statements
For the Years Ended December 31

	1986[2]	1987	1988	1989	1990
NET BILLINGS	$116,230	$289,097	$458,903	$609,733	$681,283
COST OF GOODS					
Beg. finished goods inventory	-0-	$101,050	$133,710	$ 65,507	$ 29,597
Cost of goods mfg.	184,198	220,955	249,222	396,758	481,989
Goods available	$184,198	$322,005	$382,932	$462,265	$511,586
End. finished goods inventory	101,050	133,710	65,507	29,597	18,539
COST OF GOODS SOLD	$ 83,148	$188,295	$317,425	$432,668	$493,047
GROSS PROFIT	$ 33,082	$100,802	$141,478	$177,065	$188,236
OPERATING EXPENSES					
Selling	$ 16,871	$ 44,107	$ 60,178	$ 77,470	$ 98,844
Administrative	14,632	32,244	51,548	72,162	81,240
EARNINGS BEFORE TAX	$ 1,579	$ 24,451	$ 29,752	$ 27,433	$ 8,152
PROVISION FOR INC. TAX	$ 505	$7,717	$9,666	$9,362	$ 2,420
NET INCOME	$ 1,074	$ 16,734	$ 20,086	$ 18,071	$ 5,732

[1]A Sub-chapter S Corporation having filed articles of incorporation with the State of Iowa 1 March 1986.
[2]1986 figures are for 10 months.

"Let me tell you exactly what my position on this is," Martha said. "We have worked 12 hours a day, six days a week for five years so that we could have a profitable business to pass along to Zachary. We can't put all that in jeopardy just because some idiot *might* overload his trailer, or *might* go 60 miles per hour over railroad tracks every day, and then *might* sue us because the tongue comes off! It would be his own fault! Besides, it would be just as likely to break in his own driveway as it would going up a hill in front of a station wagon full of kids."

"Honey, you might be absolutely right. It may be that nothing would ever go wrong. It also may be that if we send out letters that say, 'Guess what? Your trailer might break,' that we might be *increasing* our chances of getting sued. But we have to do the right thing."

"The right thing? You want to do the right thing?" Martha lowered her voice to a whisper. "Then make sure you can stay in business and pay your employees and have something besides debt to passs along to your son."

When she left the room, there was silence.

Finally, Lars said, "Steve, I'm sorry if I upset Mar—"

"Don't worry about it. She'll cool off. She's mad that I didn't go to her right away and talk with her alone about it first."

"Of course she is," Barbara said. "But she's also worried about Zack. She told me yesterday that she has a hard time justifying all the hours

Figure C25-2   Balance Sheets

Johnson Utility Trailer, Inc.
Comparative Balance Sheets
As of December 31

	1986	1987	1988	1989	1990
			ASSETS		
Current Assets:					
Cash	$ 381	$ 4,261	$ 5,009	$ 3,617	$ 984
A/R, Net	$9,685	$24,091	$ 47,802	$ 58,432	$ 64,722
Inventories:					
Finished goods	$101,050	$133,710	$ 65,507	$ 29,597	$ 18,539
Work in progress	8,328	14,228	14,786	13,253	14,709
Raw materials	10,631	7,609	8,885	12,601	15,761
Total Current	$130,075	$183,899	$141,989	$117,500	$114,715
Total Long-Term/Fixed	$ 78,088	$ 85,941	$129,971	$160,638	$126,874
Total Assets	$208,163	$269,840	$271,960	$278,138	$293,486
			LIABILITIES		
Current	$133,132	$183,172	$149,838	$115,735	$138,267
Long-Term	63,957	58,860	74,228	96,438	83,522
Total Liabilities	$197,089	$242,032	$224,066	$212,173	$221,789
			EQUITY		
Capital Stock	$ 10,000	$ 10,000	$ 10,000	$ 10,000	$ 10,000
Retained Earnings	1,074	17,808	37,894	55,965	61,697
Total Equity	$ 11,074	$ 27,808	$ 47,894	$ 65,965	$ 71,697
Total Liability & Equity	$208,163	$269,840	$271,960	$278,138	$293,486

she has spent doing the books instead of keeping an eye on Zack. Sometimes teenagers—well, we can talk about that later."

Steve sat down and looked at his father. "Dad, what should I do?"

"If I were you, I'd have a very frank discussion with the best product liability attorney I could find. And I would meet with your insurance man and find out what your coverage is exactly. And I would also be prepared to make some tough management decisions. If you are having cash flow problems now, you better get your house in order. The only thing we know for sure is that tough times are ahead."

Barbara started cleaning the kitchen table. She stopped long enough to stand behind her son and rub his shoulders. Steve listened to her bracelets hit each other. "This always helps your father," she said. "It seems like the end of the world now, but I'm sure you'll do the right thing, Stevie. Life goes on. The important thing is to be able to live with yourself."

Steve looked at the empty Nike box next to Zack's plate. Why did Martha spend all that money on a pair of tennis shoes for Zack when she knew that things were tight? But this mess is not *her* fault, he told himself. *I'm* the one who has to decide if we can afford to solve this problem.

Or, if we can afford not to.

When his mother started clearing the table again, Steve stood up. He saw the lights on in the shop, and he went to talk with Martha.

Question

1. What should Steve Johnson do? If Steve had consulted you, what advice would you offer?

DIAPER DAN
Environmental Regulations Create Demand

As career switches go, few have been as bold as Daniel Gold's. Two years ago, as a Manhattan lawyer, he was operating in the high-octane arena of corporate takeovers. His days were filled with proxy contests, greenmail strategies, and junk-bond machinations. But like a refugee from *The Bonfire of the Vanities,* he abandoned his Fifth Avenue law office for an earthier field of play. Now Gold is better known as Diaper Dan.

It happened that Gold was looking to get out of law anyway and start a business of his own. And if he needed a push, the collapse of the junk-bond market provided one. In seven-and-a-half years of legal work he had reviewed thousands of prospectuses, and he had a few ideas about what businesses he might want to try. He had a couple of false starts: in April 1989 he started his first business, Vision Capital Associates Inc., a venture capital consulting firm that still exists but has no active clients. That summer he opened a West Hampton, N.Y., restaurant called Crabby Dan's, but after one week of operation he closed it because he was unable to secure a permit. Restless and anxious for a big hit, Gold continued to cast about for business opportunities. The idea that most fascinated him was hatched as he roamed malls and department stores. "There were baby carriages everywhere," he says. "I figured there was a birth boom under way, and I thought there might be something in the baby market."

In his orderly, lawyerly way, Gold went to a library and did some research. Indeed, the country was in the midst of a boom. Births had risen steadily from 3.7 million in 1986 to 3.8 million in 1987 and then to 3.9 million in 1988. By 1989, when Gold began his research, they were topping 4 million and fast approaching the magnitude of the postwar explosion's peak years.

What particularly intrigued Gold, however, was that most of the media coverage also mentioned diapers. Some 17.1 billion paper and plastic diapers are sold each year in the United States, Gold learned, and they end up in the trash. More than 1 billion tons of wood pulp and 70 tons of plastic are used annually to make a product that lasts a few hours. With the average disposable-diapered tyke going through some 8,000 diapers before being toilet trained, each contributes nearly 2 tons of refuse to the country's overburdened landfills. The disposables make up only about 2% of municipal solid waste, but they have come to symbolize a throwaway society run amok. Cotton diapers, on the other hand, are the original curbside recyclables. And given the solid-waste space shortage, the debate has reached such a pitch that a number of state legislatures are on the verge of taxing disposables or banning them outright. If there was a market begging to be served, Gold's research showed, this was it.

Since their introduction in the mid-1960s, disposable diapers had captured 85% to 90% of the market. They had become a $3.5-billion industry for Procter & Gamble (Pampers and Luvs), Kimberly-Clark (Huggies), and Weyerhaeuser

Source: Jay Finegan, "Diaper Dan," *Inc.*, Vol. 13, No. 3 (March 1991), pp. 80–89. Reprinted with permission, *Inc.* magazine, March 1991. Copyright 1991 by Goldhirsh Group, Inc., 38 Commercial Wharf, Boston, MA 02110.

(private labels), and they had driven countless diaper-delivery services out of business. Only about 200 remained, mostly mom-and-pop outfits with a handful of trucks.

But as environmentally concerned new parents began turning to cloth diapers, the surviving services were swamped with demand. The landfill brouhaha had a big hand in the revival, and so did new technology. Cloth diapering was easier than ever—Velcro tabs on the covers had replaced safety pins—and new deodorants minimized diaper-pail odor. Moreover, Gold notes, there was a return to basics among upscale mothers older than 30 having their first child, a sense that it was stylish and more healthful for the baby to wear natural fibers. Diaper services had always been cheaper than disposables, about $10 to $14 a week versus $15 to $20. But now it was a matter of choice, not economics.

Right from the start, Gold knew he wouldn't be content with just running a few diaper vans around the capital area. His background suggested something more ambitious. He had completed college in just two years. At California Western School of Law, in San Diego, he had served as editor of the *California Western International Law Journal* and won awards in national moot-court competition. He had gone on from there to pick up an M.B.A. and was already at work on a master's degree in taxation. "A headhunter told me to quit going to school," he says with a laugh. "He said my parents were already proud of me."

He had spoken to several venture capitalists about investing in the company, but no one took him seriously. "You're a lawyer, Dan," one said, shrugging. "What do you know about the diaper business?" Convinced that start-ups spend too much time and money trying to raise financing, Gold simply obtained a $50,000 bank loan on his personal guarantee and added $25,000 of his own cash.

With a total capitalization of $75,000, he was hardly able to invest the kind of money required for high-volume laundry equipment. He decided to do something unusual in the industry—farm out the dirty diapers to an outside party. After exploring his options, he settled on Virginia Linen Service, part of a company that has 13 operations in six eastern states and the District of Columbia. Virginia Linen Service, rigged with a state-of-the-art, continuous-batch "tunnel" washing-and-drying system, was a 10-minute drive from Diaper Dan's own location, in Washington's Maryland suburbs. In addition, Virginia Linen had some experience laundering diapers, having done it for years before the advent of disposables.

Last March Gold locked up a three-year contract with the company to handle his and only his diapers within a 50-mile radius of the Washington Monument. There's only one catch. "It's an exclusive provided he builds the volume that makes it worth our while," says Virginia Linen's owner and chief executive, Donald Struminger. "If he doesn't build that volume, then he will not have an exclusive contract. He has not yet reached the point where we'd be satisfied to continue, but he is moving along on the projection curve that we set when we made the agreement."

Finally, Gold planned to introduce a name-brand Diaper Dan's diaper for retail sale. Most cloth diapers sold in the United States are manufactured domestically by Dundee Mills and Gerber Childrenswear. India, Pakistan, Peru, and Venezuela produce cotton diapers. But Gold was convinced that the best, the most absorbent, and the cheapest diapers came from China. Chinese cotton products exported to the United States are restricted by U.S. textile quotas, but Gold already had contacted a U.S. agent about securing for him a reliable supply of Chinese diapers.

With his plan complete, Gold got down to work. At the outset, he analyzed the other diaper services in the Washington area and listed customers' complaints. Foremost was a health matter. People seemed concerned about getting back strangers' diapers. Gold resolved that by hanging a net in each client's diaper pail. His delivery person can simply yank out the net, fasten it with a giant safety pin (engraved with the customer's account number), and toss it in the van. The diapers can be washed right in the net and returned clean and folded to the same family. Another complaint was that women were mistrustful of male delivery people. Gold solved that one by planning to employ as many female drivers as possible.

Gold and partner Dana Goldman set up operations in a 3,000-square-foot warehouse space in an industrial park just off the Capital Beltway —for a mere $250-a-month rent—and by last June they were ready to roll. They had thousands of Chinese diapers, a driver, and a 12-foot van that had been carefully customized to segregate dirty diapers from clean ones and from the ancillary products. The truck is decorated with a Dapper Dan-style logo—a baby sporting a top hat and a cane, like an infant Fred Astaire.

Gold set conservative projections. He forecast 400 customers by the end of his first year, with an average of 600 in the second, and 1,000 the third year. If those numbers held true, and if the add-on products sold as well as he expected, revenues would rise from $442,500 the first year to $1.7 million in the third, with before-tax income climbing from $35,125 to $362,037.

Questions

1. Which laws described in Chapter 26 of the textbook may be applicable to this business venture?

2. Is Gold's exclusive agreement with the laundry wise? Why or why not?

3. What trademarks, patents, or copyrights may be involved in this business?

4. What types of taxes would you expect Gold's business will be paying? Be specific.

APPENDIX A

PRESENT VALUE OF $1

n	1%	2%	3%	4%	5%	6%	7%	8%	9%	10%
1	.990	.980	.971	.962	.952	.943	.935	.926	.917	.909
2	.980	.961	.943	.925	.907	.890	.873	.857	.842	.826
3	.971	.942	.915	.889	.864	.840	.816	.794	.772	.751
4	.961	.924	.888	.855	.823	.792	.763	.735	.708	.683
5	.951	.906	.863	.822	.784	.747	.713	.681	.650	.621
6	.942	.888	.837	.790	.746	.705	.666	.630	.596	.564
7	.933	.871	.813	.760	.711	.665	.623	.583	.547	.513
8	.923	.853	.789	.731	.677	.627	.582	.540	.502	.467
9	.914	.837	.766	.703	.645	.592	.544	.500	.460	.424
10	.905	.820	.744	.676	.614	.558	.508	.463	.422	.386
11	.896	.804	.722	.650	.585	.527	.475	.429	.388	.350
12	.887	.789	.701	.625	.557	.497	.444	.397	.356	.319
13	.879	.773	.681	.601	.530	.469	.415	.368	.326	.290
14	.870	.758	.661	.577	.505	.442	.388	.340	.299	.263
15	.861	.743	.642	.555	.481	.417	.362	.315	.275	.239
16	.853	.728	.623	.534	.458	.394	.339	.292	.252	.218
17	.844	.714	.605	.513	.436	.371	.317	.270	.231	.198
18	.836	.700	.587	.494	.416	.350	.296	.250	.212	.180
19	.828	.686	.570	.475	.396	.331	.277	.232	.194	.164
20	.820	.673	.554	.456	.377	.312	.258	.215	.178	.149
21	.811	.660	.538	.439	.359	.294	.242	.199	.164	.135
22	.803	.647	.522	.422	.342	.278	.226	.184	.150	.123
23	.795	.634	.507	.406	.326	.262	.211	.170	.138	.112
24	.788	.622	.492	.390	.310	.247	.197	.158	.126	.102
25	.780	.610	.478	.375	.295	.233	.184	.146	.116	.092
30	.742	.552	.412	.308	.231	.174	.131	.099	.075	.057
40	.672	.453	.307	.208	.142	.097	.067	.046	.032	.022
50	.608	.372	.228	.141	.087	.054	.034	.021	.013	.009

PRESENT VALUE OF $1 (*Continued*)

n	11%	12%	13%	14%	15%	16%	17%	18%	19%	20%
1	.901	.893	.885	.877	.870	.862	.855	.847	.840	.833
2	.812	.797	.783	.769	.756	.743	.731	.718	.706	.694
3	.731	.712	.693	.675	.658	.641	.624	.609	.593	.579
4	.659	.636	.613	.592	.572	.552	.534	.516	.499	.482
5	.593	.567	.543	.519	.497	.476	.456	.437	.419	.402
6	.535	.507	.480	.456	.432	.410	.390	.370	.352	.335
7	.482	.452	.425	.400	.376	.354	.333	.314	.296	.279
8	.434	.404	.376	.351	.327	.305	.285	.266	.249	.233
9	.391	.361	.333	.308	.284	.263	.243	.225	.209	.194
10	.352	.322	.295	.270	.247	.227	.208	.191	.176	.162
11	.317	.287	.261	.237	.215	.195	.178	.162	.148	.135
12	.286	.257	.231	.208	.187	.168	.152	.137	.124	.112
13	.258	.229	.204	.182	.163	.145	.130	.116	.104	.093
14	.232	.205	.181	.160	.141	.125	.111	.099	.088	.078
15	.209	.183	.160	.140	.123	.108	.095	.084	.074	.065
16	.188	.163	.141	.123	.107	.093	.081	.071	.062	.054
17	.170	.146	.125	.108	.093	.080	.069	.060	.052	.045
18	.153	.130	.111	.095	.081	.069	.059	.051	.044	.038
19	.138	.116	.098	.083	.070	.060	.051	.043	.037	.031
20	.124	.104	.087	.073	.061	.051	.043	.037	.031	.026
21	.112	.093	.077	.064	.053	.044	.037	.031	.026	.022
22	.101	.083	.068	.056	.046	.038	.032	.026	.022	.018
23	.091	.074	.060	.049	.040	.033	.027	.022	.018	.015
24	.082	.066	.053	.043	.035	.028	.023	.019	.015	.013
25	.074	.059	.047	.038	.030	.024	.020	.016	.013	.010
30	.044	.033	.026	.020	.015	.012	.009	.007	.005	.004
40	.015	.011	.008	.005	.004	.003	.002	.001	.001	.001
50	.005	.003	.002	.001	.001	.001	.000	.000	.000	.000

PRESENT VALUE OF $1 (*Continued*)

n	21%	22%	23%	24%	25%	26%	27%	28%	29%	30%
1	.826	.820	.813	.806	.800	.794	.787	.781	.775	.769
2	.683	.672	.661	.650	.640	.630	.620	.610	.601	.592
3	.564	.551	.537	.524	.512	.500.	.488	.477	.466	.455
4	.467	.451	.437	.423	.410	.397	.384	.373	.361	.350
5	.386	.370	.355	.341	.328	.315	.303	.291	.280	.269
6	.319	.303	.289	.275	.262	.250	.238	.227	.217	.207
7	.263	.249	.235	.222	.210	.198	.188	.178	.168	.159
8	.218	.204	.191	.179	.168	.157	.148	.139	.130	.123
9	.180	.167	.155	.144	.134	.125	.116	.108	.101	.094
10	.149	.137	.126	.116	.107	.099	.092	.085	.078	.073
11	.123	.112	.103	.094	.086	.079	.072	.066	.061	.056
12	.102	.092	.083	.076	.069	.062	.057	.052	.047	.043
13	.084	.075	.068	.061	.055	.050	.045	.040	.037	.033
14	.069	.062	.055	.049	.044	.039	.035	.032	.028	.025
15	.057	.051	.045	.040	.035	.031	.028	.025	.022	.020
16	.047	.042	.036	.032	.028	.025	.022	.019	.017	.015
17	.039	.034	.030	.026	.023	.020	.017	.015	.013	.012
18	.032	.028	.024	.021	.018	.016	.014	.012	.010	.009
19	.027	.023	.020	.017	.014	.012	.011	.009	.008	.007
20	.022	.019	.016	.014	.012	.010	.008	.007	.006	.005
21	.018	.015	.013	.011	.009	.008	.007	.006	.005	.004
22	.015	.013	.011	.009	.007	.006	.005	.004	.004	.003
23	.012	.010	.009	.007	.006	.005	.004	.003	.003	.002
24	.010	.008	.007	.006	.005	.004	.003	.003	.002	.002
25	.009	.007	.006	.005	.004	.003	.003	.002	.002	.001
30	.003	.003	.002	.002	.001	.001	.001	.001	.000	.000
40	.000	.000	.000	.000	.000	.000	.000	.000	.000	.000
50	.000	.000	.000	.000	.000	.000	.000	.000	.000	.000

PRESENT VALUE OF $1 (*Continued*)

n	31%	32%	33%	34%	35%	36%	37%	38%	39%	40%
1	.763	.758	.752	.746	.741	.735	.730	.725	.719	.714
2	.583	.574	.565	.557	.549	.541	.533	.525	.518	.510
3	.445	.435	.425	.416	.406	.398	.389	.381	.372	.364
4	.340	.329	.320	.310	.301	.292	.284	.276	.268	.260
5	.259	.250	.240	.231	.223	.215	.207	.200	.193	.186
6	.198	.189	.181	.173	.165	.158	.151	.145	.139	.133
7	.151	.143	.136	.129	.122	.116	.110	.105	.100	.095
8	.115	.108	.102	.096	.091	.085	.081	.076	.072	.068
9	.088	.082	.077	.072	.067	.063	.059	.055	.052	.048
10	.067	.062	.058	.054	.050	.046	.043	.040	.037	.035
11	.051	.047	.043	.040	.037	.034	.031	.029	.027	.025
12	.039	.036	.033	.030	.027	.025	.023	.021	.019	.018
13	.030	.027	.025	.022	.020	.018	.017	.015	.014	.013
14	.023	.021	.018	.017	.015	.014	.012	.011	.010	.009
15	.017	.016	.014	.012	.011	.010	.009	.008	.007	.006
16	.013	.012	.010	.009	.008	.007	.006	.006	.005	.005
17	.010	.009	.008	.007	.006	.005	.005	.004	.004	.003
18	.008	.007	.006	.005	.005	.004	.003	.003	.003	.002
19	.006	.005	.004	.004	.003	.003	.003	.002	.002	.002
20	.005	.004	.003	.003	.002	.002	.002	.002	.001	.001
21	.003	.003	.003	.002	.002	.002	.001	.001	.001	.001
22	.003	.002	.002	.002	.001	.001	.001	.001	.001	.001
23	.002	.002	.001	.001	.001	.001	.001	.001	.001	.000
24	.002	.001	.001	.001	.001	.001	.001	.000	.000	.000
25	.001	.001	.001	.001	.001	.000	.000	.000	.000	.000
30	.000	.000	.000	.000	.000	.000	.000	.000	.000	.000
40	.000	.000	.000	.000	.000	.000	.000	.000	.000	.000

PRESENT VALUE OF AN
ANNUITY OF $1 FOR *n PERIODS*

n	1%	2%	3%	4%	5%	6%	7%	8%	9%	10%
1	.990	.980	.971	.962	.952	.943	.935	.926	.917	.909
2	1.970	1.942	1.913	1.886	1.859	1.833	1.808	1.783	1.759	1.736
3	2.941	2.884	2.829	2.775	2.723	2.673	2.624	2.577	2.531	2.487
4	3.902	3.808	3.717	3.630	3.546	3.465	3.387	3.312	3.240	3.170
5	4.853	4.713	4.580	4.452	4.329	4.212	4.100	3.993	3.890	3.791
6	5.795	5.601	5.417	5.242	5.076	4.917	4.767	4.623	4.486	4.355
7	6.728	6.472	6.230	6.002	5.786	5.582	5.389	5.206	5.033	4.868
8	7.652	7.326	7.020	6.733	6.463	6.210	5.971	5.747	5.535	5.335
9	8.566	8.162	7.786	7.435	7.108	6.802	6.515	6.247	5.995	5.759
10	9.471	8.983	8.530	8.111	7.722	7.360	7.024	6.710	6.418	6.145
11	10.368	9.787	9.253	8.760	8.306	7.887	7.499	7.139	6.805	6.495
12	11.255	10.575	9.954	9.385	8.863	8.384	7.943	7.536	7.161	6.814
13	12.134	11.348	10.635	9.986	9.394	8.853	8.358	7.904	7.487	7.103
14	13.004	12.106	11.296	10.563	9.899	9.295	8.746	8.244	7.786	7.367
15	13.865	12.849	11.938	11.118	10.380	9.712	9.108	8.560	8.061	7.606
16	14.718	13.578	12.561	11.652	10.838	10.106	9.447	8.851	8.313	7.824
17	15.562	14.292	13.166	12.166	11.274	10.477	9.763	9.122	8.544	8.022
18	16.398	14.992	13.754	12.659	11.690	10.828	10.059	9.372	8.756	8.201
19	17.226	15.679	14.324	13.134	12.085	11.158	10.336	9.604	8.950	8.365
20	18.046	16.352	14.878	13.590	12.462	11.470	10.594	9.818	9.129	8.514
21	18.857	17.011	15.415	14.029	12.821	11.764	10.836	10.017	9.292	8.649
22	19.661	17.658	15.937	14.451	13.163	12.042	11.061	10.201	9.442	8.772
23	20.456	18.292	16.444	14.857	13.489	12.303	11.272	10.371	9.580	8.883
24	21.244	18.914	16.936	15.247	13.799	12.550	11.469	10.529	9.707	8.985
25	22.023	19.524	17.413	15.622	14.094	12.783	11.654	10.675	9.823	9.077
30	25.808	22.397	19.601	17.292	15.373	13.765	12.409	11.258	10.274	9.427
40	32.835	27.356	23.115	19.793	17.159	15.046	13.332	11.925	10.757	9.779
50	39.197	31.424	25.730	21.482	18.256	15.762	13.801	12.234	10.962	9.915

PRESENT VALUE OF AN ANNUITY
OF $1 FOR *n* PERIODS (*Continued*)

n	11%	12%	13%	14%	15%	16%	17%	18%	19%	20%
1	.901	.893	.885	.877	.870	.862	.855	.847	.840	.833
2	1.713	1.690	1.668	1.647	1.626	1.605	1.585	1.566	1.547	1.528
3	2.444	2.402	2.361	2.322	2.283	2.246	2.210	2.174	2.140	2.106
4	3.102	3.037	2.974	2.914	2.855	2.798	2.743	2.690	2.639	2.589
5	3.696	3.605	3.517	3.433	3.352	3.274	3.199	3.127	3.058	2.991
6	4.231	4.111	3.998	3.889	3.784	3.685	3.589	3.498	3.410	3.326
7	4.712	4.564	4.423	4.288	4.160	4.039	3.922	3.812	3.706	3.605
8	5.146	4.968	4.799	4.639	4.487	4.344	4.207	4.078	3.954	3.837
9	5.537	5.328	5.132	4.946	4.772	4.607	4.451	4.303	4.163	4.031
10	5.889	5.650	5.426	5.216	5.019	4.833	4.659	4.494	4.339	4.192
11	6.207	5.938	5.687	5.453	5.234	5.029	4.836	4.656	4.487	4.327
12	6.492	6.194	5.918	5.660	5.421	5.197	4.988	4.793	4.611	4.439
13	6.750	6.424	6.122	5.842	5.583	5.342	5.118	4.910	4.715	4.533
14	6.982	6.628	6.303	6.002	5.724	5.468	5.229	5.008	4.802	4.611
15	7.191	6.811	6.462	6.142	5.847	5.575	5.324	5.092	4.876	4.675
16	7.379	6.974	6.604	6.265	5.954	5.669	5.405	5.162	4.938	4.730
17	7.549	7.120	6.729	6.373	6.047	5.749	5.475	5.222	4.990	4.775
18	7.702	7.250	6.840	6.467	6.128	5.818	5.534	5.273	5.033	4.812
19	7.839	7.366	6.938	6.550	6.198	5.877	5.585	5.316	5.070	4.843
20	7.963	7.469	7.025	6.623	6.259	5.929	5.628	5.353	5.101	4.870
21	8.075	7.562	7.102	6.687	6.312	5.973	5.665	5.384	5.127	4.891
22	8.176	7.645	7.170	6.743	6.359	6.011	5.696	5.410	5.149	4.909
23	8.266	7.718	7.230	6.792	6.399	6.044	5.723	5.432	5.167	4.925
24	8.348	7.784	7.283	6.835	6.434	6.073	5.747	5.451	5.182	4.937
25	8.442	7.843	7.330	6.873	6.464	6.097	5.766	5.467	5.195	4.948
30	8.694	8.055	7.496	7.003	6.566	6.177	5.829	5.517	5.235	4.979
40	8.951	8.244	7.634	7.105	6.642	6.233	5.871	5.548	5.258	4.997
50	9.042	8.305	7.675	7.133	6.661	6.246	5.880	5.554	5.262	4.999

PRESENT VALUE OF AN ANNUITY
OF $1 FOR *n* PERIODS (*Continued*)

n	21%	22%	23%	24%	25%	26%	27%	28%	29%	30%
1	.826	.820	.813	.806	.800	.794	.787	.781	.775	.769
2	1.509	1.492	1.474	1.457	1.440	1.424	1.407	1.392	1.376	1.361
3	2.074	2.042	2.011	1.981	1.952	1.923	1.896	1.868	1.842	1.816
4	2.540	2.494	2.448	2.404	2.362	2.320	2.280	2.241	2.203	2.166
5	2.926	2.864	2.803	2.745	2.689	2.635	2.583	2.532	2.483	2.436
6	3.245	3.167	3.092	3.020	2.951	2.885	2.821	2.759	2.700	2.643
7	3.508	3.416	3.327	3.242	3.161	3.083	3.009	2.937	2.868	2.802
8	3.726	3.619	3.518	3.421	3.329	3.241	3.156	3.076	2.999	2.925
9	3.905	3.786	3.673	3.566	3.463	3.366	3.273	3.184	3.100	3.019
10	4.054	3.923	3.799	3.682	3.570	3.465	3.364	3.269	3.178	3.092
11	4.177	4.035	3.902	3.776	3.656	3.544	3.437	3.335	3.239	3.147
12	4.278	4.127	3.985	3.851	3.725	3.606	3.493	3.387	3.286	3.190
13	4.362	4.203	4.053	3.912	3.780	3.656	3.538	3.427	3.322	3.223
14	4.432	4.265	4.108	3.962	3.824	3.695	3.573	3.459	3.351	3.249
15	4.489	4.315	4.153	4.001	3.859	3.726	3.601	3.483	3.373	3.268
16	4.536	4.357	4.189	4.033	3.887	3.751	3.623	3.503	3.390	3.283
17	4.576	4.391	4.219	4.059	3.910	3.771	3.640	3.518	3.403	3.295
18	4.608	4.419	4.243	4.080	3.928	3.786	3.654	3.529	3.413	3.304
19	4.635	4.442	4.263	4.097	3.942	3.799	3.664	3.539	3.421	3.311
20	4.657	4.460	4.279	4.110	3.954	3.808	3.673	3.546	3.427	3.316
21	4.675	4.476	4.292	4.121	3.963	3.816	3.679	3.551	3.432	3.320
22	4.690	4.488	4.302	4.130	3.970	3.822	3.684	3.556	3.436	3.323
23	4.703	4.499	4.311	4.137	3.976	3.827	3.689	3.559	3.438	3.325
24	4.713	4.507	4.318	4.143	3.981	3.831	3.692	3.562	3.441	3.327
25	4.721	4.514	4.323	4.147	3.985	3.834	3.694	3.564	3.442	3.329
30	4.746	4.534	4.339	4.160	3.995	3.842	3.701	3.569	3.447	3.332
40	4.760	4.544	4.347	4.166	3.999	3.846	3.703	3.571	3.448	3.333
50	4.762	4.545	4.348	4.167	4.000	3.846	3.704	3.571	3.448	3.333

PRESENT VALUE OF AN ANNUITY OF $1 FOR *n* PERIODS (*Continued*)

n	31%	32%	33%	34%	35%	36%	37%	38%	39%	40%
1	.763	.758	.752	.746	.741	.735	.730	.725	.719	.714
2	1.346	1.331	1.317	1.303	1.289	1.276	1.263	1.250	1.237	1.224
3	1.791	1.766	1.742	1.719	1.696	1.673	1.652	1.630	1.609	1.589
4	2.130	2.096	2.062	2.029	1.997	1.966	1.935	1.906	1.877	1.849
5	2.390	2.345	2.302	2.260	2.220	2.181	2.143	2.106	2.070	2.035
6	2.588	2.534	2.483	2.433	2.385	2.339	2.294	2.251	2.209	2.168
7	2.739	2.677	2.619	2.562	2.508	2.455	2.404	2.355	2.308	2.263
8	2.854	2.786	2.721	2.658	2.598	2.540	2.485	2.432	2.380	2.331
9	2.942	2.868	2.798	2.730	2.665	2.603	2.544	2.487	2.432	2.379
10	3.009	2.930	2.855	2.784	2.715	2.649	2.587	2.527	2.469	2.414
11	3.060	2.978	2.899	2.824	2.752	2.683	2.618	2.555	2.496	2.438
12	3.100	3.013	2.931	2.853	2.779	2.708	2.641	2.576	2.515	2.456
13	3.129	3.040	2.956	2.876	2.799	2.727	2.658	2.592	2.529	2.469
14	3.152	3.061	2.974	2.892	2.814	2.740	2.670	2.603	2.539	2.477
15	3.170	3.076	2.988	2.905	2.825	2.750	2.679	2.611	2.546	2.484
16	3.183	3.088	2.999	2.914	2.834	2.757	2.685	2.616	2.551	2.489
17	3.193	3.097	3.007	2.921	2.840	2.763	2.690	2.621	2.555	2.492
18	3.201	3.104	3.012	2.926	2.844	2.767	2.693	2.624	2.557	2.494
19	3.207	3.109	3.017	2.930	2.848	2.770	2.696	2.626	2.559	2.496
20	3.211	3.113	3.020	2.933	2.850	2.772	2.698	2.627	2.561	2.497
21	3.215	3.116	3.023	2.935	2.852	2.773	2.699	2.629	2.562	2.498
22	3.217	3.118	3.025	2.936	2.853	2.775	2.700	2.629	2.562	2.498
23	3.219	3.120	3.026	2.938	2.854	2.775	2.701	2.630	2.563	2.499
24	3.221	3.121	3.027	2.939	2.855	2.776	2.701	2.630	2.563	2.499
25	3.222	3.122	3.028	2.939	2.856	2.776	2.702	2.631	2.563	2.499
30	3.225	3.124	3.030	2.941	2.857	2.777	2.702	2.631	2.564	2.500
40	3.226	3.125	3.030	2.941	2.857	2.778	2.703	2.632	2.564	2.500
50	3.226	3.125	3.030	2.941	2.857	2.778	2.703	2.632	2.564	2.500

APPENDIX C

TIME VALUE OF MONEY
(Finding the Present Value of a Dollar)

Orientation: In this appendix the concept of time value of money is explained briefly—that is, a dollar today is worth more than a dollar received a year from now. Thus, if we are to logically compare projects and financial strategies, we must move all dollar flows back to the present.

THE DEPARTURE POINT

The beginning point for all that we do in finding the present value of future cash flows is represented in the following equation:

$$FV_n = PV(1+i)^n$$

where FV_n = the future value of the investment at the end of n years,
PV = the present value or original amount invested today,
i = the (discount rate) interest rate,
n = the number of years until the cash flow is to be received or paid

We would use this equation to answer the following question:

If you invested $500 today (present value, or $PV = \$500$) at an annual interest rate of 8 percent ($i = 8\%$), how much money would you have (future value, or FV_n) in five years ($n = 5$)?

Assuming that interest compounds annually (you earn interest on the interest each new year), the answer would be:

$$FV_n = \$500(1+.08)^5$$
$$= \$500(1.4693)$$
$$= 734.65$$

Thus, if we invested $500 today at 8 percent, compounded annually, we would have $734.65 at the end of five years. This procedure is called the *compounding of a dollar.*

THE PRESENT VALUE OF A DOLLAR

Determining the present value, that is, the value in today's dollars of a sum of money to be received in the future, involves nothing other than reversing the compounding process just described. The differences in these techniques come about merely from the investor's point of view.

Restructuring the equation shown above to solve for the present value of a dollar, PV, we have:

$$PV = \frac{FV_n}{(1+i)^n}$$
$$= FV_n\left(\frac{1}{(1+i)^n}\right)$$

where PV is now the present value of a future sum of money; FV_n is the future value of the money to be received in year n; and i is the interest rate. Thus, the present value of $1,200 to be received in 7 years, assuming an interest rate of 10 percent, would be:

$$PV = FV_n\left(\frac{1}{(1+i)^n}\right)$$

$$= \$1,200\left(\frac{1}{(1+.10)^7}\right)$$

$$= \$1,200\,(.5132)$$

$$= \$615.79$$

Rather than solving for the present value by using the above equation, we may instead use Appendix A, where the computations within the above brackets have already been performed and are called the *present value interest factors* for year n and interest rate i, frequently represented $PVIF_{i,n}$. That is,

$$\left(\frac{1}{(1+i)^n}\right) = PVIF_{i,n}$$

So if we want to calculate the present value of $2,000 received in 12 years, where the interest rate is 14 percent:

$$PV = \$2,000\,(PVIF_{14\%,12\,years})$$

Looking in Appendix A in the row for 12 years and the column for the interest rate of 14 percent, we find the present value interest factor to be 0.208. So,

$$PV = \$2,000\,(0.208)$$

$$= \$416$$

Hence, the present value of $2,000 to be received in 12 years would be $416, assuming an interest rate of 14 percent. In other words, we would be indifferent between receiving $416 today or $2,000 to be received in 12 years.

THE PRESENT VALUE OF AN ANNUITY

An annuity is a series of equal dollar payments for a specified number of years. That is, a 10-year annuity of $200 means that we will receive or pay $200 each year for 10 years. Alternatively, we could say that an annuity involves depositing or investing an equal sum of money at the end of each year for a certain number of years and allowing it to grow at the stated interest rate.

If we wanted to find the present value, PV, of a three-year annuity of $600 (received each year) at an interest rate of 13 percent, we could do so as follows:

$$PV = \frac{\$600}{(1+.13)^1} + \frac{\$600}{(1+.13)^2} + \frac{\$600}{(1+.13)^3}$$

Using the present value interest factors from Appendix A, we may find the present value as follows:

$$PV = \$600\,(PVIF_{13\%,1\,yr}) + \$600\,(PVIF_{13\%,2\,yrs})$$
$$+ \$600\,(PVIF_{13\%,3\,yrs})$$
$$= \$600\,(0.885) + \$600\,(0.783) + \$600\,(0.693)$$
$$= \$531 + \$469.80 + \$415.80$$
$$= \$1,416.60$$

We could have also found the $1,416.60 as follows:

$$PV = \$600\,(0.885 + 0.783 + 0.693)$$
$$= \$600\,(2.361)$$
$$= \$1,416.60$$

Also, rather than having to look up the three present value interest factors individually, it would be nice if we had an interest factor table that would give us the interest factors for an entire annuity rather than for only individual years. Such a table, called the *Present Value Interest Factors for an Annuity*, is provided in Appendix B. Letting $PVIFA_{i,n}$ represent the present value interest factor for an annuity of n years at an interest rate of i, and letting the annual amount each year be defined as PMT, the equation for finding the present value of an annuity would be as follows:

$$PV = PMT\,[PVIFA_{i,n}]$$

Thus, if we want to find the present value of a 15-year annuity in the amount of $3,000 each year, where the interest rate is 18 percent, the solution would be as follows:

$$PV = PMT[PVIFA_{i,n}]$$
$$PV = \$3,000[PVIFA_{18\%,15\ yrs}]$$

Looking in Appendix B for 15 years and an 18 percent interest rate, we find the interest factor for the annuity to be 5.092. Thus, the present value of the annuity is $15,276, computed as follows:

$$PV = \$3,000[5.092] = \$15,276.$$

The foregoing explanation of finding present values will enable you to find the present value of future dollars in solving finance problems important to the owner of a small company. However, while you can certainly use table values such as those shown in Appendix A and Appendix B, an even better approach is a good financial calculator or a computer spreadsheet.

GLOSSARY

A

ABC method a method of classifying inventory by value

accounting return on investment the ratio of average annual profits to the average book value of an investment

accounts payable credit extended by suppliers

accounts receivable turnover the number of times accounts receivable "roll over" during a year

accrual method of accounting a method of accounting that matches revenues when they are earned against the expenses associated with those revenues

accrued expenses expenses that have been incurred, but not paid

acid-test (quick) ratio a measure of liquidity that excludes inventories

advertising the impersonal presentation of a business idea through mass media

advisory council a group that advises, rather than governs, a corporation

Age Discrimination in Employment Act of 1967 federal legislation requiring employers to treat applicants and employees equally, regardless of age

agency a relationship whereby one party, the agent, represents another party, the principal, in dealing with a third party

agency power the right of a partner to bind all members of the firm

agents distribution intermediaries who do not take title to the goods they distribute

aging schedule a categorization of accounts receivable based on the length of time they have been outstanding

Americans with Disabilities Act federal legislation guaranteeing equal access to employment for disabled people, if they can perform with "reasonable accommodations"

application software computer programs that perform specific tasks

articles of partnership a document that states explicitly the rights and duties of partners

793

artisan entrepreneur a person who starts a business with primarily technical skills, and little business knowledge

asset-based lending financing secured by working-capital assets

asset-based valuation approach a method of assessing the value of a business by examining the value of its assets

assorting the process of bringing together homogeneous lines of goods into a heterogeneous assortment

attitude an enduring opinion that is based on a combination of knowledge, feeling, and behavioral tendency

attractive small firm any small firm that provides substantial profits to its owner(s)

attributes sampling plan a system that checks sample items on a pass/fail basis to determine the acceptability of an entire lot

average collection period the average time taken to collect accounts receivable

average pricing a pricing approach that uses average cost as a basis to set price

B

bad-debt ratio a ratio of bad debts to total credit sales that is used to determine the efficacy of a firm's credit policies

bait advertising an insincere offer to sell in order to lure customers and switch them to more expensive products

balance sheet a financial statement that shows a firm's assets and liabilities at a specific point in time

batch manufacturing production that falls between the volume and variety ranges of job shops and repetitive manufacturing

benefit variables variables that distinguish market segments according to the benefits sought by customers

blue-sky laws state laws that protect investors from securities fraud

board of directors the governing body elected by the stockholders of a corporation

brand a means of identifying a product, expressed in verbal or symbolic terms

break-even analysis a method of evaluating investments that compares cost and demand to determine the point at which total sales revenue equals total costs

breakdown process a forecasting method that begins with a macro-level variable and systematically works down to the sales forecast.

breaking bulk an intermediary process that makes large quantities of product available in smaller amounts

brokers distribution intermediaries who do not take title to the goods they distribute

budget a document that expresses future plans in monetary terms

buildup process a forecasting method that identifies all potential buyers in a market's submarkets and then adds up the estimated demand

business angels private investors who finance new, risky, small ventures

business format franchising a franchise relationship where the franchisee obtains an entire marketing system and ongoing assistance and guidance from the franchisor

business incubator a facility that provides shared space, services, and management assistance to new businesses

business interruption insurance coverage of lost income and certain expenses while rebuilding the business

business plan a document containing the basic business idea and all the related operational, marketing, and financial considerations in starting a new business

business policies fundamental statements that serve as guides to management practice

buyout purchasing an existing business

C

C corporation a type of corporation that is taxed as a separate legal entity

capitalization rate a figure used to assess the earnings-based value of a business, the capitalization rate is determined by the riskiness of the current earnings and the expected growth rate of these earnings

cash budget a budget strictly concerned with the receipt and payment of dollars

cash conversion period the time period required to complete the working-capital cycle, converting inventories and accounts receivable into cash

cash flow from operations collections from customers; payments to suppliers; cash expenses such as marketing and administrative expenses and interest payments; and cash tax payments

cash flow statement a financial statement that shows changes in a firm's cash position over a given period of time

cash flows from financing activities the amount of cash flows to or from a firm's creditors and investors, excluding interest payments

cash flows from investment activities the amount of cash used for investments by a firm

cash flows from operations collections from customers and payments related to operations, interest, and taxes

cash method of accounting transactions are recognized only when cash is received or payment is made

cash-flow-based valuation a method of assessing the value of a business determined by a comparison of the expected and required rates of return on the investment

cell the intersection of a row and a column on a spreadsheet

central processing unit (CPU) the electronic components that perform calculations and control the flow of information in a computer

chain of command the superior-subordinate relationships in an organization structure

channel of distribution the system of intermediaries that distribute a product

chattel mortgage a loan for which certain items of inventory or other moveable property serve as collateral

circulating capital the sum of a firm's current assets (cash, accounts receivable, and inventories) and current liabilities (accounts payable and short-term notes) (also called working capital)

Civil Rights Act of 1964 federal legislation prohibiting discrimination based on race, color, sex, religion, or national origin

Clean Air Act federal legislation that regulates air pollutants

client/server model a system whereby the client (the user's personal computer) obtains data from a central computer, but processing is done at the client level

code of ethics official standards of behavior for employees

cognitive dissonance the tension that occurs immediately following a purchase decision, when a customer has "second thoughts" about the purchase

coinsurance clause the insured is required to maintain a specific level of coverage or to assume a portion of any loss

common carriers transportation intermediaries that are available for hire to the general public

communications control program software that controls the flow of information between computers

competitive advantage a marketing idea that is seen by the target market as better than a competitor's idea

computer-aided design (CAD) using sophisticated computer systems to design new products

computer-aided manufacturing (CAM) using computer-controlled machines to manufacture products

consumer credit credit granted by retailers to final consumers who purchase for personal or family use

consumerism a movement that stresses the needs of consumers and the importance of serving them honestly and well

contract carriers transportation intermediaries that contract with individual shippers

contracts agreements that are legally enforceable

copyright the exclusive right of a creator to reproduce, publish, and sell his or her own works

corporate refugee a person who leaves big business to go into business for him or herself

corporation an organization that exists as a legal entity

corporation charter the document that establishes a corporation's existence

corrective maintenance the major and minor repairs necessary to restore equipment to good condition

cost of capital the rate of return a firm must earn on its investments in order to satisfy its debt holders and owners

credit an agreement to delay payment for a product or service

credit bureau an organization that serves its members—retailers and other firms in a given community—by summarizing their credit experience with particular individuals

credit insurance protection against abnormal bad-debt losses

cultural business pattern a system of beliefs and practices pertaining to the business operations of a family firm. The types of patterns are paternalistic, laissez-faire, participative, or professional

cultural configuration the total culture of the family

firm that is made up of the firm's business, family, and governance patterns

cultural family pattern a set of beliefs and behaviors pertaining to family relationships in a family firm. The types of patterns are patriarchal, collaborative, or conflicted.

cultural governance pattern a set of beliefs and behaviors pertaining to the governance of a family firm. The types of patterns are paper board, rubber-stamp board, advisory board, or overseer board.

culture a group's social heritage, including behavior patterns and values

current assets assets that will be converted into cash within a company's operating cycle

current ratio the measure of a company's relative liquidity

customer profile a description of potential customers

customer-satisfaction strategy a marketing plan that emphasizes the goal of customer service

customized software computer programs designed or adapted for use by a particular company or type of business

D

database program a computer program used to manage a file of related data

daywork compensation based on increments of time

debt capital business financing provided by a creditor

debt ratio the percentage of a firm's assets that are financed by debt

delegation of authority a superior grants to subordinates the right to act or make decisions

demographic variables characteristics that describe customers and their purchasing power

design patent a type of patent that covers the appearance of a product and everything that is an inseparable part of the product

desktop publishing producing high-quality printed documents on a personal computer

direct channel a distribution channel without intermediaries

direct forecasting a forecasting method that uses sales as the predicting variable

direct method a measurement of cash flows from operations that begins with the cash flows collected from customers and subtracts all cash outflows

disclosure document financial data required by the Federal Trade Commission to be made available to all investors

discounted cash flow techniques methods of comparing the present value of future cash flows with the value of the initial investment

discounted payback method a capital budgeting method that uses the present value of future cash flows to determine a project's payback period

dishonesty insurance coverage to protect against employee dishonesty and their other crimes

distributed processing using two or more computers in combination to process data

distribution the physical movement of products and the establishment of intermediary channels to guide and support this movement

distribution function when small businesses link producers and customers

double-entry system a self-balancing accounting system that uses journals and ledgers and requires that each transaction be recorded twice in the accounts

dual distribution distribution that involves more than one channel

Dun & Bradstreet a company that researches and publishes business information

E

earnings before interest and taxes a business' profits before interest and taxes are paid (also called operating income)

earnings-based valuation approach a method of assessing the value of a business based on its potential future income

economic competition when competing businesses vie for sales

economic order quantity the quantity to be purchased that minimizes total inventory costs

educational refugee a person who tires of an academic program and decides to go into business

elastic demand a change in the price of a product or service produces a significant change in the quantity demanded

elasticity of demand the effect of a change in price on the quantity demanded

electronic data interchange (EDI) the exchange of data between businesses through computer links

electronic mail (E-mail) text messages transmitted from one computer to another

employee stock ownership plans (ESOPs) agreements that give employees a share of ownership in the business

employer's liability insurance coverage against suits brought by employees

entrepreneur a person who starts up and/or operates a business

entrepreneurial team a group of two or more people who function together as entrepreneurs

environmentalism concern with protecting the environment from damage

Equal Access to Justice Act legislation that requires the federal government to reimburse legal expenses for small firms that win cases against regulatory agencies

equity all owners' investments in a company, and the profits retained in the firm (also called net worth)

ethical issues practices and policies involving questions of right and wrong

evaluative criteria the features or characteristics of products or services that are used to compare brands

evoked set a term used to describe brands that a person is both aware of and willing to consider as a solution to a purchase problem

executive summary an overview of the entire business plan

external equity equity ownership of a company that comes initially from the owner's investment

external locus of control believing that one's life is controlled to a greater extent by luck, chance, or fate than by one's own efforts

F

facsimile machine (fax) a device that transmits copies of physical documents across standard telephone lines

factoring obtaining cash before payments are received from customers by selling accounts receivable to a finance company

failure rate the proportion of businesses that close with a loss to creditors

family and business overlap the intersection of family concerns and business interests in a family business

Family and Medical Leave Act of 1993 federal legislation requiring unpaid leave for maternity or other specified emergency leaves

family business ownership or involvement of two or more family members in the life and functioning of a business

family council an organized group of family members who gather periodically to discuss family-related business issues

family retreat a gathering of family members, usually at a remote location, to discuss family business matters

favorable financial leverage investing at a rate of return that exceeds the interest rate on borrowed money

fax modem a circuit board installed in a computer that allows the user to transfer documents directly from a computer to a fax machine

feminist refugee a woman who experiences discrimination and elects to start a firm in which she can operate independently of male chauvinists

file server the computer that stores the programs and common data that are shared by computers on a local area network

financial plan a section of the business plan that specifies financial needs and sources of financing and presents projections of revenues, costs, and profits

fixed asset turnover the ratio of sales to fixed assets

fixed assets relatively permanent assets that are intended for use in the business, not for sale

foreign refugee a person who leaves his or her native country and later becomes an entrepreneur

forfaiting a bank's discounted purchase of promissory notes received by an exporter

formal venture capitalists individuals who formally create a firm for the purpose of investing in new growth companies

founders entrepreneurs who bring new firms into existence

franchise the privileges contained in a franchise contract

franchise contract the legal agreement between franchisor and franchisee

franchisee the party in a franchise contract whose power is limited by the franchising organization

franchising a marketing system in which one party conducts business as an individual owner according to methods and terms specified by another party

franchisor the party in a franchise contract who specifies the methods and terms to be followed by the other party

free-flow pattern a type of retail store layout that is visually appealing and gives customers freedom of movement

fringe benefits items such as vacations and health insurance that supplement monetary compensation of employees

FTA the Free Trade Agreement, signed in 1989 by the United States and Canada, which calls for the elimination of most tariffs and other trade restrictions between the two countries by 1998

G

general liability insurance coverage against suits brought by customers

general managers entrepreneurs who function as administrators of their businesses

general partner the partner with unlimited liability in a general or limited partnership

general-purpose equipment machines that serve many functions in the production process

geographic information systems (GIS) computer programs that connect a physical map with a customer file database

grid pattern a block-like type of retail store layout that provides good merchandise exposure and simple security and cleaning

growth trap a cash shortage resulting from rapid growth

H

hardware the equipment components of a computer system

headhunter a firm that locates qualified candidates for executive positions

high-potential venture a firm that has great prospects for growth

housewife refugee a woman who starts her own business after her family is grown or when she can free herself from household duties

I

Immigration Reform Act federal legislation requiring that employees are either U.S. citizens or aliens authorized to work in the U.S.

income statement a financial statement that shows the profit or loss from a firm's operations over a period of time

income tax expense a firm's tax liability

indirect channel distribution channel with one or more intermediaries

indirect forecasting a forecasting method that uses variables related to sales to project the sales forecast

indirect method a measurement of cash flows from operations that begins with net income and adds back expenses that did not result in a cash outflow

inelastic demand a change in the price of a product or service does not produce a significant change in the quantity demanded

informal capital an investment in entrepreneurial ventures by private individuals

input device any device that is used to enter data or commands into a computer

inspection scrutinizing a product or service to determine if it meets quality standards

inspection standards specification of desired product quality levels and allowable tolerances

installment account credit that normally requires a down payment toward the purchase price, with the balance of payments made over a specified time period

institutional advertising advertising intended to raise public awareness of a business establishment

interest expense the interest amounts owed to lenders on borrowed money

internal control a system of checks and balances that enhances the accuracy and reliability of a firm's financial statements

internal equity equity that comes from the retention of profits within a company

internal locus of control believing that one's success depends upon one's own efforts

internal rate of return the rate of return a firm expects to earn on a project

inventory turnover the number of times inventories "roll over" during a year

J

Job Instruction Training a system designed to make on-the-job training more effective

job shops manufacturing operations where many small, unique, short-run jobs are performed

just-in-time inventory system a system of reducing inventory levels to an absolute minimum

K

key-person insurance coverage that protects against the death of key personnel of a firm

L

laws of motion economy guidelines for increasing the efficiency of human movement and tool design

leasing employees leasing personnel from a company that handles paperwork and benefits administration

legal entity a business organization that is recognized by the law as a separate legal being

legal plan a section of the business plan describing the legal form of organization—proprietorship, partnership, or corporation—and relevant legal considerations

letter of credit an agreement that assures a seller of prompt payment

licensing a legal agreement allowing a product to be produced in return for royalties

limited partner a partner who is not active in the management of a limited partnership and who therefore has limited personal liability

limited partnership a partnership of at least one general partner and one or more limited partners

line activities activities that contribute directly to the primary objectives of a small firm

line of credit an informal agreement or understanding between the borrower and the bank as to the maximum amount of credit the bank will provide the borrower at any one time

line organization a small, simple structure in which each person in a firm reports to one supervisor

line-and-staff organization an organization structure that includes staff specialists who perform specialized services or act as management advisers in special areas.

liquidation value approach a method of assessing the value of a business based on money available if the firm were to liquidate its assets

liquidity the ability of a firm to meet maturing financial obligations as they come due

local area network (LAN) an interconnected group of computers and related devices that are capable of communicating and sharing information within a limited geographical area

logistics the physical movement activities of distribution (also called physical distribution)

long-range plans a firm's basic plans for the long-term future (also called strategic plans)

long-term debt debt with a repayment term of more than twelve months

M

magnetic disk drive a device that transfers data from magnetic disks to the computer's memory and vice versa

mainframe a large, multi-user computer

major industries as classified by the U.S. Department of Commerce, the eight largest groups of businesses

make-or-buy decision a firm's choice between making or buying the component parts for the products it makes

management functions planning, leading, organizing, and controlling operations

management plan a section of the business plan describing a firm's "key players"—the active investors, management team, and directors—and their experience and qualifications

management team managers and other key persons who give a company its general direction

marginal firm any small firm that provides insignificant profits to its owner(s)

market a group of customers or potential customers who have purchasing power and unsatisfied needs

market segmentation the process of dividing a market into several smaller groups with similar needs

market-based valuation approach a method of assessing the value of a business based on the sale prices of comparable firms

marketing plan a section of the business plan that describes potential customers and competitors and outlines marketing strategy

marketing research the gathering, processing, reporting, and interpreting of marketing information

master franchising a master franchisor has a continuing contractual relationship with a franchisor to sell its franchises (also called subfranchising)

material requirement planning (MRP) controlling the timely ordering of production materials by using computer software

merchant middlemen intermediaries who take title to the goods they distribute

methods improvement finding work methods that reduce physical effort, shorten execution time, and/or lower cost

microcomputer a small computer used by only one person at a time (also called personal computer)

micromotion study a refined time study in which a worker's motions are videotaped

microprocessor a miniaturized CPU mounted on a silicon chip

minicomputer a medium-sized computer capable of processing data input simultaneously from a number of sources

modem a device that converts digital data to analog and vice versa, used in computer communication over telephone lines

modified book value approach a method of assessing the value of a business that adjusts the firm's book value to reflect differences between the historical cost of an asset and its current value

motion study a detailed observation of all the motions that a worker makes to complete a job under a given set of physical conditions

motivations goal-directed forces within humans that organize and give direction to tension caused by unsatisfied needs

mouse a hand-controlled input device that directs an arrow on the computer screen

multimedia a combination of text, graphics, audio, and video in a single presentation

multisegmentation strategy a business recognizes the different preferences of individual market segments and develops a unique marketing mix for each segment

multitasking the ability of a computer to carry out more than one function at a time

N

NAFTA the North American Free Trade Agreement, which eliminates Mexican tariffs on U.S.-made products

National Labor Relations Act federal legislation requiring employers to avoid discrimination based on union affiliation and to bargain with a union if desired by a majority of employees in the bargaining suit

need for achievement a desire to succeed where success is measured against a personal standard of excellence

needs the starting point for all behavior

negotiable instruments credit instruments that can be transferred from one party to another in place of money

net change in cash flows the net change in cash flows resulting from operations, investment, and financing activities

net present value the present value of future cash flows from an investment, less the initial investment outlay

net profits after taxes the income that may be distributed to a company's owners or reinvested in the company

net worth all owners' personal investments in a company, including both amounts paid and the profits retained in the firm (also called equity)

network card a circuit card required for personal computers on a local area network

network control program software that controls access to a local area network

networking the process of developing and engaging in mutually beneficial relationships with peers

niche marketing choosing marketing segments not adequately served by competitors (also called target marketing)

Nutrition Labeling and Education Act legislation that requires producers to list nutritional information on food product packaging

O

Occupational Safety and Health Act (OSHA) federal legislation requiring a workplace that protects the health and safety of employees

open charge account the customer obtains possession of goods (or services) when purchased, with payment due when billed

operating income profits before interest and taxes are paid (also called earnings before interest and taxes)

operating income return on investment (OIROI) a measure of operating profits relative to assets

operating plan a section of the business plan describing the facilities, labor, raw materials, and processing requirements of a new business

operating profit margin profits derived from operations, divided by sales

operating system the system that controls the flow of information in and out of a computer and links the hardware to application programs

operations management planning and control of the production process

operations process the activities necessary to accomplish the work a firm was created to perform (also called production process)

opinion leader a group leader who plays a key communications role

opportunistic entrepreneur a person who enters business with both sophisticated managerial skills and technical knowledge

opportunity cost the rate of return an owner could earn on a similar investment

other assets assets that are neither current nor fixed

output device a computer device that allows processed data to be viewed or transmitted

owner's equity capital money the owners invest in a business

P

Paperwork Reduction Act legislation that created OIRA to reduce paperwork and simplify regulatory rules for small businesses

parental (paternal) refugee a person who leaves a family business to prove his or her own entrepreneurial capabilities

partnership a voluntary association of two or more persons to carry on, as co-owners, a business for profit

patent the registered right of an inventor to make, use, and sell an invention

payback period the length of time before an initial cash investment is recovered

penetration pricing a strategy of setting lower than normal prices in order to hasten market acceptance or to increase existing market share

percentage-of-sales technique a method used to forecast asset and financing requirements

perception the individual processes that ultimately give meaning to the stimuli that confront consumers

perceptual categorization the perceptual process of grouping together similar things in an effort to manage huge quantities of incoming stimuli

perpetual inventory system a system of maintaining a current record of inventory items

personal computer a small computer used by only one person at a time (also called microcomputer)

personal selling promotion delivered in a personal, one-on-one manner

physical distribution the physical movement activities of distribution (also called logistics)

physical inventory system a system for periodic counting of inventory items

piggyback franchising the operation of a retail franchise within the physical facilities of a host store

plant patent a patent that covers any distinct and new variety of plant

pledged accounts receivable a firm's accounts receivable are used as collateral for a loan

pre-emptive rights the rights of stockholders to buy new shares of a stock before it is offered for public sale

precipitating events occurrences, such as job termination, which move individuals to become entrepreneurs

prestige pricing setting a high price to convey the image of high quality or uniqueness

preventive maintenance inspections and other activities intended to prevent machine breakdowns

price a seller's measure of what he or she is willing to receive in exchange for transferring ownership or use of a product or service

price line a range of several distinct prices at which merchandise is offered for sale

primary data new information that is gathered through various methods

private carriers shippers who own their means of transport

private placement selling a firm's capital stock to selected individuals

pro formas a business's projected financial statements

procedures specific methods to be followed in business activities

process layout a type of factory layout that groups similar machines together

product the total "bundle of satisfaction" that is offered to customers in an exchange transaction

product advertising advertising designed to make potential customers aware of a particular product or service and of their need for it

product and trade name franchising a franchise relationship granting the right to use a widely recognized product or name

product item the lowest common denominator in the product mix—the individual item

product layout a type of factory layout that arranges machines in sequence according to their role in the production process

product line the sum of the individual product items that are related

product mix the collection of product lines within a firm's ownership and control

product mix consistency the similarity of product lines

product strategy the manner in which the product component of the marketing mix is used to achieve the objectives of a firm

production process the activities necessary to accomplish the work a firm was created to perform (also called operations process)

productivity the efficiency with which inputs are transformed into outputs

products and services plan a section of the business plan that gives a description of the product or service to be provided and an explanation of its merits

professional manager one who uses systematic, analytical methods of management

profit revenues minus expenses

profit retention the reinvestment of profits into a business

profits before tax the amount of a firm's profits before paying taxes

promotion persuasive communication between a business and its target market

promotional mix the blend of promotional methods—personal selling, advertising, and sales promotion—for a target market

proprietorship a business owned and operated by one person

prospecting a systematic process of continually looking for new customers

publicity information about a firm, its products, or services appearing as a news item

purchase order a written order issued to a supplier to buy something

purchase requisition a formal, documented request from an employee or department for something to be bought for a business

purchasing the process of obtaining materials, merchandise, equipment, and services needed to meet production and/or marketing goals

purchasing group an unincorporated group of firms who purchase liability insurance for the group

Q

quality the features and characteristics of a product or service that enable it to satisfy needs

quality circle a group of employees who meet periodically to identify, analyze, and solve work-related

problems, particularly those involving product or service quality

R

random-access memory (RAM) the memory area in a computer where data are temporarily stored for processing

read-only memory (ROM) the memory area that contains permanent operating instructions for a computer

real estate mortgage a long-term debt with real estate held as collateral for the loan

reciprocal buying a firm's policy of selling to businesses from which it buys

reference group a group that influences individual behavior

Regulatory Flexibility Act legislation protecting small firms from excessive federal regulation by simplifying rules and reducing paperwork

reorder point the level at which additional quantities of merchandise should be ordered

repetitive manufacturing production of a large quantity of a standardized product during long production runs

replacement value approach a method of assessing the value of a business based on the cost to replace the firm's assets

retail inventory valuation method an inventory control system by which retailers estimate inventory cost from marked selling prices

return on equity the rate of return a firm's owners earn on their investment (also called return on net worth)

return on net worth the rate of return a firm's owners earn on their investment (also called return on equity)

revolving charge account a line of credit on which the customer may charge purchases at any time, not exceeding an established credit limit

revolving credit agreement a legal commitment by the bank to lend up to a maximum amount of credit

risk the chance that a situation may end with loss or misfortune

risk management efforts designed to preserve assets and the earning power of the firm

risk premium the difference between the average annualized return and the risk-free rate of return on a given investment

risk-retention group an insurance company started by

a homogeneous group of entrepreneurs or professionals to provide liability insurance for its members

S

S corporation a type of corporation that is taxed as a partnership

safety stock a level of stock maintained as protection against stockouts

sales forecast the prediction of how much of a product or service will be purchased by a market for a defined time period

sales promotion all promotional techniques that are neither personal selling nor advertising

SBA standards size standards, determined by the Small Business Administration (SBA), used to determine eligibility for loans or government contract bidding

secondary data information that has been previously compiled

Section 1244 stock stock that protects the stockholder in the event of corporate failure

segmentation variables the parameters used to distinguish one form of market demand from another

self-insurance earmarking part of a firm's earnings as a contingency for possible future losses

self-service layout a retail store layout that gives customers direct access to merchandise

serendipity the faculty for making desirable discoveries by accident

Service Corps of Retired Executives (SCORE) an organization of retired executives who will consult on current problems with small-business managers

short-range plans action plans that govern business operations for a specific time period

short-term debt money borrowed that must be repaid within twelve months, including accounts payable, accrued expenses, and short-term notes

short-term notes amounts borrowed from a bank or other lending sources, and that must be repaid within twelve months

single-entry system a simple checkbook system of accounting reflecting only receipts and disbursements

single-segmentation strategy a business recognizes the existence of several distinct market segments, but pursues only the most profitable segment

size criteria criteria by which the size of a business is measured

skimming-price strategy the practice of setting very high prices for products or services for a limited period before reducing them to more competitive levels

Small Business Development Centers (SBDCs) university-affiliated centers that provide direct consultation, continuing education, research, export services, and minority support to small businesses

Small Business Institute (SBI) a program to make student consulting resources available to small-business firms

Small Business Investment Companies privately owned banks that supply capital to small businesses

small-business marketing identifying target markets, assessing their potential, and delivering satisfaction to these markets

social classes divisions in a society with different levels of social prestige

social responsibilities a business's ethical obligations to customers, employees, and the community

society refugee a person who chooses to operate a business to escape societal expectations

software programs that provide operating instructions to a computer

span of control the number of subordinates who can be effectively supervised by one manager

special-purpose equipment machines designed to serve specialized functions in the production process

spontaneous financing short-term debts that increase as a natural consequence of an increase in the firm's sales

spreadsheet an electronic worksheet divided into rows and columns, which allows the user to perform calculations on a computer

staff activities activities that support line activities

stages in succession the process of transition of power from parent to child in a family business

standard operating procedures established methods of conducting business

startup building a business from "scratch"

statistical inference using facts known about a small group to infer something about a larger group

statistical quality control using statistical methods to make decisions regarding the quality of production lots

statute of frauds a law under which specific agreements must be made in writing

stock certificate a document that stipulates the number of shares owned by a stockholder

strategic decision a decision regarding the direction a firm will take in relating to its customers and competitors

strategic plans a firm's basic plans for the long-term future (also called long-range plans)

subfranchising a master franchisor has a continuing contractual relationship with a franchisor to sell its franchises (also called master franchising)

supercomputers the largest and fastest computers, which process huge amounts of data

supply function when small businesses act as suppliers and subcontractors for larger firms

surety bonds protection against the failure of another firm or individual to fulfill a contractual obligation

System A franchising a producer/creator grants a franchise to a wholesaler

System B franchising a wholesaler is franchisor

System C franchising a producer/creator is franchisor and a retailer is franchisee

system software programs that control the internal functioning of a computer

T

target marketing choosing marketing segments not adequately served by competitors (also called niche marketing)

telecommunications the process of exchanging data between remote computers

telecommuting working at home by using a computer link to the business location

Telephone Consumer Protection Act legislation that offers consumers protection from intrusive telemarketing

template a form preprogrammed into a computer, in which the user fills in blanks with specific data

term loan money lent on a five- to ten-year term, corresponding to the length of time the investment will bring in profits

terminal emulation a communications mode that allows personal computers to telecommunicate with mainframes

throughput the amount of work that can be done by a computer in a given amount of time

time study measurement of the time taken by a worker to complete a task

times interest earned the ratio of operating income to interest charges

total asset turnover a measure of the efficiency with which a firm's assets are used to generate sales

total cost the sum of the cost of goods or services sold, the selling expenses, and general administrative expenses

total fixed costs costs that remain constant as the quantity sold varies

total quality management (TQM) a quality-focused approach to managing a firm's operations based on popular Japanese quality control methods

total variable costs costs that vary as the quantity marketed varies

trade credit credit extended by nonfinancial firms to customers that are also business firms

trade dress elements of a firm's distinctive image not covered as a trademark or patent

trade-credit agencies privately owned and operated organizations that collect credit information on business firms

trademark an identifying feature used to distinguish a manufacturer's product

transfer of ownership the final step in conveyance of power from parent to child in a family business

two-bin method a simple visual technique for showing the reorder point of stock

Type A startup ideas providing customers with an existing product or service that is not available in their market

Type B startup ideas providing customers with a new product or service

Type C startup ideas providing customers with an improved product or service

U

underlying values unarticulated ethical beliefs that provide a foundation for ethical behavior

unity of command direction is received from only one supervisor

unlimited liability liability that extends beyond the assets of the business

unsegmented strategy a business defines the total market as its target market

utility patent a type of patent that covers a new process or protects the function of a product

V

variables sampling plan a quality control method that compares actual product measurements with target measurements

venture capitalist an investor or investment group that invests in new-business ventures

voice mail a computerized system for storing telephone messages

W

warranty an expressed or implied promise that a product will do certain things or meet certain standards

weighted cost of capital the cost of capital adjusted to reflect the relative costs of debt and equity financing

Windows IBM-compatible software that creates an Apple-like operating environment

Women's Business Ownership Act legislation that removes discriminatory barriers and encourages opportunities for women-owned businesses

word processing creating and manipulating text and graphics on a computer

work group software computer programs that help coordinate the efforts of employees working on a common project

work sampling a method of work measurement that estimates the ratio of actual working time to idle time

workers' compensation insurance coverage that obligates the insurer to pay employees for injury or illness related to employment

Workers' Compensation Laws state laws requiring employers to pay medical costs and wage losses arising from work-related injuries or illnesses

working capital the sum of a firm's current assets (cash, accounts receivable, and inventories) and current liabilities (accounts payable and short-term notes) (also called circulating capital)

working-capital cycle the day-to-day flow of resources through a firm's working-capital accounts

working-capital management the management of current assets and current liabilities

workstations powerful personal computers able to carry out more than one function at a time

WYSIWYG what you see is what you get

Z

zoning ordinances local laws that regulate land use

INDEX

ACKNOWLEDGMENTS

200   © Nik Wheeler
201   © 1987 Charles Gupton/Stock, Boston, Inc.
209   © 1991 Steve Weinrebe/Stock, Boston, Inc.
214   Courtesy of Mark Dulaney
223   © 1986 Bill Denison/Uniphoto Picture Agency
232   © G.B. Steinmetz/Photo Network
237   © Mark Ferri
243   Leo de Wys Inc./Brian King
256   © Bruce Ayers/Tony Stone Images
265   © 1992 Joe Stewardson
272   © 1992 John Zich
275   © Ilene Ehrlich
276   © Henley & Savage/Uniphoto Picture Agency
280   © 1992 Gabe Palmer/The Stock Market

Part 4 © Michael Wilson
298   © Michael Carroll
302   © 1993 The Lyons Group/Photo by Mark Perlstein
306   Photo by Levy/Gamma Liaison
314   © Garry D. McMichael/Photo Researchers, Inc.
315   © 1992 C. Thatcher
326   © John Madere
335   © J. Craig Sweat
344   Courtesy of BATUS Group of Companies—John
      Breuner Co.
356   © Steve Firebaugh
360   David Strick/Onyx Enterprises, Inc.
371   (left and right) Courtesy of David Shellenberger
376   Courtesy of Specialty Advertising Association
381   Courtesy of Lawrence Chan and Stratus Corporation
383   © Paul Damien/Tony Stone Images
386   © 1989 Robert Holmgren
392   © Uniphoto Picture Agency
395   © 1992 Randy Hampton/Black Star

Part 5 © Michael Wilson
410   © Gregory Edwards
421   © Robert E. Daemmrich/Tony Stone Images
429   © Duane Hall
432   T. Michael Keza/Nation's Business
438   Courtesy of Jon Wehrenberg and Larson Advertising
440   © Chriss Wade

448   © Mark Sherman/Photo Network
451   © Michael Gallacher
460   T. Michael Keza/Nation's Business
462   (left) © 1993 Steve Jennings
466   © Joe Stewardson
474   © Mark Sherman/Photo Network
485   © 1992 Duane Hall
490   T. Michael Keza/Nation's Business
493   Courtesy of Barry & Dan Schacht
499   T. Michael Keza/Nation's Business

Part 6 © Michael Wilson
506   © 1989 Bob Mahoney
510   © Barbara Filet/Tony Stone Images
542   Courtesy of Donald Weck, LOVE AT FIRST BITE
545   (left) © Michael Heron/The Stock Market
545   (right) © Superstock
560   © Tim Redel
562   Courtesy of Stuart Hall
583   © 1986 Alan Goldsmith/The Stock Market
591   © Mark Richards
598   TRW, Inc.
600   Xerox Corporation
610   From The Wall Street Journal—Permission, Cartoon
      Features Syndicate
620   © Les Wollam
625   © 1992 Chromosohm/Sohm/Uniphoto Picture
      Agency
630   © Bruce Zake
638   © Ron Sherman/Uniphoto Picture Agency

Part 7 © Michael Wilson
648   Courtesy Reell Precision Manufacturing Corporation
651   Ted Thai/Time Magazine
652   © Tom Tracy/The Stock Market
656   © 1989 Michael Melford
666   © Roark Johnson/Gamma Liaison
681   Courtesy of Trent & Company
684   © 1993 Ferguson & Katzman
      Background of line illustrations and end-of-chapter
      material © Michael Wilson